EMPLOYMENT LAW

General Editor
Jane Moffat

OXFORD
UNIVERSITY PRESS

OXFORD

UNIVERSITY PRESS

Great Clarendon Street, Oxford OX2 6DP

Oxford University Press is a department of the University of Oxford.
It furthers the University's objective of excellence in research scholarship
and education by publishing worldwide in
Oxford New York
Auckland Bangkok Buenos Aires Cape Town Chennai
Dar es Salaam Delhi Hong Kong Istanbul Karachi Kolkata
Kuala Lumpur Madrid Melbourne Mexico City Mumbai Nairobi
São Paulo Shanghai Taipei Tokyo Toronto

Oxford is a registered trade mark of Oxford University Press
in the UK and in certain other countries

Published in the United States
by Oxford University Press Inc, New York

A catalogue record for this title is available from the British Library

Library of Congress Cataloguing in Publication Data
(Data available)

ISBN 18-4174181-7

Typeset by Hewer Text, Edinburgh
Printed in Great Britain
on acid-free paper by
Antony Rowe Limited, Chippenham

AUTHORS

Gary Byrne is a partner in BCM Hanby Wallace, Solicitors where he is head of the employment law department. Gary was educated at University College Dublin (BCL) and qualified as a solicitor in 1977. He was one of the founding partners of Byrne, Collins, Moran. Gary lectures extensively on employment law and is a regular speaker at, amongst others, the Irish Management Institute and the Institute of Personnel and Development. He is a consultant on employment law to the Law School of the Law Society of Ireland. Gary is the author of *Transfer of Undertakings: Employment Aspects of Business Transfers in Irish and European Law*. He is a fellow of the Chartered Institute of Arbitrators.

Michael Kennedy is a partner in BCM Hanby Wallace, solicitors. Michael was educated at University College Dublin (BCL). He qualified as a solicitor in 1987 and became a partner in the firm in 1995. He is Secretary of the Irish Society for Labour Law and is a member of the Dublin Solicitors Bar Association Litigation Committee (dealing with litigation issues in an employment context). Michael is a member of the Law Society's Employment and Equality Committee. He has lectured widely on employment law issues and is a regular speaker on the Law Society's Continuing Legal Education programme while he has also addressed the Irish Centre for Commercial Law Studies. He is a contributor to *Practical Employment Law* published by Thomson Professional Information.

Michelle Ni Longain is a partner in BCM Hanby Wallace, solicitors. Michelle obtained her degree at Queens University Belfast and practised in both Northern Ireland and England and Wales before joining BCM Hanby Wallace in 1999, becoming a partner in 2001. Michelle is a regular speaker to, amongst others, students in the Law Society of Ireland Law School and legal practitioners on the Continuing Legal Education programme. Michelle specialises in employment, equality and administrative law matters.

Geoffrey Shannon is a solicitor and Deputy Director of Education in the Law Society of Ireland. Geoffrey lectures on the Professional Practice course and has written extensively in the field of health and safety in the workplace.

CONTENTS

CONTENTS

CONTENTS

CONTENTS

CONTENTS

TABLES OF LEGISLATION

TABLE OF STATUTES

TABLE OF ORDERS, RULES AND REGULATIONS

UK LEGISLATION

INTERNATIONAL MATERIALS

LIST OF CASES

LIST OF CASES

xl

LIST OF CASES

CHAPTER 1

CONTRACTS OF EMPLOYMENT

1.1 INTRODUCTION

The legal relationship between an employer and a person carrying out work comes mainly within the scope of the law of contract. Legislation has had a very considerable impact on employment relationships in recent times. To a lesser extent the law of tort will impinge on the relationship. Contracts of employment are no different from other contracts and require the four essential ingredients:

    (a)   offer;

    (b)   acceptance;

    (c)   consideration; and

    (d)   intention to create legal relations.

With the exception of merchant seamen under the Merchant Shipping Act, 1894 and articles of apprenticeship there is no requirement in law that an employment contract be wholly or partly in writing. Prudent employers will specify the essential terms of contracts of employment in writing and in many cases provide a comprehensive statement of the terms and conditions of a contract of employment. In May 1994 the Terms of Employment (Information) Act, 1994 came into force. It requires employers to furnish employees with certain of the terms and conditions of an employment contract in writing. The Act does not have regard to contract law in a couple of respects. First it allows that the terms and conditions of employment be furnished after the employment relationship has been entered into—which could well give rise to difficulty if there is a dispute over the terms as the contract will have been entered into and any disputed term might be deemed to be an attempted unilateral variation. Secondly, reference is made to amendment and the notification of amendments to employees. No mention is made of the necessity to have consent to contractual amendments or variations.

While the modern employment relationship appears to be dominated by legislation it is still very much underpinned by the law of contract. Those charged with the implementation and enforcement of legislative remedies such as unfair dismissal frequently have regard to the terms agreed between the parties, particularly where a dispute might be resolved or helped to be resolved by reference to what was specifically agreed between the parties.

In providing a written statement of terms and conditions of employment employers and employees may use either a letter of appointment or a more comprehensive detailed document. The majority of employment situations may be accommodated by a comprehensive letter of appointment which should make things administratively easier for the employer and transparent and understandable for the employee. Over the years there has been an element of snobbery in the drafting of contracts. Senior executives tend to get more detailed contracts, many of which, however, fail to recognise the potential difficulties and cost of a parting of the ways with such a senior executive, frequently omitting terms such as probationary period.

1.2 EMPLOYEES IN IRISH LAW—CONTRACT OF SERVICE/ CONTRACT FOR SERVICES

1.2.1 INTRODUCTION

Tax and social welfare law and virtually all Irish employment statutes draw a distinction between an employee and an independent contractor. The employee works under a contract of service. The independent contractor provides services under a contract for services. Persons carrying out work for an employer not readily fitting into one of these two categories may be deemed to be employees of a third party or sub-contractor or contracted to an employment agency. Given that a person must establish 'employee' status in order to qualify to benefit under most employment statutes the status of persons carrying out work has frequently come under legal consideration. Status is a question of fact determined in light of the rules of legal interpretation as set out below. While the distinction should be relatively easy to draw it has proven in many instances to be extremely difficult to do so. It has been dubbed the 'elephant test'; instantly recognisable when one sees it but difficult to describe accurately.

Regardless of what label parties seek to put on their relationship the courts will look at the factual situation and decide as a matter of law what type of contractual relationship exists.

The leading precedent cases on the approach to be applied to determine the correct status in law are the cases of:

- *Graham v Minister for Industry and Commerce* [1993] IR 156
- *Ready Mixed Concrete (South East) Ltd v Minister of Pensions and National Insurance* [1968] 2 QB 497
- *Roche v Kelly* [1969] IR 100
- *Market Investigations Ltd v Minister for Social Security* [1969] 2 QB 173
- *Global Plant v Secretary of State for Social Security* [1971] 3 WLR 269
- *Massey v Crown Life Insurance Co* [1978] ICR 590
- *Airfix Footwear Ltd v Cope* [1978] IRLR 396
- *Young and Woods Ltd v West* [1980] IRLR 201
- *Mara (Inspector of Taxes) v Hummingbird* [1982] ILRM 421
- *Re Sunday Tribune Ltd* [1984] IR 505
- *Lee v Chung* [1990] IRLR 236
- *McDermott (Inspector of Taxes) v Loy* 29 July 1982, High Ct (unreported)
- *O'Coindealbhain (Inspector of Taxes) v Mooney* [1990] 1 IR 422
- *Hall (Inspector of Taxes) v Lorimer* [1994] IRLR 171
- *Henry Denny & Sons (Ireland) Ltd (t/a Kerry Foods) v Minister for Social Welfare* [1998] ELR 36
- *Express and Echo Publications v Tanton* [1999] IRLR 367

1.2.2 WRITTEN EVIDENCE OF TERMS

In *O'Coindealbhain (Inspector of Taxes) v Mooney* [1990] 1 IR 422 the employment relationship was set out in a written contract. Blayney J was heavily influenced by the existence of the written contract and stated:

'Where the agreement creating the relationship between the parties is expressed in writing, . . . the entire agreement between the parties is to be found in the writing so it is the unique source of their relationship: it follows that it is from its terms alone that the nature of the relationship can be determined.'

That statement is questionable as to do literally as he suggests would be to remove the legal assessment of the status of the contract, possibly ignore facts of the relationship not dealt with in the written document and leave status as a matter of fact to be determined only by the parties in drawing up their agreement. The better approach was neatly summarised in a similar case, *McDermott (Inspector of Taxes) v Loy*. Barron J (who was quoted and agreed with by Blayney J in *O'Coindealbhain*) held that:

'The facts as found support the proposition that the respondent is in business on his own account.'

In *Re Sunday Tribune* [1984] IR 505 Carroll J stated:

'The court must look at the realities of the situation in order to determine whether the relationship of employer and employee in fact exists regardless of how the parties describe themselves.'

In *Henry Denny & Sons (Ireland) Ltd (t/a Kerry Foods) v Minister for Social Welfare* [1998] ELR 36 the Supreme Court considered a situation where the contract between the parties provided inter alia as follows:

'*Independent Contractor*
'The demonstrator is and shall be deemed to be an independent contractor and nothing in this agreement shall be construed as creating the relationship of master and servant or principal and agent. It is further agreed that the provisions of the Unfair Dismissals Act 1977 shall not apply to the contractual relationship that exists between Kerry Foods and the demonstrator.'

Keane J in referring to that clause of the contract held that the social welfare appeals officer was 'entirely correct in holding that he should not confine his consideration to what was contained in the written contract but should have regard to all the circumstances of Ms Mahon's employment'. He went on to hold that Ms Mahon, the demonstrator concerned, was an employee engaged under a contract of service contrary to what was specifically provided in the written agreement. In his concurring judgment Murphy J referred to the views of Blayney J in *O'Coindealbhain v Mooney* (above) and went on to state:

'[T]he terms and conditions governing the engagement of Ms Mahon were not "the unique source" of the relationship. . . . I am satisfied that the Appeals Officer was correct in his conclusion that he was required to consider "the facts or realities of the situation on the ground" to enable him to reach a decision . . . whether the respondent was an employee or an independent contractor. In seeking to ascertain the true bargain between the parties rather than rely on the labels ascribed by them to their relationship the Appeals Officer was expressly and correctly following the judgment of Carroll J *In The Matter of the Sunday Tribune Limited*.'

The existence of a written document specifying the nature of the relationship will not alter the nature of the relationship but it may well influence the determination of a court or tribunal as to the status of the person carrying out the work, where such status is unclear or where there is a fine balance as to which category the relationship falls into. In *Young and Woods Ltd v West* [1980] IRLR 201 the Court of Appeal held:

'[T]he label which the parties choose to use to describe their relationship cannot alter or decide their true relationship although in deciding what that relationship is the expression by them of their true intention is relevant but not conclusive. The legal relationship between the parties must be classified not by appearance but by reality.'

1.2.3   TESTS TO BE APPLIED

The law has developed from setting out fixed tests to differentiate one type of contract from another into a wider and broader approach in modern times in determining which type of contract exists.

In *Ready Mixed Concrete v Minister of Pensions and National Insurance* [1968] 2 QB 497 the court had to assess whether an owner/driver of a Ready Mixed concrete truck was an employee or an independent contractor. The court held that a contract of service exists if:

(1) 'A worker provides his own work or skill for payment in performing some service for the employer.' *This element of personal service and the facility of assigning the duties to another person to perform is particularly inconsistent with the status of employee.*

(2) 'He agrees to be sufficiently subject to the other party's control to make that other party his employer.' *Clearly a genuine independent contractor has more control over how, what, where, when and why he does the work.*

(3) 'The other provisions of the contract are consistent with it being a contract of service.' *This aspect is the one that has particularly given rise to a widening of the test in modern times. The modern employee has more perks and benefits associated with his employment than was the case in the past and these will be assessed to see whether or not they are consistent with one status or another. Some of the matters that would be considered under this heading will be the right to paid holidays, sick leave, pension, trade union membership, staff concessions etc.*

1.2.4   A MATTER OF DEGREE

It should be noted about the above tests that none of them is ever likely to be conclusive. They are merely measurements by which the *degree* of control, personal service and other provisions are examined to see whether it is more likely that the contract falls into one category or another.

In *Hall (Inspector of Taxes) v Lorimer* [1994] IRLR 171, Lorimer was a freelance vision-mixer involved in producing television programmes. He worked for a large range of different companies, usually only for a day or two at a time. He dealt with many companies on a repeated basis but each separate assignment was quite short with no set or usual lapse between each assignment. He did not use any of his own equipment; he always used the equipment of the companies employing him. He did not contribute to the programmes he produced and nor did he stand to make any profit or loss on those programmes. However, he did stand to lose money if his client company went into liquidation or failed to pay him. The Inland Revenue assessed him as an employee and he appealed the assessment. He was successful in his appeal. In determining the matter the Court of Appeal made a number of comments worthy of quotation as follows:

'There is no single path to determining whether or not the contracts from which a person derives his earnings are contracts of service or contracts for services. An approach which suits the facts and arguments of one case may be unhelpful in another . . . it is not a mechanical exercise of running through items on a check-list to see whether they are present in, or absent from, a given situation. The object of the exercise is to paint a picture from the accumulation of details. The overall effect can only be appreciated by standing back from the detailed picture which has been painted, by viewing it from a distance and by making an informed considered qualitative appreciation of the whole . . . The indicia set out . . . in *Market Investigations Ltd v Minister of Social Security* [[1969] 2 QB 173]were not intended to lay down an all-purpose definition of employment and are not appropriate in every case. For example that test does not mention the duration of the particular engagement or the number of people by whom the individual is engaged. In a case involving a person carrying on a professional vocation the extent to which the individual is dependent upon or independent of a particular paymaster for the financial exploitation of his talents may well be significant.'

1.2.5 EMPLOYMENT APPEALS TRIBUNAL APPROACH

1.2.5.1 Kirwan v Dart Industries

While the Employment Appeals Tribunal ('EAT') must apply the law as interpreted by the courts it has tended to take a more comprehensive and broader approach. One of the leading EAT determinations is that of *Kirwan v Dart Industries Ltd and Leahy* M1 UD 1/80. Dart Industries Ltd were an international organisation producing Tupperware. The Leahys were distributors in a certain part of Ireland. Mrs Kirwan worked for the Leahys selling Tupperware through an organised dealership. The dealers organised Tupperware parties at the homes of members of the public. The products were transported by the dealers to the home of the member of the public and displayed at the premises to persons who had been invited. When goods were purchased the dealer was paid and in turn paid the distributor, less a commission. In the case of the dealer therefore it was a case of no sale no pay. Dealers were trained by distributors and, in order to assist in the training and running of the business, successful dealers were appointed managers. Mrs Kirwan was a manager, and both acted as a dealer organising parties and assisted in the training and recruiting of dealers in respect of which she was paid an overriding commission arising from their efforts. She was provided with a car, taxed and insured, but she discharged the maintenance and running costs of the vehicle. She was under no continuing obligation to do any particular hours of work. PAYE tax was not deducted. Managers were at liberty to take whatever holidays they wished but to properly carry out their functions it was necessary to take one week's holiday out of season and two weeks in season. Paid holidays were not given.

The EAT considered the relationship between the claimant and both of the respondents under the following headings:

(a) Control.

(b) Was the claimant carrying out the job on her own behalf? Was she in business on her own account?

(c) Was there a personal obligation to perform the work?

(d) Was the relationship between the claimant and the respondent such as would allow her to do other work in her spare time which would be inconsistent with the status of employee?

Having considered these tests the EAT held that the claimant was an employee of the second-named respondent but not of the first-named respondent.

1.2.5.2 McCurdy v Bayer Diagnostics Manufacturing Ltd

In another EAT case, that of *McCurdy v Bayer Diagnostics Manufacturing Ltd* [1994] ELR 83, the EAT took a very broad approach in assessing the status of the claimant who was a medical doctor engaged by the respondent company over some twenty-one years. In addition to doing work for the company the claimant ran his own medical practice. The money received from the company was not dealt with through the PAYE or PRSI system; it was treated as income of his practice. There existed a written document specifying the duties to be performed and requiring among other things that Dr McCurdy 'fulfil and obey all the lawful directions and orders of the company from time to time'. The document also used such terminology as 'the company will employ the doctor' and that Dr McCurdy would 'serve the company' and that he would be paid 'a salary . . . payable in arrears by equal monthly instalments on the 1st day of each month'.

The company invited tenders for the medical services as provided by Dr McCurdy and obtained them at, what appears from the report, to be considerably less cost. The company terminated the employment relationship with Dr McCurdy who then claimed unfair dismissal. The company contended that he was never an employee but was at all times a self-employed independent contractor. The EAT held as follows:

'(1) Having regard to the degree of skill involved on the part of a doctor a manufacturing company's control of such a person would be less than that which would be exercised over other employees.' *This indicated that Dr McCurdy failed the control test, the degree of control indicating that he was self-employed.*

'(2) The claimant was integral to the running of the respondent company in that the service he provided enhanced the efficiency of the running of the company.' *The work Dr McCurdy did for Bayer Diagnostics indicated that he was an integral part of that business rather than that such work was done by him in a personal capacity for his own benefit. This indicated a relationship of employee rather than independent contractor.*

'(3) The fact that the claimant was not paying income tax under the PAYE system was not of itself a bar to his being an employee.'

On the basis of this reasoning the EAT held that Dr McCurdy was an employee of Bayer Diagnostics and not an independent contractor. Compensation was awarded. This decision was subsequently, and not surprisingly, reversed on appeal by the Circuit Court.

1.2.6   THE DEEMED EMPLOYEE

1.2.6.1   The Labour Force case

Applying the above-mentioned tests persons carrying out work were classified as being either employees or self-employed persons until 1970 when judgment issued in the British case of *Construction Industry Training Board v Labour Force Ltd* [1970] 3 All ER 220. Labour Force was engaged in supplying labour to the construction industry. When builders required labour the company agreed to supply workmen at certain rates which were payable by the builders to Labour Force. The workmen were then paid by Labour Force depending on the hours they worked. The relationship was a three-cornered one. The builders provided the work and controlled and directed how it was to be done. The workers carried out the work under the direction of the builders but without any contractual link to them and while holding a contractual link with Labour Force. Labour Force placed the workers, paid them when work was obtained and worked with them in order to ensure that they got work wherever it was available from time to time. Labour Force, however, had no control over the work carried out by the workmen. The builders had the right to terminate the workers' employment. The Construction Industry Training Board applied a levy to Labour Force. This levy was payable if Labour Force had employees engaged in the construction industry. Labour Force argued that they had no employees. They argued that their contracts with the workers were commercial contracts, not contracts of service. The court had to examine the three-cornered relationship and to determine whether or not Labour Force was subject to the levy. The court examined the nature of the relationships between the parties and held:

(a) no contract of any kind was made between the builders and the workmen;

(b) as no contractual relationship was formed between the builders and the workmen Labour Force contracted as principals with the workmen who were paid on agreed terms for the work carried out by them for the builders;

(c) in all the circumstances of the case the contracts into which the workers entered with Labour Force were not contracts of service; and

(d) the contracts entered into by the workers were not contracts of service or contracts for services but contracts sui generis, since the workers had agreed with Labour Force Limited to render services to third persons, the contractors. (See also *Meechan v Secretary of State for Employment* [1997] IRLR 353.)

1.2.6.2   Minister for Labour v PMPA Insurance Co Ltd

That case was followed in Ireland in *Minister for Labour v PMPA Insurance Co Ltd* [1986] JISLL 151. In that case the Minister prosecuted PMPA for alleged breaches of the Holidays (Employees) Act, 1973. PMPA employed a temporary typist. The temporary typist was engaged by PMPA under the terms of an agreement in writing that they made with Alfred Marks Bureau (Ireland) Limited. The contract provided that payment would be made to the Bureau and deemed the Bureau to be the employer of the temporary typist. The contract also provided that supervision, direction and control was assigned to and was the responsibility of PMPA. The question for the court was whether or not a named temporary typist was an employee of PMPA at the time she carried out work for them. Barron J made reference to the *Labour Force* case and held:

> 'I do not regard the facts as establishing any contract express or implied between . . . [PMPA] . . . and the employee. In this view I am supported by the English decision to which I have referred.'

The High Court considered the effect of the *PMPA* and *Labour Force* decisions in *O'Rourke v Cauldwell* [1998] ELR 287.

1.2.6.3   Employment agencies

The Oireachtais has sought to close this 'loophole' in recent legislation, notably the Unfair Dismissals (Amendment) Act, 1993, the Terms of Employment (Information) Act, 1994, the Maternity Protection Act, 1994, the Protection of Employment Order, 1996 (SI 370/ 1996) and the Organisation of Working Time Act, 1997, by deeming persons working for an employer through another body or agency to be employees of the person for whom they are doing the work. The attempts to close the loophole are, however, crude. In order to bring the supplier of labour within the legislation they must be deemed to be an '*employment agency*' within the meaning of the Employment Agency Act, 1971. The definition of an employment agency in the 1971 Act is, however, very wide. It does not require that the supplier of labour be actually trading as an employment agent or licensed as one. The definition appears to be sufficiently wide to encompass companies who carry out sub-contract work and in doing so use workers who may then be deemed to have a direct relationship with the client company. The definition is so wide that many employers may genuinely be sub-contracting work and services and not realise that the persons carrying out the work and providing the services are capable of being deemed to be employees. This is bound to give rise to particular problems in the area of unfair dismissal. It may also give rise to genuine and innocent breaches of the 1994 Act and substantial liabilities, financial and otherwise, under the 1997 Act.

Section 13 of the Unfair Dismissals (Amendment) Act, 1993 provides:

> '*Where, whether before, on or after the commencement of this Act, an individual agrees with another person, who is carrying on the business of an employment agency within the meaning of the Employment Agency Act 1971, and is acting in the course of that business, to do or perform personally any work or service for a third person (whether or not the third person is a party to the contract and whether or not the third person pays the wages or salary of the individual in respect of the work or service), then, for the purposes of the Principal Act, as respects a dismissal occurring after such commencement . . . the individual shall be deemed to be an employee employed by the third person under a contract of employment . . . and any redress under the Principal Act for unfair dismissal of the individual under the contract shall be awarded against the third person.*'

Similar definitions appear in the legislation referred to above. The definition of employment agency in the 1971 Act, s 1 provides as follows:

> '*[T]he business of an Employment Agency means the business of seeking, whether for reward or otherwise, on behalf of others, persons who will give or accept employment and includes the obtaining or supplying for reward of persons who will accept employment from or render services to others.*'

A decision was given by the EAT under the 1993 Act on this particular point in the case of *Bourton v Narcea Ltd and AIBP* UD186/94. AIBP is a large meat-processing company with a number of factories. The meat business is seasonal. An essential part of meat processing is the boning of sides of beef. Boning is largely seasonal work. As meat processors do not require boners all year round they tend to hire them in from specialist companies engaged in the sub-contracting of boning work such as Narcea Limited. Boners are generally nomadic and may travel to other countries to ply their trade during quiet times in Ireland or when rates of pay are better in those countries. Narcea supplied boners to AIBP. The boners worked in AIBP plants under the supervision of AIBP's employees to ensure a high quality of work. They also, however, had their own Narcea supervisor. Bourton was an employee of Narcea engaged under a contract of service subject to PAYE and PRSI and worked in a number of meat plants, latterly an AIBP plant where he became involved in a row with an AIBP employee. The AIBP employee was disciplined. The management of the plant requested Narcea management not to deploy Bourton in that plant. Narcea management sought to place Bourton in another plant. He refused. He claimed constructive dismissal. He initially brought his claim against Narcea and during the hearing it was decided to adjourn to allow that AIBP be joined under the provisions of the 1993 Act, s 13. When AIBP was joined, the EAT examined the definition of employment agency in the 1971 Act and held that Narcea, while contracting to do work itself for AIBP, was, in the course of seeking that business, 'supplying for reward . . . person who . . . render services'. The unfair dismissal claim then proceeded against the joint respondents, Narcea Limited and AIBP. While Bourton failed in his actual claim against AIBP due to a service problem under the 1993 Act it was held that the relationship between Narcea and AIBP conferred on Bourton the status of an employee of AIBP pursuant to the provisions the Unfair Dismissals (Amendment) Act 1993, s 13.

Given that in many cases the so-called 'agency' will retain a degree of control and may well actually dismiss the 'employee' it may well prove to be a practical impossibility for the deemed 'employer' to justify such a dismissal as being fair. Section 13 is a clumsy attempt to remedy an injustice by implying a contractual relationship between parties who may never have considered making an agreement between them. An employment relationship created by s 13 will have no express terms. How then will it operate within the requirements of the statute?

1.2.6.4 Conclusion

It is possible that the deemed employer under s 13 will not know of the existence of the deemed employee until a problem arises. If the 'contractual' employer acts unfairly towards the employee and the employee then claims against the 'deemed' employer, the 'deemed' employer will find it almost impossible to defend a dismissal in which he played no part and will more than likely lose such claim and be liable for the remedies available to the employee under the legislation. The concept of the deemed employee is a purely statutory creation for the purposes only of those statutes which specifically provide for the concept to apply. The concept does not create an employer/employee relationship but merely confers statutory obligations on a particular employer in particular circumstances.

1.2.7 PARTNERSHIPS

Partners are not employed by or with each other but may, as a partnership, have employees. A partnership or the business of a partnership may constitute an undertaking for the purposes of the Transfer of Undertakings Directive. As between themselves partners are deemed to be self-employed and not to have contracts of service with each other as in *DPP v McLaughlin* [1986] IR 355, where the High Court examined an employment relationship where the crew of a ship engaged on a voyage basis were rewarded on the basis of varying shares depending on the size of the catch on each voyage less expenses of the trip. McLaughlin was the owner of the boat and he, in consultation with the crew, determined the precise proportions to be applied. The court held that the relationship between the members of the crew and the owner/skipper of the boat was not that of employer and employee but as self-employed partners engaged in a common enterprise. Where partners in their capacity as members of the partnership carry out work for clients they do so in the capacity of independent contractors. See also *Ellis v Ellis & Co* [1905] 1 KB 324 and *Cowell v Quilter Goodison* [1989] IRLR 392.

1.2.8   SHAREHOLDERS/DIRECTORS—EMPLOYEE STATUS

Difficulties may arise where a shareholder and/or director of a company is sought to be classified as an employee for the purposes of the contract or, more commonly, for statutory purposes. This is dealt with in more detail in Chapter 6: Unfair Dismissal Law. See also the following cases:

- *Buchan and Ivey v Secretary of State for Employment* [1997] IRLR 80
- *Fleming v Secretary of State for Trade and Industry* [1997] IRLR 682
- *Secretary of State for Trade and Industry v Bottrill* [1998] IRLR 120

1.3   PRE-CONTRACTUAL MATTERS

There are three matters that will arise prior to a contract of employment being entered into and they may need to be examined closely in any dispute over the details of the contract itself.

1.3.1   ADVERTISEMENT

Jobs are frequently advertised and, as applicants rely on an advertisement, the wording of the advertisement is important as it will be deemed to form part of the overall contract. Regard should be had in advertisements to equality law. Employment equality legislation makes specific reference to advertisements. The Court of Appeal in *Pedersen v London Borough of Camden* [1981] IRLR 173 held that in construing the terms of an employee's contract as to his duties the EAT was entitled to look at surrounding circumstances and, in particular, to the advertisement which led him to apply for the job in question. See also *Financial Techniques (Planning Services) Ltd v Hughes* [1981] IRLR 32.

1.3.2   INTERVIEWS

What is discussed at interview may be extremely important. Both parties may make representations to each other which could be deemed to form part of any subsequent contract. A misrepresentation may give rise to a cause of action. The parties should take careful note of what transpires at interview. Employers will normally do this but it is less easy for an interviewee to do so. Where interviewees ask questions about a job at interview they should carefully note the answers and, if necessary, confirm the answers they have received and upon which they are relying in accepting the position subsequently (see *McNally v Welltrade International Ltd* [1978] IRLR 497). Anyone carrying out an interview will have to ensure compliance with the terms of the Employment Equality Act, 1998 and to avoid discriminatory or potentially discriminatory questions about marital status, disability, age and the other areas of discrimination covered by the 1998 Act—this is dealt with in more detail in Chapter 7: Employment Equality and Discrimination Law.

1.3.3 CONDITIONS PRECEDENT

1.3.3.1 Generally

Employers frequently require that certain conditions be satisfied before a contract becomes effective. In practice, however, given the nature of these conditions precedent employers tend to make the offer and allow it to be accepted subject to these conditions being satisfied. The satisfaction of the conditions can give rise to difficulties. The usual conditions are set out below.

1.3.3.2 References

It would be unusual for a job applicant who is in employment to advise his employer that he is applying for another position. The proposed new employer will, however, require a reference. A reference cannot be sought or furnished until the candidate has made a commitment to the new employer. It is not unusual for a reference to issue and when the new employer checks out the reference or speaks with the old employer finds that the recommendation is not possibly as fulsome as he might have wished or some element not dealt with in the reference arises, such as attendance record. If the prospective employer then decides not to proceed he is in a very difficult position. The employee might well be able to argue that the condition has in fact been satisfied. References may also give rise to liability in tort.

Is an employee or former employee entitled to a reference? There is no general requirement in law that an employer furnish a reference. The contract of employment is usually silent on the question. It has been argued that it is an implied term of a contract of employment that an employer will provide a reference at the employee's request. In *Lawton v BOC Transhield Ltd* [1987] IRLR 404 it was held that an employer was free to decline to give a reference. That places employees in a very difficult position. That position is likely to be compounded by recent decisions on an employer's liability where he does actually furnish a reference.

The well-known case of *Hedley Byrne & Co Ltd v Heller & Partners Ltd* [1964] AC 465 provided that a person who carelessly provides a reference (albeit not a job reference), which is misleading is liable if the person receiving the reference suffers loss in consequence of his reliance on that reference. In *Lawton* the judge held that a duty of care was owed in respect of a job reference to ensure that it was honest, accurate and not negligently written. Liability in respect of references was comprehensively dealt with in the House of Lords decision in the case of *Spring v Guardian Assurance plc* [1994] IRLR 460. In *Coote v Granada Hospitality Ltd* [1998] IRLR 656 the European Court of Justice considered an employee's entitlement to a reference where the employee was refused a reference and claimed that such refusal offended article 6 of the Equal Treatment Directive 76/207/EEC. The Directive requires that there be no discrimination on grounds of sex in relation to a number of situations including selection criteria and access to all jobs or posts. Member States are required to take the measures necessary to ensure that laws, regulations and administrative provisions comply with the Directive and also to ensure that persons who believe themselves to have been discriminated against can pursue their claims by judicial process. Ms Coote was employed by Granada from December 1992 to September 1993. She brought a sex discrimination complaint alleging that she had been dismissed because of pregnancy. The complaint was settled. Subsequently Ms Coote encountered difficulties in finding employment and claimed that Granada had failed to provide an employment agency with a reference which she believed was a reaction to her complaint and was an action which itself constituted unlawful victimisation contrary to the UK Sex Discrimination Act 1975. The Employment Appeal Tribunal in the UK referred questions to the European Court of Justice which held as follows:

- Article 6 of the Equal Treatment Directive provides that Member States introduce into their national legal system such measures as are necessary to enable all persons who consider themselves the victims of discrimination to pursue their claims by judicial process.

- This requires Member States to ensure judicial protection for workers whose employer, after the employment relationship has ended, refuses to provide references as a reaction to legal proceedings brought to enforce compliance with the principle of equal treatment.

- By virtue of article 6 of the Directive all persons have the right to obtain an effective remedy in a competent court against measures which they consider interfere with the equal treatment provisions of the Directive.

- The principle of effective judicial control laid down in article 6 would be deprived of an essential part of its effectiveness if the protection which it provides did not cover measures which an employer might take as a reaction to legal proceedings brought by an employee.

- Fear of such measures where no legal remedy was available against them might deter workers who consider themselves victims of discrimination from pursuing their claims by judicial process which would be liable seriously to jeopardise implementation of the aim pursued by the Directive. Therefore protection against retaliatory measures by an employer taken after the employment relationship has ended falls within the scope of the Directive.

1.3.3.3 UK approach

The UK Court of Appeal has offered some clarification for employers about the position in relation to references in its decision in *Bartholomew v London Borough of Hackney* [1999] IRLR 246. Mr Bartholomew was suspended pending investigations into alleged financial irregularities while employed by Hackney Council. Mr Bartholomew, in the meantime, had presented a complaint to an employment tribunal alleging racial discrimination by Hackney Council. During the course of the hearing of his complaints the parties reached a settlement under which Mr Bartholomew agreed to take voluntary severance and to withdraw his complaint. It was also agreed as part of the settlement that the disciplinary action would come to an end. The following year another prospective employer, who had offered a job to Mr Bartholomew, sought a reference for him from Hackney Council. The reference stated that he had taken voluntary severance following the deletion of his post and that at the time of leaving he was suspended from work due to a charge of gross misconduct, and that disciplinary action had commenced which said disciplinary action automatically lapsed when he left Hackney Council. On receiving the reference the prospective employer withdrew the offer of employment given to Mr Bartholomew following on which he made a claim for damages against his former employers alleging that they were in breach of their duty of care in providing a reference which, though factually correct, was unfair. The Court of Appeal held against him stating:

'The defendants were not in breach of the duty of care owed to the plaintiff former employee in providing a reference for a prospective employer which referred to the fact that, at the time of plaintiff's voluntary severence, he was suspended from work because of a charge of gross misconduct and that the disciplinary action had lapsed automatically with the end of his employment, but which gave no details as to the nature of the gross misconduct, the fact that he strongly denied the charge and the terms of the voluntary severence. An employer is under a duty of care to provide a reference which is in substance, true, accurate and fair. The reference must not give an unfair or misleading impression overall, even if its discrete components are factually correct. However the duty of care owed by an ex-employer to an ex-employee in accordance with *Spring v*

Guardian Assurance plc does not mean that a reference must in every case be full and comprehensive. In the present case though the form of the reference might have been improved upon in some respects it was not, as a whole, unfair, inaccurate and false. Had the defendants omitted all reference to the suspension they might have considered themselves as failing in their duty not to be unfair or misleading to the recipient of the reference.'

The law relating to references was gone into in some detail in the UK case of *Kidd v Axa Equity and Law Life Assurance Society* [2000] IRLR 301.

1.3.3.4 Medical evidence

In commercial life it is quite common for employers to require an employee only to submit to medical examination after the offer has been made and accepted. There is no reason why a prospective employee should not be asked to undergo a medical prior to an offer being made. The medical will be confidential and will not become known to the candidate's then employer. Disputes may arise as to whether or not a medical condition will impact on the employment relationship in the future. Employees may consider themselves fully fit to carry out duties, whereas the employer, having become aware of a medical condition, may take a different view. Employers can avoid such disputes by ensuring that medicals are carried out prior to the making of an offer of employment. The status of a pre-employment medical carried out by a medical adviser nominated by the employer is unclear in Ireland. In the UK the Court of Appeal has held that a medical practitioner retained by an employer to carry out pre-employment medicals does not owe a duty of care to the job applicant even if it is reasonably foreseeable that negligence by the doctor might lead to the applicant losing the opportunity for employment.

In *Kapfunde v Abbey National plc* [1998] IRLR 583 Mrs Kapfunde applied to Abbey National for a permanent post in a branch where she was already employed on a temporary basis. She completed a standard confidential medical questionnaire disclosing a condition which had led to her being absent from work in the past. The questionnaire was then passed to a GP retained by Abbey National who gave, as his opinion, that Mrs Kapfunde's medical history indicated that she was likely to have a higher than average level of absence and assessed her as not suitable for employment. Acting on that advice the company rejected the application. Mrs Kapfunde brought negligence proceedings against Abbey National and the doctor claiming damages for the economic loss she suffered as a result of not getting the job. The Court of Appeal held:

(a) The medical practitioner did not owe a duty of care to the plaintiff.

(b) A medical practitioner retained by a company to carry out pre-employment medical assessments is not under a duty of care to a job applicant in assessing suitability for employment even though it is reasonably foreseeable that the applicant might suffer economic loss if a careless error in the doctor's assessment leads to the loss of the opportunity of employment. In order for a duty of care to exist there must be some relationship of sufficient proximity between the plaintiff and the person alleged to be subject to such duty from which the duty may be derived. The fact that a person's actions are likely to cause damage to the plaintiff if he fails to take due care is not sufficient by itself to create a duty of care.

(c) The existence of a duty not to make negligent misstatements and the identity of the person to whom the duty is owed depend upon the circumstances in which the statement is made. A duty of care will generally be owed to the person to whom the statement is made and who relies on it. In the case of a medical report this is normally the person who commissions the report, not the subject of it.

(d) In the present case there was no special relationship between the defendant doctor and the plaintiff such as to give rise to a duty of care. The plaintiff did not rely on the doctor's report; it was not a report to her and she never even saw it.

(e) The Court of Appeal distinguished this case from the House of Lords decision in *Spring v Guardian Assurance plc* [1994] IRLR 460 on the basis that the duty in *Spring* was derived from the pre-existing relationship between the employer and the former employee. There was no pre-existing relationship between the defendant doctor and the plaintiff from which duty of care to the plaintiff could be derived in *Kapfunde*.

In giving its decision the Court of Appeal overruled the High Court decision in *Baker v Kaye* [1997] IRLR 219 which had held that a doctor retained by a company to examine a potential employee owed a duty of care to the potential employee. See also *X (minors) v Bedfordshire County Council* [1995] 2 AC 633.

1.3.3.5 Union membership

The pre-contractual closed shop is lawful under the common law and under European law. Where an employer operates a closed shop it is essential that the closed shop provision is explained to candidates and forms part of the employment offer. Union membership should be documented either prior to the offer being made or the acceptance being deemed valid.

1.3.3.6 Requirements of writing

A contract will be made up of both express and implied terms. As referred to above it is now a requirement of legislation that certain terms be expressed in writing.

Prior to 1973 there was no obligation on an employer to put terms and conditions of employment in writing. Prudent employers did and have always done so without there being any legal obligation. The Minimum Notice and Terms of Employment Act, 1973 provided that details of certain terms and conditions of employment (as specified in the legislation) were to be made available to employees on request. Under the terms of the Unfair Dismissals Act, 1977 it was provided that an employer should make known to an employee in writing the procedure that would be adopted in the event of dismissal being proposed or taking place.

1.3.3.7 Terms of Employment (Information) Act, 1994

The Council of the EC adopted Directive 91/533/EEC on 14 October 1991 obliging employers to inform employees of conditions applicable to a contract of employment or employment relationship. As a result of the Directive the Oireachtais enacted the Terms of Employment (Information) Act, 1994 in May 1994 which provides as follows:

(a) the legislation applies as between employers and employees. It also applies to persons employed through employment agencies who are deemed for the purposes of this legislation to be employed by the party paying the wages;

(b) the legislation only applies to those employees normally expected to work at least eight hours per week;

(c) the legislation does not apply to employees with less than one month's service;

(d) an employer is obliged to provide an employee with a statement in writing no later than two months after the commencement of employment containing the following particulars:

(i) the full names of both employer and employee;

(ii) the address of the employer;

(iii) the place of work or, alternatively, a statement specifying that the employee is required or permitted to work at various places;

(iv)   the title of the job or nature of the work;

(v)   the date of commencement of the contract of employment;

(vi)   in the case of temporary contracts, the expected duration or in the case of a fixed term contract the date on which the contract expires;

(vii)   the rate or method of calculation of the employee's remuneration and details as to at what intervals the payment of remuneration will be made;

(viii)   any terms or conditions relating to hours of work including overtime;

(ix)   any terms or conditions relating to paid leave (other than paid sick leave);

(x)   any terms or conditions relating to sick leave or for payment due to incapacity as a result of injury;

(xi)   details of pensions or pension schemes;

(xii)   the period of notice which the employee is required to give and entitled to receive whether by statute or contract. If a specified period of notice is not provided for then the method or manner by which notice is to be calculated is to be specified;

(xiii)   reference must be made to any collective agreements which directly affect the terms and conditions of the employee's employment including, where the employer is not a party to such agreements, particulars of the bodies or institutions by whom they were made. This requirement only applies to contracts entered into after the commencement of the Act—May 1994;

(xiv)   it is further provided that if after the commencement of the Act (May 1994) an employee is required to work outside the State for a minimum period of one month the following details are to be given to the employee or added to the above-mentioned statement:

– the period of employment outside the State;

– the currency in which the employee is to be remunerated in respect of that period;

– any benefits in cash or kind for the employee while working outside the State; and

– the terms and conditions applying to the employee's repatriation; and

(xv)   employers are obliged to notify employees of any changes in their terms and conditions of employment as soon as possible after the change but no later than one month thereafter;

(e)   where a contract has been entered into prior to the commencement of the Act an employee is entitled to ask for a statement such as is required above and the employer must furnish the statement within two months of the request; and

(f)   any complaints by an employee of contravention of the Act by employers may be referred to a rights commissioner. The rights commissioner may require the employer to provide the particulars and also, if appropriate, may order payment of compensation not to exceed a maximum four weeks' remuneration. Remuneration is to be calculated in accordance with the formula provided for under the Unfair Dismissals Acts. Reference must be made to a rights commissioner no later than six months after the date of termination of the contract of employment. Appeals from the rights commissioner are to the EAT within six weeks (forty-two days) of the date on which the recommendation was communicated to the party appealing.

None of the above legislation can or does affect the law of contract in so far as it applies to employment relationships.

The European Court of Justice considered the scope of Directive 91/533 in *Kampelmann v Landschaftsverband Westfalen-Lippe* [1998] IRLR 333.

1.4 IMPLIED TERMS

There are four sub-categories of implied terms as follows.

1.4.1 TERMS IMPLIED BY STATUTE

Terms implied by statute include the right not to be unfairly dismissed, the right to redundancy payments in the event that employment is terminated in a situation of redundancy, equality, safety from sexual harassment etc.

1.4.2 TERMS IMPLIED BY CUSTOM OR PRACTICE

As to terms which may be implied by custom or practice, see *Spring v Guardian Assurance plc* [1994] IRLR 460. Such rights include the right to suspend, the right to sick pay, selection for redundancy etc. In *DP Refinery (Westernport) Pty Ltd v Shire Hastings* (1978) 52 AJLR 43 the court set out the test that will normally be applied before a term may be implied into a contract as follows:

(a) the term must be reasonable and equitable;

(b) it must be necessary to give business efficacy to the contract, so no term will be implied if the contract is effective without it;

(c) it must be so obvious that it goes without saying;

(d) it must be capable of clear expression; and

(e) it must not contradict any express term of the contract.

1.4.3 COLLECTIVE AGREEMENTS

In unionised employment employers usually copy written collective agreements to new employees and make it clear to them that these agreements form part of their terms and conditions of employment. Subsequent variation of or addition to contractual terms by agreement between a trade union and an employer may be of particular relevance, particularly where the employee objects to the terms. A trade union cannot bind all of its members where some of those members made it quite clear that they did not wish to or intend to be bound (see *Goulding Chemicals Ltd v Bolger* [1977] IR 211).

The position was somewhat altered by a Supreme Court decision arising from the provisions of the Postal and Telecommunications Act, 1983 which provided for the formation of An Post and Bord Telecom. The Act provided at s 45(2) that conditions of service could only be changed in accordance with a collective agreement negotiated with any recognised trade union or staff association. The plaintiffs'/respondents' terms and conditions were changed after the company had entered into a collective agreement with their representative trade union. The plaintiffs, however, had not consented to the change as constituting an alteration in their contractual terms and conditions. The Supreme Court held in favour of the defendant/appellant, Bord Telecom Eireann, holding that where a collective agreement had been concluded with a representative trade union which had the effect of changing the plaintiffs' terms and conditions of employment the plaintiffs were bound by the change by virtue of the provisions of the subsection referred to (see per Blayney J in *O'Cearbhaill v Bord Telecom Eireann* [1994] ELR 54.

1.4.4   TERMS IMPLIED BY LAW

Terms will be implied where necessary to give commercial efficacy to a contract of employment. As referred to above this arises usually in the context of courts analysing specific agreed terms which may not have been comprehensive enough to cover what was intended to be covered or where a dispute has arisen as to their meaning. The Supreme Court examined the circumstances in which a term might be implied into a contract of employment in *Sweeney v Duggan* [1997] 2 ILRM 211. In that case the plaintiff had been injured but the company he worked for had been placed in voluntary liquidation and was unable to pay its debts. The plaintiff sought to sue the managing director personally and sought to imply into his contract of employment a duty on the employer to insure him for personal injury and then to hold the defendant liable for breach of that implied term. In its judgment the Supreme Court referred to the leading cases of *The Moorcock* (1889) 14 PD 64 and *Shirlaw v Southern Foundries [1926] Ltd* [1939] 2 KB 206, and held that there were two principal situations where the courts will independently of a statutory requirement imply a term which has not been expressly agreed by the parties:

(a)   on the basis of the presumed intention of the parties; and

(b)   as a matter of law independently of the intention of the parties as a necessary legal incident of a definable category of contract.

The court rejected the plaintiff's case that a term requiring insurance should be implied into the particular contract concerned.

Implied terms include the usual terms such as the employer's duty of care and an employee's duty to perform and conduct himself properly and to take reasonable care in the performance of his work. Employees have an implied duty of fidelity to their employer. This duty of fidelity is frequently pleaded in dismissal cases where employers seek to argue that the necessary 'trust and confidence' that must exist in order to properly underpin a contract of employment has been irreparably damaged by the actions of the employee.

The duty of fidelity was initially most comprehensively laid down in the case of *Boston Deep Sea Fishing & Ice Co v Ansell* (1888) 39 Ch D 339. Ansell received a secret commission when placing contracts with shipbuilders and this was deemed to be a breach of a duty of fidelity to his employer. The duty of fidelity frequently arises in the context of restrictive covenants which are dealt with in more detail at **1.5.17** below. The duty of fidelity was examined in *Soros and Soros v Davison and Davison* [1994] IRLR 264. Mr and Mrs Davison were employed by Mr and Mrs Soros as butler/chauffeur and cook/housekeeper. They were dismissed and an industrial tribunal found the dismissal to have been unfair. After the finding of unfair dismissal the Davisons sold information about their employment to a national newspaper. Soros instituted proceedings to restrain them from disclosing information which was claimed to be in breach of an alleged implied term in their contracts of employment and of an alleged duty of confidence arising from the relationship of employer and employee. While much of the case was taken up with legal argument on the effect of post-dismissal conduct on an unfair dismissal claim, and available remedy, reference was made to the general duty of confidentiality and the fact that it survived termination of a contract whether the dismissal is fair or unfair.

In modern cases the duty of fidelity is more often referred to as the duty of *'trust and confidence'*. This is a mutual duty on both the employer and the employee and if either party is in breach it entitles the other party to terminate and may entitle them to damages—see

16

1.5.18.5 below. The implied duty of mutual trust and confidence is outlined in detail in *TSB Bank plc v Harris* [2000] IRLR 157.

1.5 EXPRESS TERMS

The principal express terms that should be contained in any document setting out the terms and conditions of a contract of employment are set out below.

1.5.1 PARTIES

While it may seem self-evident, confusion often arises as to who the employer actually is. It is particularly important to specify who the employer is where an individual might be trading as a limited company, a partnership, or a subsidiary company within a group of companies. It may happen that an employee is employed by one company or individual but is paid through the account of another. It is important for the employer to specify who is the actual employer in such circumstances. In *Clifford v Union of Democratic Mineworkers* [1991] IRLR 518 the Court of Appeal held that the question as to by whom an employee is employed is a question of law which will often depend not only on construction of relevant documentary evidence but also on evaluation of the facts. In *O'Rourke v Cauldwell (t/a Recruitment and Engineering Design Services Ltd)* [1998] ELR 287 a dispute arose as to whether the plaintiff had entered into a contract of employment with a recruitment agency or the client of the recruitment agency.

1.5.2 DATE OF COMMENCEMENT

With most statutory entitlement being dependent on length of service, as would pension entitlement, it is most important to specify what the commencement date of the employment is deemed to be. It is particularly important where an employee is made an offer and cannot take up the employment for some time because of commitments to his previous employer or otherwise.

1.5.3 JOB FUNCTION

Employers normally seek to avoid disputes over what work an employee may be required to do. They therefore frame job specifications or job descriptions in as wide a manner as possible. That, however, may give rise to difficulties if a redundancy was later to be considered, in which event employees could argue that their job function obliged them to carry out duties different from those duties which had become redundant. In *Haden v Cowen* [1982] IRLR 314 Cowen's contract included a provision that he was required 'to undertake at the direction of the company any and all duties which reasonably fall within the scope of [his] capabilities'. Cowen was subsequently made redundant. In justifying redundancy his employers focused on the duties he was carrying out at the time the decision was made. It was held by the EAT that it was not sufficient to show merely that the requirements of the employer for employees to carry out work of the kind on which the employee was actually engaged had ceased or diminished. It was necessary for the employer to show that such diminution or cessation covered any work that the employee could have been required to do under the contract of employment. The Court of Appeal did hold, however, that there had been a diminution in work for persons carrying out the particular kind of work which Cowen was contracted to do and he was therefore redundant. Employers should also have regard to the possibility of requiring an employee to carry out work for a subsidiary or associated company.

See also *Cresswell v Board of Inland Revenue* [1984] IRLR 190 where staff of the Inland Revenue sought a declaration that a changeover to computerisation without their consent was breach of an implied term in their contract of employment that they could not be required to change the manner in which their stipulated tasks had been habitually performed either at all or in such a manner as to make these tasks different in nature from those previously performed. The court held that employees must adapt to new methods and techniques provided that the employer ensured that there was the necessary training or retraining to assist them in performing such methods or techniques. Employees had no implied right to remain in perpetuity doing one defined type of work even if this resulted in less job satisfaction. A loss of job satisfaction by itself provided no cause of action.

The general common law rule is that an employer is not contractually obliged to provide work for the employee (see *Collier v Sunday Referee Publishing Co* [1940] 2 KB 647 and *Turner v Sawdon & Co* [1901] 2 KB 653). Exceptions to that general rule will be where the employee's remuneration depends on performance, eg commission (see *Re Rubel Bronze & Metal Co* [1918] 1 KB 315), and where performance of work is linked to reputation and ability to use and improve one's skills and talents (*Marbe v George Edwards (Days Theatre) Ltd* [1928] 1 KB 269).

1.5.4   HOURS OF WORK

Apart from setting out the basic hours of work an employer should make reference to breaks, shifts and overtime, particularly where an employee may be required to work beyond the normal hours on a regular basis. A specific reference should be made to payment for overtime, whether payment is to be made or not to be made. In *Green v Roberts* [1992] IRLR 499 reference was made to the manner in which hours of work should be calculated in the event of there not being a specific provision. This case followed *Deane v Eastbourne Fishermen's and Boatmen's Protection Society and Club Ltd* [1977] IRLR 143 and *Larkin v Cambos Enterprises (Stretford) Ltd* [1978] ICR 1247, where a simple averaging out of hours actually performed over a period that covered most variations in the contract was sufficient. Where averaging out may not give a fair result see *Opie v John Gubbins Insurance Brokers Ltd* [1978] IRLR 540. Where salary is reduced by an employer for good commercial reason but possibly in breach of terms of a contract of employment see *Burdett-Coutts v Hertfordshire County Council* [1984] IRLR 91; *Millar v Hamworthy Engineering Ltd* [1986] IRLR 461 and *Rigby v Ferodo Ltd* [1987] IRLR 516.

Regard must also be had to hours of work set by statute such as:

- Protection of Young Persons (Employment) Act, 1977
- Conditions of Employment Acts, 1936–1944
- Shops (Hours of Trading) Act, 1938

There is no right in law to lay off staff or place them on short time due to a temporary shortage or downturn in work and so it is best to provide for this right in the contract of employment (see *Devonald v Rosser* [1906] 2 KB 728).

1.5.5   PLACE OF WORK

Place of work may give rise to difficulties both in respect of the department or area in which an employee works and geographical location, or as to working in different geographical locations. The first situation was dealt with in the case of *White v Reflecting Roadstuds Ltd* [1991] IRLR 331. White originally worked in the rubber-mixing department of the company which attracted the highest level of pay but involved the hardest physical work and longest hours. White had difficulty with the work and asked to be moved to lighter work. He could not be moved and remained in the mixing department. His attendance, however, deteriorated and other staff complained about the effect his absence was having upon them in earning their entitlement to team bonuses. After warning White was transferred from the mixing department to the pressing department which resulted in a considerable drop in pay. He resigned and claimed constructive dismissal on the basis that the move from mixing to pressing constituted a fundamental breach of his contract. The contract included an express term covering job flexibility which provided that:

> '[T]he company reserves the right when determined by requirements of operational efficiency to transfer employees to alternative work and it is a condition of employment that they are willing to do so when requested.'

The EAT held:

(a) Where organisation and reorganisation are concerned it is for management to reach the decisions provided they do so responsibly and give effect to their decisions within the legal framework of a clear contractual term on mobility or job transfer. Even where there is an express clause a purely capricious decision would not be upheld. There must be reasonable or sufficient grounds for requiring the employee to move; otherwise the employer would be in breach of the specific term of the clause which had implied into it the obligation to act responsibly and reasonably.

(b) A reduction in pay as a result of a contractually allowed transfer is not a breach of a fundamental implied term that there would be no unilateral reduction in pay. There is clear binding authority that where an employer acts within the contract of employment the fact that thereby there is caused a loss of income to the employee does not render the employer's act a breach of contract.

On geographical mobility it may be taken that a similar onus lies on an employer to act reasonably and responsibly even where there is a geographical mobility clause in the contract. Geographical mobility was considered in *Parry v Holst & Co Ltd* [1968] ICR 317 where the employee's contract provided for mobility between different workplaces and he was refused a redundancy payment when his current workplace closed and he refused to transfer to another. In *Wilson-Undy v Instrument & Control Ltd* [1976] ICR 508 an employee accepted a job as part of a mobile workforce but he stipulated at the time of his appointment that he was not prepared to work at any sites beyond daily travelling distance of his home. When work at his site finished he claimed a redundancy payment. He refused to transfer to another site which was not within daily travelling distance from his home. He was held to be entitled to his redundancy payment. The Court of Appeal in the UK refused to allow an employer to use the mobility provisions of a contract to establish that a place of work was in a particular location where that sought to defeat an entitlement of the employee—in this case a redundancy entitlement—*High Table Ltd v Horst* [1997] IRLR 513.

Lou Macari was appointed manager of Celtic Football Club in 1993. It was a term of his contract that he reside no further than 45 miles from the centre of Glasgow while carrying out his duties. Mr Macari did not do so. This was held to be a material breach of his contract in failing to comply with the lawful and legitimate instruction of his employers entitling the employers to terminate the contract (see *Macari v Celtic Football and Athletic Co Ltd* [1999] IRLR 787).

1.5.6 EXCLUSIVE SERVICE

Employees have the right to work for another employer in their spare time provided this does not conflict with their duties, including fidelity and confidentiality, to their employers (*Nolan v Irish Snack Foods Ltd* UD 303/79; *Conroy v Travenol Laboratories* UD 47/81 and *Mulchrone v Feeney* UD 1023/82). See also *Fairbrother v Stiefel Laboratories* UD 665/85, an interesting decision of the EAT. Dr Fairbrother held the position of Director of Research and

Development. His wife, who had no link with Stiefel Laboratories, was a trained pharmacist who formed her own company and launched a product which competed with a product manufactured by Stiefel. Dr Fairbrother's employment contract contained clauses designed to protect confidentiality and trade secrets. There was no allegation that Dr Fairbrother had breached these provisions but, given his position of responsibility and control and his wife's activities, there was a conflict of interest which could have been resolved by Mrs Fairbrother ceasing her activities. Dr Fairbrother could not oblige her to do so. In those circumstances the company resolved the conflict by terminating Dr Fairbrother's employment. The EAT held the dismissal to be fair.

See also *ECI European Chemical Industries Ltd v Bell* [1981] ILRM 345 where an interlocutory injunction was granted to restrain a chemist from joining a competitor in breach of a restraint of trade clause in his contract.

1.5.7 PROBATION

Unfair dismissal legislation provides that a probationary period cannot exceed one year. Probationary periods are useful to employers in unionised employment as employees tend not to be deemed by unions to be 'permanent' until they have completed the probationary period. It is also useful to employers employing senior employees who might have a lengthy notice period, in the event of the employment continuing, to have a probationary period although it may be difficult to attract senior employees where they lack job security in the early stages of their employment. The wording of probationary periods may sometimes give rise to a possible construction that the probationary period is in itself a fixed term within the contract. If a contract were to state, for example, 'The first six months of this contract shall be a probationary period' this might give rise to a claim on early termination, eg after one month, that the employee is entitled to be paid the balance of five months' salary. There has in fact been a District Court finding to this effect. The position, however, seems to be at common law that the employer has an implied right to terminate during the probationary period on the giving of specified or reasonable notice (*Dalgleish v Kew House Farm Ltd* [1982] IRLR 251). A prudent employer will provide that during a probationary period the employment may be terminated on specified notice often shorter than the notice required to terminate the contract when employment has become permanent. See also *Doyle v Grangeford Precast Concrete Ltd* [1998] ELR 260 where the employer sought to impose a probationary period in a written document produced to the employee for his signature after he had commenced employment. The employee obtained an interlocutory injunction pending the outcome of his claim for damages.

1.5.8 TERM OF CONTRACT

Term of contract is relevant only in relation to fixed term or specified purpose contracts which are dealt with more specifically at **1.6** below.

1.5.9 SALARY/REMUNERATION

Precision is necessary in setting out the various components of a remuneration package. Basic salary tends not to cause difficulty. However, bonuses and commission do. Employers normally seek to have bonuses described as discretionary where employees will require first to establish that they have a right to bonus and, secondly, that where there is a bonus or commission system in place its terms are specifically set out so that the employee can enforce payment in the event of any dispute arising. Reference should be made to what entitlement will be in the event of either party terminating during the course of a bonus/commission period. The method in which remuneration may be paid is dealt with in the

Payment of Wages Act, 1991 which is dealt with in Chapter 5. This legislation repealed the Truck Acts, 1743–1896.

1.5.10 COMPANY CAR

Again it is in an employer's interest to provide that a company car is furnished at the discretion of the employer either in terms of the basic entitlement or in terms of the make, model and renewal terms. The provision of a company car may give rise to consideration as to vicarious liability for the employer both in the normal use of the vehicle and for the employee outside the hours of work (see *Smith v Stages* [1989] 1 All ER 833). For cases where employees may be entitled to car allowances and they are varied or withdrawn see *Keir and Williams v County Council of Hereford and Worcester* [1985] IRLR 505.

1.5.11 HOLIDAYS

Holidays are governed in Ireland by the contract and since September 1997 the Organisation of Working Time Act, 1997. All contracts should make reference to this entitlement and, if extra days' holidays are to be conferred, they should be deemed to be in addition to the statutory entitlement which is to annual leave and public holidays. As the legislation vests in the employer the right to determine when holidays are to be taken it will normally suffice for a contract of employment to refer to the mechanics of taking holidays as being governed by the legislation. Employers and employees cannot contract out of the terms of the 1997 Act.

1.5.12 SICK PAY

1.5.12.1 Generally

There is no general right in law to be paid while absent from work due to illness. An entitlement to sick pay may, however, be implied from the custom and practice of the employment. *Halsbury's Laws of England* (4th edn) vol 16, para 24 states in relation to non-statutory sick pay:

'Whether any such private sick pay is payable, its amount, its duration, and its relationship with statutory sick pay or any other benefit depends entirely on the terms of the individual employee's contract, since there is no rule of law that it either is or is not payable. The relevant term may be expressed in the contract and this is common; if not so expressed a term may be implied. In the absence of an expressed term there is however no presumption that a term is to be implied. It is rather a case of considering all the evidence in the particular case, including the normal method of remuneration, custom and practice, and any pronouncement by the employer.'

In *Howman & Son v Blyth* [1983] IRLR 139 the court considered whether or not an employee should have implied into his contract of employment an entitlement to sick pay. There had in the past been a term expressly provided for in all contracts of employment within the company that employees would be entitled to sick pay. The onus was on the employers to show that the respondent had either expressly or by implication agreed to vary his contract to lose this right and it was held that such variation was not proven. On the question of implication of terms the court stated:

'Where the relationship between the parties requires that there should be some agreed term which has not in fact been agreed but both parties would not have agreed what that term would be if they had been asked, the Court is free to imply a reasonable term. In the present case there was undoubtedly a contractual obligation to pay sick pay but there was no agreed term as to the duration of the sick pay.'

As there had to be some contractual term regulating the duration it was legitimate to imply a reasonable term. See also *Marrison v Bell* [1939] 2 KB 187 and *Mears v Safecar Security Ltd* [1983] 1 QB 54.

1.5.12.2 Implied entitlement

The question of an implied entitlement to sick pay was raised in the context of an employee seeking injunctive relief to restrain a disciplinary hearing, and other reliefs in the case of *Charlton v HH The Aga Khan's Studs Société Civile* [1999] ELR 136. The disciplinary investigation was initiated against the plaintiff and she sought eight interlocutory injunctions restraining her employer from continuing the enquiry into the disciplinary matters and other reliefs. During the course of the disciplinary enquiry the plaintiff became ill. Her employers refused to make payments to her in respect of sick pay claiming they had no contractual obligation to do so and suggesting that she rely on social welfare entitlements. In the course of her judgment Laffoy J commented:

> 'It is common case that the terms of the plaintiff's employment with the defendant are not contained in a written contract. It is also common case that it is not an express term of the plaintiff's employment with the defendant that she is entitled to be paid her salary while absent from work due to illness or incapacity. The plaintiff's contention is that her entitlement to sick pay is an implied term of her contract of employment. Her case is that it has always been the position in the defendant's Studs that long-standing employees were paid their salary in full when they were absent through illness and that this custom is part of her terms of employment. This is disputed by the defendant.'

Laffoy J went on to state that the plaintiff had established a fair issue to be tried that there was an implied sick pay term in her contract of employment and ordered that her salary be paid pending the resolution of the matters in dispute and for so long as she remained ill provided that she furnished to the employer a weekly illness report. See also *Wandsworth London Borough Council v D'Silva* [1998] IRLR 193.

1.5.12.3 Drafting the sick pay clause

In drafting clauses relating to sick pay entitlement reference may well be made also to VHI entitlements and to income continuance plans which may cover payment to an employee after the employer's obligation to pay sick pay has ceased. In *Adin v Sedco Forex International Resources Ltd* [1997] IRLR 280 the Court of Session in Scotland held against an employer who sought to dismiss an employee who was entitled to claim under short-term and long-term disability plans but by reason of the dismissal was prevented from obtaining the benefit of the plans. Even though the employer had no restrictions on the circumstances in which it could dismiss the employee the court refused to allow such a dismissal in the circumstances of the dismissal acting to defeat the entitlement under such policies. The Court of Session accepted that where an employee is off work due to illness and in receipt of sick pay there was an implied term in the contract that the employee would not be dismissed on grounds of sickness or for an arbitrary reason since to do so would be to subvert the employee's entitlements to payments while sick. In *Hill v General Accident Fire and Life Corporation* [1998] IRLR 641 the court did state, however, that the employer was not in breach of the employee's contract of employment in dismissing on grounds of redundancy while the employee was off work ill and in receipt of sickness benefit with a prospective entitlement to long-term sickness benefit under an ill-health policy. The court held that there was no implied term that the employers would not use their contractual powers of dismissal where that would frustrate an accruing or accrued entitlement to sickness benefit or ill health and early retirement. The court refused to accept that there was an implied term that gross misconduct was the only cause that would warrant dismissal of an employee who was in receipt of sick pay. The court examined the implied term of mutual trust and confidence and held that an employer would be prohibited from terminating a sick employee's employment 'solely with a view to relieving themselves of the obligation to make such payment for a specious or arbitrary reason or for no cause at all. To do so would be to subvert the employee's entitlement to payment while sick'.

This decision is arguably only of use to an employee who can prove that the actual reason for dismissal was to deny him his entitlement to short-term or long-term sickness benefit and is unlikely to avail an employee where an employer dismisses for cause, eg misconduct or redundancy. The practice of courts in the UK has been to prevent employers from terminating employment due to incapacity if the effect of the termination would be to deny the employee rights to third party benefits such as an insured permanent health scheme or income continuance. The *Hill* case was reviewed and partly affirmed in *Villella v MFI Furniture Centres Ltd* [1999] IRLR 468 where the UK High Court held that termination of the plaintiff's employment in that case would have been a breach of an implied contractual term that the employers would not terminate employment except for cause 'in circumstances which would deprive the plaintiff of the continuing entitlement to disability benefit in the course of payment or due to him'. The court in that case felt that such an implied limit on the employer's power to dismiss was necessary in order to give *"business efficacy"* to the contract which allowed for disability benefit to be made available to the employee.

Employers should ensure that their terms or conditions for sick pay or sick leave and the manner in which those conditions operate do not exclude pregnancy or maternity-related illness, as to do so would be in breach of the Employment Equality Act, 1998 and the EU Directive on equal treatment (see *Todd v Eastern Health and Social Services Board* [1997] IRLR 410).

1.5.13 PENSION

Pension should always be referred to where it is part of the employment relationship. It may be best to simply refer to the pension entitlement being subject to the terms of the trust deed and rules and being dependent on the operation of the scheme by the trustees. Most schemes allow for the termination of the scheme or the suspension of payments by the principal employer which effectively allows an employer to discontinue pension entitlement under the contract. Schemes must in turn comply with the Pension Act, 1990. Care must be taken to ensure that employees are not excluded from pension schemes in situations where they may be able to claim entitlement by virtue of direct or indirect discrimination. Employers may inadvertently create a situation of indirect discrimination fully believing that they have no obligation to provide a pension in line with the general common law position in that regard but where they provide pension to workers of a different type or class and are held to have indirectly discriminated against those excluded from the pension scheme, pension entitlement may follow—see the European Court of Justice decision in *Magorrian and Cunningham v Eastern Health and Social Services Board and Department of Health and Social Services* [1998] IRLR 86 and *Hill and Stapleton v Revenue Commissioners* [1998] ELR 225.

1.5.14 RETIREMENT AGE

Many employers omit to make reference to retirement age because it is provided for in the pension scheme. Given that most statutory remedies subsist until an employee reaches 65 or 66 years of age, unless there is a specified contractual retirement age, employers should specify the actual age. That age may in turn be subject to variation within the terms of the pension scheme. The possibility of such variation should also be referred to by the employer. See *Buckley v Ceimici Teo* UD 528/80 where, at the time the claimant commenced employment, there was no contractual provision and the normal retirement age was 70 years. His employment was terminated when he reached 65 which was the pension age. The claimant maintained he was entitled to continue working until the normal retirement age of 70. The respondents, however, were in a position to produce documentary evidence that the normal retirement age had changed to 65 years and that the claimant was aware of this. The dismissal was held to be fair.

The issue of age, retirement age and fitness to work was considered by the High Court in *Donegal County Council v Porter* [1993] ELR 101. The respondents were employed by the county council as part-time firemen. When they commenced service the retirement age was 60. In recent years the policy of Donegal County Council, in common with other fire authorities in Ireland and Britain, has changed in favour of compulsory retirement at age 55 for firemen. Firemen engaged in recent years have a contractual provision to this effect. The reason for this is because the work has become more hazardous and stressful and requires more agility and flexibility. In December 1985 the Department of the Environment issued a Directive recommending the introduction of a retirement age of 55 and compulsory annual medical examination for all operational personnel.

The respondents' contracts provided for retirement at age 60 and they never at any time agreed to an alteration or variation in their contract. The county council subsequently retired them at age 55 which the court held was an attempt to unilaterally alter the contract and was in breach of contract unless it could be justified in some other lawful way which it was not.

The council put forward a strong plea with expert evidence that employees should retire at 55 and made reference to the Safety, Health and Welfare Act, 1989, s 61. The court held, in dismissing the claim of the county council to be entitled to compulsorily retire firemen at 55, that there is a statutory duty to observe but it can be observed

> 'by a much less draconian measure than dismissal at the age of 55 and one which does not involve a blatant disregard for the Council's contractual obligations . . . they can comply with their statutory obligation in requiring . . . the respondents to undergo medical examination from such age and at such frequency as they consider necessary to assure all persons concerned of the physical fitness of the men in the fire-fighting services . . . this is consistent with the terms implicit in the men's contract of service— while fit and capable they have a contractual expectation of service to age 60—if not fit and capable there are "substantial grounds justifying dismissal".'

1.5.15   GRIEVANCE PROCEDURE

In the interest of good industrial relations and to avoid industrial action taking place without the employer at least having an opportunity to consider the matters at issue, employees should be bound to process any grievance they have in a specified manner. Grievance procedures may be constructed quite simply by proving an *obligation* on employees to raise their grievance at the next level supervisor, manager etc and, if the matter is not determined at that stage, appeal to a further higher level. For senior executives grievances should be referable to either the managing director or board of directors. Sexual harassment policies frequently make reference to grievance procedures and require that any problem in relation to alleged sexual harassment should be treated as a grievance although the nature of sexual harassment complaints may be required to be dealt with in somewhat different manner and will require particular undertakings of confidentiality.

1.5.16   DISCIPLINARY PROCEDURE

With a very heavy emphasis on the following of procedures in the processing of disciplinary action, and in particular dismissals, laid down by courts and tribunals over the years, employers should have a specified disciplinary procedure. There is no requirement to have an over-elaborate procedure, simply a procedure specifying the following:

(a)   what will be done in the event of a complaint or allegation being made;

(b)   how many stages are likely to be followed in each event;

(c)   the right of the employer to choose the appropriate stage and/or penalty depending on the nature of the matter at issue;

(d)   the right of representation; and

(e)   whether there is a right to appeal against the imposition of disciplinary penalty—it should be kept in mind that the EAT does not have regard to appeals against dismissal in assessing whether the original dismissal was fair or unfair.

1.5.17   RESTRICTIVE COVENANTS

1.5.17.1   Introduction

Restrictive covenants and the right of employees to compete with their employers after they leave employment, and the law relating to the proprietary interests of an employer in trade secrets and information imparted to an employee while in employment all raise very considerable practical difficulties in the area of employment law and contract law. In order to understand how the respective parties' rights and entitlements are to be treated regard must be had both to the common law position and the changes effected by the provisions of the Competition Act 1991. Both of these areas are dealt with below.

At common law an employer is entitled to expressly protect, and by terms and conditions implied in the contract to have the law protect, his trade secrets and confidential information and, in certain circumstances, to limit the ability of an employee to compete after employment has terminated. Traditionally the common law categorised such restrictions as restraints on trade and took the view that they were prima facie unlawful unless they could be shown to be reasonable in protecting an interest that is entitled to be protected, is reasonable in its intended duration and reasonable in respect of its geographic scope or product scope.

1.5.17.2   Fidelity and loyalty

The common law courts will imply a duty of fidelity and obligations of loyalty in all contracts of employment. This duty is one of the most basic elements of the employment relationship. In 1888 it was held that a company's managing director who received a secret commission for the placing of contracts was in breach of an implied duty of good faith to his employer. He had the employing company make contracts with a third party company in which he was a shareholder, thereby receiving benefit from the employing company, albeit indirectly, and was held to be liable to his employer to account for such money earned and, in failing to do so, to be in breach of contract (*Boston Deep Sea Fishing & Ice Co v Ansell* (1888) 39 Ch D 339). In *Redding v Attorney-General* [1951] AC 507 a British Army sergeant turned a blind eye to a criminal practice which resulted in him making substantial money in respect of which the House of Lords, per the judgment of Lord Oaksey commented:

> 'I do not think that there is any difficulty in imputing to a servant an implied promise that he will account to his master for any moneys he may receive in the course of his master's business, or by the use of his master's property, or by the use of his position as his master's servant.'

This duty has been held to include an obligation not to compete with the employer while in his employment. The duty clearly applies to the normal hours of work but does it also apply to spare-time work? In *Thomas Marshall (Exporters) Ltd v Guinle* [1978] 3 WLR 116 the court considered a situation where, during working hours, the managing director was trading in competition with the employing company, and held his actions to be unlawful.

In *Hivac Ltd v Park Royal Scientific Instruments Ltd* [1948] 1 Ch 169 the employer succeeded in preventing competing activity during the employee's free time as they were held to be entitled to protect confidential information. Contrasted with that is the case of *Nova Plastics Ltd v Froggatt* [1982] IRLR 146 where a manual worker was held not to be in breach of duty where he worked for a competitor of the employer in his spare time. This implied contractual duty of good faith was held to only apply during the currency of the contract of employment. The EAT has upheld dismissals as being fair where the employee has breached or threatened to breach the contractual duty of good faith and loyalty. In *Preece v Irish Helicopters Ltd* UD 236/84 the employee had a specific provision in his terms and conditions of employment not to compete with the employing company. In the course of its determination the EAT commented:

> 'An employer is entitled to insist that an employee does not interest himself in a company which will compete with the business of the employer. Failure of the claimant to commit himself not to do anything while in the respondent's employment in pursuit of his own interest which might conflict with the interest of his employer was reasonably construed as a breach of duty or loyalty.'

In *Mulchrone v Feeney* UD 1023/82 the EAT upheld a dismissal of an employee working for a direct competitor in her spare time. The EAT has taken contrasting positions in situations where an employer has dismissed an employee in fear of potential breach of the duty of fidelity. In *Goggin Carroll & Co v Dineen* UD 106/85 an employee who had a relationship with a person working in a competing business was offered an alternative position in another branch of the employing company but refused it as a result of which she was dismissed. The EAT held that the dismissal was unfair as 'the fear of an inadvertent slip is not grounds for dismissal'. In *Coffey v Alcan Metal Centres (Dublin) Ltd* UD 603/90 the respondent was a substantial company with two main competitors in Dublin. The pricing or rebating of products was highly sensitive and if leaked to either competitor, it was submitted, could have caused considerable damage to the employing company. The respondent's brother and fiancé worked for the company. Both left within a short period of time to join one of the two competitors. The claimant subsequently married her fiancé. The company explained its concerns to the employee about the possibility of breach of confidence while not aware of any actual breach of confidence. Discussions were had about what could be done to avoid a dismissal. No suitable alternative position was available. The claimant was dismissed. The EAT held that where an employer had a real and significant concern bona fide derived from circumstances which could reasonably justify such concern, and the circumstances did not reasonably permit the adoption of an alternative solution to that of dismissal then dismissal was justified. See also *Fairbrother v Stiefel Laboratories (Ireland) Ltd* UD 665/85.

When the contract comes to an end the duty also comes to an end unless the contract contains a specific provision whereby the parties have agreed that restrictions will continue to apply. That is not the case, however, where the employer is seeking to protect confidential information or trade secrets. An employee working out his notice, or on 'garden leave' whereby he is still employed and still in receipt of remuneration but is not required to work, remains under the contractual duty of good faith (see *J A Mont (UK) Ltd v Mills* [1993] IRLR 172).

1.5.17.3 Confidential information and trade secrets

While the common law duty and many restrictive covenants provide for the protection of an employer's confidential information and trade secrets, in determining the enforcement of these terms, the information sought to be protected must be examined to see if it has the necessary quality of confidentiality; if not it will not enjoy the protection sought to be conferred on it no matter how clear the duty or the terms of the restriction.

Faccenda Chicken Ltd v Fowler [1986] IRLR 69 set out the proposition that something which may properly be categorised as a trade secret and is known, or should be known to the former employee as being such, remains protected after the employment has ceased even in the absence of the employer pointing out to the employee the precise limits of what he seeks to protect as confidential or binding the employee on foot of a written agreement.

In *Lancashire Fires Ltd v S A Lyons & Co Ltd* [1997] IRLR 113 the second-named defendant had worked for the plaintiffs and had become familiar with trade secrets. He left and set up his own business. The Court of Appeal held that given his position in the plaintiff company the second defendant must have known that the information he exploited after he left their employment was properly a trade secret belonging to the plaintiff and therefore he was in breach of an obligation of confidence in using the process for his own benefit.

See also *Printers and Finishers Ltd v Holloway* [1965] 1 WLR 1; *Sun Printers Ltd v Westminster Press Ltd* [1982] IRLR 292 and *British Railways Board v Natarajan* [1979] ICR 326.

1.5.17.4   What is protected

It is not essential that an employer has a written or express term in a contract of employment to protect confidential information and trade secrets. The common law will protect confidential information and trade secrets if it can be shown that the information sought to be protected is of such a nature that confidentiality must apply to it or that it be treated as a trade secret. In *Faccenda Chicken Ltd v Fowler* the Court of Appeal examined various types of information and set out the principles that would apply in its protection and held as follows:

(a)   In the absence of any express term in a contract of employment the obligations of an employee in respect of the use and disclosure of information are the subject of implied terms.

(b)   While the employment subsists the obligations protecting the employer's information are included in the general implied common law term imposing a duty of good faith and fidelity on an employee.

(c)   When the employment ceases the obligation not to use or disclose information covers only information that is of a sufficiently high degree of confidentiality as to amount to a trade secret. The obligation does not continue to cover all of the information covered prior to termination. In determining what constitutes a trade secret no hard and fast criteria can be laid down but the following will be taken into account:

    (i)   the nature of the employment—as some employments may impose a higher obligation than others;

    (ii)   the nature of the information itself—some matters clearly qualify as trade secrets, others may be less obviously so; and

    (iii)   whether the employer impressed on the employee the confidentiality of the information. While the employer cannot prevent use or disclosure merely by telling the employee that the information is confidential his attitude may provide evidence that is of use in determining the question as to how confidential the information actually is.

The distinction between trade secrets and what is merely confidential during the currency of the employment and usable by the employee when employment ends was also considered in *Roger Bullivant Ltd v Ellis* [1987] IRLR 491. See also *Cantor Fitzgerald (UK) Ltd v Wallace* [1992] IRLR 215 dealt with at **1.5.17.10** below.

The UK High Court drew a distinction between two types of knowledge that may be acquired by an employee in the course of employment, one of which is protected, the other which is not, in the case of *SBJ Stephenson Ltd v Mandy* [2000] IRLR 233. Mr Mandy had been employed by a firm of insurance brokers (SBJ) and his contract contained a clause restricting him from disclosing or using information of which he became possessed while in the service of the company. Mr Mandy sought to take business from SBJ when he left and joined another insurance broker. The information used was the identity of SBJ clients and knowledge of their renewal dates, cover, premiums etc. The judge drew a distinction between *'objective knowledge'* which is the property of the employer and *'subjective knowledge'* which is the employee's own property. In this case, however, the judge stated that what the employee innocently remembered of SBJ's business

> 'may be objective knowledge or subjective knowledge. Therefore, whether the recollected identity of customers is capable of legitimate protection has to be decided on the evidence of the case. The fact that the employee could remember the customers and go to them to obtain information which the covenant purported to protect could not in itself make the covenant too wide and therefore invalid.'

The court granted SBJ an injunction against Mr Mandy in the particular circumstances of that case.

1.5.17.5   Whistle blowers

'Whistle blowers' are protected in law. It is not possible to prevent the disclosure of wrongdoing under a duty of confidence. Given the interest of the media in business, and the possibility of employees disclosing information to the media, as stated in *Faccenda Chicken* an employer cannot choose what to describe as 'confidential'. The information must have the necessary element of secrecy or confidentiality attaching to it in order to be protected. Even if the information has the necessary element of confidentiality attaching to it to qualify under the *Faccenda Chicken* test disclosure may be legitimate where it is in the public interest that such information should be disclosed. In *National Irish Bank Ltd v RTE* [1998] 2 ILRM 196 the Supreme Court upheld the disclosure by RTE of confidential information in the public interest. The court balanced the public interest in the maintenance of confidentiality and the public interest in defeating wrongdoing and held that where the publication of confidential information could be of assistance in defeating wrongdoing then the public interest in such publication may outweigh the public interest in the maintenance of confidentiality. Keane J stated:

> 'The authorities . . . make it clear that where someone is in possession of confidential information establishing that serious misconduct has taken place or is contemplated the courts should not prevent disclosure to persons who have a proper interest in receiving information.'

Disclosure of such information will only be allowed to appropriate persons or authorities and whistle blowing will not be allowed indiscriminately. The dissemination of such information cannot be to the world at large. See also *Gartside v Outram* (1857) 26 LJCH 113 and *Initial Services Ltd v Putterill* [1968] 1 QB 396 and *Re A Company Application* [1989] ICR 44. In *Camelot v Centaur Communications Ltd* [1998] IRLR 80 Camelot obtained a restraining order preventing Centaur from publishing certain financial information which had been made known to a journalist employed by Centaur. Camelot sought the return of documents in the possession of Centaur to its system, identifying the source of the leak whom they believed to be an employee of theirs. They wanted to identify the source and dismiss the employee as otherwise their activities would continue to suffer damage and in order to protect all of their confidential information from disclosure. In the UK the Contempt of Court Act 1981 restricts the entitlement to the return of information and/ or the making of disclosure of a source. The Court of Appeal, however, held that it was proper to make an order requiring Centaur to return the confidential documents to enable Camelot to identify the employee responsible for leaking the information and dismiss him. The court stated inter alia:

> '[A]n employer has a legitimate and a continuing interest in enforcing an obligation of loyalty and confidentiality against an employee who has made unauthorised disclosure and use of documents acquired by him in his employment.'

1.5.17.6 Restrictions on competing with employer after termination of employment

There is no common law restriction on a former employee competing with his employer or soliciting the employer's clients and customers in the absence of a specific contractual restriction on doing so. However, if an employee breaches the employer's proprietary rights in confidential information or trade secrets in the course of competing with the former employer, the employer can prevent the unlawful use of such information or trade secrets thereby limiting the damage that might be done by such competition. While employees are entitled to retain information in their heads and to use their established personal contacts and relationships, copying customer lists or details is a breach of the employer's proprietary rights. In *Robb v Green* [1895] 2 QB 315 Green copied the names and addresses of customers from his employer's books intending to solicit them after he left employment. The court held that he had a duty not to breach the employer's proprietary rights in the information contained in its books and Green was restrained from using the information he had obtained. This may be contrasted with *Diamond Stylus Co Ltd v Bauden Precision Diamonds Ltd* [1973] RPC 675, where the employee left employment and solicited his former employer's customers on the basis of information he had retained in his head. The number of customers was quite small and he was able to recall all of the necessary details. The employer failed to obtain an order restricting him. In *Laughton v Bapp Industrial Supplies Ltd* [1986] ICR 634 two employees in their own time and on their own stationery wrote to their employer's customers advising them that they were setting up a business and, while not directly soliciting business, made it clear that they would be available to do business with them. It was held that there was no breach of the duty of fidelity.

The rights and entitlements of employers and employees must be distilled from the three sources of law on this topic, the common law, the law of contract and a relatively limited intervention of statute law.

1.5.17.7 Soliciting business

There is no common law restriction on former employees canvassing or soliciting business being done or previously done by their former employer. Restrictions on soliciting the business of a former employer may apply where the employer can show that protected confidential information or trade secrets have been violated or, alternatively, where there is a specific contractual commitment against soliciting business. Even where there is such a specific written provision it can be difficult to define what is meant by 'soliciting' or 'solicitation'. The parties may be clear what they mean but the use of such terminology can lead to difficulties and requires great care in draftsmanship. Where possible the use of such a term should be qualified by expressly stating what it means rather than leaving it to a court to define the term.

As to whether 'solicitation' means actively seeking business from customers of the former employer or whether ex-employees can be restrained when they are approached by the customers (ie when the customer makes the initial contact,) see the contrasting decisions in *John Michael Design plc v Cooke* [1987] 2 All ER 332 and the unreported Court of Appeal decision in *Merrill Lynch Pierce Fenner v Besman* (5 December 1985). The limits of the common law or implied protections of employers are set out in the Court of Appeal decision in *Wallace Bogan & Co v Cove* [1997] IRLR 453. The three defendants were solicitors who left the plaintiff firm, each giving four weeks' notice of termination and informing the plaintiffs that they intended setting up together on their own account. They were then placed on garden leave for the notice period by the plaintiffs. After leaving the employment of the plaintiffs the defendants wrote to clients with whom they had dealings while employed with the plaintiffs informing them of the existence of the new firm, the type of work undertaken and offering to act for them if they wished. A number of clients left the plaintiffs and transferred their instructions to the new firm. The contracts under which the defendants had been employed by the plaintiffs did not contain any express covenants restricting their dealings with former clients after their employment terminated. The plaintiffs sought to get such undertakings in writing after the defendants had given notice but the defendants refused to give them. The plaintiffs applied for an injunction in the High Court in order to prevent the defendants from canvassing or soliciting their clients. An interlocutory injunction was granted by the High Court on the basis that there was a serious issue to be tried as to whether there should be implied into the contracts of service between solicitors and the firms employing them an obligation after their contracts terminate not to canvass or solicit customers of the employing firm with whom they had dealt. The judge in the High Court went on to say that he believed 'solicitors are regarded by the law as having a more onerous obligation imposed on them because of the special position which they occupy in relation to the client'. On appeal the Court of Appeal reversed the decision, discharged the injunction and, in dismissing the plaintiff's claims, held:

> 'In the absence of an express covenant there is no general restriction on ex-employees canvassing or doing business with customers of their former employers. This rule applies to solicitors as much as to any other trade or profession. In the eye of the law all are equal. Although in canvassing their former employer's clients solicitors are taking advantage of a professional connection with those clients, that connection is no different in principle from the trade connection that, for instance, milk roundsmen may acquire with their employer's customers. Clients and customers alike represent the employer's goodwill which the employer is entitled to protect by an express covenant in reasonable restraint of trade but which is not protected for them by an implied term if they do not bother to extract an express covenant forbidding solicitation after employment has ended. In the present case there was no express covenant restricting the defendant solicitors' dealings with former clients after their employment terminated. Therefore after leaving the plaintiffs and together setting up a new firm they were not in breach of any contractual obligation in writing to the plaintiff's clients and canvassing their business.'

In *International Consulting Services (UK) Ltd v Hart* [2000] IRLR 227 Mr Hart had a restriction in his contract which provided that for a period of twelve months following the termination of his employment he would not 'canvass, solicit, approach, deal or contract with any company, firm or person who at any time during the 12 months immediately preceding the date of termination is or was' negotiating with ICS or was a client or customer or in the habit of dealing with ICS. ICS were dealing with a prospective customer during Mr Hart's employment and after he left he took up a course of dealing with that company. ICS sought to restrict him from doing so. Mr Hart argued that simply because ICS were negotiating with that company they did not have a legitimate interest to protect in restraining him and, further, that a restriction that stopped him dealing with third parties with whom ICS were simply 'negotiating' was too vague to be enforceable. The High Court rejected his claims and granted ICS an injunction. The court stated that 'negotiations' must mean more than a customer simply expressing an interest in dealing with a company and stated:

> 'What is required is a discussion between the parties about the terms of a contract which both parties have in view and which is a real possibility. In most cases, whether there have been negotiations will be clear on the facts. Where it is not the court has to make up its mind as part of the ordinary process of interpreting a contract.'

If solicitation arises from the abuse of documentation or information in respect of which the former employer can claim a proprietary interest, as in *Robb v Green* [1895] 2 QB 315, solicitation would be restricted if the use of the information upon which the solicitation was based was to be restricted.

1.5.17.8 Poaching staff

Not all staff of a business are liable to cause significant commercial damage if they leave the employment, but if such staff were to leave and join up with staff that are more obviously liable to cause difficulty, the problems for the transferee can be greatly compounded. Some employers seek to protect their business by the inclusion in contracts of employment of key staff of a restriction preventing such key staff from poaching or enticing away from the employer other staff whom the key people may need to assist them in the event that they leave the employment and become engaged in a competing enterprise. These clauses are not directed against the staff sought to be enticed away but rather are intended to be enforceable against the departing staff who need such people to assist them in their new enterprise. The validity of such clauses is unclear. In the context of non-solicitation clauses, the Court of Appeal has cast doubt upon the validity of clauses restraining employees from poaching their former employer's staff. In *Hanover Insurance Brokers Ltd v Schapiro* [1994] IRLR 82 the court refused to enforce a restrictive covenant under which the employee agreed, for twelve months after termination of employment, not to 'solicit or entice any employees of the company to the intent or effect that such employee terminates that employment'. The court pointed out that 'the employee has the right to work for the employer he wants to work for, if that employer is willing to employ him'. While the court accepted that the goodwill of the employer's business depended upon its staff, it distinguished staff from assets of the company 'like apples or pears or other stock in trade'. The court held:

> 'the restriction as drawn would apply to all employees of Hanover, irrespective of expertise or juniority and would apply to those who were employees at the time of the solicitation or enticement, even if they had only become employees after all the defendants had left Hanover's service.'

The *Hanover* case was a decision of the Court of Appeal at interlocutory stage. The Court of Appeal effectively reversed its finding in *Hanover Insurance Brokers* in the later case of *Dawnay Day & Co Ltd v De Braconier D'Alphen* [1997] IRLR 442 when the court held:

> 'The judge was also entitled to hold that the clause in the managers' service agreements prohibiting them for a year after their employment terminated from soliciting or enticing away anyone who, during the managers' employment, was a director or senior employee of the company, was not unreasonable. An employer's interest in maintaining a stable trained workforce is one which can properly be protected within the limits of reasonableness by means of a non-solicitation covenant, although it does not follow that it will always be so. The employer's need for protection arises because the ex-employee may seek to exploit the knowledge which he has gained of employees' qualifications, rates of pay and so on. In the present case the managers had acquired confidential information of that kind and, in the circumstances, the one year restriction was justified. It could not be accepted the reference to "senior employee" was so uncertain that the covenant should be regarded as unenforceable on that ground alone. The broad classification was clear and there was no reason to suppose that applying it would present any undue difficulty to anyone with knowledge of the kind of business carried out by the company in the present case. Moreover it was not clear what other formula could be adopted if something more precise and detailed was required.'

See also *Alliance Paper Group plc v Prestwich* [1996] IRLR 25. In *SBJ Stephenson Ltd v Mandy* [2000] IRLR 233, which is referred to in more detail at **1.5.17.4** above, the UK High Court considered a clause restraining Mr Mandy from soliciting employees of the company and held that the stability of the workforce was a legitimate interest which the company was entitled to protect, having invested a great deal in training and because the staff were its prime asset. The clause in that case was upheld as being legitimate and necessary to protect that legitimate interest of the employer.

1.5.17.9 Restrictive covenants permitted in contract

The general common law principle as referred to at **1.5.17.7** above is that the law will not uphold restraints on normal trade. The law will, however, allow the restriction in specific contractual terms where the following circumstances exist.

1.5.17.10 Where employer has legitimate interest to protect

This is an area that gives rise to practical difficulty and may tend to be overlooked. Many employers believe that if there is a general prohibition on certain conduct then the former employee cannot engage in such conduct. That is not the case. The employer must isolate and define the interest that is being or may be damaged by the employee; restricting general competition will not be sufficient (see *Herbert Morris Ltd v Saxelby* [1916] AC 688 and *Office Angels Ltd v Rainer-Thomas & O'Connor* [1991] IRLR 214).

While it is clear that, at common law, employers are entitled to protect, by way of restraint, a proprietary right such as a customer base, this does not mean that former employees can always be lawfully prevented from taking the company's customers with them when they leave. In *Cantor Fitzgerald (UK) Ltd v Wallace* [1992] IRLR 215, the English High Court held that an employer could not claim a proprietary interest in, and protect for itself, the customer connection an employee builds up during the course of employment where, in truth, that client connection is a function of the employee's personal qualities, such as personality, temperament and ability to get on with people. In that case, the court declined to enforce a restrictive covenant restraining bond dealers from working in a competing business after their employment terminated, because the court found that the skills and art of the job of producing clients lie in the make-up of the person performing it. In that case the court found that 'there was no magic about the job [the former employees] were doing'. The court heard evidence to the effect that it would not take long to train replacements for the former employees, that replacements could master the technique in three months. The court accepted that it would take longer 'to build up a reputation; and in the end it is that reputation, the speed, ease of dealing with, manner of dealing, trustworthiness in the sense of giving confidence to [clients] . . . that matters'. The court took the view that 'once the technique and procedure have been learned, the rest of the maturity as a broker depended on the personality and character of the individual . . . consequently, some would be better brokers than others because their personality and particular qualities suited the job of broking'. The court held that there was no proprietary right in any of these matters which an employer could claim to protect for himself as part of his business. The plaintiff claimed a proprietary right by virtue of the customer connection, built up while the employee was in his employment and before. The court, however, held that this customer connection was nothing more than those personal qualities to which reference is made above. It is, however, of interest to note that the court distinguished other types of employee 'such as the milk roundsman or the hairdresser [as] a very different category from the defendants'. The court accepted that

> 'just as the milk roundsman may endear himself to the housewives on his round, so an assistant in a ladies hairdressing establishment may well endear herself, either by her personality or by her skill, to the customers of the establishment who come there for service and that constitutes part of the goodwill of the employer's business which the employer is fully entitled to protect'.

However, the court stated that, in such cases, 'a goodwill is built up which attaches to the business and in addition, of course, when dealing with a milkman, for example, he is selling product also'. In that way, the court distinguished between brokers, relying solely on 'speed, ease of dealing with, manner of dealing, trustworthiness in the sense of giving confidence to [clients]' and ladies hairdressers, relying on 'personality or . . . skill'. The distinction is, to say the least, subtle. See also *Wallace Bogan & Co Ltd v Cove* [1997] IRLR 453.

In *Marshall v NM Financial Management Ltd* [1996] IRLR 20 Mr Marshall was employed as a commission agent under a contract which provided that he would only get renewal commissions after his employment terminated if he had at least five years' service at the date of termination, did not work in competition with the company or was aged 65 at termination. The court held that this provision was in reality a restriction on competition, was far broader than was necessary to protect any legitimate interest of the company in seeking to protect its existing clients, and was therefore void as being an unlawful restraint of trade. See also the linked case, involving the same parties, where one of the consequences of the striking down of the restraint was considered in *Marshall v NM Financial Management Ltd* [1997] IRLR 449 which is dealt with at **1.5.17.14** below. See also *Scully UK Ltd v Lee* [1998] IRLR 259 where Mr Lee was subject to a restriction that he not work with a company involved in certain types of business in which the employing company was involved. The court held that the restriction was such that it was not limited to a business which was in competition with his employers. There was no intention to limit the restriction to competing businesses in the wording of the restriction and the court found no reason to imply such a restriction. The restrictive covenant was therefore too wide and was struck down. This was against the background that the employee wished to work with a company which was not competing with the previous employer but used certain equipment and carried out certain processes similar to those manufactured and sold by the previous employer, albeit not in competition with it. This, not surprisingly, was held to be too wide. In this case also the High Court judge, in striking down provisions of the restrictions, severed them from the balance of restrictions which were upheld against the employee.

The concept of 'legitimate interest' was also examined and applied in the cases of *International Consulting Services (UK) Ltd v Hart* [2000] IRLR 227 and *SBJ Stephenson Ltd v Mandy* [2000] IRLR 233.

1.5.17.11 Restraint must be reasonable in terms of conduct sought to be restricted

Such conduct or activity must relate to the conduct or activity the employee engaged in while working with the employer and not be any wider (see *Stenhouse Ltd v Phillips* [1974] AC 391).

1.5.17.12 Duration of restriction must be reasonable

A thread running through all of the recent cases on restrictive covenants and their duration, is the assessment by the courts of the time it will take for the employer to take the necessary steps to protect the goodwill of the business and measuring the reasonableness of the restrictions sought to be imposed against such necessary time period or, alternatively, only allowing the restriction to continue for whatever time is determined to be, or have been, necessary to allow the employer to take steps to limit the damage done by the departure of the employee (see *Cantor Fitzgerald (UK) Ltd v Wallace* [1992] IRLR 215 at **1.5.17.10** above). If, therefore, a restriction were to be stated to last for two years but the court held that only six months was necessary to adequately protect the goodwill, the restriction is likely to be struck down as being unreasonable. If an employee is prevented from working in a competitive area for even a short time after leaving the employer, the impact of the employee's departure will be greatly lessened. It is hard to conceive of a situation where an employer would need more than one year to minimise the effect of an employee's departure and, if the effect is to be long term, the employer can do a lot in that period to protect his interests into the future. In many cases six months or less might well suffice. (See also *Dentmaster (UK) Ltd v Kent* [1997] IRLR 636.)

1.5.17.13 Geographical extent of restriction must be reasonable

In *Commercial Plastics Ltd v Vincent* [1965] 1 QB 623 it was held that where an employer had a worldwide restrictive covenant, but only operated in the UK, the covenant was geographically too wide and was unenforceable. A restriction on competing within a 25-mile radius of the employer's business may be too wide if the employer's customers are all within a 20-mile radius. In *Spencer v Marchington* [1988] IRLR 392 the court held that 'a restriction is too wide to be enforced if its area was more than was adequate to protect the employer's legitimate business interests'. In *Marley Tile Co v Johnson* [1982] IRLR 75 the employee was subject to a restrictive covenant covering more than 2,000 customers in the area of Devon and Cornwall. The restriction related to 'within any area in which you have been employed by the employer at any time during the twelve months before . . . termination'. It happened that Johnson was promoted during that twelve-month period which meant that, in two separate periods within the twelve months, he had operated in two different areas. The court held that the combined area thereby restricted was too wide in that Johnson could not possibly have known of, or come into contact with, more than a small percentage of the company's customers in the area. Lord Denning stated in the course of the judgment:

> 'Taking the size of the area, the number of customers, the class of products—because Marley have many lines other than roofing and tiling—it seems to me that the covenant is too wide to be reasonable.'

The courts will look at geographical restrictions, not just as to their extent but also as to whether they are appropriate or necessary. In *Office Angels Ltd v Rainer-Thomas & O'Connor* [1991] IRLR 214 the court examined a restriction precluding the defendants from opening an office of an employment agency anywhere within an area of about 1.2 square miles, including most of the City of London, for a period of six months and held that it was not appropriate or necessary for the protection of the plaintiff's connection with their clients holding:

> 'The area restriction was not an appropriate form of covenant because it would do little to protect the plaintiff's connection with their clients. The client's orders were placed over the telephone and it was of no concern to them where the office was located. It was unlikely therefore that the restriction would serve to prevent the defendants from attracting the custom of clients with whom they had dealings during their employment with the plaintiffs.'

In *Howlis & Co v Stocks* [2000] IRLR 712 the UK Court of Appeal examined a restriction on an assistant solicitor restraining him from setting up a competing business within 10 miles of the firm's office. Taking into account the geographical extent of that 10 miles and the cities and towns covered by it the County Court judge and the Court of Appeal on appeal held that the ambit of the covenant covering a 10-mile radius was reasonable.

1.5.17.14 Blue pencil clauses

It is frequently provided in contracts that if any particular provision of the agreement is held to be unenforceable then first the unenforceable clause is to be severed from other covenants and, secondly, the court is called upon to substitute what it considers to be reasonable. These two elements must be considered in drafting or seeking to rely on restrictive covenants and supportive clauses. The general principle is that severance will not be applied by the courts as enunciated in *Mason v Provident Clothing and Supply Co Ltd* [1913] AC 724, where it was held that there should only be severance if the enforceable part is clearly severable. This line was followed in *Living Design (Home Improvements) Ltd v Davidson* [1994] IRLR 69 where the Court of Session held, per Lord Coulsfield, that:

> '[T]here should be severance only if the enforceable part is clearly severable and even so, only where it is of trivial importance or technical and not part of the main import or substance of the clause. In the present case I think it very doubtful whether the offending part of the clause could be said not to be part of its main import and substance and it is certainly not trivial.'

See also *Attwood v Lamont* [1923] KB 571. In *J A Mont (UK) Ltd v Mills* [1993] IRLR 172, Simon Brown LJ indicated:

> 'as a matter of policy, . . . the Court should not too urgently strive to find within restrictive covenants, ex facie too wide, implicit limitations such as alone could justify their imposition'.

Simon Brown LJ went on to state that, in the event that the courts proved too amenable to limiting restrictive covenants which were, on their face, too wide, 'what possible reason would employers ever have to impose restraints in appropriately limited terms?'

In *Marshall v NM Financial Management Ltd* [1997] IRLR 449 the Court of Appeal, having already held that a restriction within a clause was unreasonable and unenforceable, was then asked to consider whether the balance of the clause, which gave rise to a commission entitlement, should stand. The court held:

'[T]he plaintiff . . . was entitled to enforce those parts of a contractual clause providing for payment of post-termination renewal commission which will not void an unreasonable restraint of trade. That part of the clause was excised did not mean the whole of the clause should be struck out. A party who has been freed from an invalid restraint of trade can enforce the remainder of the contract without it unless the invalid restraint forms "the whole or substantially the whole consideration" for the promise. The contract will be upheld even if the consideration for the promise of the promisee includes an invalid restraint. It will be struck down in its entirety only if, in substance and regardless of its form, it is an agreement for an invalid restraint.'

In *Marshall* the court was anxious to avoid removing a clause and by what was left consequentially imposing on the parties a condition that was radically different from what was originally contemplated. In severing the restriction on being paid renewal commissions in certain circumstances the court was anxious that it not deprive Mr Marshall of the payment. The court held that he had earned the commissions and was entitled to them without the burden of the restrictions attaching.

In *Sadler v Imperial Life Assurance Co of Canada Ltd* [1988] IRLR 388 it was held that severance could be effected if the following conditions were met:

(a) the unenforceable provision is capable of being removed without the necessity of adding to or modifying the wording of what remains;

(b) the remaining terms continue to be supported by adequate consideration;

(c) the removal of the unenforceable provision does not so change the character of the contract that it becomes *'not the sort of contract that the parties entered into at all'*; and

(d) that the severance must be consistent with the public policy underlying the avoidance of the offending term.

The courts have always had an understandable reluctance to rewrite a contract that at least one of the parties got wrong in the first place, but will allow severance where appropriate. In *Hinton and Higgs (UK) Ltd v Murphy* [1989] IRLR 519 Lord Dervaird observed:

'It has often been said that the courts will not make contracts for the parties. Here however as it seems to me the parties have agreed in advance they will accept as continuing to bind them such part of the arrangements which they have made as the court finds by deletion only to be alterations which permit the restriction to be regarded as reasonable . . . I do not see why the court should refuse to perform that role, not being one of rewriting the contract but of selecting that version of it which the parties have inter alia made with each other and enabling the bargain as so modified to stand.'

See also *Scully (UK) Ltd v Lee* [1998] IRLR 259 where the question of severance was considered. Severance was applied by the High Court judge and while the High Court was overruled by the Court of Appeal, the Court of Appeal allowed that severance could take place in certain circumstances.

Many agreements contain a provision that by signing the document the employee accepts that the restrictions contained therein are reasonable. The courts have no difficulty in ignoring these provisions. The courts have been invited to defeat such provision by accepting the argument of economic duress but the simple answer was given in *Hinton and Higgs* where the court held such a clause to be an attempt to oust its jurisdiction and therefore unenforceable.

In *Wincanton Ltd v Cranny* [2000] IRLR 716 the employee was restricted from being involved 'in any capacity . . . in any business of whatever kind within the UK which is wholly or partly in competition with any business carried on by the company'. The Court of Appeal held that this was too wide a restriction and therefore unenforceable. Sedley LJ sent out a strong message to lawyers drafting these contracts when he stated:

> '[T]hese are clauses drafted with the comprehensive particularity of a conveyancer and one of the morals of the many decided cases in this field of law is that those who live by this mode of drafting may find, when it comes to litigation, that they perish by it. Unlike leasehold covenants, restrictive employment covenants need particularity in those parts which limit their scope rather than in those which expand it.'

1.5.17.15 Employer's repudiation of contract

An employer who repudiates a contract or is involved in fundamental breach will normally be unable to rely on restrictive covenants in that contract which effectively crystallised as a result of the employer's breach. In *Cantor Fitzgerald International v Callaghan* [1999] IRLR 234 the defendants were employed by the plaintiffs as dealer brokers. Their contracts contained restrictive covenants aimed at preventing them working for competitors for a specific period. As part of an improved salary package aimed at retaining their services, the plaintiffs made non-forgivable loans to the staff with an assurance that there would be no tax liability during the period of the loan. Due to an error by the company the Revenue was misinformed about the nature of the loans and raised a tax charge on the loans. One of the plaintiffs' directors tried to sort out matters and to make money available to the staff to deal with the tax liabilities. Another director, however, intervened and decided not to advance money to meet the tax liabilities as an incentive to the employees to work harder. The employees handed in a joint written notice of termination intending to go to work for a competitor. In defending a claim by the company to enforce the restrictive covenants in their contracts the employees contended that the company could not rely on the restrictions as they were in repudiatory breach of contract in refusing to pay them the money to meet their tax liabilities on the loans which they had been assured would be tax-free. The High Court held against them but, on appeal, the Court of Appeal held that the employer was in fundamental breach in refusing to pay the employees sums due under their salary packages in connection with assurances given to them about tax liabilities. The Court of Appeal held that this was a deliberate refusal by an employer and not a mere failure or delay in paying agreed remuneration. The court held that consequently the entire foundation of the contract of employment was undermined and the injunction was discharged.

1.5.17.16 'Springboard' injunctions

Injunctive relief may be granted to employers where a departing employee seeks to use or rely on trade secrets or confidential information belonging to the former employer as a springboard to allow a more immediate advantage in setting up the competing business than might otherwise be available if the employee were to act lawfully and only use information, the use of which is permitted in law. The Court of Appeal held in *Roger Bullivant Ltd v Ellis* [1987] IRLR 491 that it is unlawful for an employee setting up a business on his own account to use confidential information belonging to his former employers as a springboard to establish himself in competition with them and such use will be restrained by injunction; but any such injunction should be limited to the period during which the unfair advantage may be expected to continue. In many cases where injunctions are granted they are granted on an interlocutory basis which means that they remain in effect until the full trial of the action. Depending on how long the case takes to come to full hearing will therefore determine how long the restriction remains in force rather than, in line with normal legal principle, remaining in force only as long as it should. In *Roger Bullivant* Mr Ellis set up a competing business and, on leaving the plaintiffs, took with him a large number of documents including a card index listing the company's trade contacts. The documents were recovered on the execution of an Anton Piller order and the employers then applied for and were granted an injunction restraining the former employees until after judgment in an action for damages, from entering into or fulfilling contracts made with or through any person whose name appeared on the card index. The injunction was granted by the High Court until the trial of the full action. The Court of Appeal was asked to decide whether the injunction ought to have been granted at all and if so whether it ought to have been granted until the trial of the action or for a more limited period. In its decision the Court of Appeal made the following statement:

(1) 'The principle established in *Robb v Green* [[1895] 2 QB 315]that an employee's duty of fidelity would be broken if he makes or copies a list of the employer's customers for use after his employment ends or deliberately memorises such a list even though there is no general restriction on an ex-employee canvassing or doing business with customers of his former employer, should be steadfastly maintained. The principle is one of no more than fair and honourable dealings. The plaintiffs were entitled to an injunction restraining use of the information contained in the card index.'

(2) 'An injunction to prevent unfair advantage being taken of the springboard that may be gained by the misuse of confidential information should not normally extend beyond the period for which the unfair advantage may reasonably be expected to continue. The law does not restrain lawful competition and in restraining unlawful competition it seeks to protect the injured and not punish the guilty. In the present case as the restrictive covenant contained in the contract was for a period of one year after termination they could not reasonably expect, and the law could not reasonably allow, a longer period and therefore regardless of when the full trial was to take place the restriction should only apply for that period of one year.'

1.5.17.17 Competition Act, 1991

The enforceability of restrictive covenants was altered by the provisions of the Competition Act, 1991.

Section 4(1) of the Act provides inter alia, as follows:

'*All agreements between undertakings, decisions by associations of undertakings and concerted practices which have as their object or effect, the prevention, restriction or distortion of competition in trade of any goods or services in the state or any part of the state are prohibited and void.*'

While not specifically aimed at employment contracts (and indeed, many commentators are of the view that the Act is an inappropriate means of controlling the employer/employee relationship), the Competition Authority has, in a number of cases, considered employment contracts which include restrictions placed on employees or former employees.

1.5.17.18 Notice on employee agreements

The Competition Authority, on 15 September 1992, issued a Notice on Employee Agreements and the Competition Act, which was published in Iris Oifiguil on 18 September 1992. The Notice was issued on foot of a number of requests regarding the status of employee contracts or agreements under the Competition Act. The Authority indicated its position relating to such agreements as follows:

(a) In general, employees are not deemed to be undertakings within the meaning of the Act, as employees normally act on behalf of an undertaking and do not therefore constitute an undertaking themselves.

(b) Accordingly, an agreement between an employer and an employee is not, in the Authority's view, an agreement between undertakings and therefore does not fall within the ambit of s 4(1) of the Competition Act. Such an agreement is not therefore notifiable to the Authority.

(c) Once an employee leaves an employer and establishes his/her own business, the Competition Authority then regards such an individual as an undertaking. In such circumstances an agreement with a former employer will be regarded as an agreement between undertakings, which is within the scope of s 4(1).

(d) While a single agreement between an individual and a former employer containing a non-competition clause might not have a substantial impact on competition, the effect of a network of such agreements could greatly restrict competition by foreclosing the market and the Authority stated its view that it would be difficult for such an agreement to satisfy the requirements specified for the grant of a licence under the Act.

In issuing this notice, the Competition Authority acknowledges that it is adopting a similar position to that taken by the European Commission in *Suiker-Unie v Commission* [1975] ECR 1663 (Case 40/73) concerning article 85.1 of the EC Treaty (upon which s 4(1) is based). The guiding principle adopted by the Commission in that case was that of economic unity—where an employee is in the employment of an employer, they are effectively deemed to operate as one economic unit. However, once the employee leaves that employment, the economic interests of the parties are no longer similar and the employee may be regarded as a separate and independent undertaking.

The further implications of the notice are that the Competition Act does not apply to employees who are competing during their employment, or employees who subsequently leave that employment and take up new employment with a new firm.

1.5.17.19 Apex v Murtagh

The leading decision of the Competition Authority on employer/employee agreements is *Apex Fire Protection v Murtagh* [1993] ELR 201. Mr Murtagh had been in the employment of Apex and left that employment to establish his own business. His contract of employment included a covenant which prevented him, for a period of two years after termination, from soliciting persons who were customers of Apex for two years prior to termination, and also included a confidentiality clause preventing him from disclosing information. Apex sought an injunction to prevent Mr Murtagh from breaching the terms of this contract, and notified the agreement to the Competition Authority requesting a certificate, or in the alternative, a licence.

Section 4 was used by Mr Murtagh as a defence in the Circuit Court. The injunction was granted on the basis that damages were not an adequate remedy, and pending the Competition Authority decision. It should be noted that this was a motion for an injunction only and was not a hearing of the case on its merits and cannot be taken to reflect judicial opinion on the interpretation of the Competition Act, 1991.

The Competition Authority, in its decision which issued in June 1993, refused a certificate or a licence in this case.

The Authority distinguished between a non-competition clause (which prevents an individual from entering the market on his own account) and a non-solicitation clause. In relation to the non-solicitation clause, Apex had argued that the restraints were justified because of the knowledge which their former employee had acquired during the course of his employment with the company and it further argued that the company was entitled to protect itself by virtue of the employment and training which it had provided to Mr Murtagh.

The non-solicitation clause was held to be overly restrictive and in the course of the hearing, Apex agreed to modify the clause to limit its applicability.

In relation to the confidentiality clause, Apex gave an assurance that the clause would only be used to protect confidential business information, and the Competition Authority accepted this, notwithstanding that the clause itself referred to 'any information'.

The Competition Authority held that the restrictions imposed went beyond what was required to protect the legitimate interests of the company and emphasised that any restrictions imposed should not exceed what was absolutely necessary to protect the interests of the company.

The clause was held to be in breach of s 4(1) because of the two-year time restraints which, the Competition Authority felt, were excessive. The Authority stated that while the European Commission had allowed a two-year period for the transfer of the goodwill of a business, the same period could not apply to employment contracts. The following conclusions can be drawn from the *Apex* decision

- A business which is owned and controlled by an ex-employee can constitute an undertaking, bringing the contract with the former employer within the ambit of the Act.

- Trade secrets and direct customer connections constitute legitimate proprietary interests of an employer which may warrant protection.

- The legality of restraints in any agreement depends on the facts of each individual case and the position of the employee in the firm.

- The decision in *Apex* implies that a one-year restraint is acceptable in order to allow the former employer to re-establish customer goodwill, following on the departure of the former employee.

- With regard to confidentiality clauses, the decisions of the Competition Authority to date have shown no notable deviation from the common law position. The *Apex* case makes it clear that it is necessary that an employer should be able to entrust confidential information to employees and the employer should be able to rely on such information being used only on the terms on which it is disclosed.

In the subsequent case of *Cambridge v Imari*, Competition Authority Decision no 24, the Authority held a part-owner and managing director of Imari, who was also an employee of the company, to be an undertaking within the meaning of the Competition Act.

1.5.18   NOTICE

1.5.18.1   Generally

Notice is probably one of, if not the, most important provisions in a contract of employment as far as an employer is concerned. In the absence of agreed notice an employer is obliged to give 'reasonable' notice. What is or is not reasonable may well be open to dispute allowing or obliging the parties to resort to the courts. An agreed or specified notice period will avoid litigation in this regard at least. Where a person is dismissed with notice paid for the notice period and not required to work it the employment does not come to an end until the end of the period of notice (see *Adams v GKN Sankey Ltd* [1980] IRLR 416).

Prior to 1977 a dismissed employee had only one form of legal remedy available, the breach of contract action known as wrongful dismissal. In order for an employee to succeed in a claim of wrongful dismissal it is necessary to show that a term of the contract was breached by the employer. It is rare to find a term in a contract that prevents or limits an employer's right to terminate. The most notable exceptions are specified purpose or fixed term contracts. Most contracts of employment are of indefinite duration and will continue in force until terminated by either party. The rights of both parties to terminate at common law are similar. A contract may be terminated on the giving of the requisite notice provided for in the contract. If notice is not specifically provided for in the contract, the common law implies the right of either party to terminate on the giving of reasonable notice. Following the normal common law principle of endeavouring to place the parties in no better position than they would have been had the contract been properly terminated an employee's damages will be limited to what he would have earned if proper notice had been given in accordance with the terms of the contract (*Sanders v Ernest A Neale Ltd* [1974] ICR 565; *Ridge v Baldwin* [1964] AC 40; and *Hill v C A Parsons & Co Ltd* [1972] Ch 305).

A prudent employer will provide a specific period of notice which will normally obviate any dispute and avoid a wrongful dismissal action unless the employer specifically refuses to honour the notice entitlement of the employee.

Notice provisions are one of the matters covered by the requirement to give details of terms and conditions of employment in writing contained in the Terms of Employment (Information) Act, 1994.

1.5.18.2 Contract silent as to notice

If a contract is silent as to notice entitlement it is a matter for the courts to assess what they consider to be reasonable notice in all the circumstances of the employment (see Dix and Crump, *Contracts of Employment* (6th edn) pp 137–38). In determining what notice would be reasonable in any particular case the courts will have regard to the following criteria:

(a) job function—the more senior a person is in an organisation the more likely he is to be held to be entitled to a longer period of notice;

(b) length of service;

(c) age and experience of the employee; and

(d) custom and practice in the particular employment if such exists (see *Produce Brokers Co Ltd v Olympia Oil and Cake Co Ltd* [1916] 2 KB 296). It is sometimes thought that reasonable notice will relate to the frequency at which remuneration is paid, eg monthly or weekly. That is not the case. Neither, as stated above, will regard be had to statutory notice entitlement as provided for in the Minimum Notice and Terms of Employment Act, 1973. If payment is made in lieu of notice this will normally suffice to cover an employee's entitlement as it would equate to the amount that he would expect to receive from a court in any event.

The absence of a notice provision in the contract will not be construed by the courts as granting employment for life (see *Salt v Power Plant Co Ltd* [1936] 3 All ER 322; and *McClelland v Northern Ireland General Hospital Services Board* [1957] 2 All ER 129). Even where the term 'permanent' is used or where a job is described as 'permanent and pensionable' this does not mean that it cannot be terminated by reasonable notice (*Walsh v Dublin Health Authority* [1998] ILTR 82; and *Grehan v North Eastern Health Board* [1989] IR 422).

1.5.18.3 Length of notice period

In *Lyons v M F Kent & Co (International) Ltd (in liquidation)* [1996] ELR 103 the High Court considered the length of notice to which an employee was entitled at common law. The court first held that the aged common law doctrine of *'general hiring'*, which implied employment for fixed periods of one year at a time, had fallen into disuse but that in any event it did not apply in the instant case. In considering what constituted *'reasonable'* notice in all the circumstances of this particular case Costello J was of the view that he got little assistance from decided cases because each case must depend on its own facts. He held that the modern world is far different even from the world of twenty years ago. In considering what was reasonable the court took the following into account:

(a) the plaintiff's status within a group of companies;

(b) the fact that he was engaged in very substantial work abroad;

(c) he carried very considerable responsibilities related to the size and nature of the contracts in which he was involved and the work took place in foreign countries;

(d) he was a professionally qualified person; and

(e) he was required to work abroad even though he was Irish and was based with his family in Ireland.

Costello J asked what would be said by the 'officious bystander' in the particular circumstances of this case and he considered it unlikely that a person would leave his profession in this country and travel abroad without at least a minimum of six months' notice and, in this case, considered twelve months' notice to be appropriate.

1.5.18.4 Clear and unequivocal

In order for notice to be valid it must be clear and unequivocal with a specific expiry date or be stated to occur on the happening of a specific event. Notice does not have to be in writing—unless specifically provided for in the contract—see *Hughes v Gwynned County Council* [1977] ICR 436. Calculation of notice is the period starting on the day after notice is given. If therefore an employee is told during the course of a working day that his employment is to terminate the notice does not start to run until the following day (see *West v Kneels Ltd* [1986] IRLR 430). Notice may be given at any time and during periods of illness or leave, but not maternity leave, as notice given during a period of maternity leave is deemed to be void under maternity legislation which is dealt with in more detail in Chapter 8: Maternity Rights of Employees.

Regard must also be had to the provisions of the Minimum Notice and Terms of Employment Act, 1973 (as amended). Section 4 sets out specific notice that an employer is required to give to an employee who is covered by the legislation. The notice is based on a sliding scale starting with one week's notice for those employed for up to two years with a maximum entitlement of eight weeks' notice for those employed for fifteen years or more. In all cases the notice required to be given by the employee is one week's notice. If the contractual notice is less than the statutory notice there would be a breach of the statute unless the statutory notice is given. If the contractual notice is longer than the statutory notice it will be deemed to include the statutory notice so two periods of notice do not have to be given and they can run concurrently rather than consecutively. The requirements of giving valid notice under the 1973 Act are dealt with by the Supreme Court in *Bollands Ltd (in receivership) v Ward* [1988] ILRM 382. See also *Waterford Multiport Ltd (in liquidation) v Fagan* [1999] ELR 185 and *Irish Leathers Ltd v Minister for Labour* [1986] IR 177. If an employee is dismissed by reason of misconduct he loses his entitlement to notice under the 1973 Act as per s 8 (see *Leopard Security Ltd v Campbell* [1997] ELR 227).

1.5.18.5 Expiry of notice period

Where a person is dismissed with notice, paid for the notice period and not required to work it, the employment does not come to an end until the end of the period of notice (see *Adams v GKN Sankey Ltd* [1980] IRLR 416). Regard should also be had to the statutory date of dismissal as defined under the Unfair Dismissals Acts, 1977–1993 which effectively provide that the date of dismissal shall be the date notice expires whether the notice is given or not and whether it is worked or whether payment in lieu is made (Unfair Dismissals Act, 1977, s 1). Where the employee is deemed to have lost his right to notice this provision would not have effect and the date of dismissal would be the last day worked. This is particularly relevant where long periods of notice, such as three months or more, are allowed for in a contract. This can cause difficulty in the transfer of an undertaking. A transferee might therefore take the view, mistakenly, that an employee with less than one year's continuous service would not have the right to claim unfair dismissal against the transferee in the event of his employment terminating and his seeking to initiate a claim under unfair dismissal legislation. Given that notice is added to the actual period of employment the notice period may carry the employee over the threshold of the one year's continuous service even though he may have only worked for the transferor for a relatively short period of time and not be an obvious employee covered by the Transfer of Undertakings Directive and Regulations at the time of transfer. With a six-month notice provision an employee is effectively covered by unfair dismissal legislation on the expiry of six months at work. An employer may place an employee on what is known as 'garden leave' during a notice period whether that notice is given by the employer or the employee.

In *Marshall (Cambridge) Ltd v Hamblin* [1994] IRLR 260 the employee had given notice and the employer cut it short but made payment in lieu of notice. The employee was entitled, as part of his contract, to commission on vehicles sold. The payment of commission was described by the contract as being 'at the absolute discretion of the company'. Commission at times constituted as much as 75 per cent of the employee's earnings. It was held that the employee had no right to work out his notice. Until such time as the notice period expired the contract of employment continued and the employer was entitled to utilise a term of that contract to bring the employment to an end at an earlier date and, where it was specified in the contract, make a payment in lieu of the remuneration that would have been earned during the notice period. The position was held not to be affected by the fact that the employee derived a major part of his remuneration from a discretionary commission payment. It was not accepted that it was an implied term of the employee's contract that the employers would not prevent the employee from placing himself in a position whereby the employer's discretion could be exercised and that the employers were in breach of that term in refusing to allow him to work out his notice.

It was held in *Marshall* that the nature of the payment in lieu fell within the category of what damages the employee might be entitled to for breach of contract. As there was no contractual entitlement to the commission there was no entitlement to be paid it during the notice period. The courts will not have regard to the provisions of the Minimum Notice and Terms of Employment Acts, 1973–1991 unless that legislation has been specifically incorporated into the contract. Notice provision might also cover a right to temporarily suspend the employment contract with or without pay due to shortage of work, during the currency of an investigation or because of a requirement for the employee to work for short-time.

1.5.18.6 Punitive damages—and duty of trust and confidence

The mutual duty of trust and confidence resting on both the employer and the employee has been outlined in a number of cases (see *TSB Bank plc v Harris* [2000] IRLR 157). If the employee is in breach this generally entitles the employer to terminate the contract but it would be rare that the employer would have the right to seek damages from the employee unless some specific and measurable damage was caused wilfully by the employee. If the employer is in breach the employee may leave and claim that he has been constructively dismissed. In some cases the actual reason for, or manner of, dismissal may be without foundation or substance, improper and consequently damaging to the employee. In general punitive damages or damages for distress or inconvenience are not available following a dismissal regardless of the manner in which the dismissal is carried out. Damages are limited to recoverable losses which cover all incidents of remuneration to which the employee was contractually entitled. It is well established that punitive damages cannot be awarded against the employer, the leading case being *Addis v Gramophone Co Ltd* [1909] AC 488, which has been affirmed in the more recent cases of *Bliss v South East Thames Regional Health Authority* [1987] ICR 700 and *O'Laoire v Jackel International Ltd* [1991] ICR 718.

A significant move away from the general principle was made, albeit in exceptional circumstances, in the case of *Malik v Bank of Credit and Commerce International SA (in compulsory liquidation)* [1997] IRLR 462. The plaintiffs were bank managers dismissed on grounds of redundancy by the provisional liquidators of BCCI. They claimed that their mere association with BCCI at the moment of its liquidation and the fraudulent practices which subsequently came to light caused them considerable personal disadvantage and stigma in the marketplace. They contended that there was an implied term in their contracts of employment that the employer would not, without reasonable and proper cause, conduct itself in a manner calculated to be likely to destroy or seriously damage the relationship of confidence and trust that must exist between an employer and an employee and in their circumstances, in light of such a breach, they were entitled to punitive, or what were described as 'stigma', damages. The Court of Appeal held:

(a) the managers were not entitled to damages for breach of contract in respect of losses which allegedly resulted from the stigma attaching to them as former employees of BCCI and the adverse effect that had on their employment prospects; and

(b) *'stigma damages'* cannot be recovered where an employee claims that his reputation has been damaged by the employer's breach of an implied term.

1.5.18.7 Principles of punitive damages awards

The Court of Appeal held that there were three well-established principles to be derived from the precedent cases as follows:

(a) an employer has no obligation to employ or pay an employee for longer than the period of notice for which the contract provides;

(b) damages are not recoverable for the manner of the breach, an award of exemplary damages being confined in practice to certain specific claims in tort; and

(c) damages are not recoverable for damage to or loss of an existing reputation. However, this principle does not apply where loss is sustained as the foreseeable consequence of a breach of contract in specific contracts such as apprenticeships or the promotion or preservation of a reputation, eg advertising or the opportunity to appear in a prestigious place or part for an actor.

In so holding the Court of Appeal stated that the object of the employment contracts in *Malik v Bank of Credit and Commerce International* was to employ, not to promote or preserve existing reputations or to prepare for future employment. The House of Lords on appeal reversed the finding of the Court of Appeal in relation to stigma damages and held as follows.

● The Court of Appeal had erred in holding the appellants could not bring claims for damages for financial losses allegedly suffered because the stigma attaching to their reputations as former employees of BCCI put them at a disadvantage in the labour market. The court had wrongly decided the case on the basis that there is a positive rule debarring recovery of damages for injury to an existing reputation.

● Damages for loss of reputation caused by breach of contract may be awarded provided that a relevant breach of contract can be established and the requirements of causation, remoteness and mitigation can be satisfied. If conduct by the employer in breach of the implied term of trust and confidence prejudicially affects an employee's future prospects so as to give rise to continuing financial losses and it was reasonably foreseeable that such a loss was a serious possibility, in principle damages in respect of the loss should be recoverable.

● The observations in *Addis v Gramophone Co Ltd* [1909] AC 488 could not be read as precluding the recovery of damages where the manner of dismissal involved a breach of the trust and confidence term and that caused financial loss. *Addis* was decided in the days before this implied term had been adumbrated. Now that the term exists, and is normally implied in every contract of employment, damages for its breach should be assessed in accordance with contractual principles. There is no basis for distinguishing in this respect between wrongful dismissal following a breach of the trust and confidence term, constructive dismissal following a breach of the trust and confidence term and a breach of the trust and confidence term which, as in the present case, only becomes known after the contract had ended for other reasons.

- An employer which operates its business in a dishonest and corrupt manner is in breach of the implied contractual term of trust and confidence. In agreeing to work for the employer an employee, whatever his status, cannot be taken to have agreed to work in furtherance of a dishonest business.

- In the present case therefore, on the assumption that BCCI had operated its business in a corrupt and dishonest manner, it was in breach of the implied term of trust and confidence. Since it was arguable that the employees might be able to establish as a matter of fact that the corruption associated with the bank undermined their employment prospects causing them financial loss there was a good cause for action and the appeal would be allowed.

1.5.18.8 Employer's wrongdoing

In a follow-on case to *Malik v Bank of Credit and Commerce International* the UK High Court has clarified an employer's obligations in relation to its own wrongdoing and has stated that there is no duty on an employer to disclose its breaches of contract. In *Bank of Credit and Commerce International SA v Ali* [1999] IRLR 226 the defendant and others were made redundant by BCCI as part of a restructuring. They received ex gratia payments which they accepted 'in full and final settlement of all or any claims whether under statute, common law, or in equity of whatsoever nature that exist or may exist'. Following *Malik* Ali and others wished to make claims against BCCI for stigma damages. The bank contended that they could not do so by virtue of the terms of the severance agreement they had signed. The employees argued that they were unaware of the bank's wrongdoing at the time they signed and that the agreement was invalid because the bank had failed to disclose that it was insolvent in carrying on a dishonest business and that had they known this they would not have signed the agreement. The High Court held that the agreement the employees signed 'was not invalidated by the employer's failure to disclose to the employees that, at the time the agreement was signed, it was carrying on a dishonest business and was insolvent'. The court went on to state:

> 'Since the agreement was a "compromise" rather than a "release" the employer did not owe the employees a duty to disclose its prior misconduct or breaches of contract before entering into the agreement. In the case of a release there is a duty of disclosure on the party obtaining the release of such claims against him but there is no such obligation in the case of a compromise. The essential difference between a compromise and a release is that in the case of a compromise there is a release of claims for valuable consideration and in the case of a release there is no such consideration. . . . [T]he employer was not under a duty by reason of the implied term of trust and confidence in an employment contract, to disclose, when it entered into the compromise agreement, that it had committed breaches of the contract. . . . [T]hat the employees did not know at the time they signed the compromise agreement that they had common law claims against the bank did not amount to a unilateral mistake such as to entitle the employees to impugn the agreement. The agreement was designed to afford the employer protection against any further claims by the employees and the employer agreed to make an additional payment for obtaining this protection. The fact that the employees did not focus on the claims covered by the agreement could not lead to any re-opening of the bargain. The real complaint of the employees was that, with the knowledge acquired since the collapse of the employer of the extent of its wrongdoing and, since the commencement of the proceedings in *Malik*, of the possibility of substantial claims and damages in respect

of the loss occasioned to them by such wrongdoing they now repent of what they see as a bad bargain and wish to be free of it. Such a complaint cannot vitiate a contract or give grounds for relief.'

1.5.19   SEARCH CLAUSE

Any attempt to search employees without their consent would constitute assault and battery. It may also constitute false imprisonment and/or give rise to defamation claims. Employers frequently provide therefore in contracts of employment that they have the right to search employees, their baggage, locker, vehicles etc. Given that there would be a considerable practical problem if an employee refused to be searched the employer may seek to resolve that difficulty in advance by further providing in such a clause that in the event of the employee refusing to submit to search this will be treated as misconduct (or gross misconduct if that is the definition in common use within the employment) and process the refusal through the disciplinary procedure. Employers frequently emphasise that they take a very serious view of such a refusal and dismissal is a possibility in such events.

1.5.20   PATENTS, COPYRIGHTS AND INVENTIONS

The common law position on patents, copyrights and inventions is set out in *Sterling Engineering Co Ltd v Patchett* [1955] 1 All ER 369 and *British Syphon Co Ltd v Homewood* [1955] 2 All ER 897. The Copyright Act, 1963 (as amended by the Copyright (Amendment) Act, 1987) provides at s 10 that the copyright in material made in the course of a person's employment belongs to the employer and not to the author. In some instances it can be difficult to ascertain whether the material sought to be copyrighted, and which relates to business of the employer and the work done by the employee, was actually created or made in the course of the employment, such as when created or made in the employee's spare time (see *Byrne v Statist Co* [1914] 1 KB 622 and *Stevenson Jordan and Harrison Ltd v Macdonald and Evans* [1952] ILTR 101). There is an exception contained in s 10(2) in respect of journalists (see *Beloff v Pressdram Ltd* [1973] 1 All ER 241 and *Re Sunday Tribune Ltd* [1984] IR 505).

An employer is also entitled to protect inventions under the terms of the Patents Acts 1964 and 1992. The position is less clear under the Patents Acts as there is no specific provision in the Acts determining when employees' inventions might be the property of their employers. Disputes can be decided by the Controller of Patents, Designs and Trademarks, originally under s 53 of the 1964 Act, and now s 96 of the 1992 Act, subject to appeal to the High Court as provided in that section. If the employee is obliged to carry out research and development work resulting in an invention the employer is likely to be deemed to be the owner of the patent thereby arising and the employee is deemed to hold the patent on trust for the employer in such circumstances (see *British Reinforced Concrete Ltd v Lind* (1917) 34 RPC 101; *Sterling Engineering Co Ltd v Patchett* and *Electrolux Ltd v Hudson* [1977] FSR 312).

A former employee can of course also be restrained from breaching an employer's rights in a registered design or a trade mark as with any person who breaches such rights. Employers may have rights under the Trade Marks Act, 1996 and any attempt by a former employee to breach the employer's rights under that legislation or proprietary rights arising thereunder can be restrained as would be the case with any person. An employer or transferor is also entitled to have computer programs protected under the terms of the European Communities (Legal Protection of Computer Programs) Regulations, 1993 which were implemented to give effect to Council Directive 91/250/EEC. Computer databases are also protected under EC Directive 96/9/EC.

1.5.21 SHARE OPTIONS

Most employers who offer share options do so on foot of detailed share option schemes. The contract may therefore simply refer to the availability of share options at the discretion of the employer and subject to the employer's share option scheme. Reference should in particular be made to the position that will pertain in the event of the employee's job function or geographical location changing or otherwise providing that the option will be available during the currency of the contract. Provision should be made for the position that would pertain on termination. In *Micklefield v SAC Technology Ltd* [1990] IRLR 218 the contract provided that the option holder must continue to be employed in order to exercise the option granted and the holder shall be deemed to have waived his right to damages for loss of option rights as part of any claim for compensation for loss of office. The court held that this was in the nature of an exclusion clause which applied to exempt the employers from liability to pay compensation for loss of rights under the option scheme in the event of termination of employment. Micklefield was held not to be entitled to recover damages for loss of his option rights even where he could show that he had been wrongfully or unfairly dismissed just prior to the date when the option became exercisable.

In contrast, the UK Employment Appeal Tribunal awarded compensation based on loss of value in share options forgone as a result of a dismissal in *Leonard v Strathclyde Buses Ltd* [1998] IRLR 693. In *Levett v Biotrace International plc* [1999] IRLR 375, Mr Levett was entitled to participate in a share option scheme which provided that the options would lapse immediately if the option holder became 'subject to the company's disciplinary procedures' leading to the termination of his contract. Mr Levett's employment was subsequently terminated. Mr Levett claimed that the termination was in breach of his contract and this was conceded at hearing by the company. In those circumstances the Court of Appeal held that the strict interpretation of the rule disqualifying Mr Levett from share options only applied where employment was lawfully terminated and applied the general rule of construction of a contract that a party to a contract cannot rely on its own wrong.

1.5.22 BULLYING AND HARASSMENT

It is well-established practice now that employers must meet their obligations to employees to create a work environment free of bullying and harassment by putting in place a policy or policies designed to prevent such bullying or harassment occurring in the first place and not just to deal with incidents when they arise. Failure to have such a policy can lead to liability being imposed on the employer the first time such an incident arises. Policies of this sort are rarely included in the text of a letter of appointment or contract but rather are contained in a separate document which is appended to or referred to and incorporated in the contract. The comprehensive grounds of discrimination contained in the Employment Equality Act, 1998 have heightened the need for comprehensive policies covering not just bullying, intimidation, harassment and sexual harassment but also any form of detrimental treatment by the employer or by fellow employees, of any person on any of the grounds specified in that Act including age, gender, race etc (see *Saehan Media Ireland Ltd v A Worker*, a Labour Court recommendation reported at [1999] ELR 41). The US Supreme Court has given two decisions following comprehensive judgments in the Court of Appeals in two harassment cases which analysed the employer's obligation to create a proper work environment and the operation of policies to do so in *Faragher v Boca Raton* [1997]–282 June 26, 1998 and *Burlington Industries Inc v Ellerth* [1997]–69 June 26, 1998.

1.5.23 E-MAIL, INTRANET AND INTERNET USE

Employers are conscious of the significant risks and legal liabilities that may arise where their employees use e-mail, intranet or internet facilities as part of their work. Employers have been held liable for defamation (see *Western Provident Association v Norwich Union*, 1997 (unreported) and a range of other possible legal liabilities such as sexual or racial harassment, copyright infringement, spreading of viruses, accessing of pornography and waste of computer capacity and employer's time. Increasingly employers are adopting policies setting out the rules and regulations relating to use of electronic information and equipment and again these policies are usually contained in a document separate from the actual letter of appointment or contract of service but referred to therein and incorporated as part of the contract or employment relationship.

1.5.24 RESIGNATION OF DIRECTORSHIPS OR OFFICES ON TERMINATION OF EMPLOYMENT

Resignation of directorships or other offices should be catered for in a contract of employment. In any event the Companies Act, 1963, s 182 provides that shareholders may by ordinary resolution remove any or all of the directors of a company from the board before their period of office expires. This provision takes effect notwithstanding anything in the articles of association or a contract of service. The power could be overwritten by the provisions of a shareholders' agreement governing how votes will be cast in respect of the removal of a director. Neither can a director for life be removed by this provision from a private company as per s 182(1).

1.5.25 PROPER LAW

The proper law of a contract is of particular importance where an employee may be required to work abroad. The employment by a foreign employer of a foreign citizen in Ireland is covered by unfair dismissal legislation (see *Scheel v Kelly Engineering Ltd* UD 535/86 and *Roder v Liebig International Ltd* UD 144/79). See also *McIlwraith v Seitz Filtration (GB) Ltd* [1998] ELR 105 where the claimant had a written contract of employment with the respondent company which was based in the UK. The contract provided that the area of work was the Republic of Ireland and Northern Ireland. The contract was stated to be subject to the laws of the United Kingdom. When the claimant claimed unfair dismissal here in the Republic of Ireland the respondent claimed that the contract provided that it be governed by the laws of the UK. The EAT held that such provision was void as being contrary to the Unfair Dismissals Act, 1977, s 13 and, as the UK was a party to the Convention on the Law Applicable to Contractual Obligations 1980 which became law in Ireland through the Contractual Obligations (Applicable Law) Act, 1991, article 6 of the Convention allowed the employee to choose the applicable law and he was therefore entitled to claim under the Unfair Dismissals Acts in the Republic of Ireland.

1.5.26 MISCELLANEOUS

There is almost no limit to the number of provisions that may be included in a contract of employment. Where lawyers are asked to draft a 'standard' contract of employment great care should be taken to ensure that the contract meets the actual needs of the specific employer and with the specific work sought to be done. Provisions that might be included in this regard are:

- attendance and punctuality;
- particular safety regulations;
- responsibility for property, tools or machinery;
- deportment, wearing of uniforms;
- severance of obligations;

- survival of obligations;
- waiver, where certain conduct may be tolerated from time to time it should be deemed not to be a waiver of any specific provision of the contract;
- requirement to hold a driving licence;
- right of residence in employer's property, this, under the law of landlord and tenant, merely creates a licence and not a tenancy;
- return to employer of all property, notes, copies etc on termination of the contract;
- reconstruction in receivership or liquidation and any surviving rights;
- maternity leave entitlements particularly where these are over and above statutory entitlement;
- compassionate leave;
- parental leave also subject to statutory entitlement;
- work standards;
- insider dealing; and
- holding of stocks and shares;

1.6 FIXED TERM AND SPECIFIED PURPOSE CONTRACTS

1.6.1 INTRODUCTION

Much confusion has arisen in recent times regarding the use and operation of fixed term and specified purpose contracts. They may be classified as one type of contract. In a fixed term contract the actual period of employment is specified. A specified purpose contract is identical except that the exact period of the contract cannot be measured but its life is measured by reference to the occurrence of an event or the cesser of a purpose.

At common law these contracts do not cause particular difficulty. If an employer agrees to employ a person for a specified period of time then, in the absence of a fundamental breach of contract, the employer cannot be absolved from that obligation except by the agreement of the employee. If A agrees to hire B for five years and after two years decides he has had enough of B, B must be paid the balance of the contract. B has of course the normal common law duty to mitigate his loss but, in the absence of mitigation, his loss must be measured at the full value to him of the balance of the contract. A prudent employer will therefore seek to put into such a contract a provision allowing for early termination. This may seem to be a contradiction in terms but the Court of Appeal held in *Dixon and Constanti v BBC* [1979] IRLR 114 that the words 'fixed term contract' referred to a contract for a specified term even though the contract is determinable by notice within that term.

1.6.2 ADVANTAGES AND DISADVANTAGES

An employer may enter into a fixed term or specified purpose contract in order to grant security of tenure to an employee which should tempt him to remain in the employment. While the contractual theory is all very well, if an employee were to abandon his employment under such a contract there is little or nothing the employer can do to remedy the problems thereby caused. While the employer could claim that there was a cost in having to seek a replacement that cost would have been, in theory at least, incurred on the normal ending of the contract anyway. The cost of hiring a replacement will be met in the main by the money saved in not having to pay the departed employee. If, however, an employer were to be engaged in a special project which was in some way delayed or put in jeopardy the employer may well be able to seek compensation from the employee who has breached the agreement to remain for the fixed term or until the cesser of the purpose. In practice, however, employers' prospects of actually recovering compensation are minimal.

Highly skilled employees may well seek fixed term or specified purpose contracts to give themselves security of tenure. Employers must be aware of the risks of using such contracts if they do not reserve unto themselves the right to terminate on notice within the life of the contract.

1.6.3 UNFAIR DISMISSALS LEGISLATION

1.6.3.1 Introduction

Most of the difficulty of using fixed term or specified purpose contracts has arisen under unfair dismissal legislation. The Unfair Dismissals Act, 1977 provides that the legislation shall not apply on the expiry of a fixed term contract or the cesser of the purpose of a specified purpose contract provided the following conditions are adhered to:

(a)   the contract is in writing;

(b)   the contract specifies that the Act will not apply on the ending of the period of the cesser of the purpose; and

(c)   the contract is signed by the parties.

Many employers have taken it as automatic that if they draw up a fixed term or specified purpose contract and comply with the above-mentioned conditions the employee has no right to claim unfair dismissal when the contract comes to an end. That may not be the case. If, on the ending of such a contract, an employee claims unfair dismissal the EAT will require to determine whether the contract was genuinely a fixed term or specified purpose contract or was in reality an open-ended employment dressed up as being for a fixed term or specified purpose. The leading EAT case on this point is *Fitzgerald v St Patrick's College, Maynooth* UD 244/78 reported in Kerr and Madden, *Cases and Commentary on Unfair Dismissals*, p 86.

1.6.3.2 Fitzgerald v St Patrick's College

The facts of *Fitzgerald v St Patrick's College, Maynooth* UD 244/78 were that a vacancy for a permanent junior lecturer arose in the college. Before a permanent appointment could be made certain procedures had to be followed. While these procedures were being followed a temporary appointment of Ms Fitzgerald was made by way of a fixed term contract for one academic year. The first attempt to make a permanent appointment failed and the permanent appointment was deferred. Ms Fitzgerald was reappointed for a further academic year as a temporary lecturer on foot of a fixed term contract for that academic year containing the necessary terms to provide for the exclusion of the Act. On the expiry of the contract and its non-renewal Ms Fitzgerald claimed unfair dismissal.

The college claimed that this was a case of a fixed term contract complying with the conditions of the 1977 Act and she had therefore no right to claim.

The EAT held first that there had been a dismissal on the expiry and non-renewal of the fixed term contract. The EAT further held that the mere fact that the appointment was temporary could not of itself, regardless of other factors, constitute substantial grounds for or justify the non-renewal. What the EAT did was to look at the employer's reasoning behind entering into the temporary contract in the first place. Normally, if an employer has a commercial justification for entering into a fixed term or specified purpose contract this will suffice to deem that contract to be genuine. The EAT will also, however, look at what was happening at the time the contract expired and the reasons as to why it was not renewed. In cases of genuine fixed term or specified purpose contracts an employer should have no difficulty in showing how circumstances had changed or that the temporary need catered for at the time of entering into the contract had in some way been satisfied. In *Fitzgerald* the EAT held:

'If the mere expiry of a fixed term contract of employment were to be regarded as a substantial ground for the non-renewal of the employment the Unfair Dismissals Act could be rendered abortive in many cases. An employer could side-step its provisions by employing his employees on fixed term contracts only. Then to get rid of an employee on whatever grounds, be they trivial or substantial, fancy full or solid, fair or unfair, he need only wait until that employee's fixed term contract expired and then refuse to renew it. The threat of non-renewal of his contract might well be enough to make many an employee submit to oppressive conditions or treatment at the hands of an employer.'

In *Fitzgerald* the EAT found that the reasons offered, which were essentially only the deemed temporary nature of the contract, did not constitute substantial grounds to justify dismissal under the 1977 Act.

1.6.3.3 Unfair Dismissals (Amendment) Act, 1993

Some confusion has arisen by virtue of the provisions of the Unfair Dismissals (Amendment) Act, 1993 in so far as it refers to fixed term contracts. It does not in any way affect the EAT's interpretation referred to above or the status of fixed term or specified purpose contracts. It merely deals with continuity of service between successive fixed term or specified purpose contracts. It is another attempt to prevent employers getting around the provisions of the legislation by employing people on what may appear to be genuine contracts and terminating, allowing a break to develop and then re-employing such persons. The break in continuity would mean that until at least one year of the renewed period has elapsed the employee would not have unfair dismissal protection. What the 1993 Act does is confirm continuity where the gap is three months or less between successive contracts, apparently no matter what the employee was doing in that three-month gap provided that the two contracts are similar.

It should be kept in mind of course that if an employer terminates a fixed term or specified purpose contract early, on notice as provided for in the contract, the employee will have the right to claim unfair dismissal provided he has at least one year's service. This is whether or not the three exclusions mentioned at **1.6.3.1** are contained in the contract, given that one of the exclusions relates to the time of the expiry of the term or cesser of the purpose which of course could not be applicable on early termination.

1.6.3.4 Case law

The following cases on fixed term contracts are instructive:

O'Mahony v Trinity College [1998] ELR 159

1. The claimant understood the nature and term of the post being offered to him at the time he signed his contract.

2. Expectation or hope of renewal does not create legal entitlement.

3. The EAT will not involve itself in deciding that the post could or should have continued for reasons as argued by the claimant.

4. The post to which the claimant was appointed ceased to exist and the claimant was not replaced—the employer was not seeking to avoid the Unfair Dismissals Act by entering into the fixed term contract.

Orren v Western Health Board UD 268/96

1. Appointment in an acting capacity.

2. A number of consecutive fixed term contracts.

3. Obligation on employer to comply with the Local Authorities (Officers and Employees) Act, 1926, s 6 and ss 15–18 of the Health Act, 1970.

4. Claimant not successful in open competition; post offered to another doctor.

5. Delay in appointing successful candidate. Claimant's employment terminated.

6. Unfair to terminate employment of claimant until the post is filled by successful candidate—compensation awarded.

Buckley v Southern Health Board UD 110/96

1. Temporary post pending filling post on a permanent basis.

2. Succession of fixed term consecutive contracts.

3. Application of 1926 Act, s 26 and 1970 Act, ss 15–18.

4. Position held by Dr Buckley was temporary.

5. Formal requirements of fixed term contracts not followed. Some contracts not signed, letters of confirmation not issued—this did not of itself entitle Dr Buckley to consider that her temporary status had changed.

6. Ultra vires for the health board to unilaterally confer permanent status on Dr Buckley.

7. Unfair Dismissals (Amendment) Act, 1993 extended protection to temporary officers and Dr Buckley was covered by the Act *but* substantial grounds existed to justify the termination of the temporary contract and the 'replacement' of Dr Buckley by a permanent appointee appointed in accordance with the 1926 and 1970 Acts.

Cahill v Teagasc [1996] ELR 215

1. Employed as student supervisor.

2. Employer believed the post not to be permanent having a policy that people took the job for a year or two while looking for a permanent job.

3. First took up the position in September 1991.

4. In January 1993 was asked to sign a fixed term contract to expire in September 1993 when he signed another contract for a further year to September 1994.

5. Employment was then terminated.

6. Claimant stated it was his intention to remain in the job 'for a number of years'.

7. The EAT took the view that there was a dismissal on the expiry of the last fixed term contract and that the purpose of the employer entering into the written contracts in question was to avoid liability under the Unfair Dismissals Acts which is prohibited by the 1993 Act, s 3(2)(b).

1.7   COMPANY DIRECTORS

A service contract for a director, whether an employee or independent contractor, may not be longer than five years in duration. Any term longer than five years must be approved by the shareholders. In the case of the director of one or more companies in a group, the approval must come from the shareholders in the holding company. Before approval may be given a written note of the terms must be available for inspection for at least fifteen days prior to the general meeting at which the vote would be taken. Terms of any contract which contravene these requirements are void and the contract may be terminated by the company at any time on giving reasonable notice. Similar provisions apply to termination payments to directors that might exceed the equivalent of five years' remuneration. See the Companies Act 1963, ss 187–189 and the Companies Act, 1990, s 28.

Section 50 of the Companies Act, 1990 requires that every shareholder is entitled to inspect a copy of each director's service contract and that such a copy must be kept at the registered office, principal place of business or where the shareholders' register is kept. Similar provisions relate to subsidiaries of holding companies.

1.8 CONTRACTUAL PROVISION OR WORK PRACTICE?

1.8.1 GENERALLY

The line between what is a contractual entitlement, which may not be varied without consent, and what is a work practice, which may be changed by the employer, is unclear in Irish law. Despite the existence of a vast body of modern case law on employment law and an impressive number of textbooks now available there has been very little analysis of what exactly constitutes a contractual term or condition and what is merely at the discretion of the parties to give, take away or alter as they see fit. What is clear is that what is contractual may not be changed or varied unilaterally but only by agreement whether that is implied, by acquiescence, or otherwise (see *Cowey v Liberian Operations Ltd* [1966] 2 Lloyd's Rep 45). What is actually written down by the parties, no matter how comprehensive, cannot cover all of the incidents of a contract of employment or employment relationship. In practice many employers use relatively simple and understandable letters of appointment and provide for the application of additional terms and conditions as may be contained in other documentation such as union management agreements. Issues will, however, arise on a regular basis which will fall to be determined on whether or not the employer or employee has a legal right, entitlement or obligation. If, for example, an employee were to be provided with a company car it might be described in a written document as being provided at the discretion of the employer which would normally allow the employer the right to remove the car from the employee. On the other hand, a contract might simply state that the employee will be provided with a vehicle, or make no reference to the vehicle and the employer simply makes it available, in which event it would be expected that the employee would be deemed to have an implied contractual right to be provided with the substantial benefit of a car. What then if the employer changed the make or model of the vehicle or provided the employee with a new but less luxurious vehicle? Is the employer in breach of contract? One would expect that it would be relatively easy to answer such a question. It is not. In order to answer the question it must be determined whether or not the point in issue relates to a term or condition of the contract of employment or otherwise.

Some assistance in determining what is a term or condition and what is a work practice is afforded by the judgment of O'Hanlon J in *Kenny v An Post* [1988] IR 285. This case involved a claim by the plaintiffs to a contractual right to a fifteen-minute break paid at the ordinary overtime rate. There was a slight complicating factor in that the contracts of An Post staff carried certain guarantees in relation to conditions of service provided for in the Postal and Telecommunications Act, 1983, s 45 when An Post and Bord Telecom were created out of what was previously the one employing authority, the Department of Posts and Telegraphs.

Mr Kenny and his colleagues were employed as postal sorters. In 1969 they had agreed with their supervisor that on the 8.00 pm to 11.30 pm shift they would be allowed a fifteen-minute paid break. In 1983 An Post decided that the privilege of the paid break would be withdrawn and no payment was made thereafter in relation to the taking of the break. No issue was taken by the employees trade union but the plaintiffs instituted proceedings claiming that An Post was in breach of contract or, alternatively, had failed to continue in operation all conditions of service as required by the 1983 Act, s 45.

Evidence was given that the supervisor came up with the idea of allowing the staff a fixed break in order to lessen the disruption to work caused by small groups leaving at irregular intervals to deal with calls of nature. The supervisor's suggestion was discussed with staff representatives drawn from the union representing the men, was agreed, and was introduced as a work practice from that time. The matter was raised for discussion a number of years later and in or about 1983 a decision was taken by another supervisor to discontinue the practice of having the entire workforce cease work for a fifteen-minute period paid at overtime rates. O'Hanlon J said he had to consider whether An Post (a) were in breach of contract, or (b) in breach of the duties imposed upon them by the 1983 Act, in seeking to implement and enforce the change in working practices.

1.8.2 WRITTEN AGREEMENT

1.8.2.1 Kenny v An Post

O'Hanlon J referred to the fact that the fifteen-minute break in *Kenny v An Post* [1988] IR 285

> 'was never made the subject of any formal written agreement or . . . of any exchange of letters or other written communication between the employers and the employees or their representatives. Nor did it go any higher than the supervisors who did not seek formal sanction from the Department of Posts and Telegraphs'.

It was argued for the plaintiff that the decision had been implemented and continued over many years and must by implication be regarded as having become one of the terms of employment of the employees concerned. In reaching his decision on whether or not the term was contractually binding O'Hanlon J had regard to what he described as 'collective bargaining' which resulted in agreements not normally intended to create legal relations rather than contractually binding commitments and stated:

> 'Alteration of, and adjustment to, work practices may have to take place constantly in the sphere of employment where large numbers of people are working on the premises and it seems to me that where a particular change in the terms of employment is intended to be regarded as binding contractually the parties should take some positive steps to achieve this objective.'

He went on to state that he was not satisfied on the evidence that the supervisors had authority from the Department of Posts and Telegraphs to change the contract between the Department and their employees but at the same time he accepted that the supervisors 'must be regarded as having authority to adapt the work practices in the sorting office to the particular needs of the work situation'. He stated, however, that he 'would not be prepared to hold that they [the supervisors] had authority to bring about changes in the entitlement to remuneration for overtime on a contractual basis so that the employer was to be henceforth bound to pay for time not worked by the employee'.

Section 45 of the 1983 Act sought to preserve employees' 'conditions of service' when their employment contracts transferred from the Department of Posts and Telegraphs to An Post. O'Hanlon J was not satisfied that the right to the paid work break came within the meaning of the term 'conditions of service'. In this regard he stated:

> '[I]t is not clear to me that when the Act refers to "conditions of service" it includes within its ambit conditions of service which were not legally enforceable as terms of the contract of employment, but were merely customs and usages practised in a particular section. On the view I have taken of the arrangement . . . the work practice in question was one which the employer was entitled to terminate unilaterally at any time . . . without being involved in any breach of the contractual rights of the workers.'

1.8.2.2 Cresswell v Board of Inland Revenue

In *Cresswell v Board of Inland Revenue* [1984] 2 All ER 713; [1984] IRLR 190 the plaintiffs were employees of the UK Inland Revenue involved in the administration of the PAYE tax scheme. The case arose following the computerisation of the scheme, which had previously been operated by the plaintiffs on a manual basis. In the course of the change from manual to computerised systems a dispute arose, as a result of which the plaintiffs refused to operate the first phase of computerisation but indicated their willingness to continue the previous manual operation. The employers would not allow the use of the manual method of operation and indicated that they would not pay the plaintiffs while they refused to work the computerised system. The contracts were not brought to an end but payment was suspended until such time as the plaintiffs returned to operating the computerised system.

The employees took the position that their employers were acting in breach of contract in requiring them to operate the computerised system. They claimed the work which they were employed to perform involved dealing manually with files, records and correspondence, and maintained it was an implied term of their contracts of employment that they could not be required to perform tasks or carry out functions other than those expressly stipulated in their contracts or their terms and conditions of service and/or such as were habitually carried out by custom and practice. It fell to the High Court to determine what the contractual positions of the employer and the employees were and to determine whether the plaintiffs were entitled to refuse to follow the instruction given to them.

The court did not analyse in any detail what is meant by a term or condition of employment or how it might be possible to distinguish a contractual term or condition from a work practice but gave assistance in its judgment as follows:

'The defendants were not in breach of the plaintiffs' contracts of employment in requiring them to carry out their job duties associated with the administration of the PAYE scheme by means of a new computerised system instead of the traditional manual method of working. Although the content of some of the jobs in question had been considerably altered by computerisation the degree of such alteration was nothing like sufficient to fall outside the original description of the proper functions of the grade concerned.' (See also *O'Neill v Merseyside Plumbing Co Ltd* [1973] ICR 96.)

'An employee is expected to adapt himself to new methods and techniques introduced in the course of his employment. On his side, the employer must provide any necessary training or retraining. It is a question of pure fact in each particular case whether the retraining involved the acquisition of such esoteric skills that it would not be reasonable to expect the employee to acquire them. Nowadays, however, it cannot be considered esoteric or unusual to ask an employee to acquire basic skills as to retrieving information from a computer or feeding information into one.' (See also *North Riding Garages v Butterwick* [1967] 2 QB 56.)

'In the present case after computerisation of the PAYE scheme each of the jobs in question was the same as it was before though in part done in a different way. Computerisation merely introduced up-to-date methods for dealing with bulk problems. Though there may have been some loss of job satisfaction on the part of the employees concerned that was regrettable but by itself provided no cause for action. Moreover, in the present case, there was no suggestion that the plaintiffs themselves or anybody else in any similar category affected by computerisation had found any real difficulty in accepting the necessary instruction in the use of the computerised system or putting it into practice.'

'The defendants had not committed any act in breach of contract in refusing to allow the plaintiffs to continue working manually and in refusing to pay them as long as they refused to work the new computerised system.'

1.8.2.3 O'Cearbhaill v Bord Telecom Eireann

The Supreme Court also considered the question of terms and conditions of employment in *O'Cearbhaill v Bord Telecom Eireann* [1994] ELR 54. This was another case where s 45 of the Postal and Telecommunications Act, 1983 was considered and, while the case related to whether or not a collective agreement could alter terms and conditions without the express agreement of the individual employees, Blayney J observed that neither of the parties was able to refer the court to any case in which the question of what constitutes conditions of service was considered. He did not consider that *Kenny v An Post* or *O'Rourke v Talbot (Ireland) Ltd* [1984] ILRM 587 threw any light on the question and stated:

> '[T]he matter must be approached on first principles. It seems to me that conditions of service are conditions which one would expect to find in a contract of employment between an employer and an employee. Any terms which would be normal to include in such a contract would be entitled to be so described.'

Blayney J went on to pose the question:

> 'Would a term dealing with an employee's prospects of promotion come into this category? In my opinion it would not. It does not concern the immediate relationship between the employer and employee as would, for example, the rate of pay, hours of work, length of holidays, sick-leave, pension rights etc. It relates rather to the general manner in which the employer's business is structured and managed. If an employer were to make it the subject of the contract of employment of individual employees he would be unable to change it without the consent of each of them. No employer would be prepared to restrict his freedom in this way. For this reason it seems to me that it would be wholly inappropriate to include a prospect of promotion in the contract of employment and so it could not be considered as being a condition of service. It is simply an incident of a person's employment depending entirely on how the employer's business is structured and subject to change since the employer is under no obligation not to alter the structure of his business.'

1.8.2.4 Rafferty v Bus Eireann

Kelly J delivered a very useful High Court judgment on terms and conditions of employment and work practices on 21 November 1996 in the case of *Rafferty, Ward and the National Bus & Rail Union v Bus Eireann and Irish Bus* [1997] 2 IR 424. In the course of his judgment Kelly J referred to *O'Cearbhaill*. Commenting on Blayney J's views Kelly J took the view

> '[T]hat in the totality of the relationship between employer and employee certain aspects of it may truly be described as conditions of service whereas other aspects are not. Even though these other aspects may have important implications for both employer and employee they are nonetheless not to be regarded as conditions of service. . . . Accordingly there is a difference in law between conditions of service and work practices.'

In *Rafferty* Kelly J was asked to consider whether or not the respondents could change rostering arrangements, abolish certain duties and replace them with other duties. The plaintiffs took issue with the changes and complained that they were unilateral alterations in terms and conditions of employment. The respondents submitted that as a result of serious financial difficulties they had to achieve cost savings and that the changes they sought to impose were not contractual alterations but changes in work practices which are effectively at the discretion of the employer to order in the best interests of the business. Kelly J cited the *O'Cearbhaill* and *Cresswell* cases, the latter of which he appeared to feel was particularly apposite having regard to the facts in *Rafferty*. He accepted that the requirements to be imposed on Mr Rafferty and his colleagues required them to undertake duties which they had not formerly done, but took the view that after the proposed changes the principal occupation of Mr Rafferty and his colleagues, who were bus drivers, 'remains that of driving'. He concluded as follows:

'The position therefore is that in my view Irish Bus is correct in saying that the changes which it seeks to bring about are ones which involve work practices rather than changes in conditions of service. These alterations do not affect the rate of pay, hours of work, length of holidays, sick leave or pension rights. Neither do they in my view alter the basic or core work of a bus driver. These altered duties will only fall to be executed at times where drivers would otherwise be idle and yet remunerated. In each case these duties will constitute a small part of the overall work which will remain bus driving. I therefore conclude that the proposed alterations relate to work practices rather than conditions of service.'

1.8.3 WORSENING OF TERMS AND CONDITIONS OF SERVICE

The employees in *Rafferty, Ward and the National Bus and Rail Union v Bus Eireann and Irish Bus* [1997] 2 IR 424 had similar statutory assurances to the employees in *O'Cearbhaill v Bord Telecom Eireann* [1994] ELR 54 and *Kenny v An Post* [1988] IR 285 in that under the Transport (Reorganisation of Coras Iompair Eireann) Act, 1986 three new operating companies were formed and the employment of the applicants was transferred from the holding company to one of the operating companies. Section 14(5) of the Act provided that employees could not, after the transfer, 'receive a lesser scale of pay or be brought to less beneficial conditions of service' than those they enjoyed prior to the transfer, unless the changes were made in accordance with a collective agreement. In deciding whether or not that section was triggered Kelly J made an interesting observation as to what might constitute worsening of terms and conditions. What might constitute worsening of terms or conditions or a detriment to an employee may be a very subjective decision. Kelly J held that s 14(5) was not triggered because the provision did not prohibit an alteration or change in conditions of service 'unless it brings about a worsening in the employee's position'. He then posed the question:

'What worsening is brought about here? Can an employee complain that his conditions of service are worsened when his employer re-orders his working arrangements so as to ensure that the employee is not idle whilst being paid? That is what these changes hope to achieve in an ailing company. I do not believe that any such complaint would be legitimate. The position would of course be different if Irish Bus sought to require the drivers to receive a lesser scale of pay or to carry out work during times when they would not be paid. But merely to require them to work during a time when they are being paid cannot give rise to a legitimate claim under s 14 on the grounds that formerly they did not have to work during such times. It follows that even if the proposed changes are ones which alter conditions of service rather than work practices they do not give rise to a complaint under s 14 since they do not worsen the drivers' conditions of service.'

1.8.4 VARIATION OF CONTRACT

Once it is established that a provision is a term or a condition of a contract of employment is it the case that the employer cannot then make any change or variation to the contract? It is a basic tenet of contract law that the terms of a contract cannot be varied except by agreement of the parties. A change or variation in the contract cannot be unilateral. Neither party can impose any change they desire. The change must occur by agreement whether that agreement is express or implied, tacit or by acquiescence.

1.8.5 VARIATION BY THE PARTIES

The law of contract has had great difficulty with the scope of what constitutes variation by one of the parties. While the basic rule expressed above seems to be quite straightforward judges have come across many situations in commercial agreements where an element of unilateral variation or modification becomes necessary in order to give commercial efficacy to the contract. Their desire to see the bargain of the parties carried out can sometimes override specific terms of an agreement which may defeat that purpose, albeit unwittingly. Robert Clarke in *Contract Law in Ireland* (3rd edn), p 407 states:

> 'Post-contractual representations which purport to have the effect of abrogating or modifying contractual terms present acute difficulties, due in the main to a failure on the part of judges to use and define terms like . . . "variation" . . . with any degree of precision.'

In *Tradax (Ireland) Ltd v Irish Grain Board Ltd* [1984] IR 1 the Chief Justice stated that the power to imply terms must *'be exercised with care'*.

The courts will not make a bargain that was badly made in the first place. In normal commercial contracts that doctrine is not difficult to adhere to. In employment contracts, however, the situation is different. The relationship between the parties is radically different from a normal commercial contract. The parties are bound together throughout their working day and, possibly for one or both, throughout their working lives. The consequences of any difficulty will tend to be considerably worse for the employee than for the employer which may be a firm or company.

If a term is so obvious that common sense would hold that it must be included in a contract then the courts are likely to hold that it is part of the contract. Clarke also refers to *Shirlaw v Southern Foundries [1926] Ltd* [1939] 2 KB 206 where it was stated:

> '[W]here . . . that which in any contract is left to be implied and need not be expressed is something so obvious that it goes without saying; that, if while the parties were making their bargain, an officious bystander were to suggest some express provision for it in their agreement they would hastily suppress him with a common "oh of course".'

The Supreme Court had followed *Shirlaw* in *Sweeney v Duggan* [1997] 2 ILRM 211 in refusing to imply a term into a contract of employment that an employer should carry insurance against negligence of personal injury to an employee. (See also *The Moorcock* (1889) 14 PD 64 and *Spring v National Amalgamated Stevedores and Dockers Society* [1956] 1 WLR 585.)

In *Wandsworth London Borough Council v D'Silva* [1998] IRLR 193 the council had a code of practice on staff illness which included procedures for monitoring and reviewing absence. A review process was triggered when employees reached a certain level of absence. The council proposed changing the method of triggering such a review and the staff objected to such a change. The staff maintained that the code of practice formed part of their contractual terms and conditions and could not be changed by the employer unilaterally. The employers argued that the relevant provisions of the code were not contractually binding and that, even if they were, the contracts expressly allowed the employers to amend those provisions unilaterally. In making this latter argument the employer was relying on a clause which stated inter alia 'from time to time variations in your terms of employment may occur and these will be separately notified to you or otherwise in-corporated in the documents to which you have reference'. The Court of Appeal held that the provisions in the employer's code of practice on staff sickness were not contractually binding and could be altered by the employers unilaterally. The court stated:

> 'Whether a particular provision in an employer's code of practice is contractually binding depends upon whether it should properly be regarded as conferring a right on employ-ees or as setting out no more than good practice which managers were intended to follow.'

In the present case the language of the provisions in question did not provide an appropriate foundation on which to base contractual rights. They did no more than provide guidance for both supervisors and employees as to what was expected to happen in certain circumstances. They did not set out what was contractually required to happen. The whole procedure in its initial stages was designed to be flexible and informal in a way which was inconsistent with contractual rights being created. Therefore the employers were entitled to amend the provisions unilaterally. See also *Doyle v Grangeford Precast Concrete Ltd* [1998] ELR 260 where the employer took on an employee and later gave him the letter of appointment which contained a probationary clause. Probation had not previously been discussed or agreed. The High Court held that this was a breach of trust and that the employer was not entitled to unilaterally impose a new contractual provision. Interlocutory relief was granted to the employee pending the outcome of his action for damages. The employee subsequently obtained damages measured at six months' remuneration in lieu of notice. .

1.8.6 VARIATION BY THIRD PARTY OR AGENT—TRADE UNIONS

The most common form of variation other than one expressly agreed between employer and employee is variation agreed with a trade union acting on behalf of specific employees or employees generally.

1.8.7 COLLECTIVE AGREEMENTS

In unionised employment employers normally copy collective agreements to new employees and make it clear to them that these agreements form part of their terms and conditions of employment. Collective agreements may be varied by the main parties, being the employer and the trade union, from time to time and the question may arise as to how that variation affects the employees. In the main employees will in practice accept terms or conditions negotiated on their behalf by their trade union and, even where a vote may be taken on such changes, those voting against the changes are likely to accept them and to continue working under such changed terms and conditions. There is unlikely therefore to be any doubt as to whether or not the contract has been changed. If there is a doubt in most cases that doubt can be removed by the application of the common law doctrine of 'acquiescence' where a party will be estopped from denying a term if they have acquiesced in its application and, in particular, where they have benefited from the operation of the term. Variation of, or addition to, contractual terms by agreement between a trade union and an employer may be problematic, particularly where the employee objects to the change. A trade union cannot bind those of its members who have made it clear that they did not wish or intend to be bound.

In *Goulding Chemicals Ltd v Bolger* [1977] IR 211 the Supreme Court took a straightforward traditional common law line on the change or variation to a contract and the need for the consent of the contracting parties. Bolger and some of his workmates had made it quite clear that they did not intend to be bound by a change even where the majority of their colleagues in the trade union voted for a change. The Supreme Court in that case had no difficulty in construing each employee's individual contract as requiring the consent of that individual employee be it express, implied or by acquiescence. Bolger and his workmates had made it very clear that they were not to be bound in any of these ways and were held therefore not to be bound.

In *Gray Dunn & Co Ltd v Edwards* [1980] IRLR 23 it was held that where employers negotiate a detailed agreement with a recognised union they are entitled to assume that all unionised employees know of and are bound by its provisions, where the employees had not made it clear that they had no intention to be bound. It was held in *Dal v A S Orr* [1980] IRLR 413 that an agreement between employer and union that employees' hours of work should be changed will effectively vary their contracts and will not amount to a fundamental breach of contract entitling the employees to claim constructive dismissal where the employers have reserved the right to alter the hours of work in the contract of employment. In *Scott v*

Formica Ltd [1970] IRLR 104 it was held that if there is to be an important variation in the contract of employment resulting from a collective agreement this variation must be brought to the employee's attention in some way such as the issue of an amended statement of terms and conditions, a slip in the employee's pay packet or an address by management or a union official; otherwise the variation will not become part of the contract. The question of whether collective agreements are legally binding in themselves is dealt with at **1.11** below. In *Whent v T Cartledge Ltd* [1997] IRLR 153 rates of pay were linked to a collective agreement agreed between a transferor and trade unions. Following the transfer of the undertaking the question arose as to whether or not the transferee was obliged by rates of pay set under the terms of the collective agreement. In the course of its decision the EAT held (at p 154):

> '[T]he terms of a collective agreement can be incorporated into and become legally binding terms of individual contracts of employment and that unilateral abrogation of or withdrawal from the collective agreement does not affect the latter.'

See also *Robertson v British Gas Corporation* [1983] IRLR 302.

1.8.8 CUSTOM AND PRACTICE

In contracts of employment many terms are implied by operation of custom and practice of the employment. In order for a term to be implied by custom and practice it must be *'notorious'* as in the case of *O'Reilly v Irish Press* [1937] ILTR 194 where it was held that for a custom to be implied into a contract it must be:

> 'so notorious, well known and acquiesced in that in the absence of agreement in writing it is to be taken as one of the terms of the contract between the parties'.

In *DP Refinery (Westernport) Pty Ltd v Shire Hastings* (1978) 52 AJLR 43 the court set out the test that will normally be followed before a term may be implied into a contract as follows:

(a) the term must be reasonable and equitable;

(b) it must be necessary to give business efficacy to the contract, so no term will be implied if the contract is effective without it. (See also *Whent v Cartledge* [1997] IRLR 153 at p 157);

(c) it must be so obvious that it goes without saying;

(d) it must be capable of clear expression; and

(e) it must not contradict any express term of the contract.

1.8.9 EXPRESS CONTRACTUAL RIGHT TO VARY

It is possible to provide within the terms of a contract that the employer reserves the right to alter or vary terms but courts and tribunals will not allow that right to be exercised in an unfettered manner. They will require both business efficacy and reasonableness to apply. In *BBC v Beckett* [1983] IRLR 43 it was held that the right to demote an employee for a disciplinary offence was limited by an implied term that the employers would not exercise such a right in other than a reasonable manner. Such a clause will also be construed strictly against the employer (see *Lister v Fram Gerrard Ltd* [1973] ITR 610). Express contractual right to vary, while not specifically provided for in the contract, may be implied by construction of one or other of the terms of the contract as in *Parry v Holst & Co Ltd* [1968] ITR 317 where it was held that where an employee's contract provides for mobility between different workplaces he cannot claim a redundancy payment when his current workplace closes and he refuses to transfer to another.

In *Simmonds v Dowty Seals Ltd* [1978] IRLR 211 it was held that whether there has been a consensual variation of the terms of the employment depends on the evidence in the particular case. An agreement to vary the terms of a contract is not required to be in writing to have legal effect. Where an employee stays silent and works on under changed terms without objecting, this may amount to an implied agreement to the variation in his terms. This view should be adopted with caution and mainly in respect of terms like pay changes of immediate effect. Changes of future import like workplace should be regarded even more circumspectly—see also *Jones v Associated Tunnel Link Co Ltd* [1981] IRLR 477 and *Wandsworth London Borough Council v D'Silva* [1998] IRLR 193.

1.9 TIME LIMITS ON VARIATION

1.9.1 GENERALLY

Courts and tribunals will be slow to bind a party to a particular term or variation in terms to that party's detriment where they are satisfied that on the facts of the case a change was agreed but it was not the purpose or intention of one of the parties, usually the employee, that the change be binding on him without any limit in time.

1.9.2 CO-OPERATION NOT VARIATION

Where a rearrangement of terms of work is based upon co-operation and not contract, the variation of contract so as to bind the employee to the new arrangement will not be inferred, see *Turriff Construction Ltd v Bryant* [1967] ITR 292. In *Saxton v National Coal Board* [1970] ITR 196 it was held that where an employee with twenty years' service accepts a reduced working week for a short period of months while his workplace runs down prior to closure, consensual variation of his contract is not to be inferred. Courts will not allow employers to slip in change unknown to an employee as in *Stepney Cast Stone Co Ltd v MacArthur* [1979] IRLR 181, in which the court held that where an employer wishes to make a fundamental change in an employee's terms and conditions it must bring it clearly to the employee's notice or it will not amount to consensual variation.

1.9.3 CONTINUING CONTRACT OR NEW CONTRACT?

In *Meek v Port of London Authority* [1918] 2 Ch 96 it was held that employees who accepted promotion to a higher grade of employment were held to have entered into a fresh contract of service. It is unlikely, given the modern authorities, that a court or tribunal would today hold that such a change within the scope of a contract of employment constituted the termination of one contract and the commencement of another, but even if a court or tribunal was to follow that line of reasoning the likelihood is that the court would find that the new 'contract' would be identical in all respects to the 'old' contract with the addition of the new term. The introduction, however, of such new terms is not merely a legal or contractual matter but it may well have practical implications for the parties' relationship into the future. Frequently disputes arise following a consensual variation in a contract in circumstances which might well have been anticipated at the time of the variation but to which the parties gave insufficient thought. If, for example, an employee was to be promoted from a post that he had held for a considerable period of time, for example, promotion from shop floor to management, little or no thought might be given to the consequences for the parties if the employee failed to perform in the new role. May the employee revert to the old job? If someone else has been recruited to fill the shop floor job that might well be a practical impossibility. Does the failure to perform in the new role lead to the destruction of the entire relationship? Such issues are relevant to variation in terms and conditions of employment and variation of contracts; however, the parties effecting the variation may not anticipate such difficulties arising and therefore find themselves embroiled in a dispute as to what should happen when the event occurs. Employers and employees should seek to anticipate what possible difficulties might arise and to cater for them at the time the variation is agreed and put into effect, otherwise disputes will almost inevitably arise.

1.10   TRADE DISPUTES

It should be kept in mind at all times that even where the employer is legally correct in taking action, or where the employees are seeking a change which they cannot enforce in law, employees may, where appropriate, engage in a trade dispute and use their industrial powers of persuasion to seek to bring about the changes they require or to prevent the employer from imposing changes the employer may require.

1.11   COLLECTIVE AGREEMENTS AND CONTRACTS OF EMPLOYMENT

1.11.1   INTRODUCTION

In practice many terms and conditions of employment are negotiated between employers and trade unions on a collective basis. Two issues arise in relation to collective agreements, the first of which is how they might be binding in respect of individual contracts and the incorporation, alteration or variation of terms or conditions of employment through a trade union. In *O'Rourke v Talbot (Ireland) Ltd* [1984] ILRM 587 the plaintiffs through their trade union had negotiated with the company on the redeployment of certain employees as a result of financial difficulties encountered by the company. In the course of the negotiations the employees sought a written assurance from the company in relation to job security for the future. The company produced a document which gave 'an assurance that compulsory redundancy' would not be introduced. A further document was sought by the employees giving guaranteed protection against compulsory redundancy up to a certain date. This 'guarantee' was given by management. Barrington J held that productivity agreements similar to the first agreement in this case, which contained the assurances that there would be no compulsory redundancies, were agreements of a sort that 'did not contemplate legal relations, at any rate so far as all their clauses were concerned but were meant to be binding in honour on the management and the trade union'. He went on to hold, however, that given the circumstances of the second commitment wherein the word 'guarantee' was used and taking the view that 'the representatives of management did not think that they were entering into a legally binding arrangement' that he was 'satisfied however that not only were the men looking for something which was legally binding but that management knew this' and thereby held that the second commitment was legally binding.

In reaching his conclusion Barrington J considered the leading British and Irish precedents on the legal status of collective agreements (*Edwards v Skyways Ltd* [1964] 1 WLR 349; *Ford Motor Co Ltd v AEF* [1969] 2 QB 303 and *Goulding Chemicals Ltd v Bolger* [1977] IR 211) and went on to hold that the agreement sought to be upheld by the plaintiffs was a commercial agreement legally binding on the parties. The way in which collective agreements are incorporated in individual contracts of employment is referred to in *Becton Dickinson v Lee* [1973] IR 1.

It should also be kept in mind that the terms of the collective agreement may apply to employees who are not members of the trade union with which the agreement was concluded. This may arise in a number of ways. The employee may have commenced employment and been advised that his terms and conditions would be governed, at least in part, by the terms of the collective agreement (see *Singh v British Steel Corporation* [1974] IRLR 131), or the employee may have left or been expelled from his trade union at a time when the collective agreement was in being. It should also be noted that a trade union cannot bind all of its members where some of those members have made it clear that they did not intend or wish to be bound (*Goulding Chemicals Ltd v Bolger*).

1.11.2 LEGALITY OF COLLECTIVE AGREEMENTS

The Supreme Court in *Goulding Chemicals Ltd v Bolger* [1977] IR 211 considered a situation where agreement was reached between the company and representative trade unions as to the manner in which a plant would be closed and the amounts of redundancy payments the employees were to be paid. The trade unions arranged for a vote to be taken on the proposals and a majority of the members of the various unions supported the company's proposals and accepted them. The company then acted on the acceptance by the majority and treated it as an acceptance by the entire workforce. The company had negotiated on a collective basis and then proceeded to act in relation to each individual employee's contract of service on the basis of what was collectively negotiated. The defendants were part of the minority of the workforce who had voted against the proposals. They made their objections clear to their employers. The agreement reached between the company and the trade unions restricted unions' and employees' rights to picket. The defendants engaged in a picket. The company sought to restrain them on a number of grounds, one of which was that they were bound by the collective agreement concluded with their trade union. Two issues had to be considered. The first was whether or not collective agreements of the sort concluded in this case were legally binding on the parties to the agreement and, secondly, whether a collective agreement binds the employees who are members of the unions involved in concluding the agreement. The judgments in *Goulding* refer extensively to *Edwards v Skyways* [1964] 1 WLR 349 and *Ford Motor Co Ltd v AEF* [1969] 2 QB 303.

In *Edwards* agreement was reached between the employer and the employees that an ex gratia payment would be paid in the event of redundancy. In that case the court held that the agreement was binding on the parties. As the subject matter was business relations there was an intention to agree and, further, that where there is a difference between the parties the onus of proof lies on the party who asserts that no legal effect was intended and this onus was not discharged in the *Edwards* case.

In the *Ford Motor Co* case it was held that collective agreements negotiated between a large industrial company and various trade unions were, due to the contents which were stated to be mainly aspirational, and the fact that the parties were seeking to order their day-to-day relations rather than impose legal obligations on each other, not legally binding as there was no intention to create legal relations the court stating:

> 'Agreements such as these, composed largely of optimistic aspirations presenting grave practical problems of enforcement and reached against a background of opinion adverse to enforceability, are, in my judgment not contracts in the legal sense and are not enforceable at law.'

In *Goulding* the Supreme Court expressed reservations about the *Ford Motor Co* decision (per Kenny J at p 237). The Supreme Court analysed the nature of the particular agreement reached and held that it was 'a business-like document and had all the appearances of being intended to create legal relations'.

1.11.3 TESTS APPLIED

In *O'Rourke v Talbot (Ireland) Ltd* [1984] ILRM 587 Barrington J also referred to *Edwards v Skyways* and the reference at p 355 of that report to the leading textbooks on the law of contract, which maintain that the test of intention to create or not to create legal relations is an 'objective' test, and held that in the case before him the conditions of the objective test had been met and that Talbot could not rebut the presumption that the agreement they reached with the trade unions and the workforce was one intended to create legal relations, and that the agreement was binding on the company and that they were in breach of agreement in making the plaintiffs redundant prior to the date after which employment had been guaranteed. The conclusion reached by the Supreme Court in *Goulding Chemicals Ltd v Bolger* on the general issue of whether or not a collective agreement is legally binding was effectively that regard must be had to the circumstances in which the agreement was concluded and its contents which might suggest it was not intended to be legally binding but concluded on the first issue as per O'Higgins CJ (at p 231):

'I would regard the agreement resulting from the acceptance of these proposals as being similar in effect to that dealt with in *Edwards v Skyways Ltd* and, there being nothing to suggest the contrary, in my view a valid contract is thereby created between these unions and the plaintiff.'

He went on to refer to 'this valid enforceable agreement'. Kenny J (at p 236) stated:

'An agreement between parties is enforceable by the law unless the agreement itself or the surrounding circumstances show that the parties did not intend to enter into legal relations.'

In reviewing the authorities Kenny J stated: 'I have considerable doubts about the correctness of the decision in the *Ford Motor Company* case'. In relation to the agreement concluded between the company and trade unions within Goulding Chemicals Limited he said:

'It seems to me that the six-point agreement was intended to create legal relations and was intended to be a contract between the plaintiffs and the unions engaged in the negotiations . . . when an apparent agreement in relation to business relations is entered into the onus on the party who asserts that it was not intended to have legal effect is a heavy one. In my opinion the six-point statement and its acceptance created a valid enforceable contract between the plaintiffs and the unions who took part in the negotiations.'

On the second issue, as to whether or not in the circumstances of this particular case, where the defendants rejected an agreement accepted by the majority membership of the trade unions concerned, and made this rejection clear to their employers, the Supreme Court considered whether they were or should be bound by the terms of the agreement which in itself the court had found to be binding on the company and trade unions. In this regard O'Higgins CJ stated (at p 231):

'I find it hard to accept . . . the defendants can be bound by an agreement which they have expressly repudiated and opposed. It seems to me that to hold them bound would be contrary to all principle.'

On this point Kenny J stated (at p 237):

'Membership of a corporate body or of an association does not have the consequence that every agreement made by that corporate body or association binds every member of it. None of the defendants are parties to the agreement and as they consistently opposed it no question of their being bound by acquiescence can arise.'

See also *Holland v London Society of Compositors* (1924) 40 TLR 440 and *Young v Canadian Northern Railway Co* [1931] AC 83.

If a collective agreement is legally binding then in itself it constitutes a contract by which employer and employee, and in certain circumstances the trade union, will be legally bound to each other. Even if the collective agreement is not in itself legally binding it may be incorporated into the contract of employment as referred to in *Whent v Cartledge Ltd* [1997] IRLR 153 referred to at **1.8.7** above and the cases of *Robertson v British Gas Corporation* [1983] IRLR 302 and *National Coal Board v National Union of Mineworkers* [1986] IRLR 439.

1.11.4   TRANSFER OF UNDERTAKINGS

Whent v Cartledge was related to the transfer of an undertaking. Prior to the transfer the employees had their rates of pay determined under the terms of a collective agreement by a body known as the NJC. The individual contracts of employment provided that the employees' pay would be that set by the NJC. On 11 April 1994 the undertaking was transferred. On 21 April 1994 the transferee wrote to the trade union concerned withdrawing recognition and from the agreement stating that any collective agreements relating to employees transferred would no longer have effect. The employees were individually advised of the discontinuance of 'any formal or implied recognition arrangements or collective agreements or related arrangements' which were stated to no longer have any effect and to have ended with immediate effect. The employees claimed that despite these letters their pay was still to be ascertained by reference to the rates agreed and established from time to time by the NJC for their respective grades. The transferee contended that pay for the relevant employees was frozen at the level last fixed before the employers withdrew from the collective agreement.

The EAT held:

> 'The transferee employers were still bound by the NJC agreement so far as incorporated in individual contracts of employment notwithstanding their withdrawal from the collective agreement. Until the transfer it was undisputed that the appellants' contracts incorporated the result of the annual round of negotiations and there were no grounds for holding that the transfer caused any change in the meaning of the words.'

In *Whent v Cartledge* the industrial tribunal, whose decision was overturned by the EAT, had reasoned that 'it cannot be right that an employer is bound ad infinitum by the terms of the collective agreement negotiated by bodies other than themselves'. The EAT described that as a 'fallacious reasoning' and stated:

> 'The employer was not bound ad infinitum since it could at any time without breach of contract negotiate variations of contract with individual employees or terminate their contracts on due notice and offer fresh ones. In any event there was no reason why the parties should not if they choose agree that matters such as remuneration be fixed by processes in which they do not themselves participate.'

1.12   APPLYING CONTRACTUAL TERMS

Even where a contract is clear as to its provisions and an employer seeks to apply the provision to the letter, the courts may intervene to restrict the employer and require the employer to act 'reasonably' in all the circumstances of the employment relationship. In *Bass Leisure Ltd v Thomas* [1994] IRLR 104 Mrs Thomas had worked for Bass in their Coventry depot for more than ten years. When the depot closed she was offered relocation in a depot some 20 miles away. She reluctantly agreed to try the new post but because of the disruption to her life she decided not to continue working there. She terminated her employment and sought a redundancy payment. Her employers rejected her claim and sought to rely on a paragraph in her contract which gave the employer the right to transfer any employee either temporarily or permanently to a suitable alternative place of work and went on to state that domestic circumstances would be taken into account in reaching a decision if relocation was involved. The EAT analysed the clause and, while holding that the actual wording of the clause favoured the employee, considered whether strict reliance on the terms of the contract would work an injustice on the employer. In *United Bank v Akhtar* [1989] IRLR 507 the Court of Appeal implied a term into the contract that the literal contractual rights of the employer would not be applied in an oppressive or unfair manner which is the line most likely to be followed by Irish courts.

CHAPTER 2

RESTRAINING DISMISSALS: INJUNCTIONS

2.1 NO SPECIFIC PERFORMANCE OF CONTRACT OF EMPLOYMENT

2.1.1 GENERAL RULE

It is well established that, generally, the courts will refuse to order the specific performance of a contract of employment. The courts are loath to compel employer and employee to continue to work together in circumstances where one or other no longer wishes to maintain the relationship and where it would not be possible for the courts to supervise the relationship. Indeed, as recently as December 1999, Kelly J, speaking with regard to the *American Cyanamid* (*American Cyanamid Co v Ethicon Ltd* [1975] AC 396) principles (which determine the circumstances in which the courts will generally grant injunctions by reference to (a) whether there is a serious issue to be tried; (b) the balance of convenience; and (c) the adequacy of damages in a particular case), stated that:

> '[T]hese principles have a wide but not a universal application. In a small number of cases special rules which are not encompassed by these principles apply. One such type case arises in the field of contracts of employment. Normally courts will not grant an injunction to restrain breaches of covenant in a contract of employment if that would amount to indirect specific performance of such a contract or would *perpetuate a relationship based on mutual trust which no longer exists*' (*Reynolds v Malocco* (Irish Times Law Report, 18 January 1999).

2.1.2 EXCEPTIONS TO THE RULE

However, the rule is not absolute. In a judgment delivered on 29 November 1971, in *C H Giles & Co Ltd v Morris* [1972] 1 All ER 960, Megarry J stated:

> 'Such a rule is plainly not absolute and without exception, nor do I think that it can be based on any narrow consideration such as difficulties of constant superintendence of the court.'

Indeed, some days earlier, on 10 November 1971, the Court of Appeal had already granted an interlocutory injunction, restraining an employer from dismissing an employee (*Hill v C A Parsons & Co Ltd* [1972] Ch 305). Mr Hill was a senior engineer in the employment of the defendants. In May 1970, a closed shop arrangement was put in place, whereby all of the defendants' employees had to become members of a particular trade union. Mr Hill refused to join the union and received one month's notice of dismissal. He successfully obtained an interlocutory injunction restraining the termination of his contract of employment. Lord

Denning MR made reference to the general rule that an employee cannot claim specific performance of the contract of employment. However, he then stated:

> 'The rule is not inflexible. It permits of exceptions. The court can, in a proper case, grant a declaration that the relationship still subsists and an injunction to stop the master treating it as at an end.'

He went on to state:

> 'It may be said that, by granting an injunction in such a case, the court is indirectly enforcing specifically a contract for personal services. So be it. Lord St Leonards LC did something like it in *Lumley v Wagner* [(1852) 1 De G M & G 604] and I see no reason why we should not do it here.'

The circumstances in *Hill* were special. Mutual confidence still existed between employer and employee and the attempt to dismiss Mr Hill was made only by reason of the intervention of a third party, the trade union. Further, damages would not have been an adequate remedy. The Court of Appeal held that Mr Hill was entitled to six months' notice. During that six-month period, the Industrial Relations Act 1971 came into operation in Britain and gave employees the right not to be unfairly dismissed. If the proper notice had been given to Mr Hill it was probable that his employment would have continued until the coming into operation of Part II of the 1971 Act, in which case his rights would thereafter have been safeguarded and he would not have been obliged to join the union. Sachs LJ described the case as 'highly exceptional'. It was subsequently stated to be 'unusual, if not unique'.

In 1978, Kenny J refused to grant injunctions to plaintiff civil servants, restoring them to their positions, in circumstances where they had been suspended without pay. He took the view that restoring the plaintiffs to their positions would amount to specific performance of contracts for personal services and refused to make such orders, stating that 'it is settled law that the courts never specifically enforce a contract for personal services' (*Yeates v Minister for Posts and Telegraphs* [1978] ILRM 22).

In *Shiels v Clery & Co [1941] Ltd* 13 October 1979, High Ct (unreported) the High Court refused 'to thrust upon the company a servant whom they did not wish to employ'.

However, at the same time, McWilliam J acknowledged that the rule against specifically enforcing contracts of employment is not rigid. In *Lift Manufacturers Ltd v Irish Life Assurance Co Ltd* [1979] ILRM 277 the judge, echoing the sentiments of Megarry J in *Giles & Co Ltd v Morris*, stated that where there does not seem to be any reason for the court to supervise performance of a contract, the principle against enforcement does not apply.

2.2 THE TRUST AND CONFIDENCE ISSUE

2.2.1 INTRODUCTION

In *Hill v C A Parsons & Co Ltd* [1972] Ch 305 the court stated that, as personal confidence between the parties continued to exist, one of the main grounds for refusing an injunction (that it was wrong to enforce a contract based on a confidential relationship in the absence of personal confidence) was not applicable. This 'trust and confidence issue' was to be central to developments in the UK for almost twenty years.

In November 1984, in *Irani v Southampton and South-West Hampshire Health Authority* [1985] IRLR 203, the English High Court granted the plaintiff an injunction restraining the defendants from implementing a notice purporting to terminate the employment relationship. The defendants were purporting to dismiss Mr Irani, arguably in breach of contractual procedures, from his post as a part-time ophthalmologist, by reason of irreconcilable differences which had arisen as between Mr Irani and the consultant in charge of the clinic in which he worked. The court pointed out that the decision to dismiss was based on incompatibility with the consultant and that there was no criticism of the plaintiff's conduct or professional competence. In fact, the court was satisfied 'that the defendant authority [had] perfect faith in the honesty, integrity and loyalty of Mr Irani'.

2.2.2 THE FENNELLY CASE

Within a matter of months, the Irish High Court followed suit. In *Fennelly v Assicurazioni Generali SpA and General Underwriting Agencies Ireland Ltd* [1985] 3 ILTR 73 ('*Fennelly*') the defendant purported to dismiss the plaintiff by reason of redundancy on the grounds of a massive down-turn in business. The plaintiff claimed that he was employed under a fixed term contract for a period of twelve years and, in that context, Costello J held that there was a fair question for trial. Turning to the issue of the balance of convenience, as between the parties he stated that, pending a hearing, 'the plaintiff [would] be left without a salary and nothing to live on' and that his situation 'would be little short of disastrous'. Costello J held that the balance of convenience was in Mr Fennelly's favour and stated that it would be 'unjust' to leave him in a situation where he would 'be virtually destitute with a prospect of damages', pending a trial of the action. The judge stated that, in view of the 'very special circumstances' pertaining, he would order the defendant to pay the plaintiff's salary and bonus until the trial of the action and went on to state:

'I accept that the court should not require an employer to take on an employee where serious difficulties have arisen between them or where there is no work for the employee but in this case the parties have obviously the highest regard for one another. I will take an undertaking that the plaintiff will be prepared to carry out such duties as the defendant will ask of him until the trial. If they would make use of him until the trial of the action, the plaintiff should attend and carry out such duties as they give him. They might prefer not to give him any duties and put him on leave of absence. That is for the defendant but they must continue to pay his salary until the trial.'

2.2.3 UK CASE LAW

Following *Irani v Southampton and South-West Hampshire Health Authority* [1985] IRLR 203, the UK Court of Appeal accepted that the court could order specific performance of a contract of employment, on condition that the employer retained trust and confidence in the employee (*Powell v London Borough of Brent* [1987] IRLR 466). Mrs Powell was employed by the defendants as a senior benefits officer. She applied for promotion to a post as Principal Benefits Officer (Policy and Training). She was one of several candidates interviewed and, after the interviews were concluded, she was informed by telephone that she had been successful in her application for the post. She took up her new position, but at the same time one of the other candidates submitted a grievance concerning his unsuccessful application. The defendants took the view that the selection procedure might have been in breach of their equal opportunity code of practice and, within days of her having taken up her new position, Mrs Powell was informed that it was not possible to appoint her. Approximately two months later, it was decided to readvertise the post. Mrs Powell sought an injunction restraining the defendants from so doing and requiring them to treat her as if she were properly employed by them in the post. The Court of Appeal granted the injunction sought and Ralph Gibson LJ offered the following guidance, with regard to the requirement for subsisting trust and confidence:

'For my part I am not able to derive much assistance from the words "complete confidence" for the purposes of this case . . . Sufficiency of confidence must be judged by reference to the circumstances of the case, including the nature of the work, the people with whom the work must be done and the likely effect upon the employer and the employer's operations if the employer is required by injunction to suffer the plaintiff to continue in the work.'

In the later case of *Ali v London Borough of Southwark* [1988] IRLR 100, Millett J stated that:

'[T]he court will intervene by way of injunction in an employment case to restrain dismissal only where it is satisfied that the employer still retains confidence and trust in the employee or, if he claims to have lost such trust and confidence, does so on some irrational ground.'

2.3 A 'WORKABLE' ORDER/A JUST RESULT

2.3.1 INTRODUCTION

Ralph Gibson LJ, when analysing the circumstances in which interlocutory relief will be granted so as to restrain a dismissal in *Powell v London Borough of Brent* [1987] IRLR 466, stated that it must be

'clear on the evidence not only that it is *otherwise just* to make such a requirement but also that there exists sufficient confidence on the part of the employer in the servant's ability and other necessary attributes for it to be reasonable to make the order.'

In August 1990 the UK High Court appeared to focus on what was just and rejected the submission that unless trust and confidence remain, an injunction to preserve the contract of employment should never be granted. In *Robb v London Borough of Hammersmith and Fulham* [1991] IRLR 72 the defendants acknowledged that they had dismissed the plaintiff, in breach of his contract, having failed to comply with the contractual disciplinary procedures. The plaintiff made applications for an injunction restraining the dismissal, in circumstances where it was made clear that it was not sought to require the defendants to reinstate him so that he could actually perform his duties, but rather that he be treated as suspended on full pay, pending compliance with the contractual disciplinary procedure. The defendants' submission that an injunction to preserve the contract of employment should never be granted unless trust and confidence between employer and employee remain, was described by the court as 'far too sweeping'. Morland J stated:

'If an injunction is sought to reinstate an employee dismissed in breach of contract, so that when reinstated, he can actually carry out the job for which he was employed, clearly trust and confidence are highly relevant. Without his employer's trust and confidence in his ability to perform his job, his position as an employee would be unworkable.'

However, Morland J went on to state:

'In my judgment, although the courts will only rarely grant the plaintiff injunctive relief against his employer, the all important criterion is whether the order sought is workable.'

Thus, while the judge accepted that 'trust and confidence are highly relevant', the absence of such trust and confidence should not prevent the granting of an injunction where such injunction would be 'workable'. He pointed out that the plaintiff was not seeking reinstatement so that he could actually perform his duties and responsibilities. He was seeking an order to restore the position as it was before the defendants unilaterally aborted the disciplinary procedure and unlawfully terminated his contract. In such circumstances, the defendants' lack of trust and confidence in the plaintiff's capability to do his job had no relevance to the 'workability' of the disciplinary procedure.

2.3.2   SHORTT v DATA PACKAGING LTD

Fennelly v Assicurazioni Generali SpA and General Underwriting Agencies Ireland Ltd [1985] 3 ILTR 73 stood alone, as the sole example in this jurisdiction, of an exception to the rule against specific performance of contracts of employment for a further nine years. Then, in January 1994, Mr Terence Shortt, the managing director of Data Packaging Ltd, was informed by telephone, by the chairman of the company, that owing to a restructuring of the company, he was to be made redundant. Later that same day, he received a letter confirming that his employment was being terminated 'with immediate effect' and he was directed to vacate his office that evening. Keane J was satisfied that 'in accordance with the tests required for the granting of an interlocutory injunction', Mr Shortt had made out 'a fair issue to be tried as to the legality of the purported termination'. Mr Shortt claimed that only the directors of the company had the power to dismiss him, that the directors had made no decision to that effect, given that he was a director and would have been aware of such decision. He claimed that his removal from office was ineffective in that it was in breach of the principles of natural justice and that his purported removal was by virtue of an alleged redundancy which he said was spurious and unsubstantiated. He claimed that the real reason for his dismissal lay in 'differences between himself and his employers'. Keane J was satisfied that damages would not constitute an adequate remedy, 'where the plaintiff [would] have to await the trial of the action in circumstances where he [was] totally without remuneration and where a trial [would] inevitably, be some time away'. The judge held that the balance of convenience was in favour of the granting of an injunction (*Shortt v Data Packaging Ltd* [1994] ELR 251).

The issue of continuing trust and confidence was not even addressed in *Shortt*. While it should have been possible for the plaintiff to contend that he continued to enjoy the defendant's trust and confidence, given that Data Packaging Ltd had purported to terminate his employment on grounds of redundancy, the issue was not addressed by Keane J and an injunction was granted, in circumstances where the plaintiff spoke of 'differences between himself and his employers'.

2.3.3   PHELAN v BIC (IRELAND) LTD

A case with striking similarities to *Shortt v Data Packaging Ltd* came before the High Court three years later—*Phelan v BIC (Ireland) Ltd, Biro BIC Ltd, Société BIC SA and Robert MacDonald* [1997] ELR 208. Mr Phelan was the managing director of BIC (Ireland) Ltd. Like Terence Shortt, he was summarily dismissed, purportedly on grounds of redundancy. He claimed that the termination of his office was in breach of the rules of natural justice and in breach of contract, that the decision to remove him was ultra vires the powers of a company and contravened the provisions of the Redundancy Payments Acts. Costello J, making reference to the 'old rule' that the court should not grant specific performance of a contract of employment, stated that the rule 'should be subject to qualifications and in a number of cases, the courts have granted interlocutory relief where it was in the interest of justice to do so'. Costello J was satisfied that Mr Phelan had 'made out and established serious issues'. He stated that damages would not be an adequate remedy, although he acknowledged that it was 'not a case in which the plaintiff [was] destitute as in *Fennelly*'. During the course of the hearing, it had transpired that Mr Phelan would get a pension, while he had also received two months' salary in lieu of notice. His shareholding was valued at £300,000. However, Costello J stated that he had 'never come across a case where a managing director was dismissed in such a way, other than in cases of serious misconduct'. He took the view that Mr Phelan had made out a case for exemplary damages and expressed the view that, 'if the case is established, the judge may not grant damages as it is not adequate compensation but would allow the plaintiff to stay on as managing director'. He granted an interlocutory injunction restraining the defendant from implementing the purported termination of the plaintiff's appointment as managing director. Costello J made no reference whatever to the issue of trust and confidence but he ordered that the defendant pay the plaintiff's salary until the trial of the action and such other emoluments to which the plaintiff might be entitled, including his pension and the use of his motor car.

2.3.4   FURTHER CASE LAW

There followed a number of similar applications to the court. In *Boland v Phoenix Shannon plc* [1997] ELR 113 Barron J held that there was a fair issue to be tried and that 'the balance of hardships' was in the plaintiff's favour. He concluded that damages would not be an adequate remedy, that while the plaintiff, a chartered accountant, who had been operations director and vice president of the defendant, 'has his profession and to that extent, should be in a position to earn . . . in practical terms his dismissal will leave him in the same situation as the plaintiff in *Fennelly's* case'. Without addressing the trust and confidence issue, Barron J granted an injunction restraining the dismissal.

In *Harte v Kelly* [1997] ELR 125 the defendants conceded that there were fair issues to be tried. Laffoy J found that there had been 'a total breakdown of trust and confidence between . . . the plaintiff and the first defendant'. She went on to state:

'In my view, the entitlement to the type of order granted in the *Fennelly* case is not limited to a situation in which the plaintiff will establish that he will face penury if such an order is not made. The rationale of the decision is that it is unjust to leave a person who alleges that his dismissal has been wrongful without his salary pending the trial of the action and merely with his prospect of an award of damages at the trial of the action. The prospect of the destitution of the plaintiff pending the trial of his action was certainly a factual consideration in the *Fennelly* case. However, in the two later cases [*Shortt v Data Packing Ltd* [1994] ELR 251 and *Boland v Phoenix Shannon plc* [1997] ELR 113], which concerned the alleged wrongful dismissal of a managing director and of an operations director and vice-president respectively, there was no consideration of matching the totality of the income of the plaintiff to his outgoings or commitments nor was there any consideration of the value of his assets or his spending pattern, matters which the court has been invited to consider in the instant case.'

Laffoy J held that

'it would be an unjust situation to leave [the plaintiff] without approximately half his net income pending the trial of the action and only with the prospect of an award of damages at the trial. In short . . . damages would not be an adequate remedy in the circumstances'.

She made an order directing the company to pay Mr Harte's salary and other benefits, from the date on which he claimed relief, until the trial of the action.

Within days of delivering judgment in *Harte*, Laffoy J made a similar order in *Courtenay v Radio 2000 Ltd (t/a Classic Hits 98FM)* [1997] ELR 198. Laffoy J held that there were fair issues to be tried and that the balance of convenience lay in favour of granting the injunction. She expressed the view that:

'[R]elief should be granted if it would perpetrate an injustice to leave a person who alleges that he has been wrongfully dismissed without his salary, and only with the prospect of an award of damages at the trial of the action, pending the trial of the action. In that case the defendant claimed that, as the plaintiff "was employed to present live broadcasts and given that trust and confidence in the plaintiff no longer [existed] on the part of the defendant, it would be inappropriate for the court to grant the [injunctions] sought by the plaintiff and, in any event, to do so would be to result in an unworkable situation".'

In all of these circumstances, Laffoy J granted an injunction restraining the defendant from implementing the plaintiff's purported dismissal until the trial of the action but, 'having regard to the attitude evinced on the part of the defendant', she refused to reinstate the plaintiff to his position as a radio presenter, while she also refused to prevent the defendant from appointing another person to the plaintiff's position, pending the trial of the action.

2.3.5 'JUSTICE' PREVAILS?

Thus, by the end of July 1997, it seemed that employees seeking to restrain dismissals were no longer required to establish 'very special circumstances'. Clearly, the possibility of destitution was no longer a prerequisite to the award of an injunction, nor was it necessary to establish that trust and confidence still existed, as between the parties. Once an employee could establish that it would be unjust to leave him without a salary and only with the prospect of an award of damages, the employee need only satisfy the *American Cyanamid* principles in order to secure an injunction restraining a dismissal.

It will be appreciated that in all of the cases to which reference is made above—*Fennelly v Assicurazione Generali SpA and General Underwriting Agencies Ltd* [1985] 3 ILTR 73; *Shortt v Data Packaging Ltd* [1994] ELR 251; *Phelan v BIC (Ireland) Ltd* [1997] ELR 208; *Boland v Phoenix Shannon plc* [1997] ELR 113; *Harte v Kelly* [1997] ELR 125; and *Courtenay v Radio 2000 Ltd* [1997] ELR 198—the court restrained the employer from dismissing the employee and ordered the employer to pay the plaintiff during the period leading to the trial of the action. The courts are reluctant ever to order the employer to allow the employee to return to work, but will order the employee to undertake to perform such duties as may be required by the employer during the period leading up to the trial. An order of such nature is often described as a 'Fennelly Order'.

While the courts are reluctant to put employees back at work, that is not to say that they will never do so and, indeed, two recent cases, *Martin v Nationwide Building Society* [1999] ELR 241 and *Howard v University College Cork*, 25 July 2000 (unreported) are illustrative of a willingness on the part of the courts to make orders compelling employers to allow employees to continue to work where justice requires the making of such orders (see **2.9** below).

2.4 FENNELLY REVISITED—'EXCEPTIONAL CASES'

2.4.1 O'MALLEY v ARAVON SCHOOL

On 13 August 1997 *O'Malley v Aravon School Ltd* came before the High Court. The plaintiff was the Principal of the defendant school. She and her husband commenced their association with the school as far back as 1970. They lived on school property with their dependent children. During the early 1990s problems arose between the board of the defendant and Mrs O'Malley's husband in relation to his performance as the then Principal. Ultimately, he resigned as Principal and his wife, the plaintiff, was appointed in his place (following a period when they had acted as joint Principals). Mr O'Malley continued to teach at the defendant's school. An agreement was executed as between the plaintiff, her husband and the defendant, embodying the new arrangements. It appears that those arrangements broke down, as far as the school authorities were concerned, during the first half of 1997. The board's concerns were brought to the attention of the plaintiff and her husband. They attended at a meeting on 5 June, when Mr O'Malley addressed the issues of concern and then left. Following the meeting, Mr O'Malley and the plaintiff were dismissed. Mrs O'Malley sought an injunction to restrain the dismissal. The matter came before the then President of the High Court, Costello P, on 13 August 1997. He stated, with regard to applications for specific performance of contracts of employment:

'The principles are well established. One of the most important principles is whether, at the trial, should the plaintiff succeed, an injunction would be granted. If the court decides that, at the trial, the plaintiff would not get an injunction, then she should not get an injunction, at this stage.'

Costello P made reference to *Hill v C A Parsons & Co Ltd* [1972] Ch 305, but stated that in order to rely on the principles enunciated in that case:

'The plaintiff has to establish that her case is one of the exceptional cases. There have been exceptions. *Fennelly* was one, but in that case, I pointed out that I accept that the court should not require an employer to keep the employee, where there are serious differences. Here, the board has lost confidence. The whole essence of the contract is based on confidence and trust. It would be wrong to order the school to retain the employee. The plaintiff has failed to bring herself within the exception. She will not get an order for specific performance at the trial. I will not grant interlocutory relief, because I do not think that at the trial of the action, an injunction will be granted.'

2.4.2 O'MALLEY DISTINGUISHED

Obvious and immediate difficulties arose in attempting to reconcile *O'Malley* with judgments, all delivered within the six-month period preceding *O'Malley* (in *Phelan v BIC (Ireland) Ltd* [1997] ELR 208; *Boland v Phoenix Shannon plc* [1997] ELR 113; *Harte v Kelly* [1997] ELR 125; and *Courtenay v Radio 2000 Ltd* [1997] ELR 198). It was acknowledged during the *Phelan* hearing that the plaintiff would get a pension, that he had received two months' salary in lieu of notice and had a shareholding valued at £300,000. Barron J took the view that Brian Boland '[had] his profession and to that extent, should be in a position to earn'. Peter Harte was in receipt of £3,000 per month net of tax, his share of royalty payments. Mrs O'Malley had been associated with Aravon School for approximately twenty-seven years. She and her husband resided on school property, as did the dependent children. Apart from their school salaries, neither Mrs O'Malley nor her husband had any other sources of income.

Clearly, Costello P was not prepared to grant injunctive relief, in the absence of subsisting trust and confidence, as between the parties. His position, in that context, was in direct conflict with that of Laffoy J (while it could hardly be argued that trust and confidence existed as between Brian Boland and Phoenix Shannon plc).

Costello P's statement to the effect that if the judge, at an interlocutory hearing, decides that the plaintiff would not get an injunction at the trial of the action, then the plaintiff should not get an interlocutory injunction, is certainly evocative of the House of Lords, in *American Cyanamid Co v Ethicon Ltd* [1975] AC 396, where the Law Lords stated:

'[U]nless the material available to the court at the hearing of the application for an interlocutory injunction fails to disclose that the plaintiff has any real prospect of succeeding in his claim for a permanent injunction at the trial, the court should go on to consider whether the balance of convenience lies in favour of granting or refusing the interlocutory relief that is sought.'

The UK Court of Appeal had interpreted this statement in *Powell v London Borough of Brent* [1987] IRLR 46, where the defendants had sought to prevent the plaintiff from taking up a post as Principal Benefits Officer and to readvertise the post. Ralph Gibson LJ stated:

'It was common ground . . . in this court that the expression "permanent injunction at the trial" means no more in this case than an injunction prohibiting the defendants from treating the plaintiff otherwise than in the post as Principal Benefits Officer on the ground that she was not contractually appointed to it. The injunction which will be sought at the trial, as with the case of the interlocutory injunction sought by this appeal will not prevent Brent Council from exercising any powers they may have which will in law effectively terminate the contract of employment.'

In any event, at the end of 1997, *O'Malley* stood in direct conflict with all of the other cases that had come before the court during the previous twelve months. Tom Mallon BL and Marguerite Bolger BL in 'Injuncting the Contract of Employment', which was published in the December 1997 issue of *The Bar Review* at p 113, attempted to distinguish *O'Malley*, on the grounds that Mrs O'Malley had been dismissed, 'with at least some regard to principles of natural justice':

> 'It is arguable that *O'Malley* can be distinguished from the line of cases in which trust and confidence had been shattered by the fact that the plaintiff had been dismissed with at least some regard to principles of natural justice. The grounds for her employer's dissatisfaction were put to her, she was given an opportunity to respond and careful consideration was given to her response. The existence of at least some recognition of an employee's rights to fair procedures is in stark contrast to the summary manner in which the successful plaintiffs in *Shortt, Harte, Courtenay* and *Phelan* were dismissed.'

However, it is clear that Mr Mallon and Ms Bolger were uncomfortable with that view of *O'Malley*. They went on to state:

> 'On the other hand, the procedures applied were minimum and the court could have taken the same approach as had been taken in cases where virtually no procedures were applied without any great inconsistency in the developing line of case law.'

They did make reference to the fact that 'Costello P also seemed to be very influenced by his belief that the trial judge would not be prepared to grant a permanent injunction'.

2.5   O'MALLEY IGNORED

2.5.1   DOYLE v GRANGEFORD PRECAST CONCRETE LTD

Doyle v Grangeford Precast Concrete Ltd [1998] ELR 260 came before the High Court, on appeal from the Circuit Court, on 19 January 1998. Mr Doyle was employed by the defendant as safety officer, on terms agreed in July 1997. In September 1997 he received a letter of appointment, setting out terms and conditions of employment, which contained terms which were not included in the original agreement. Mr Doyle refused to sign the letter of appointment and the defendant terminated his employment. The Circuit Court granted injunctive relief, requiring the defendant to pay Mr Doyle's salary (and other benefits) pending the hearing of the action. The matter came before O'Donovan J on appeal from the Circuit Court. He stated:

> 'In my view, an employer is entitled to terminate the employment of an employee for good or bad reasons or, indeed, for no reason at all provided, however, that the employee is given proper notice of termination.'

He went on to state:

> 'In my view, the cases of *Fennelly* . . . *Shortt* . . . and *Harte* . . . are all authorities for the proposition that I can grant an injunction to an employee, who challenges the legality of a dismissal on the basis that the termination of his employment was unlawful, where that person is facing short term impecuniosity, even though, at the end of the day, that person is likely to end up with an award of damages, rather than reinstatement. Moreover, I am satisfied that the decisions in the *Shortt* and *Harte* cases established that it is not necessary for trust and confidence to be present to justify the granting of interlocutory relief. The same conclusion can, I think, be drawn from the decision of Costello J in *Phelan*. . . . In this regard, I find it difficult to reconcile the decision of Costello J in *O'Malley* . . . with the other decisions to which I

have referred because that decision would appear to be inconsistent with those decisions . . . in all the circumstances, I intend to ignore the decision in *O'Malley.'*

O'Donovan J was satisfied that the plaintiff 'would be somewhat stricken in his financial circumstances were he to await the outcome of the trial . . . without any salary' and he ordered the defendant to pay Mr Doyle's salary pending the trial. Issue No 5 of the 1998 Employment Law Report states that the matter came on for full hearing on 26 February 1998 and judgment was delivered on 4 March 1998. The plaintiff was awarded six months' remuneration in lieu of notice. The defendant was allowed a discount for the remuneration paid to the plaintiff since the granting of the injunction in December 1997.

2.5.2   HEGARTY v P J HEGARTY AND SONS

On the day after O'Donovan J delivered his judgment in *Doyle*, Shanley J delivered judgment in *Hegarty v P J Hegarty and Sons*, 20 January 1998 (unreported). In that case the plaintiff claimed that he had been removed from his position as contracts director with the defendant, in breach of natural and constitutional justice. However, he 'concentrated on seeking to have the defendant pay his salary to the trial of the action and less on an order restraining the defendant from acting on the decision to dismiss him'. Shanley J, referring to 'the application to restrain the defendant from acting on the decision to dismiss', stated as follows:

'In substance that application is for specific performance requiring the defendant to retain the plaintiff's services as contracts manager, in circumstances where the defendant has deposed to a breakdown of trust and confidence. I would not, in those circumstances, consider that there were any grounds for the order sought. It would be quite unwise to try to force the defendant who has lost trust and confidence to take the plaintiff back. Just to balance the matter, it is equally clear that the plaintiff has lost trust and confidence in the defendant and having regard to what is said in his affidavit, it is clear that the plaintiff would not be comfortable resuming his employment.'

Thus, it is clear that Shanley J was of the view that the court should not restrain an employer from dismissing an employee in circumstances where trust and confidence have broken down. However, he went on to deal with the issue of 'whether in the context of a claim for wrongful dismissal [he] should order the defendant to continue to pay the plaintiff's salary as accruing', as a separate issue. In that context, having found that there was a serious issue to be tried (albeit, 'one of the thinnest cases of a serious issue that I have come across'), Shanley J went on to deal with the issue of the adequacy of damages, stating that he was 'satisfied that damages would not be an adequate remedy if it is found that the plaintiff has not been validly dismissed' and, in that context, he made specific reference to 'the effect of the action complained of on the plaintiff's reputation'. He stated that, in considering the balance of convenience, he must 'consider whether it would be more oppressive on the plaintiff to refuse the application than on the defendant to grant it'. He addressed the issue of impecuniosity and acknowledged that:

'[T]he court is not confined to considering a situation where the plaintiff is indigent and has such outgoings as require the payment of some sum by way of salary. Instead, the court can match the totality of the plaintiff's income to his outgoings and can consider the overall value of his assets and spending pattern and having regard to the overall picture can require a defendant to pay a plaintiff's salary pending trial even if the plaintiff is not indigent.'

Shanley J made a most unusual order, directing 'the payment of half the plaintiff's salary only, net of tax' to the trial of the action, with a view to ensuring that the plaintiff be able to maintain himself and that 'no injustice will arise'. While he had refused to 'restrain the defendant from acting on the decision to dismiss', he accepted the plaintiff's undertaking 'to do such work as he may be asked to do'. While the reality in most, if not all, of these cases is that the plaintiff does not return to work pending a trial of the action, it is submitted, nonetheless, that it is difficult to reconcile a refusal to 'restrain [an employer] from acting on [a] decision to dismiss', with an order compelling that employer to continue to pay the employee.

2.5.3 O'SHAUGHNESSY v BOSTON SCIENTIFIC IRELAND LTD

On 18 January 1999 *O'Shaughnessy v Boston Scientific Ireland Ltd* came before the court. The plaintiff was employed as human resources manager by the defendant. Having successfully completed a six-month probationary period, she was told by the Director of Human Resources, in August 1998, that he had received very negative feedback about her and that he wanted her out of the company by 1 November 1998. She claimed the purported justification for her removal was 'clouded in secrecy' in that, while there were intimations of dissatisfaction, no single complainant was identified and the specifics of their alleged complaints were similarly obscured. The company claimed that when Ms O'Shaughnessy was confronted with regard to the perceived problems with her 'style', she had said she would leave but asked for time to repair the 'damage done' and that it was agreed that she would be allowed to leave the company gracefully. While Ms O'Shaughnessy claimed that she was being forced out, the company claimed that she had agreed to leave of her own volition. When, ultimately, Ms O'Shaughnessy refused to leave, her employment was terminated, on 19 November 1998. She sought an injunction restraining the dismissal.

O'Sullivan J ordered the company to pay the plaintiff's salary as it fell due and to discharge all other incidents of the plaintiff's employment until the trial of the action. He granted an injunction restraining the defendant from giving effect to the purported dismissal of the plaintiff and from appointing anybody to her position 'on a permanent basis'.

O'Sullivan J stated:

'I am satisfied that the plaintiff has raised a substantial issue, primarily in relation to the question of whether the plaintiff agreed to go or, as alleged, she was dismissed.'

The defendant's counsel urged O'Sullivan J not to grant an interlocutory injunction unless he was satisfied that there was a possibility that the trial judge might grant a permanent injunction. O'Sullivan J stated:

'In my view, the court must decide as to whether there is a fair or substantial question and once it does so, should move smartly to the other issues.'

In relation to the question of whether damages would be an adequate remedy, O'Sullivan J stated:

'The plaintiff is entitled to the dignity of employment and the satisfaction and fulfilment that it will give her. Money is not adequate. Damages will not be adequate in this particular case.'

In this context, O'Sullivan J was echoing the sentiments of Ralph Gibson LJ in *Powell v London Borough of Brent* [1987] IRLR 466, where he stated that the plaintiff

'could be compensated, of course, for loss of earnings [during the period leading to the trial of the action] but she would have lost the satisfaction of doing this more demanding and rewarding job and I accept that damages for estimated future financial loss would not be full compensation to her.'

He went on to state that:

'it would be disagreeable and difficult for this plaintiff to be returned now to her old work at her old place of work and to be denied the satisfaction and challenge to be doing the work which she was selected . . . to do. She will get no damages for the frustration and unhappiness thereby caused, nor for the loss of the chance to continue to get better by experience in her post and thereby to increase the likelihood that Brent Council will not dismiss her if she succeeds in showing that she was validly appointed.'

O'Sullivan J made no reference to trust and confidence while deciding that the issue of 'a permanent injunction at the trial' should be answered by simply deciding as to whether there is a fair or substantial question.

2.5.4 DISTINGUISHING BETWEEN ORDERS FOR PAYMENT OF SALARY AND FOR REINSTATEMENT

Some weeks later, on 9 February 1999, Macken J drew a clear distinction between ordering payment of an employee's salary and ordering the reinstatement of the employee, in *Lonergan v Salter-Townshend, the Irish Council for Disabled Persons and the Minister for Justice, Equality and Law Reform* [2000] ELR 15. The plaintiff claimed that he had been appointed to the post of Chief Executive Officer of the second-named defendant and that his subsequent removal from the post was unlawful. He stated 'unequivocally' that he was dependent on his salary to meet general day-to-day expenses and Macken J found that he had established that he was likely to suffer irreparable loss and damage if deprived of that salary. However, the judge also found that it was 'clear that the plaintiff . . . does not enjoy the wholehearted support of all members of the board' of the second-named defendant. In those circumstances, she ordered the second-named defendant to continue to pay the plaintiff his salary, but did 'not consider it appropriate to make an order reinstating the plaintiff, save that, in return for the continuation of his salary' she directed that he 'may be requested . . . to carry out work . . . and if he is not requested to carry out such work, this will not in any way affect his entitlement to be paid his salary until the hearing of the action'. While it is clear that, once again, the absence of trust and confidence did not inhibit the granting of the injunction, Macken J, in distinguishing between an order requiring an employer to pay an employee and an order reinstating the employee in his position was simply articulating the reality, in cases of this nature. From the beginning (*Fennelly v Assicurazioni Generali SpA* [1985] 3 ILTR 73), the court has restrained dismissal but, in the vast majority of cases, has stopped short of reinstating plaintiff employees, rather ordering that the employees comply with the employer's requirements, in terms of actually doing work, during the period leading to the trial of the action. Invariably, the employee is not required to work by the employer during that time.

2.6 UNFAIR DISMISSALS ACTS, 1977–1993

2.6.1 COMMON LAW POSITION DISTINGUISHED

On a practical note, while the attractions of an injunction, from the point of view of a plaintiff, are obvious, practitioners should bear in mind the outcome of *Doyle v Grangeford Precast Concrete Ltd* [1998] ELR 260, before seeking injunctive relief. Section 15(3) of the Unfair Dismissals Act, 1977 provides as follows:

> '*Where the hearing by a Court of proceedings for damages at common law for wrongful dismissal of an employee has commenced, the employee shall not be entitled to redress under this Act in respect of the dismissal to which the proceedings relate.*'

It will be apparent that all of these cases relate to an alleged breach of the contract of employment or a failure on the part of an employer to comply with the principles of natural and constitutional justice. The plaintiff's contractual rights or his constitutional right to fair procedures are inevitably at issue. As O'Donovan J stated in *Doyle*:

'an employer is entitled to terminate the employment of an employee for good or bad reasons or, indeed, for no reason at all provided, however, that the employee is given proper notice of termination' (and, it is submitted, only in circumstances where fair procedures are followed).

However, it is unlikely that a court will ever restrain a dismissal on the grounds that the dismissal was not merited or that a lesser sanction should have been imposed. It is difficult to envisage the granting of a permanent injunction or, indeed, the making of an award of exemplary damages. Thus, an employee who seeks a remedy for unlawful dismissal at common law ('wrongful dismissal') can only expect an award of damages for breach of contract and, apart from cases where the employee has a contractual right to more than twelve months' notice, it is difficult to envisage the making of an award of damages amounting to more than one year's remuneration. Indeed, awards of more than six months' remuneration are exceptional. Mr Doyle was awarded six months' remuneration, less money received by him, during the period leading to the trial. An employee claiming unfair dismissal has the potential to secure an award of up to two years' gross remuneration. This fact should always be borne in mind in deciding how best to proceed (and by counsel, when drafting proceedings claiming injunctive relief).

2.6.2 FRAMING PROCEEDINGS FOR INJUNCTIVE RELIEF

Counsel will normally be extremely careful in framing proceedings for injunctive relief, so as to ensure that a plaintiff might not be considered to have taken part in a 'hearing by a court of proceedings for damages at common law'. To that end, proceedings in cases of this nature invariably seek declarations and injunctions, but rarely embody a claim for damages for breach of contract. In this way, it is intended to keep open the door to the Employment Appeals Tribunal (under the Unfair Dismissals Acts) but the judgment of Murphy J in *Philpott v Ogilvy & Mather Ltd* [2000] ELR 225 raises serious questions about the extent to which such approach will prove effective in the future. Delivering judgment in *Philpott* (on 21 March 2000), Murphy J refused to grant declaratory and/or interlocutory relief to the plaintiff because he (the plaintiff) had not claimed damages for wrongful dismissal. He stated as follows:

'If the traditional relief at common law for unfair dismissal was a claim for damages then the plaintiff may also have been entitled to declarations and injunctions in aid of his common law remedy. But if such equitable relief has no independent existence apart from the claim for damages for wrongful dismissal then, it seems to me, that there is no other free standing relief which can be claimed at law or in equity.'

In coming to this conclusion, Murphy J relied on the judgment of the Supreme Court in *Parsons v Iarnrod Eireann* [1997] ELR 203 and, while such interpretation of *Parsons* would almost certainly reduce the popularity of the application for declaratory/injunctive relief in employment cases, Murphy J's judgment must be viewed beside that of Budd J in *Cassidy v Shannon Castle Banquets and Heritage Ltd* [2000] ELR 248, which was delivered less than nine months previously (on 30 July 1999) and illustrates an entirely different interpretation of *Parsons*. Budd J took the view that *Parsons* 'is authority for the proposition that declaratory relief is available unless precluded by the option having been taken of making a claim under the Unfair Dismissals Act'. He pointed out that in *Parsons* the plaintiff, having claimed unfair dismissal, had 'forfeited his right to bring an action for damages for wrongful dismissal' and he went on to point out that it was in those circumstances that 'the declaratory relief sought could avail him nothing' and was 'quite properly refused'. Thus, while Murphy J is of the view that declaratory/injunctive relief may only be sought in conjunction with a claim for damages for wrongful dismissal, Budd J appears to be of the view that a plaintiff is only prohibited from seeking such declaratory/injunctive relief in circumstances where a recommendation has been made by a rights commissioner in respect of a claim by the employee for redress under the Unfair Dismissals Acts or the hearing of a claim by the Employment Appeals Tribunal has commenced. These cases are analysed at greater length at **2.10** below. Until such time as this dichotomy is resolved, practitioners should carefully advise their clients with regard to the ramifications of the Unfair Dismissals Act, 1977, s 15(3) while the choice of remedy in employment cases will have to be carefully considered, for fear of exposing a client to an order for High Court costs, alternatively depriving the client of the possibility of securing a substantial award for compensation under the Unfair Dismissals Acts.

2.6.3 IMPLICATIONS OF UNSUCCESSFUL APPLICATION

Practitioners should also bear in mind that an unsuccessful injunction application may also have extremely serious implications for a plaintiff employee. Injunction applications, by their very nature, often embody a claim that the purported termination of the employment relationship was unlawful and without effect and that the relationship continues to subsist. Thus, where a plaintiff fails to secure an injunction on, say, the grounds that the balance of convenience did not favour the granting of the injunction, the employee will probably be in a situation where he is a plaintiff in a High Court action in which it is claimed that the employment relationship subsists. Consequently, he may have difficulty in claiming unfair dismissal before the EAT while the efficacy of the dismissal is the subject of a 'live' High Court action. If the employee decides to abandon the High Court action, he will have a substantial exposure to costs. In this way, an employee who makes an unsuccessful application for an injunction may find that he is 'trapped' in the High Court and cannot gain access to the potentially more lucrative forum that is the EAT, without incurring considerable cost.

2.7 REDUNDANCY

2.7.1 SCOTTISH CASE LAW

The Scottish Court of Session recently granted 'the first mainstream employment law decision in which an injunction has been issued prohibiting a private sector employer from dismissing an employee in breach of the terms of a redundancy selection procedure' (see Industrial Relations Law Report, vol 27, no 2, February 1998). In *Anderson v Pringle of Scotland Ltd* [1998] IRLR 64 Mr Anderson was a longstanding employee of the respondent company. In 1997 it was decided that some 290 employees would have to be made redundant. An agreement with the union, the GMB, included a redundancy procedure which provided for selection for redundancy on the basis of last in, first out. However, the employers decided not to operate that procedure but instead to use a selective scheme. On that basis, Mr Anderson would be one of those made redundant whereas, on the basis of last in, first out, he would not have been selected for redundancy. Neither Mr Anderson nor the GMB had agreed to the employer proceeding in accordance with the selective scheme and Mr Anderson sought to restrain the company from so doing. The Court of Session held that he was entitled, in terms of his contract of employment, to require the employer to operate the last in, first out method of redundancy selection provided for under the agreement with the union and, correspondingly, not to operate the selective scheme, which the company wished to adopt. The court held that the whole of the employer/union agreement had been incorporated into Mr Anderson's contract of employment, so that the selection criteria for redundancy set out in the agreement were to be treated as provisions having contractual force between the employee and the employer. Lord Prosser stated:

> 'As a general proposition, it is trite that the courts will not oblige master and servant to continue in that relationship together and that even where termination of employment is wrongful, the appropriate remedy will be damages, rather than, for example, reinstatement. But general propositions need not be read as universal propositions.'

He continued:

'I am satisfied that in principle it is a matter of circumstances rather than of law that interdict will usually be refused. Whatever may be the outcome on fuller pleadings or after proof, I am prepared at this stage to see the case as one where (as in *Irani*) the mechanisms of dismissal rather than the principle of dismissal may be the heart of the matter. In the contemporary world, where even reinstatement is a less inconceivable remedy, intervention before dismissal must in my view be seen as a matter of discretion, rather than an impossibility. If there were any question of mistrust, the position would no doubt be very different; but at least on the material before me, I am not persuaded that there is any true analogy between the respondents' preference for other employees and the need for confidence which is inherent in the employer/employee relationship. It may be very inconvenient or difficult for the respondents to abide by the priorities they have agreed to; but they can hardly call it unfair to be held to their own bargain. Perhaps because fairness cannot readily be categorised, such exceptional cases as there have been give no very clear picture of the criteria for intervention. But I have come to the view that in this case and having regard to the terms of the interdict sought, the petitioner has a prima facie case for suspension and interdict.'

Having concluded that the balance of convenience favoured 'maintaining the status quo' Lord Prosser granted an interim order prohibiting the employer from selecting employees for redundancy on any basis other than length of service.

2.7.2   ENGLISH CASE LAW

The decision in *Anderson v Pringle of Scotland Ltd* conflicts squarely with the earlier decision of the English High Court in *Alexander v Standard Telephones and Cables Ltd* [1990] IRLR 55. In that case Aldous J refused to grant an injunction, in almost identical circumstances to those pertaining in *Anderson*. Again, the plaintiff employees sought to rely on a collective agreement which provided for selection for redundancy on the basis of last in, first out. The employer served redundancy notices on workers who were selected on the grounds of relative skills and flexibility. The court accepted that the plaintiffs had an arguable case that the redundancy procedure contained in the collective agreements required selection for redundancy on the basis of last in, first out. It was also agreed that the collective agreements formed part of the contract of employment. However, the court held that, even assuming that the plaintiffs' dismissals were wrongful, they had no real prospect of succeeding at trial in obtaining an injunction restraining the employers from dismissing them or giving effect to their purported dismissals. Aldous J stated that, as a matter of principle, the courts have refused to grant injunctions to restrain a breach of contract for personal service which would compel an employer to provide work for an employee he does not wish to employ. He stated that, once an employer has lost confidence in an employee, nothing a court says or orders will correct that view and the relationship of employer and employee will have broken down. Referring to *Irani v Southampton and South-West Hampshire Health Authority* [1985] IRLR 203 and *Powell v London Borough of Brent* [1987] IRLR 466, he stated that those cases were different in that there was work for the plaintiffs. He stated that the evidence established that if the plaintiffs were maintained in employment, others would have to be made redundant and that, unlike the plaintiffs in *Irani* and *Powell*, it could not be said that the employer in this case had complete confidence in the plaintiffs, as it had less confidence that they could do the work than the other members of the workforce who were retained. He stated that the relationship of employer and employee had broken down and that the employer believed that it did not have any work for the employees to do and would suffer some detriment if the plaintiffs' employment was continued, as employees who were considered more capable of doing that work would have to be dismissed.

2.7.3 CONCLUSION

The direct conflict between the English court and the Scottish court is stark and it is submitted that the reasoning of the Scottish court is preferable. As one UK commentator has pointed out:

> 'The contractual relationship of trust and confidence should not be treated as a function of the business cycle. It is no more appropriate to regard confidence in the employee as no longer existing because of a redundancy situation than it would be to regard that confidence as restored by an upturn in the order book. The issue for the court is whether the necessary trust and confidence to continue the employment relationship exists so as to allow a remedy for a legal wrong, not whether the employer has even more confidence in someone else' (IRLR, vol 27, no 2, February 1998).

While these cases are instructive in the context of redundancy, it will be clear, from the earlier sections of this chapter, that the Irish courts will grant injunctive relief, even in circumstances where trust and confidence no longer exist as between employer and employee.

2.8 THE INJUNCTION—PRE-DISMISSAL

2.8.1 INTRODUCTION

Recent decisions of the High Court illustrate that the court will intervene and grant an injunction to prevent an employer from taking steps to terminate an employee's contract of employment, other than in accordance with a contractual disciplinary procedure and/or the principles of natural justice.

2.8.2 AUDI ALTERAM PARTEM

In *Maher v Irish Permanent plc (No 1)* [1998] ELR 77 the plaintiff worked as a branch manager for the defendant. He was suspended from that position on 30 August 1996, pending the outcome of an investigation by the defendant into alleged misconduct including sexual harassment. Following an investigation and oral hearing, he was notified that a decision to dismiss him was warranted, but such decision would not be finalised for one week to allow him to make representations. The plaintiff instituted High Court proceedings seeking, inter alia, an order restraining the defendant from taking further steps to terminate his employment, save in accordance with the defendant's disciplinary procedure and the principles of natural justice. He contended that every stage of the procedure initiated by the defendant was tainted with unfairness.

Laffoy J found that 'the defendant embarked on and conducted the investigation into the allegations with due promptness' and, indeed, 'strove to conduct the investigation fairly and with due regard to proper procedures', up to a point. Then, on 20 September 1996, the defendant wrote to the plaintiff advising of its intention to convene a meeting on 27 September 1996, when the staff who had made allegations would be present and the plaintiff would be afforded an opportunity to question them. The plaintiff's solicitors wrote to the defendant demanding, inter alia, copies of the statements made by the staff members and seeking confirmation that they would be allowed to represent the plaintiff at the proposed hearing. The defendant failed to furnish the plaintiff with the copy statements, while Laffoy J found that it 'was not made clear to the plaintiff until the morning of the hearing that he would be allowed legal representation, if he attended at the hearing. This was far too late given that the plaintiff resided in Killarney, his solicitor practised in Cork and the meeting was to be held in Limerick'. Neither the plaintiff nor his representative attended at the meeting. Laffoy J stated:

'The stance adopted by the defendant in relation to the meeting of 27 September 1996 in advance of that meeting imperilled a fair hearing and a fair result. In the absence of the plaintiff and his legal representative, the hearing was not a fair hearing because only one side of the story emerged and there was no one to rebut, or to attempt to rebut, that version. That one-sided hearing could not and did not present a fair result. In my view, the blame for this cannot be ascribed to the plaintiff.'

Following the 27 September meeting, the defendant decided to dismiss the plaintiff, with effect from 9 October 1996. Laffoy J stated that:

'The decision to dismiss, being based on a hearing which contravened the most elementary requirement of fair procedures, in that it was conducted in the absence of the person against whom the allegations were made, cannot stand. Accordingly, the plaintiff's employment with the defendant did not terminate on 9 October 1996 and subsists.'

She made an order restraining the defendant from taking any further steps to terminate the plaintiff's employment, save in accordance with the defendant's disciplinary procedure and the principles of natural justice.

It may interest practitioners to note that, in October 1997, Mr Maher again sought interlocutory relief, in the context of the Irish Permanent's disciplinary enquiry (*Maher v Irish Permanent plc (No 2)* [1998] ELR 89). He sought an injunction restraining Irish Permanent from investigating allegations based on hearsay or admitting hearsay evidence at hearing and from considering allegations of serious misconduct in respect of which he had previously received a final written warning. Costello P refused the relief sought.

2.8.3   BIAS

In *Charlton v HH The Aga Khan's Studs Société Civile* [1999] ELR 136 the plaintiff had been in the employment of the defendant for twenty-seven years and for the thirteen-year period leading up to June 1998, she acted as secretary to the manager of the defendant's studs in Ireland, a Mr Drion. In July 1998 she was advised by the defendant's personnel manager, Mr Faughnan, that it was his intention to hold an enquiry 'into matters relating to [her] involvement in the improper use of [the defendant's] resources and/or property'. She was advised that an enquiry, conducted by Mr Faughnan, would take place on 4 August 1998, at which he would be enquiring, in particular, into her role in the improper use of the studs' resources by certain individuals, including Mr Drion and certain companies and institutions. Ms Charlton claimed, inter alia, that Mr Faughnan, who had been head of security while Mr Drion was the manager of the defendant's studs, was 'at the very least complicit' in the activities he purported to enquire into and that he was not an appropriate person to conduct the enquiry and that there was at best a real risk of an inference of bias or prejudgment on his part. In those circumstances, she sought an order restraining the defendant from continuing the enquiry. Mr Faughnan, in a replying affidavit, contended that it was only in the event of the plaintiff failing to provide satisfactory explanations in response to his queries that the question of disciplinary sanction would fall for consideration and that he would not be the decision-maker in such a contingency, since his sole function was to carry out an investigation and to prepare a report, which he would in turn furnish to his employer. He denied any bias or pre-judgment on his part and he asserted that the plaintiff had not been denied natural justice at any stage, particularly since she was not as then involved 'in a disciplinary process'.

Laffoy J stated:

'In my view, there is a fair issue to be tried on the plaintiff's challenge to the continuance of the enquiry . . . there is undoubtedly a fair issue to be tried as to the true nature of the enquiry, whether it is merely an investigation or is a disciplinary process. There is also a fair issue to be tried as to whether, if the enquiry is conducted by Mr Faughnan, the plaintiff can be assured of a hearing in accordance with the principles of natural and constitutional justice, which is her entitlement and, in particular, whether Mr Faughnan could conduct the enquiry without infringing the *audi alteram partem* principle and the principle *nemo iudex in causa sua*. The plaintiff contends that it is crucial to her defence that she should be in a position to examine or cross-examine Mr Faughnan, having regard to his day-to-day involvement in the matters at issue in the enquiry. On this ground alone, it seems to me that there is a fair issue to be tried as to whether Mr Faughnan should step aside and let somebody else conduct the enquiry.'

Laffoy J went on to conclude that given that dismissal had been 'signalled as a possible outcome', in this case damages would not be an adequate remedy if Ms Charlton was subjected to an enquiry which was subsequently found to have contravened the principles of natural and constitutional justice. The judge stated that the balance of convenience clearly favoured granting an injunction to restrain the prosecution of the enquiry, until the issues between the parties in relation to the conduct of the enquiry had been determined at the trial of the action. She made an order restraining the defendant, its servants or agents from prosecuting the enquiry, pending the trial of the action.

While not directly related to tenure and consequently not specifically relevant in the context of this chapter, it might interest practitioners to note that Laffoy J also ordered the defendant to pay sick pay to the plaintiff, while she continued to produce certificates from a medical practitioner of her unfitness for work, the plaintiff having claimed that it was an implied term of her contract of employment that she would be entitled to sick pay, for a reasonable period, while absent from work on medical grounds. See further Chapter 1 at **1.5.12.2**.

2.8.4   MAINTENANCE OF THE STATUS QUO

In *Howard v University College Cork*, 25 July 2000 (unreported) the plaintiff—Professor and Head of the Department of German at University College Cork—sought injunctions restraining the defendant from 'taking any steps' whatsoever to remove her from her post as Head of Department or towards appointing anybody else to the post and from interfering with or prohibiting her from performing her role and functions in that post. Ms Howard was unhappy with the manner in which the college had purported to investigate allegations of impropriety with regard to her conduct (in circumstances where it had been alleged that she was guilty of harassment and bullying) and she told the court that she was 'apprehensive' that the defendants would remove her from the post of Head of Department. The defendants submitted that the post of Head of the Department of German did not involve employment as such because it was inevitably associated with a position on the staff of the Department, such as professorship, and accordingly the person exercising the functions of the Head of Department was not, in performing that role, an employee and therefore termination of that post did not involve dismissal from employment, as it is ordinarily understood. In those circumstances, it was submitted on behalf of the defendants that principles of natural and constitutional justice were not relevant when considering the termination of the post of Head of the Department of German and need not be observed. The plaintiff, on the other hand, submitted that she was employed as Head of Department and that the governing body could not act capriciously, or unilaterally, but must observe fair procedures and, in particular, must give the holder of the office reasonable notice of the intention to consider the change and the reasons therefor. Having concluded that there were fair questions to be tried and that damages would not adequately compensate the plaintiff, O'Donovan J went on to find that the balance of convenience, as between granting or refusing the injunctive relief sought by Ms Howard, demanded that the status quo be maintained. He did so in circumstances where the defendants had suggested that their Department of German 'was in crisis' and that the only way to resolve the problem was to consider the appointment of a new Head to the Department. In that context, O'Donovan J expressed a view that 'whether or not there are significant problems within the Department of German at University College Cork and if there are, who is to blame for them, is not a relevant consideration' at the hearing of an application for interlocutory relief and is 'a problem for the trial judge'. He expressed the view that 'the appointment of a new Head of the Department in advance of the hearing, while the question as to whether or not the plaintiff is entitled to retain the post is still, as it were "up in the air" is likely to cause greater difficulties within the Department'. He went on to state that:

'If a new Head of the Department were appointed in advance of the hearing, it would place an intolerable burden on the trial judge because, instead of having to decide the fairly straightforward question as to whether or not the plaintiff was entitled to retain her role as Head of the Department, he or she would then have to choose between two identified persons and, possibly remove someone [from] a post to which that [person] had been appointed only a very short time previously.'

It was in all of those circumstances (and where the defendants had conceded that the plaintiff was entitled to remain as Professor of German) that O'Donovan J decided to grant injunctions to the plaintiff. He rejected the defendants' submission that an injunction would cause them irreparable harm or amount to discrimination in favour of the plaintiff, stating that he could not 'accept that maintaining a situation which has obtained for the last six years could have that effect'.

2.8.5 DEVELOPMENTS IN SCOTLAND

Recently, developments in this jurisdiction have been mirrored in Scotland. Reference is made at **2.7.1** above to *Anderson v Pringle of Scotland Ltd* [1998] IRLR 64, where Lord Prosser expressed the view that 'intervention before dismissal must be seen as a matter of discretion, rather than an impossibility'.

The recent decision of the Scottish Court of Session, Outer House, in *Peace v City of Edinburgh Council* [1999] IRLR 417, reinforces that view. Mr Peace had been employed by Edinburgh Council (and their statutory predecessors as local education authority) since about 1970. On 28 June 1997 he was suspended pending investigation of allegations of professional misconduct (of such nature as might lead to his dismissal, if held to be well founded). He claimed that, for the purposes of his contract of employment, disciplinary proceedings had to follow terms agreed in about 1975 by the Scottish Joint Negotiating Committee for Teaching Staff in School Education, as supplemented by local agreements, under which all material stages of the procedure have to take place before elected members of the authority. Edinburgh Council was purporting to proceed, pursuant to the provisions of disciplinary procedures first published in August 1997, under which initial investigations are committed to a senior officer of the council, with an appeal lying to a committee of elected members of the authority. The court held that Mr Peace was entitled to seek an injunction ('interdict') restraining the council from proceeding with disciplinary procedures, where the selection of those procedures was in breach of his contract of employment. Lord Penrose, having considered a long line of English and Scottish decisions, in this context, concluded that:

'Modern employment contracts may include a range of provisions which may be enforced as between employer and employee during the subsistence of the employment without prejudice to any general rule that the courts will not enforce implement or continuing implement of a working relationship as such between the employer and the employee.'

He concluded that the English cases, *Hill v C A Parsons & Co Ltd* [1972] Ch 305 and *Irani v Southampton and South-West Hampshire Health Authority* [1985] IRLR 203, point 'at least to an effective jurisdiction to control by injunction certain anticipated breaches of contracts of employment while the employment relationship subsists. Where the parties are in agreement that the contract of employment subsists and should subsist, albeit in a qualified form, there is no reason in principle or in the common sense for declining to enforce provisions which can be put into effect without requiring any greater degree of contact and mutual co-operation in the carrying out of obligations derived from the employment than the parties themselves are prepared to accept'.

He stated that, in the case before him

'suspension is accepted. There is no current requirement to work either imposed on the petitioner, or demanded by him and resisted by the respondents. Disciplinary procedures are intended. Subject to any remaining issue of relevance, the question is whether those prescribed by binding contract can be enforced in the face of a desire by the respondents to adopt an alternative scheme. The issue, so far as it is material to categorise it for present purposes, is simply one of selection between competing mechanical provisions.'

2.9 THE 'FENNELLY ORDER' AND SPECIFIC PERFORMANCE

2.9.1 GENERALLY

Delivering judgment in *Fennelly v Assicurazioni Generali SpA and General Underwriting Agencies Ireland Ltd* [1985] 3 ILTR 73, Costello J stated that 'the court should not require an employer to take on an employee where serious difficulties have arisen between them'. While the court has eroded the requirement for trust and confidence in the many injunction cases which have followed *Fennelly*, there remains a reluctance to compel employer and employee to work together. The court has tended towards the 'Fennelly Order' in the many cases that have arisen in this area since the mid-1990s—prohibiting the employer from dismissing the employee and compelling the employer to continue to remunerate the employee but allowing the employer to choose as to whether or not to avail of the employee's services. Indeed, when Macken J (in *Lonergan v Salter-Townshend* [2000] ELR 15) restrained the Irish Council for People with Disabilities and the Minister for Justice, Equality and Law Reform from appointing any person other than David Lonergan to the position of Chief Executive Officer of the Council, the editor of the Employment Law Report spoke of 'an unusual order' (Employment Law Report, vol 11, no 1, February 2000). Some weeks earlier, O'Sullivan J made an order restraining Boston Scientific Ireland Ltd from appointing anybody other than the plaintiff as human resources manager 'on a permanent basis' in *O'Shaughnessy v Boston Scientific Ireland Ltd*. The orders made in these cases go beyond the standard 'Fennelly Order', in that the employer was not only restrained from dismissing the employee but was also restrained from appointing a third party to do the employee's work (although in *O'Shaughnessy* the employer was only restrained from appointing somebody to the plaintiff's position 'on a permanent basis'). However, in extreme cases, the court will go further and, contrary to the view expressed by Costello J in *Fennelly*, will 'require an employer to take on an employee where serious difficulties have arisen between them'. Thus, University College Cork ('UCC') was restrained from 'taking any steps towards appointing a person, other than [Ms Howard] to the post of Head of the Department of German' and 'from interfering with or prohibiting [Ms Howard] from performing her role and functions as Head of the Department' (or so the judgment of O'Donovan J in *Howard v University College Cork*, 25 July 2000 (unreported) would suggest). However, in that case, Ms Howard, as Professor of German, would have continued to work in UCC's Department of German, irrespective of whether or not O'Donovan J had decided to restrain UCC from removing her from her post as Head of Department and if the court order is viewed in that light, then it might well be argued that it was not a question of 'requiring an employer to take on an employee where serious difficulties have arisen' but rather requiring an employer to allow an employee to continue to perform certain functions during the ordinary course of the employment. That said, it is clear that the court will 'reinstate' an employee, where it is considered appropriate to do so, in the interests of justice.

2.9.2 THE SUSPENDED EMPLOYEE

In *Martin v Nationwide Building Society* [1999] ELR 241 the plaintiff was a manager of the defendant's Cavan town branch. On 3 November 1998 he was suspended from his position, on full pay, so as to enable the defendant to proceed through a disciplinary process, in circumstances where issues had arisen relating to the plaintiff's involvement in his brother's auctioneering business. At the outset, the plaintiff was informed that the suspension would last for a period of five days, but by the time that he made application for interim relief, he had been suspended for over fourteen weeks. On 12 February 1999 Laffoy J granted an interim injunction, restraining the Nationwide Building Society from prosecuting a proposed disciplinary enquiry against the plaintiff, and Mr Martin then sought an interlocutory injunction. He contended, inter alia, that the suspension should not be permitted to continue 'having regard to the length of time which [had] passed since the commencement of his suspension and since the investigation process took place' and he sought 'an order for reinstatement back into his position as manager at the defendant's branch office in Cavan town'.

The interlocutory application came before Macken J, who delivered her judgment on 18 May 1999. With regard to the *Fennelly* line of cases, she stated that she was

'not satisfied that these cases are on the point insofar as the facts in this case are concerned. In the present case, the plaintiff, although suspended, is on full pay. Moreover, even in the cases where reinstatement has been sought at an interlocutory stage, the cases make it clear that if the employee does not enjoy the wholehearted support or confidence of his employer, the court will be very slow indeed to reinstate the employee pending the full action'.

However, she stated that this case was different and had nothing to do 'with purported dismissal'. She was satisfied that the delay in dealing with the complaint or allegation against the plaintiff had been 'inordinate and unjust'. She stated that the plaintiff was 'entitled to have such matters dealt with within a reasonably speedy timescale' and referred to Laffoy J's decision in *Charlton v HH The Aga Khan's Studs Société Civile* [1999] ELR 136 in that context. In these circumstances, and notwithstanding the fact that Macken J acknowledged that 'the defendant [did] not appear to have wholehearted trust in the plaintiff', she ordered that the building society 'do all things necessary to permit the plaintiff to carry out his duties and responsibilities as manager of the branch at Cavan town' and that it be 'restrained from treating the plaintiff as other than in the act of employment as manager of the branch at Cavan town'. Thus, Macken J reinstated Mr Martin in his position (while the building society was also restrained from appointing anybody else to that position or from having any other person discharge Mr Martin's functions and responsibilities).

While Macken J distinguished *Martin* from the *Fennelly* line of 'dismissal cases', she was clearly of the view that a court should be 'very slow indeed' to reinstate a dismissed employee who does not enjoy 'the wholehearted support or confidence of his employer', but did not feel so constrained, when dealing with a suspended employee.

2.10   THE FUTURE—EQUITABLE RELIEF STANDING ALONE OR DEMISE OF EMPLOYMENT INJUNCTION?

2.10.1   INTRODUCTION

It will be apparent from the above that it is difficult to fashion a common thread from the line of injunction cases post-*Fennelly*. It is clear that subsisting trust and confidence is no longer an essential prerequisite to the granting of an injunction (although the comments of Costello J in *Fennelly v Assicurazioni Generali SpA* [1985] 3 ILTR 73 and *O'Malley v Aravon School Ltd*; Kelly J in *Reynolds v Malocco*, Irish Times Law Report, 18 January 1999; and Macken J in *Martin v Nationwide Building Society* [1999] ELR 241 suggest that many judges remain 'very slow' to grant injunctions in the absence of such continuing trust and confidence). Certainly, a plaintiff is no longer required to show long-term impecuniosity when seeking interlocutory relief. The case law suggests that it is the requirements of justice, in any particular case, that will now determine whether or not an injunction will be granted, while the 'dignity of employment and the satisfaction and fulfilment' to be derived from a job are factors that may influence the court.

The attractions of the injunction are obvious. A successful plaintiff will continue to receive remuneration, pending a trial, while the employer will normally be prohibited from replacing the employee during that time (although in *O'Shaughnessy v Boston Scientific Ireland Ltd* the defendant was only restrained from appointing anybody else to the plaintiff's position 'on a permanent basis' and was not restrained from temporarily appointing a replacement). Further, employees who do not enjoy the protection afforded by the Unfair Dismissals Acts are not prohibited from seeking injunctive relief. On 13 February 1999 the Irish Times reported that a Ms Martina Keating, a goldsmith and gemologist, had been granted an interim injunction restraining her dismissal or suspension by Weir and Sons Ltd. It seems that Weir and Sons Ltd had purported to dismiss Ms Keating, 'less than a month after she commenced employment'.

While an employee who is intent on challenging the efficacy of a dismissal but who is not covered by the provisions of the Unfair Dismissals Acts may have no option but to make application for an injunction, those employees who do enjoy the protections afforded by unfair dismissal legislation must bear in mind those issues raised in that context, at **2.6** above. As stated, proceedings claiming injunctive relief rarely include a claim for damages at common law, given that the Unfair Dismissals Act, 1977, s 15, as amended, prohibits an employee from claiming a statutory remedy for unfair dismissal, in circumstances where the hearing by a court of proceedings for damages at common law for wrongful dismissal has commenced. As the levels of compensation which are awarded under the Unfair Dismissals Acts will almost invariably exceed the levels of compensation that might be awarded by way of damages at common law, a dismissed employee will always be loath to 'close the door' on an unfair dismissal claim. In that light, the two conflicting High Court judgments, to which reference is made at **2.6** above, are of significant interest, when viewed in the context of possible future developments in this area.

2.10.2   CASSIDY v SHANNON CASTLE BANQUETS AND HERITAGE LTD

In *Cassidy v Shannon Castle Banquets and Heritage Ltd* [2000] ELR 248 the plaintiff, an archaeologist employed by the defendant, was dismissed for gross misconduct, on foot of an allegation of sexual harassment. He instituted proceedings seeking an order (sic) that the purported dismissal was in breach of natural and constitutional justice and, accordingly, that such purported dismissal was without efficacy and invalid (while it appears that he also sought a declaration to the effect that he was and continued to be employed by the defendant as project manager pursuant to a contract of service).

Counsel for the defendant contended that the plaintiff was not entitled to declaratory relief. Relying on the judgment of the Supreme Court in *Parsons v Iarnrod Eireann* [1999] ELR 203, it was submitted that the traditional relief at common law for wrongful dismissal was a claim for damages and, whereas the plaintiff may have had an entitlement to declarations, these were in aid of the common law remedy and had no existence apart from it. However, Budd J stated that *Parsons* is 'authority for the proposition that declaratory relief is available *unless precluded by the option having been taken of making a claim under the Unfair Dismissals Act'*. He went on to state as follows:

'While in the distant past an action at common law for a declaration was unknown, since the Judicature Acts the common law courts followed the chancery practice of making declaratory judgments as an equitable remedy. In a number of Irish cases the courts have granted such declarations in purported dismissal cases. For example *Garvey v Ireland* [1981] IR 76 and *O'Donnell v Dun Laoghaire Corporation* [1991] ILRM 301. In the present case the plaintiffs are seeking an order that the purported dismissal was in breach of natural and constitutional justice and accordingly that such purported dismissal is without efficacy and invalid. It seems to me that, if the procedure to terminate the plaintiff's employment was invalid, then a declaration is the appropriate relief. Such a declaration does not coerce a reinstatement, which might be illogical or unnecessary, but it is declaratory of the plaintiff's rights and position. It also enables the defendant to proceed, if it wishes, in accordance with law to conduct a further inquiry and to afford the plaintiff an opportunity to vindicate his name.'

2.10.3   PHILPOTT v OGILVY & MATHER LTD

Budd J's judgment in *Cassidy v Shannon Castle Banquets and Heritage Ltd* was delivered on 30 July 1999 and within nine months, Murphy J, relying on the very same passage from the judgment of Barrington J in *Parsons v Iarnrod Eireann*, interpreted it as meaning that declaratory relief 'has no independent existence apart from the claim for damages for wrongful dismissal'.

In *Philpott v Ogilvy & Mather Ltd* [2000] ELR 225 the plaintiff sought an injunction restraining the defendant from giving effect to his purported dismissal. He also sought a mandatory injunction requiring the defendant to pay his salary as it fell due and to discharge all other incidents of his employment. It was acknowledged that no reasons had been given for his dismissal, while the court was satisfied that he had been denied a 'contractual right to notice'. In that context, counsel for the defendant pointed out that his client 'had not invoked disciplinary issues' and submitted 'that the only issue is that of damages. There is, accordingly, no issue which requires injunctive relief'. Counsel for the plaintiff relied on the long line of injunction cases, *Shortt v Data Packaging Ltd* [1994] ELR 251; *Phelan v BIC (Ireland) Ltd* [1997] ELR 208; *Boland v Phoenix Shannon plc* [1997] ELR 113; *Harte v Kelly* [1997] ELR 125; and *Lonergan v Salter-Townshend* [2000] ELR 15, in support of the claim for interlocutory relief, but Murphy J noted that all of those cases 'apply to purported dismissal *for reasons given or arising out of disciplinary procedures.*' He went on to point out that the plaintiff was seeking:

'a declaration that he is and continues to be in the defendant's employ pursuant to a contract of service and that the purported summary termination of that contract of service was and is without efficacy and constitutes an unlawful repudiation of the plaintiff's contract on grounds particularised in the endorsement of claim'.

Referring to the judgment of Barrington J in *Parsons v Iarnrod Eireann*, he stated as follows:

'In the present case, the plaintiff has not elected to pursue a remedy under the Unfair Dismissals Act, 1977. He had not been in employment for the requisite period under the Unfair Dismissals Act. However, *Parsons* has a relevance insofar as the pleadings are concerned. The plaintiff seeks a declaration that he is and continues to be a creative director in the defendant's employ pursuant to contract of service and looks for further declarations and injunctions. In respect of damages he seeks aggravated/exemplary damages in defamation, misrepresentation, negligent misstatement, deceit and want and infringement of the plaintiff's constitutional right to earn a livelihood.

'Significantly, there is no claim for damages for wrongful dismissal.

'In such circumstances, it seems to me that *Parsons* has application. If the traditional relief at common law for unfair dismissal was a claim for damages then the plaintiff may also have been entitled to declarations and injunctions in aid of his common law remedy. But if such equitable relief has no independent existence apart from the claim for damages for wrongful dismissal then, it seems to me, that there is no other free standing relief which can be claimed at law or in equity.'

Murphy J went on to make reference to *Phelan v BIC (Ireland) Ltd* [1997] ELR 208 and Costello J's statement to the effect that, where there are allegations of misconduct, natural justice requires that 'the [employee] be informed of the allegations of misconduct before the action is taken' and he stated that, given that the defendants had made no allegation of misconduct against Mr Philpott, he (Mr Philpott) was not entitled to the relief claimed. Indeed, Murphy J seemed to suggest that employees are only entitled to natural justice in misconduct cases and it is respectfully submitted that that cannot be so and that employees are also entitled to natural justice in other types of case (eg capability cases—see *Bolger v Showerings (Ireland) Ltd* [1990] ELR 184).

2.10.4   CONCLUSION

The *Cassidy/Philpott* debate is now the key to the future of the employment injunction. While it seems certain that disgruntled employees will continue to make application for declaratory/injunctive relief, until such time as the Supreme Court elaborates on the reasoning in *Parsons v Iarnrod Eireann* [1997] ELR 203 such applications will continue to be perceived as fraught, serving to bring employment disputes to an early conclusion but not for the fainthearted, while the remedies afforded by the Unfair Dismissals Acts will always be more attractive than their common law equivalents.

CHAPTER 3

ORGANISATION OF WORKING TIME ACT, 1997

3.1 INTRODUCTION

The Organisation of Working Time Act, 1997 (implementing the terms of European Council Directive 93/104) was signed by President Robinson on 7 May 1997. The provisions of the Act came into effect on foot of the Organisation of Working Time Act, 1997 (Commencement Order), 1997 (SI 392/1997) which provided for the implementation of various sections of the Act at different times. This chapter provides a brief summary, identifying the principal changes introduced by the Act.

3.2 DEFINITIONS

The following definitions (see s 2) are significant:

' "*Collective agreement*" *means an agreement by or on behalf of an employer on the one hand, and by or on behalf of a body or bodies representative of the employees to whom the agreement relates on the other hand.*'

' "*Contract of employment*" *means*
(a) a contract of service or apprenticeship, and
(b) any other contract whereby an individual agrees with another person, who is carrying on the business of an employment agency within the meaning of the Employment Agency Act, 1971, and is acting in the course of that business, to do or perform personally any work or service for a third person (whether or not the third person is a party to the contract),
whether the contract is express or implied and if express, whether it is oral or in writing.'

Practitioners should bear in mind the fact that the Employment Agency Act, 1971 makes clear that 'the business of an employment agency' includes the 'supplying for reward . . . of persons who will render services to others'.

' "*Employee*" *means a person of any age, who has entered into or works under (or, where the employment has ceased, entered into or worked under) a contract of employment.*'

' "*Employer*" *means in relation to an employee, the person with whom the employee has entered into or for whom the employee works under (or, where the employment has ceased, entered into or worked under) a contract of employment, subject to the qualification that the person who under a contract of employment referred to in paragraph (b) of the definition of "contract of employment" is liable to pay the wages of the individual concerned in respect of the work or service concerned, shall be deemed to be the individual's employer.*'

'*"Rest period"* *means any time that is not working time.'*

'*"Working time"* *means any time that the employee is—*
(a) at his or her place of work or at his or her employer's disposal, and
(b) carrying on or performing the activities or duties of his or her work,
and work shall be construed accordingly.'

The Act does not apply to members of the Gardaí or the Defence Forces.

Part II, which governs minimum rest periods and other matters relating to working time, does not apply to a person:

(a) engaged in sea fishing;

(b) engaged in other work at sea;

(c) engaged in the activities of a doctor in training;

(d) employed by a relative or a member of that relative's household and whose place of employment is a private dwellinghouse or a farm in or on which he or she and the relative reside; or

(f) the duration of whose working time (saving any minimum period of such time that is stipulated by the employer) is determined by himself or herself, whether or not provision for the making of such determination by that person is made by his or her contract of employment (and in that context, the Directive spoke in terms of 'managing executives or other persons with autonomous decision-taking powers').

The following areas are dealt with in the Act:

- Maximum weekly working time and rest breaks (Part II).
- Holidays (Part III).
- Public holidays (Part III).
- Records (Part IV).

3:3   MAXIMUM WEEKLY WORKING TIME AND REST BREAKS

Since 1 March 1998 (and allowing for a 'phase-in period': see below), the maximum average working week is forty-eight hours. The forty-eight hours may be averaged according to the following rules:

- For employees generally, four months.
- For employees where work is subject to seasonality, a foreseeable surge in activity or where employees are directly involved in ensuring continuity of service or production, six months.
- For employees who enter into a collective agreement with their employers which is approved by the Labour Court, twelve months.

The maximum forty-eight-hour week became effective in the third year following the commencement of the 1997 Act. During the first year (from 1 March 1998), employees were permitted to work up to sixty hours and during the second year (from 1 March 1999) a fifty-five hour week was permitted, subject to a requirement for employees to sign a written agreement with their employers.

In a judgment delivered by the High Court in England on 3 March 1999, *Barber v RJB Mining (UK) Ltd* [1999] IRLR 308, the court held that the UK Working Time Regulations 1998 (SI 1998/1833) introduced a forty-eight-hour limit in all relevant contracts of employment. Gage J took the view that: 'Parliament intended that all contracts of employment should be read so as to provide that an employee should work no more than an average of forty-eight hours in any week during the reference period', and he distinguished this right from the statutory obligation on employers to prevent employees from working hours over and above the forty-eight-hour threshold. The editor of the Industrial Relations Law Reports views the decision as being highly significant:

> 'It means that employees who are being asked to work in excess of the limit on working time can bring a claim in the ordinary courts for a declaration of their rights and can seek to enforce their rights by means of an injunction prohibiting the employer from requiring them to work in excess of the limit imposed by the Regulations.'

It remains to be seen whether an Irish court will interpret the 1997 Act as conferring such contractual rights on employees, in circumstances where it is envisaged that contraventions of the Act will be addressed by way of complaint to a rights commissioner, in the first instance.

The Act also provides that, from 1 March 1998, every employee has a general entitlement to:

(a) eleven hours daily rest per twenty-four-hour period;

(b) one period of twenty-four hours rest per week preceded by a daily rest period (eleven hours); and

(c) rest breaks—fifteen minutes where up to four-and-a-half hours have been worked and thirty minutes where up to six hours have been worked which may include the first break.

3.4 HOLIDAYS

There is now no qualifying period for holidays, and all employees, regardless of status or service, qualify for paid holidays. All time worked qualifies for paid holiday time. Under the Act the minimum holiday entitlements for employees were increased on a phased basis over the leave years 1997–98 to 1999–2000. The minimum holiday entitlements for employees who work at least 1,365 hours per year was increased from three weeks to four weeks (with pro rata increases for other employees) over that phased period, starting in the 1997–98 leave year.

The Act also contains provisions dealing with the calculation of an employee's holiday pay and places the obligation on the employer to ensure that the employee takes his full statutory leave allocation within the leave year, or within the six months thereafter. In addition, an employee is entitled to an unbroken period of two weeks' holiday, which may include one or more public holidays, following eight months' work.

3.5 PUBLIC HOLIDAYS

There are nine public holidays in the calendar year. In respect of a public holiday the employee is entitled to whichever of the following his employer determines:

(a) a paid day off on that day;

(b) a paid day off within a month of that day;

(c) an additional day of annual leave; or

(d) an additional day's pay.

If an employer does not nominate one of the options above, the employee will automatically be entitled to a paid day off on the day of the public holiday.

'Wholetime' employees have an immediate entitlement to public holiday benefits. 'Non-wholetime' employees must have worked at least forty hours in the five weeks ending on the day before the public holiday to qualify for public holiday benefit.

Employees absent from work immediately before the public holiday will not be entitled to benefit from the public holiday in the event of the following absences:

(i)   an absence in excess of fifty-two weeks by reason of occupational injury;

(ii)   an absence in excess of twenty-six weeks by reason of illness or injury;

(iii) an absence in excess of thirteen weeks by virtue of a reason not referred to above but being an absence authorised by the employer, including lay-off; or

(iv)   an absence by reason of strike.

3.6   RECORDS

Employers are obliged to keep records of holidays and public holidays for a period of three years. These records must be available for inspection by labour inspectors of the Department of Enterprise, Trade and Employment. Records should also be maintained to show as evidence in the event of a rights commissioner or Labour Court investigation of an employee's complaint.

CHAPTER 4

PARENTAL LEAVE ACT, 1998

4.1   INTRODUCTION

On 8 July 1998 the Parental Leave Act was signed by the President and it came into effect on 3 December 1998. It implements EU Directive 96/34/EC in the following way.

The Act (as amended by the European Communitites (Parental Leave) Regulations, 2000 (SI 231/2000)) confers an entitlement to parental leave and 'force majeure leave' on qualifying employees.

For the purposes of the Act the following definitions apply (s 2):

'*"Contract of employment'* *means—*
(a) a contract of service or apprenticeship, or
(b) any other contract whereby an individual agrees with another person, who is carrying on the business of an employment agency within the meaning of the Employment Agency Act, 1971, and is acting in the course of that business, to do or perform personally any work or service for a third person (whether or not the third person is a party to the contract),
whether the contract is express or implied and if express, whether it is oral or in writing'. (See *Bourton v Narcea Ltd and AIBP* UD 186/94).

'*"Employee'* *means a person of any age who has entered into or works under . . . a contract of employment.'*

'*"Employer''* *means in relation to an employee—*
   '*(a) means the person with whom the employee has entered into or for whom the employee works under (or, where the employment has ceased, entered into or worked under) a contract of employment, subject to the qualification that the person who under a contract of employment referred to in paragraph (b) of the definition of ''contract of employment'' is liable to pay the remuneration of the individual concerned in respect of the work or service concerned shall be deemed to be the individual's employer, and*
   (b) includes, where appropriate, the successor or an associated employer of the employer.'

4.2   ENTITLEMENT TO PARENTAL LEAVE

The natural or adoptive parent of a child is entitled to a period of fourteen working weeks' parental leave to enable him or her to take care of the child.

The period of parental leave must end not later than the day on which the child reaches its fifth birthday, or in the case of an adopted child who had reached three years of age but not eight years of age on or before the date of the making of the adoption order, not later than the expiration of the period of two years beginning on that date.

Parental leave is only available to employees with one year's continuous service with the employer from whose employment the leave is taken (subject to one exception: see below).

An employee is entitled to parental leave in respect of each child of which he or she is the natural or adoptive parent.

Where a person is both a natural and adoptive parent of a particular child, that person is only entitled to parental leave as the natural parent.

Parental leave is non-transferable between the parents of a child.

Where the employee will not have completed the requisite one year's continuous service on the latest day for commencing a period of parental leave, but will have completed three months on the latest day for commencing pro rata leave, the person will be entitled to one week for each month of continuous employment completed at the time of commencement.

4.3   MANNER IN WHICH PARENTAL LEAVE MAY BE TAKEN

Parental leave may be taken as:

(a)   a continuous period of fourteen weeks, or

(b)   any combination of days or hours with the agreement of the employer or an industry-wide collective agreement.

In *O'Neill v Dunnes Stores* [2000] ELR 306 the EAT, upholding the decision of a rights commissioner, determined that 'whilst a continuous period of fourteen weeks is an absolute entitlement for an employee, in order for the employee to be entitled to take uncontinuous leave, it must be pursuant to an agreement between the employer and the employee'. Thus, an employee who wishes to avail of leave by way of 'a number of periods of days[and/or]hours' (pursuant to s 7(6) of the Act) may only do so with the permission of the employer.

In the context of the determination of the EAT (and notwithstanding the manner in which the case is reported in the Employment Law Reports), it is to be noted that the determination, when considered in isolation, is ambiguous and unclear. It sets out the respondent's argument and allows the reader to have some understanding of the appellant's argument. However, having failed to make any reference to the decision of the rights commissioner in the case, the findings of the EAT are articulated only to the extent that the determination states that 'the Tribunal upholds the decision of the Rights Commissioner'. The decision of the rights commissioner has never been reported. All of that said, it is clear that the appellant sought to rely on 'a spirit and intention of the Act which was other than the interpretation made by Mr Flemming, Rights Commissioner', while the EAT refused to 'go behind the expressed provisions of the Act', preferring to uphold Mr Flemming's decision.

Parental leave taken as days or hours should equate to the hours the employee worked in an agreed fourteen-week period before the parental leave period or in the absence of agreement, fourteen times the average number of hours per week the employee worked in each of the periods of fourteen weeks ending immediately before commencement of each week in which leave is taken.

Where an employee is entitled to parental leave in respect of more than one child (not being children of a multiple birth) the leave in total cannot exceed fourteen weeks in any period of twelve months, without the employer's consent.

Holidays (apart from public holidays), if they fall within a period of parental leave, must be taken at such other time as determined by the employer pursuant to the Organisation of Working Time Act, 1997, s 20.

In respect of public holidays, where entitlement arises during a period of parental leave a day is added to the period of parental leave in respect of each such public holiday.

4.4 NOTICE PROVISIONS

A minimum of six weeks' notice in writing of intention to take parental leave must be given to the employer, specifying the date of commencement, the duration, the manner in which it is proposed to be taken and the notice shall be signed by the employee. Not less than four weeks before taking the leave the employer and the employee must sign 'a confirmation document'.

The employer and the employee are obliged to retain the notice and the confirmation document (or copies of the same, as the case may be).

There are interesting provisions in relation to establishing proof of parenthood. In respect of an adopted child, the employer is entitled to call for evidence of the dates of birth of the child and of the making of the adoption order. In respect of any other child, the employer can call for 'evidence in relation . . . to the employee being a parent of the child and the date of birth of the child'. The employer is only entitled to evidence which is 'reasonably' required, but no detail is given as to what might be covered by such 'reasonable' requirements.

4.5 POSTPONEMENT, CURTAILMENT AND VARIATION OF LEAVE BY THE PARTIES

Once a confirmation document has been signed, the employee is not entitled to work during the agreed period of parental leave, but the parties may agree to postpone, curtail or vary the leave at any time. Curtailed leave may be taken at another time, by agreement.

4.6 POSTPONEMENT BY EMPLOYER

Employers may postpone parental leave entitlement for no more than six months, by notice in writing (to be retained by the parties) of not less than four weeks, following consultation with the employee, where the taking of parental leave would have a substantial adverse effect on the business, profession or occupation by reason of:

(a) seasonal variations in the volume of the work concerned;

(b) the unavailability of a person to carry out the duties of the employee in the employment;

(c) the nature of those duties;

(d) a number of employees in the employment

(e) the number of employees in the employment whose periods, or part of whose periods, of parental leave will fall within the period specified by that employee in their notice; or

(f)   'any other relevant matters',

and on condition that no confirmation has been signed by the parties.

An employer may not postpone the commencement of parental leave more than once, unless a ground for the postponement is seasonal variation in the volume of work concerned, in which circumstances, the leave may be postponed twice—being leave in respect of a particular child.

Postponed leave will give rise to a deferred entitlement, beyond the normal expiry date.

4.7   CONDITION OF TAKING PARENTAL LEAVE

Entitlement to parental leave is subject to the condition that it must be used to take care of the child concerned.

Where an employer 'has reasonable grounds for believing that an employee . . . who is on parental leave is not using the leave for the purpose of taking care of the child concerned' he can terminate the leave by no less than seven days' notice in writing, whereupon the employee must return to work.

Where an employer 'has reasonable grounds for believing that the employee is not entitled to . . . parental leave', the employer may refuse the leave by notice in writing.

In both of the above cases, the employer must give the employee written notice of intent, advising the employee of the right to make representation, within seven days, which representation the employer must consider.

Notices must be retained by the parties.

4.8   FORCE MAJEURE LEAVE

4.8.1   MEANING

Force majeure leave arises where for urgent family reasons owing to an injury or illness the immediate presence of the employee 'at the place where the [injured or ill] person is, whether at his/her home or elsewhere is indispensable'.

4.8.2   CASE LAW

4.8.2.1   Quinn v J Higgins Engineering Galway Ltd

In *Quinn v J Higgins Engineering Galway Ltd (t/a APW Enclosures Systems)* [2000] ELR 102 the determination of the EAT recites that the first-named appellant

> 'told the Tribunal that his three children were ill from Monday, 11th January 1999; however on Wednesday, 13th January 1999 he received a phone call in the afternoon from his wife stating that the children's condition had deteriorated and that she herself was not feeling well. During the night all four of them had very high temperatures. Mr Quinn felt that he had to stay at home from work to look after his family and on Thursday morning when a fellow worker called to bring him to work he explained the situation and told him that he would not be attending work. Mr Quinn brought his wife and three children to the doctor on Thursday morning. There was a meningitis scare in

the area at the time. He got medication from the doctor and he phoned his employment to state that he would not be in. Mr Quinn stated that the illness lasted throughout the weekend, the family were very ill on Friday and by Sunday they had started to improve. He said he could not ask anybody to come to the house to look after them because of the meningitis scare.

'During cross-examination Mr Quinn told the Tribunal that because his wife and children were ill his presence was required in the home, his family could not have done without him.

'He discussed the "meningitis scare" with the doctor and was relieved when the doctor discounted such as being the cause of the family's illness, but stated that the doctor said that they "needed minding".'

The EAT found that:

'The applicant's circumstances on Thursday, 14th January 1999 were such as to constitute urgent family reasons for the purpose of the Parental Leave Act rendering his presence indispensable. In reaching this conclusion we accept as reasonable the claimant's belief on 14th January that he could not ask anyone else to assist him because he did not want to expose family or neighbours to a risk of meningitis.

'However, we are satisfied that after his visit to the doctor the appellant, on his own evidence, had been advised by the doctor that his wife and children did not suffer from meningitis. Accordingly, while accepting his evidence as to the continuing illness of his wife and children on Friday 15th January 1999 we are not satisfied that his absence on that date satisfied the requirements as set out in the Act for force majeure leave.'

In these circumstances, the EAT determined that the appellant was entitled to leave with pay for Thursday, 14 January 1999 but that he had no such entitlement in respect of Friday, 15 January 1999.

The EAT used the words 'applicant', 'claimant' and 'appellant' interchangeably in the determination.

4.8.2.2   Carey v Penn Racquet Sports Ltd

In *Carey v Penn Racquet Sports Ltd* [2001] ELR 27 the employee was 'a single mother caring for an eight-year-old child'. The determination of the EAT recites that:

'She did not come to work on 11th June 1999 as her eight-year-old child was sick. During the very early morning she noticed that she was sick and she did not know if she had a temperature. When she got up for work she noticed that the child had rash on her two legs and she decided to stay at home and observe her. The rash was getting worse and she took her to the doctor, 3 miles away. [The employee] lives alone, is a single parent and is 18–20 miles from Mullingar. The doctor advised her to get calamine lotion and to keep an eye on her daughter. She then had to travel 10 miles to a chemist in Ballymahon. She felt it was best to stay with her child that day and that her presence was indispensable.

'During cross-examination [the employee] said that between 12 am and 6 am she had been concerned about her child. She said she would not be in a position herself to diagnose whether her condition may be serious. She was due to start work at 8 am that day and sometimes she worked on the 4 am shift. She took the child to the doctor at around 10 am or 11 am and asked her sister to ring the respondent.'

The EAT determined:

'that the applicant was concerned about her child's health on 11th June 1999. She became aware very early in the morning that her daughter was sick. She did not know if she had a temperature. She did not call the doctor. When she got up she noticed a rash on the child's legs. She took the child to the doctor at around 10.30 am. According to her evidence she could not be sure of the time. Again, according to her own evidence she did not panic. The first mention of meningitis was at the hearing before the rights commissioner. There was conflicting evidence as to the time she had to start work. She had a child minder.'

The EAT, by a two to one majority, determined that 'the particulars of [the] case [did] not fall within the meaning of the Act, as urgent, immediate and indispensable'.

The matter came before the High Court on 24 January 2001. Carroll J stated that, '[w]hile it [was] not spelt out in the determination of the Tribunal, it [seemed] clear that the reason the force majeure leave was refused was that the rash turned out to be not serious'. The judge went on to state:

'[T]he Tribunal should not have approached the matter on that basis. This was judging with hindsight the urgency of the family reasons and the question of whether the employee's presence with her child was indispensable. The matter should have been looked at from the plaintiff's point of view at the time the decision was made not to go to work. Also the plaintiff could not be assumed to have medical knowledge which she did not possess.'

It is to be noted that the defendant did not contest the matter and did not appear in court.

Carroll J held that it was a mistake of law to decide the issue on the basis of the ultimate outcome of the illness and, accordingly, she held that the plaintiff was entitled to one day of paid force majeure leave for Friday, 11 January 1999.

4.8.3   MISCELLANEOUS REQUIREMENTS

Force majeure leave may be taken in respect of the following people:

(a)   child;

(b)   spouse or person with whom the employee is living as husband or wife;

(c)   a person to whom the employee is in loco parentis;

(d)   a brother or sister; or

(e)   a parent or grandparent.

By its very nature notice cannot be given of force majeure leave but the employee is obliged 'as soon as reasonably practicable thereafter' to give a written notice to the employer of the date on which the leave was taken and giving a statement of facts as to why it was taken.

Force majeure leave may consist of one or more days but shall not exceed three days in any period of twelve consecutive months or five days in any period of thirty-six consecutive months.

Where an employee is absent on force majeure leave for part of a day it is deemed to be a full day.

4.9   EMPLOYMENT RIGHTS

While on parental leave employees have to be treated as benefiting from all of their employment rights and entitlements other than remuneration and pension benefits, and absence cannot be treated as part of any other type of leave including sick leave, annual leave, maternity leave and force majeure leave.

In the context of the above, the decision of the European Court of Justice in *Lewen v Denda* [2000] IRLR 67 is of interest. In that case, the court held that article 119 of the EC Treaty precludes an employer from entirely excluding women on parental leave from the benefit of a Christmas bonus without taking account of the work done in the year in which the bonus is paid, or of periods of maternity leave during which they were prohibited from working, where that bonus is awarded retroactively as pay for work performed in the course of that year (and the case turned primarily on the differentiation as between payments which might be regarded as 'retroactive pay' and payments which might be regarded as incentives to work hard in the future/rewards for future loyalty). The court stated that a worker who exercises a statutory right to take parental leave is in a special situation, which cannot be compared to that of a man or woman at work, since such leave involves suspension of the contract of employment and, therefore, of the respective obligations of the employer and the worker. Therefore, Community law does not preclude a refusal to pay a Christmas bonus to a woman on parental leave where the award of such a bonus is subject to the sole condition that the worker must be in active employment when it is awarded. Article 119 of the EC Treaty precludes an employer, when granting a Christmas bonus, from taking periods during which mothers are prohibited from working into account, so as to reduce the benefit pro rata. However, Community law does not preclude an employer, when granting a Christmas bonus to a female worker who is on parental leave, from taking periods of parental leave into account, so as to reduce the benefit pro rata.

Probation, training or apprenticeship may be suspended during parental leave.

An employee on force majeure leave retains all entitlements including remuneration and pension and again such absence cannot be treated as part of any other leave.

4.10 RIGHT TO RETURN TO WORK

There is a general right to return to work, for the same employer (or the employer's successor) in the same job, under the same contract, but if it is not 'reasonably practicable for the employer to permit the employee to return to work . . . the employee shall be entitled to be offered . . . suitable alternative employment'.

4.11 DISPUTES

Disputes are dealt with at first instance by a rights commissioner and, on appeal, to the EAT with appeal to the High Court on a point of law thereafter.

4.12 REDRESS

The rights commissioner or EAT may order 'appropriate' redress including the grant of leave or an award of compensation, not exceeding twenty weeks' remuneration.

Decisions/determinations of a rights commissioner or the EAT are enforced by the Circuit Court.

It should be noted that the Act does not oblige an employer to pay an employee while on parental leave although it leaves it open for employers to do so. Many believed that the EU Directive would lead to paid parental leave but this has not happened.

4.13   REGULATIONS

The following regulations have been made under the Parental Leave Act:

(a)   Parental Leave (Disputes and Appeals) Regulations, 1999 (SI 6/1999); and

(b)   Parental Leave (Maximum Compensation) Regulations, 1999 (SI 34/1999).

CHAPTER 5

PAYMENT OF WAGES ACT, 1991

The Payment of Wages Act, 1991 ('the 1991 Act') came into operation on 1 January 1992.

5.1   INTERPRETATION: s 1

The 1991 Act governs the payment of wages to an employee by an employer and, in that context, the meanings of 'contract of employment' and 'wages' are particularly important.

5.1.1   CONTRACT OF EMPLOYMENT

For the purposes of the 1991 Act, 'contract of employment' means:

'A contract of service or of apprenticeship, and any other contract whereby an individual agrees with another person to do or perform personally any work or service for a third person (whether or not the third person is a party to the contract) whose status, by virtue of the contract, is not that of a client or customer of any profession or business undertaking carried on by the individual, and the person who is liable to pay the wages of the individual in respect of the work or service shall be deemed, for the purposes of this Act, to be his employer, whether the contract is express or implied and if express, whether it is oral or in writing.'

5.1.2   EMPLOYEE

'Employee' means:

'A person who has entered into or works under (or, where the employment has ceased, entered into or worked under) a contract of employment and references in relation to an employer, to an employee shall be construed as references to an employee employed by that employer; and for the purpose of this definition, a person holding office, or in the service of, the State (including a member of the Garda Síochána or the Defence Forces) or otherwise as a civil servant, within the meaning of the Civil Service Regulation Act, 1956, shall be deemed to be an employee employed by the State or the Government, as the case may be and an officer or a servant of a local authority for the purposes of the Local Government Act, 1941, a harbour authority, a health board or a vocational education committee shall be deemed to be an employee employed by the authority, board or committee, as the case may be.'

5.1.3   EMPLOYER

'Employer' in relation to an employee means:

> 'The person with whom the employee has entered into or for whom the employee works under (or, where the employment has ceased, entered into or worked under) a contract of employment.'

In *Sullivan v Department of Education* [1998] ELR 217 the Employment Appeals Tribunal held that the Department of Education employs teachers for the purposes of the 1991 Act. While it is generally accepted that teachers are employed by the manager or board of management of the schools in which they are employed, the EAT refused to accept that that is the case under the Payment of Wages Act. The EAT stated:

> 'When it comes to the question of remuneration, for the Department to say it is not the employer would effectively mean that as far as the question of remuneration would go the teacher would have no employer which is inconceivable. If a deduction is made from a teacher's salary the school is likely to say that it, having no role in the question of payment of remuneration, cannot be considered to have made such deduction and the Department may say that it is not the employer for the purposes of any aspect of the teacher's employment. It is inconceivable that all of the teachers in the country should not have the benefit of the Payment of Wages Act, 1991. It is difficult to see how the Board of Management could, short of ordering the Department to make a deduction, actually make a deduction from any particular teacher's remuneration.

> 'In all the circumstances we are satisfied there are sufficiently close ties and controls exercised by the Department in relation to individual teachers. We are satisfied that the Department is the employer for the purposes of the Payment of Wages Act, 1991.'

While the reasoning of the EAT is based on a certain attractive logic, it is difficult to view the Department as other than a 'paying agent', in circumstances where the EAT accepted that 'the board of management or other managing authority of a school may well have a role in the day to day running of the school and indeed in engaging teachers, interviewing etc'. Certainly, it is difficult to argue that the Department is the 'person with whom the [teacher] has entered into or for whom the [teacher] works under a contract of employment'. In reality, all of the incidents of the employment relationship pertain as between teacher and school, while the Department of Education funds that relationship. So, the Department could fund an award made against a school under the 1991 Act and removing the Department from the employment relationship need not give rise to a situation where 'all of the teachers in the country should not have the benefit of the . . . Act'.

5.1.4   WAGES

'Wages', in relation to an employee, means:

> 'Any sums payable to the employee by the employer in connection with his employment, including—
> (a)   any fee, bonus or commission, or any holiday, sick or maternity pay, or any other emolument, referable to his employment, whether payable under his contract of employment or otherwise, and
> (b)   any sum payable to the employee upon the termination by the employer of his contract of employment without his having given to the employee the appropriate prior notice of the termination, being a sum paid in lieu of the giving of such notice.'

In the English case of *Saavadra v Aceground Ltd* [1995] IRLR 198 the UK Employment Appeal Tribunal held that a restaurateur who retained part of the service charges for himself, was making unlawful deductions from the wages of his employees. The EAT stated that what is 'properly payable to those who give service' is 'that which is paid for service'.

Provided, however, that the following payments shall not be regarded as wages for the purposes of this definition:

(a) any payment in respect of expenses incurred by the employee in carrying out his employment;

(b) any payment by way of a pension, allowance or gratuity in connection with the death, or the retirement or resignation from his employment, of the employee or as compensation for loss of office;

(c) any payment referable to the employee's redundancy;

(d) any payment to the employee otherwise than in his capacity as an employee; and

(e) any payment in kind or benefit in kind.

5.1.5 MISCELLANEOUS DEFINITIONS

'Cash', 'the Minister', 'strike', 'industrial action' and 'the Tribunal' are also defined for the purposes of the Act, in s 1.

5.2 MODES OF PAYMENT OF WAGES: s 2

Section 2 provides that 'wages may be paid by and only by one or more of the ... modes' set out in the section, including cheque, draft, postal order, credit transfer and cash.

The section makes special provision governing the mode of payment of wages, when, owing to a strike or other industrial action affecting a financial institution, cash is not readily available to the employee.

The section creates an offence and provides for a fine not exceeding £1,000.

5.3 REPEAL OF TRUCK ACTS, 1831–1896 AND RELATED ENACTMENTS: s 3

Apart from repealing the Truck Acts, s 3 also repealed the Payment of Wages Act, 1979 and contains transitional arrangements relating to cash and non-cash payment of wages under the 1979 Act.

5.4 STATEMENTS OF WAGES AND DEDUCTIONS FROM WAGES: s 4

Section 4 requires employers to furnish employees with written statements of wages and deductions, 'at the time of the payment' (except in the case of credit transfers, when the statement should be given to the employee 'as soon as may be thereafter'). The employer is obliged to 'take such reasonable steps as are necessary to ensure' confidentiality in this context.

The section creates an offence, and provides for a fine not exceeding £1,000.

5.5 REGULATION OF CERTAIN DEDUCTIONS MADE AND PAYMENTS RECEIVED BY EMPLOYERS: s 5

5.5.1 DEDUCTIONS PERMITTED BY STATUTE AND CONTRACT

Section 5(1) prohibits an employer from making a deduction from the wages of an employee (or receiving any payment from an employee) unless

> '(a)   . . . required or authorised . . . by virtue of . . . statute or . . . instrument . . .
>
> (b)   . . . required or authorised . . . by virtue of a term of the employee's contract of employment included in the contract before, and in force at the time of, the deduction or payment, or
>
> (c)   in the case of a deduction, the employee has given his prior consent in writing, to it.'

In *Curust Hardware Ltd v Elaine Dalton* [1993] ELR 10 the employee was contractually obliged to give one month's notice of termination of employment. She received an offer of a new job and was required to start work in two weeks. She gave notice to her employer on a Monday that she would be leaving the job on the following Friday week (less than two weeks' notice). On termination of her employment, she collected her P45 and wages and found that one month's pay, plus her bonus for the previous month, had been deducted. Her employer stated that the deduction was made because she failed to give one month's notice as was specified in her contract of employment but agreed that the contract did not specify the withholding of payment if notice was not given (although the employer claimed that the employee had been told this at her interview). The EAT held that while the contract of employment provided for one month's notice to be given by either party on the termination of the contract, there was no express provision in the contract that a deduction from wages could be made for failure to give notice. The EAT stated:

> '[T]he remedy for default on a term of a contract lies in contract law and such a remedy would have its basis in compensation rather than penalty. In the Minimum Notice and Terms of Employment Acts, 1973–1991 there is no provision for a penalty to be imposed on either the employee or employer for failure to comply with the Act. There is, however, a provision for payment of compensation by an employer to an employee for any loss sustained by the employee as a result of the employer's failure to give notice'.

The EAT determined that the deduction in this case contravened the 1991 Act and ordered Curust to pay Ms Dalton for the period worked by her and also to pay her bonus and holiday pay.

In *John Grimes v Iarnrod Eireann/Irish Rail* (PW3/95), the EAT stated that it

> 'is prepared to consider that the signature of an employee on the contract of employment might indicate that the employee is subscribing and indicating his consent to matters which are not referred to specifically in the contract of employment document proper but in a separate document, such as the booklet dealing with applicable grievance and disciplinary procedures and which is drawn to the employee's attention prior to his signing the actual contract of employment'.

5.5.2 ACTS OR OMISSIONS/SUPPLY OF GOODS AND SERVICES

5.5.2.1 Generally

Section 5(2) further restricts an employer from making deductions from wages in respect of:

> '(a) any act or omission of the employee, or
>
> (b) any goods or services supplied to or provided for the employee, by the employer, the supply or provision of which is necessary to the employment.'

Such deductions may only be made where:

> '(i)   ... required or authorised ... by ... the contract of employment ...
> (ii)   ... fair and reasonable.'

In *Jerome Lynch v Clonlara Wholesalers* (PW3/98) the employee was suspended, without pay, for a period of four weeks, in circumstances where, having previously received a final warning, he allegedly used foul and abusive language in a threatening manner in dealing with his store manager. The EAT determined that a four-week suspension without pay was too harsh and was not 'fair and reasonable' in all the circumstances, as required by the Act. The EAT found 'that the appellant did use foul and abusive language' and held 'that a reduced sanction of one week's suspension without pay would be fair and reasonable in all the circumstances'. It ordered the company to repay three of the four weeks' pay which had been deducted from Mr Lynch's wages.

5.5.2.2   Notice of contractual term

Under s 5(2)(iii) deductions may also be made where:

> 'before the time of the act or omission or the provision of the goods or services, the employee has been furnished with a copy of the contractual term, where it is in writing, or otherwise a notice in writing of the existence and effect of the term.'

In *Murphy v Ryanair plc* [1993] ELR 215 the employee (Mr Murphy) was employed as a pilot by Ryanair plc. He gave evidence to the EAT of the duty requirements that he had to fulfil. These included the requirement that he have at least fourteen hours' rest before he flew one of the company's planes. At 2.30 pm on a Saturday early in March 1992, he was asked to fly a scheduled flight, which would finish at 11.30 pm. He refused to comply with this request on the grounds that it would prevent him from having the maximum fourteen hours' rest between one flight and the next. He was told that if he did not fly the plane, he would be suspended. Following a meeting with his employer, he was suspended for one week, without pay. The EAT held that:

> '[U]nder s 5(2)(iii) of the Payment of Wages Act, 1991, an employee must be furnished with a written copy of such a term, or written notice to that effect, before the act or omission if wages are to be deducted.'

The EAT went on to find that 'the deduction of pay in the circumstances outlined, was not in accordance with the provisions of the Payment of Wages Act, 1991 [and] that the employee [was] entitled to the payment in the normal way of the amount that was deducted'.

5.5.2.3   Notification requirements

Further requirements will arise, depending on the nature of the deduction. Section 5(2)(iv) provides:

> 'where the deduction is in respect of the employee's act or omission, the employee must be furnished with particulars in writing, of the act, or omission and the amount of the deduction, at least one week before the making of the deduction.'

In *John Grimes v Iarnrod Eireann/Irish Rail* (PW3/95) the EAT stated as follows:

> 'The clear intendment behind the 1991 Act is to introduce certainty surrounding the making of deductions from the wages of employees so that employers and employees will know in advance the nature and amount of deductions. In those circumstances, it is important that s 5(2)(iv) be strictly construed and in those circumstances the EAT finds that any notice not specifying the amount of the deduction expressly and clearly is a defective notice.'

In that case, the EAT refused to accept that a letter, which made reference to 'one day's suspension', but made no reference whatever to a monetary amount, could constitute 'particulars in writing of . . . the amount of the deduction'. The EAT refused to 'place reliance' on evidence that Mr Grimes would have been aware of the amount that was to be deducted, in the context of the day's suspension from negotiations that took place prior to the suspension being effected, reiterating that:

> 'the intendment of the 1991 Act is to introduce certainty in and about the whole area of deductions from the wages of employees and clearly the Act intends that the most satisfactory way of doing this is to provide for the issuing of a notice at least one week in advance, containing certain prescribed details so as to remove any uncertainty'.

However, in *Lynch v Clonlara Wholesalers* (PW3/98), the EAT stated that 'no binding case law that the statutory requirements [at s (5)(2)(i) and (iv) of the Act] are strict was cited to the EAT'. In those circumstances, the EAT found that there had been 'compliance with the spirit, if not with the black letter of the Act', in circumstances where the employee had received a letter, informing him that he was going to be 'suspended without pay' for four weeks. The EAT found that 'while the amount of the deduction [was] not specified in figures, it [was] ascertainable. Accordingly . . . the spirit of the requirement [that the employee be furnished with particulars in writing of the amount of the deduction] [had] been complied with'.

5.5.2.4 Amount of deductions and time limits

Section 5(2)(v)–(vii) provide:

> '(v) where the deduction is in respect of compensation for loss or damage sustained by the employer as a result of an act or omission of the employee, the amount of the deduction cannot exceed the amount of the loss or the cost of the damage;
> (vi) where the deduction is in respect of necessary goods or services supplied to the employee by the employer, the amount deducted cannot exceed the cost to the employer of the goods or services;
> (vii) the deduction (or the first in a series of deductions) must be made not later than six months after the act or omission becomes known to the employer or after the provision of the goods or services.'

Payments can only be received by employers from employees in respect of an act or omission or the supply of necessary goods or services, in circumstances where all of the conditions set out above, in relation to such deductions, are satisfied in respect of such payment.

5.5.3 EXCLUDED DEDUCTIONS

5.5.3.1 Reimbursement for overpayments

Section 5(5)(a) provides that the section does *not* govern deductions made by an employer from the wages of an employee (or, where appropriate, payments received by an employer from an employee), in the following circumstances:

> 'reimbursement of overpayments of wages or expenses, where the amount of the deduction or payment does not exceed the amount of the overpayment.'

In *Department of Defence v Cathal O'Riordan* (PW3/92), the EAT found that it had no jurisdiction to determine the case, when deductions were made from Mr O'Riordan's wages following a period of sick leave. Evidence was given to the effect that Mr O'Riordan had been removed from the Department's sick pay scheme for disciplinary reasons. However, while he was out sick the Department continued to pay his wages, by reason of an administrative error. It seems that he assumed that he was receiving sick pay. When he returned to work, the Department stopped his pay until the money received by him, while he was out sick, had been recouped. The EAT stated:

'The principal question that arises here, however, is did the payment of the wages to the respondent while out sick constitute an overpayment of wages, made for any reason by the employer to the employee? The word "overpayment" means "to pay too much". It follows then that where the employer has paid too much as in this case, the matter is caught by s 5(5) and the EAT has no jurisdiction to determine the case and the appeal is allowed.'

5.5.3.2   Disciplinary proceedings

Section 5(5)(b) provides that the section does not apply to deductions made:

'in consequence of disciplinary proceedings held by virtue of a statutory provision'.

In *Grimes v Iarnrod Eireann/Irish Rail* (PW3/95) the employee was suspended for one day, without pay, as a result of disciplinary proceedings taken against him. Inter alia, it was submitted on behalf of Iarnrod Eireann, that the day's pay constituted a deduction 'in consequence of . . . disciplinary proceedings . . . held by virtue of a statutory provision'. Iarnrod Eireann argued that, because disciplinary proceedings are required to be conducted according to the rules of fairness of procedures, by the Unfair Dismissals Act, the disciplinary proceedings invoked in this case constituted disciplinary proceedings held pursuant to or by virtue of a statutory provision. The EAT had no hesitation in rejecting that argument and stated:

'They were ordinary disciplinary proceedings not held specifically under the aegis of any statute or statutory regulation such as the Garda Síochána Discipline Regulations and the connection that (Iarnrod Eireann) sought to draw with the Unfair Dismissals Acts, 1977–1993 was not a direct connection and that part of the Act dealing with statutorily held disciplinary proceedings appears to the Tribunal to require a direct connection between the Act under which disciplinary proceedings are held and the proceedings themselves.'

In *Lynch v Clonlara Wholesalers* (PW3-98) the EAT refused to accept that, where there are no disciplinary procedures agreed between employer and employee, the Code of Practice on Disciplinary Procedures set out in the schedule to) the Industrial Relations Act 1990 Code of Practice on Disciplinary Procedures (Declaration) Order 1996 (SI 117/1996) governs the employment relationship. Article 14(d) of the Code provides that disciplinary action 'may include, inter alia, suspension without pay'. The EAT stated that:

'taking into account the use of the word "may" in that article and the fact that the code is merely a guideline on disciplinary procedures, the Tribunal holds that Article 14(d) of the Code of Practice and the disciplinary action mentioned therein cannot be the "disciplinary proceedings pursuant to a statutory provision" referred to in s 5(5)(b) of the Payment of Wages Act, 1991'.

The EAT went on to state that to accept such argument

'would be to allow a procedural guideline to supersede a statutory provision and to deny the employee in this case, and indeed, most, if not all, employees, the very protection which the Act sets out to provide for them. Where a deduction is to be made from the wages of an employee for "any act or omission of the employee", s 5(2) imposes a firm duty on the employer to ensure that the employee has prior knowledge of the fact that a deduction can be made, that the amount of the deduction is fair and reasonable and that the employee has timely notice of the amount of the deduction and the reason(s) for it. To accept [the Code of Practice] argument would set these protections at nought.'

5.5.3.3   Other exclusions

Section 5(5) further provides that the section does not govern deductions made:

'(c)   in pursuance of a requirement imposed by virtue of any statutory provision to make deductions with a view to making payments to a public authority;

> (d)   in pursuance of any arrangements whereby deductions are made by the employer with a view to making payments to a third person of amounts due to that third person by the employee, consequent on the employer receiving a notice in writing from the third person, to that effect and the payment is made to the third person, in compliance with the said notice and on condition that the employee has given his prior consent in writing, either to the embodiment of such arrangement in a contract with his employer or otherwise;
>
> (e)   in consequence of the employee having taken part in a strike or other industrial action.'

In *Beaumont Hospital v McNally* (PW29–33/96) the hospital refused to pay the employees in respect of hours during which they engaged in a protest. There was some disagreement between the parties as to whether there was a total cessation of work and, consequently, the EAT did not make a finding that there was a strike as defined. However, the EAT did determine that the employees had engaged in 'industrial action' as defined, and consequently determined that it had no jurisdiction 'to address the rights or wrongs of the dispute'.

Section 5(5) further provides that the section does not govern deductions made:

> '(f)   for the purposes of satisfying an Order of a Court or Tribunal requiring the payment of any amount by the employee to the employer;
>
> (g)   for the purpose of satisfying an Order of a Court or Tribunal requiring the payment of any amount by the employer to the Court or Tribunal or a third party out of the wages of the employee.'

In the UK, the Employment Appeal Tribunal has held that where a deduction falls within one of these categories, a tribunal has no jurisdiction to hear a complaint about such a deduction. In the context of a dispute with regard to the lawfulness of such deduction, the appropriate procedure is not to make a complaint about the deduction to a tribunal, but to institute appropriate proceedings in the civil courts for alleged breach of contract and recovery of the sum deducted (*SIP (Industrial Products) Ltd v Swinn* [1994] IRLR 323).

5.5.4   DEFICIENCY IN OR NON-PAYMENT OF WAGES

5.5.4.1   Statutory provisions

Section 5(6) provides as follows:

> 'Where—
>
> (a)   the total amount of any wages that are paid on any occasion by an employer to an employee is less than the total amount of wages that is properly payable by him to the employee on that occasion (after making any deductions therefrom that fall to be made and are in accordance with this Act) or
>
> (b)   none of the wages that are properly payable to an employee by an employer on any occasion (after making any such deductions as aforesaid) are paid to the employee, then, except insofar as the deficiency or non-payment is attributable to an error of computation, the amount of the deficiency or non-payment shall be treated as a deduction made by the employer from the wages of the employee on the occasion.'

5.5.4.2   Reduction in wages

In the British case, *Morgan v West Glamorgan County Council* [1995] IRLR 68, the Employment Appeal Tribunal in the UK held that an employee whose salary was reduced consequent upon a demotion, which was imposed in breach of contract, is entitled under the UK Wages Act 1986 to the shortfall in pay, because a deduction in wages, made as a result of an error of law is not an 'error of computation' so as to fall outside the protection provided by the Act. Mummery J stated that an 'error' is 'a mistake, something incorrectly done through ignorance or inadvertence'.

'Computation of wages [is] a matter of reckoning the amount, of ascertaining the total amount due by a process of counting and calculation. That does not cover a deliberate decision to demote an employee and reduce his salary and although that decision was itself the result of an erroneous or mistaken view of the legal and factual position, the reduction in salary and consequent deduction from the wages paid to the employee was attributable to that decision and not to any error of computation.'

However, in this country, the EAT has ruled that a reduction in wages does not constitute a 'deduction' for the purposes of the 1991 Act. In *Mary Redmond v South Eastern Health Board* (PW47/96 TE6/96) ('*Redmond No 2*'), Mrs Redmond claimed that she had, 'at one time been paid £90 indicating that her wages had been reduced by £10 per week when she was furnished with her written contract of employment which cited her pay as £80'. While the determination is lacking in factual detail, it seems that the dispute arose by reason of confusion in relation to the appropriate hourly rate of pay. In 1995 the same Mrs Redmond had presented a complaint under the 1991 Act, in circumstances where she claimed that she was an employee of the South Eastern Health Board and, for that reason, refused to accept 'wages' from a third party. The circumstances of that case are outlined at **5.5.4.4** below and it will be noted that the EAT determined that Mrs Redmond was an employee of the health board. Bearing that fact in mind, it would appear that Mrs Redmond was then furnished with a written contract of employment by the health board and that that contract 'cited her pay as £80, ie £2 per hour'. Mrs Redmond claimed that she used to receive £90 per week, but she 'could not show that the £90 was a payment in excess of £2 per hour.' The health board claimed that 'the rate had always been £2 per hour and had not changed'. The EAT stated as follows:

'The Tribunal's jurisdiction under the Payment of Wages Act, 1991 arises from an appeal from the Rights Commissioner recommendation and is only under s 5 of the Act. This jurisdiction covers deductions from wages but not the situation when an employer reduces wages. A reduction in wages is not covered by the legislation. The EAT has no jurisdiction derived from this legislation then in what constitutes an alteration in the conditions of employment, ie a reduction in wages, but does not constitute a deduction in wages.'

With respect to the EAT, it is difficult to accept this reasoning. Section 5(6) clearly states that where the total amount of any wages that are paid on any occasion is less than the total amount of wages 'that is properly payable' then the amount of the deficiency shall be treated as a deduction. While Mrs Redmond might not have been able to establish that £90.00 was 'properly payable' to her each week, it does seem clear from s 5(6) that the EAT did have jurisdiction to decide on the issue of whether the 'reduction' constituted a lawful or unlawful deduction for the purposes of the 1991 Act. While it is clear that non-payment of wages constitutes a 'deduction' for the purposes of the 1991 Act, the position under the UK Wages Act was not so clear and was the subject of conflicting decisions, until 1991, when the Court of Appeal held that the Act covered 'any claim by an employee that . . . his employer failed to pay him at the appropriate time, the full amount of the wages as defined . . . which he ought then to have been paid' (*Delaney v Staples* [1991] IRLR 112). However, the later case of *Bruce v Wiggins Teape Stationery Ltd* [1994] IRLR 536, is of more interest in this jurisdiction. In that case, the UK Employment Appeal Tribunal ruled that a 'reduction' in wages is a 'deduction' in wages for the purposes of the UK Wages Act, in circumstances where the employer unilaterally reduced an overtime rate. It is clear from *Redmond No 2* that the EAT here has not followed the UK Tribunal, on this particular point, although it is submitted that the reasoning of the UK Tribunal is to be preferred.

The recent English decision in *Hussman Manufacturing v Weir* [1998] IRLR 288 is also interesting in that context. Mr Weir was moved from a night shift to a day shift, pursuant to the provisions of his contract of employment. As a consequence, his weekly wages were reduced by £17, being the amount that he had been receiving by way of pay for unsocial hours. The UK Employment Appeal Tribunal heard that a reduction in income, which is a consequence of a lawful act, does not in itself amount to an unauthorised deduction from wages. The wages 'properly payable' to the employee, once he was moved to the day shift were those payable to all persons working on that shift.

5.5.4.3   Reduced rate of pay from outset

What is the position where an employee 'continues to receive the same amount (and the same composition) of wages from the outset'? In *Sullivan v Department of Education* [1998] ELR 217 the complaint concerned the amount that was properly payable to the claimant, a secondary school teacher. Ms Sullivan was a graduate of UCC and held a BA single honours degree in French and English. Part of her remuneration comprised of a degree allowance. The level of such allowance was dependent on whether the recipient held an honours or a pass degree. Part of Ms Sullivan's degree course had been taken at honours level and part had been taken at pass level. The Department of Education only paid the higher level of allowance to teachers with degrees where all subjects were taken to honours level in the final examinations. The EAT was 'satisfied that the BA (single honours) programme was in all respects an honours degree programme and could not in any respect be considered to be a pass degree programme'. In those circumstances, the EAT was 'satisfied that there was no justification for the Department to have applied . . . the qualification allowance appropriate to the primary degree (pass)'. The EAT went on to hold that Ms Sullivan was entitled to compensation in respect of the 'non-payment' of the appropriate degree allowance. The EAT made some very interesting observations in this context:

> '[T]he Tribunal considers that if an employee does not receive what is properly payable to him or her from the outset then this can amount to a deduction within the meaning of the 1991 Act. We take "payable" [in the definition of 'wages'] to mean properly payable. The definition of "wages" goes on to give examples of types of payments which can amount to "wages" and states that the payments can amount to wages "whether payable under [his] contract of employment or otherwise. . . .". Although in our view it is not simply a matter of what may have been agreed or arranged or indeed paid from the outset but, in the view of the Tribunal, all sums to which the employee is properly entitled.

> 'An employee may not be aware of his or her full entitlements and an employer may have a greater awareness of the employee's entitlements in terms of pay etc and it would be highly unjust for an employee to lose a claim under the Payment of Wages Act, 1991 for an unlawful deduction simply because an employer, being aware of the employee's proper entitlement, chose, unknown to the employee, to pay less than that from the outset.'

While this argument is undeniably interesting, it is surely inconsistent with the basic principles of the law of contract. It suggests that an employer is not entitled to recruit an employee on terms as agreed between them and seeks to introduce a 'compulsory collective agreement' on parties, in circumstances where they may have voluntarily entered into an independent arrangement. If an employee is recruited, at a specific rate of pay, how can the employee unilaterally demand a higher rate and claim that a failure to pay that higher rate equates to an unlawful deduction from wages, under the Payment of Wages Act?

5.5.4.4   Indirect payments

In *Mary Redmond v South Eastern Health Board* (PW14/95) ('*Redmond No 1*'), the EAT had to determine the nature of the relationship between Mrs Redmond and the health board. Mrs Redmond provided 'home help' to elderly patients on the instructions of the health board. She was not regarded by the health board as an employee. Health board payments were made directly to the individual patients and there was a dispute as to whether the patients always endorsed the cheques or whether Mrs Redmond lodged them directly to her own bank account. Either way, Mrs Redmond refused to accept the cheques in June 1994 and claimed that the health board had contravened the provisions of the 1991 Act. It was submitted on behalf of the health board that no unlawful deduction had been made from Mrs Redmond's wages, but that she had refused to accept payment. It was further submitted that the EAT did not have jurisdiction under the Act to consider whether or not she was an employee in the absence of such an unlawful deduction. The EAT determined that Mrs Redmond was employed by the health board and that:

'as an employee [she] was entitled to insist that she be paid directly. [She] was entitled to refuse to accept payment as it was not tendered to her in the correct form in the first instance. In the circumstances, this amounts to an unlawful deduction within the meaning of s 5 of the Payment of Wages Act, 1991 and [she] is entitled to payment in respect of all such deductions, to date, for work done.'

5.5.4.5 Conditional payments

In *Dominic Dineen v Mid Western Health Board* (PW16/97) the board agreed to pay the employee an extra £5 per week, on condition that he sign an authorisation form (for Paypath) and on the understanding that it had been agreed with his union that the payment of the £5 per week would be discontinued in the case of individual staff members who failed to return the completed authorisation form by a specified date. Mr Dineen received the extra £5 per week for a period, but ultimately it was discontinued by reason of his failure to complete the authorisation form. He claimed that the board had contravened the provisions of the 1991 Act. The EAT stated as follows:

'The £5 was a pay increase negotiated on the appellant's behalf by his trade union, but conditional on his completing an authority for "Paypath". Admittedly the increase was paid in advance of completing the formalities for "Paypath" but the agreement expressly provided that it would be "discontinued" in respect of any employees who failed to sign the necessary authorisation. After the date provided by that agreement . . . the £5 was no longer "properly payable" to him because he had failed to complete his side of the bargain.

'If the £5 was not "properly payable" to him under the agreement, its non-payment to him cannot be said to be a deduction. That it was originally paid to him and later discontinued is a complication, but this complication arose following an agreement reached with the trade unions, who insisted upon that sequence. Having regard to the terms of the [union/management] agreement, this complication does not take from the essential point that the payment was subject to a condition with which the appellant did not comply'.

5.6 COMPLAINTS BY EMPLOYEES IN RELATION TO CONTRAVENTIONS OF s 5 BY THEIR EMPLOYERS: s 6

5.6.1 GENERALLY

Section 6 governs complaints in relation to unlawful deductions. Complaints are entertained by rights commissioners. Section 6(2) provides:

'Where a rights commissioner decides . . . that the complaint is well-founded . . . the commissioner shall order the employer to pay to the employee compensation of such amount . . . as he thinks reasonable in the circumstances, not exceeding—
(a) the net amount of the wages . . . that—
   (i) in case the complaint related to a deduction, would have been paid to the employee in respect of the week immediately preceding the date of the deduction if the deduction had not been made, or

> (ii)   in case the complaint related to a payment, were paid to the employee, in respect of the
> week immediately preceding the date of payment, or
> (b)   if the amount of the deduction of payment is greater than the amount referred to in
> paragraph (a) twice the former amount.'

This provision does not seem to have ever been specifically addressed by the EAT. It prevents a rights commissioner from awarding compensation amounting to more than twice the net amount of the wages that would have been paid to the employee in respect of the week immediately preceding the date of the deduction, if the deduction had not been made. Yet, in *Redmond No 1*, the EAT held that Mrs Redmond was 'entitled to payment in respect of all . . . deductions' made over a lengthy period. In *Sullivan v Department of Education* [1998] ELR 217 the EAT found that Ms Sullivan was 'entitled to compensation calculated by reference to the differential amounts between primary degree (pass) qualification allowance amount and primary degree (1st and 2nd honours) amount for the relevant period', where the relevant period ran from 1 September 1991 to 1 July 1994. A close reading of the relevant provision (s 6(2)) reveals that the EAT cannot make awards of such nature, as the level of such awards surely exceeds the maximum compensation that can be awarded under the Act.

A rights commissioner cannot give a decision under the 1991 Act at any time after the commencement of the hearing of proceedings in a court brought by the employee concerned in respect of the deduction or payment, while an employee cannot recover any amount in proceedings in a court in respect of such a deduction or payment at any time after a rights commissioner has given a decision in relation to the deduction or payment. Section 6(4) provides:

> 'A rights commissioner shall not entertain a complaint under this section, unless it is presented to
> him within the period of six months beginning on the date of the contravention to which the
> complaint relates or (in a case where the rights commissioner is satisfied that exceptional
> circumstances prevented the presentation of the complaint within the period aforesaid) such
> further period not exceeding six months as the rights commissioner considers reasonable.'

A complaint is presented by way of notice in writing to a rights commissioner. It is for the rights commissioner to pass the complaint to the employer.

5.6.2   TIME LIMITS

In *Dineen v Mid Western Health Board* (PW16/97) the health board claimed that the complaint was not made within the requisite six-month period. The EAT rejected the argument, stating:

> 'The claim was dealt with by a rights commissioner and there is no record of the time
> limit being raised at that stage. The Tribunal, on appeal, cannot go behind the face of the
> recommendation before it and the respondent did not lodge an appeal on those grounds.
> Moreover, the "deduction" complained of . . . is of a continuing nature and the time limit
> does not arise.'

In *Byrne v P J Quigley Ltd* [1995] ELR 205 the EAT considered s 7(2) of the Unfair Dismissals (Amendment) Act, 1993, which also allows the rights commissioner (or the EAT) to extend the period for claiming unfair dismissal in circumstances where they are 'satisfied that exceptional circumstances prevented' the making of the claim during the requisite six-month period. In that case, the EAT stated as follows:

> 'In the view of the Tribunal, (subject to the reservations of Mr O'Donnell on 2(a) and
> 2(b) in his dissenting opinion . . .) there are two, if not three elements involved:
>
> (1)   the words "exceptional circumstances" are strong words and should be contrasted
> with the milder words "reasonably practicable" in the claimant's written submission
> or "reasonable cause" which permit the extension of time for lodging a redundancy

claim under s 12(2)(b) of the Redundancy Payments Act, 1971. ''Exceptional'' means something out of the ordinary. At the least, the circumstances must be unusual, probably quite unusual, but not necessarily highly unusual.

(2) (a) In order to extend the time the EAT must be satisfied that the exceptional circumstances ''prevented'' lodging the claim within the general time limit. It is not sufficient if the exceptional circumstances caused or triggered the lodging of the claim.

(2) (b) It seems to follow that the exceptional circumstances involved must arise within the first six months, ''the period aforesaid''. If they arose later, they could not be said to ''prevent'' the claim being initiated within that period.'

In *Sullivan v Department of Education* [1998] ELR 217 the complaint related to Ms Sullivan's salary during the entirety of her teaching career, from 1 September 1991 to the date of the hearing. However, as a result of agreement reached in the context of the 'Revised Teachers' PCW Proposals', which were concluded, prior to the hearing, in PCW negotiations, the Department had committed to treating qualifications such as Ms Sullivan's, as a primary degree. In that context, the Department had agreed to backdate the primary degree allowance, in such cases, to 1 July 1994. Nonetheless, Ms Sullivan insisted on proceeding with her complaint, claiming that ''an unlawful deduction continues in respect of the period from which she commenced work until, at least, 1994''. The EAT acknowledged that ''that is the period we are concerned with and we have to consider the matter in that light''. It seems clear, from the record number of the case, that Ms Sullivan presented her complaint in early 1997. In those circumstances, it is difficult to understand how the EAT might have awarded compensation ''in respect of the period from which she commenced work until, at least, 1994''. It seems manifest that Ms Sullivan could not have made a complaint, in that context, within the requisite six- (or twelve-) month period.

5.7 APPEAL FROM DECISION OF RIGHTS COMMISSIONER: s 7

Section 7 provides for a right of appeal to the EAT:

'*An appeal under this section shall be initiated by a party by his giving, within six weeks of the date on which the decision to which it relates was communicated to him—
(a) a notice in writing to the EAT . . . and
(b) a copy of the notice to the other party concerned.*'

The Minister may, at the request of the EAT, refer a question of law to the High Court, while parties to proceedings before the EAT may appeal to the High Court on a point of law. The decision of the High Court is 'final and conclusive'.

The Payment of Wages (Appeals) Regulations, 1991 (SI 351/1991) govern appeals under this section.

5.8 ENFORCEMENT OF DECISIONS OF RIGHTS COMMISSIONER AND DETERMINATIONS OF EAT: s 8

A decision of a rights commissioner or a determination of the EAT under this Act may be enforced as if it were an order of a Circuit Court, made in civil proceedings by the judge of the Circuit Court for the place where the person in whose favour the decision or determination was made ordinarily resides.

The rights commissioner or the EAT may provide that a decision/determination shall be carried out before a specified date. Otherwise, the decision/determination will be deemed to provide that it shall be carried out within six weeks from the date on which it is communicated to the parties concerned.

5.9 POWERS OF AUTHORISED OFFICERS: s 9

Section 9 empowers the Minister to appoint 'authorised officers' for the purpose of ensuring compliance with the Act and gives the officers power to enter premises, conduct inspections and make enquiries, demand information and copy documents.

The section creates an offence and provides for a fine not exceeding £1,000.

5.10 PROVISIONS IN RELATION TO OFFENCES: s 10

Section 10 empowers the Minister to prosecute offences arising under the Act.

5.11 VOIDANCE OF CERTAIN PROVISIONS IN AGREEMENTS: s 11

Section 11 provides:

> 'A provision in an agreement (whether a contract of employment or not and whether made before or after the commencement of this Act) shall be void insofar as it purports to preclude or limit the application of, or is inconsistent with, any provisions of this Act.'

It is clear from decisions of the EAT, dealing with the Unfair Dismissals Act, 1977, s 13, which is almost identical to this section, that agreements reached in full and final settlement of a potential claim under the Act do not contravene the section. See *Gaffney v Fannin Ltd* UD 1/89 and *McGrane v Avery Label Ltd* UD 573/88 (both reproduced in Madden and Kerr, *Unfair Dismissal Cases and Commentary* (2nd edn, 1996) at pp 29 and 30 respectively.

5.12 MISCELLANEOUS

Sections 12–14 deal with the laying of regulations before the houses of the Oireachtas, expenses of the Minister and the short title and commencement of the Act.

CHAPTER 6

UNFAIR DISMISSAL LAW

6.1   INTRODUCTION

In 1977 the Unfair Dismissals Act ('the 1977 Act') was enacted creating a new form of remedy for dismissed employees. This legislation has brought about major changes in employment law and practice.

The legislation is based on two fundamental principles:

(a)   substantial grounds must exist to justify the termination of a contract of employment; and

(b)   fair procedures must be followed in effecting the termination.

6.2   WHO IS COVERED BY UNFAIR DISMISSAL LEGISLATION?

Not all employees are covered by the legislation. Those who are covered are those who satisfy the basic requirements of having:

(a)   one year's continuous service with the employer. This means fifty-two weeks' continuous service as defined by the rules of continuity contained in the Minimum Notice and Terms of Employment Act, 1973, Sch 1. One year's continuous service is not required where employees can show that they were dismissed by reason of trade union membership or activity, pregnancy or because they exercised their statutory rights to maternity leave (see *Maxwell v English Language Institute* [1990] ELR 226), additional maternity leave or time off for ante- and post-natal care. One year's service is not necessary where the employees are dismissed for seeking to exercise their rights to adoptive leave (see Adoptive Leave Act, 1995, s 25). Holiday leave is not included in the calculation of service under unfair dismissal legislation and, in particular, in establishing whether the employee has the necessary one year's service to bring a claim (see *Twomey v O'Leary Office Supplies Ltd* [1997] ELR 42);

(b)   those who are normally expected to work for at least eight hours per week (see Worker Protection (Regular, Part-time Employees) Act, 1991). The 'normal expectation' includes time spent 'on call'. Therefore persons such as midwives and firemen may be covered by the legislation even though they do not actually work eight hours or more in each week (see *Bartlett v Kerry County Council* UD 178/78 and *Limerick Health Authority v Ryan* [1969] IR 194). It should be noted also that in calculating continuity of service weeks in which an employee is not normally expected to work at least eight hours are excluded from the calculation. That does not mean that continuity is broken, merely that the week is not actually calculated in the total service;

(c) employees who have not reached the normal retirement age for the employment in question. Where there is no normal retirement age specified by the employer, employees are excluded from the legislation on reaching the social welfare pensionable age which is 66. Difficulty may arise in determining what the contractual pension age is if the contract is silent. Nowadays, with pension ages dropping, it is important for employers to specify what the actual retirement age is rather than seek to imply the retirement age because it is provided for in a pension scheme (see *Buckley v Ceimici Teo* UD 528/80). See also the judgment of Flood J in *Donegal County Council v Porter* [1993] ELR 101 where the county council sought to unilaterally reduce retirement age for firemen from 60 to 55 but failed in their attempt to do so.

In *Tipperary (North Riding) County Council v Doyle* [1996] ELR 93 the Employment Appeals Tribunal stated that it had received clear documentary evidence from the council of the policy in practice of compulsory retirement for part-time firemen going back some four decades, and therefore the retirement age of 55 was a condition of the employment of Mr Doyle at all times and distinguished the case on that basis from *Donegal County Council v Porter*. In contrast, in *Scally v Westmeath County Council* [1996] ELR 96 the EAT held that, on the evidence, the fireman in that case came within the ambit of *Donegal County Council v Porter* and that his compulsory retirement on reaching age 55 was an unfair dismissal.

An unusual retirement age of 20 years was sought to be relied upon by the employer in the case of *Kiernan v Iarnrod Eireann* [1996] ELR 12. The claimant was employed as a 'boy porter'. Shortly before his twentieth birthday he was advised that his employment would terminate on reaching 20 years of age as that was the maximum age limit for a boy porter. He was told that he could apply for other positions within the company, which he did, but was unsuccessful. The claimant submitted that when he took up employment he was not told he would be required to retire at 20. He had received a copy of the company's rule book but it made no mention of an obligation to retire at that age. The EAT, in finding in favour of the claimant, stated 'when the employer relies on the normal retirement age provisions of the Unfair Dismissals Acts the precise age of retirement should be given to the employee in writing'. Failure to notify the claimant in writing that 20 was the normal retirement age for his grade rendered the dismissal unfair.

6.3   WHO IS EXCLUDED?

There are certain categories of persons excluded from the legislation. The full list of exclusions is contained in the 1977 Act, s 2, as amended by the Unfair Dismissals (Amendment) Act, 1993 ('the 1993 Act'), s 3. The main excluded categories are:

(a) persons employed in the defence forces and Gardaí;

(b) FAS trainees who are not employed (see *Fallon v Athlone Bowl & Leisure Ltd* [1997] ELR 67 and *Morey v Rock Foundation* [1997] ELR 236);

(c) civil servants (see *Central Bank of Ireland v Gildea* [1997] ELR 238; *McLoughlin v Minister for Social Welfare* [1958] IR 1 and *Murphy v Minister for Social Welfare* [1987] IR 295);

(d) officers of local authorities and VECs (see *O'Callaghan v Cork Corporation* in Kerr and Madden, *Unfair Dismissals Cases and Commentary*, p 182); and

(e) officers of health boards, but temporary officers are not excluded by virtue of the 1993 Act amendment.

6.4   DEFINITIONS

There are some fundamental definitions provided for in unfair dismissal legislation of particular importance in understanding the application of the legislation.

6.4.1   EMPLOYEE

As may be seen in the references in **6.2** above only employees may claim under unfair dismissal legislation. The legislation only covers persons who are engaged under a contract of service. The distinction between a contract of service and a contract for services is fundamental to most employment law.

6.4.2   EMPLOYEE/INDEPENDENT CONTRACTOR

It is well established that regardless of what label parties seek to put on their relationship the courts will look at the factual situation and decide as a matter of law whether a contract was a contract of service or a contract for services (see *Macken v Midland Community Radio Services Ltd* [1992] ELR 143 and *Phelan v Coillte Teoranta* [1993] ELR 56). In *Duncan v O'Driscoll* [1997] ELR 38 a 'share fisherman' was held to be a partner and not an employee. It can also be difficult to establish if a controlling shareholder is an employee of the company he owns. Ownership does not disqualify the person from being held to be an employee but is a factor, and sometimes a very relevant factor, to be taken into account (see *Lee v Lee's Air Farming Ltd* [1961] AC 12; *Secretary of State for Trade and Industry v Bottrill* [1998] IRLR 120; *Buchan and Ivey v Secretary of State for Employment* [1997] IRLR 80; and *Fleming v Secretary of State for Trade and Industry* [1997] IRLR 682).

6.4.3   AGENCY-SUPPLIED STAFF

6.4.3.1   Statutory provisions

Section 13 of the Unfair Dismissals (Amendment) Act, 1993 was enacted in order to provide that staff placed in a business by an employment agency are deemed to be the staff of the business in which they are placed for the purposes of unfair dismissal legislation. The section provides as follows:

> 'Where, whether before, on or after the commencement of this Act, an individual agrees with another person, who is carrying on the business of an employment agency within the meaning of the Employment Agency Act 1971, and is acting in the course of that business, to do or perform personally any work or service for a third person (whether or not the third person is a party to the contract and whether or not the third person pays the wages or salary of the individual in respect of the work or service), then, for the purposes of the Principal Act, as respects a dismissal occurring after such commencement . . . the individual shall be deemed to be an employee employed by the third person under a contract of employment . . . and any redress under the Principal Act for unfair dismissal of the individual under the contract shall be awarded against the third person.'

The definition of employment agency in the Employment Agency Act, 1971, s 1 provides as follows:

> '[T]he business of an Employment Agency means the business of seeking, whether for reward or otherwise, on behalf of others, persons who will give or accept employment and includes the obtaining or supplying for reward of persons who will accept employment from or render services to others.'

The Terms of Employment (Information) Act, 1994 contains a similar provision relating to agency-supplied employees. That confers a liability under that legislation to provide details of basic terms and conditions of employment. That legislation will cause very considerable knock-on effects. If one were to comply with the legislation, one would in effect be accepting that the person is an employee and that the terms and conditions in place are a matter over which one has control. Compliance with the legislation would effectively put employers in a position that they would have enormous difficulty arguing under this legislation and, indeed, in other respects that the person is other than an employee.

6.4.3.2 Case law

In the first case heard by the EAT dealing with the 1993 Act, s 13, *Bourton v Narcea Ltd and AIBP* M318 UD186/94, Mr Bourton was a full-time employee of Narcea Limited. Narcea provided boning services to the meat industry. Bourton was a boner working for Narcea. Narcea entered into commercial contracts with meat companies to bone meat at a piece rate. The money was paid to Narcea and Narcea in turn paid wages to its staff, including Bourton, subject to PAYE and PRSI. Narcea had the right to, and in practice did, move its employees from one meat plant to another as the work required. While working in a meat plant owned by AIBP Bourton became involved in a skirmish with an AIBP employee. Disciplinary action was taken against the AIBP employee and Narcea was requested not to allow Bourton to return to the particular factory. Bourton had a disagreement with Narcea and claimed unfair dismissal. During the course of the first hearing of his claim it was decided to adjourn the matter in order to join AIBP as a possible deemed employer under s 13. Bourton actually settled his dispute with Narcea and continued with his case against AIBP who at all times denied that he was an employee. AIBP made the case that they would not apply disciplinary procedures to a person who was not their employee. This raises practical and procedural problems with deemed employees under s 13. In the event, given the particular wording of the 1993 Act, Bourton did not have the necessary one year's service with AIBP and on that ground alone his claim failed. The EAT's comments indicated, however, that in all other respects Bourton came within the definition of a deemed employee in s 13. There is a similar provision contained in the UK Race Relations Act 1976 at s 7(1) which provides that for the purposes of that legislation the section

> 'applies to any work for a person ("the principal") which is available for doing by individuals ("contract workers") who are employed not by the principal himself but by another person who supplies them under a contract made with the principal'.

In *Harrods Ltd v Remick* [1997] IRLR 9 Ms Remick was employed as a consultant by Shaeffer Pens (UK) Limited who have a sales counter in Harrods. Employees require to be approved by Harrods for working in the store. Ms Remick's store approval was withdrawn by Harrods because she was considered to have failed to adhere to the store's dress code, as a consequence of which she was dismissed by Shaeffer Pens (UK) Limited. She claimed discrimination on grounds of race. The EAT held that staff employed by concessionaires at Harrods were contract workers who worked 'for' Harrods within the meaning of s 7 of the Race Relations Act. The case hinged on the meaning of the word 'for' as Ms Remick had to prove that she was working 'for' Harrods, even though not employed by them. Harrods claimed that Ms Remick did not work for them within the meaning of the Act. In holding for Ms Remick the EAT asked for whose benefit the work was carried out and held that it was a question of fact and degree in each case whether the particular work which was available for doing was work 'for' a principal. The EAT stated:

> 'in the present case the work in question was work "for" Harrods in that it was work done in the store for the benefit of Harrods and ultimately under Harrods' control as Harrods could grant, refuse or withdraw store approval for the worker to do the work available. The fact that the applicants as employees also worked for their employer did not prevent the work which they did from being work "for" Harrods within the meaning of s 7'.

6.5 FIXED TERM AND SPECIFIED PURPOSE CONTRACTS

The legislation allows for the exclusion of dismissals resulting from the ending of a fixed term contract at its expiry and the conclusion of a specified purpose contract on the cesser of the purpose. In order for these exclusions to apply the following conditions must exist:

(a)   the contract must be in writing;

(b)   the contract must specifically exclude the legislation; and

(c)   the contract must be signed by both parties.

In *Sheehan v Dublin Tribune Ltd* [1992] ELR 239 the employer had failed to specify in a fixed term contract the exclusion of the Unfair Dismissals Act and the EAT held that, in the absence of such specific exclusion as required by the legislation, the exclusion of fixed term contracts provided for in the legislation cannot be relied upon by the employer. Further, as no substantial ground had been shown to justify the dismissal the dismissal was held to be unfair.

Many employers use fixed term contracts in the mistaken belief that they are under no obligation to renew on the expiry of the term. Non-renewal will amount to dismissal. The employer can only rely on justification for the non-renewal or dismissal where it can be shown that the contract was a genuine fixed term or specified purpose contract. The employer must be able to show that there was a commercial justification for using such a contract in the first place.

At common law these contracts do not cause particular difficulty. If an employer agrees to employ a person for a specified period of time then, in the absence of a fundamental breach of contract, the employer cannot be absolved from that obligation except by the agreement of the employee. If A agrees to hire B for five years and after two years decides to terminate the contract, B must be paid the balance of the contract. B has, of course, the normal common law duty to mitigate his loss but, in the absence of mitigation, his loss must be measured at the full value to him of the balance of the contract. A prudent employer will therefore seek to put into such a contract a provision allowing for early termination. This may seem to be a contradiction in terms but the Court of Appeal held in *Dixon and Constanti v BBC* [1979] IRLR 114 that the words 'fixed term contract' referred to a contract for a specified term even though the contract is determinable by notice within that term.

An employer may enter into a fixed term or specified purpose contract in order to grant security of tenure to an employee which should tempt him to remain in the employment. While the contractual theory is all very well, if an employee were to abandon his employment under such a contract, there is little or nothing the employer can do to remedy the problems thereby caused. While the employer could claim that there was a cost in having to seek a replacement that cost would have been, in theory at least, incurred on the normal ending of the contract anyway. The cost of hiring a replacement will be met in the main by the money saved in not having to pay the departed employee. If, however, an employer were to be engaged in a special project which was in some way delayed or put in jeopardy the employer may well be able to seek compensation from the employee who has breached the agreement to remain for the fixed term or until the cesser of the purpose. In practice, however, employers' prospects of actually recovering compensation are minimal.

Highly skilled employees may well seek fixed term or specified purpose contracts to give themselves security of tenure. Employers must be aware of the risks of using such contracts if they do not reserve unto themselves the right to terminate on notice within the life of the contract.

Most of the difficulty of using fixed term or specified purpose contracts has arisen under unfair dismissal legislation (see *Orren v Western Health Board* UD 268/96 and *Buckley v Southern Health Board* UD 110/96).

See also **1.6** on fixed term and specified purpose contracts in Chapter 1: Contracts of Employment.

6.6   DISMISSAL

6.6.1   GENERALLY

In order to succeed with a claim under the legislation, the employee must be able to show that he was actually dismissed. A person who has voluntarily resigned his position, or whose contract has come to an end by reason of frustration, could not establish a dismissal and cannot proceed with an unfair dismissal claim. The leading cases on frustration are *Marshall v Harland and Wolff* [1972] IRLR 90; *Egg Stores (Stamford Hill) Ltd v Leibovici* [1976] IRLR 376; and *Nolan v Brooks Thomas Ltd* UD 179/79.

In order for there to be an actual dismissal the employer must have evinced an intention to terminate the contract of employment. Where an employer has used unclear language or ambiguous terminology, an objective test is applied to the words used to see if they were capable of being construed by a reasonable person as indicating a dismissal (see *Tanner v D T Kean Ltd* [1978] IRLR 110). In some cases employers have used crude or abusive language (see *Maher v Walsh* UD 683/83). In *Futty v D & D Brekkes Ltd* [1974] IRLR 130 Futty had a reputation for turning 'banter into acrimony'. One day his foreman got fed up with him and said 'If you do not like the job, f . . . off'. Futty maintained his interpretation of those words was 'you are dismissed'. The company thought he had left in a 'huff' and would come back. He did not. The EAT considered the words actually spoken and also interpreted them 'not in isolation—but against a background of the fish dock'. They held that bad language was not uncommon and 'once the question of dismissal becomes imminent bad language tends to disappear and an unexpected formality seems to descend upon the parties'. The foreman's words were held to be no more than 'a general exhortation to get on with his job'. (See also *Wallace-Hayes v Skolars Hairdressing School Ltd* [1991] ELR 108).

6.6.2   INDEFINITE SUSPENSION

In *Deegan v Dunnes Stores Ltd* [1992] ELR 184 the claimants had been placed on indefinite suspension for refusing to sign undertakings in relation to certain management requirements. The EAT held that:

> 'indefinite suspension amounted to dismissal and that the dismissal in this case was unfair as it was too severe a penalty but that the claimants had contributed to their dismissal through their lack of co-operation which gave rise to the undertaking requirement in the first place'.

6.6.3   APPEAL

Dismissal subject to an appeal will still be a dismissal. In *Michelle Kenny v Warner Music (Ireland) Ltd* UD 389/92 the employee was dismissed for misconduct and was written to advising her of her proposed dismissal subject to a right of appeal against the decision. She was advised that if she invoked her right of appeal she would be suspended on full pay until such time as the outcome of the appeal was known. The employee initiated her right of appeal, the appeal was heard and her dismissal was set aside. She refused to resume work and claimed unfair dismissal based on the original decision which had not been effected by the employer following the outcome of the appeal. The EAT held that she was dismissed and that the dismissal was unfair.

This may be contrasted with the UK case of *Martin v Yeomen Aggregates Ltd* [1983] ICR 314 where there was an angry exchange between a director and the employee who refused to carry out an instruction. In the course of the exchange the director dismissed the employee. A few minutes later the director realised that he had acted improperly and revoked the dismissal advising the employee that he was suspended without pay for two days. The employee, however, treated himself as having been dismissed and claimed unfair dismissal. The EAT held, following *Tanner v Kean* [1978] IRLR 110, that there had been no dismissal, adding that it was a matter of common sense vital to industrial relations that either an employer or an employee should be given an opportunity of recanting from words spoken in the heat of the moment.

The *Kenny* case seems also to have taken the opposite line to that taken by the House of Lords in *West Midlands Co-operative Society Ltd v Tipton* [1986] IRLR 112 which in turn approved *Savage v J Sainsbury Ltd* [1980] IRLR 109.

The Industrial Relations Act 1990 (Code of Practice on Grievance and Disciplinary Procedures) (Declaration) Order 2000 (SI 146/2000), while not legally binding, recommends that disciplinary procedures include a right of appeal against a dismissal decision. In *O'Leary v Eagle Star Life Assurance Company of Ireland Ltd* UD 99/2002 the EAT held that failure to provide an appeal for a dismissed employee can be a factor in determining the fairness or otherwise of the dismissal.

6.6.4   TERMINATION

In order for a contract to properly terminate where notice is given the notice must specify the date of termination, or be given in such a way that the date is ascertainable. A warning of dismissal at some future date may not amount to a dismissal (see *Morton Sundour Fabrics Ltd v Shaw* [1967] 2 ITR 84).

Issuing a P45 does not of itself terminate employment. See *P J O'Flanagan v Houlihan (t/a Anner Hotel)* UD 579/1983 and *McKenna v Bursey Peppard Ltd* [1997] ELR 87, and also *Ennis v Carroll, David Carroll and Scale Force Ltd* UD 586/99 where the employee was offered and sought her P45 but this was held not to have been an indication of dismissal, and the UK case of *Villella v MFI Furniture Ltd* [1999] IRLR 468 . Failure to allow an adopting parent to return to work is a deemed unfair dismissal by virtue of the provisions of s 26 of the Adoptive Leave Act, 1995.

6.6.5   NON-RENEWAL OF FIXED TERM CONTRACT

The expiration of a contract of employment for a fixed term without its being renewed constitutes a dismissal. The dismissal by virtue of non-renewal may not be automatically unfair. See *Hade v Brunswick Press Ltd* 291 UD 377/84 when the non-renewal of a fixed term contract was held to be dismissal but the dismissal was held to be by reason of redundancy.

6.6.6   CONSTRUCTIVE DISMISSAL

6.6.6.1   Generally

The third category is the category known as constructive dismissal which is defined in s 2 of the 1977 Act as:

> 'The termination by the employee of his contract of employment with his employer, whether prior notice of the termination was or was not given to the employer, in circumstances in which, because of the conduct of the employer the employee was or would have been entitled, or it was or would have been reasonable for the employee to terminate the contract of employment without giving prior notice of termination to the employer.'

Where an employee terminates his employment because of an employer's conduct towards him, and that conduct is deemed sufficiently serious, the employee may be entitled to claim constructive dismissal. The equivalent UK provision is more restrictive as far as employees are concerned and does not provide that it might be 'reasonable for the employee to terminate the contract of employment'. The UK cases tend therefore to focus on constructive dismissal more akin to fundamental breach at common law. The Irish cases are broader and more wide-ranging in the types of conduct dealt with. The leading Irish case is probably that of *Byrne v RHM Foods (Ireland) Ltd* UD 69/79. Following the termination of employment of the manager for whom the claimant worked, the claimant noticed a considerable deterioration in her working conditions and particularly her relationship with the managing director, who had assumed the duties of her former boss. She was given no work to do and was effectively isolated. While she had her own office, her telephone was cut off and later her filing cabinets were removed. As a result of the stress she suffered, the claimant had to receive medical treatment and subsequently claimed constructive dismissal. The EAT in its determination in her favour stated:

> 'We appreciate that following an upset in the upper management level in any company difficulties can arise but no explanation or contact was made with the claimant who was left in her office for a period of approximately three weeks' continuous isolation without knowledge of what was going on or contact by any person and in our view it is reasonable and understandable that her confidence and trust in her employer should be undermined to the extent that she could tolerate it no longer. We are of the opinion that the Managing Director should have communicated in person or otherwise with the claimant so as to reassure her during this period concerning her position and thereby maintain reasonable confidence and trust which an employee is entitled to have in an employer.'

The employer's failure to pay tax and PRSI contributions on behalf of the employee was held to be sufficient grounds to entitle the employee to succeed with a claim of constructive dismissal in *Branigan v Collins* UD 28/77.

6.6.6.2 Reduction in pay

A unilateral reduction in pay, even for good reasons and to a relatively small extent, may be a material breach of a fundamental element in the contract of employment (see *Industrial Rubber Products v Gillon* [1977] IRLR 389). The employer may, however, have a contractual right to vary the employee's income (see *White v Reflecting Roadstuds Ltd* [1991] IRLR 331). A refusal to pay overtime payments for overtime hours worked was held to be a breach going to the root of the contract of employment entitling the employee to claim constructive dismissal in *Stokes v Hampstead Wine Company Ltd* [1979] IRLR 298.

6.6.6.3 Working environment

In *Waltons & Morse v Dorrington* [1997] IRLR 488 a secretary employed by a firm of solicitors claimed constructive dismissal as a result of the problems she encountered with smokers in the office. A limited smoking policy was adopted by the firm but this did not lead to a sufficient improvement for Mrs Dorrington. She succeeded with a constructive dismissal claim. The EAT held that the employer was in breach of an implied term in her contract of employment that the employer would 'provide and monitor for employees, so far as is reasonably practicable, a working environment which is reasonably suitable for the performance by them of their contractual duties'.

6.6.6.4   Lack of pay rise

A lack of pay rises may not entitle an employee to claim constructive dismissal depending on the circumstances (see *Murco Petroleum Ltd v Forge* [1987] IRLR 50). In the Irish case of *Riddell v Mid-West Metals Ltd* M962 UD 687/80 the employee's terms and conditions were changed in that he received a lesser bonus than he had been led to believe he would receive and he was required to carry his own motoring expenses which he had not previously been required to do. The EAT noted, however, the remuneration was reviewable under the terms of the contract and, given the fact that the claimant did not seek to engage in negotiations on the issues causing him concern, took the position that he could not accept the proposal and terminated his employment. His claim failed (see *Conway v Ulster Bank* UD 474/81 referred to at **6.6.6.10** below.

6.6.6.5   Change in job functions

Removal of job functions or changes imposed by the employer may give rise to an entitlement to claim constructive dismissal (see *Coleman v S & W Baldwin* [1977] IRLR 342). If, however, an employer for good commercial reason directs an employee to transfer to other suitable work on a purely temporary basis at no diminution in salary and it is made clear that it is only a temporary arrangement, the employee may not be entitled to claim constructive dismissal.

6.6.6.6   Change of location

An imposed change of location, where the employee is not contractually obliged to work at the new location, may give rise to a constructive dismissal claim as in *Bass Leisure Ltd v Thomas* [1994] IRLR 104. See also *Rank Xerox Ltd v Churchill* [1988] IRLR 280.

6.6.6.7   Change in working hours

Where an employer has the contractual right to alter hours of work and shift systems, doing so did not constitute a breach of contract and did not give rise to a constructive dismissal claim in the case of *Dal v A S Orr* [1980] IRLR 413.

6.6.6.8   Unmerited warnings

In *Walker v Josiah Wedgewood & Sons Ltd* [1978] IRLR 105 it was held that the giving of an unjustified warning or series of warnings can give rise to a legitimate complaint of constructive dismissal if the employee makes a case that the warnings were given, not with a view to improving his conduct and performance, but with a view to disheartening him and driving him out. A tribunal in such a case would have to fully investigate the merits of the warnings complained of.

6.6.6.9   Sexual harassment or abuse in workplace

In *O'Doherty v John Paul Hennessy Junior and Harrow Holdings Ltd* [1993] ELR 161 the claimant alleged that she had been subjected to sexual harassment by a member of the first-named respondent's family. She stated that she had complained to her manager. Nothing was done about her allegations. She left her employment and claimed constructive dismissal. The EAT held that the actions complained of by the claimant amounted to sexual harassment, which justified her in terminating her employment, amounting to constructive dismissal. This case seems to tie in neatly with the Labour Court requirement of employers that they have in place a procedure for dealing with claims of sexual harassment. The absence of such a procedure has, on a number of occasions, been used by the Labour Court to confer liability on an employer for an allegation of sexual harassment even where the employer may have been unaware of the allegations. Had the employer in *O'Doherty* had a procedure in place for dealing with claims of sexual harassment one must presume that this claim would have been dealt with and the outcome might have been considerably different.

In *Kennedy v Foxfield Inns Ltd* [1995] ELR 216 the claimant gave evidence of reporting her manager for rudeness and name-calling in front of customers, standing on her foot and slapping her on the back, as a result of which she decided she could no longer work with the company. She handed in a letter of resignation giving her reasons for leaving. The manager called her to his office and apologised for any offence claiming he had 'only been messing'. In evidence to the EAT, however, the manager denied any verbal or physical abuse and denied apologising. The general manager of the employer gave evidence that he was shocked on reading the claimant's letter of resignation and had instructed the manager in question to conduct an investigation. The EAT held in all the circumstances the claimant's decision to terminate her employment was reasonable and that she had been constructively dismissed.

In *Holmes v O'Driscoll* [1991] ELR 80 the claimant was a trainee machinist. The employer had poked her in the arm with clippers and warned her to get on with her work, an action he allegedly repeated later in the day. The claimant became upset, left work and claimed that she had been constructively dismissed. The EAT held she was entitled to treat herself as constructively dismissed and that her dismissal was unfair.

The mutual bond of trust and confidence is dealt with quite comprehensively in *Woods v WM Car Services (Peterborough) Ltd* [1981] IRLR 347 and *United Bank v Akhtar* [1989] IRLR 507.

6.6.6.10 Conduct of employee

Where an employee has a difficulty with his employer he will be required to act reasonably himself and seek to resolve the matter internally before resorting to a claim of constructive dismissal. In *Conway v Ulster Bank Ltd* UD 474/81 the claimant was employed at the Sligo branch of the bank. After she became engaged to an account holder she was given two weeks' notice of proposed transfer to Ballina. In that notice period she submitted her resignation and claimed constructive dismissal. The employer had in place a detailed grievance procedure which had not been invoked by the claimant. In holding against the claimant the EAT stated:

'By majority the Tribunal considered that the claimant did not act reasonably in resigning without first having substantially utilised the grievance procedure to attempt to remedy her complaints. An elaborate grievance procedure existed but the claimant did not use it. It is not for the Tribunal to say whether using this procedure would have produced a decision more favourable to her but it is possible.'

See also *Beatty v Bayside Supermarket* UD 142/87; *Harrington v Julias Ltd* UD 140/82 and *Corcoran v Amusements Eden Quay Ltd* UD 681/80.

In *Olsson v John Quinn & Co* [1992] ELR 91 the claimant alleged assault by the head barman and continuing difficulties with him. When the difficulties were not resolved the claimant left his employment and claimed unfair dismissal. The EAT dismissed his claim, holding that it was not reasonable for him to leave his employment in the manner in which he did since his employer did not know of the incident which triggered his walk-out.

The EAT took an apparently different view in *Gallery v Blarney Woollen Mills Ltd* [1990] ELR 143. Following the takeover of the shop managed by the claimant she was unhappy with a lack of clarity about her position and felt she was being undermined in a number of ways. She sought written confirmation of the terms and conditions of her employment and confirmation that the company had full confidence in her. She was unhappy with the response and demanded a written response. She was asked to attend a meeting but refused to do so. She claimed the company's conduct amounted to constructive dismissal and she resigned. She succeeded in her claim despite the EAT considering the *Conway* and *Beatty* cases referred to above. In *Gallery* the EAT held that 'the respondent company acted unreasonably in its dealings with the claimant and she became frustrated leaving her with no option but to resign'.

In *Madden v Western Regional Fisheries Board* M1356 UD 857/82 the claimant was suspended without pay, and his solicitor wrote to state that it was being treated as a constructive dismissal. The EAT noted that there were procedures in existence for dealing with staff problems but that the claimant did not avail of them. The EAT noted that the employee's conditions of service allowed for suspension without pay pending an investigation. The EAT stated that it would have sympathy for the claimant if he had no alternative under his contract, but as he had the right to appeal the suspension and have the matter resolved in accordance with the terms of the contract or availing of the rights commissioner services under the Industrial Relations Acts, in not doing so he had not made out a case that he was constructively dismissed.

It has been established that a constructive dismissal is not automatically unfair (see *Savoia v Chiltern Herb Farms Ltd* [1982] IRLR 166) but it will obviously be very difficult for an employer who claims he did not dismiss a person to then argue, once dismissal has been established, that substantial grounds existed to justify doing what he claimed he did not do. There may, however, be certain circumstances in which the employer may wish to make that argument. In *Cawley v South Wales Electricity Board* [1985] IRLR 89 the UK EAT said that the considerations of fairness under the legislation and the concept of constructive dismissal are effectively 'two sides of the same coin'. If the employer's behaviour is unreasonable enough to amount to constructive dismissal it would normally almost automatically follow that the dismissal has to be unfair.

6.7 RESIGNATIONS

The common law rule regarding notice given by either party is that once notice is given it cannot unilaterally be withdrawn. The giving of notice is itself not a dismissal because it may be withdrawn by agreement and the dismissal does not come about until notice has expired. If, however, either party seeks to withdraw notice and the other party does not agree, a dismissal will occur and difficulties may be caused for employees where they have resigned and they seek to overturn their resignation. A leading common law case is *Riordan v War Office* [1959] 1 WLR 1046 where Diplock J stated:

> 'This was sufficient notice given by the plaintiff terminating his employment . . . once given it could not be withdrawn save by mutual consent.'

Even where an employer claims that an employee has resigned, some steps should be taken to ascertain why the employee resigned, some effort made to get the employee to stay, as otherwise the employer's actions might be construed as either a constructive dismissal or an actual dismissal. In *Maxwell v Coruscate Ltd (t/a Glenview Hotel)* [1992] ELR 122 the claimant had a dispute with the head chef about being told to 'get out of the kitchen'. He then asked for his P45 and entitlements and was again told to 'get out'. He then packed up and was leaving the hotel when the chef told him he had not sacked him, that he had walked out and was therefore entitled to nothing. Some days later the claimant went back to see the owner of the hotel, who was unaware that he had been dismissed, and when the claimant told him the story said that there was nothing he could do about it and referred him back to the head chef. The claimant sought out the head chef and offered him a sick note for his absence but the head chef was not interested in dealing with him any further. The EAT held that on the evidence the claimant had been dismissed. See also *Dodd and Murphy v Houston and Morrow* UD 257/259/78.

Not all apparent resignations will be held to be effective. In *Barclay v City of Glasgow District Court* [1983] IRLR 313 it was held that Barclay had resigned but was known to be mentally defective and his employers were not therefore entitled to treat his words of resignation as notice of termination. In *Sothern v Franks Charlesly & Co* [1981] IRLR 278 it was held that there may be exceptions to the resignation rules as in the case of an immature employee or a decision taken in the heat of the moment which may not in fact be an effective resignation at all. A refusal by the employer to allow the employee to retract or revoke or remain in employment will in those circumstances be deemed to be a dismissal.

6.8   DATE OF DISMISSAL

The date of dismissal is of particular relevance to an employee's entitlement to bring a claim and possibly also to the time at which a claim should be brought. Unlike in Britain, the date of dismissal in Ireland may be artificial, being a date other than the date on which the actual employment terminated. Section 1 of the 1977 Act provides that the statutory date of dismissal shall be the later of:

(a)   the earliest date that would be in compliance with the provisions of the contract; or

(b)   the earliest date that would be in compliance with the provisions of the Minimum Notice and Terms of Employment Act, 1973 (as amended): see Chapter 1: Contracts of Employment.

It may be seen therefore that the date of dismissal is the date upon which notice expires, being the longer of either the statutory or the contractual notice entitlement. This is the case even where the employee does not actually work out the notice period. The situation might be altered if the contract specifically allowed for payment in lieu of giving notice as opposed to an accommodation reached between the parties where the payment is made in lieu of the employee actually working out the notice (see *Ogden v Harp Textiles* UD 112/79 and *O'Reilly v Pullman Kellog Ltd* UD 340/79). Holiday entitlements are not added to a period of service to determine length of service (see *Maher v B & I Line* UD 271/78 and *Twomey v O'Leary Office Supplies* [1997] ELR 42).

In constructive dismissal cases an employee may opt to give notice or not as the case may be. The date of dismissal will be the date notice expires and not a deemed date where, for example, the employee gives no notice or gives lesser notice than he might be obliged to give under the contract or the 1973 Act (see *Stamp v McGrath* UD 1243/83).

6.9   REMUNERATION

6.9.1   CALCULATION OF REMUNERATION

The calculation of remuneration is important in the assessment of the maximum value of a claim, being actual loss attributable to a dismissal, and the ability to make these calculations is of vital importance in negotiating prior to the hearing of a dismissal claim.

Section 7(1)(c) of the 1977 Act allows for the award of compensation to an employee held to have been unfairly dismissed and caps the amount awarded at the equivalent of 104 weeks' remuneration. The subsection further provides that the compensation is awardable *'in respect of any financial loss incurred . . . and attributable to the dismissal as is just and equitable having regard to all the circumstances'*.

Section 7 defines 'remuneration' as including *'allowances in the nature of pay and benefits in lieu of or in addition to pay'*. Remuneration has been held to include not only basic payments to an employee but the value of the loss of benefits in kind. Remuneration has been held to include such diverse items as:

(a) basic pay or salary;

(b) overtime payments;

(c) bonuses;

(d) commission;

(e) tips;

(f) benefits in kind such as:

(i) clothing allowances;

(ii) subsidised telephone costs;

(iii) private use of company car;

(iv) professional and social subscriptions;

(v) VHI; and

(vi) pension contributions—it is the employer's pension cost only that is calculated.

Tribunals do not allow for loss of benefits such as preferential loans or mortgages. These are facilities made available to employees that they may or may not avail of. Employees doing identical work, one of whom avails of a maximum mortgage entitlement and the other who avails of a nil mortgage entitlement, could not be deemed to have different rates of remuneration for unfair dismissal purposes (see *Bunyan v United Dominions Trust (Ireland) Ltd* UD 66/80).

When assessing remuneration for the purposes of calculating the maximum award allowable under the legislation regard is had to the gross amount of such payment.

6.9.2 ASSESSMENT OF LOSS

For the purposes of compensation loss is a matter for assessment. The 1977 Act defined financial loss in s 7 as including

> *'any <u>actual</u> loss and any estimated <u>prospective</u> loss of income attributable to the dismissal and the value of any loss or diminution attributable to the dismissal of the rights of the employee under the Redundancy Payments Acts or in relation to superannuation.'*

In case of share options the share option scheme under which the employee gets the entitlement to the shares may provide that there is no compensation for loss of share options when employment terminates as in *Micklefield v SAC Technology Ltd* [1990] IRLR 218. However, in calculating unfair dismissal compensation under the UK legislation, the UK Employment Appeal Tribunal awarded compensation where employees lost the value of share options as a result of being dismissed at a particular time in *Leonard v Strathclyde Buses Ltd* [1998] IRLR 693. The EAT interpreted the words 'actual loss' to mean precisely that. Any benefit gained by the employee following dismissal, including unemployment benefit, was deducted from the loss of income arising from the dismissal in order to arrive at 'actual loss'.

If an employee successfully mitigated his loss immediately following a dismissal he was liable to receive a nil compensation award in the event of succeeding with an unfair dismissal claim until the enactment of the 1993 Act, s 6 as referred to below.

The reason why an employee might not have a loss is usually related to the fact that he was successful in mitigating the loss, but could arise for other reasons such as illness and an inability to earn at the time of and after the dismissal. In *Coyle v Tipper House Trust Ltd* UD 904/93 the EAT held that the dismissal of the claimant was unfair but made no compensatory award under the 1977 Act as the claimant had been unfit for work since his dismissal and it could not be said when, if ever, he would be fit for work in the future and he therefore had no loss. That was made prior to the enactment of the 1993 Act which allowed for the awarding of up to one month's remuneration in cases where there is no loss. See also *Cadbury Ltd v Doddington* [1977] ICR 982.

The 1993 Act made two important changes in respect of actual loss. The changes are contained in s 6. The first change was to provide that if an employee incurred no financial loss he could in any event be awarded compensation up to a maximum equivalent of four weeks' remuneration. The second substantial change made by s 6 was to provide that in calculating actual financial loss regard should not be had to social welfare benefits or income tax rebates.

6.10 CONTINUITY OF SERVICE

As has been seen at **6.2** above, one year's continuous service is necessary in order to establish the right to claim under the Act. The one year is reckoned from the date of dismissal working backwards until one reaches a break in continuity. It is possible under the rules of continuity to work during a period which is not recognisable but which does not actually break service.

Service under the age of 16 years is not computable. Probationary service is computable. Once a person is established as an employee it does not matter what designation he carries such as casual, permanent, semi-permanent, temporary etc once he satisfies the rules of continuity of service. The rules for calculation of continuity are set out in the Minimum Notice and Terms of Employment Act, 1973, Sch 1. Service is deemed to be continuous unless otherwise broken. Continuity is not broken by normal periods of absence such as illness, holidays, maternity leave or even strikes or lockouts. All of these periods may, however, not be actually recognisable as periods of service.

The rules provide that continuity is not broken where an employee is dismissed and 'immediately' re-employed. There is no definition of immediate but in *Howard v Breton Ltd* UD 486/84 re-employment a week after dismissal was sufficiently immediate to preserve continuity but a different decision was arrived at in the earlier case of *Mulhall & Sons v Dunphy* UD 710/81. A break of three months between periods of employment was deemed not to be sufficient to come within the expression 'immediate' re-employment contained in the Minimum Notice and Terms of Employment Act, 1973, Sch 1, para 6 in the case of *Myles v O'Kane* [1991] ELR 217.

It is sometimes thought that the issue of a P45 constitutes the termination of an employee's employment. That is not the case. The issue of a form P45 or termination papers of any other sort is merely indicative, but if other facts show that the employment was not brought to an end within the normal rules of notice of termination then the employment will be deemed continuous (see *Allison v Incorporated Law Society and Cullen* UD 492/86 and *O'Flanagan v Houlihan* UD 579/83). In *McKenna v Bursey Peppard Ltd* [1997] ELR 87 the claimant was absent from work due to illness and when he furnished a fitness certificate from his doctor it was refused by the employer, who sought a more detailed form of certification. Pending that issue being sorted out the employee sought and obtained his P45 in order to claim social welfare entitlements. Dismissal as a fact was in dispute and the EAT held by a majority that the claimant was entitled to seek his P45 to claim social welfare benefit but there had been no dismissal, or constructive dismissal, by the employer.

Lay-off does not break continuity but where a lay-off exceeds twenty-six weeks, the period in excess of twenty-six weeks is not computable as a period of service. What actually constitutes a lay-off is a question of fact. It may be argued on behalf of an employee, who has been absent from the place of work for some time or who is seeking to link two apparently separate periods of service with one employer, that there was actually a lay-off covering the gap. In some of the more traditional industries the term 'lay-off' or 'laid off' is used and the word terminate would be more appropriate.

6.11 EMPLOYEES WORKING OUTSIDE IRELAND

The legislation does not apply to the dismissal of an employee who ordinarily works outside the State unless:

'(i)   he was ordinarily resident in the State during the term of the contract, or
(ii)   he was domiciled in the State during the term of the contract, and the employer—
   (I)   in case the employee was an individual, was ordinarily resident in the State during the term of the contract, or
   (ii)   in case the employer was a body corporate or an unincorporated body of persons had, its principal place of business in the State during the term of the contract.'

See s 2(3) of the Unfair Dismissals Act, 1977. The first part of the definition excludes from the legislation employees working outside Ireland and not ordinarily resident here during the term of the contract. What constitutes residence in the State will effectively be determined by the employee's base during the performance of the contractual obligations. If an employee lives and works outside the State during the currency of a contract of employment he will not be in a position to claim unfair dismissal on the termination of his contract.

In *Dignam v Sisk Nigeria Ltd* UD 125/83 and *D'arcy v General Electric Technical Services Company Inc* UD 542/86 both claimants were Irish nationals working outside the State and, in both cases, the employer's principal place of business was outside the State and the claimants were held not to be entitled to claim under the legislation.

Non-nationals are entitled to claim under the legislation if they work for Irish companies, and non-nationals working for foreign companies in Ireland are also covered by the legislation (see *Roder v Liebig International Ltd* UD 144/79 and *Kay v Nobrac Carbon Ltd* Circuit Court No 63, 18 December 1985—see Kerr and Madden, *Unfair Dismissals Cases and Commentary*, p 116).

A comprehensive assessment of entitlement to claim in respect of work carried on outside the State is set out in the British case of *Wilson v Maynard Shipbuilding Consultants* [1977] IRLR 419, albeit in the context of somewhat different British legislation. In determining the practice to be taken into account the Court of Appeal laid down the following tests:

(a)   An employee either works in Great Britain or outside it. He only does one or the other and not both. If he carries out some of his work in Great Britain that appears to be sufficient to entitle him to claim.

(b)   The key factor is what is envisaged under the contract and not what happens in practice.

(c)   It is necessary to look at the whole period contemplated by the contract at the time it was made. It is not sufficient to look at what happened the short time before the contract was terminated which may not be representative of what the parties had in mind at the time the contract was formed.

(d)   In the absence of special factors an employee's base is to be his ordinary workplace.

(e)   An employee's base may be determined by looking at his headquarters, where he starts and finishes his travels, where he lives, where he is paid and in what currency and where he makes his tax and social security payments.

It is only necessary to use the base test if the ordinary workplace cannot be established otherwise from the terms of the employment contract (see *Carver v Saudi Arabian Airlines* [1999] IRLR 991).

In *Zimmerman v Der Deutsche Schuliverein Ltd* [1999] ELR 211 the claimant, who was a German civil servant, had been appointed as principal of a German school in Dublin. The claimant brought a claim against the school for unfair dismissal and the EAT had to consider the question of its jurisdiction holding that the terms of the Rome Convention on the Law Applicable to Contractual Obligations 1980 and s 13 of the 1977 Act, which renders void any contractual provision seeking to limit or exclude the effect of that Act, applied so that it had jurisdiction to hear the claim.

See also **1.5.25** on Proper Law in Chapter 1: Contracts of Employment.

6.12   DIPLOMATIC IMMUNITY

Employees of embassies and foreign governments in Ireland cannot bring dismissal claims against their employers (see *Government of Canada v Employment Appeals Tribunal* [1991] ELR 57).

6.13   PROBATION

There are apparently complicated provisions relating to probation and training in the legislation. The 1977 Act allows for the exclusion of persons on probation or training but only where the period of such is less than one year, in which case all of the distinctions appear to be largely academic. The fact that employees are on probation or undergoing training has therefore no effect on continuity or status and is entirely recognisable. Employers should at all times have regard to the statutory date of dismissal where employees are being trained or are undergoing probationary assessment in order to ensure that the employment does not extend to or beyond the one-year period in which event, if they were to terminate the employment, they may find themselves having to show that substantial grounds existed to justify the termination in circumstances where they believed otherwise.

6.14   APPRENTICES

A contract of apprenticeship may be defined as one in which the apprentice agrees to serve the employer and to learn from him and the employer agrees to instruct the apprentice in his trade, profession or business and to maintain him during the continuance of that relationship. The general view is that an employer may terminate an apprenticeship if the apprentice's conduct is such that the employer can no longer instruct him. Certain apprenticeship agreements are capable of being construed as fixed term or specified purpose contracts and both parties should have regard to the specific terms of an apprenticeship or training contract which is something that is frequently overlooked.

Apprentices' rights are curtailed under the 1977 Act, s 4 which provides that the Act shall not apply in relation to the dismissal of a person who is or was employed under a statutory apprenticeship if the dismissal takes place within six months after the commencement of the apprenticeship or within one month after the completion of the apprenticeship.

What is the meaning of a statutory apprenticeship? Section 1 of the 1977 Act defines statutory apprenticeship as being apprenticeship 'in a designated industrial activity within the meaning of the Industrial Training Act, 1967'.

The effect of s 4 of the 1977 Act is that apprentices are not protected for the first six months of their employment and for a period of one month following completion of the apprenticeship. This means that once an apprentice has completed six months of an apprenticeship he is covered by the legislation where otherwise he might be thought to require the one year's continuous service (see *MacNamara v Castlelock Construction & Development Ltd* UD 808/84). It must be stressed, however, that this relates only to statutory apprentices.

It appears that the employers of non-statutory apprentices, eg solicitors, are not in a position to allow a period of one month to elapse after the apprenticeship has ended. Non-statutory apprenticeships should be treated as specified purpose contracts where the employer wishes to be adequately protected from unfair dismissal claims.

In *Boal v IMED Ireland Ltd* [1995] ELR 178 the employee was employed under a statutory apprenticeship for six years. His contract was terminated one month after the completion of the apprenticeship. The employers claimed that they had informed the claimant on a number of occasions during the six years of his apprenticeship that they would not be retaining him on the ending of his apprenticeship. The EAT held that the claimant was employed under a contract of statutory apprenticeship and was therefore excluded from cover of the Unfair Dismissals Acts and his claim was dismissed.

In *O'Callaghan v Denis Mahony Ltd* UD 177/79 the claimant worked as an apprentice from 1974 to 1978 when his apprenticeship came to an end. When given notice of expiration of the apprenticeship the claimant requested a month's extension of time and this was granted. He planned on emigrating to Australia but encountered some delays as a result of which a further extension of time was granted to him. Eventually the respondent company dismissed the claimant on the basis that it maintained it could not longer afford to retain him as an employee. The EAT took the view that the respondent company could not rely on s 4 of the 1977 Act. The dismissal was in any event held to be fair. It should not be taken therefore that because the one-month period has elapsed the employer is under any obligation to give permanent employment to the former apprentice. Tribunals will look sympathetically on a situation where an apprentice ceases to hold that status and becomes a different type of individual and where the employer may reach temporary accommodation with him. Employers should, however, make their position very clear in this regard.

See also *Rooney and Byrne v Abbey Homesteads Ltd* UD 712/80 and UD 2/81 heard as one case and also *Farrell v J D Brian Motors Ltd* UD 341/87.

6.15 UNFAIR DISMISSALS

6.15.1 CATEGORIES

For the purpose of the legislation dismissals are divided into two categories:

(a) dismissals deemed to be automatically unfair; or

(b) dismissals deemed to be not unfair.

Section 6(2) of the 1977 Act as amended by the 1993 Act, s 5 sets out the categories of 'automatically' unfair dismissal which are:

(i) An employee's membership (or proposed membership) or activity on behalf of a trade union where the times in which he engages in such activities are outside his hours of work or are at permitted times during his hours of work. In *White v Betson* [1992] ELR 120 the EAT held that the coincidence of the employer having received correspondence from a trade union prior to the termination of the claimant's employment and the making of the decision to dismiss was such that the claimant was dismissed because of his trade union membership and, accordingly, the dismissal was unfair.

In *O'Riordan v Killine Eyewear Ltd* [1991] ELR 89 the EAT held that the coincidence of a clear intention by the claimants to join a trade union, the fact that this was known to the respondent and the making of the decision to terminate their contracts of employment were such that the dismissal was held to be by reason of trade union membership and held to be unfair.

(ii) The employee's religious or political opinions.

(iii) Because the employee is engaged in civil or criminal proceedings against the employer or is a party or a witness to such proceedings whether they are actual, threatened or proposed, or where the employee has made any complaint or statement to the prosecuting authority connected with the case.

(iv) The race, colour or sexual orientation of the employee.

(v) The age of the employee (see *Kerrigan v Peter Owens Advertising and Marketing Ltd* UD 31/97) where the claimant was declared redundant by the company for a number of reasons, one of which was his age. While the EAT held that there was no redundancy situation at the time of dismissal it determined that the claimant's dismissal arose wholly or mainly from his age in contravention of the 1977 Act, s 6(2), as amended, and awarded compensation.

(vi) The employee's membership of the travelling community.

(vii) The pregnancy of the employee or matters connected therewith—this provision must be cross-referenced to maternity legislation. Reasons connected with pregnancy have been held to include miscarriages and hypertension (see *George v Beecham Group* [1977] IRLR 43 and *Elegbede v The Wellcome Foundation* [1977] IRLR 383).

The 1977 Act provides however that the dismissal of a pregnant employee will not be unfair if the employee was unable by reason of the pregnancy or matters connected therewith:

(a) to do adequately the work for which she was employed, or

(b) to continue to do such work without contravention by her or her employer of a provision of a statute or instrument made under statute, and

(c) there was not at the time of the dismissal any other employment with her employer that was suitable for her and in relation to which there was a vacancy, or she refused an offer by her employer of alternative employment on terms and conditions corresponding to those of the employment to which the dismissal related, being an offer made so as to enable her to be retained in the employment notwithstanding her pregnancy.

An employer may therefore dismiss a pregnant employee who is incapable of doing her work provided he has sought out a suitable alternative vacancy and there is not one, or she refuses a reasonable offer of one (see *Matthews v Ophardt Products Ltd* UD 550/83). See also *Hallissey v Pretty Polly (Killarney) Ltd* UD 362/84 and *McCarthy v Sunbeam Ltd* [1991] ELR 38. Regard must be had in all such cases to the provisions of the Maternity Protection Act,

1994, which makes provision in s 18 for health and safety leave for a pregnant employee in certain circumstances, and the Safety, Health and Welfare at Work (Pregnant Employees etc) Regulations, 2000 which place a duty on every employer to carry out a risk assessment and to make the employee aware of the results of that risk assessment (see *Coffey v Byrne* [1997] ELR 230).

6.15.2 ENGAGING IN INDUSTRIAL ACTION

Section 5(2) of the 1977 Act as amended provides:

> *'The dismissal of an employee for taking part in a strike or other industrial action shall be deemed for the purposes of this Act to be an unfair dismissal if:*
> *(a)* *one or more employees of the same employer who took part in the strike or other industrial action were not dismissed for so taking part or;*
> *(b)* *one or more of such employees who were dismissed for so taking part were subsequently permitted to resume their employment on terms and conditions at least as favourable to the employees as those specified in the said paragraph (a) or (b) and the employee was not.'*

In *Tuke v Coillte Teo* [1998] ELR 324 the claimants engaged in industrial action together with a number of colleagues. The dispute was resolved with some of their colleagues but the claimants became subject to disciplinary procedures ultimately leading to their dismissal. The dismissal was held to be unfair on the following grounds:

(a) even though the claimants' actions were unreasonable they did constitute in-dustrial action within the meaning of the Unfair Dismissals Act, 1977;

(b) the claimants were dismissed because of their industrial action;

(c) two employees who took part in the industrial action had been allowed to resume their employment while the claimants who also took part remained dismissed. Accordingly s 5(2) of the 1977 Act meant that the claimants had been unfairly dismissed;

(d) reinstatement was not the appropriate form of redress because the claimants' behaviour had been unreasonable and they were the authors of their own misfortune; and

(e) the claimants were to be re-engaged. Remuneration was not to commence until the date of the re-engagement and the respondent was not to be penalised with any claim for back pay.

6.16   REDUNDANCY

6.16.1   STATUTORY DEFINITION

The statutory definition of redundancy is to be found in the Redundancy Payments Act, 1967, s 7(2) (as amended by s 4 of the Redundancy Payments Act 1971) and provides that:

> *'an employee who is dismissed shall be taken to be dismissed by reason of redundancy if the dismissal is attributable wholly or mainly to:*
> *(a)* *the fact that his employer has ceased, or intends to cease, to carry on the business for the purposes of which the employee was employed by him, or has ceased or intends to cease, to carry on that business in the place where the employee was so employed; or*
> *(b)* *the fact that the requirements of that business for employees to carry out work of a particular kind in the place where he was so employed have ceased or diminished or are expected to cease or diminish; or*

(c)   *the fact that his employer has decided to carry on the business with fewer or no employees, whether by requiring the work for which the employee had been employed (or had been doing before his dismissal) to be done by other employees or otherwise; or*

(d)   *the fact that his employer has decided that the work for which the employee had been employed (or had been doing before his dismissal) should henceforward be done in a different manner for which the employee is not sufficiently qualified or trained; or*

(e)   *the fact that his employer has decided that the work for which the employee had been employed (or had been doing before his dismissal) should henceforward be done by a person who is also capable of doing other work for which the employee is not sufficiently qualified or trained.'*

This definition is quite broad, broader than the equivalent UK definition. Part of the reason for such a broad definition is that the 1967 and 1971 Acts sought to confer on a wide constituency of employees the right to a statutory redundancy payment. In more recent times statutory redundancy payments have become less financially attractive.

6.16.2   REDUNDANCY AND UNFAIR DISMISSAL

In 1977, when the statutory remedy of unfair dismissal was created, the Unfair Dismissals Act 1977 provided, at s 6(4)(c), that a dismissal is deemed not to be an unfair dismissal if it resulted wholly or mainly from the redundancy of the employee. Redundancy is therefore an absolute defence to a claim of unfair dismissal, provided the employee has been fairly selected for redundancy. Strict adherence to the definition of redundancy is required from employers if an employee is to be held to be dismissed by reason of redundancy. Redundancy defences are closely scrutinised by the EAT. An example of a failure, on the part of an employer, to strictly adhere to the definition is to be found in *Keenan v Gresham Hotel Company Ltd* UD 478/88 where the EAT stated, in the context of s 7(2)(g) of the Redundancy Payments Act, 1967, as referred to above, that an employer, who dismisses employees on the grounds that his workforce requirements 'are expected to cease or diminish', must establish that the cesser or diminution was 'expected to occur at or within a very short time after the time of the alleged redundancy'. It is not enough for an employer to claim that his workforce requirements are expected to cease or diminish 'at some distant time in the future'.

6.16.3   'IMPERSONALITY' REQUIREMENT

An essential feature of a redundancy dismissal is the requirement that the function be redundant, not necessarily the person, and that there be an element of 'impersonality' about the dismissal as held by the EAT in *Moloney v Deacon & Sons Ltd* [1996] ELR 230. In that case the claimant had been dismissed for what was claimed to be a reason of redundancy. The company made a number of submissions to the EAT, including a written note of the reasons for discontinuation of employment, one of which was that the claimant did not satisfactorily complete a statutory probationary period, and made reference to a final warning letter. Reference was also made to a claim for back pay which Mr Moloney had withdrawn, having been found to have made a false statement. In the circumstances the EAT stated 'one of the essential features of redundancy is impersonality. One of the reasons given for dismissal refers to the claimant's personality'. This was held not to be a genuine redundancy situation.

6.16.4   CONDUCT OF THE EMPLOYER IN EFFECTING REDUNDANCIES

6.16.4.1   Introduction

With the exception of collective redundancies, which are dealt with at **6.16.9** below, there are limited procedural requirements imposed on employers in Ireland in effecting re-

134

dundancy dismissals. There are no specific requirements for prior consultation or the following of procedures, such as are laid down in relation to collective redundancies. The rules of natural justice do not apply where a dismissal results from redundancy. In *Hickey v Eastern Health Board* [1991] 1 IR 208; [1990] ELR 177 the Supreme Court held that, since the appellant had not been dismissed for any fault, or any failure to perform her duties properly, the rules of natural justice which are relevant to dismissal of a person for misconduct did not apply to her case.

In that case the appellant was a qualified state registered nurse working as a part-time temporary nurse in a hospital run by the health board. Ultimately Hickey was advised that her employment was being terminated as the health board's budget allocation had been reduced and the hospital was not in a position to retain her services. In the High Court it was found that her dismissal was not based on any fault or misconduct on her part and that therefore the relevant rules of natural justice did not apply. The Supreme Court upheld the decision of the High Court. While Hickey complained that she did not receive any hearing and therefore the decision to declare her redundant was tainted, she also complained that other employees with shorter service had been retained and that this would be a matter germane to the hearing to which she claimed she was entitled. The Supreme Court took the view that the decision to make Hickey redundant was not 'arbitrary or capricious or induced by a wrong motive' and went on to hold:

(a) the rights of an employee in regard to dismissal do not depend on whether such employee is a servant or an officer but rather on the reasons for and circumstances surrounding the dismissal; and

(b) since the appellant had not been dismissed for any fault or any failure to perform her duties properly the rules of natural justice relevant to dismissal of a person for misconduct did not apply to her case.

6.16.4.2 Reasonableness

The decision in *Hickey v Eastern Health Board* was made prior to the enactment of the Unfair Dismissals (Amendment) Act, 1993. The 1993 Act provides that reasonableness of an employer's conduct is now an essential factor to be considered in the context of all dismissals, including redundancy dismissals. Section 6(7) of the 1977 Act (as inserted by the 1993 Act, s 5(g)) provides that:

> 'in determining if a dismissal is an unfair dismissal, regard may be had . . . to the reasonableness or otherwise of the conduct (whether by act or omission) of the employer in relation to the dismissal, and . . . to the extent (if any) of the compliance or failure to comply by the employer, in relation to the employee . . . (with any dismissal procedure) . . . or with the provisions of any code of practice.'

In *Roche v Richmon Earthworks Ltd* UD 329/97 (see also *Vokes v Bear* [1973] IRLR 363) the company encountered financial difficulties and reorganised its staff, as a result of which the claimant was made redundant. Roche contested the circumstances surrounding the redundancy and the fact that she was advised of her redundancy without any prior notification, discussion or consultation. The EAT held that the dismissal was unfair and stated 'the failure to hold any selection process or consultation with the claimant rendered it so'.

Thus, it is important that employers act reasonably, in the context of redundancy dismissals and, in that regard, it is to be expected that rights commissioners and the EAT will require that, while an employer is not bound by the actual rules of natural justice, some sort of 'hearing' by way of prior notification or consultation with the employee, should take place prior to the decision being made.

6.16.4.3   Considering options to redundancy

The sort of steps required to be taken by an employer before reaching a decision that an employee is, or an employee's functions are, redundant and that he be dismissed by reason of redundancy or selected for dismissal by reason of redundancy should be on the lines of the following.

Employers should consider all options other than termination of employment. Reasonableness dictates that employers should not immediately opt for redundancies, without first addressing possible alternatives. Full and proper regard must be had to all possible options in order to avoid having to dismiss employees and not simply to determine the way in which redundancies are to be effected. Employers should record the decision-making process, which gives rise to the possibility of redundancies. When a business experiences financial problems, discussions or meetings regarding the problem should be minuted and proposals on dealing with the problem should be recorded. The consideration given to all options should be noted, so that a tribunal or a court can see, at a future date, that the employer did not simply opt for redundancy, to the detriment of the employee.

See the decision of the EAT in *St Ledger v Frontline Distribution Ireland Ltd* UD 56/94 in Kerr and Madden, *Unfair Dismissals Cases and Commentary* (2nd edn) p 413. See also *Curling v Securicor Ltd* [1992] IRLR 549 where the contracts of employment of staff contained a mobility clause requiring the employees to work from various locations to be decided or changed at the company's discretion.

Alternative employment should be considered by any reasonable employer. While there is no legal obligation to give an employee an alternative job if the job for which he was employed has become redundant the general concept of reasonableness will cover examining other options to termination of employment by reason of redundancy. Where, for example, redundancies are being considered, by reason of 'the fact that the requirements of [the] business for employees to carry out work of a particular kind . . . have ceased or diminished the employer must consider whether the employees might be employed to do some other work in the employer's business'. Again, such considerations should be minuted/noted, in advance of arriving at a final decision. Similarly, where qualifications or training are the criteria, an employer should carefully consider whether an employee might be retrained, with some assistance or retraining, so as to reach the standard required.

Employers should ensure that consultation takes place either with a recognised trade union (see *Mugford v Midland Bank plc* [1997] IRLR 208) or directly with the employee if there is no trade union (see *Freud v Bentalls* [1982] IRLR 443). Even if *Hickey v Eastern Health Board* [1991] 1 IR 208; [1990] ELR 177 was to be followed strictly, natural justice and consultation are different concepts. On the issue of lack of consultation rendering a redundancy dismissal unfair, see *Trafford v Sharpe and Fisher (Building Supplies) Ltd* [1994] IRLR 325.

6.16.4.4   Future developments?

It is likely that the EAT will, in light of the addition of the 'reasonableness' requirement added to unfair dismissal legislation by the 1993 Act, follow the development of British law which has moved from the position of not requiring consultation (*Holister v MFU* [1979] IRLR 238) to the requirement that for an employer to act reasonably it must warn and consult any employees affected by a redundancy situation or their representative (*Polkey v AE Dayton Services Ltd* [1987] IRLR 503). The only exception allowed in UK law to the requirement to warn and consult in a redundancy situation is where to engage in consultation would be a useless or futile exercise (see *Polkey v AE Dayton Services Ltd* and *Duffy v Yeomans and Partners Ltd* [1994] IRLR 642). It was held in *Mugford v Midland Bank plc* that consultation with a trade union is likely to be sufficient in most cases to satisfy the test for determining a fair dismissal by reason of redundancy; individual consultation is not a prerequisite.

6.16.5 SELECTION FOR REDUNDANCY

Where a redundancy situation comes about within an employment those employees to be made redundant are those whose functions are redundant. If an employer's needs for a number of employees to perform one, or similar functions, diminishes, then the situation will require that the employer select one or more employees, from the body or group of employees affected by the general situation, to be made redundant and the others retained. Where this situation arises the employer is under an obligation to select fairly employees for redundancy, where the circumstances constituting the redundancy apply equally to one or more employees in similar employment as per the 1977 Act, s 6(3) which provides:

> 'Without prejudice to the generality of subsection (1) of this section, if an employee was dismissed due to redundancy, but the circumstances constituting the redundancy applied equally to one or more other employees in similar employment with the same employer who have not been dismissed, and either:
>
> (a) the selection of the employee for dismissal resulted wholly or mainly from one or more of the matters specified at subsection (2) of this section or another matter that would not be a ground justifying dismissal; or
>
> (b) he was selected for dismissal in contravention of a procedure (being a procedure that has been agreed upon by or on behalf of the employer and by the employee or a trade union or an excepted body under the Trade Union Acts 1941 and 1971, representing him, or has been established by the custom and practice of the employment concerned) relating to redundancy and there were no special reasons justifying a departure from that procedure, then the dismissal shall be deemed, for the purposes of this Act, to be an unfair dismissal.'

The subsection may be paraphrased as providing the following.

The concept of selection for redundancy only arises where the circumstances constituting the redundancy apply to more than one employee. It may happen that an employee, who finds himself made redundant, points to another employee who carries out different functions for the employer and seeks to argue that that other employee, or other employees from a group of employees who carry out different functions, should have been made redundant instead of him. That is not the statutory concept of unfair selection. The statutory concept is based on the requirement that the statutory definition of redundancy as referred to above must apply equally to two or more employees of that employer but where the requirement to reduce the workforce requires that some employees within that group be retained and others dismissed by reason of redundancy.

The selection may not be for one of the prohibited reasons set out in the 1977 Act which are pregnancy, trade union activity or membership of a trade union, race, colour, age, sexual orientation or membership of the travelling community.

A fair selection procedure must be followed in the sense of applying selection criteria which may, as far as possible, be objectively justified and applied in a fair manner, which will require some level of discussion or consultation with the employee to be affected by the application of such selection criteria.

An employer, faced with the possibility of having to effect redundancies, should approach the employees or their trade union. They should be invited to put forward alternative proposals and those proposals should be carefully considered by the employer. If the employer concludes that the proposals are without merit, the employees or their union should be so advised (and told why) and only then should notice be served on the employees.

For an interesting decision on what constitutes redundancy and how individual employees within a business may come within the definition of redundancy, see the UK Employment Appeal Tribunal decision in *Church v West Lancashire NHS Trust* [1998] IRLR 492.

6.16.6   SELECTION CRITERIA

6.16.6.1   General

Neither redundancy legislation nor unfair dismissal legislation sets out the criteria to be adopted by an employer in selecting employees to be made redundant. It is a matter for each employer to choose the criteria to be applied in the selection process. Those criteria will, however, come under close scrutiny in the event that the employee claims unfair selection for redundancy. It is important that the employer be in a position to, as far as possible, justify objectively the criteria chosen and the rating under each criterion of the employee selected.

6.16.6.2   Views of the EAT

The EAT set out its views in *Boucher v Irish Productivity Centre* [1990] ELR 205. The EAT accepted that the dismissal of each of the claimants was made in the context of a genuine redundancy situation applying within the company which resulted in a need to reduce the workforce by five people. The EAT accepted that the employer had to select five people for redundancy from amongst a group of individuals who had different background skills and contributions to make to the company, and that the company wished to ensure that, after the redundancies, there would remain a core of skills sufficient to maintain the services provided and therefore the survival of the company. The employer was not obliged to follow any procedure agreed with a trade union but was held to have an overriding obligation to act fairly in relation to the criteria applicable.

The EAT held that redundancy dismissals were subject primarily to the provisions of the 1977 Act, s 6(1), as amended, which provides:

> '*Subject to the provisions of this section the dismissal of an employee shall be deemed for the purposes of this Act to be an unfair dismissal unless, having regard to all the circumstances, there were substantial grounds justifying the dismissal.*'

The EAT then laid down the following general principles on the approach it will take in determining on claims of unfair selection for redundancy.

(a)   The onus is on the employer to justify the selection for redundancy of the employees claiming unfair dismissal, and each of them—it is not sufficient to establish an overall umbrella context such as redundancy within which the decision was made. In the selection of each individual employee for redundancy the EAT will examine the assessments involved and used as a means for selection and will require to be satisfied that reasonable criteria were applied to all the employees concerned and that the selection for redundancy of an individual employee in the context of such criteria was fairly made. The legislation establishes the right of each individual employee to be fairly treated in such an important matter.

(b)   In the absence of agreement being reached with a trade union under the provisions of s 6(3)(b) of the 1977 Act the dismissals must be considered under s 6(1) as referred to above.

(c)   The existence of a general redundancy situation does not deny the individual employee the right to be fairly assessed for selection.

In *Boucher v Irish Productivity Centre* the employer put forward various criteria to justify retaining a balance of skills and assessed the individuals on variables, such as income earned, credit for research, time and versatility etc. These matters were not put to each of the claimants as part of the selection process; they were unaware of the criteria for selection being used and were denied the right to make a constructive contribution to the selection process. For that reason the EAT considered the procedure to be unfair and held each of the dismissals to be unfair.

The Supreme Court had held in *Hickey v Eastern Health Board* [1991] 1 IR 208; [1990] ELR 177 that the right to be heard enshrined in natural justice did not apply in a redundancy situation. The *Hickey* case did not, however, involve selection for redundancy but rather the factual redundancy simpliciter of the function carried out by the employee. The employer in that case did not have to carry out a balancing act or decide on criteria to be applied in the selection process. Both *Boucher* and *Hickey* were decided prior to the enactment of the 1993 Act which imposed the 'reasonableness' requirement on redundancy dismissals. *Boucher* indicates a view very much in line with what was later required by the 1993 Act and *Hickey* must be seen as limited to a particular situation not related to the concept of a fair dismissal under unfair dismissal legislation. (See in general cases on selection for redundancy in Kerr and Madden; *Unfair Dismissals Cases and Commentary* (2nd edn) chapter 10).

6.16.6.3   Objectivity of selection process

Selection only arises where the employee was employed in similar employment to one or more other employees with the same employer who were not dismissed. The Act does not go so far as to say that employees must be in identical employment but the reality is that those in stand-alone positions, particularly in management positions, find it very difficult to argue that they were unfairly selected for redundancy. Where two or more employees are engaged in similar employment the employer is obliged, in the absence of the following criteria specifically agreed with the trade union, to adopt some sort of objective criteria for differentiating between one employee and another. In theory there is nothing to prevent employers using any of a wide range of objective criteria such as ability, attendance record, disciplinary record, skill levels. All things being equal, and with no objective criteria to select between one employee and another, an employer will be expected to resort to the 'last in, first out' rule of thumb. See *O'Connor v SSIH (Ireland) Ltd* UD 50/83.

In *Kirwan v Iona National Airways Ltd* UD 156/87 the claimant was selected for redundancy due to alleged low productivity. The selection was held to be unfair on the basis that his low productivity had never been addressed to him and he had not been advised that he had low productivity that might impact on his future with the company.

In *Daniels v County Wexford Community Workshop (New Ross) Ltd* [1996] ELR 213 the company employed a consultant to recommend improvements to its operations. One of the recommendations was the appointment of a manager with a third level qualification. The claimant was the manager of organisation but did not have a third level qualification. She maintained that she was more than qualified to run the company in view of her extensive experience and years of service and, while the company acknowledged her contribution and resolved to make a position available to her under the same conditions, she was unhappy that one element of the new job was demeaning to her and refused it. She was made redundant, to be replaced by the person with third level qualifications. The EAT held that this was a valid redundancy on the 'qualification' ground.

In *Dawson v Eir Imports Ltd* UD 616/83 it was established that there was no 'last in, first out' rule in operation in the employment and nor was there any union/management agreement. The employee was selected on the basis of her competence, having been determined not to be as competent as other members of staff. The EAT stated:

> 'Following an assessment of the comparative performance of all similar staff the claimant was selected. The respondent retained the employees whom he thought could best contribute to the company, the claimant's performance was judged to be the weakest. The criteria used in the absence of any other procedures were appropriate in the circumstances. The respondent was competent to make the assessment having regard to the small number of staff and his close contact with them. . . . the principles of natural justice did not require the respondent to give the claimant details of this assessment and his not doing so resulted in no injustice. We are of the view that the selection was reasonable and not unfair.'

On the difficulties of selection criteria in selecting a secretary in a professional firm for redundancy which was held to be unfair, see *Lynch v Baily P/A Bastow Charleton* [1995] ELR 65.

In *Fox v Des Kelly Carpets Ltd* [1992] ELR 182 one of the reasons for selecting Mr Fox for redundancy was the fact that he had received a verbal warning and the EAT held that the dismissal was unfair 'as a more junior person had been retained. The employer was estopped from using alleged misconduct as a reason for selection for redundancy since the employment of the claimant continued after the said alleged misconduct'.

6.16.7 NOTICE OF REDUNDANCY

It is important to note that while the Redundancy Payments Acts require two weeks' notice of termination of employment (see Redundancy Payments Act, 1967, s 17(1)) long-serving employees will have more substantial notice entitlements under the Minimum Notice and Terms of Employment Acts (see Minimum Notice and Terms of Employment Act, 1973, s 4(2) for the actual notice periods). Contractual notice entitlements should also be borne in mind as they must be complied with also in order to avoid claims of wrongful dismissal. It will suffice to give the longest period of notice which will itself subsume and cover the other periods of notice—it is not necessary to give cumulative or total notice periods.

6.16.8 REDUNDANCY PAYMENT

6.16.8.1 Calculation of earnings

Employees who are qualified to receive a statutory redundancy payment under the Redundancy Payments Acts will have the actual amount calculated in accordance with the provisions of the 1967 Act, Sch 3, which also sets out the manner in which continuous and recognisable service and normal weekly remuneration are to be calculated. All earnings of an employee in excess of £15,600 are to be disregarded in making the statutory redundancy payments (see the Redundancy Payments (Lump Sum) Regulations, 1994 (SI 64/1994). This means that in calculating a week's pay, if an employee earns £300 or less gross per week, then his actual weekly remuneration is used in formulating the amount due. If he earns in excess of £300 gross per week, the payment is based on a notional £300 maximum gross per week. The formula for making the payment is as follows:

(a) half a week's pay for each year of continuous and recognisable employment between the ages of 16 and 41 years;

(b) a full week's pay for each continuous and recognisable year of employment over the age of 41; and

(c) an additional one week's normal earnings.

6.16.8.2 Extra-statutory payments

It is common practice in Ireland for employees and trade unions to negotiate extra-statutory redundancy payments, usually calculated as a set number of weeks' pay—with no ceiling on the amount of a week's pay—for each year of service. In the case of long service employees a cap is sometimes applied, eg no more than two years' remuneration payable. These extra-statutory redundancy payments will be subject to tax, whereas statutory redundancy payments are tax free. Section 15 of the 1993 Act allows for a break in statutory service, for unfair dismissal and minimum notice purposes, where an employee receives and retains a redundancy payment from the transferor at the time of a transfer. This may work an injustice on an employee who may be offered a payment by his former employer, the transferor, quite possibly in gratitude for excellent service, accept the payment in good faith and later finds himself dismissed by the transferee. If such dismissal takes place within the period of one year from the date of transfer the employee might not have the necessary one year's service required under unfair dismissal legislation to maintain a claim against the new employer, the transferee, if s 15 were to apply to break his service at the time of the transfer. Such employees are not in reality redundant at all. The payments they receive from their former employer could constitute statutory redundancy payment and an ex gratia payment. Strictly speaking, under redundancy legislation there is a case to be made that they are redundant in that their former employer has ceased to trade but there clearly should be continuity of employment where there is no break and a new employer takes over regardless of what payment they might have received. If they receive only an ex gratia payment, which might be colloquially termed a 'redundancy' payment, does this break their service—probably not. Section 15 must be read in its reference to a redundancy payment as meaning a statutory redundancy payment within the meaning of the Redundancy Payments Acts.

The UK EAT got around a similar provision in UK legislation in *Ross v Delrosa Caterers·Ltd* [1981] ICR 393 where an employee was given proper notice of termination, agreed to continue working with the new owner, was paid redundancy payment together with money in lieu of notice and holiday entitlement, and then took up working with the new employer doing the same work until she was downgraded and her wages reduced. She resigned and complained to an industrial tribunal that she had been constructively dismissed. The tribunal stated that her continuity had been broken by the receipt of the redundancy payment and she could not maintain what appeared to be an otherwise valid claim. On appeal, the EAT allowed the appeal and said that on a proper consideration of the relevant statutory provsions (which are similar to s 15 of the 1993 Act) that 'there had been no dismissal of the employee by the company and the payment made by the company to the employee which must be regarded as having been made under a mistake of fact or of law had no relevance to the new employer's liability to pay compensation for unfair dismissal by reference to a continuous period of employment'.

6.16.9 COLLECTIVE REDUNDANCIES

6.16.9.1 Introduction

The provisions of the Protection of Employment Act, 1977 and the Protection of Employment Order, 1996 (SI 370/1996) (see *Rockfon A/S v Specialarebejderforbundet i Danmark* [1995] ECR 1-4291) must be followed when an employer employing at least twenty people proposes to make at least five employees redundant, in any period of thirty consecutive days. EU Directive 75/129/EEC defines collective redundancies as being 'dismissals effected by an employer for one or more reasons not related to the individual workers concerned' where the number of redundancies comes within the following scale.

    (a)   *Over a period of thirty days*: at least ten redundancies in establishments (SI 370/1996) normally employing more than twenty and less than 100 workers;
at least 10 per cent of the number of workers in establishments normally employing at least 100 but less than 300 workers; or
at least thirty redundancies in establishments normally employing 300 workers or more; or

    (b)   *Over a period of ninety days*: at least twenty redundancies irrespective of the number of workers normally employed in the establishment in question.

As with the Transfer of Undertakings Directive, the Collective Redundancies Directive does not apply to redundancies consequent on the closure of an establishment as a result of bankruptcy or winding-up proceedings.

The original Collective Redundancies Directive was amended by Directive 92/56/EEC which expanded the consultation procedures contained in the original Directive.

6.16.9.2 Protection of Employment Act, 1977

Directive 75/129/EEC became law in Ireland on the enactment of the Protection of Employment Act, 1977. The term 'redundancy' in the Act is linked directly to the Redundancy Payments Acts, 1967–1991 and s 6(3) contains a comprehensive definition of the term 'establishment'. In the 1977 Act collective redundancies are defined in s 6(1) as follows:

> 'where in any period of 30 consecutive days the number of such dismissals is:
> (a) at least five in an establishment normally employing more than twenty and less than 50 employees;
> (b) at least ten in an establishment normally employing at least 50 but less than 100 employees;
> (c) at least 10 per cent of the number of employees in an establishment normally employing at least 100 but less than 300 employees; and
> (d) at least 30 in an establishment normally employing 300 or more employees.'

The Directives apply to all employees with a contract of service regardless of the length of time they are employed or the hours they work. If, therefore, employees under Irish legislation are not entitled to a statutory redundancy payment (or do not have the right to claim unfair dismissal, by virtue of not having the requisite continuous service required to make claims under that legislation) they must still be counted as employees for the purposes of the Collective Redundancies Directives and the domestic Irish law implementing same. Part-time employees are also included by virtue of there being no minimum hourly requirement as is required in respect of other statutes, notably the requirement that an employee must normally be expected to work at least eight hours before being covered by unfair dismissal and minimum notice and redundancy legislation, all of which was amended by the addition of the eight-hour threshold as provided for in the Worker Protection (Regular Part-Time Employees) Act, 1991, s 2(1).

6.16.9.3 Protection of Employment Order, 1996

The provisions of Directive 92/56/EEC became law in Ireland on the amendment of the 1977 Act by the Protection of Employment Order, 1996 which added to the category of persons covered by the law on collective redundancies by providing that persons are deemed to be employees under the same deeming provision as is contained in the Unfair Dismissals (Amendment) Act, 1993, s 13 as discussed above. See also the 2000 amendments in the European Communities (Protection of Employment) Regulations 2000 (SI 488/2000)

Definitions of 'employer' and 'employees' representatives' are also provided for in the statutory instrument. While there are no specific exclusions provided for in the 1977 Act or the 1996 Order, the Directive does not apply to redundancies resulting from the expiry of a fixed-term contract or specified-purpose contract on the cesser of the purpose. Employees employed by public administrative bodies or by establishments governed by public law in terms of civil service establishments are also excluded from the scope of the Directive (see *Griffin v South West Water Services Ltd* [1995] IRLR 15). The crews of sea-going vessels are also excluded. The definition of 'establishment' is also expanded to mean an employer or a company or a subsidiary company or a company within a group of companies which can independently effect redundancies. The statutory instrument also provides that in mitigating the circumstances of redundancies an employer must have recourse to 'social measures' aimed inter alia at aid for redeploying or retraining employees who are to be made redundant.

6.16.9.4 Emergency circumstances

The European Court of Justice allowed that an employer may, in certain emergency circumstances or where force majeure applies, avoid the provisions of the Collective Redundancies Directive as held in *Dansk Metalarbejderforbund v Nielsen* [1985] ECR 553.

The employer, Nielsen, informed trade unions of financial difficulties in February 1980. On 14 March 1980 it informed the appropriate bankruptcy court that it was suspending payment of its debt and the trade unions then advised their members to stop work. On 25 March 1980, Nielsen was declared insolvent and the following day the employment of the employees was terminated by reason of redundancy. The trade union, the Dansk Meta-larbeijderforbund, argued that as soon as the employer experienced financial difficulties it should have anticipated the need for collective redundancies and applied the terms of the Directive. The European Court of Justice rejected the trade union's claim and refused to hold the employer liable for failing to have foreseen collective redundancies and failing to implement the procedures of the Directive. In its judgment, however, the European Court of Justice made reference to article 1(2)(d) of the original Directive 75/129/EEC, which has now been deleted by article 1 of Directive 92/56/EEC.

6.17 STRIKES AND LOCK-OUTS

Where the employee participated in a strike or lock-out and one or more other participants were not similarly dismissed or were subsequently offered reinstatement or re-engagement and the claimant was not, the dismissal will be deemed to be unfair. Section 4 of the 1993 Act has amended the 1977 Act in relation to strikes and lock-outs to extend the provisions to situations where the employee may have been taken back but on terms not as favourable as employees who did not take part in the strike or lock-out.

The original 1977 provision simply protected employees against victimisation of being the only one to be dismissed or the only one not to be taken back following a strike or lock-out. The 1993 amendment extended this to a situation where they were taken back but after return were treated less favourably than people who remained throughout. The 1993 Act provided not only that better terms and conditions should apply to employees taken back after a strike or lock-out if they had been afforded to others but also that reinstatement or re-engagement should be deemed to have commenced on the earliest date on which reinstatement or re-engagement was offered to the majority of other employees who are the subject of the lock-out or took part in the strike or other industrial action. See also *Tuke v Coillte Teoranta* [1998] ELR 324.

In *Butler v MB Ireland* UD 1058/82 the company maintained that the claimant was dismissed because of misconduct surrounding the taking of official action. The EAT, however, held on the evidence that 'the paramount reason for the termination was the action taken by the claimant . . . ie the strikes'. The EAT then referred to the 1977 Act, s 5 and found that the dismissal was unfair. Compensation was awarded and reduced by 33 per cent due to the contribution of the claimant to his own dismissal. This case also shows that s 5 will apply to unofficial action as well as official action.

6.18 PROCEDURAL FAIRNESS

6.18.1 GENERAL

The 1977 Act made no reference to procedures that might or might not be followed by an employer prior to effecting a dismissal. Courts and tribunals, however, implied into the concept of 'fairness' under the 1977 Act the requirement that an employer not only have substantial grounds as is required by the legislation but also carry out the dismissal in a manner that was procedurally fair. This is a reflection of the constitutional right to fair procedures.

The 1993 Act enshrines procedural requirements in the legislation by providing at s 5(b) that in determining fairness the decision-maker shall have regard to:

(a)   the reasonableness or otherwise of the conduct (whether by act or omission) of the employer in relation to the dismissal, and

(b)   the extent, if any, of the compliance or failure to comply by the employer in relation to the employee with the procedure referred to in s 14(1) of the 1977 Act which provides for the furnishing to employees of the disciplinary procedure that will be followed in the event of dismissal being contemplated. Regard will also be had to an employer's failure to comply with any code of practice drawn up under the terms of the 1993 Act itself.

6.18.2   CASE LAW

6.18.2.1   Employment Appeals Tribunal

The EAT has always taken the view that if an employer acts in a manner that is procedurally unfair the dismissal itself will be held to be unfair. In *Caulfield v Verbatim Ltd* UD 938/93 the claimant was dismissed by reason of excessive absence from work. While the dismissal was held to be fair, the trade union representative gave a dissenting opinion stating:

'Regardless of the guilt or otherwise of the claimant . . . the procedures used by the company to effect the decision to dismiss must, in my view, be open and transparent, and the company's behaviour must be seen to be reasonable. . . . In this case those criteria were not met . . . the procedures used by the company in dismissing the claimant were seriously flawed. Where the behaviour of the employer is seen as being unreasonable in this context I believe the Tribunal must find the dismissal to be unfair whether the employee is guilty or not of the offence for which the employer seeks to dismiss her.'

6.18.2.2   Supreme Court

In *Gallagher v Revenue Commissioners* [1995] ELR 108 the Supreme Court held that the requirements of fair procedures encompassed the following:

(a)   Given the consequences for the applicant in the event of a decision adverse to him the employer was obliged to act judicially and adopt procedures which were fair and reasonable. While tribunals exercising quasi-judicial functions are given a certain latitude in the exercise of their functions and in determining the requirements of natural justice and fair procedures in the circumstances of the case they may not act in such a way as to imperil a fair hearing or a fair result.

(b)   Mere administrative difficulties in securing the attendance of witnesses before a tribunal or inquiry are not a sufficient ground for depriving a person charged before the tribunal of the right to cross-examine witnesses as to facts which are essential to the establishment of the charges against him.

(c)   As far as the applicant was concerned the charges against him were substantial. The failure of the employer to require direct evidence . . . deprived the applicant of the opportunity of hearing this evidence, or challenging it by means of cross-examination. This was contrary to the requirements of natural justice and the requirements of fair procedures.

(d)   In a preliminary application in *Gallagher* the High Court, per Blayney J had held that having regard to the nature of the charges which could result in the respondent's dismissal in the event of an adverse decision he was entitled to legal representation at the disciplinary hearing. Against that Barr J had held in the case of *Aziz v Midland Health Board* [1995] ELR 48 that a doctor who was under investigation for an alleged failure to attend for duty had no general right to legal representation at a quasi-judicial disciplinary hearing. The Supreme Court judgment in *Georgopoulus v Beaumont Hospital Board*, 4 June 1997 (unreported) indicates that the courts are likely to require that if an employee seeks to be legally represented in a case where his employment is in jeopardy refusal by the employer rendered the procedure unfair.

6.18.2.3   House of Lords

The House of Lords considered procedural fairness in the leading case of *Polkey v Edmund Walker (Holdings) Ltd* [1988] AC 344 and held that procedural fairness was necessary in order to justify a dismissal as being fair. Employers must give employees fair warning and opportunity to improve before making any decision to dismiss. The House of Lords also laid down the fundamental test for courts and tribunals that they cannot ask whether or not the decision would have been any different if the appropriate procedural steps had been followed. They must judge what the employer did at the time he did it, not what he might have done or what the outcome might have been had he taken other steps. The House of Lords did go on, however, to qualify this view by stating that if the decision-maker was in a position to conclude that the employer had acted reasonably even though procedures had not been followed, in the exceptional case where procedures would have made no difference it is possible to conclude that the dismissal was fair.

6.18.2.4   Irish case law

The EAT here in Ireland prefers to stick with the basic importance of fair procedure, but where an employer's procedural default arises in a case where a dismissal was in any event clearly justified the EAT tends to award compensation and reduce the amount of compensation by a significant percentage measure of the employee's contribution to his own dismissal, in some cases as high as 100 per cent. See *Sheehan v HM Keating & Sons Ltd* [1993] ELR 12; *Murray v Meath County Council* UD 43/78; and *Condron v Rowntree Mackintosh Ltd* UD 195/79.

In *Gearon v Dunnes Stores Ltd* UD 367/88 the EAT held that fair procedures had not been followed and concluded:

> 'The right to defend herself and have her arguments and submissions listened to and evaluated by the respondent in relation to the threat to her employment is a right of the claimant and is not the gift of the respondent or this Tribunal . . . the right is a fundamental one under natural and constitutional justice, it is not open to this Tribunal to forgive its breach.'

In *White v Cadbury (Ireland) Ltd* UD 44/79 the claimant was dismissed for failing to refuse to submit to a search properly requested in accordance with his conditions of employment. In essence the facts of what occurred were not in dispute. The evidence, however, showed that the decision to dismiss was taken following reports of the incident of refusal and not after any further investigation had been carried out involving White himself and the hearing with him. The EAT held:

> 'The denial to the appellant of the opportunity to make or present his counter arguments prior to . . . [the] decision to dismiss him was, in our opinion, a breach of his fundamental right to be confronted with the evidence against him and to make counter arguments, explanations, pleas etc as may be relevant. We are accordingly of the opinion that the denial of this fundamental right to the appellant had the inevitable result of rendering this dismissal an unfair dismissal and we determine accordingly.'

Given the accepted conduct of Mr White the EAT determined to award him compensation but reduced his compensation by 100 per cent attributable to his contribution to his own loss.

6.18.3 EMPLOYEE SUBJECT TO CRIMINAL CHARGES

The making of criminal charges against an employee and the processing of such criminal charges may complicate an employer's disciplinary procedure. Frequently such disciplinary procedures are delayed or suspended while the criminal charges are being processed. This is often done at the behest of the employee, usually on the grounds that as he has the right to remain silent in the criminal case this right may be compromised if he is required to defend himself in a disciplinary case. Given that the criminal case would involve the individual losing his liberty it will take precedence. What then happens to the disciplinary process if the employee is acquitted of the criminal charges? In the High Court decision in *Mooney v An Post* [1994] ELR 103 Keane J stated that the 'acquittal of criminal charges does not preclude employers from considering whether an employee should or should not be dismissed because of circumstances which gave rise to the charges.' *McGrath v Commissioner of An Garda Síochána* [1991] 1 IR 69 considered.

6.18.4 IMPORTANCE OF PARTICULAR CIRCUMSTANCES

The requirements of procedural justice may vary depending on the particular circumstances of each case. The late Shanley J gave an interesting decision in *A Worker v Hospital* [1997] ELR 214 in which he considered the procedural requirements of a disciplinary investigation where a hospital employee was accused by a patient, who was suffering from a schizophrenic condition and was said to be mentally fragile, of sexually abusing her. The employee sought to cross examine the patient in the course of the investigation but medical experts on behalf of the hospital advised that a validation interview take place and that she only be interviewed about the allegations by a person specially trained in interviewing mentally handicapped people. The plaintiff had the facility of nominating a suitable expert to assess the complainant in the presence of the hospital's experts but the complainant herself would not be produced for questioning by the plaintiff in the course of the investigation. The allegations of the complainant would therefore be conveyed by experts and would of necessity contain hearsay. The plaintiff sought an interlocutory injunction restraining the defendant from commencing and determining a disciplinary charge against him without him being afforded the opportunity to hear and test, by cross-examination, the evidence of the complainant. Shanley J refused to grant an injunction holding:

'1. The requirements of natural justice must depend on the circumstances of each case and the nature of each particular inquiry. In considering the question of the admissibility of hearsay evidence all the facts must be examined and the rights and interests of all the parties must, as far as it is practicable, be safeguarded.' [*Southern Health Board v CH* 11 March 1996, Supreme Court (unreported) followed].

2. In determining the question as to the admissibility of hearsay evidence in the present case the court would seek to balance the risk of serious damage to the complainant's health if she were forced to give evidence against the risk that a serious injustice would be done to the plaintiff if she did not.

3. Injustice to the plaintiff could be avoided by directing that further validation of the complainant's complaints be carried out in the presence of the complainant's doctor by an expert nominated by the plaintiff. Such validation to be carried out in advance of the hearing and any report produced to be the property of the plaintiff.

4. Where as normally applications for interlocutory injunctions should be decided by reference to the principles of whether or not a serious issue was to be tried, the balance of convenience and the adequacy of damages, there are exceptional cases where those principles would have no application and the instant case was such a case.'

The EAT requirement for fair procedures focused on sales, budgets and forecasts and the employee's failure to meet his sales targets. The absence of adequate warnings rendered the dismissal unfair in the case of *Pritchard v Oracle Ireland Ltd* [1992] ELR 24.

The EAT also places very considerable importance on the following of agreed procedures within an employment (see *Mellett v Tara Mines Ltd* [1997] ELR 79). Such procedures are usually disciplinary procedures but may include grievance procedures—see **6.19** below.

6.19 GRIEVANCE PROCEDURES

Grievance procedures are commonly contained in contracts of service or union/management agreements or works rules books and may be very relevant to dismissal cases which may focus on the manner of operation of the grievance procedure by either the employer or the employee (see *Conway v Ulster Bank* referred to in **6.5.6.10** above on constructive dismissal). Even where a formal grievance procedure is not in place one may be implied as in *W A Goold (Pearmak) Ltd v McConnell* [1995] IRLR 516 and *Waltons & Morse v Dorrington* [1997] IRLR 488 where the EAT held in considering an appeal from the industrial tribunal:

> 'The industrial tribunal was also entitled to find that the employers had failed properly to address the employee's grievance and therefore were in breach of the implied contractual term enunciated by the EAT in *W A Goold (Pearmak) Ltd v McConnell* that the employer will reasonably and promptly afford employees a reasonable opportunity to obtain redress of any grievance.'

6.20 WARNINGS

6.20.1 GENERALLY

In cases other than fundamental breach, such as dishonesty, gross misconduct, etc warnings are a necessity in order to show that fair procedures were followed. An employee is entitled to know that his job is in jeopardy. Many employments provide for detailed disciplinary procedures with variation dependent on the nature of the 'offence'. There is no particular format set out for a warning but it should be clear and unequivocal and the employee should be made fully aware of the cause of the complaint whether it be his conduct, lack of competence or other reason with the consequences clearly spelt out to the employee in the event that the warning is not heeded. The employee must also be given reasonable time and opportunity to improve. The EAT laid down principles relating to warning in *Richardson v H Williams Ltd* UD 17/79 where it stated:

> 'Where an employee has been given a justified warning that unless his work improved in a specific area and that his job would be in jeopardy otherwise then it follows that he must be given:
> (1) a reasonable work situation within which to concentrate on such defects;
> (2) a reasonable time in which to effect such an improvement; and
> (3) the employer must in a fair and reasonable way monitor his progress and reaction in relation to such warning.

> 'If an employee improves in the complained of area to the reasonable satisfaction of the employer and such defect is not repeated then such a warning cannot be solely relied upon for dismissal for other reasons.'

Warnings must be clear and unequivocal and not simply hints or broad statements (see *O'Donoghue v Emerson Electric (Ireland) Ltd* UD 177/86). The claimant was the managing director of an American multi-national. His superiors had indicated on a number of occasions their dissatisfaction with the performance of the company. However, he did not receive a clear and unequivocal warning of possible dismissal. His dismissal was held to be unfair.

In *Evode Industrial Ltd v Hearst and O'Shea* UD 396/397/79 the EAT held that in cases of dishonesty no warning is necessary.

Tribunals will not allow a situation where warnings remain effective for an indefinite period. This will depend greatly on the nature of the warning but, in the main, tribunals will allow the clearing of an employee's record after a lapse of a period of time without the employer having any further cause for complaint. Some employments allow that warnings will lapse or be expunged after a specified period of time. In *Gibbons v Donnolly Mirrors Ltd* UD 196/82 the claimant was dismissed following warnings. However, the company grievance procedure allowed, in certain circumstances, that warnings would be expunged after a period of six weeks. The company felt, however, that although warnings were expunged they should remain on file and could not be ignored in the event of subsequent misconduct. The EAT held that this was not made clear to the claimant or his union who were entitled to believe that the warnings had been expunged and the dismissal was held to be unfair.

There have been cases where senior management were involved where courts and tribunals have held that the need for warnings and opportunities to improve was less apparent or necessary than in relation to less senior employees. There have also been cases where inadequacy of performance was so extreme that it was deemed to be irredeemable in capability in respect of which warnings would not be effective. See *Grant v Ampex Great Britain Ltd* [1980] IRLR 461; *James v Waltham Holy Cross UDC* [1973] IRLR 202 and *Cooke v Thomas Linnell & Sons Ltd* [1977] IRLR 132.

6.20.2 PERFORMANCE-RELATED PROBLEMS

For employers seeking to justify a dismissal for a performance-related problem the employers should be in a position to explain the problem and how they dealt with it under the following headings:

(a) They must be able to give an explanation as to how the problem came to light. It is not safe to presume that the problem suddenly materialised, particularly where an employee has service of any appreciable length.

(b) The employers must be able to show that they carried out a thorough investigation as to the reasons why performance fell short of what was normally required. Again it is not sufficient simply to show that there was a failure of performance and that disciplinary action resulted. It may later transpire that there was an obvious reason for the shortfall in performance. A thorough investigation will, or should, unearth such a difficulty at an early state.

(c) There must be a clear warning to the employee that he is falling short of the employer's requirements. Emphasis on what is required of him should be made at this stage. Employers should avoid vagueness and, while a blunt warning may appear harsh, it is in both parties' interests that there be no misunderstanding as to what was actually meant.

(d) The employers must be able to show that the employee was counselled as to the need to improve and that assistance was offered to help the employee to improve.

(e) The employers must be able to show that they monitored the response to the warning, not simply that the employee was left to his own devices until the employer came back at a later stage and expressed further dissatisfaction and imposed further disciplinary sanction.

(f) If there is no improvement the employer must be able to show that he investigated as to why the warning, counselling and assistance had not given rise to the required improvement.

(g) There must at some stage, if a dismissal was the result, have been a final warning that is clear and unequivocal as to:

(i) what the problem was;

(ii) what was required of the employee;

(iii) the consequences of failing to meet the required standards; and

(iv) when those consequences could be expected to result. An employer should not simply demand that the standards be met by a specific date but rather that the standards be met on an ongoing basis and maintained into the future; and

(h) The employer must have available evidence of the failure to meet the requirements of the final warning, that that evidence was put to the employee and the employee was allowed facility of responding and making a case against dismissal before the final decision to dismiss was made.

6.21   TARGETS

As to employments where targets are set for the measurement of work and performance, see *Nagle v Mulcahy Group West Ltd* UD 621/81 where the employee was not given sufficient opportunity to improve. The EAT held that the claimant should have been clearly instructed as to the targets expected and warned of the consequences of not reaching those targets. Where an employee reaches a required target and then proceeds to deteriorate in respect of subsequent targets the EAT may well require the employer to revert to the first stage of a warning procedure. See *Sweeney v Canada Life Assurance Ireland Ltd* UD [1994] where the employee was warned of the consequences of failure to meet targets, met the targets and, in the next year for which targets were set, fell below target. The EAT held that once the claimant had reached the target following warning the employer should have recommenced from the initial stage of the disciplinary process in the event of further shortcomings. Where employers encounter persistent highs and lows on target or budget achievement, warnings might be worded in such a way as to make it clear to the employee that reaching targets on an inconsistent basis is unsatisfactory and be advised as to the consequences of future failures which may not require the employer to revert to the first stage of a procedure. In *Murphy v Kilkenny Marble Works Ltd* UD 608/83 the claimant was dismissed for failure to reach specified sales targets. In examining the facts of the situation the EAT held that the targets themselves were unreasonable and the dismissal was unfair for that and for other specified procedural reasons. In *Hanlon v Smith Dolphins Barn Ltd* UD 883/82 the EAT held that increases in targets, which the claimant subsequently failed to meet, were not reasonable and the dismissal was held to be unfair. See also *Pritchard v Oracle Ireland Ltd* [1992] ELR 24.

6.22   SUSPENSION

Suspension may arise in the context of removing an employee from the workplace during the course of an investigation or, alternatively, as a disciplinary sanction. Suspension without pay may not be resorted to unless the employer has a contractual right to do so. In the context of suspension pending investigation, suspension without pay might well be deemed to be prejudgment of the outcome of the investigation. Suspension should only be for a limited time. Indefinite suspension will not be tolerated by the courts. See *Flynn v An Post* [1987] IR 68 where the Supreme Court held that prolonged suspension was unfair and that the power of suspension must be construed as permitting suspension to continue only for the period of time in which it was not reasonably practicable to hold a full hearing or investigation.

It was held in *D & J McKenzie Ltd v Smith* [1976] IRLR 345 that an employer is not entitled unilaterally to suspend an employee unless there is some provision, express or implied, in the contract of employment permitting him to do so. In *Deegan v Dunnes Stores Ltd* [1992] ELR 184 the claimants had been placed on indefinite suspension for refusing to sign undertakings in relation to certain management requirements. The EAT held that:

'indefinite suspension amounted to dismissal and that the dismissal in this case was unfair as it was too severe a penalty but that the claimants had contributed to their dismissal through their lack of co-operation which gives rise to the undertaking requirement in the first place'.

6.23   DISCIPLINARY HEARING

6.23.1   GENERAL REQUIREMENTS

The requirements to be followed in a disciplinary hearing were set out by the Supreme Court in *Connolly v McConnell* [1983] IR 172. It was held:

'When a person holds a full-time pensionable office from which he may be removed, and thus be deprived of his means of livelihood and of his pension rights the domestic tribunal or body having the power to remove him are exercising quasi-judicial functions. Therefore they may not remove him without first according to him natural justice. He must be given the reasons for his proposed dismissal and an adequate opportunity of making his defence to the allegations made against him—*audi alteram partem*. The members of the Tribunal must be impartial and not be judges in their own cause—*nemo iudex in causa sua*. They must ensure that the proceedings are conducted fairly. In determining whether the Tribunal is impartial a member is not to be regarded as impartial if his own interest might be affected by the decision: and this interest is not necessarily to be confined to pecuniary interest.'

While the *McConnell* case dealt with an officer of a trade union the quotation referred to encapsulates the thinking of the EAT. In *Ryan v CIE* UD 27/84 the EAT held:

'Whatever the seriousness of the allegations made against an employee there is a duty on the employer to:
(1)   Fully investigate the circumstances surrounding the alleged offence.
(2)   Complete such an investigation *prior* to taking disciplinary action.
(3)   Offer the employee and his union or legal advisor the opportunity of defending the charge.
(4)   Create an environment of parity between the employee and his accusers at any oral hearing of inquiry/appeal.'

6.23.2   CRIMINAL INVESTIGATIONS

In *Ryan v CIE* UD 27/84 the EAT also dealt with a situation where an employer wished to investigate at the same time as the Gardaí had become involved in a criminal investigation of the same or similar facts. The EAT stated in *Ryan*:

'In addition it has been established in a previous unfair dismissal claim involving the same employer, *Kelly v CIE* UD 28 [1978], that involvement of the Gardaí in a criminal investigation should properly have resulted in the suspension of the company's internal investigations in so far as they required the appellant/accused person to comment on the allegations the subject of the criminal charge unless the accused person consents with the knowledge and agreement of his legal representative where such a representative has been instructed.'

In *Burlington Sportswear Fabrics Ltd v O'Connor* UD 103/83 the dismissal involved allegations of fighting. A number of statements had been taken by the employer in the course of investigation but not all of these statements were put to the claimant and he did not therefore have an opportunity to comment on them regardless of what his comment might have been. The dismissal was held to be unfair.

Even if an employee is convicted of a criminal offence arising from the facts which are of concern to his employer, the employer cannot dismiss without carrying out an investigation and having a disciplinary hearing (see *Cranston v Independent Newspapers Ltd* UD 90/84). While this dismissal was held to be unfair because there was no separate management investigation and hearing the claimant was held to have contributed 100 per cent to his dismissal.

In *Redmond v Lever Brothers (Ireland) Ltd* UD 655/82 a criminal prosecution against the claimant was dropped when the prosecution entered a 'nolle prosequi'. The company, however, carried out its own investigation and dismissed the claimant. The EAT held that the respondent had good grounds to find the claimant's explanations unsatisfactory and that accordingly the bond of mutual trust had been broken and the dismissal was held to be fair.

6.23.3   DISHONESTY

Dishonesty during the course of a disciplinary hearing or investigation may itself constitute a breach of trust. In *Cody v Marlowe Cleaners Ltd* UD 120/83 the company was in the course of investigating allegations against the claimant when he sought to have other employees make false statements to protect him. The EAT held that this exacerbated the situation and, while expressing reservations about the original set of facts under investigation, the EAT held 'the attempt to conceal the matter by deceit constituted substantial grounds justifying the dismissal'.

6.23.4   EFFECT OF DELAY

Delay in carrying out an investigation may render the ultimate decision unfair if the delay prejudices the employee. In *Marley Homecare Ltd v Dutton* [1981] IRLR 380 Mrs Dutton was a part-time cashier at one of the company's stores. The employers regularly carried out test purchases. On 20 December 1979 a report was made that there were suspected irregularities regarding Mrs Dutton's operation of the till. Certain purchases did not show up on the till roll and yet Mrs Dutton's cash did not exceed the total shown on the till roll. Further test purchases were carried out on 16 January 1980. It was alleged that one of these tests was not registered on the till roll and, again, the cash did not exceed the amount recorded as taken. Mrs Dutton was interviewed on 23 January 1980. She was unable to put forward any explanations as to what had happened in relation to the test purchases and stated that she could not remember what had happened on the occasions in question. She was summarily dismissed for gross misconduct and not complying with the company's cash-handling procedures. Dismissal was held to be unfair on the basis that a seven-day delay between the date of the last test purchase and the date on which the employee was confronted by the employers was such as to be unreasonable in the circumstances of the case because, at that stage, the employee could not identify the matters at issue and was unable to properly defend herself. Had she been confronted at a time when she might have identified the purchases in question it was impossible to say that the employee could have had no explanation. In the course of this decision it was suggested that if the employer had matters to investigate other than the alleged offending test purchases the employer could have suspended the employee on full pay while carrying out that investigation. The employee then would be in no doubt as to the occasion on which the alleged misconduct occurred and would have some chance of recalling what had happened and properly defending herself.

6.24   REPRESENTATION—LEGAL REPRESENTATION

The EAT put a very substantial emphasis on an employee's right to be represented at a disciplinary hearing. Employers should always commence a disciplinary hearing by first advising the employee of the seriousness of the matter at issue and, secondly, the right to representation. There does not exist any right to legal representation—see *State (Smullen) v Duffy* [1980] ILRM 46, which was a case not involving a dismissal but the expulsion of a child from a school, in which the Supreme Court held that there was no automatic right to legal representation even though the consequences for the person of the decision affecting him were particularly serious. It is unlikely that the courts would follow that view in a dismissal case; however, it could prove difficult in a hearing before the EAT if an employer refused to allow legal representation and the employee was not a member of a trade union and had no competent available representation other than a lawyer.

See *Flanagan v University College Dublin* [1988] IR 724; [1989] ILRM 469; the High Court decision in *Gallagher v Revenue Commissioners* [1991] ILRM 632 and the Supreme Court appeal in that case ([1995] 1 ILRM 241) and the comments of Laffoy J in *Maher v Irish Permanent plc* [1998] ELR 77 at p 89 which stand in contrast to the High Court decision in *Aziz v Midland Health Board* [1995] ELR 48 at p 50 where Barr J held 'there is no general right to legal representation at a quasi-judicial disciplinary hearing' and refused an order to the applicant where he had claimed inter alia that unfair procedures had been followed by the respondent in a number of respects, one of which was the refusal to afford him the right to legal representation at a domestic enquiry which resulted in his suspension and subsequent dismissal. The Supreme Court seemed to accept a right of legal representation in *Georgopolous v Beaumont Hospital Board* 4 June 1997 (unreported).

6.25   STANDARD OF PROOF

6.25.1   GENERALLY

Where an employer has carried out a comprehensive investigation having regard to fair procedures how far does he have to go in establishing the guilt or innocence of the employee in order to justify a decision to dismiss?

Dismissals related to dishonesty or procedural irregularities provide a good illustration of the standard of proof required of an employer in establishing substantial grounds justifying dismissal. Every dismissal case is approached under two headings:

(a)   How was the dismissal effected? The procedures adopted in effecting dismissal are extremely important, and even with the existence of a substantial reason justifying dismissal, improper procedures may render such dismissal unfair. In the case of dishonesty dismissals warnings will rarely be required and the procedural focus will be on the manner of investigation carried out prior to making the decision to dismiss and the preservation of the job of the employee.

(b)   Why was the dismissal effected? In dishonesty cases the employee will normally take it that he is being dismissed for theft and very often challenges his dismissal on that basis. As will be seen below tribunals and courts are not concerned with right and wrong fact and fiction. Such would be an objective view. Tribunals take a subjective view in that they must place themselves in the shoes of the employer at the time the decision was made and consider whether, in all the circumstances of the case, the employer had reasonable grounds for believing what he believed prior to making his decision to dismiss.

6.25.2   UK CASE LAW

The seminal precedent case on dismissals of this nature is the British case of *British Home Stores Ltd v Burchell* [1978] IRLR 379.

Miss Burchell was dismissed for allegedly being involved with a number of other employees in acts of dishonesty relating to staff purchases. The acts concerned countersigning each other's staff purchases when this should have been done by another member of staff, a purchase by one of the employees appearing as a purchase by Miss Burchell, and an incident involving the purchase by another employee of a pair of expensive sunglasses which were charged by Miss Burchell at the cost of a less expensive type. During the company's investigations of these incidents Miss Burchell was implicated in statements made by a fellow employee. Management, in investigating these allegations, did not confront Miss Burchell with the employee who made such statements. It was put to the EAT on behalf of Miss Burchell that the employer should have confronted Miss Burchell with this employee and allowed her the opportunity of challenging the statements. Management had simply transmitted the statements to Miss Burchell without advising her who had made them or confronting her with the employee. The EAT held that it was not unreasonable on the part of the employer to resist such a confrontation. When the matter was put to Miss Burchell in general terms with an implication that she had acted dishonestly her reaction was to deny the allegation saying, 'You'll have to prove it'. She did not give any further explanation. It was put to the EAT on behalf of Miss Burchell that to effect a dismissal for a reason of this sort the employers were obliged to conclusively prove that Miss Burchell had been guilty of dishonesty.

The EAT held that the function of a tribunal faced with a problem of this sort is to decide every time whether the employer who discharged the employee on the ground of the misconduct in question (usually, though not necessarily, dishonest conduct) entertained a reasonable suspicion amounting to the belief in the guilt of the employee of that misconduct at that time. *First* there must be established by the employer the fact of that belief—that the employer did believe it. *Secondly*, the employer must show that in his mind reasonable grounds upon which to sustain that belief existed. *Thirdly*, the employer must prove that at the stage at which he formed his belief on those grounds he had carried out as much investigation into the matter as was reasonable in all the circumstances of the case. It is not relevant that the tribunal would itself have shared that view in those circumstances. It is not the function of the tribunal to examine the quality of the material which the employer had before him to see whether it was the sort of material, *objectively* considered, which would lead to a certain conclusion on the balance of probability or whether it was the sort of material which would lead to the same conclusions only upon the basis of being 'sure' in a criminal context or such as to put the matter 'beyond reasonable doubt'. The test and the test all the way through is reasonableness. A conclusion *on the balance of probabilities* will in any surmisable circumstance be a reasonable conclusion.

6.25.3 IRISH CASE LAW

The leading Irish EAT case is that of *Hennessy v Read and Write Shop Ltd* UD 192/78.

In that case the claimant worked as a shop assistant for the respondents. The claimant asked her manageress for a discount on a doll for her daughter who also worked in the shop. It was agreed that the discount would be from £8.49 to £7.50. The manageress heard the claimant asking her daughter if she had paid for the doll and the daughter replied that she had. The manageress was somewhat concerned about the transaction and the following day (Sunday) she went into the shop and checked the till rolls but could not find an entry of £7.50 or an approximate figure. Enquiries were carried out by the manageress and manager and as a result of these the claimant's daughter was dismissed from her employment on the following Tuesday and the claimant was dismissed the following Wednesday. The EAT, in considering the evidence on foot of which the employer's decision was made, stated:

> 'the Employment Appeals Tribunal is not a criminal court. It does not apply itself to establishing the guilt or innocence in the criminal sense of an employee dismissed fundamentally because of the employer's belief that at the time of dismissal a monetary transaction had been improperly handled by the employee resulting in a loss to the employer in financial terms and particularly in loss of confidence in the capacity of the employee to maintain a position of trust.'

In deciding whether or not the dismissal of the claimant was unfair a test of reasonableness is applied to:

(a) the *nature and extent of the enquiry* carried out by the respondent prior to the decision to dismiss the claimant, and

(b) the conclusion arrived at by the respondent that on *the basis of the information resulting from such enquiry* the claimant should be dismissed.

In the course of the investigation the claimant had first confirmed that she had handled the transaction and recalled her daughter paying for the doll. She examined the till roll and agreed that there was no entry for £7.50 on the roll. The employer stated to her that if she agreed that she handled the transaction and if she further agreed that there was no entry of £7.50 on the till roll he had no alternative but to draw the conclusion that there was collusion between the claimant and her daughter and that he would be forced to dismiss her. The EAT further stated:

> 'in deciding whether or not the dismissal of the claimant was unfair we applied the test of reasonableness to the nature and extent of the inquiry made by the respondents prior to the decision to dismiss the claimant. We applied the same test to the conclusion arrived at by the respondent that on the basis of the information resulting from such inquiry the claimants should be dismissed'.

The EAT held:

> 'we are satisfied that the claimant was an employee in a position of trust in the company . . . we are unanimous in our opinion that on the basis of the information resulting from the inquiry the conclusion arrived at by the respondents that the claimant should be dismissed was fair and reasonable in all the circumstances'.

For a further exposition of the standards required of an employer in effecting such a dismissal, see *Dunne v Harrington* M259 UD 166/77.

In *Looney & Co Ltd v Looney* UD 843/84 the EAT stated:

> 'It is not for the Tribunal to seek to establish the guilt or innocence of the claimant nor is it for the Tribunal to indicate or consider whether we in the employer's position would have acted as [he] did in his investigation or concluded as he did or decided as he did. To do so would be to substitute our own mind and decision for that of the employer. Our responsibility is to consider against the facts what a reasonable employer in [his] position

and circumstances at that time would have done and decided and to set this up as a standard against which [his] actions and decision be judged.'

In *Georgopoulus v Beaumont Hospital Board* 4 June 1997 (unreported) the Supreme Court ruled on the standard of proof to apply in a dismissal case, and held that as the case was a civil case it did not involve allegations of criminal offences and the standard of proving a case beyond reasonable doubt is confined to criminal trials and has no application in procedures of a civil nature. The Supreme Court accepted that the charges against the plaintiff in that case were particularly serious and had serious implications for his reputation but held that this did not require that the facts upon which the allegations were based should be established 'beyond all reasonable doubt' and that they could be dealt with on the 'balance of probabilities'. The court held that the degree of probability required should always be proportionate to the nature and gravity of the issue being investigated.

6.26   ABSENCE/SICKNESS DISMISSALS

6.26.1   GENERALLY

One of the commonest forms of dismissal is that relating to an employee's attendance record, usually involving a high level of absence due to illness. Even after a number of years in which courts and tribunals have laid down guidelines as to how such dismissals should be handled, this form of dismissal still causes considerable problems due, in the main, to a prevailing belief among employers, employees and trade unions alike that an employee may not be dismissed while medically certified absent or may not be dismissed due to a high level of medically certified absence or that an employee may be dismissed simply because he has a high level of absence.

Unlike most forms of dismissal, this area does not involve any fault on the part of the employee. In scrutinising such a dismissal a court or tribunal must balance the employee's welfare against the demands of the business, which is frequently a difficult task. The 1977 Act says very little other than the general statement in s 6(4)(a) that a dismissal shall not be unfair if it results wholly or mainly from the capability of the employee for performing work of the kind which he was employed by the employer to do.

On the basic principles of such dismissals the jurisprudence is clear as in *Reardon v St Vincent's Hospital* UD 74/79 which is one of the earliest Irish EAT cases to tackle the problem. In this case Mr Reardon was employed as a kitchen porter in St Vincent's Hospital. He had a serious problem with many prolonged absences, all due to illness and all covered by medical certificates. The employers wrote to Mr Reardon on several occasions informing him that his sick leave record was a source of concern and inconvenience and that if it did not improve the question of his continued employment would have to be reviewed. Mr Reardon's sick leave record did not improve and his employers decided to terminate his employment. It was argued on behalf of Mr Reardon that, as all absences were due to illness and covered by medical certificates, it was unfair of the employers to dismiss him. It was further stated on his behalf that his health had improved since his dismissal and as his doctor had, prior to the dismissal, suggested that a change of duties away from the kitchen might help, the employers should have transferred Mr Reardon away from the kitchen. The employers submitted that they did not have any suitable alternative vacancy for Mr Reardon. The EAT held that the dismissal was not unfair. The question was whether Mr Reardon was capable under s 6(4) of the 1977 Act of doing the work for which he was employed. In the view of the EAT Mr Reardon and the kitchen did not agree. The employers, following the doctor's recommendations, considered the possibility of moving him to another job but did not have a suitable alternative. The employers acted reasonably in dismissing Mr Reardon and the EAT emphasised that it was not Mr Reardon's fault that he was not capable of doing his job.

Before effecting such a dismissal, in common with all other forms of dismissal, an employer is obliged to afford fair procedures to an employee and warn the employee of the possibility that the employment *may* be terminated. The employer must afford to the employee all reasonable opportunities to improve on the attendance record but if it is clear that it is beyond the capacity of the employee to improve the attendance record the employer may dismiss if there is no other alternative, including contrived tolerance of the absence.

6.26.2 ILLNESS RECORDS GIVING RISE TO DISMISSAL

There are two main types of illness record which give rise to dismissal and each must be approached separately.

6.26.2.1 Frequent intermittent absences

The first type of such illness record is of a large amount of absences covering a considerable number of small periods where the absence is medically certified to be for a number of different reasons.

The leading case on this type of dismissal is the English case of *International Sports Co Ltd v Thomson* [1980] IRLR 340. Mrs Thomson was dismissed for persistent absenteeism. For the last eighteen months of her employment she was absent on average for about 25 per cent of the time. Most of her absences were covered by medical certificates which referred to a large number of conditions such as dizzy spells, anxiety, nerves, bronchitis, virus infections, cystitis, dyspepsia and flatulence. The employers had an absence tolerance level of 8 per cent. When Mrs Thomson exceeded this level she was warned. In all a total of four warnings were given to her, the last one stating that if there was no improvement in her attendance record dismissal would result. Before deciding to dismiss the company consulted a general practitioner employed by them. After looking at the employee's medical certificates the doctor advised no useful purpose would be served by examining the employee because she had not had an illness which could be subsequently verified. There did not appear to be any common link between the various illnesses and the doctor saw little point in examining the woman when the symptoms of the illnesses would undoubtedly have passed. At first instance an industrial tribunal held against the employers on the grounds that they had not acted reasonably in dismissing the employee for persistent sickness absence without carrying out a full and proper investigation including examination of the employee prior to making their decision. On appeal, the EAT overruled that decision and held

> 'where an employee has an unacceptable level of intermittent absences due to minor illness what is required is firstly that there should be a *fair review by the employer of the attendance record* and the reasons for it and secondly *appropriate warnings* after the employee has been given an *opportunity to make representations*. If there is then no adequate improvement in the attendance record in most cases the employer will be justified in treating the persistent absences as a sufficient reason for dismissing the employee. It would be placing too heavy a burden on an employer to require him to carry out a formal medical investigation in such a case. Even if he did such an investigation would rarely be fruitful because of the transient nature of the employee's symptoms and complaints. There is no rule of law or practice to support the proposition that employers are bound to investigate the bona fides of medical certificates issued. It cannot realistically be said that any reasonable employer would investigate the position in order to query the authenticity or genuineness of medical certificates before reaching a decision. This is a case where the reasonable employer was entitled to say "enough is enough".'

The employers had investigated the employee's attendance record and issued warnings. The dismissal therefore was held to be fair.

156

In a similar case, *Rolls Royce Ltd v Walpole* [1980] IRLR 343, the employee had very high absence levels due to various illnesses, all medically certified. Over the last three years of his employment his rate of absence was 44 per cent, 55 per cent and 44 per cent. The employee was given various warnings and subsequently dismissed on the grounds of his attendance record and claimed that he was unfairly dismissed. An industrial tribunal upheld his complaint on the sole ground that, as he was in no way to blame for his record of illness, there was automatically a failure on the part of the employers to discharge the burden of establishing a fair dismissal. The decision was successfully appealed by the employers to the EAT and the matter was remitted to another industrial tribunal for rehearing. The second industrial tribunal also found the dismissal to be unfair on the grounds that the company should have obtained an up-to-date medical report from its own doctor or, alternatively, given the employee an opportunity of providing medical evidence of his own. The company appealed against this decision and the EAT held that the industrial tribunal had erred and that the dismissal was in fact fair. It held that medical examination would not have made any difference to the employer's decision. It was not suggested that the employee was suffering from any *underlying condition* rendering him more susceptible to illness than his fellow employees. Had the employer's doctor examined him when he was suffering from the conditions in respect of which his own doctor had given certificates then the employer's doctor would simply have found that he was suffering from those conditions. If the employer's doctor had examined him when he was back at work he would have found him fit and able to do his work. The employers had followed fair procedures and their decision was within the range of reasonable responses such as a reasonable employer might adopt.

6.26.2.2 Continuing problem or underlying condition

The second type of illness absence is either frequent short absences or lengthy absences related to *one continuing problem or underlying condition*. In this sort of case the employer in reviewing the position would normally be expected to obtain medical advice to find out:

(a) whether or not the problem will persist, and

(b) what is the likelihood of the employee being able to attend on a more regular basis in the future.

This sort of problem was addressed in the leading Irish EAT case of *Mooney v Rowntree Mackintosh Ltd* UD 473/474/475/478/90 which in fact addressed both types of absence problem but in relation to the latter stated:

'faced with the problem of prolonged absence due to illness an employer will seek to obtain a medical report on the employee's condition in order that he may evaluate the likelihood of his returning to work in the reasonable future or of his ability of ever being able to perform the work which he was employed to do and possibly consider alternative employment if he is not able to do such work. In any event having equated himself with the true medical position at the particular time he will be in a position to relate the needs of his business with the employee's need to recover from his illness and make an assessment of whether he can any longer keep the employee's position open for him.'

6.26.3 ONUS OF PROOF

The High Court dealt with an absence case in *Bolger v Showerings (Ireland) Ltd* [1990] ELR 184. The High Court upheld the dismissal of Mr Bolger by reason of absence from work and stated in allowing the appeal:

(a) for a dismissal on grounds of incapacity to be deemed fair the onus is on the employer to show that:

(i) it was the incapacity which was the reason for the dismissal;

(ii)   the reason was substantial;

(iii)   the employee received fair notice that the question of his dismissal for incapacity was being considered; and

(iv)   the employee was afforded an opportunity of being heard;

(b)   where there is no dispute between employer and employee as to the incapacity of the employee because of ill health it is not necessary for the employer to await the results of medical tests before deciding to dismiss the employee; and

(c)   in this case the appellant had substantial grounds for the dismissal and the dismissal had been reasonable in all the circumstances.

6.26.4   MANAGEMENT DECISION

It should be noted that in seeking medical advice employers should always keep in mind that the decision to terminate is not a decision to be made by a doctor but is one to be made by management in light of medical advice. In *Bergin v Easons Cash & Carry (Wholesale) Ltd* UD 669/81 the EAT addressed a case where the employee had in the last year of her employment a considerable record of sick leave, and from 3 July 1981 to the date of her dismissal on 25 September 1981, was on continuous sick leave. The employee's absence caused the employers concern because her medical certificates did not indicate the exact nature of her illness and when she would be likely to return to work. The employee was interviewed on 4 September 1981 and was asked to obtain more definite information on when she would be returning to work. It was pointed out to her that her job could not be kept open for her indefinitely and if she did not know when she would be returning her employment would have to be terminated. The employee promised to get a report from her doctor. A further meeting took place on 15 September 1981 when the employee was warned that her job would not be kept open indefinitely and was asked to contact the company doctor to arrange a medical examination. She was warned that if it was unfavourable she would be expected to return to work in a month. The employers refused to alter their decision to dismiss as they were relying on the report from their own doctor. At the hearing of the claim there was no dispute on the facts other than that the employee stated that her job did not involve any 'heavy cleaning work'. On the evidence the EAT held that the dismissal was unfair. The employers had given no reason for the dismissal other than the company doctor's report. The company doctor was not familiar with the work carried out by the employee and no effort was made by the employers to elaborate on what the employee meant by 'heavy cleaning work'. The employee had complied with the request of management and obtained a medical opinion from her own doctor which, when submitted, was totally ignored by management even though it stated that her condition was improving and it was anticipated that she would be returning to work in a month. The decision to dismiss had been abdicated by the employers to the company doctor who was not fully conversant with the facts. As the dismissal decision was one properly made by management in light of medical advice the dismissal was held to be unfair.

6.26.5   UP-TO-DATE MEDICAL OPINION

In *McLoughlin v Celmac (Ireland) Ltd* UD 799/84 the decision to dismiss was taken without getting an up-to-date medical opinion with regard to the employee's possible future availability for work. The EAT held that the employer should have had up-to-date medical evidence prior to making the decision to dismiss and the dismissal was held to be unfair.

In *Walsh v Arthur Guinness Son & Co (Dublin) Ltd* UD 871/85 the claimant had been warned about his unsatisfactory attendance and could not give an indication as to when he thought he would be fit for work. It was decided to dismiss him. He then made a submission through his trade union that he had been informed by his doctor that he would be fully fit to resume work in the very near future. The company went ahead with the dismissal. The EAT held it was unfair because the employers did not take steps to ascertain the fitness of the employee prior to making the decision to dismiss. This appears to be a clear case where, had the employee been examined by a doctor, it could have resolved the 'crystal ball gazing' that the company engaged in prior to making the decision to dismiss.

6.26.6 NEED TO DISMISS

One very important factor often overlooked by employers in making a decision to dismiss by reason of incapacity is the need to dismiss. Some employers take the view that because an employee has a poor attendance record, that justifies dismissal. That is not the case. The dismissal must be related to the requirements of the business. There will be many instances where employers are able to make alternative arrangements and can tolerate high levels of absence. They must therefore in all absence-related cases be able to show that dismissal was necessary for good commercial reasons. In *McGrane v Mater Private Nursing Home* UD 369/85 the claimant was dismissed by reason of her high level of absence. The EAT noted that there was no pressure on the employer to replace the employee and there was effectively no reason to dismiss. The dismissal was held to be unfair. In *McElhinney v Templemore Co-operative Society Ltd* UD 434/82 the EAT commented:

> 'In cases of ill health the basic question that has to be determined in every case is whether in all the circumstances the employer can be expected to wait any longer and, if so, how much longer. The nature of the illness, the likely length of the continuing absence, the need of the employers to have done the work which the employee was engaged to do—and these presumably will vary with the size of the employing organisation. In some cases four to six weeks may justify dismissal, in others six months may not. What is reasonable will depend on the circumstances.'

In *Cummins v Jurys Hotel Group plc* [1994] ELR 21 Ms Cummins was dismissed due to prolonged absence. There was medical opinion to the effect that her medical problems might be aggravated by the type of work she did for the company. The company did not have any suitable alternative work available for the claimant and dismissal was held to be fair.

In *Boyle v Marathon Petroleum (Ireland) Ltd* UD 787/93 the claimant had been out of work due to illness for over two years and the medical opinion was that he would not be fit to return to work. He was accepted under an income continuance plan. Under the terms of such plans beneficiaries usually have to remain legally employed by the employer, which occurred here. A replacement employee was recruited and the claimant's position was filled. Some two years later he sought to return to work on the basis that he was now fit. The company advised him that there was no position for him as his pre-accident position had been filled and there was no other work available. He claimed unfair dismissal. On the evidence the EAT came to the conclusion that the claimant's contract of employment was frustrated at a date earlier than when he informed the respondent he was fit to return to work and, as frustration automatically terminates a contract of employment, there was no dismissal.

It may happen that the employee is actually fit at the time the decision to dismiss is made in circumstances where the decision is made due to the history or pattern of absences (see *Lynock v Cereal Packaging Ltd* [1988] IRLR 510).

6.26.7 EMPLOYEES INJURED OR ALLEGEDLY INJURED AT WORK

Absence from work may in some cases be caused by actual or alleged negligence of the employee causing injury or illness which in turn results in absence from work. In such circumstances an employer is entitled to dismiss given the incapacity of the employee. In *Caulfield v Waterford Foundry Ltd* [1991] ELR 137 the employee suffered a back injury at work and this made him unfit to do the heavy work required in the place of employment. His dismissal was held to be fair as he was not fit for any work in the respondent company. The UK Employment Appeal Tribunal had held in *London Fire and Civil Defence Authority v Betty* [1994] IRLR 384 that even if the ill health had been caused by the employer's treatment of the employee's negligence and/or duty of care it was still open to the employer to fairly dismiss the employee due to incapacity if such was the case.

6.26.8   INCOME CONTINUANCE/PERMANENT HEALTH INSURANCE

Many employers effect insurance policies to cover their employees during a period of prolonged absence due to illness. Normally these policies have a deferred period of six months or twelve months during which the employee will not receive benefit but on the completion of that period is entitled to apply to be covered. It is normally a condition of these policies that the employee remain an employee while in receipt of payments. If the employers therefore were to terminate the employment they would defeat the employee's rights under such a policy. That itself may give rise to a common law breach of contract action, probably based on an implied term that the existence of the policy gave the employee an implied right to remain in the employment, albeit ill, for the deferred period in order not to defeat his entitlement. Once accepted under the policy the money is paid by the insurer to the employer who processes it through the payroll in the normal way and passes the net amount to the employee. If the employee were to regain his health and seek to return to work after a prolonged absence while covered by such a policy the employer may have a problem, having effectively treated the employee for all practical purposes as having left employment.

The situation was considered in *McGrath v Euro Container Shipping plc* UD 819/92. In September 1990 the claimant became incapacitated and was accepted for permanent health insurance cover. He kept in sporadic contact with the company about his illness. The claimant was fit to return to work in April 1992 when his permanent health insurance payment ceased. The company had, while he was absent from work, 'no longer regarded him as an employee'. The EAT held that he was not dismissed and was at all material times an employee.

In *Adin v Sedco Forex International Resources Ltd* [1997] IRLR 280 the Court of Session in Scotland held against an employer who sought to dismiss an employee who was entitled to claim under short-term and long-term disability plans but by reason of the dismissal was prevented from obtaining the benefit of the plans. Even though the employer had no restrictions on the circumstances in which it could dismiss the employee, the court refused to allow such a dismissal in the circumstances of the dismissal acting to defeat the entitlement under such policies. The Court of Session accepted that where an employee is off work due to illness, and in receipt of sick pay, there was an implied term in the contract that the employee would not be dismissed on grounds of sickness or for an arbitrary reason since to do so would be to subvert the employee's entitlements to payments while sick. In *Hill v General Accident Fire and Life Corporation* [1998] IRLR 64 the court did state, however, that the employer was not in breach of the employee's contract of employment in dismissing the employee on grounds of redundancy while he was off work ill and in receipt of sickness benefit with a prospective entitlement to long-term sickness benefit under an ill-health policy. The court held that there was no implied term that the employers would not use their contractual powers of dismissal where that would frustrate an accruing or accrued entitlement to sickness benefit or ill health and early retirement. The court refused to accept that there was an implied term that gross misconduct was the only cause that would warrant dismissal of an employee who was in receipt of sick pay. The court examined the implied term of mutual trust and confidence and held that an employer would be prohibited from terminating a sick employee's employment 'solely with a view to relieving themselves of the obligation to make such payment for a specious or arbitrary reason or for no cause at all. To do so would be to subvert the employee's entitlement to payment while sick'. This decision is arguably only of any use to an employee who can prove that the actual reason for dismissal was to deny him his entitlement to short-term or long-term sickness benefit and is unlikely to avail an employee where an employer dismisses for cause, eg misconduct or redundancy. It remains to be seen whether this decision or similar decisions could be extended to cover a situation where an employee is dismissed due to non-performance or inability to perform by reason of illness. Employers should ensure that their terms or conditions for sick pay or sick leave and the manner in which those conditions operate do not exclude pregnancy or maternity related illness, as to do so would be in breach of the Employment Equality Act, 1998 and the EU Directive 76/207/EEC on equal treatment (see *Todd v Eastern Health and Social Services Board* [1997] IRLR 410).

6.26.9 LIGHT WORK

Where illness or incapacity is partial, rendering the employee unfit to do the work for which he was employed, but resulting in him still being in a position to do some work, an employer is under no obligation to provide alternative or light work unless there is a suitable alternative vacancy available. See *Gurr v Office of Public Works* UD 919/87 and *Corless v Steiner (Galway) Ltd* UD 535/82 where the EAT stated:

'We are satisfied that the respondent was not unreasonable in deciding that there was no alternative employment available for the claimant. There is no legal obligation on an employer to provide light work for an employee.'

The EAT will, in any event, examine the facts of a dismissal to see if an employee could have been accommodated without undue difficulty. In *Caulfield v Waterford Foundry Ltd* [1991] ELR 137 it was held that all employees of the foundry, being general operatives, could be called upon to do heavy work at any time. There were therefore no jobs in the foundry for which the claimant was fit on the basis of the medical report submitted. As the claimant was not fit for any work in the respondent company the dismissal was justified on grounds of incapacity.

6.26.10 DISCLOSURE OF OUTCOME OF MEDICAL EXAMINATION

In *Lawless v Dublin County Council* UD 335/89 the employer's medical officer examined the claimant and concluded that he was unfit for further work and should be retired on health grounds. The claimant was not advised by the doctor that he was intending to recommend his retirement and the claimant was not appraised of the outcome of the examination by the respondent's medical officer. The EAT held:

'Having heard the evidence presented the Tribunal is satisfied, while the respondent appears to have acted on a bona fide medical report, that because of the seriousness of the recommendation contained in that report a single medical report was not adequate. It is our view that a second report or indeed a specialist opinion should have been obtained before Mr Byrne contemplated his decision. It is our further view that there was an obligation on the respondent because of the medical report they had received to inform the claimant of the report and that his position was under review.'

The question of fitness for work was dealt with in some detail by the High Court in *Porter v Donegal County Council* [1993] ELR 101. The Department of the Environment introduced a requirement that all firemen should retire at age 55. The claimants at the time they were taken on had a normal retirement age of 60. The county council forcibly retired the employees who then claimed unfair dismissal. The justification for the forced retirement was the Department of Environment requirement and the practice that given the nature of the work, firemen should not be required to work after age 55. In holding that the dismissals were unfair because of the unilateral imposition of a new retirement age Flood J held that the employer could have resolved the problem of possible unfitness by requiring the employees to undergo regular medical examinations. He effectively held, albeit in an obiter dictum, that the employer had an implied right to require the employees to undergo a medical examination. An employer cannot normally oblige an employee to undergo a medical examination but in this case it was accepted that the employer might be in a position to suspend the employee from duty until such time as the employee had satisfied the employer as to his fitness.

6.26.11 ABUSE OF SICK LEAVE

Abuse of sick leave by working or otherwise acting inconsistently with being out sick and on sick leave may justify dismissal for misconduct or dishonesty. The general principles are well set out in *Lynch v P V Doyles Hotel Ltd* UD 89/89 and *Gildea v James Doherty (Production) Letterkenny Ltd* UD 680/84. The actual conduct of the employee will come under close scrutiny and the employer's grounds for believing that the employee had acted improperly will be examined carefully in situations such as this. In *Malone v Burlington Industries (Ireland) Ltd* UD 947/82 the claimant was seen on his farm while medically certified ill. He was met near his hay shed. A tractor and trailer were loaded with bales of hay and the tractor's engine was still running nearby to him. When asked if he was working the claimant stated he was 'doing a bit'. At the EAT hearing the claimant denied he had been working and said that the tractor had not been running but was on loan from a neighbour and had broken down. The managers who met the claimant assumed from the scene that he had been doing heavy work. The EAT held, however, that it was not satisfied that the claimant's activities were in conflict with his declaration of inability to work for the company. It pointed out that there was a difference between being fit for industrial work for an eight-hour shift and 'doing a bit' around a farm or household. The dismissal was held to be unfair.

In *Hardy v Cadbury Ireland Ltd* UD 727/83 Hardy was dismissed because, while absent on sick leave, it was alleged that he was collecting clothes at a charge and bringing them to the drycleaners. His dismissal for breaching the sick pay scheme was upheld as being fair.

In absence cases procedures may be effectively redundant if the employee is accepted as actually being unfit. In *Fahy v Comhlucht Siuicre Eireann Teoranta* UD 607/82 it was held that fair procedures had not been following by the employer; however, the evidence was that the claimant was still unable to work at the time of the hearing and the decision would have been the same even if fair procedures had been followed and the dismissal was held to be fair. This contrasts with the dissenting opinion in *Caulfield v Verbatim* UD 938/93 referred to at **6.18.2.1** above.

6.27 COMPETITION/CONFLICT OF INTEREST

6.27.1 GENERALLY

An employer is entitled to dismiss where it is established that an employee is competing against him or acting against his interests and in breach of his duty of fidelity. An employer is entitled to defend himself against unfair competition from his employee and take whatever reasonable steps are necessary in order to achieve that end (see *Davidson and Maillou v Comparisons* [1980] IRLR 360). In *Harris and Russell Ltd v Slingsby* [1973] IRLR

221 it was held that an employer cannot dismiss an employee who was seeking employment with a competitor unless the employer had grounds to show that the employee was doing so in order to abuse his confidential position. If an employee forms the intention of leaving to set up in competition that does not of itself justify termination (see *Laughton and Hawley v Bapp Industrial Supplies Ltd* [1986] IRLR 245). That case should be contrasted with *Marshall v Industrial Systems and Controls Ltd* [1992] IRLR 294 where the managing director of the company was dismissed after it was discovered that he had planned with another manager to set up in competition and take away some of the company's best business. The managing director had also tried to induce another key employee to join in the new venture.

The Irish cases are interesting on this whole question. In *Preece v Irish Helicopters Ltd* UD 236/84 the employee had signed an acknowledgement in his terms and conditions of employment that he would not 'assist or support any activity by myself or with others which may be in conflict with or in competition with or contrary to the interests of Irish Helicopters Limited'. The company received information that the claimant was involved in setting up another company and seeking a licence. The claimant was interviewed. He was evasive and admitted nothing. He was asked to sign an undertaking that if he was in any way connected with the application for a licence he would withdraw from it. He refused to sign any such undertaking. The board of the company took the view that his failure to sign the undertaking had damaged the trust and confidence necessary between them. He was dismissed. The EAT held:

> 'An employer is entitled to insist that an employee does not interest himself in a company which will compete with the business of the employer. Failure of the claimant to commit himself not to do anything while in the respondent's employment in pursuit of his own interest which might conflict with the interest of his employer was reasonably construed as a breach of duty or loyalty.'

The dismissal was held to be fair.

In *Mulchrone v Feeney* UD 1023/82 the employee worked for a confectioner in Westport. In her spare time she worked part-time for a direct competitor. She was dismissed because her employer believed that she 'was undermining his business and also that there was a danger she could be passing on trade secrets'. The EAT held, having regard to the size of the town of Westport, the direct competition in a limited market and the inadvertent possibility of the claimant passing on information, that the dismissal was justified.

6.27.2 FAMILY CONNECTIONS

In *Goggin Carroll & Co v Dineen* UD 106/85 the employers traded as insurance brokers in the town of Charleville, Co Cork. The employee was an office worker. The employers became aware that the employee's boyfriend was setting up a competing business in the town. While the employers had complete confidence that the employee would not knowingly breach confidentiality, they were concerned that information of a confidential nature could be inadvertently passed on. She was offered an alternative position in another branch some 30 miles away. She refused the offer and was dismissed. The EAT held that the dismissal was unfair as 'the fear of an inadvertent slip is not grounds for dismissal'.

The EAT took a different view in a more recent case, *Coffey v Alcan Metal Centres (Dublin) Ltd* UD 603/90. The respondent was a substantial company with two main competitors in Dublin. The pricing or rebating of products was highly sensitive and, if leaked to either competitor, could have caused considerable damage to the company. The appellant's brother and fiancé worked for the company. Both left within a short period of time to join one of the two competitors. The claimant subsequently married her fiancé. The company explained their concerns to the claimant about the possibility of breach of confidence while not aware of any actual breach of confidence. Discussions were had with the claimant about what could be done to avoid a dismissal. The company did not believe it had any other option. The claimant was unable to put forward any other option. The claimant was dismissed. The EAT held that where an employer had a real and significant concern held bona fide derived from circumstances which could reasonably justify it and that the employer's own circumstances did not reasonably permit the adoption of an alternative solution to that of dismissal, dismissal was justified.

A similar decision was reached in *Fitzgerald v Regsimm Ltd (t/a Doherty Print)* [1997] ELR 65 where the claimant, who was employed as a printer, became a director of a company owned by his brother who had himself left the employing company and set up a business in direct competition with the employer. The claimant denied his directorship, which the employer confirmed on foot of a Companies Office search. The claimant then claimed he had no involvement in the company but was a director only for legal reasons. The EAT held that the employer was justified in terminating the claimant's employment due to the breakdown of trust and confidence and the claimant's involvement in a competing company.

In *Fairbrother v Stiefel Laboratories (Ireland) Ltd* UD 665/85 the claimant was employed as director of research and development in a pharmaceutical company manufacturing dermatological products for skin disorders. The claimant's contract contained detailed confidentiality provisions. It came to the employer's attention that the claimant's wife, who was a trained pharmacist, had set up her own company and had launched a new protective cream for sensitive skin. The company pointed out to the claimant the possibility of a conflict of interest. As the conflict could not be resolved the claimant was dismissed. The dismissal was held to be fair. The EAT stated:

'We accept that the claimant's wife cannot be restrained from using her own knowledge to set up a business but having regard to her husband's position of responsibility, authority and control in the respondent company we consider that the claimant had obligations to ensure the wellbeing of his own company and to act in its best interest by discouraging his wife from promoting a product which the respondents felt was competing with their own product. We accept that the respondents were mainly concerned with the protection of their legitimate interests and the extent of those interests depends on the nature of the business and the employee's position within it. In reaching our conclusions it is not necessary for us to determine whether or not there was a conflict of interest . . . the only point at issue is whether the respondents acted reasonably in treating the claimant's failure to have his wife's product withdrawn as a reason for his dismissal. The claimant was made aware of the likely consequences if the conflict of interests was not resolved and he was given every opportunity to resolve it.'

6.27.3 BEHAVIOUR INCONSISTENT WITH EMPLOYER'S BUSINESS

In *O'Donoghue v Carroll Group Distributors Ltd* UD 942/82 the claimant was dismissed for acting in a manner inconsistent with the employer's business. The claimant drove a van to work. The side of the van had two non-smoking stickers prominently displayed on it. The van was normally parked outside the employer's depot. It was in plain view of customers and fellow employees. Some of the claimant's fellow employees objected to the stickers. The claimant was asked to remove the stickers but refused. She was then asked to park her van on the public road or at the rear of the premises. She refused. She was then dismissed. The EAT held that the dismissal was fair, stating:

'We take the view that the stickers were a cause of serious embarrassment to the respondent and could have been detrimental to its business. We feel that the claimant refused a reasonable and important request and left the respondent with no option but to dismiss her.'

6.28   CRIMINAL CONVICTIONS

Criminal convictions may justify dismissal if the offence is connected with the employment (see *Singh v London County Bus Services* [1976] IRLR 176). The criminal act may affect the reputation of the business (see *Robb v Mersey Insulation Co Ltd* [1972] IRLR 18).

In *O'Leary v Thomas Crosbie & Co Ltd* UD 1118/83 the claimant was convicted of indecent assault and subsequently dismissed from his employment. The EAT held:

> 'The critical factor in this case is whether or not the claimant's criminal conduct was such as to render him unsuitable for his employment with the respondent or unacceptable to other employees. The Tribunal is not satisfied that the latter onus was fully discharged by the respondent. Accordingly the respondent not having fully discharged the onus the Tribunal takes the view that the claimant must succeed on the primary issue namely that the dismissal was unfair.'

6.29   LACK OF COMPETENCE AND POOR PERFORMANCE

6.29.1   TEST OF INCOMPETENCE

There are effectively two tests used in incompetence or poor performance dismissal cases, being:

(a)   Does the employer have an honest belief of the employee's incompetence?

(b)   Does the employer have reasonable grounds to sustain such a belief?

These tests were referred to in *McDonnell v Rooney (t/a Spar Supermarket)* [1992] ELR 214.

In *Cooke v Thomas Linnell & Sons Ltd* [1977] IRLR 132 it was held:

> 'When responsible employers have genuinely come to the conclusion over a reasonable period of time that the manager is incompetent we think that it is some evidence that he is incompetent. When one is dealing with routine operations which may be more precisely assessed there is no real problem. It is more difficult when one is dealing with such imponderables as the quality of management which as a last resort can only be judged by those competent in the field.'

In *Taylor v Alidair Ltd* [1978] IRLR 82 Lord Denning summarised the test of incompetence as being:

> 'Whenever a man is dismissed for incapacity or incompetence it is sufficient that the employer honestly believed on reasonable grounds that the man is incapable and incompetent. It is not necessary for the employer to prove that he is in fact incapable or incompetent.'

It is a matter for employers to set their own standards and they may therefore insist on levels of competence or higher standards than might pertain in comparable organisations.

6.29.2   MONITORING OF EMPLOYEE

The employer's actions will be examined carefully both in terms of procedure and the substantive action taken to remedy and monitor the poor performance.

It was held in *James v Waltham Holy Cross UDC* [1973] IRLR 202 that:

> 'the employer should be very slow to dismiss upon the grounds that the employee is incapable of performing the work which he is employed to do without first telling the

employee of the respects in which he is failing to do his job adequately, warning him of the possibility or likelihood of dismissal on this ground and giving him an opportunity to improve his performance'.

In *Dowling v Niteout Ltd* UD 938/82, having examined the work done, the conclusion reached by the employer that the employee was incompetent was unfair given that the employer had not properly trained the employee for the job in respect of which he had been determined to be incompetent. Dismissal was unfair.

Regular monitoring of an employee's performance is important (see *O'Brien v Professional Contract Cleaners Ltd* [1991] ELR 143). The claimant had been warned, accepted the warnings and improved her performance. She was subsequently dismissed. The EAT held on the evidence that at the time of the dismissal she was adequately performing her duties and the employer had not kept himself fully appraised of her competence and the dismissal was held to be unfair.

It was held in *Sutton and Gates (Luton) Ltd v Boxall* [1978] IRLR 486:

> 'Where the poor performance is something over which the employee himself has control he should be warned probably several times and given plenty of opportunity to improve his performance. If it reaches the stage where it becomes obvious that he is incapable the employer, provided he handles the matter sensibly, is entitled to dismiss. But, in such circumstances, the employer should not dismiss without giving the employee a final opportunity to explain.'

6.29.3 INTRANSIGENT EMPLOYEES

In the case of intransigent employees who do not accept warnings, or do not accept that there is any justification for warnings, and who give no indication that they will heed the warning, dismissal may be justified at an earlier stage than otherwise. See *Retarded Children's Aid Society Ltd v Day* [1978] IRLR 128 where Lord Denning stated:

> 'In some cases it may be proper and reasonable to dismiss at once, especially with a man who is determined to go his own way. It should be kept in mind of course that the employee must be advised that their conduct will lead to dismissal. If they then refuse to do anything about their conduct it appears that dismissal is justified at an early stage rather than at a later stage.'

6.29.4 TEMPORARY APPOINTMENT

In *Williams v Willis Oil Tool Ireland Ltd* UD 59/83 the employee was promoted to a senior position which he occupied together with another senior employee, both being under assessment to get the job in due course. The other employee was chosen and Mr Williams' employment was terminated. The dismissal was held to have been unfair. The EAT held that the appointment to the joint position was expressed to be temporary and the claimant therefore had a reasonable expectation that he could revert to his old position if he did not get the new job on a permanent basis. Failure to do so was a dismissal and an unfair dismissal.

6.30 CONDUCT

In *Parsons v Liffey Marine Ltd* [1992] ELR 136 the claimant had a medical certificate stating him to be unfit for work for a period of one week. He was offered a certificate by his doctor for a period of two weeks but stated that he wanted to go back to work and the certificate for one week would suffice. At the end of that one week, however, the claimant had a continuing problem and, rather than return to the hospital, he altered the date of the certificate. The employers claimed that this was a serious breach of trust. The EAT, however, ordered his re-engagement, the dismissal being held to be unfair on the grounds that 'while the Tribunal did not condone the claimant's actions in altering the certificate he had nonetheless ultimately admitted to this. The penalty of dismissal was disproportionate to the offence and was accordingly unfair'.

In *O'Mahony v Whelan (t/a Pallet Providers)* [1992] ELR 117 a scuffle took place close by a rotary saw which, while it had been switched off, was still moving. The employer, having investigated the matter, took the view that he could not take the risk that such an incident would not occur again and as there was a rule that fighting in the workplace would result in instant dismissal, he dismissed the claimant. The EAT held that the summary dismissal of the claimant was warranted as a recurrence of the incident could result in serious injury. The respondent was justified in making a rule which protected his workplace and a breach of this rule was a serious offence.

In *Costello v Gerard F May Roofing Ltd* [1994] ELR 19 the company issued a circular about the times at which holidays could be taken. The claimants ignored the circulars and booked holidays at a time when the employer had prohibited holidays. Their employment was terminated upon taking the holidays in contravention of their employer's instruction. The EAT held that the claimants were aware of the employer's position with regard to the taking of holidays and in disregarding the circulars were responsible for the resulting dismissals and their claims failed.

In contrast, in *Conroy v Iggy Madden Transport Ltd* [1991] ELR 29 the employer claimed that it had a standard holiday period and the claimant took her annual holidays against management wishes. The claimant, however, contradicted this and stated that she had been told, when she was originally offered the job, that she could take her annual leave at her own discretion. The EAT held that the dismissal was unfair as it was too severe a penalty for the claimant having taken holidays against the management's wishes.

The employer's terms and conditions were upheld in *McKenna v Farrell Brothers* [1991] ELR 77 where the claimant's contract had a requirement that he work overtime on request. He had done so for a period but subsequently refused to work overtime despite having been told that his refusal would cause problems in meeting orders. He persisted in his refusal and was dismissed and the dismissal was held to be a fair dismissal as the claimant was in breach of his contract by refusing to work overtime.

In *Creed v KMP Co-Op Society Ltd* [1991] ELR 140 the claimant worked in a meat factory. One of the terms of employment was that 'fighting, provoking or instigating a fight when on company premises' warranted immediate dismissal. Following an investigation of an incident where the claimant was claimed to have thrown a piece of fat, which was dangerous behaviour and which the employer decided could lead to further horseplay and accidents, the claimant was dismissed. The EAT held that it was a fair dismissal, the employer having 'acted reasonably in all the circumstances. A thorough investigation was carried out by the respondent. The claimant did not act aggressively but his action caused risk of injury to others. Having regard to the dangerous environment the dismissal was not unfair'.

In *McArdle v Superquinn* [1991] ELR 171 the employer had in place strict requirements on checkout register procedures and impressed upon the staff the importance of the procedures and that breach of them was a dismissible offence. During a series of test purchases the claimant was observed to fail to register a number of items on different occasions and her explanations were deemed to be unacceptable. The EAT held the dismissal to be fair, the employer having acted reasonably in all the circumstances following a thorough investigation of the explanations given by the claimant and having afforded her sufficient time, information and opportunity to enable her to explain her actions.

In *O'Keefe Weber v Terence Casey & Co* [1997] ELR 71 the claimant was employed as a secretary and typing was her main function. The respondent became aware that she was doing typing unrelated to her work. The principal returned to the office unexpectedly and discovered the claimant occupied at the unofficial work whereupon she was dismissed summarily for breach of trust. The dismissal was held to be fair.

6.31 PENALTY

Even where fair procedures are followed carefully and the employer has decided that the employee's behaviour was sufficiently serious to justify a severe penalty, the EAT will require the employer to assess a range of penalties and not just dismissal or retention in employment. Employers are frequently asked at hearing by EAT members whether they considered any penalty other than dismissal. In *Bolger v Dublin Sport Hotel Ltd* UD 45/85 the claimant was dismissed for working for another employer on a day when he should have been at work for the respondent but had failed to attend. The EAT held that the dismissal was unfair because dismissal was not the appropriate penalty. It was held that the employer should have considered alternatives such as suspension without pay and/or a final written warning. While the claimant's conduct was clearly serious the EAT still determined that he should be re-engaged. See also *Fitzpatrick v Superquinn Ltd* UD 462/84.

It is a well-established principle that in determining whether a dismissal is unfair regard cannot be had to matters of which the employer was unaware at the time of dismissal. Any such facts, which later came to light, could not have formed part of the reason for dismissing the employee and therefore cannot be assessed in determining the basic fairness or otherwise of the decision (see *Devis & Sons Ltd v Aitkins* [1977] IRLR 314). The effects of rigid adherence to that principle could possibly work an injustice where, immediately after the dismissal, information came to light that may have been relevant, such as absolute proof of the employee's guilt or the employee engaging in another form of misconduct possibly unknown to the employer at the time the decision was made. The EAT mitigates the effect of the rule by taking into account other facts not known at the time of dismissal in consideration or remedy if any should be afforded to the employee. Section 7(1)(c) of the 1977 Act makes reference to awards of compensation and provides that compensation shall be in such amount 'in respect of any financial loss incurred . . . as is just and equitable having regard to *all* the circumstances'. In *Devis & Sons Ltd v Aitkins* the employee succeeded but received no compensation because he had contributed 100 per cent to his dismissal. The contribution was measured having regard to misconduct which came to light after the decision, which was held to be unfair, was made. In that case the House of Lords held:

(a) evidence of misconduct discovered since dismissal is irrelevant and inadmissible in deciding whether a dismissal is fair;

(b) in assessing compensation tribunals are entitled to take into account misconduct which came to light after the dismissal; and

(c) there is no inconsistency in coupling a finding of unfair dismissal with an award of no compensation.

See *Fitzpatrick v Polygram Records Ltd* [1994] ELR 24.

6.32 CONTRACTING-OUT AND SETTLEMENT OF CASES

6.32.1 CONTRACTING-OUT

It is not possible for an employee to contract out of his rights under unfair dismissal legislation. Section 13 of the 1977 Act provides:

'a provision in an agreement (whether a contract of employment or not and whether made before or after the commencement of this Act) shall be void in so far as it purports to exclude or limit the application of or is inconsistent with any provisions of this Act.'

If an employee were to reach an agreement with his employer at the time of a dismissal whereby the employer paid an amount of money to the employee which he stated to be in full and final discharge and settlement of all or any claim the employee may have the question must be asked as to whether or not such an agreement is defeated by s 13. It may well be. The circumstances in which the agreement was entered into will be examined.

In *Shortt v Data Packaging Ltd* [1996] ELR 7 the EAT heard evidence of the offer and payment of an ex gratia payment on condition that a letter of waiver was signed. The claimant was advised that he would not receive the money unless the waiver was signed. He stated he would sign the waiver on a without prejudice basis. The EAT held that on the evidence of the meetings leading up to the signing of the waiver and of the signing of the document it had jurisdiction to hear the claimant's claim.

Agreements entered into after the initiation of proceedings are rarely set aside under s 13 as to do so would be to defeat the settlement of cases and, in terms of outcome, a very substantial amount of cases are actually settled. In *Fitzgerald v Pat the Baker* [1999] ELR 227 the claimant resigned from his employment because he was demoted and then signed a document accepting a payment which was stated to then preclude him from taking a claim against the employer. The claimant signed the document without professional advice. He then brought a claim for constructive dismissal. The employer sought to rely on the document, claiming that the claimant was precluded from bringing his claim as a result of what he had signed. The EAT drew a distinction between settlements of cases which followed negotiations, usually with professional advice, and settlements essentially imposed by one party on the other without negotiation or professional advice. The former are within the jurisdiction of the legislation and are valid whereas the latter are void under the legislation.

6.32.2 DUPLICATION OF CLAIMS

Section 15 of the 1977 Act provided that where an employee gave notice in writing to a rights commissioner or tribunal of intention to claim under the 1977 Act the employee could not then recover damages for wrongful dismissal at common law. Where proceedings for damages at common law for wrongful dismissal were initiated a claim could not then be brought under the 1977 Act. In both cases it was the initiation and notification of the claim that brought about the bar to the alternative remedy even where the claim initiated or notified was not proceeded with. That situation was changed in s 10 of the 1993 Act, which provides that the bar will only apply where a recommendation has actually been made by a rights commissioner, the hearing of a claim by the EAT has commenced or where the common law court proceedings have commenced. It is possible therefore for an employee to initiate claims for unfair dismissal and wrongful dismissal but be deemed to have abandoned one of the remedies under s 10 at the time specified. Section 15 of the 1977 Act was considered by the Supreme Court in *Parsons v Iarnrod Eireann* [1997] ELR 203. The plaintiff had sought declaratory orders relating to the defendant's internal appeals and decision to dismiss and also claimed in those High Court proceedings 'damages for wrongful/unfair dismissal'. The Supreme Court held:

(a) The effect of s 15 was not to oust the jurisdiction of the High Court but to provide an employee with an additional statutory remedy. However, the Unfair Dismissals Act, 1977 provides that employees must choose between suing for damages at common law for wrongful dismissal and claiming relief under the Unfair Dismissals Act.

(b) The traditional relief at common law was a claim for damages and whereas the plaintiff may have had an entitlement to declarations, such declarations were in aid of his common law remedy and had no independent existence apart from it.

Section 15 of the 1977 Act also provided that a person who accepts redress under the Anti-Discrimination (Pay) Act, 1974, s 9 or 10 cannot accept any redress under the Unfair Dismissals Act, 1977, s 7, as amended by the 1993 Act.

Apart from legal procedures there was the possible duplicity of proceedings where an employee brought an unfair dismissal claim and also referred the dispute regarding the dismissal to the Labour Court under the terms of the Industrial Relations Acts. The EAT had, in a number of cases, indicated an unwillingness to rule on a dismissal where the Labour Court had dealt with the matter, and vice versa, but the problem of duplicity has now been resolved by virtue of the provisions of the 1993 Act, s 7, which amends the 1977 Act, s 8, and provides that a dispute in relation to a dismissal cannot be referred under the Industrial Relations Acts, 1946–1990 where a recommendation has been made by a rights commissioner under unfair dismissal legislation or a hearing by the EAT has commenced. It also provides that if the matter has been referred under the Industrial Relations Acts and a recommendation has been made by a rights commissioner under that legislation or a hearing by the Labour Court has commenced then the employee cannot seek redress under unfair dismissal legislation.

6.32.3   REMEDIES/REDRESS

6.32.3.1   Generally

Unfair dismissal legislation provides for three possible remedies as follows:

(a)   reinstatement;

(b)   re-engagement; or

(c)   compensation.

6.32.3.2   Reinstatement

Reinstatement is to the position which the employee held immediately before the dismissal on the same terms and conditions as he enjoyed. The 1993 Act provides that if terms and conditions have been improved after the employee was dismissed and prior to the reinstatement order taking effect the employee must enjoy the improved or more beneficial terms and conditions. An employee who is reinstated will be entitled to back pay for the period he was out of work and all other benefits and perquisites to be brought up to date. The employee retains continuity of service if reinstated. For this reason tribunals have reinstated employees even where the employee may have been partly to blame for the original dismissal. In such cases the tribunal may vary the strict application or under-standing of reinstatement by providing that part of the period the employee was out of work should be treated as a period of unpaid suspension.

6.32.3.3   Re-engagement

Re-engagement is where the tribunal orders that the employee resume work in the position he held immediately before his dismissal or in a different position which might be 'reasonably suitable . . . on such terms and conditions as are reasonable having regard to all the circumstances'. Re-engagement is very close to reinstatement but does not of itself guarantee continuity and payment of lost salary, perquisites and benefits. The tribunal may order re-engagement on the condition that continuity of service is not broken.

6.32.3.4   Compensation

Compensation is the most common form of remedy and usually preferred by the parties. Remuneration is not simply basic salary but includes 'allowances in the nature of pay and benefits in lieu of or in addition to pay'. The term remuneration includes salary and all other cash payments such as commissions, bonuses and non-cash items such as company car, value of employer's contribution to pension scheme, share options, VHI and any other benefit provided to the employee at the employer's cost. Remuneration does not include expenses which are incurred in the carrying out of duties.

Remuneration may be awarded under the legislation up to a maximum of 104 weeks' gross entitlement.

Compensation itself may only be calculated on the basis of actual loss incurred by the employee as a result of the dismissal as opposed to damages. The Supreme Court considered the issue of contribution and the EAT's discretion in calculating loss in *Carney v Balkan Tours Ltd* [1997] ELR 102 and stated:

'1.   The Employment Appeals Tribunal in determining the payment to be made by the respondent to the appellant of compensation by way of redress for unfair dismissal in respect of financial loss incurred by her and attributable to that dismissal were entitled to have regard to her contribution to the dismissal as one of the relevant circumstances in determining the amount to be so paid.'

2.   'The discretion conferred on the Tribunal by s 7 is very wide. Section 7(2)(d) coupled with the discretion conferred upon the adjudicating tribunal in its widest terms would lead to the inference that the legislature intended that the body determining the nature or extent of the redress to which the employee was entitled should look at all the circumstances of the case including the conduct of the parties prior to the dismissal.'

6.32.3.5   Assessment of loss

Employees have an obligation to mitigate their loss once they are dismissed. Compensation may be reduced or may not be awarded at all if an employee has failed to mitigate his loss. Under the 1993 Act social welfare entitlement received following dismissal may not be taken into account in calculating actual loss. The actual loss of an employee will be examined carefully by a tribunal or court before making any compensatory award and a fairly strict line is taken in compensation being awarded only where there is real loss. An example of this is in *Coyle v Tipper House Trust Ltd* UD 904/93 where the employee won his unfair dismissal claim but was awarded no compensation under the legislation (it being prior to the 1993 Act), nor was he able to recover under the Minimum Notice and Terms of Employment Act, 1973, having had no loss. The employer's case was that the employee was redundant but this was rejected by the EAT. The EAT had heard evidence that, at the time of the dismissal and shortly thereafter, the claimant was unfit for work on medical grounds. His future prognosis was unclear. The EAT held, in the circumstances, of his unfitness and, in allowing his claim under the Unfair Dismissals Acts, made no award under that legislation 'as the Tribunal was told that the claimant has been unfit for work since his dismissal and it cannot be said when he will be fit for work, if ever, in the future. As the claimant was not available for work in the notice period due to illness his claim under the Minimum Notice and Terms of Employment Acts, 1973–1991 is dismissed.'

The 1993 Act also provides that if an employee has been held to have been unfairly dismissed and has no loss a basic award of up to four weeks' remuneration may be made.

6.32.3.6   Taxation of termination payments

All payments made to employees related to the termination of employment, whether paid at the time of termination or thereafter, are subject to taxation of termination payments. Taxation applies whether the payments are agreed as part of a settlement or an ex gratia payment and also where awarded by a rights commissioner, EAT, Circuit Court, High Court, or Supreme Court. The taxation of such payments was originally provided for under the terms of the Income Tax Act, 1967, ss 114 and 115 as amended by subsequent Finance Acts. The applicable provisions are now contained in Chapter 5 of the Taxes Consolidation Act, 1997.

While the ceiling of 104 weeks' remuneration is based on the gross remuneration figure, compensation and actual loss are based on the net figure as the difference is not a loss to the employee. An example of the calculation of remuneration gross and net is as follows:

	€ Gross	€ Net
Salary	30,000	20,000
VHI	500	500
Car	3,000	2,000
Employer's Pension Contribution	5,000	5,000
Annual bonus	4,000	2,000
Telephone rental	500	500
Accommodation	4,000	2,500
Total remuneration	47,000	32,500

6.33   TAXATION

The basic rules on taxation of termination payments are as follows:

(a)   basic exemption available to all employees on each and every occasion of termination of employment, €10,160; and

(b)   €765 for each full year of service.

These deductions may be applied by the employer without Revenue consent.

Section 15 of the Finance Act 2002 also allows for an additional allowance of €10,000 which is available in whole or in part once every ten years. Effectively therefore over a ten-year period an individual can use up this allowance to the maximum of €10,000. This allowance, however, will not be available if the individual is a member of an occupational pension scheme with the right to receive a lump sum from such a scheme. The individual, however, can irrevocably give up the right to receive the lump sum from the pension scheme and therefore avail of this allowance. If the individual receives or is entitled to receive a pension lump sum then this €10,000 allowance is reduced by the amount of the pension lump sum – most lump sums will be in excess of €10,000 which makes the exercise academic but if it was less than €10,000 then there would be a balancing allowance available to the individual.

To mitigate the effects of the above reliefs there is a further relief available to employees in respect of the taxation of termination payments. This is available as an alternative to the entitlements referred to above and it is as follows:

Standard capital superannuation benefit which is calculated as follows:

$$\frac{A \times B}{15} - C$$

Where:

A = average remuneration for the final three years of service.
B = number of complete years of service.
C = any tax-free lump sum received or receivable under an appropriate Revenue approved pension scheme.

On the basis of the above the amount of relief is calculated. Tax is then applied to the taxable portion as if it was income in the year in which it was received. This will be at the standard rate or may, depending on the employee's income in that particular year, push the income into a higher tax bracket. To mitigate the effect of this the Revenue Commissioners allow the application of what is known as top-slicing relief which is computed as follows:

$$A - (P \times T)$$

Where:

A = the additional tax which would be payable if the taxable lump sum were treated as income earned in the year of assessment over and above the amount which would have been payable if the lump sum were not taxable.

P = the taxable lump sum.

T = the average rate of tax chargeable in respect of the income of the employee for the five preceding years.

6.34 CLAIMS UNDER UNFAIR DISMISSAL LEGISLATION

6.34.1 TIME LIMITS

An employee may bring an unfair dismissal claim to a rights commissioner or the EAT within six months of the date of dismissal, extendable to twelve months under the 1993 Act where appropriate. In *Hogan v Quaid* [1996] ELR 210 the claimant's employment was terminated on 23 April 1994 and she lodged an unfair dismissal claim on 14 December 1994. She claimed that she thought there would be an offer of part-time employment so she had not lodged her claim. She was also unaware of the six-month time limit. On the evidence the EAT held that the circumstances did not prevent the claimant lodging her claim within six months of the date of her dismissal and declined jurisdiction under the provisions of s 8(2), as amended, of the Unfair Dismissals Acts, 1977–1993. See also *O'Neill v Miller* [1996] ELR 202.

If the employee chooses to lodge a claim with a rights commissioner the employer may object and require that the hearing be carried out by the EAT. The time limits remain the same.

6.34.2 DOCUMENTATION

There are pre-printed forms available for the making of claims to both the rights commissioner and the EAT. Once the claim form is served on the employer the employer must revert to the rights commissioner within twenty-one days advising of the objection or willingness to participate in the hearing. In the case of EAT hearings an appearance form will be forwarded by the tribunal to the employer and the employer must complete this and return it to the tribunal and file it on the employee or employee's representative within fourteen days of receipt. Completion and service of all documentation is essential; otherwise the employer may not be entitled to participate in the hearing although the tribunal has a discretion to extend the time for the filing of an appearance form on application.

The EAT has issued guidelines on its procedures which are set out at **6.35.1** below.

6.35 EMPLOYMENT APPEALS TRIBUNAL

6.35.1 GUIDELINES FOR PERSONS REPRESENTING PARTIES BEFORE EAT

Guidelines have been prepared for the assistance of those who appear on behalf of clients before the EAT.

The EAT was established to provide a speedy, inexpensive and relatively informal means for resolution of disputes under the various legislation that comes within the Tribunal's scope. All practitioners should bear this principle in mind when preparing and presenting cases and should avoid 'legalisms'.

- Practitioners trained in the adversarial method should remember that the EAT often uses the inquisitorial method and may raise matters that have not been raised by either of the parties.

- While the EAT is empowered to take evidence on oath, it is not essential to take sworn evidence, and evidence may be presented in a less formal manner. By and large, the EAT endeavours to limit the application of the oath to cases where it is necessary.

- Where cross-examination is considered necessary, practitioners are reminded that such cross-examination should be brief and to the point and they should also bear in mind that, at the end of the cross-examination, there may be further questions from EAT members. Re-examination, if required, may follow the members' questions.

- The EAT does not necessarily enforce the strict rules of evidence. The 'best evidence' rule does not always apply and hearsay evidence may be admitted by the EAT, subject to the rules of fair procedure.

- Parties should endeavour to reach agreement on uncontroversial issues of fact (wages, length of service etc). If possible, parties should try to reach a wider agreement so as to net down the issues to be decided by the EAT.

- There are no paper pleadings lodged in the EAT. However, the parties are expected to set out their respective cases in writing on the forms completed by the parties prior to hearing. A flexible approach, however, is taken to these papers and parties will not necessarily be confined to what is contained in them. This approach by the EAT is, however, governed by the rules of fair procedure.

- Documents to be used by the parties should be prepared in a booklet or booklets and sufficient copies should be made for the EAT and the other party.

- Both parties are entitled to make opening statements. Apart from outlining a party's case, these statements will help to eliminate areas of disagreement and bring the focus of the EAT onto the net issues involved.

- Witness summonses may be obtained on application to a sitting division of the EAT. Parties should bear in mind that it is the EAT which requires the attendance of a witness, and the issue of a summons is a matter within the EAT's discretion. Applications should be made in good time so as to allow the witness reasonable opportunity to make arrangements to attend. If the venue of the hearing requires a witness to travel some distance, this is a matter to which the EAT shall have regard in deciding whether to issue a summons. Professional witnesses and witnesses who are not closely involved with either party should not be unnecessarily detained.

- The EAT does not have power to order discovery of documents. It is, however, empowered to order a person to attend at a time and place and to bring such documents as are specified. An application for such a summons should state the nature of the documents involved with some particularity.

- By their very nature, adjournments cause delays to the EAT's schedule of hearings. While consideration will be given to all applications, the following conditions should at least be met when applying for an adjournment:

  * good cause should be shown as adjournments are only granted for very grave reasons;

  * the application should be at the earliest opportunity after receipt of the notice of hearing, save where the EAT for just cause dispenses with this requirement; and

  * the written consent of the other party must be obtained. Where same is not forthcoming or cannot be procured easily, the EAT nevertheless requires the application to be made at the earliest possible date.

- The EAT may not award costs against any party unless, in its opinion, a party has acted frivolously or vexatiously. Such costs are confined to a specified amount in respect of travelling expenses and any other costs or expenses reasonably incurred by that other party in connection with the hearing, but shall not include any amount for the attendance of counsel or solicitors, officials of a trade union, or of an employers' association.

6.35.2 STATUTORY FORMS TO BE USED IN APPLICATION TO EAT

T1-A: To be used for direct claims to the EAT under the following Acts:

- Redundancy Payments Acts, 1967–1991
- Minimum Notice and Terms of Employment Acts, 1973–1991
- Unfair Dismissals Acts, 1977–1993
- Worker Protection (Regular Part-time Employees) Act, 1991
- Organisation of Working Time Act, 1997

T1-B: This form is to be used for appeals of a rights commissioner's recommendation to the EAT under the following legislation:

- Unfair Dismissals Acts, 1977–1993
- Payment of Wages Act, 1991
- Terms of Employment (Information) Act, 1994
- Maternity Protection Act, 1994
- Adoptive Leave Act, 1995
- Protection of Young Persons (Employment) Act, 1996

T1-C: Replacing Form RP51C, this form is to be used for appeals to the EAT under the Protection of Employees (Employers' Insolvency) Acts, 1984–1991.

RP51B: This form is to be used for appeals against a decision of the Minister for Enterprise, Trade and Employment or a deciding officer in a matter of redundancy under the Redundancy Payments Acts, 1967–1991

T2: This form is to be used by a respondent against whom a claim has been lodged to enter a notice of appearance before the EAT.

All enquiries and forms to:

Employment Appeals Tribunal,
Davitt House,
65A Adelaide Road,
Dublin 2.

Telephone: (01) 6312121 or
                 1890 220222 LoCall from outside (01) area

Fax: (01) 6764810

CHAPTER 7

EMPLOYMENT EQUALITY AND DISCRIMINATION LAW

7.1 EVOLUTION OF IRISH EMPLOYMENT EQUALITY LAW

7.1.1 SOURCES OF IRISH EMPLOYMENT EQUALITY LAW

The sources of Irish employment equality law are:

- The Constitution
- Article 119 (now article 141) of the EC Treaty
- Council Directive 75/117/EEC
- Council Directive 76/207/EEC
- Anti-Discrimination (Pay) Act, 1974
- Employment Equality Act, 1977
- Employment Equality Act, 1998

The Employment Equality Act 1998 ('the 1998 Act') adds to the scope of equality legislation and replaces both the 1974 Act and the 1977 Act.

7.1.2 THE CONSTITUTION

The adoption of the Irish Constitution in 1937 allowed an aggrieved employee to seek redress under the terms of the Constitution in addition to any relevant statutory or common law rights (see Curtin, *Irish Employment Equality Law* (1989)). The Constitution does not contain any general prohibition on sex discrimination but Article 40.3 provides for certain personal rights as follows:

> '(i) *The State guarantees in its laws to respect and, as far as practicable, by its laws to defend and vindicate the personal rights of the citizen.*
> (ii) *The State shall, in particular, by its laws protect as best it may from unjust attack and, in the case of the injustice done, vindicate the life, person, good name, and property rights of every citizen.'*

The first significant case dealing with this sub-article of the Constitution was *Ryan v Attorney General* [1965] IR 294 in which Kenny J held that there existed a number of unspecified rights in addition to those specifically mentioned in Article 40.3. Kenny J found, which decision was upheld by the Supreme Court on appeal, that there existed a right to bodily integrity. In *Murtagh Properties v Cleary* [1972] IR 330 the plaintiff publicans applied for an interlocutory injunction restraining the picketing of their premises by members of a trade union who objected to the employment of female staff as part-time bar waitresses. The trade union contended that such employment was a breach of an agreement between an employer's association and a trade union. None of the women in question was a member of the union. It emerged that while there were some female members of the union, who were employed in the grocery and provision business, employment in licensed premises was confined to males. The plaintiffs contended (inter alia) that the Constitution recognised a right to earn a livelihood without discrimination on the grounds of sex and that that right was infringed when an employer who was willing to employ a woman was prevented from doing so by persons objecting solely on the grounds of sex. Kenny J concluded that the framers of the Constitution intended that in so far as the right to adequate means of livelihood was involved, men and women were to be regarded as equal. It followed that a policy or internal rule under which anyone sought to prevent an employer from employing men or women on the ground of sex only was prohibited by the Constitution. Kenny J confined his decision to finding that the women had the right to have an 'opportunity' to earn a livelihood. Such a personal right did not extend to the right to receive pay equal to that of their male colleagues.

7.1.3   THE EC TREATY

7.1.3.1   Introduction

The EC Treaty was signed in Rome on 25 March 1957 by six European countries in order to create the Common Market. The preamble of the Treaty made it clear that the objective of the Community was to foster the development of an even closer union through a co-operative effort devoted to economic and social progress. The social aims of the Treaty were to a large extent merely regarded as a consequence of the economic aims, rather than as an end in itself (see Curtin, *Irish Employment Equality Law*). Article 119 of the Treaty contains the only specific obligation which was created by the chapter of the Treaty dealing with social provisions and gives expression to the principle that men and women should receive equal pay. The practical position was that at the time of the negotiation of the Treaty, there were substantial differences in the scope of labour and social legislation in the Member States. In particular, France had enacted domestic provisions more favourable to female workers and which were more costly for employers. It was feared by France that the ability of other countries to compete in its market once the Common Market had been established would make its products uncompetitive having regard to this extra cost. In order to protect French industry against unfair competition from those Member States who had not enacted provisions dealing with equal pay, article 119 was included. The article was seen for many years as aspirational, rather than conferring any rights.

7.1.3.2   Article 119

Article 119 provides as follows:

> '*Each Member State shall, during the first stage ensure and subsequently maintain the application of the principle that men and women should receive equal pay for equal work.*'

For the purposes of this article, 'pay' means the ordinary, basic or minimum wage or salary and any other consideration, whether in cash or in kind, which the worker receives, directly or indirectly in respect of his employment from his employer.

'Equal pay without discrimination based on sex' means that:

> '*(a)   pay for the same work at piece rates shall be calculated on the bases of the same unit of measurement; and*
>
> *(b)   pay for work at time rates shall be the same for the same job.*'

7.1.3.3   The Defrenne case

It was only during the 1970s that the equal pay guarantee in article 119 was developed and its legal effect recognised. The European Court of Justice in Case 43/75 *Defrenne v Sabena* [1976] ECR 455 gave teeth to the provisions of article 119. The court stated that:

> 'The aim of Article 119 is to avoid a situation in which undertakings established in States which have actually implemented the principle of equal pay suffer a competitive disadvantage in intra-Community competition as compared with undertakings established in States which have not yet eliminated discrimination against women workers as regards pay. Secondly, this provision forms part of the social objectives of the Community which was not merely an Economic Union, but is at the same time intended, by common action, to ensure social progress and see the constant improvement of the living and working conditions of their peoples, as emphasised by the Preamble to the Treaty.'

Ms Defrenne had been an air hostess with the Belgian airline, Sabena, and had lodged a series of claims with the Belgian courts claiming backdated equal pay and equal pension entitlements. She failed before the relevant national courts on all her claims before the reference to the European Court of Justice. Ms Defrenne was successful and the Court of Justice not only held that the right contained at article 119 was partly directly effective, but also that it was a right enforceable against private as well as public employers in so far as it was directly effective in the Member State. The provisions of article 119 in the Treaty of Rome are now contained in article 141 of the Treaty of Amsterdam, which incorporated equal treatment measures into the EC Treaty.

7.1.3.4   The Treaty of Amsterdam

The Treaty of Amsterdam adds to the article 119 provisions. Article 141(3) adds a requirement that the Community adopt measures to provide equal treatment and opportunity in occupation and employment. Article 141(4) permits positive action by Member States. It does not require positive action.

7.1.4   THE EQUAL PAY DIRECTIVE

It was contended that the terms of article 119 only provided that equal pay should be paid in circumstances where equal work was carried out. It was contended that this did not extend to giving a right to equal pay in situations where a woman carried out work equal in value to the work carried out by a male employee. The Equal Pay Directive (75/117/EEC) resolved this interpretation problem and article 1 of the Directive explains that the concept of 'same work' contained in the first paragraph of article 119 includes cases of work to which equal value is attributed. The courts have decided that the Directive in no way affects the concept of 'pay' contained in the second paragraph of article 119, but simply restates the principle of equal pay. It was stated that the Directive did no more than explain in greater detail the concept of equal work already used in article 119. In *Jenkins v Kingsgate (Clothing Productions) Ltd* [1981] ECR 911 the court declared that article 1 of the Directive was 'principally designed to facilitate the practical application of the principle of equal pay outlined in article 119 of the Treaty' and that it 'in no way alters the scope of the content of that principle as defined in the Treaty'. The Directive identifies both equal work and work of equal value on an equal basis to a claim for equal pay and gives an equal and independent right to found such a claim on either basis.

7.1.5   THE EQUAL TREATMENT DIRECTIVE

The object of the Equal Treatment Directive (76/207/EEC) is to implement in the Member States the principle of equal treatment for men and women in relation to access to employment, vocational training, promotion and working conditions. The purpose of the 1998 Act is articulated in article 1, and article 2 defines the principle of equal treatment and its limits. Article 3 provides that in relation to access to employment, no discrimination whatsoever on grounds of sex is permitted and Member States are also required to take active measures necessary to abolish laws, regulations or administrative practices contrary to the principle of equal treatment. Provisions contrary to this principle which appear in collective agreements, individual contracts of employment, company rules or the articles of professional associations must either be void or be declared void or amended. Article 6 of the Directive obliges Member States to introduce judicial remedies under their national legislation so all persons who consider themselves wronged may pursue their claims by judicial process.

7.1.6   NEW EQUAL TREATMENT DIRECTIVE

7.1.6.1   Introduction

The Council adopted Directive 2000/78/EC establishing a general framework for equal treatment in employment and occupation on 27 November 2000. The Directive arises out of article 13 of the EC Treaty as modified by the Amsterdam Treaty. Its purpose is to combat discrimination based on religion or belief, disability, age or sexual orientation.

The Employment Equality Act, 1998, which came into force in Ireland on 18 October 1999, prohibits discrimination on all but one of those grounds. It does not make particular reference to belief as a separate category to religious belief. The Act also prohibits discrimination on other grounds, to a total of nine. The grounds are gender, marital status, family status, sexual orientation, religion, age, disability, race and membership of the traveller community.

This Directive is part of a three-pronged article 13 anti-discrimination package. A directive on race discrimination has also been adopted (Directive 2000/43/EC of 29 June 2000), together with an action programme to support the efforts of Member States to combat discrimination across the EU.

7.1.6.2   Areas covered by the Directive

The areas covered by Directive 2000/78/EC are access to employment, self-employment and occupation, promotion, vocational training, employment and working conditions and membership of certain bodies. The areas covered by the Irish Employment Equality Act are access to employment, conditions of employment, training or experience for or in relation to employment, promotion or regrading, classification of post and membership of certain bodies. Discrimination on the ground of pay is prohibited in more limited circumstances.

The Directive does not cover discrimination on the grounds of gender, which has been covered in earlier European Directives, 76/207/EEC and 86/613/EEC. The provisions cover self-employment and membership of professional bodies as well as salaried employment. Paragraph 22 of the preamble to the Directive provides that the Directive is without prejudice to national laws or marital status and the benefits dependent on marital status. The Irish Employment Equality Bill, 1997 was referred to in the Commission's proposal for the Directive in respect of the provisions in respect of disability. In respect of harassment in the workplace the proposal for some reason referred to the Employment Equality Act rather than the Bill. This is interesting because the provisions of the Bill in respect of disability were overturned by the Supreme Court in a material respect, which was to provide that employers are only required to provide reasonable accommodation for persons with disabilities if same have a 'nominal cost'. No such provision is contained in the Directive. The nominal cost provision will be superseded by the Directive when implemented.

7.1.6.3 Measures to be taken to accommodate disability

Article 5 of the Directive provides that employers shall take appropriate measures, where needed in a particular case, to enable a person with a disability to have access to, participate or advance in employment, or to undergo training, unless such measures would impose a disproportionate burden on the employer. This burden shall not be disproportionate when it is sufficiently remedied by measures existing within the framework of disability policy in the Member State concerned.

The preamble qualifies this provision as follows.

Paragraph 7 of the preamble states that the Directive does not require the recruitment, promotion, maintenance in employment or training of an individual who is not competent, capable and available to perform the essential functions of the post concerned or to undergo the relevant training, without prejudice to the obligation to provide reasonable accommodation for persons with disabilities.

Paragraph 20 of the preamble states that appropriate measures should be provided, ie effective and practical measures to adapt the workplace to the disability, for example, adapting premises and equipment, patterns of working time, the distribution of tasks or the provision of training or integration resources.

Paragraph 21 provides that, to determine whether the measures in question give rise to a disproportionate burden on the employer, account should be taken in particular of the financial and other costs entailed, the scale and financial resources of the organisation or undertaking, and the possibility of obtaining public funding or any other assistance.

This is quite different from a nominal cost test. The Irish nominal cost test has not yet been interpreted by an equality officer or Labour Court; however, it has been argued that it may not relate to the financial resources of the employer, but be an absolute, rather than a relative test. It is clear that the Directive requires a relative test to be applied. The equivalent provisions of the Disability Discrimination Act 1995 in the UK in respect of reasonable adjustment, which mirror the Irish reasonable accommodation provision, require the financial resources and size of the undertaking to be taken into account in determining what is reasonable. It is suggested that, when the Directive is implemented, the nominal cost test can no longer apply, at least as an absolute test.

7.1.6.4 Right of redress

Article 9 of the Directive specifically provides that persons who consider themselves wronged may pursue their claims through an administrative and/or judicial procedure to enforce their right to equal treatment even after an employment relationship has ended. This reflects the European Court of Justice's decision in 1998 in the case of *Coote v Granada Hospitality Ltd* [1998] IRLR 656, where it was held that there was an obligation on Member States to introduce into national law measures necessary to ensure protection for workers from retaliatory action taken by employers after the employment relationship had ceased. No such provision has yet been enacted in Ireland.

7.1.6.5 Burden of proof

Article 10 of the Directive provides that the burden of proof reverts to the defendant once the plaintiff has established facts from which it may be presumed that there has been direct or indirect discrimination. This does not apply to criminal proceedings. European Communities (Burden of Proof in Gender Discrimination Cases) Regulations, 2001 (SI 337/2001) provide for a shift in the burden of proof in gender discrimination cases only.

There is no such provision in the Employment Equality Act, 1998 or amending statutory instrument in respect of the burden of proof in respect of allegations of discrimination on the grounds of religion or belief, disability, age or sexual orientation. As previously mentioned at **7.1.6.1**, the separate ground of belief is not a ground within the 1998 Act and will have to be added once the directive is implemented. A further statutory instrument will also be required to provide for the shifting burden of proof, similar to SI 337/2001.

7.1.6.6 Victimisation

Article 11 of the Directive prohibits victimisation, which is prohibited in the Irish Employment Equality Act, 1998.

7.1.6.7 Implementation

The Directive provides that Member States are required to transpose the Directive into national law by 31 December 2003. A further three-year period may be taken by Member States to implement the provisions on age and disability discrimination in order to take account of particular conditions.

7.1.6.8 Harassment

Article 2(3) of the Directive provides that harassment shall be deemed to be a form of discrimination within the meaning of article 2(1), when unwanted conduct related to any of the grounds takes place with the purpose or effect of creating an intimidating, hostile, degrading, humiliating or offensive environment. This differs from the Irish Employment Equality Act provision in respect of harassment on grounds other than gender. Part of the definition of harassment on grounds other than gender is that any act or conduct of a person including, without prejudice to the generality, spoken words, gestures or the production, display or circulation of written words, pictures or other material constitutes harassment of a person by another person if the action or conduct is unwelcome to the person and could reasonably be regarded, in relation to the relevant characteristics of the person, as offensive, humiliating or intimidating to the person. It incorporates an objective and subjective element. It does not, unlike the Directive, make reference to the environment created by the conduct, but rather to the effect on the person.

7.1.6.9 Age discrimination

The Directive contains provisions in respect of age discrimination which substantially mirror the provisions contained in the Irish Employment Equality Act and it is therefore unlikely that any amendments to those provisions will be required to implement the Directive.

7.1.6.10 Racial or ethnic discrimination

The Council has adopted a directive, Directive 2000/43/EC of 29 June 2000, implementing the principle of equal treatment between persons irrespective of racial or ethnic origin.

The Directive's purpose is to lay down a framework for combating discrimination on the grounds of racial or ethnic origin, but not national origin, with a view to putting into effect in the Member States the principle of equal treatment. This is provided for in article 1. Article 3(2) provides for the exception in respect of difference of treatment based on nationality.

The Directive provides at article 3(2) for definitions of direct and indirect discrimination. The definition of direct discrimination is consistent with that in the 1998 Act, which contains the relevant provisions on direct discrimination on the grounds of race in Ireland.

Section 6(1) and (2)(a), when read together, provide that for the purposes of the 1998 Act, discrimination shall be taken to occur where one person is treated less favourably than another is, has been or would be treated, on the ground that the persons are of different race, colour, nationality or ethnic or national origins.

As stated above, the ground of nationality is not contained within the Directive.

7.1.6.11 Indirect discrimination

The definition of indirect discrimination in article 2(2)(b) differs from that in the 1998 Act and is more favourable to complainants.

Article 2(2)(b) of the Directive provides:

> *'indirect discrimination shall be taken to occur when an apparently neutral provision, criterion or practice would put persons of a racial or ethnic origin at a particular disadvantage compared with other persons, unless that provision, criterion or practice is objectively justified by a legitimate aim and the means of achieving that aim are appropriate and necessary.'*

This definition is similar to that now contained in the 1998 Act in respect of discrimination on the ground of gender. The 1998 Act has been amended by the European Communities (Burden of Proof in Gender Discrimination Cases) Regulations, 2001 (SI 337/2001). These regulations give effect to Council Directive 97/18/EC of 15 December 1997 on the burden of proof in cases of discrimination based on sex. They not only address the question of burden of proof but, at regulation 4, amend the definition of indirect discrimination on the grounds of gender as provided in s 22(1) of the 1998 Act.

Prior to the amending regulations, indirect discrimination on the gender ground as defined in s 22(1) of the 1998 Act occurred when:

> *'where a provision (whether in the nature of a requirement, practice or otherwise) which relates to any of [the grounds] or to membership of a regulatory body—*
> *(a) applies to both A and B,*
> *(b) is such that the proportion of persons who are disadvantaged by the provision is substantially higher in the case of those of the same sex as A than in the case of those of the same sex as B, and*
> *(c) cannot be justified by objective factors unrelated to A's sex,*
> *then, for the purposes of this Act, A's employer or, as the case may be, the regulatory body shall be regarded as discriminating against A on the gender ground contrary to sections 8 and 13 of the Act which prohibit discrimination in access to employment, conditions of employment, training or experience for or in relation to employment, promotion or regrading, classification of posts and membership of certain bodies.'*

Subsection (c) is amended to 'is not appropriate and necessary and cannot be justified by objective factors unrelated to A's sex'.

No amendment has been made to the provision in respect of indirect discrimination on all grounds other than gender, contained in the 1998 Act, s 31(1). That definition, in respect of the race ground, provides that:

> *'Where a provision (whether in the nature of a requirement, practice or otherwise) relating to employment—*
> *(a) applies to all the employees or prospective employees of a particular employer who include C and D or, as the case may be, to a particular class of those employees or prospective employees which includes C and D,*
> *(b) operates to the disadvantage of C, as compared with D, in relation to any of the matters specified [access to employment etc, as above] in respect of discrimination on the gender ground,*
> *(c) in practice can be complied with by a substantially smaller proportion of the employees or prospective employees having the same relevant characteristic as C when compared with the employees or prospective employees having the same relevant characteristic as D,*
> *(d) cannot be justified as being reasonable on all the circumstances of the case, then, subject to*

[provisions that do not relate to the race ground] for the purpose of this Act the employer shall be regarded as discriminating against C, contrary to section 8, on whichever of the discriminatory grounds give rise to the relevant characteristics. There are similar provisions in respect of a membership of a Regulatory body.'

Irish legislation at present therefore permits the justification of indirect discrimination on the grounds of race as being reasonable in all the circumstances of the case.

On implementation of the Directive, indirect discrimination on the grounds of race can only be justified where it can be shown that the indirectly discriminating provision, criterion or practice is objectively justified by a legitimate aim and the means of achieving that aim are appropriate and neccssary.

This will require amendment such as the amendments introduced by the European Community (Burden of Proof in Gender Discrimination Cases) Regulations, 2001, and that provision itself will require enhancement, as it makes no reference to the requirement that there be a legitimate aim. It will become much more difficult for employers or such bodies to justify indirect discrimination on the race ground.

The Directive must be implemented by 19 July 2003. There is no provision for extending this deadline.

7.1.7   ANTI-DISCRIMINATION (PAY) ACT, 1974

7.1.7.1   Introduction

The Anti-Discrimination (Pay) Act, 1974 ('the 1974 Act') came into operation on 31 December 1975 and introduced the principle of equal pay for like work into Irish law. It was repealed when the Employment Equality Act, 1998 came into effect on 18 October 1999. It complied with the terms of the Equal Pay Directive and article 119 of the EC Treaty. It established a legal right to equal pay for men and women employed on 'like' work by the same employer (or an associated one). The device used to achieve the aim of the 1974 Act was to imply into the contract of the person employed a term conferring an entitlement to equal pay.

7.1.7.2   Employment Equality Act, 1998—remuneration provisions between women and men

Where 'A' and 'B' are persons of opposite sex, the Act provides at s 19(1):

'it shall be a term of the contract under which A is employed that, subject to this Act, A shall at any time be entitled to the same rate of remuneration for the work which A is employed to do as B who, at that or any other relevant time, is employed to do like work by the same or an associated employer.'

At s 19(3) the Act provides:

'where B's employer is an associated employer of A's employer, A and B shall not be regarded as employed to do like work unless they both have the same or reasonably comparable terms and conditions of employment.'

Men and women employed on like work at the same place by the same employer, or in the same area by two associated employers, are entitled to the same remuneration. Remuneration means any consideration in cash or kind received directly or indirectly by an employee from the employer in respect of his employment, excluding pension rights. The case law which developed around the previous legislation, the Anti-Discrimination (Pay) Act, 1974, will continue to assist in interpreting the equal remuneration provisions of the 1998 Act.

7.1.7.3　Case law

The Labour Court in *Linson Ltd v ASTMS* DEP 2/77 held that remuneration covered all benefits based on the wage or salary received by an employee. The definition must also be taken to include bonus payments, marriage gratuities, house purchase loans, and benefits in kind such as company cars and VHI cover. Prior to the 1998 legislation it also included pension rights, which are expressly excluded in the definitions section of that Act.

In *Garland v British Rail Engineering Ltd* [1982] ICR 420 the European Court of Justice held that the provision of travel concessions for retired male employees constituted discrimination against retired female employees who did not receive the same facilities. The travel concession was not a legal obligation forming part of the contract between the employer and employee (pensioner) but as a concessionary right which nonetheless was held to constitute remuneration within the meaning of article 119 of the EC Treaty. In Ireland the Labour Court held, before the 1998 Act, that the provision of pension benefits came within the scope of the 1974 Act (see *Clery & Co [1941] Ltd v O'Brien* EP17/84).

The full scope of the necessity for equal treatment is well illustrated in the case of *Meyers v Adjudication Officer* [1995] IRLR 498 where the European Court of Justice considered the availability of what is known as 'family credit' under the UK Social Security Act 1986. Family credit is an income-related benefit awarded to supplement the income of low-paid workers who are responsible for a child. Ms Meyers' application for family credit was rejected on the grounds that her income was greater than the level conferring the entitlement. Ms Meyers argued, however, that in order to be able to work she had to incur childcare costs and that, in failing to permit her to deduct such childcare costs for the purposes of calculating her income to qualify for the benefit, she had been discriminated against as a single parent since it is easier for couples to arrange their working hours so that children may be looked after by one of them. She claimed that this constituted indirect discrimination on grounds of sex since most single parents are women. While the ECJ did not comment on whether there was discrimination—which was referred back to the national court—it did hold that a benefit such as family credit, which is concerned with both access to employment and working conditions, is not excluded from the scope of the Directive even though it is a State social security measure, and to confine the concept of an employment benefit or working condition solely to those working conditions which are set out in the contract of employment or applied by the employer in respect of a worker's employment, is not sufficiently wide to meet the terms of the Directive which cover the wider concept of an 'employment relationship'.

Under the 1974 Act it was not necessary for a person seeking to establish a comparison of like work to compare themselves to a male or female in a contemporaneous employment. The position remains unchanged by the 1998 Act. In *McCarthy's v Smith* [1980] IRLR 210 Mrs Smith was paid less per week than a man who had, until some four months before she took up the job, held the same position. The European Court held that she could claim equal pay to that of her predecessor but left it to be decided as a question of fact in every case whether or not a pay differential was due to sex discrimination or whether it could be explained by the operation of other facts unconnected with sex.

7.1.7.4　Red circling

An employer may pay different rates of pay to male and female employees justified by objective criteria where this can be factors unrelated to sex. Red circling may be allowed in circumstances where an employee's rate of pay could be said to be above the normal rate for the job. Such a person could be red circled, thereby disallowing comparisons. This may happen, for example, if a long-serving male employee were to suffer a partially incapacitating illness and then be moved to a less demanding job. If he is allowed to retain his higher rate of pay on humanitarian grounds, then it is possible to red circle him for comparison purposes (see *Minister for Transport v Campbell* [1996] ELR 106 and *Department of Tourism v 4 Workers* [1997] ELR 1).

7.1.7.5 Reference of disputes

Under the 1998 Act, a dispute over entitlements to equal pay may be referred by either party to the Director of Equality Investigations, who may refer the case for mediation to an equality mediation officer or investigate the case and hear evidence in private. Any party to a dispute may then appeal to the Labour Court if dissatisfied with the decision, or if the recommendation has not been implemented. Appeal to the High Court is allowed but only on points of law.

7.1.7.6 Time limits

Even though action under the 1998 Act is based on contract, the ordinary limitation period of six years under the Statute of Limitations, 1957 does not apply. Section 8(4) and (5) of the Act provide that arrears of remuneration may only be backdated three years from the date on which the relevant dispute was referred to an equality officer.

The 1974 Act was repealed by and replaced with the 1998 Act.

7.1.8 EMPLOYMENT EQUALITY ACT, 1977

The Employment Equality Act, 1977 ('the 1977 Act') derived from the Equal Treatment Directive. The Act provided for equal treatment as regards access to employment, conditions of employment other than remuneration or conditions relating to occupational pension schemes, training, promotion and regrading. The Act also made unlawful certain discriminatory practices in relation to employment committed by bodies such as employment agencies, vocational training organisations, employers' organisations, trade unions and professional bodies. The Act also provided for a prohibition on the display or publication of discriminatory advertisements.

Discrimination was defined in s 2 of the Act as occurring in any of the following cases:

(a) where by reason of his sex, a person is treated less favourably than a person of the other sex;

(b) where because of his marital status a person is treated less favourably than another person of the same sex;

(c) where because of his sex or marital status a person is obliged to comply with a requirement relating to employment or membership of a body referred to in s 5 which is not an essential requirement for such employment or membership and in respect of which the proportion of persons of the other sex or (as the case may be) of a different marital status but of the same sex able to comply is substantially higher; or

(d) where a person is penalised for having in good faith, made a reference under the 1977 Act or the 1974 Act.

7.2 EMPLOYMENT EQUALITY ACT, 1998

7.2.1 CONSTITUTIONALLY REPUGNANT PROVISIONS

The Employment Equality Bill, 1996, passed all stages in both houses of the Oireachtas on 26 March 1997. The President referred the Bill in its entirety to the Supreme Court under Article 26 of the Constitution on 3 April 1997, to determine whether or not any provisions of the Bill were inconsistent with the Constitution. The Supreme Court held that three aspects of the Employment Equality Bill, 1996 were so repugnant.

In December 1997 a revised version was published which essentially amended the 1996 Bill only to the extent necessary to take account of the Supreme Court's objections. The Act was finally passed into law in early 1998 and came into effect on 18 October 1998.

In the 1998 Act, the provisions found to be unconstitutional in the Employment Equality Bill, 1996 have been replaced as follows:

(a) Sections 16(3) and 35 have been drafted so that the employer is obliged to bear the cost of special treatment or facilities, arising from the employment of a person with a disability, only in so far as these costs are nominal in nature. The term 'nominal' has not been defined and it is not clear whether or not it will be defined in relation to the resources of the employer on a case by case basis, or as some absolute definition of the term. The 1996 Bill had required an employer, in certain circumstances, to provide special treatment or facilities to a person with a disability unless the employer could show undue hardship. The Supreme Court held that the costs associated with the provision of such treatment or facilities constituted an unjust attack on the property rights of the employer.

(b) Section 15 and the definition of 'proceedings' have been redrafted so that vicarious liability is applied only in respect of civil proceedings. The 1996 Bill applied the principle of vicarious liability in both civil and criminal proceedings which was found to be unconstitutional.

(c) Section 63(3) of the 1996 Bill, which had allowed for the use of a certificate as evidence of an offence, was also found to be unconstitutional, contrary to Article 38.1 of the Constitution. No similar provision appears in the 1998 Act.

7.2.2   PROVISIONS OF THE 1998 ACT

The 1998 Act replaced the Anti-Discrimination (Pay) Act, 1974 and the Employment Equality Act, 1977. The substantial body of case law which had developed under the earlier legislation remains binding in so far as the legislative provisions they interpret are consistent with the 1998 Act. New grounds of discrimination were created, new areas of discrimination were identified and, for the first time, statutory definitions of sexual harassment and indirect discrimination were created.

The Act prohibits discrimination in relation to:

(a) access to employment;

(b) conditions of employment;

(c) training or experience for or in relation to employment;

(d) promotion or regrading; or

(e) classification of post.

The discrimination outlawed by the legislation is on the following grounds:

(i) gender;

(ii) marital status;

(iii) family status;

(iv) sexual orientation;

(v) religion;

(vi) age;

(vii) disability;

(viii) race/nationality/ethnic or national origins; and

(ix) membership of the traveller community.

7.2.3 GENDER

7.2.3.1 UK case law

An interesting claim was brought to the EAT in the UK in *Fire Brigades Union v Fraser* [1997] IRLR 671. An allegation of sexual harassment was made against Mr Fraser and he was suspended from duty pending investigation. Both Mr Fraser and the female employee concerned were members of the Fire Brigades Union. The union decided to support the female employee in the investigation and refused to pay for a solicitor to represent Mr Fraser at the disciplinary hearing. The EAT held that the union had discriminated against Mr Fraser on grounds of sex by refusing to afford him access to representation or legal assistance for the purpose of disciplinary proceedings. The EAT held that the industrial tribunal was entitled to draw an inference of sex discrimination from the union's failure to provide a satisfactory explanation for denying Mr Fraser the right to representation. In a dissenting judgment the President of the EAT held that there was no material on which the industrial tribunal could conclude that the union's behaviour was gender related and therefore the inference which the tribunal drew, that a woman would have been treated differently, was unjustified. He was of the view that the industrial tribunal had effectively decided that the union had behaved unfairly and drew from that an inference that the union had been guilty of sex discrimination. He was clearly of the view that this was not a gender issue.

A UK employment tribunal made an equally interesting finding in *Armstrong v Prison Officers' Association*, case no 2401194/94. A trade union refused representation at disciplinary hearings to a female member who complained of sexual harassment by a male colleague, also a member of the union. The woman member claimed that the union's failure to represent her was unlawful sex discrimination, both direct and indirect. The tribunal found against her, holding that she was refused representation because she was not the accused, not because she was a woman. They found that the union's actions and inactions were not influenced by reasons of gender.

7.2.3.2 Irish case law

In *A Worker v Mid Western Health Board* [1996] ELR 1 the Labour Court determined:

(a) to establish discrimination on gender grounds, a complainant must show *both* less favourable treatment and that such treatment arises from the sex of the complainant;

(b) there is no discrimination if nurses are assigned to different tasks because of their gender. The legislation is only contravened if the assignments are less favourable treatment because of gender; and

(c) a decision to assign a particular task to a nurse of a particular sex is not less favourable treatment if the task is within the range of responsibilities for which the nurse was employed.

See also *Martin Smyth v Eastern Health Board* [1996] ELR 72.

In *Field v Irish Carton Printers* [1994] ELR 129 a free taxi service was provided to female employees on shift work when public transport was not available. The male claimant sought to be included in the taxi arrangement but this was refused. He brought a claim under the employment equality legislation seeking to prove that he was engaged on like work to a female comparator and for the purposes of the 1974 Act was denied remuneration in the form of provision of a free taxi service. He also claimed he was discriminated against because he was male in relation to a condition of employment under the 1977 Act. The equality officer held:

(1) The claim was admissible under the Anti-Discrimination (Pay) Act, 1974 as provision of a taxi service is a benefit-in-kind and consequently remuneration.

(2) The company had not established a 'real need' for the agreement negotiated with the trade union representing the female employees.

(3) The taxi service was provided for the protection of female staff and there were no legitimate 'grounds other than sex' to justify the provision of taxis.

(4) The taxi facility should be made available to the claimant.

7.2.4 MARITAL STATUS

Section 2 of the 1998 Act defines marital status as meaning single, married, separated, divorced or widowed persons. The inclusion of single persons for the first time in the definition of marital status will preclude employers from making certain benefits available to employees because they are married. If, for example, health benefits are to be provided for single employees only but where employees are married the benefit is extended to the spouse and possibly also the children, this would constitute discrimination on grounds of marital status but for s 34(1)(b) of the Act, which is set out below.

In *Eagle Star Insurance Co (Ireland) Ltd v A Worker* [1998] ELR 306 the company operated a staff discount scheme whereby staff and their spouses were entitled to discounted motor policies for themselves. The worker concerned was a single man with a female partner who was a named driver on his policy. Because of the terms of the company scheme the discount was not available in respect of his female partner. He claimed that this was discrimination on grounds of his marital status under the Employment Equality Act, 1977. The company argued inter alia that a single person does not have a 'marital status' and that there was no discrimination under the 1977 Act. The equality officer at first instance found in favour of the employee on the basis that the company treated married persons more favourably than single persons by providing them with discounted policies in respect of their spouses. If the claimant was married he would have benefited from the company scheme; however, as he was single he was denied the benefit and this constituted discrimination under the 1977 Act. A sum of £1,000 by way of compensation for stress was awarded. On appeal the Labour Court found that the 'advantage of the married employee amounts to less favourable treatment of the single, or non-married employee, including the claimant'. The court upheld the recommendation of the equality officer including the award of £1,000 for stress. See also *Ormiston v Gypsum Industries* [1993] ELR 1 which dealt with VHI benefit.

In examining such benefits and the extension of the benefits to members of an employee's family, s 34(1)(b) of the 1998 Act states:

'(1) *In relation to the discriminatory grounds . . . nothing in this Part . . . shall make it unlawful for an employer to provide— . . .*
(b) *a benefit to or in respect of a person as a member of an employee's family.'*

7.2.5 FAMILY STATUS

Family status is defined as where a person has responsibility for someone else under the age of 18. Employers must examine recruitment practices in light of the various discriminatory grounds created by the 1998 Act and this is one particular area that requires examination. If a person who has a child fails to secure a job at interview, that person may now claim discrimination and the employer may have to explain the reasons why the applicant failed to get the job, which previously an employer was not normally in law required to do. It is, however, the usual result of equality claims even under previous legislation. In *An Employee v An Employer* [1995] ELR 139 the female employee concerned had been employed by the employer until she resigned on marriage in 1972. She had subsequently worked with the employer from time to time on a temporary basis. She applied for a permanent job but was unsuccessful. She claimed that the recruitment manager had told her that the reason for her failure to obtain a permanent position was because of her inflexibility due to her domestic background, she being separated and having two children. She claimed that she had been discriminated against on the basis of her employer's perception that she was inflexible and not transferable due to her childcare responsibilities and was discriminated against on the grounds of her sex and/or marital status. The employer contested the grounds of non-selection stating that it related to her overall suitability and not as alleged by the claimant. The equality officer held in favour of the claimant stating:

> 'The status of male candidates or female candidates who did not have the same childcare responsibilities would not have been similarly perceived by the employer as irreconcilable with the capacity to give a commitment to a permanent career position. The claimant was discriminated against within the meaning of s 2 of the Employment Equality Act, 1977 and contrary to s 3 thereof.'

7.2.6   SEXUAL ORIENTATION

7.2.6.1   European Court of Justice

Protection against discrimination on grounds of sexual orientation does not expressly exist in European law, UK law or US law. The protection is, however, available under the 1998 Act. The European Court of Justice considered the issue of sexual orientation in *Grant v South-West Trains Ltd* [1998] IRLR 206. Lisa Grant was a clerical worker, employed by South-West Trains who lived in a stable relationship with a same-sex partner. Staff of SWT were provided with free and reduced rate travel concessions which extended to 'your spouse and dependants'. Privilege tickets were also granted to 'a married member of staff for one legal spouse . . . and . . . for one common law spouse (of the opposite sex) subject to a statutory declaration being made that a meaningful relationship has existed for period of two or more years'.

Ms Grant requested travel concessions for her female partner but this was turned down because her partner was not of the opposite sex. Ms Grant claimed that the rejection of her request was contrary to the principle of equal pay for men and women established by article 119 of the EC Treaty and article 1 of the Equal Pay Directive.

The European Court of Justice held as follows:

> 'A refusal by an employer to grant travel concessions to a person of the same sex with whom a worker has a stable relationship does not constitute discrimination based directly on the sex of the worker prohibited by Article 119 of the EC Treaty or the Equal Pay Directive. Even where such concessions are allowed to the person of the opposite sex with whom a worker has a stable relationship outside marriage.

> 'A condition which applies in the same way to female and male workers cannot be regarded as constituting discrimination directly based on sex. In the present case the travel concessions are refused to a male worker living with a person of the same sex just as they are to a female worker if she is living a person of the same sex.

> 'Discrimination based on sexual orientation does not constitute discrimination based on the sex of the worker within the meaning of Article 119. European Community law does not cover discrimination based on sexual orientation. The reasoning of the Court in *P v S*

and Cornwall County Council [1996] IRLR 347 that discrimination based on a worker's gender re-assignment is based essentially on the sex of the person concerned and is therefore prohibited, is limited to the case of a worker's gender re-assignment and does not apply to differences of treatment based on a person's sexual orientation.

'European Community law does not regard stable relationships between two persons of the same sex as the equivalent of marriages or stable relationships outside marriage between two persons of the opposite sex. Consequently Community law does not require an employer to treat the situation of a person who has a stable relationship with a partner of the same sex as equivalent to that of a person who is married or has a stable relationship outside marriage with a partner of the opposite sex.'

7.2.6.2   UK and Irish case law

Grant v South-West Trains Ltd was followed by the High Court in the UK in *R v Secretary of State for Defence, ex parte Perkins* [1998] IRLR 508. In that case the High Court stated that the decision of the European Court of Justice in *Grant* was 'that Community law does not cover or render unlawful discrimination based on sexual orientation'. In this particular case Mr Perkins was discharged by the Royal Navy because of his homosexual orientation. His claim that this breached UK and European law on discrimination was rejected in light of the *Grant* decision.

See also *Smith v Gardner Merchant Ltd* [1998] IRLR 510 which was a sexual harassment case where the applicant claimed that the harassment occurred because of his sexual orientation. While following the *Grant* decision the Court of Appeal also held that Mr Smith was entitled to pursue a sexual harassment case albeit on other grounds, ie because he was male not because he was a male with a particular sexual orientation.

In the Irish case of *A Worker v Brookfield Leisure Ltd* [1994] ELR 79 the claimant was dismissed from her job in a leisure centre after it was claimed that she had been seen kissing another woman in the changing rooms of the leisure centre. The claimant denied the allegation. Following her dismissal the claimant claimed against her employer under the Employment Equality Act, 1977 and argued that she was dismissed by the respondent because of her sexual orientation on the basis that the respondent was aware that she was a lesbian and that this did not adversely affect her until such time as the allegations, which she denied, were made. The claimant argued that if she had not been homosexual or if she had been a male employee she would not have been dismissed, and argued that discrimination on the grounds of sexual orientation was prohibited by the 1977 Act. She further argued that lesbianism was a characteristic unique to females and thus any action against such females was a breach of the 1977 Act. The Labour Court, however, dismissed the claim on the basis that the unfair treatment she did suffer did not arise from any attribute of her sex but of her sexual orientation and, in all probability, a man would have suffered the same treatment for a similar display of his sexual orientation. That decision is now overruled.

A very similar decision was made by the UK Court of Appeal in *Pearce v Mayfield Secondary School* [2001] IRLR 669 where, on appeal, it was held that homophobic harassment and abuse of a lesbian teacher by pupils was not discrimination contrary to the UK's Sex Discrimination Act 1975. It was held that a homosexual man would have received similar abuse to that meted out to Ms Pearce, a lesbian woman, who was called a 'lesbian', 'dyke', 'lesbian shit', 'lemon', 'lezzie' or 'lez'. The Court of Appeal held that her harassment resulted from her sexual orientation, or the perception of it. The court said that there was nothing to suggest that, apart from the actual words of abuse, a male homosexual teacher would have been treated any differently by the pupils, or that the course adopted by the school authorities in the face of the problem was less favourable to the applicant than the course which would have been adopted to deal with identical harassment directed at a homosexual male. Such a decision could not now be made in Ireland, as discrimination on the grounds of sexual orientation is expressly prohibited. Section 2 of the 1998 Act defines 'sexual orientation' as meaning:

'Heterosexual, homosexual or bisexual orientation'.

7.2.6.3 Transsexuals

It should be noted that, unlike the UK where specific regulations have been enacted, transsexuals are not specifically covered by the legislation and persons who undergo a sex change may, depending on the nature of the work and the possible requirement for a person of a particular sex, have difficulty if their employment is terminated because of their change of status from male to female, or female to male as the case may be. The case of *P v S and Cornwall County Council* [1996] IRLR 347 suggests that transsexuals must in fact be protected under domestic law on gender discrimination, although the case arose in the context of the UK Sex Discrimination Act 1975. The effect of this ruling was that it applied immediately in the public sector, as a directly enforceable European directive. The private sector position was less clear. In *Chessington World of Adventures Ltd v Reed* [1998] IRLR 56 the EAT in the UK held that discrimination against transsexuals was to be regarded as unlawful discrimination on the grounds of sex contrary to the UK sex discrimination legislation. By analogy with sexual harassment and pregnancy discrimination a new category of discrimination was created. It is very likely that this decision will be followed in Ireland, in interpreting the Employment Equality Act, 1998.

The European Court of Justice held that where Mr P was hired as a male employee in 1991, subsequently had a gender reassignment and became a woman, her consequential dismissal was a breach of the Equal Treatment Directive. The court held:

'Where such discrimination arises . . . from the gender reassignment of the person concerned, he or she is treated unfavourably by comparisons with persons of the sex to which he or she was deemed to belong before undergoing gender reassignment.'

The Advocate General's opinion in this case is very helpful in clarifying the concepts of discrimination.

7.2.7 RELIGIOUS BELIEF

Religious belief includes having no religious belief. The Department of Education pays salaries of chaplains employed in community schools. Such payment was challenged as being in breach of Article 44.2.2 of the Constitution by which the State guarantees 'not to endow any religion' in *Campaign to Separate Church and State Ltd and Murphy v Minister for Education* [1996] ELR 164. Costello J held in that case:

(1) The purpose of the payment is to recompense the recipient for the service which is rendered and not to endow religion and as so is constitutionally licit.

(2) A further purpose of the payment is to fulfil the State's obligation to respect the parental rights and facilitate their exercise and it therefore does not infringe the Constitution.

(3) The prohibition against endowment of religion must be construed as permitting state aid to assist in the religious formation of children in accordance with their parents' wishes and accordingly the payment of chaplains in schools is not unconstitutional.

(4) The payment to hospital chaplains does not infringe Article 44 because the purpose of the payment is to assist in caring for the spiritual and religious needs of hospital patients (which the State acknowledges that as human persons they possess) and not for the purpose of endowing any religion and is accordingly constitutionally valid.

191

Religious discrimination has been prohibited in Northern Ireland since 1976 and a substantial body of case law has been developed there. It is likely to be considered with interest, if not closely followed, by the Director of Equality Investigations in interpreting the 1998 Act.

7.2.8 AGE

Where persons are aged between 18 and 65 no discrimination is permitted on grounds of age. Again, this will cause considerable difficulty for employers in recruitment. Older people who fail to secure jobs as against younger competition may bring discrimination claims. Unlike US law the 1998 Act does not simply protect workers over the age of 40; it prohibits discrimination between employees/applicants who are of different ages. Young employees/applicants, who are not promoted/appointed because they are assumed to be immature or too young for responsibility, may also bring discrimination claims. The EAT held that selection for redundancy on the grounds of age constituted unfair dismissal in *Kerrigan v Peter Owens Advertising and Marketing Ltd* UD 31/97 where the claimant gave evidence to the EAT that the grounds for his redundancy included his age. The EAT rejected the company's claim that a redundancy situation existed and stated 'from the evidence produced we determine that the claimant's dismissal arose wholly or mainly from his age in contravention of s 6(2) of the Unfair Dismissals Act, 1977 as amended'.

An equality officer held against Ryanair in proceedings brought by the Equality Authority under the 1998 Act, s 85 at the end of 2000—*Equality Authority v Ryanair* DEC-E/2000/14. Ryanair advertised for a 'young and dynamic professional' in the Irish Times. It was held that they breached the age discrimination provisions of the Act. This provision does not require the employer to intend to discriminate. The question for the equality officer is whether or not the advertisement could be reasonably understood to indicate an intention to discriminate. The equality officer held that the advertisement could be reasonably understood to indicate that intention. The proceedings were brought by the Equality Authority. It had not sought an injunction, nor had it brought proceedings against the publisher of the advertisement, the newspaper. The equality officer recommended that the Equality Authority should, in further cases, consider making use of its powers under the Act to seek an injunction preventing a recruitment process going ahead where it appears to be discriminatory, and take action against both the publisher and the employer, as appropriate.

7.2.9 DISABILITY

7.2.9.1 Generally

The ground of disability does not apply where the person is not willing to do, or fully capable of doing, the job in question. However, in the case of a person with a disability fully capable of doing the job it may be construed as including doing the job with the assistance of special services or facilities. An employer may, however, where an employee is restricted in his ability to do a job by reason of a disability, pay a different rate of pay to that person for that reason. On the other side of the coin, the employer is allowed to provide special treatment or facilities to a person with a disability which they do not have to extend to other persons who are not similarly disabled. In relation to the provision of facilities or special treatment, the employer does not have to go to expense or cost *'other than costs of a nominal value'*. It remains to be seen what yardstick will be applied in this regard. Section 2 of the 1998 Act contains a comprehensive definition of disability as meaning:

'(a) *the total or partial absence of a person's bodily or mental functions, including the absence of a part of a person's body;*

(b) *the presence in the body of organisms causing, or likely to cause, chronic disease or illness;*

(c)   the malfunction, malformation or disfigurement of a part of a person's body;

(d)   a condition or malfunction which results in a person learning differently from a person without the condition or malfunction; or

(e)   a condition, illness or disease which affects a person's thought processes, perception of reality, emotions or judgment or which results in disturbed behaviour.'

This is a very wide-ranging medical definition and may cover a very considerable number of physical and mental conditions, both of job applicants and existing employees.

7.2.9.2   UK case law

Several UK cases relating to existing employees are instructive; however, the definition of disability in the UK legislation is more restrictive than in the Irish 1998 Act, whereas the UK concept of reasonable adjustment is unfettered by 'nominal cost', unlike the Irish concept of reasonable accommodation. In *Morse v Wiltshire County Council* [1998] IRLR 352 Mr Morse was employed as a road worker. Following a road traffic accident he was left with a 20 per cent disability involving limited movement and grip in his right hand, stiffness in his right leg and susceptibility to blackouts. The occupational health physician recommended that when Mr Morse returned to work he not operate in certain areas and with certain equipment or drive vehicles. Subsequently a redundancy situation arose in the county council and the relevant department took the view that it required to retain only the most flexible workforce, particularly in order to carry out its obligation to provide a winter road service. That required fully qualified drivers. Mr Morse was restricted from driving a vehicle due to his disability. He was selected for redundancy on the grounds of his lack of flexibility. He complained that this was a breach of the Disability Discrimination Act 1995. That Act contains a requirement that an employer make reasonable adjustments in the method of operation to accommodate disabled persons and that the employer in this case had not taken the steps 'reasonably to avoid dismissing a disabled employee' and was in breach of the legislation.

In *Kenny v Hampshire Constabulary* [1999] IRLR 76 the Employment Appeal Tribunal held that only job-related arrangements need be made by the employer. In *Clark v Novacold Ltd* [1999] IRLR 318 Mr Clark had been employed in manual and physically demanding jobs but suffered a back injury involving a soft tissue spinal injury. This resulted in his absence from work. In light of the length of his absence from work he was dismissed from service. He claimed that this constituted discrimination under the Disability Discrimination Act 1995. His claim was rejected on the grounds that he was treated no differently from a person in similar circumstances, who was not disabled, would have been treated. The EAT held that the proper comparator where a disabled person is dismissed for absence related to their disability is someone who is off work for the same amount of time but for a reason other than disability. This was overturned on appeal. The Court of Appeal held that the proper comparator was an employee who was not absent from work as it was disability related absence which led to the dismissal, and therefore the comparator was an employee to whom the absenteeism reason did not or would not apply.

7.2.9.3   Irish case law

There has been one decision under the 1998 Act in respect of discrimination on the ground of disability, *William Gorry v Manpower* DEC-E/2001/017.

Manpower placed a newspaper advertisement seeking applications for the position of switchboard operator in Eircom. The complainant applied and was invited to forward his CV. He stated on his CV that he had had a slight visual impairment since birth. He was not called for interview and he alleged that he was directly and indirectly discriminated against in his application for the post on the ground of his disability, contrary to the 1998 Act. The respondent denied discrimination.

The equality officer found that the complainant established a prima facie case of direct discrimination on the basis of his qualifications and previous experience as a switchboard operator for Eircom and on the basis that it had not been alleged that there was an issue with the complainant's previous performance. The respondent defended the claim by reference to what it described as an Eircom policy of not employing ex-employees. The equality officer noted that the respondent had processed the complainant's application for employment in 1999 even though his CV at that time also referred to his health. The equality officer found that an Eircom policy of not re-employing people who previously worked for Eircom, and who had left under a specific voluntary leaving scheme, had been misapplied to the complainant. The equality officer found that the misapplication of the policy was the reason for the non-processing of the complainant's application and that the respondent did not directly discriminate against the complainant on the disability ground. The equality officer also found that the complainant had failed to establish a prima facie case of indirect discrimination on the disability ground.

The equality officer found that the respondent rebutted the complainant's prima facie case of direct discrimination on the disability ground, on the balance of probability. She also found that the complainant failed to establish a prima facie case of indirect discrimination.

7.2.10 RACE

7.2.10.1 Ethnic origins

The full definition of the term 'race' is contained in s 6(2) of the 1998 Act and defines the ground of race as being differences 'in . . . race, colour, nationality or ethnic or national origins'. The question of 'ethnic' origins was considered in some detail in *Mandla v Lee* [1983] IRLR 209 by the UK House of Lords. The Lords stated that a group may be defined by reference to its 'ethnic origins' if it constitutes a separate and distinct community by virtue of characteristics which are commonly associated with common racial origin and is a term 'appreciably wider than strictly racial or biological'. In defining an ethnic group the Lords stated that a group must regard itself, and be regarded by others, as a distinct community by virtue of certain characteristics and went on to state that it was essential in order to constitute an ethnic group that there be the following:

(a) a long shared history of which the group is conscious as distinguishing it from other groups and the memory of which it keeps alive;

(b) a cultural tradition of its own including family and social customs and manners often but not necessarily associated with religious observance. In addition there are other relevant characteristics, one or more of which will commonly be found and will help to distinguish the group from the secondary community;

(c) either a common geographical origin or descent from a small number of common ancestors;

(d) a common language, not necessarily peculiar to the group;

(e) a common literature peculiar to the group;

(f) a common religion different from that of the neighbouring groups or from the general community surrounding it; and

(g) a sense of being a minority or being an oppressed or a dominant group within a larger community.

7.2.10.2 Application of ethnic origins test

As an example of how the test in *Mandla* may be used, it was held in *Dawkins v Department of the Environment* [1993] IRLR 284 by the Court of Appeal that Rastafarians are not a separate 'racial group' within the ethnic group of the Afro-Caribbean community. The court held that, although they are a separate group with identifiable characteristics, they have not established some separate identity by reference to their ethnic origins, and that comparing Rastafarians with the rest of the Jamaican community in England or with the rest of the Afro-Caribbean community there was nothing to set them aside as a separate ethnic group. Rastafarians are likely to be protected by the religious discrimination provisions of the 1998 Act. It is likely that Mr Dawkins would have brought his claim on the grounds of religious discrimination had religious discrimination been prohibited in England, which it is not.

On the matter of nationality the Court of Appeal held in *Dhatt v McDonald's Hamburgers Ltd* [1991] ICR 226 that an application form which distinguished between British citizens and EU nationals, on the one hand, and those who were neither British citizens nor EU nationals on the other hand, did not discriminate on grounds of nationality.

In *Northern Joint Police Board v Power* [1997] IRLR 610 Mr Power applied for the post of Chief Constable of the Northern Constabulary but was not shortlisted. He claimed this was because he was English rather than Scottish. The EAT held that discrimination against an English person or a Scot based on their 'national origin' was discrimination on 'racial grounds' within the meaning of the Race Relations Act 1976. It held that the Scots and the English are separate racial groups defined by reference to national origin. Mr Power had also claimed that he had been discriminated against on grounds of his 'ethnic origins'. This argument was rejected on the grounds that the Scots and the English do not have different 'ethnic origins'.

In *Bryans v Northumberland College of Arts and Technology* [1995] COIT in England an Irish employee was a special needs lecturer at a technical college. One of his colleagues called him an 'Irish prat'. He regarded this as racial harassment and raised a grievance under the college's grievance procedure. The colleague who made the remark refused to offer an apology and the employee's manager delayed in taking action over the grievance. The employee was subsequently denied a place on a shortlist for promotion because he had persisted in pursuing his grievance. He suffered stress as a result of the remark and the delay in investigating and addressing the matter, and was absent from work through illness as a result. He brought a claim of race discrimination to a tribunal. He was awarded a total sum of £29,900 compensation for racial discrimination, having fully succeeded in his claim. The tribunal broke down the elements of the compensation between individuals and the employer. A sum of £15,000 was awarded for injury to feelings and £5,000 for aggravated damages because of the way in which the matter was dealt with. £2,000 was awarded against the college principal, £6,500 against the line manager, £1,500 against the curriculum director and £5,000 against the colleague who made the offensive remark.

7.2.11 MEMBERSHIP OF THE TRAVELLER COMMUNITY

No case law has yet developed in respect of discrimination against travellers in employment, but there have been numerous cases brought by members of the traveller community under the Equal Status Act, 2000 which provides for non-discrimination in the provision of goods and services. In those cases the concept of membership of the travelling (now 'traveller' as amended by the Equal Status Act) community has been broadly interpreted to counteract prejudice against members of the travelling community, whether settled or otherwise.

7.3 EMPLOYER POLICIES

The Supreme Court in the United States, in two decisions handed down in June 1998, *Burlington Industries v Ellerth* [1997] – 69 June 26, 1998 and *Faragher v Boca Raton* [1997] –

282 June 26, 1998 held that in claims of sexual harassment an employer who does not have a policy against sexual harassment in place, notified to staff and operational, while not being devoid of the opportunity to defend a claim of sexual harassment, would have considerable difficulty and it would make it much easier for employees to succeed in claims of sexual harassment in the absence of the existence and promulgation of such a policy. US courts have followed *Ellerth* and *Faragher* to the extent of applying the principle to race discrimination cases. Irish employers would be well advised therefore in light of the provisions of the 1998 Act to either redraft their existing sexual harassment policies to include the other grounds prohibited by the 1998 Act or bring into existence similar type policies to cover the new grounds.

7.4   FORMS OF DISCRIMINATION

In seeking to deal with all areas of employment, the 1998 Act seeks to outlaw discrimination that may be perpetrated as follows:

Discrimination by employers includes access to employment, conditions of employment, training and promotion.

Discrimination in collective agreements with regard to access to, and conditions of, employment and equal pay for like work.

Discriminatory advertising which includes advertising that might reasonably be understood as indicating an intention to discriminate. Under the terms of the 1998 Act, the new Equality Authority may apply to the courts to injunct any proposed appointment of a person to be made on foot of a discriminatory advertisement until such time as the Director of Equality Investigations has made a decision in the matter or the court otherwise orders.

Discrimination by employment agencies: Employment agencies have become a popular target of the legislators in recent years. Under the provisions of the Unfair Dismissals (Amendment) Act, 1993, persons retained through a third party company are deemed to be employees of the employer as is also provided for in the terms of the Employment (Information) Act, 1994. This has proven problematic for employers. While it may appear easy to identify an employment agency, the 1998 Act and the other legislation referred to defines an employment agency as per the provisions of the Employment Agency Act, 1971. The definition of an employment agency in the 1971 Act is very wide and is not limited to licensed employment agencies. The 1971 Act provides:

> '*the business of an Employment Agency means the business of seeking, whether for reward or otherwise, on behalf of others, persons who will give or accept employment and includes the obtaining or supplying for reward of persons who will accept employment from or render services to others.*'

To paraphrase, it can cover:

> 'The business of . . . supplying for reward . . . persons who . . . render services to others.'

In the EAT determination in *Bourton v Narcea Ltd and AIBP* M318 UD 186/94, it was held that the employees of a sub-contractor carrying out sub-contract work on a company's premises may, by virtue of the provisions of the 1993 Act, s 13, be deemed to be employees of that company. See also *Harrods Ltd v Remick* [1997] IRLR 9.

Discrimination in vocational training to include the giving of instruction to carry on any occupational activity. Section 12 of the Act prohibits educational training bodies, and what it describes as 'any person' which must include the employer, from refusing or omitting to afford access to training courses to any person. This requires careful planning by employers who make education and training available to staff to ensure that the offer is made on an open, transparent and across the board way to all relevant employees.

Discrimination by trade unions, professional and trade associations as regards membership and other benefits also became a discriminatory ground under the 1998 Act.

7.5 INDIRECT DISCRIMINATION

7.5.1 TEST FOR INDIRECT DISCRIMINATION

Discrimination may arise in an indirect way where an employer requires or applies a condition equally to men and women but the condition is one with which fewer of one gender than the other can comply. This may arise in situations where discrimination, even inadvertently, may be institutionalised as part of structures, practices or requirements.

The test is whether or not a substantially higher proportion of persons of one sex/marital status is able to comply. In seeking to avoid an allegation of indirect discrimination on the gender ground, an employer must show that the practice complained of is based on objectively verifiable factors which have no relation to the sex of the complainant. This is provided for under the 1998 Act, s 22, as amended. This concept existed in Irish law pre-October 1998 for gender and marital status only. Section 31 of the 1998 Act extends indirect discrimination to all categories of persons covered by the new discrimination grounds. An employer must be able to justify indirect discrimination on the gender ground by *objective factors* unrelated to the employee's sex. The 1998 Act has been amended by the European Communities (Burden of Proof in Gender Discrimination Cases) Regulations, 2001. These regulations give effect to Council Directive 97/18/EC of 15 December 1997 on the burden of proof in cases of discrimination based on sex. They not only address the question of burden of proof, but, at regulation 4, amend the definition of indirect discrimination on the grounds of gender as provided in the 1998 Act, s 22(1).

Prior to the amending regulations, indirect discrimination on the gender ground occurred:

'*where a provision (whether in the nature of a requirement, practice or otherwise) which relates to any of [the grounds] or to membership of a regulatory body*
(a)   *applies to both A and B,*
(b)   *is such that the proportion of persons who are disadvantaged by the provision is substantially higher in the case of those of the same sex as A than in the case of those of the same sex as B, and*
(c)   *cannot be justified by objective factors unrelated to A's sex,*
      then, for the purposes of this Act, A's employer or, as the case may be, the regulatory body shall be regarded as discriminating against A on the gender ground contrary to Sections 8 and 13 of the Act which prohibit discrimination in access to employment, conditions of employment, training or experience for or in relation to employment, promotion or regrading, classification of posts and membership of certain bodies.'

Subsection (c) is amended to 'is not appropriate and necessary and cannot be justified by objective factors unrelated to A's sex'.

No amendment has been made to the provision in respect of indirect discrimination on all grounds other than gender, contained in the 1998 Act, s 31.

Indirect discrimination on the other grounds may be justified by the employer as being *reasonable* in all the circumstances of the case. 'Reasonable' is of course less difficult for an employer to prove than 'appropriate and necessary and justified by objective factors' as provided in the amended s 22 for indirect discrimination between men and women.

7.5.2 NATHAN v BAILEY GIBSON

7.5.2.1 Background

In *Nathan v Bailey Gibson, The Irish Print Union and the Minister for Labour*, Ms Nathan was employed by Bailey Gibson in the manufacture of cartons. She applied for a post which became vacant following the retirement of a man who had operated a folder/gluer machine. Ms Nathan had assisted him on the machine for the ten years prior to his retirement. The man was a member of the IPU. In the printing industry craft workers are organised into specific unions, such as the IPU, while male non-craft employees are organised by the ITGWU and female non-craft workers by the Irish Women Workers Branch of the FWUI.

Bailey Gibson had a closed shop agreement with the IPU in relation to the machine in question, giving IPU members first call on the job when the man retired. If IPU members were unavailable a non-union member could be recruited but would be required to join the IPU and would be granted membership without any distinction whatsoever on the basis of sex.

Bailey Gibson was anxious to appoint Ms Nathan but the IPU would not agree to her appointment. A male IPU member was appointed to the vacant post. Ms Nathan claimed there had been a breach of the Employment Equality Act, 1977 by denying her access to the job and thereby indirectly discriminating against her on the grounds of her sex by making it a requirement that access to the vacant position be confined to members of the IPU which was traditionally male.

7.5.2.2 The Labour Court

The equality officer held that the company had indirectly discriminated against Ms Nathan by making it a requirement that access to the vacant position be confined to persons who held membership of the IPU. The matter was appealed to the Labour Court. The Labour Court, in dealing with the issue of indirect discrimination, ruled that in order for Ms Nathan to succeed in that argument she would have to show that there was a *causal link* between the requirement to have a union card and her sex and only then would it become a relevant consideration as to whether the proportion of men able to comply with the requirement was substantially higher. The Labour Court held that there were no conditions for membership of the IPU which discriminate against women, and while it was factually correct that more men than women have IPU membership, this was because historically males occupied the craft positions in the Irish printing industry. The agreement between the company and the IPU was craft based and when it was imposed on Ms Nathan bore no relationship to her sex. The IPU was indifferent to whether a male or a female was recruited for the job, but given the imbalance (82 per cent male membership, 18 per cent female membership) against females, the likelihood of a female being appointed was far less once the restriction of IPU membership was imposed.

The Labour Court held that the disproportionate impact on women was not causally linked to sex but historic. It was not because she was a woman that she could not become a member of the IPU; it was because she was a non-craft worker in a non-craft union and there were existing IPU members available for employment. Reference was made to *Revenue Commissioners v Kelly* EE9/87 where a requirement of a driving licence was imposed on applicants for a job. The equality officer was unable to establish any attribute of sex which would result in a lower proportion of females than males being able to comply with that requirement. The Labour Court held here that unless the IPU was discriminating between men and women the worker could not claim that the requirement to have an IPU card discriminated against her. As the employee had *failed to make a causal link* between the requirement and her sex, her claim failed.

The matter was appealed to the High Court, where Murphy J held that the Labour Court was correct in requiring a causal link between sex and the job requirement being established by the applicant.

The matter was appealed to the Supreme Court which took a different view from the Labour Court and the High Court.

7.5.2.3 The Supreme Court

The Supreme Court ([1996] ELR 114) on the issue of indirect discrimination held:

(a) The discrimination referred to in Directive 76/207/EEC and the 1977 Act covers both direct and indirect discrimination.

(b) The worker in this case was not required to prove a causal connection between the practice complained of and the sex of the complainant.

(c) It is sufficient for the worker to show that the practice complained of bears significantly more heavily on members of the complainant's sex than on members of the other sex.

(d) Once the claimant has established a prima facie case of discrimination, the onus of proof shifts to the employer to show that the practice complained of is based on *objectively verifiable factors which have no relation to the plaintiff's sex*.

7.5.2.4 Remittance to the Labour Court

Following the Supreme Court decision in her favour Ms Nathan's case was remitted to the Labour Court which reheard the claim in light of the Supreme Court ruling and a decision was issued on 14 August 1997 rejecting Ms Nathan's claim of discrimination; which is now reported at [1998] ELR 52. The Labour Court based its decision on the following:

(1) The practice engaged in by the company, which was sought to be impugned by Ms Nathan, was the recruitment of only IPU card-holding members to certain jobs. The requirement was to be a member of the IPU in order to be eligible for the job to which Ms Nathan sought access.

(2) It was not contradicted that the company, had it not had the obligation in relation to IPU membership, would have sought candidates for the position from its entire workforce including Ms Nathan.

(3) The workforce consisted of eighty-nine persons of whom sixty-one were men and twenty-eight were women. Twenty-one of the male employees were members of the IPU who would have been able to satisfy the requirement of IPU membership. The practice therefore affected twenty-eight women and forty men who were employees of the company but did not hold IPU membership. If a male worker who was not a member of the IPU applied for the post to which Ms Nathan sought access, the same requirement would have applied to him with the same result as complained of by Ms Nathan.

(4) Whereas the equality officer concluded that the impugned requirement affected more women than men because no women held an IPU card, the court found that statistically the requirement affected more men than women. Given the undisputed figures for the workforce and their respective sexes and the undisputed fact that normal recruitment at the time was from within the existing workforce 45 per cent of those who were affected by the impugned practice were male and 31.5 per cent of those affected were females. Those who could comply comprised 23.6 per cent of the workforce.

(5) The practice of requiring a worker to be an IPU member did discriminate against the women employees, including the worker in this case, but not in such numbers

as to amount to discrimination within the meaning of the 1977 Act, s 3 since it was male employees who are more significantly affected.

(6) The court referred to the fact that the position referred to was eventually filled by a male non-IPU member who, at the time Ms Nathan complained of being discriminated against, was himself also 'equally disadvantaged'.

(7) The court concluded from the statistics referred to above that the practice complained of did not bear significantly more heavily on members of the female sex but rather bore more heavily on members of the male sex. The court held that there was no evidence that the obtaining of an IPU card was made more difficult by the company for the women employees than it was for the male employees.

(8) In light of the above the court held that there were no sex based criteria operated by the company which resulted in the non-selection of Ms Nathan for the position she sought and the claim failed.

(9) The court did hold that the company was responsible for accepting the constraints of a 'closed shop' arrangement and therefore was also responsible for the effect that practice had on its employees. The practice was, however, held not to be discriminatory of females.

7.5.3 BURDEN OF PROOF

Employers must now examine all work practices carefully to ensure that they do not give rise to discrimination as a result of some inadvertent ingrained or institutionalised practice which disproportionally affects one person as against another on one of the discriminatory grounds as set out in the 1998 Act, s 6. The practice of requiring telephonists to accept transfers and assignments throughout the country at short notice was held to be discriminatory in that it was unnecessarily onerous on married persons in *Department of Posts and Telegraphs v Mullins* EE1/78 DEE2/78.

In dealing with the proportion of persons able to comply or not comply with a requirement, use of statistics has become very prevalent. While the *Nathan* decision will have eased the task of employees they must be prepared to deal with the possibility that the burden of proof will shift back to them and be in a position to deal with the requirement to make a more substantial case. In showing disproportionate impact, the starting point must be a group or pool of persons who in turn will be sub-divided in percentage terms to show disproportionate impact. Employers in turn must anticipate such arguments and themselves prepare statistical analyses. Those who cannot do so or cannot objectively justify the job requirement must reconsider what they are doing and change their ways. A recent decision of McCracken J on a claim of indirect discrimination focused on the approach to be taken to such cases and, in particular, the approach taken by the Labour Court in the wake of the Supreme Court decision in *Nathan v Bailey Gibson* [1996] ELR 114. In *Conlan v University of Limerick* [1999] ELR 155 the plaintiff was a lecturer in law in the University of Limerick. The defendant advertised the position of Professor of Law, a portion of the advertisement for which read as follows:

'Applications are invited from suitably qualified candidates holding a higher law degree, preferably at doctorate level. The successful candidate will have several years' experience at a senior academic level and be a leading published researcher in a specialised field of law.'

The plaintiff applied for the position but was not shortlisted on the grounds that there were other candidates whose qualifications and experience more closely matched the requirements of the defendants. The plaintiff claimed inter alia that in requiring that an applicant should have several years' experience at a senior academic level the defendant was indirectly discriminating against her on grounds of her sex in that this requirement meant that there would be very few females qualified for the post because there were very few females at a senior academic level. Her claims were rejected by the equality officer and the Labour Court. In referring to *Nathan v Bailey Gibson* [1996] ELR 114 McCracken J followed the principle set down in that case that initially it is for the worker to show that the practice complained of bears more heavily on one sex than on the other. Once this is established it is then for the employer to show that, notwithstanding this fact, the practice complained of is in fact based on factors which are unconnected with the sex of the worker. In this regard the onus of proof is clearly on the employer. He went on to quote Hamilton J at p 128 of that judgment where he said:

'In such a case the worker is not required, in the first instance, to prove a causal connection between the practice complained of and the sex of the complainant. It is sufficient for the worker to show that the practice complained of bears significantly more heavily on members of the complainant's sex than on members of the other sex. At that stage the complainant has established a prima facie case of discrimination and the onus of proof shifts to the employer to show that the practice complained of is based on objectively verifiable factors which have no relation to the plaintiff's sex.'

The type of analysis required to prove objectively verifiable factors was explained by McCracken J in referring to the pensions equality case, *Bilka-Kaufhaus GmbH v Weber Von Hartz* [1986] 2 CMLR 701, where it was stated at p 721:

'It falls to the national court which alone is competent to assess the facts, to decide whether, and if so, to what extent, the grounds put forward by an employer to explain the adoption of a pay practice which applies irrespective of the employee's sex, but which in fact affects more women than men can be considered to be objectively justified for economic reasons. If the national court finds that the means chosen by Bilka meet a genuine need of the enterprise, that they are suitable for attaining the objective pursued by the enterprise and are necessary for that purpose, the fact that the measures in question affect a much greater number of women than men is not sufficient to conclude that they involve a breach of Article 119.'

McCracken J had a difficulty with the manner in which the Labour Court approached the plaintiff's complaint of indirect discrimination but came to the view that, despite the apparent flaws in the approach and type of reasoning adopted, the right result was reached and he held that the Labour Court had taken an objective view of the factors relating to the requirements of the defendant and found as a fact that the defendant believed its requirements to be essential. McCracken J also quoted the decision of the ECJ in examining what are objectively justifiable and essential criteria in *Kording v Senator Fur Finanzen* [1997] ECR 5289 where the court stated:

'In . . . *Nimz* [v *Freie ünd Hansestadt Hamburg* [1991] IRLR 221] the Court took the view that it is impossible to identify objective criteria unrelated to any discrimination on grounds of sex on the basis of an alleged special link between length of service and acquisition of a certain level of knowledge or experience since such a claim amounts to no more than a generalisation concerning certain categories of workers. Although experience goes hand in hand with length of service and experience enables the worker in principle to improve performance of the tasks alloted to him, the objectivity of such a criterion depends on all the circumstances in each individual case, and in particular on the relationship between the nature of the work performed and the experience gained from the performance of that work upon completion of a certain number of working hours.'

The plaintiff's claim was dismissed on the grounds that the university had discharged the onus of proof on it in justifying the reasons put forward for setting out the requirements of the job and that the Labour Court considered those reasons objectively and reached the conclusion that they were essential requirements which had no connection with the sex of the plaintiff.

7.5.4   JOB-SHARING

Indirect discrimination also arose in *Hill and Stapleton v Revenue Commissioners and Department of Finance* [1998] IRLR 466; [1998] ELR 225. Ms Hill and Ms Stapleton were employed as clerical assistants in the Civil Service where they worked with the Revenue Commissioners. Ms Hill started as a full-time employee in 1981 and began job-sharing in 1988. Ms Stapleton was recruited in a job-sharing capacity in 1986. Each worked half the time that a full-time employee worked on a week-on/week-off basis. The Civil Service job-sharing scheme provided that while on job share each employee moved one point up the incremental pay scale with each year of service and they were paid 50 per cent of the salary applicable to the point they had reached on the scale.

After two years both employees took up full-time employment but as the scheme treated each year's job share as only equivalent to six months' full-time service they were placed on a lower point of the full-time scale than they otherwise would have been. They claimed that equating two years' job-sharing service with one year's full-time service constituted indirect sex discrimination contrary to the Anti-Discrimination (Pay) Act, 1974 and article 119 of the EC Treaty on the basis that far more female workers than male workers spent part of their working lives in a job-sharing capacity. The following questions were raised before the European Court of Justice:

(1)   Is the principle of equal pay contravened if employees who convert from job sharing to full-time work regress on the incremental scale due to the application by the employer of the criterion of service calculated by time worked in the job?

(2)   If so does the employer have to provide special justification for recourse to the criterion of service defined as actual time worked?

(3)   If so can a practice of incremental progression by reference to actual time worked be objectively justified by reference to factors other than the acquisition of a particular level of skill and experience over time?

The ECJ held:

'A system for classifying workers converting from job sharing to full-time employment comes within the concept of "pay" for the purposes of Article 119 of the EC Treaty since it determines the progression of pay due to those workers. Rules which treat full-time workers who previously job shared at a disadvantage compared with other full-time workers by applying a criterion of service calculated by length of time actually worked in a post and therefore placing them on the full-time pay scale at a level lower than that which they occupied on the pay scale applicable to job sharing must, in principle, be treated as contrary to Article 119 and the Equal Pay Directive where 98 per cent of those employed under job-sharing contracts are women. When workers convert from job sharing, where they worked 50 per cent of full-time hours and received 50 per cent of the salary for full-time work, they should expect both their hours of work and the level of their pay to increase by 50 per cent in the same way as workers converting from full-time work to job sharing would expect those factors to be reduced by 50 per cent unless a difference in treatment can be justified. The onus was on the respondents to establish before the national court that the reference to the criterion of service defined as the length of time actually worked in the assessment and the incremental credit to be granted to workers who convert from job sharing to full-time work, is justified by objective factors unrelated to any discrimination on grounds of sex. However, an employer cannot justify discrimination arising from a job-sharing scheme solely on the ground that avoidance of such discrimination would involve increased costs. Nor was it relevant that there was an established practice within the Civil Service of crediting only actual service or that the practice was said to establish a reward system which maintained staff motivation, commitment and morale.'

7.5.5   PROPORTIONALITY

In *Irish Press Newspapers v Mandate* DEP 5/95, the Labour Court was faced with a claim relating to the exclusion of part-time workers from the company pension scheme. The proportion of male employees who could comply with the requirement was 56 per cent compared with the proportion of females which was 38 per cent. The Labour Court found that the difference between the proportion of female workers and the proportion of male workers who could comply with the requirement was 'not substantial'. The court said it did not regard a difference of 18 per cent as considerable. It should be noted that 62 per cent of women could not comply with the requirement as against 44 per cent of men who could not comply with the requirement.

The European Court of Justice dealt with the question of indirect sex discrimination in *R v Secretary of State for Employment, ex parte Seymour-Smith and Perez* [1999] IRLR 253. Ms Seymour-Smith sought to claim unfair dismissal but did not have the necessary two years' continuous service required under UK unfair dismissal legislation. She sought to challenge the relevant UK legislative provision on the basis that the proportion of women who could comply with the two-year qualifying period is considerably smaller than the proportion of men so as to amount to prima facie indirect sex discrimination against women and that therefore the two-year qualifying period was contrary to the EC Equal Treatment Directive. Over the period from 1985 to 1991 the proportion of men who had two or more years of service with their current employer ranged from 72 per cent to 77.4 per cent. The proportion of women ranged between 63.8 per cent and 68.9 per cent. The female percentage as a percentage of the male percentage averaged 89.1 per cent. In 1991 it was 90.5 per cent. It was accepted that the differences found in the impact of the requirement on the sexes were statistically significant in that it could be said with confidence that they were due to social facts rather than to chance.

The ECJ held:

'In order to establish whether a measure adopted by a Member State has disparate effect as between men and women to such a degree as to amount to indirect sex discrimination the national courts must verify whether the statistics available indicate that a considerably smaller percentage of women than men is able to fulfil the requirement imposed by that measure. The best approach for determining whether a rule has a more unfavourable impact on women than on men is to consider the respective proportions of men in the workforce able to satisfy the requirement and those unable to do so and to compare those proportions as regards women in the workforce. It must be ascertained whether the statistics indicate that a considerably smaller percentage of women than men is able to satisfy the condition required, in this case two years' employment. That would be evidence of apparent sex discrimination. That could also be the case if the statistical evidence revealed a lesser but persistent and relatively constant disparity over a long period between men and women who satisfied the requirement of two years' employment. It is for the national court to determine the conclusions to be drawn from such statistics. It is also for the national court to assess whether the statistics are valid and appear to be significant or whether they illustrate purely fortuitous or short-term phenomena.'

In *Seymour-Smith* the ECJ went on to give some assistance as to the actual percentages that might be considered significant and stated:

'In the present case in 1985, the year in which the requirement of two years' service was introduced, 77.4 per cent of men and 68.9 per cent of women fulfilled that condition. Such statistics did not appear, on the face of it, to show that a considerably smaller percentage of women than men was able to fulfil the requirement imposed by the disputed rule.'

7.6   EQUAL PAY

7.6.1   EU COMMISSION CODE OF PRACTICE

To avoid both direct and indirect discrimination in pay and conditions employers should review their terms and conditions of employment in light of the recommendations set out in the EU Commission Code of Practice on the implementation of equal pay issued in July 1996.

The code is aimed at employers, whether from the public or private sector, and states that it seeks to help the parties in wage negotiations to remove all direct or indirect discrimination from collective agreements and further states that it:

> 'Also aims to assist women and men who believe their work is under-valued because of sexual discrimination *to obtain the necessary information* to resolve their problem through negotiation or, as a last resort, to bring the matter to the National Courts.'

7.6.2   THE 1998 ACT

The 1998 Act repeats the definition of 'like work' as in the 1974 Act but broadens it to allow that a comparator employee need not be employed in the same place as the claimant. As regards the time of employment the comparator must be employed at the same time as the claimant or during the previous or following three years.

In relation to work which a person employed through an employment agency is required to do, comparison as regards like work may only be made with another agency worker. A comparison may not be made with non-agency workers.

In relation to like work, the old discrepancy where it was found that work was not like work but actually superior in value, is to be ruled out now and work greater in value deemed to be within the definition of 'like work'.

Sections 19 and 20 of the 1998 Act insert an equal pay clause into every employment contract and, for the first time, expressly provide for indirect discrimination in equal pay. The definitions of equal pay in the 1974 Act are preserved, but the need for the claimant and the comparator to be employed in the same place is abolished. The notion of 'associated employer' is also preserved which has the effect of narrowing the potential pool of comparators.

Section 19(1) provides as follows:

> 'It shall be a term of the contract under which A is employed that, subject to this Act, A shall at any time be entitled to the same rate of remuneration for the work which A is employed to do as B who, at that or any other relevant time, is employed to do like work by the same or an associated employer.'

Section 19(2) provides that 'a relevant time' is any time (including a time before the commencement of the Act) during the three years which precede, or the three years which follow, the time in question.

Section 19(4) contains a prohibition on indirect discrimination in relation to equal pay and provides:

> 'Where a term of a contract or a criterion applies to employees (including A and B)—
> (a)   it applies to all the employees of a particular employer or to a particular class of such employees (including A and B);
> (b)   is such that the remuneration of those employees who fulfil the term or criterion is different from that of those who do not;
> (c)   is such that the proportion of employees who are disadvantaged by the term or criterion is

substantially higher in the case of those of the same sex as A than in the case of those of the same case as B; and

(d)   *cannot be justified by objective factors unrelated to A's sex,*
        then, for the purpose of sub-section (1), A and B shall be treated as fulfilling or, as the case may be, as not fulfilling the term or criterion, whichever results in the higher remuneration.'

Section 29 of the Act provides a similar entitlement to equal pay for members of protected groups, on non-gender grounds.

The 1998 Act is firmly based on a system of comparisons between a person who is a member of the protected group and one who is not. The need for a comparator presents particular problems for claimants seeking to attack the notion of a lesser value being placed on work that is traditionally seen as women's work. Statistics show that there is still a significant differential between male and female earnings in Ireland and one of the main reasons for this is historically to be occupational sex segregation. There are industries where women are still clustered on the assembly lines, and it may be difficult for a claimant in such circumstances to provide a male comparator.

7.6.3   ASSOCIATED EMPLOYER

Section 2(2) of the Act provides that two employers shall be taken to be associated if one is a body corporate of which the other (whether directly or indirectly) has control, or if both are bodies corporate of which a third person (whether directly or indirectly) has control. The nexus between two associated employers is that of 'control', a term which is not defined. Section 115 of the Companies Act, 1963 sets out relevant criteria determining whether a company is a subsidiary of another company and presumably such criteria applies in this context. It has been found, for example, that where two hospitals are run by the same health board, that they rank as associated employers for the purposes of the 1974 Act.

7.6.4   LIKE WORK

7.6.4.1   Statutory definition

Section 7 of the 1998 Act provides that two people shall be regarded as being employed to do like work if:

'(a)   *both perform the same work under the same or similar conditions, or each is interchangeable with the other in relation to the work;*

(b)   *the work performed by one is of a similar nature to that performed by the other and any differences between the work performed or the conditions under which it is performed by each either are of small importance in relation to the work as a whole or occur with such irregularity as not to be significant to the work as a whole; or*

(c)   *the work performed by one is equal in value to the work performed by the other, having regard to such matters as skill, physical or mental requirements, responsibility and working conditions.'*

7.6.4.2   Case law

Most of the cases which were brought under the 1974 Act were claims (under the similar provision of that Act) that the work performed by the claimant is equal in value to the work performed by the comparator. In practice, the equality officer carries out a detailed investigation (including interviews and work inspections at the place of work) in order to assess the demands placed on claimants and comparators in terms of skill, physical and mental effort, responsibility, and working conditions. In examining the work conditions, the equality officer will have regard to such matters as working times and the work environment. The decision of the equality officer in *550 Sales and Clerical Assistants (Mandate) v Penneys Ltd* EP06/94 where clerical and sales assistants (who were predominantly female) brought an equal claim against the respondent company is a useful example of the methodology employed by an equality officer. They named as comparators storemen who were all male. The equality officer (and on appeal the Labour Court) examined the very dissimilar jobs carried out by the claimants and comparators and found that the work was of equal value.

The equality officer carried out such a detailed investigation in the case of *24 Female Employees v Spring Grove Services* EP01 [1996] and found that the work of the claimants was not equal in value to the work of the comparators. The female claimants worked in the finishing area of the respondent's linen services supply factory and sought remuneration with eight named male comparators who worked in the wash house area of the same venture. The equality officer found that the demands made on the comparator, under the headings referred to above, were greater in each case. The equality officer also found that the fact that no female staff worked in the wash house area, despite it being open to female members of staff to work there, was not an issue for consideration.

The equality officer in *8 Male Employees v Eastern Health Board* EP06 [1996] emphasised the greater volume of work being performed by the comparators in finding that their work was of greater value than that of the claimants. The claimants were employed by the health board as porters whose duties included answering the telephones one night every six weeks. The claimants argued that during that time they were doing like work to the female day telephonists and were therefore entitled to the same rate of remuneration. The volume of calls handled by the comparators was not comparable with the volume handled by the claimants.

The decision of the equality officer in *Rita O'Leary v Minister for Transport, Energy and Communications* 3 February 1998, Supreme Ct (unreported) was appealed to the Labour Court, the High Court on a point of law, and then to the Supreme Court. The claimant was a communications assistant employed by the respondent at Dublin Airport. She alleged discrimination on grounds of sex as between her grade and that of radio officers. Her claim was rejected by the equality officer who found that she and her comparators did not carry out like work since the work of the comparators required additional qualifications, skills and responsibilities. Although it was not necessary to his decision, the equality officer indicated that he considered that the higher qualifications required by radio officers would have constituted valid grounds other than sex for the higher rate of remuneration associated with their grade. The claimant appealed and argued that the higher qualifications were unnecessary for the work which the comparators carried out. The Labour Court dismissed Ms O'Leary's appeal on the ground that the higher qualifications required of the comparators were necessary to comply with international broadcasting conventions. On appeal to the High Court, Barron J held that once the question of like work was decided against the applicants, their claim under the 1974 Act failed; it was not then necessary to determine the question of qualifications. On appeal, the Supreme Court determined that the essential finding of fact that the work of the comparators and the claimants was not 'like work' was made by reference to the skills and responsibilities demanded by the work rather than by reference to the qualification stipulated by others. Such qualifications might provide evidence of additional skills, but could not be evidence of the demands made by work.

The European Court of Justice in *Angestektenbetriebszrat der Weiner Gebietskrankenkasse v Wiener Gebierskenkase* [1999] IRLR 481 held that the term 'the same work' does not apply where the same activities are performed over a considerable length of time by persons the basis of whose qualification to exercise their profession is different. The case concerned psychotherapy being carried out by medical doctors and psychologists. The doctors were paid 50 per cent more than the psychologists, most of whom were women. They unsuccessfully claimed equal pay.

7.6.5 GROUNDS OTHER THAN GENDER

Grounds other than gender are referred to in cases prior to the 1998 Act as grounds other than sex. It is likely to be the case that in interpreting the 1998 Act similar principles will apply so that the wider range of discriminatory grounds provided for in the 1998 Act will be treated in similar fashion to the 'sex' ground.

Section 19(5) in relation to the gender ground, and s 29(5) in relation to non-gender grounds of the 1998 Act, provide that nothing shall prevent an employer from paying, on grounds other than a discriminatory ground, different rates of remuneration to different employees.

The European Court of Justice in *Nimz v Freie und Hansestadt Hamburg* [1991] IRLR 221 established the principle that the reasons for which some employees are paid more than others must be based on 'objective criteria unrelated to any discrimination based on sex' and that 'the objectivity of such a criterion depends on all the circumstances in each case'. The court held here that the arguments that full-time workers acquired skills necessary for their employment more quickly and that they have greater experience, were generalisations and could not amount to objective criteria unrelated to any discrimination based on sex.

An example of where certain criteria for differential wage levels was held by the Labour Court to be objective and therefore lawful, occurred in *550 Sales and Clerical Assistants (Mandate) v Penneys Ltd* [1998] ELR 94 which is referred to at **7.6.4.2** above. The rates of pay were held to be unisex and reached through different negotiating routes, one via direct negotiations with the employer and one via an industry-wide basis. It was held by the equality officer and by the Labour Court in 1996 that although the claimants were performing work of equal value to that of the comparators, there were reasons other than sex for the differences in their remuneration, ie claimants' and comparators' rates of pay had been achieved by different industrial routes. On appeal, Barron J held that the correct principle to apply is whether the difference in remuneration between the claimants and the comparators is objectively justified on economic grounds. The Labour Court found, at the rehearing, that the employer was justified in paying different rates of pay to the claimants and comparators and that the justification was objectively based on economic grounds since the increase in pay which the comparators achieved was in return for a productivity agreement which generated economic and industrial benefit to the respondent. The court held that there was no sex based ingredient in the negotiating process but that determination has again been appealed and would appear to conflict with the European Court of Justice decision in *Enderby v Frenchay Health Authority* [1993] IRLR 591.

The fact that a person of the opposite sex to the claimant is paid the same remuneration does not prevent a claimant from bringing an equal pay claim. In an English Court of Appeal decision, *Pickstone v Freemans plc* [1987] ICR 867, which was upheld by the House of Lords, it was held that article 119 of the EC Treaty permitted a woman to bring an equal value complaint even though she was employed on like work or work rated as equivalent to that of a man other than her comparator. In *C & D Food Ltd v Cunnion*, 30 July 1996, High Court (unreported) the situation was considered where both men and women were represented in the two pay grades in question. Employees in grade A were paid more highly than those in grade B. Female employees claimed that they were being discriminated against on grounds of sex as there were male employees engaged in occupations covered by grade A which were of no greater value than the employment of the claimants. The equality officer held that some of the claimants were employed on work of equal value to that of the comparators and that they should be paid equally. Both parties appealed to the Labour Court which rejected both appeals. The employer appealed the determination of the Labour Court claiming that as a matter of law, a finding that the difference in pay was not on grounds other than sex was not permissible when the evidence was that both men and women were recruited for and carried on the same occupations as the claimants and at the same wage. Barron J rejected the employer's appeal and held that in this case the comparator received more remuneration than the claimant because the employer had evaluated the male comparator's work more highly than that of the claimant. This was not a ground other than sex and the work was not more valuable. The decision as to what constituted 'like work' was for the tribunal, not the employer. If the employer's evaluation was incorrect, then unless there were grounds other than sex, the employer could not rely on it. The fact that men and women were recruited for the same job at the same wage was a matter which would be taken into account in determining the relative values of different occupations. It was relevant that the work of one of the male comparators was also done by a woman, as it was relevant that men and women did the same work as the applicants, but these factors went only to the issue of genuine belief.

In the light of the judgment of Barron J in *C & D Foods*, the determination of the Labour Court in *Mandate v Dunnes Stores* DEP 98/12 of 9 December 1998 must be questioned. The equality officer found that certain of the claimants were performing like work with that of the comparators. The equality officer in *Dunnes* found that there were grounds other than sex for the differential in their remuneration. This finding was on the grounds that the comparators were six males out of a group of twenty-four sales assistants and that the remaining eighteen sales assistants were all female. All canteen workers (the applicants) were female. On appeal, the court stated that it could find nothing in the claimants' claim to show that they were being paid less than the comparators by reason of their sex. This is not the test set out in the legislation or applied by the High Court, which seeks to prohibit not only direct, but indirect discrimination in equal pay.

7.6.6   RED CIRCLING

Where an employee's rate of pay can be said to be above the normal rate for the job, due to purely personal factors related to the individual only, such a person may be red circled, thereby disallowing comparisons. It may arise where a long serving male employee has suffered a partially incapacitating illness and has been moved to a less demanding job, but retained a higher rate of pay on humanitarian grounds. Such red circling is regarded as a genuine ground other than sex, for a difference in remuneration. In *Department of Tourism, Transport and Communications v 4 Workers* [1997] ELR 1 female claimants, who were employed as communications assistants in the accounts section of the Irish Aviation Authority, sought equal pay with that of male comparators employed in the same section at a higher rate of pay. The equality officer found the claimants and comparators were employed on like work and recommended the same rate of remuneration. On appeal, the Labour Court upheld the equality officer's finding of like work and went on to consider a defence of red circling which had not been raised before the equality officer. It was argued by the employer that the comparators had been red circled as they were the subject of a special agreement to protect their pay while they were unfit for the duties of radio officers. The Labour Court held that red circling was to be recognised, factual and acknowledged if it is to serve as a defence. The claimants appealed to the High Court ([1996] ELR 106) where Keane J held that the Labour Court had misconstrued the relevant section of the 1998 Act. Keane J held that where it was established that the discrimination was based on grounds other than sex, that the employer could not be prevented from relying on the defence even if all parties to the red circling arrangement were not aware of the circumstances which brought it into operation. He remitted the matter to the Labour Court for reconsideration which found as a matter of fact that the positions of radio officers in the accounts section had not been red circled. Any male radio officer could be transferred into that section and retain his rate of pay.

7.7   SEXUAL HARASSMENT

7.7.1   DEFINITION

One of the main difficulties with sexual harassment to date has been finding an acceptable definition. Unless an offence is properly defined it is difficult, if not impossible, to enforce. There was no statutory definition prior to the 1998 Act. There were a number of acceptable definitions which were very similar. Before examining the changes brought about by the 1998 Act it is worth looking at the development of the offence of sexual harassment.

The early definitions ranged over the following:

– the creation of a hostile working environment by statements or conduct with a gender based or sexual connotation;

– subjecting a person of the opposite sex to a detriment or less favourable treatment on grounds of sex may constitute sexual harassment;

– a single incident of sexual harassment, while it seems to contradict the dictionary definition of harassment which of itself suggests a continuing course of conduct, may amount to unlawful sexual harassment.

– for sexual harassment to be actionable, it must be sufficiently severe or pervasive to alter the conditions of the victim's employment and to create an abusive working environment.

The most frequently quoted definition in this jurisdiction is the decision of the Court of Session in the Scottish case of *Strathclyde Regional Council v Porcelli* [1986] IRLR 134 in which the court stated:

'If the form of unfavourable treatment or any material part of it which is meted out included a significant element of a sexual character to which a man would not be vulnerable, the treatment is on grounds of sex.'

Some courts and tribunals have favoured more direct and less subtle definitions such as:

– unnecessary touching or unwanted physical contact;

– suggestive remarks or other verbal abuse;

– leering at a person's body;

– compromising invitations or comments;

– demands for sexual favours; and

– physical assault.

In Ireland's only High Court judgment on sexual harassment, *Health Board v B C and the Labour Court* [1994] ELR 27 Costello J stated that sexual harassment is a term which, while it is in general use, 'has no well-established legal definition'. He then quoted the definition of sexual harassment adopted by the employers in that case in their staff handbook and commented that the definition appeared to him to 'reflect well the connotation of the phrase as it is used in everyday life in this country today'. The definition was:

' "Sexual harassment" is defined as unsolicited, unreciprocated behaviour of a sexual nature to which the recipient objects or could not reasonably be expected to consent and may include:

– unwanted physical contact;

– lewd or suggestive behaviour whether verbal or physical;

– sexually derogatory statements or sexually discriminatory remarks;

– the display of pornographic or sexually explicit material in the workplace.'

The European Commission has drawn up a code of practice on sexual harassment which defines sexual harassment as follows:

'Sexual harassment means unwanted conduct of a sexual nature, or other conduct based on sex affecting the dignity of women and men at work. This can include unwelcome physical, verbal or non-verbal conduct.

'A range of behaviour may be considered to constitute sexual harassment. The essential characteristic of sexual harassment is that it is unwanted by the recipient, that it is for each individual to determine what behaviour is acceptable to them and what they regard as offensive.'

The Commission definition does not include the requirement related to reasonableness as referred to by Costello J and which is relevant in the context of the definition in the 1998 Act referred to at **7.7.6.1** below.

7.7.2   EMPLOYMENT EQUALITY ACT, 1977

The Employment Equality Act, 1977, which set out to outlaw discrimination (other than in matters related to remuneration) on grounds of sex or marital status, provides at s 2(a) that for the purposes of the Act, discrimination shall be taken to occur:

'Where by reason of his sex, a person is treated less favourably than a person of the other sex.'

Section 3 of the Act provides that an employer

'shall not discriminate against an employee . . . in relation to . . . conditions of employment . . .

'A person shall be taken to discriminate against an employee . . . in relation to conditions of employment if he does not offer or afford to a person or class of person the same terms of employment, the same working conditions and the same treatment . . . as he offers or affords to another person or class of persons.'

Claims of sexual harassment are dealt with under the legislation by equality officers and the Labour Court with appeal thereafter to the High Court on a point of law only.

7.7.3   LABOUR COURT APPROACH

The approach of the Labour Court has been clear and does not seem to be open to much misinterpretation.

In Ireland's first reported case in 1985 (*A Garage Proprietor v A Worker* EE02/85) the court held:

'Freedom from sexual harassment is a condition of work which an employee of either sex is entitled to expect. The Court will accordingly treat any denial of that freedom as discrimination within the terms of the Employment Equality Act 1977.'

In a later decision in 1988 (*A Company v A Worker* EE02/88) the court stated:

'Freedom from sexual harassment is a condition of work which an employee of either sex is entitled to expect. The court considers that employers have a duty to *ensure* their employees enjoy such working conditions'.

The EAT also held in *Allen v Dunnes Stores Ltd* [1996] ELR 203 that there was an onus on an employer to inform, educate and instruct its employees on sexual harassment and in that particular case the employer's failure to do so was fatal to the case which was actually brought by the alleged harasser. This case is dealt with in more detail at **7.7.5.2** below.

In *British Telecommunications plc v Williams* [1997] IRLR 668 a female employee claimed sexual harassment by a male manager who conducted an appraisal interview in what she claimed was an atmosphere she found sexually intimidating and claimed that the male manager was sexually aroused during the interview. The industrial tribunal rejected the claim that the manager was aroused but concluded that the absence of a third party, the proximity of the parties in the meeting, and the excessive length of the interview contributed to an atmosphere which the female employee was entitled to find sexually intimidating and held that there had been sexual harassment. On appeal the EAT overturned the tribunal decision on the basis that having found on the evidence that the manager was not sexually aroused, the only conclusion which the tribunal was entitled to reach was that the complaint was not proved. Either the manager was behaving inappropriately towards the applicant for sexual reasons or he was not. The EAT went on to state: 'if the reason why the Tribunal concluded that the interview was sexually intimidating was because there was no woman present and the interview took place in a confined space, their conclusion had to be rejected'. It is neither required by law nor desirable in practice that employers should see that male managers are chaperoned when dealing with female staff.

7.7.4   LEGAL ACTION

Victims of sexual harassment may seek legal remedy against either the harasser or the employer if they are different parties. They may also seek their remedy against both of them. The reality is that the harasser is unlikely to be a good 'mark' for a claim and the employer then becomes the focus of any such claim. That has given rise to problems, the main problem being one of vicarious liability which was not referred to at all in the Irish legislation until the 1998 Act came into force, is reasonably well defined at common law, and gives rise to all sorts of practical and policy considerations.

7.7.5   VICARIOUS LIABILITY

7.7.5.1   Health Board v B C and the Labour Count

The relevant provision of the 1998 Act relating to vicarious liability is covered at **7.9** below. The Labour Court approach is well set out in the case later dealt with by the High Court of *Health Board v B C and the labour Court* [1994] ELR 27 (EE10/92). The facts of the case were that a female employee had been subjected to lewd and coarse comments from two male colleagues. One of the two was the prime mover in such conduct. She asked them on a number of occasions to stop or she would report them to a superior. Shortly after this, and before she reported anything, she found herself in a working area alone with the two men. One of the men physically restrained her while the other interfered with her. After a moment she was released. Later in the day she mentioned the incident to a colleague who advised her to tell a member of the supervisory staff. This she did the following morning and an immediate investigation of the incident was then held by the employer, which resulted in the suspension of one employee without pay for five weeks with a final warning regarding his future conduct, and the dismissal of the other.

The employer had issued policy guidelines to supervisory staff for dealing with sexual harassment. The claimant, through her trade union, made a claim against her employers under the provisions of the Employment Equality Act, 1977 on the basis that the single incident referred to constituted discrimination within the meaning of the Act. The union maintained that the issuing of guidelines solely to supervisory staff was insufficient. Staff generally were unaware of the procedure to follow if they were victims of sexual harassment. Employees were unaware of what is or is not acceptable in the working environment. As the employer had failed to take pro-active steps to avert sexual harassment generally and the particular act of sexual harassment complained of, liability should lie on the employer and compensation was sought.

The employers responded that they had not discriminated against the employee within the meaning of the 1977 Act. The incident which occurred was not the responsibility of the employers. The perpetrators of the incident acted outside their duties and the employer could not and should not be held liable in those circumstances. The employer took every action possible when made aware of the complaint and felt it should not be blamed for something it was not aware of and did not condone.

The Labour Court held against the employer. There was no dispute that the act complained of was a most serious case of sexual harassment, 'the persons responsible being two male employees'. The main issue the court addressed was the responsibility or liability of the employer for the actions of those two male employees. The court stated:

> 'The court wishes to state that in dealing with cases of sexual harassment it does and will take into account steps taken by employers to eliminate and prevent sexual harassment in the workplace. Whilst accepting that an employer cannot guarantee total prevention of harassment the court will look for and take note of what steps have been taken. The adoption of a code of practice, the adoption of a policy statement on the prevention of sexual harassment, the existence of guidelines as to how all staff should behave and the establishment of clear grievance procedures all constitute the kind of "reasonable steps" which employers should adopt and which will be accepted by the court as evidence of the employer's bona fides in this type of dispute. Clearly information about steps must be widely circulated in the place of work and information on the employer's attitude to acts of sexual harassment made available to all staff.

> 'In this case, the court does not consider that the action of the board in instructing supervisors and top management as to how complaints of this nature should be dealt with constituted "reasonable steps".'

The court stated its view that employers:

> 'have a duty to ensure that employees enjoy working conditions free from sexual harassment.'

The court held that in this particular case, as the employer had not taken reasonable steps to avoid sexual harassment, the employer was liable for the actions of the two employees concerned.

The health board appealed the Labour Court decision to the High Court on the grounds that the Labour Court had applied an incorrect test as to its liability for the actions of its employees. Costello J held that the Labour Court had not applied the correct test of employer liability. Costello J referred to the provisions of the Employment Equality Act, 1977 and noted that there was no express or implied provision in the Act that an employer should be automatically vicariously liable for the acts of employees and stated:

> 'I cannot envisage any employment . . . in respect of which a sexual assault could be regarded as so connected with it as to amount to an act within its scope.'

7.7.5.2   Allen v Dunnes Stores Ltd

In *Allen v Dunnes Stores Ltd* [1996] ELR 203 the claimant was employed as a security manager. His employment was terminated on grounds of gross misconduct. It was alleged that while carrying out a security check on staff bags he commented on the perfume worn by a shop assistant and attempted to kiss her. After an investigation the claimant was dismissed. The employers treated the actions of the claimant as sexual harassment. In the course of its judgment the EAT stated:

> 'Whether behaviour amounts to sexual harassment in a particular instance is determined from the point of view of the victim and what she/he regards as acceptable behaviour. Behaviour regarded as acceptable and innocent by the perpetrator, his

colleagues and others may nonetheless be unacceptable to the victim and so could constitute sexual harassment. The Tribunal, by majority on this point, holds that this puts an onus on the employer to put in place a programme to inform, educate and instruct its employees on the issue of sexual harassment. The failure of the respondent to discharge that onus in this case was fatal'.

The tribunal went on to state:

'Sexual harassment is a broad category of offence and comprises conduct of varying degrees of seriousness. There should be a range of penalties commensurate with the seriousness of the offence which can be imposed with a particular instance.'

The EAT accepted the female employee's version of events but went on to hold that the ultimate sanction of dismissal of the claimant was disproportionate to the behaviour complained of and held the dismissal to be unfair and ordered the re-engagement of the claimant. Not only must an employer have a policy in place but must actively discourage sexual harassment, take firm but fair steps to deal with any allegation of sexual harassment and process such complaints in a structured, sympathetic and confidential manner. (See also *An Employee v An Employer* [1993] ELR 75 where the employee claimed she was suffering ongoing harassment but that the employer took inadequate steps to prevent what was happening, was unsympathetic towards her and acted in an ineffective manner in respect of her.)

7.7.5.3   Reed v Stedman

In *Reed and Bull Information Systems Ltd v Stedman* [1999] IRLR 299 Mr Reed and his employers appealed a decision of an industrial tribunal which held in favour of Ms Stedman arising from complaints she brought under the Sex Discrimination Act 1975, claiming that she found working with Mr Reed to be intolerable. Ms Stedman had given evidence of comments, remarks and behaviour on the part of Mr Reed with sexual connotations which she found unacceptable. The industrial tribunal held that although no single incident was serious enough to be capable of constituting sexual harassment, there had been a series of events with a pervading sexual innuendo and sexist stance. While Ms Stedman had made no formal complaint she had complained to other members of staff and the personnel department was aware of a deterioration in her health. The tribunal took the view that there should have been an investigation into the cause of the illness and the complaints that had been made, even though the complaints were not made directly to the employer through its personnel department. The tribunal went on to hold that by failing to investigate, the employers were in breach of contract. That decision was appealed to the EAT which dismissed the appeal. The EAT was satisfied that there was a course of conduct which amounted to sexual harassment, which in turn forced Ms Stedman to leave her employment which amounted to a constructive dismissal and accordingly was an act of discrimination within the meaning of the Sex Discrimination Act.

In its judgment the EAT commented on the behaviour of Mr Reed as follows:

'There was a course of conduct which amounted to sexual harassment. The manager knew his actions which contained a sexual overtone were unwanted, yet he continued to make comments which contained sexual innuendo and to tell sexual jokes in the applicant's presence.'

On the employer's conduct or reaction to what was going on in its employment the EAT stated:

'Since the applicant had made complaints to other colleagues at work it was incumbent on the employers to investigate the matter and that their failure to investigate was enough to justify a finding of breach of trust and confidence.'

7.7.6 SEXUAL HARASSMENT IN THE 1998 ACT

7.7.6.1 Definition

Sexual harassment in the workplace is dealt with in s 23 of the 1998 Act which seeks to outlaw harassment by fellow employees, the employer or a client, customer or other business contact of the employer. Sexual harassment is defined in part in s 23(3) as being:

(a) any act of physical intimacy;

(b) any express request for sexual favours;

(c) any other act or conduct including spoken words, gestures or the production, display or circulation of written words, pictures or other material.

If the act, request or conduct is unwelcome and could reasonably be regarded as sexually, or otherwise on the gender ground, offensive, humiliating or intimidating it will constitute sexual harassment.

7.7.6.2 Defences

Section 23 provides a defence for employers if they can prove that they took such steps as were reasonably practicable to prevent the harassment and 'if and so far as any such treatment has occurred to reverse the effects of it' and to prevent fellow employees from sexually harassing the complainant.

In relation to the defence of taking 'such steps as were reasonably practicable' provided in s 15(3) of the 1998 Act the EAT in the UK held in *Balgobin v London Borough of Tower Hamlets* [1987] IRLR 401 that the employers had proved a defence to acts of sexual harassment committed by their employee where they had shown that the allegations had not been made known to management; that there was proper and adequate staff supervision; and that the employers had made known their policy of equal opportunities. The EAT also held in *Burton v DeVere Hotels* [1996] IRLR 596, where two black female waitresses were racially and sexually harassed by the comedian Bernard Manning and his audience, that an employer subjects an employee to the detriment of racial harassment if he causes or permits harassment serious enough to amount to a detriment, to occur in circumstances in which he can control whether it happens or not.

7.7.6.3 Who may commit an act of sexual harassment

It may be seen from s 23 that the harassment may be carried out by a number of persons and not just fellow employees. It may include non-employees, as in *2 Female Claimants v Boy's Secondary School* DEC-E 2001-005, where an equality officer held that a board of management of a school may be vicariously liable for sexual harassment of teachers by pupils. That is an express statement which is supportive of the position taken by the Labour Court under the 1977 Act which was silent on the specific issue of sexual harassment and obviously silent on the extent of the employer's liability for various parties. Despite these shortcomings of the 1977 Act the Labour Court had held in *A Worker v A Company* [1992] ELR 40, in circumstances where it was claimed that an outsider who was not an employee of the company but had been granted permission to use the company premises and facilities for his own business purposes, had subjected a female employee to offensive conduct of a sexual nature. In holding for the claimant and awarding her compensation the Labour Court held inter alia:

> 'The worker was objected to sexual harassment while in the employment of the company. It was irrelevant that the perpetrator of the harassment was not an employee of the company since he was on the company premises with the agreement of the employer who was in a position to protect the worker. In failing to protect the worker

against the harassment the employer had, in effect imposed discriminatory conditions of employment on the worker.'

In an equality officer's recommendation of January 2001, applying the provisions of the 1977 Act, in *2 Female Claimants v Boy's Secondary School* it was held that the board of management of a secondary school was clearly responsible for the disciplinary and working environment at the school and therefore in a position to exercise control over the behaviour of the pupils—in this case, the sexual harassment of teachers by pupils. The equality officer considered the disciplinary action taken by management against the perpetrators of the acts of sexual harassment and, in this particular case, found that the disciplinary action was what might reasonably be expected in the circumstances of the individual cases. However, the equality officer held that the school had victimised the two teachers because they had complained about the sexual harassment to the Labour Court. He recommended that the school make compensatory payments of £7,000 and £12,000, respectively, to the teachers.

As referred to at **7.3** above the US Supreme Court in two similar decisions issued on 26 June 1998, *Burlington Industries Inc v Ellerth* [1997]–69 June 26, 1998 and *Faragher v Boca Raton* [1997]–282 June 26, 1998 confirmed that an employer effectively must have a policy against sexual harassment in order to show that it meets the present-day standards of provision of a safe system of work and place of work free of sexual harassment.

7.8 HARASSMENT OTHER THAN SEXUAL HARASSMENT

The 1998 Act also seeks to outlaw harassment which occurs by reason of or as a result of the relevant characteristics which form the basis of the 1998 Act as detailed below. Harassment as defined may be carried on by a fellow employee, the employer, client, customer or other business contact and the circumstances of the harassment are such that the employer ought reasonably to have taken steps to prevent it. Harassment itself is defined in s 32 of the 1998 Act as being:

> 'any act or conduct . . . including spoken words, gestures or the production, display or circulation of written words, pictures or other material, constitutes harassment . . . if the action or other conduct is unwelcome . . . and could reasonably be regarded in relation to the relevant characteristic [of the person harassed] as offensive, humiliating or intimidating.'

Section 2 of the Act, which is the definition section, defines 'relevant characteristic' by reference to s 28(3) of the Act which, in turn, provides that the relevant characteristic is to be defined by reference to the discriminatory grounds upon which an applicant or claimant founds their allegation or claim of discrimination and the discriminatory grounds are those set out in s 6(2) of the Act as being the following grounds:

- (a) gender;
- (b) marital status;
- (c) family status;
- (d) sexual orientation;
- (e) religion;
- (f) age;
- (g) disability;
- (h) race; and
- (i) membership of the traveller community.

7.9   VICARIOUS LIABILITY UNDER THE 1998 ACT

Section 15 of the 1998 Act deals with vicarious liability of the employer as follows:

> *(1)   Anything done by a person in the course of his/her employment shall . . . be treated for the purposes of the Act as done also by that person's employer, whether or not it was done with the employer's knowledge or approval.*
>
> (2)   *Anything done by a person as agent for another person with the authority (whether express or implied and whether precedent or subsequent) of that other person shall be treated for the purposes of this Act as done also by that other person.*
>
> (3)   *In proceedings brought under this Act against an employer in respect of an act alleged to have been done by an employee of the employer it shall be a defence for the employer to prove that the employer took such steps as were reasonably practicable to prevent the employee—*
> *(a) from doing that act; or*
> *(b) from doing in the course of his employment acts of that description.'*

There have not as yet been any decisions from the Office of the Director of Equality Investigations, the Labour Court or the Circuit Court in respect of the 1998 Act, s 15 and it is therefore relevant to the case law which existed prior to 18 October 1999, when the 1998 Act took effect.

In *Health Board v B C* [1994] ELR 27, referred to at **7.7.5.1** above, Costello J was faced with a sexual assault that was in itself one of the more extreme forms of sexual harassment one may encounter. It was so extreme that Costello J had no difficulty in drawing a dividing line between the employer and the employee over which liability did not pass. The 1998 Act does not impose *automatic* vicarious liability given that there is a saver in s 15(3) as referred to above. That saver, however, requires the employer to show that he took such steps 'as were reasonably practicable'. In the *Health Board* case no steps were needed by the employer. The act spoke for itself. It was so serious and savage as to be totally unconnected with the employment. It appears now, however, that it is a matter for employers to specify that the act, no matter how extreme, must not occur before the saver referred to can be effective.

Vicarious liability is conferred where the conduct complained of was done by a person 'in the course of his or her employment'. The leading UK case on vicarious liability in sex or racial discrimination is *Jones v Tower Boot Co* [1997] IRLR 168. In that case the Court of Appeal stated that the words 'in the course of employment' should be interpreted in the sense in which they are employed in every-day speech and not restrictively by reference to the principles laid down by case law for establishing an employer's vicarious liability for the torts committed by an employee. The court held the employer to be vicariously liable for harassment of a black employee by his white colleagues, despite the fact that the harassment culminated in the branding of the black employee with hot metal, which was clearly a criminal act. The Court of Appeal held that to find otherwise would defeat the purpose of anti-discrimination laws by finding that the more serious the harassment the less likely an employer was to be held liable and an employee was to succeed in a discrimination claim. This contrasts with Costello J's finding in the *Health Board* case.

The Court of Appeal went on to state in *Waters v Commissioner of Police of the Metropolis* [1997] IRLR 589 that in applying the *Tower Boot* test no tribunal could find that an alleged sexual assault by a male police constable on a female police constable was committed in the 'course of employment' where both parties were off duty at the time of the alleged offence and the man was a visitor to the woman's room at a time and in circumstances which placed them in no different position from that which would have applied if they had been social acquaintances only with no working connections. A later UK police case of *Chief Constable of Lincolnshire Police v Stubbs* [1999] IRLR 81 clarified the 'course of employment'.

It was held that where events or circumstances may be described as 'extensions of the workplace' they may come within the definition of course of employment. A distinction was drawn between chance meetings and circumstances closely related to work. The Chief Constable was held liable for two acts of harassment of one employee by another, one of which occurred during a routine visit to a pub after work and one of which occurred during a leaving party for a fellow employee. A social setting does not therefore mean that an employer is not liable for the actions of employees.

7.10   POSITIVE ACTION

7.10.1   ACTION PERMITTED BY 1998 ACT

Section 24(1) of the 1998 Act provides that the provisions of the Act are without prejudice to measures to promote equal opportunities for men and women, in particular by removing existing inequalities which affect women's opportunities in the areas of access to employment, vocational training and promotion and working conditions. This is a very general provision and has not yet been interpreted in decisions under the 1998 Act.

Section 33 of the Act provides for further positive action on the grounds of age, disability and membership of the traveller community. Section 33(1) provides that nothing in Parts II and IV of the Act, the general provisions on discrimination and the specific provisions as to equality between other categories of persons, shall prevent the taking of measures specified in s 33(2) in order to facilitate the integration into employment, either generally or in particular or a particular workplace, of:

  (a)   persons who have obtained the age of 50 years;

  (b)   persons with a disability or any class or description of such persons; or

  (c)   members of the traveller community.

Section 33(2) provides that the measures referred to above are those intended to reduce or eliminate the effects of discrimination against any of the above persons.

Section 33(3) provides that nothing in Parts II or IV of the Act shall render unlawful the provision, by or on behalf of the State, of training or work experience for a disadvantaged group of persons if the Minister for Justice, Equality and Law Reform certifies that, in the absence of the provision in question, it is unlikely that the disadvantaged group would receive similar training or work experience.

7.10.2   ACTION PERMITTED BY EQUAL TREATMENT DIRECTIVE

The status of positive discrimination under the Equal Treatment Directive 76/207 was considered by the European Court of Justice in *Marschall v Land Nordrhein-Westfalen* [1998] IRLR 39, where the Civil Service law of the region in question provided that where 'there are fewer women than men in the particular higher grade post in the career bracket, women are to be given priority for promotion in the event of equal suitability, competence and professional performance, unless reasons specific to an individual [male] candidate tilt the balance in his favour'.

Mr Marschall applied for a promotion but failed on the basis that fewer women than men were employed in the relevant post for which he had applied and that an equally qualified woman was to be appointed to the position. The European Court of Justice was asked to consider whether Directive 76/207 allowed for positive discrimination. The court in its judgment held inter alia:

'A national rule which, in a case where there are fewer women than men at the level of the relevant post in sectors of the public service and both female and male candidates for the post are equally qualified in terms of their suitability, competence and professional performance, requires that priority be given to the promotion of female candidates unless reasons specific to an individual male candidate tilt the balance in his favour is not precluded by . . . Directive 76/207 . . . on the implementation of the principle of equal treatment for men and women as regards access to employment, vocational training and promotion and working conditions provided that:

– in each individual case the rule provides for male candidates who are as equally qualified as the female candidates a guarantee that the candidatures will be the subject of an objective assessment which will take account of all criteria specific to the candidates and will override the priority accorded to female candidates where one or more of those criteria tilts the balance in favour of the male candidate and;

– such criteria are not such as to discriminate against the female candidates.'

The court held therefore in favour of the rule under consideration and added that such a rule, since it does not guarantee absolute and unconditional priority to women, does not go beyond the limits of article 2(4) of the Directive. The court distinguished an apparently contradictory decision in an earlier case, *Kalanke v Freie Hansestadt Bremen* [1995] IRLR 660.

Article 2(1) of the Directive provides:

'For the purposes of the following provisions the principle of equal treatment shall mean that there shall be no discrimination whatsoever on grounds of sex either directly or indirectly by reference in particular to marital or family status.'

Article 2(4) provides:

'This Directive shall be without prejudice to measures to promote equal opportunity for men and women in particular by removing existing inequalities which affect women's opportunities in the areas referred to in Article 1(1).'

In *Kalanke v Freie Hansestadt Bremen* the rule at issue provided that women who had the same qualifications as men, applying for the same post were to be given priority in sectors where they were under-represented and that there was under-representation if women did not make up at least half of the staff in the relevant pay bracket in the relevant personnel group within a department. There was no exception built into the provision.

Mr Kalanke and a female colleague were shortlisted for promotion. It was accepted that they were equally qualified for the post and that women were under-represented in the relevant sector. The national rule accordingly required the post to be offered to the female. Mr Kalanke challenged the operation of the rule. In its decision the ECJ stated that the rule was contrary to article 2(1). It went on to examine whether the rule was permissible under article 2(4). The court concluded that national rules which guaranteed women absolute and unconditional priority for appointment or promotion went beyond promoting equal opportunities and overstepped the limits of the exception allowed for in article 2(4) of the Directive.

In the *Marschall* case, however, the court very much fine tuned its decision in *Kalanke* and reached an apparently different conclusion to the effect that the rule which defeated Mr Marschall's entitlement to the post was not precluded either by article 2(1) or 2(4).

7.11 EXEMPTIONS

7.11.1 INTRODUCTION

Employers may discriminate in certain circumstances as follows.

Many of the new grounds of non-discrimination listed in the 1998 Act, s 6 are already unfair grounds for dismissing an employee under the Unfair Dismissals (Amendment) Act, 1993. The 1998 Act represents the first attempt to outlaw such types of discrimination in relation to access to and conditions of employment. The prohibitions on discrimination are not without exemption and some of the prohibitions have been watered down.

7.11.2 SEXUAL ORIENTATION

Section 16(5) provides as follows:

'Nothing in this Act shall be construed as requiring an employer to recruit, retain in employment or promote an individual if the employer is aware, on the basis of a criminal conviction of the individual or other reliable information, that the individual engages, or has a propensity to engage, in any form of sexual behaviour which is unlawful.'

Section 16(6) goes on to say that subsection (5) applies in particular where the employment concerned involves access to minors or to other persons who are vulnerable. Although drafted with the laudable aim of protecting children against paedophilia, s 16(4) may be used to avoid the prohibition on discrimination on grounds of sexual orientation, particularly as no definition of 'reliable information' is given. It is, however, a drastic improvement on the provisions of s 16(4) of the 1996 Bill which provided that an employer should not be obliged to recruit or retain in employment an individual if the employer was aware:

'On the basis of a criminal conviction of the individual or other reliable information, that the individual engages, or has a propensity to engage in any form of sexual behaviour to which the employer's clients, customers or any other business contact (a) might be at risk of exposure; or (b) might reasonably object.'

7.11.3 EXCEPTIONS RELATED TO THE FAMILY, AGE OR DISABILITY

Section 34(1) provides that nothing in Part II or IV of the Act shall, in relation to the discriminatory grounds other than gender, make it unlawful for an employer to provide:

(a) a benefit to an employee in respect of events related to members of the employee's family or any description of those members;

(b) a benefit to or in respect of a person as a member of an employee's family;

(c) a benefit to an employee on or by reference to an event occasioning a change in the marital status of the employee; or

(d) to an employee who has family status a benefit intended directly to provide or assist in the provision, during working hours, of care for a person for whom the employee has responsibility as in the definition of family status.

Certain benefits are expressly protected from being unlawful, such as benefits for members of an employee's family or a benefit to an employee upon his or her marriage. Such benefit should not, however, be conferred in a way that would discriminate between persons whose circumstances are not materially different on the basis of one of the prohibited grounds of discrimination. Section 34(3) also allows discrimination on grounds of age or disability where there is clear actuarial or other evidence that 'significantly increased costs would result if the discrimination were not permitted' in those circumstances. This clearly allows discrimination to be justified on the grounds of cost, a ground that had been rejected by the European Court of Justice in the context of direct discrimination on grounds of sex. Maximum ages for recruitment are expressly allowed by s 34(5) and again the cost implications are cited as a justification for permitting what would otherwise be unlawful discrimination.

Section 34(5)(b) allows an employer to take into account (in setting a maximum age for recruitment) the fact that there may need to be a reasonable period of time prior to retirement age during which the recruit will be effective in that job. Section 34(5)(a) also allows the employer to take into account any period of time involved in training a recruit to a standard at which the recruit will be effective in that job. This may be interpreted as implying that older people will take longer to train; however, it is unlikely that an employer would succeed in such an argument and more likely to be interpreted by reference to the normal training period for the job in question. Section 34(7) also provides that it shall not constitute discrimination on grounds of age for an employer to provide different rates of remuneration, or different terms and conditions of employment if the difference is based on the relevant seniority of the staff in question.

7.11.4   SPECIAL PROVISIONS FOR EMPLOYEES WITH DISABILITIES

Section 16(3) provides that an employer shall do all that is reasonable to accommodate the needs of a person who has a disability by providing special treatment or facilities which might render the employee fully competent to undertake any duties required. 'Providing', however, only means making provision for, or allowing or availing of such treatment or facilities. It does not compel the employer to bear the financial cost of providing same.

Section 35(1) allows a special rate of remuneration to be paid to persons with a disability where, by reason thereof, they are restricted in their capacity as compared to another employee without that disability.

Section 34(3) also provides that discrimination on grounds of disability (or age) is permitted where the cost of any special treatment or facilities would give rise to a significantly increased cost. This very wide exemption was, to some extent, necessitated by the decision of the Supreme Court in relation to the constitutionality of the provisions on disability discrimination.

7.11.5   SPECIAL EXEMPTIONS FOR STATE EMPLOYEES

Section 36 allows for a series of exemptions for many State employees in relation to residence, citizenship or proficiency in the Irish language. Section 37(6) makes an extremely broad exemption (on the age or disability grounds) to the Army, Gardaí or the prison services. This exemption to the prohibition on discrimination does not relate to specific jobs, or types of jobs but to the defence forces, Garda Síochána and prison services as a whole.

7.11.6   RELIGIOUS ETHOS

Section 37(1) permits discrimination by a religious, educational or medical institution established for a religious purpose, where it is reasonable to do so in order to maintain the religious ethos of the institution or is reasonably necessary in order to avoid the undermining of that ethos. While s 37(1)(a) appears to indicate that discrimination may only take place on the religion ground, paragraph (b) of that subsection also provides that it shall not be discriminatory for such a religious, educational or medical institution to take action which is reasonably necessary to prevent an employee or prospective employee from undermining the religious ethos of the institution. What may be regarded as 'undermining' may be a very subjective assessment.

7.12 INSTITUTIONS

7.12.1 EQUALITY AUTHORITY

The Employment Equality Agency has been replaced by the Equality Authority.

A post of Director of Equality Investigation has been created and the Director has been conferred with powers of investigation to include references to mediation and the carrying out of equality audits. The Director may also assist the Circuit Court at the request of the court where a matter has been referred to the court.

7.12.2 INFORMATION

The 1998 Act states that any person who considers he has been discriminated against must be provided with certain information material to the proposed claim. The Employment Equality Act, 1998 (s 76–Right to Information) Regulations, 1999 (SI 321/1999) came into effect on the same day as the Act. They prescribe a questionnaire form to be used to obtain material information to decide whether to bring a claim or to assist in formulating and presenting a case. The reply form is also prescribed. There is no obligation on an employer to reply to the questionnaire. No time is laid down for replying to the questionnaire. Inferences may be drawn from a failure to reply, to reply adequately or for a false or misleading reply. The regulations mirror the position in the UK, where questionnaires have been found to be an invaluable tool in assisting tribunals in deciding complex discrimination cases, where evidence is often difficult to obtain.

There are provisions within this s 76 to protect confidential information and to ensure that references and testimonials can be kept confidential. There are no such provisions in the equivalent UK law.

7.12.3 ENFORCEMENT AND REMEDIES

7.12.3.1 Routes for seeking redress

The equality officers and the Labour Court continue their existing roles under the 1998 Act. In addition the Director of Equality Investigations may have cases referred to her other than those involving dismissals. The Director investigates complaints which are not resolved in mediation and gives a decision. The decision may be appealed to the Labour Court within *thirty-five days* of its issue. This is a reduction from the forty-two-day limit that was previously in effect between equality officer and Labour Court. The Director uses equality officers in the same way as formerly done by the Equality Service. The Act allows for quite extensive investigation powers for the Director and the Labour Court to secure information, interview relevant people and secure documentary evidence.

In cases of gender discrimination only, a claimant may bypass the Director and Labour Court and refer the matter directly to the Circuit Court. It seems that this provision, at s 77(3), follows the European Court of Justice decision in *Marshall v Southampton Area Health Authority (No 2)* [1993] ECR I-4367. In that case the court held that a cap on the potential award for sex discrimination was inconsistent with the right to an effective judicial process pursuant to article 6 of the Equal Treatment Directive. When gender discrimination cases are referred directly to the Circuit Court there is now no ceiling on the award that may be made by the court and s 82(3) allows that the award may exceed the normal civil jurisdiction of the Circuit Court. In cases not referred directly to the Circuit Court the compensation available under the legislation is as follows:

(a)　in an equal pay case the ordering of equal pay and maximum arrears up to equal pay for the preceding three years; and

(b)　in other cases the ordering of equal treatment or ending of the discrimination and compensation of a sum up to a maximum of two years' pay or where the person was not an employee up to £10,000.

7.12.3.2　Awards of compensation

Equality officers and the Labour Court took it upon themselves under the 1977 Act in particular to award compensation for hurt feelings even though there was no specific provision in the legislation for them to do so. Section 82 of the 1998 Act provides for full redress referred to above. The section provides that the Director of Equality and the Labour Court may make:

'an Order for compensation for the effects of acts of discrimination or victimisation which occurred not earlier than six years before the date of the referral of the case.'

The ceiling on such an award of compensation is, for an employed person, the maximum of two years' remuneration referred to above, or for a non-employee, £10,000. No guidance is given as to the level at which compensation might be ordered, nor does the existing case law give any indication as to what type of awards might be expected, particularly in respect of the new areas of discrimination.

Some guidance was given by the EAT in the UK in *Armitage, Marsden and HM Prison Service v Johnson* [1997] IRLR 162. The awards for discrimination in the UK have traditionally been higher than in Ireland. Mr Johnson had been subjected to an ongoing campaign of racial discrimination described by the industrial tribunal as 'appalling treatment'. His complaint of race discrimination against two prison officers and the prison service was upheld and he was awarded £28,500 compensation including £20,000 for injury to feelings reflecting the fact that the campaign had gone on for some eighteen months, and £7,500 aggravated damages against his employers for failure to properly deal with his complaints. £500 for injury to feelings was also awarded against both of the two prison officers personally for their victimisation and aiding the employer to discriminate.

7.12.3.3　Assessing injury to feelings

The EAT in upholding the award set out what it considered were the relevant principles for assessing awards for injury to feelings for unlawful discrimination as follows:

(1)　Awards for injury to feelings are compensatory. They should be just to both parties. They should compensate fully without punishing the tortfeasor. Feelings of indignation of the tortfeasor's conduct should not be allowed to inflate the award.

(2)　Awards should not be too low as that would diminish respect for the policy of the anti-discrimination legislation. Society has condemned discrimination and awards must ensure that it is seen to be wrong. On the other hand awards should be restrained, as excessive awards could be seen as the way of untaxed riches.

(3)　Awards should bear some broad general similarity to the range of awards in personal injury cases. This should be done by reference to the whole range of such awards, rather than to any particular type of award.

(4)　In exercising their discretion in assessing a sum, tribunals should remind themselves of the value in everyday life of the sum they have in mind. This may be done by reference to purchasing power or by reference to earnings.

(5) Tribunals should bear in mind the need for public respect for the level of awards made.

In a recent Labour Court case, *Rotunda Hospital and the Mater Hospital v Gleeson* BC9/99, DEE003, where a female doctor was not appointed to the position of consultant obstetrician/gynaecologist, an award of £50,000 was made in favour of the claimant. The claimant had been asked discriminatory questions which had not been asked of the male candidates and an offensive comment of 'sink the sisters' had been made to her. The Labour Court made reference to the fact that only two of the eight interviewers were female, as one of the matters which had led them to make a finding of discrimination on the grounds of gender. The claimant had been unsuccessful before an equality officer.

7.12.4 BURDEN OF PROOF

The European Communities (Burden of Proof in Gender Discrimination Cases) Regulations, 2001 provide for a shift in the burden of proof in gender discrimination cases only. Regulation 3(1) provides:

> 'where in any proceedings facts are established by or on behalf of a person from which it may be presumed that there has been direct or indirect discrimination in relation to him or her, it shall be for the other party concerned to prove the contrary.'

This provision explains the test usually described as a 'prima facie' case, the test adopted by equality officers in gender discrimination cases before the statutory instrument.

7.13 IMPACT OF THE 1998 ACT

7.13.1 INTRODUCTION

The main impact of the 1998 Act since its commencement has been to increase awareness and to seek to eliminate wider areas of discrimination than had hitherto been the case. Indirect discrimination must now come into sharper focus not just because there is now a statutory definition but because the grounds upon which discrimination may now occur are considerably wider than they were.

The most immediate impact should be on the following.

7.13.2 RECRUITMENT

Current practice in relation to the profile of a successful candidate, advertising the job and conducting interviews will have to change radically. The employer's current ideas as to whom it wishes to secure as the 'best' candidate will have to be looked at. Who is considered 'best'? The youngest, physically fittest individual with no family responsibilities? Not any longer. Focusing on the person who performed best at interview and is the most likely candidate is no longer sufficient. Each candidate rejected must be given thought. What is the reason for the rejection? Rejection at different stages, eg application, shortlisting, first, second or subsequent interviews, will all have to be considered in detail and non-discriminatory reasons relied on by the employer in rejecting each candidate. In *Corrib Airport Ltd v A Worker* [1994] ELR 81 the claimant applied for a job with the company and was granted an interview. She claimed that at interview she was asked about her pregnancies, her husband, her children and her child-care arrangements. She claimed the questions were asked of her about her availability and unavailability for work given her child-minding arrangements. She was concerned that the person who interviewed her seemed to be overly interested in such arrangements and concerned as to how they might impact on her ability to do the job. The company disputed much of what was claimed by the claimant. The Labour Court held:

(1) 'On the balance of probability the claimant's record accurately reflected the content, thrust and atmosphere of the interview.'
(2) 'The managing director's decision not to award the job to the claimant was largely determined by his perception that her work availability had limitations because of her child-minding responsibilities.'
(3) 'The managing director's decision not to offer the claimant the job constitutes discrimination contrary to s 2(a) of the Employment Equality Act, 1977.'

Compensation was awarded.

7.13.3   TERMS, CONDITIONS AND BENEFITS

Terms, conditions and benefits will have to be examined to ensure that they do not directly or indirectly discriminate. The provision of benefits such as health benefits for spouses may now have to be extended to partners. What then is to be done if employees change partners and request that the benefit be extended to them? If a middle-aged male is provided with motor insurance and his spouse is added to the insurance at no cost, is similar provision made for the young employee with a boyfriend or girlfriend to be added to the policy? Does s 34(1) allow the employer to make such benefit available to the spouse as a member of the employee's family?

7.13.4   HARASSMENT POLICIES

Are policies on harassment and sexual harassment in place and enforced, given prominence and included in job offers? If a problem arises is the employer's paperwork in order and sufficiently well operated to ensure that the available defences under the Act can be relied on?

7.13.5   DISCRIMINATION POLICIES

Are policies against discrimination or unequal treatment in place covering gender, marital status, family status, sexual orientation, religion, age, disability, race and membership of the traveller community?

7.13.6   POSITIVE ACTION

What positive action has the employer taken to carry out an equality audit in regard to the EU code of practice on equal pay and what steps has the employer taken to ensure that pay and other discrimination have not arisen?

CHAPTER 8

MATERNITY RIGHTS OF EMPLOYEES

8.1   MATERNITY PROVISIONS

The Maternity Protection Act, 1994 ('the 1994 Act') is the main legislation on maternity leave in Ireland. It operates in conjunction with the Safety, Health and Welfare at Work (Pregnant Employees) Regulations, 1994 (SI 446/1994) which govern safety, health and welfare protections and the European Communities (Social Welfare) Regulations, 1994 (SI 312/1994) which cover paid leave entitlements, safety and health and maternity leave. These regulations and the 1994 Act were enacted by the government to implement Directive 92/85/EEC (the Pregnant Workers' Directive) on the introduction of measures to encourage improvements in the safety and health at work of workers who have recently given birth or are breastfeeding.

The 1994 Act repealed the Maternity Protection of Employees Acts, 1981 and 1991. The provisions of the European Directive are similar to the 1981 and 1991 Acts in some respects, but enhance the rights of pregnant workers. The 1994 Act goes somewhat further than the standards of the Directive, giving enhanced rights to pregnant workers.

8.2   MATERNITY LEAVE

8.2.1   GENERALLY

Section 8 of the 1994 Act provides that a pregnant employee shall be entitled to fourteen consecutive weeks as a minimum period of maternity leave. A 'pregnant employee' is defined in the Act as an employee who is pregnant *and* who has informed her employer of her condition.

Section 9 provides that to avail of this right, the employee must notify the employer in writing of her intention to take maternity leave and must have a medical certificate confirming the expected date of confinement. 'Confinement' is defined in the Social Welfare (Consolidation) Act, 1993, s 41 as 'labour resulting in the issue of a living child, or labour after 28 weeks of pregnancy resulting in the issue of a child whether alive or dead'.

The provisions of the 1994 Act do not enhance those in the 1981 Act. They simply repeat its provisions as follows.

8.2.2   ALLOCATION OF MINIMUM PERIOD OF LEAVE

Section 10 deals with the allocation of the minimum period of maternity leave. It provides that the maternity leave shall commence when the employee decides but it must not be later than four weeks before the end of the expected week of confinement. The maternity leave will end when the employee decides but shall end no earlier than four weeks after the end of the expected week of confinement.

8.2.3   VARIATION IN ALLOCATION OF LEAVE

Section 11 provides for a variation in the allocation of maternity leave. It states that maternity leave may commence at an earlier date if there are medical grounds. A medical practitioner must provide a medical certificate to that effect and the provision of those medical certificates to the employer constitutes a notification to the employer in accordance with s 9.

8.2.4   EXTENSION OF LEAVE

Section 12 provides for the extension of maternity leave where the baby is born after the expected week of confinement. The common practice is that employees take four weeks before the baby is born and ten weeks afterwards. However, in the event that the baby arrives late and the employee has fewer than four weeks left to the end of her maternity leave, the Act provides for an extension of maternity leave by a maximum of four weeks. The section provides that the employee should notify her employer as soon as practicable of her intention to avail of the extension.

8.2.5   ADDITIONAL LEAVE

It should be noted that even if an employee has an extension of maternity leave under s 12, she is still entitled to take the 'additional maternity leave' provided for in s 14. Section 14 allows for an additional four weeks beginning immediately after the end of the maternity leave. This 'additional maternity leave' is unpaid and at the employee's own expense. The employee must notify the employer not later than four weeks before the expected date of return to work.

8.2.6   UNEXPECTED EARLY CONFINEMENT

Section 13 provides for the commencement of maternity leave on unexpected early confinement. If the baby is born four weeks or more before the due date, the employee is still entitled to fourteen weeks but the commencement date of the maternity leave will be the earlier of the date when she commenced maternity leave or the date of confinement. The employee must notify her employer within fourteen days of the date of confinement so as to comply with s 9.

8.3   PAYMENT DURING MATERNITY LEAVE

There is no provision in Irish law for maternity pay from employers to employees, unlike several other European countries. Employees on maternity leave are entitled to claim social welfare benefits, but not to receive any payment from their employers. The social welfare benefit is at the rate of 70 per cent of the employee's reckonable earnings provided that she has made the requisite PRSI contributions. The social welfare benefit is available for the fourteen weeks' maternity leave but not for the four weeks of additional leave. Parties may make their own contractual arrangements but are not compelled by law to do so. Many employees are contractually entitled to receive some form of payment from their employers during maternity leave.

8.4 PAID TIME OFF FOR ANTE- AND POST-NATAL CARE

Section 15 of the 1994 Act entitles pregnant employees to paid time off from work for ante-natal and post-natal care. Such a right existed under the 1981 Regulations, but the 1994 Act also entitles pregnant women to be paid for time off for medical appointments for examinations and tests.

The Directive required paid time off for ante-natal leave only; however, the Irish Act entitles employees to paid time off for post-natal absences also. This entitlement applies during the first fourteen weeks following the birth of the employee's child.

Section 15 does not specifically state that the period of post-natal care is for fourteen weeks after the birth of the baby. Section 15(2) provides for the making of regulations in relation to the right to time off. Regulation 5 of the Maternity Protection (Time Off for Ante- and Post-Natal Care) Regulations, 1995 (SI 18/1995) provides for the fourteen-week period.

If the employee is on maternity leave for fourteen weeks following the birth of the child, it is difficult to see how the entitlement to paid time off from work will arise. The entitlement will arise if the employee does not take the full fourteen weeks' leave or if the baby arrives late and the employee returns to work while still receiving post-natal care. If the employee has to receive post-natal care after the fourteen-week period has expired, it appears that she will not be entitled to paid time off.

8.5 DEATH OF MOTHER

Section 16 introduces a new provision, which entitles an employed father to leave where the mother has died within fourteen weeks of the birth of the child (and providing the child is born alive). The section is technical and complicated. If the mother dies before the end of the tenth week following the week of confinement, then the father's period of leave will end at the end of that tenth week. If the mother dies at any time after the expiry of the tenth week, then the father's period of leave will end at the end of the fourteenth week following the week of the confinement.

8.6 HEALTH AND SAFETY

The Safety, Health and Welfare at Work Act, 1989 and the Safety, Health and Welfare at Work (Pregnant Employees) Regulations, 2000 (SI 218/2000) require employers to carry out risk assessments in respect of their employees. The Pregnant Workers Directive requires specific risk assessment for pregnant employees.

In Ireland, because of the broad framework of the health and safety legislation, such risk assessment was required in any event, although not specifically provided for in respect of pregnant workers as a separate group of workers. The 1994 Regulations require employers to carry out a specific risk assessment for pregnant women even if there are no pregnant employees in the firm. As soon as an employer is on notice of an employee's pregnancy or the fact that she has just given birth to a child or is breastfeeding, the employer must reassess the risk in the workplace for that employee without delay. Until the risks are at an acceptable level pregnant workers and new mothers must not be exposed to these risks. The employer must move the employee to alternative work if a risk assessment shows unacceptable risks or if the employee cannot be required to perform night work. If this is not technically or objectively feasible or if the other work is not suitable or a move cannot reasonably be required on duly substantiated grounds, the employee must be granted health and safety leave and receive payment for the first three weeks of that leave. The entitlement to leave on health and safety grounds is provided for in the 1994 Act, s 18. The employee is entitled to receive three times the normal weekly pay for the twenty-one days of health and safety leave as provided for in the Maternity Protection (Health and Safety Leave Remuneration) Regulations, 1995 (SI 20/1995). For any period after the first twenty-one days, the employee will be entitled to social welfare benefits.

The health and safety leave can end when the risk no longer exists, as provided for in the 1994 Act, s 20. Employers are not entitled to dismiss employees if they are unable to work during pregnancy, just after giving birth or while breastfeeding, if that inability to work arises for health and safety reasons.

8.7 EMPLOYMENT PROTECTION AND THE RIGHT TO RETURN TO WORK

8.7.1 PROTECTIVE LEAVE

Section 21 provides that protective leave includes maternity leave, additional maternity leave, father's leave and health and safety leave. The employee's statutory and contractual rights remain in place while on protective leave. Any termination notice by an employer during that period is void. Section 22(4) provides that absence while on protective leave will not be treated as part of sick leave or annual leave and s 22(6) provides that when an employee is on health and safety leave she will not be entitled to payment for any public holidays falling during that period of absence.

8.7.2 RIGHT TO RETURN TO WORK

Section 26 of the 1994 Act reflects the provision of the 1981 Act in providing for a general right to return to work. An employee has a general right to return to the position held before the maternity leave. Similarly, if there was a transfer of undertaking while the employee was on leave, she is still entitled to return to work.

8.7.3 SUITABLE ALTERNATIVE WORK

Alternatively, s 27 provides for a right to suitable alternative work. This means that an employer is not always required to offer an employee her original job back at the end of her maternity leave. Section 27 provides that where the employee is entitled to return to work but it is not reasonably practicable for the employer to permit her to return to work she is entitled to be offered suitable alternative employment under a new contract of employment. Section 27(2) imposes two requirements in respect of the new contract of employment. It provides that the work required to be done shall be of a kind which is suitable in relation to the employee concerned and appropriate for her to do in the circumstances. It also provides that the terms and conditions relating to the place where the work is required to be done, the capacity in which the employee is to be employed and then the other terms and conditions of employment are not to be substantially less favourable to the employee than those of her contract of employment immediately before the start of her period of absence from work while on maternity leave or additional maternity leave.

This means that the suitable alternative work is work that is suitable in relation to the particular employee concerned and appropriate for her to do in the circumstances. This requires a subjective analysis of the work done and the conditions of employment of the employee before she took maternity leave. In *Tighe v Travenol Laboratories (Ireland) Ltd* (1989) 8 JISLL 124 a woman claimed that she had been unfairly constructively dismissed when she returned from maternity leave to be given production work, having previously been employed as an office worker. The EAT took on board the subjective test and said that the nature of work involved in production is so very different from office work that they did not consider it appropriate from the employee's standpoint, although the management might and did argue that the production work was appropriate for the employee in the circumstances.

The employer must show that it was not reasonably practicable to permit the employee to return to work, in order for the employer to be able to rely upon the provisions of s 27 allowing it to offer the employee suitable alternative work. The employer must be able to establish that it made reasonable attempts to be in a position to allow the employee to return to her job, which may mean the employer having to show that it sought a temporary rather than a permanent replacement for the woman while she was on maternity leave. The EAT has twice held, in *Butler v Smurfit Ireland Ltd* UD 137/88 and *O'Brien v Harringtons & Goodlass Ltd* P5/81, that temporary replacements can often be found by employers and, in both of those cases, the employer was found to have unfairly dismissed the employee when a vacancy was filled on a permanent basis during maternity leave.

8.8 NOTIFICATION OF INTENTION TO RETURN TO WORK

An employee is not entitled to return to her job or suitable alternative work unless she has complied with the provisions of the 1994 Act in respect of notification of her intention to return to work. The employer is not obliged to make enquiry of the employee in respect of her intention to return or otherwise.

It is still the employee who must notify the employer of her intention to return to work as provided in s 28. The employee must do so not later than four weeks before the date in which she expects to return to work. She must provide written notification of her intention to return to work and the date on which she expects to do so. The 1981 Act required her to then give further written confirmation. She no longer has to do this. A rights commissioner or EAT may extend the time for an employee giving notification where there are reasonable grounds for her failure to give notification or for her giving notification other than as provided for in the Act. Section 28(2) of the 1994 Act governs this. If there are no reasonable grounds, the employee's failure to give the required notification may be taken into account by a rights commissioner, tribunal or the Circuit Court in determining her rights under the Unfair Dismissals Act, 1977, the 1994 Act and any other enactment as far as the remedies of reinstatement, re-engagement or compensation are concerned.

8.9 PREGNANCY RELATED DISMISSALS

Section 23 of the 1994 Act provides that any purported termination of an employee's employment while, inter alia, absent on protective leave will be void.

Section 38(1) provides that dismissals are automatically unfair if connected with pregnancy or giving birth. This includes women made redundant during the maternity period and not offered suitable alternative employment if such is available. No qualifying period is necessary to bring a claim for unfair dismissal by reason of pregnancy or the taking of maternity leave.

The Unfair Dismissals Act, 1977 is amended by the Maternity Protection Act, 1994, s 38(4). The amendment adds the matters to be deemed to be unfair dismissal:

'the employee's pregnancy, giving birth or breastfeeding or any matter connected therewith,

'the exercise or proposed exercise by the employee of a right under the Maternity Protection Act, 1994 to any form of protective leave or natal care absence.'

8.10   PREGNANCY RELATED ILLNESS

A substantial jurisprudence has developed in the European Court of Justice in respect of the rights of employees suffering from pregnancy related illness, before and after the birth of their children and in the periods during and after the end of statutory maternity leave. An equality officer has recently applied the relevant European Court of Justice case law in deciding *McKenna v North Western Health Board* DEC-E2001. Margaret McKenna claimed that she suffered discrimination contrary to article 119 of the EC Treaty (now article 141 of the Treaty of Amsterdam) when her employer treated all of her sick leave in the same manner, despite the fact that some of her sick leave took place while she was pregnant and during her period of statutory maternity leave. The North Western Health Board's sick pay scheme provided for full pay for a period of six months and then half pay for a further six-month period. The way in which it applied its scheme meant that Ms McKenna lost salary because she was treated as having used her six months' full sick pay and therefore had her sick pay reduced to half pay. The equality officer held that her period of sickness during her pregnancy and during her statutory maternity leave could not be used to calculate the amount of sick leave she had incurred and therefore the amount of full sick pay she had received. The period of sickness during pregnancy and maternity leave was to be discounted for the purposes of calculating the six-month period of full pay.

The essence of the decision is that employers must not treat pregnancy related illness as normal illness when applying the provisions of their sick leave schemes. This is consistent with many judgments of the European Court of Justice in respect of pregnancy related illness. The decision is, however, restricted to illness prior to the birth of a child and during the period of statutory maternity leave. Again, this is consistent with the jurisprudence of the European Court of Justice and in particular the judgment in *Brown v Rentokil* [1998] ECR I-4185.

In that case the European Court of Justice said that:

'[W]here a woman is absent owing to illness resulting from pregnancy or childbirth and that illness arose during pregnancy and persisted during and after maternity leave, her absence not only during maternity leave but also during the period extending from the start of pregnancy to the start of maternity leave cannot be taken into account for computation of the period justifying her dismissal under national law. As to her absence after maternity leave, this may be taken into account under the same conditions as a man's absence, of the same duration, through incapacity for work.'

The equality officer's decision in *McKenna v North Western Health Board* approves this European Court of Justice judgment and states that the special protection cannot prevail for an indefinite period and ceases at a particular point in time. A female employee is protected from less favourable treatment that results from pregnancy throughout the pregnancy and all the way through to the end of the statutory period of maternity leave. The equality officer states that, in accordance with European jurisprudence, an employer may take full account, for the purposes of its sick leave scheme, of pregnancy related absence occurring after the statutory period of maternity leave.

A pregnant employee, or an employee suffering from pregnancy related illness during the period of her statutory maternity leave, cannot be compared to a sick man. After the end of the statutory maternity leave, an employee who was absent from work due to pregnancy related illness may be compared with a sick man and treated as a sick man absent from work for a similar period (the period after the end of the statutory maternity leave) would be treated.

8.11   RESOLUTION OF DISPUTES

Part V of the 1994 Act deals with disputes. Section 31 provides that disputes are to be referred to a rights commissioner within six months of the employer being informed of the initial circumstances of the dispute. The rights commissioner may, in exceptional circumstances, extend the six-month period to twelve months. Section 32(3) provides that the rights commissioner may award up to twenty weeks' remuneration. Section 33 provides for an appeal to the EAT within four weeks and s 34 provides for an appeal to the High Court on point of law only. The Maternity Protection (Disputes and Appeals) Regulations, 1995 (SI 17/1995) set out the procedures to be followed and incidental matters in relation to the hearing of disputes and appeals by a Rights Commissioner or the Employment Appeals Tribunal under the 1994 Act.

CHAPTER 9

INDUSTRIAL RELATIONS AND TRADE DISPUTES

9.1   COLLECTIVE AGREEMENTS AND CONTRACTS OF EMPLOYMENT

In practice many terms and conditions of employment are negotiated between employers and trade unions on a collective basis. Two issues arise in relation to collective agreements: the first is how they might be binding in respect of individual contracts and the second, the incorporation, alteration or variation of terms or conditions of employment through a trade union.

In *O'Rourke v Talbot (Ireland) Ltd* [1984] ILRM 587 the plaintiffs, through their trade union, had negotiated with the company on the redeployment of certain employees as a result of financial difficulties encountered by the company. In the course of the negotiations the employees sought a written assurance from the company in relation to job security for the future. The company produced a document which gave 'an assurance that compulsory redundancy' would not be introduced. A further document was sought by the employees giving guaranteed protection against compulsory redundancy up to a certain date. This 'guarantee' was given by management. Barrington J held that productivity agreements similar to the first agreement in this case, which contained the assurances that there would be no compulsory redundancies, were agreements of a sort that 'did not contemplate legal relations, at any rate so far as all their clauses were concerned but were meant to be binding in honour on the management and the trade union'. He went on to hold, however, that given the circumstances of the second commitment, wherein the word 'guarantee' was used, and taking the view that 'the representatives of management did not think that they were entering into a legally binding arrangement' that he was 'satisfied however that not only were the men looking for something which was legally binding but that management knew this' and thereby held that the second commitment was legally binding.

In reaching his conclusion Barrington J considered the leading British and Irish precedents on the legal status of collective agreements (*Edwards v Skyways Ltd* [1964] 1 WLR 349; *Ford Motor Co v AEF* [1969] 2 QB 303 and *Goulding Chemicals Ltd v Bolger* [1977] IR 211) and went on to hold that the agreement sought to be upheld by the plaintiffs was a commercial agreement legally binding on the parties. The way in which collective agreements are incorporated into individual contracts of employment is referred to in *Becton Dickinson v Lee* [1973] IR 1 at p 5.

It should also be kept in mind that the terms of a collective agreement may apply to employees who are not members of the trade union with which the agreement was concluded. This may arise in a number of ways. The employee may have commenced employment and been advised that his terms and conditions would be governed, at least in part, by the terms of the collective agreement (see *Singh v British Steel Corporation* [1974]

IRLR 131), or the employee may have left or been expelled from his trade union at a time when the collective agreement was in being. It should also be noted that a trade union cannot bind all of its members where some of those members have made it clear that they did not intend or wish to be bound (see *Goulding Chemicals Ltd v Bolger* [1977] IR 211).

9.2 LEGALITY OF COLLECTIVE AGREEMENTS

9.2.1 EU LAW

The second issue to be considered is whether collective agreements are in themselves legally binding as between the parties, being the employer on one side and the trade union/ employees on the other side. Apart from the case law referred to there are no legislative provisions in Ireland making collective agreements legally binding. However, article 3(2) of the Transfer of Undertakings Directive (77/187/EEC) obliges a transferee to observe terms and conditions agreed in any collective agreement after a transfer. If the collective agreement is not binding under the law of the Member State within which the parties are situate does article 3(2) make the collective agreement legally binding? The Committee on Social Affairs and Employment of the European Parliament, when considering the Yeats Report, surveyed a number of employment practices in Member States and, in relation to the issue of whether or not collective agreements were legally binding in the Member States, the following answers were given.

Belgium	Collective agreements are not legally binding. Their value depends on the strength of the trade unions.
Germany	Yes.
Denmark	Not generally legally binding.
France	No information.
Ireland	No.
Italy	Normally the main ideas of civil right are part of the collective agreements.
Netherlands	There is a tendency to consider collective agreements legally binding.
UK	No.
Luxembourg	Yes.

The conclusion in relation to Ireland is questionable.

9.2.2 CASE LAW

The Supreme Court in *Goulding Chemicals Ltd v Bolger* [1977] IR 211 considered a situation where agreement was reached between the company and representative trade unions as to the manner in which a plant would be closed and the amounts of redundancy payments the employees were to be paid. The trade unions arranged for a vote to be taken on the proposals and a majority of the members of the various unions supported the company's proposals and accepted them. The company then acted on the acceptance by the majority and treated it as an acceptance by the entire workforce. The company had negotiated on a collective basis and then proceeded to act in relation to each individual employee's contract of service on the basis of what was collectively negotiated. The defendants were part of the minority of the workforce who had voted against the proposals. They made their objections clear to their employers. The agreement reached

233

between the company and the trade unions restricted the unions' and employees' rights to picket. The defendants engaged in a picket. The company sought to restrain them on a number of grounds, one of which was that they were bound by the collective agreement concluded with their trade union. Two issues had to be considered. The first was whether or not collective agreements of the sort concluded in this case were legally binding on the parties to the agreement and, secondly, whether a collective agreement binds the employees who are members of the unions involved in concluding the agreement. The judgments in *Goulding* refer extensively to *Edwards v Skyways* [1964] 1 WLR 349 and *Ford Motor Co Ltd v AEF* [1969] 2 QB 303.

In *Edwards* agreement was reached between the employer and the employees that an ex gratia payment would be paid in the event of redundancy. In that case the court held that the agreement was binding on the parties as the subject matter was one of business relations and there was an intention to agree and, further, that where there is a difference between the parties the onus of proof lies on the party who asserts that no legal effect was intended, and this onus was not discharged in *Edwards*.

In *Ford Motor Co Ltd* it was held that collective agreements negotiated between a large industrial company and various trade unions were, owing to the contents, which were stated to be mainly aspirational, and the fact that the parties were seeking to order their day-to-day relations rather than impose legal obligations on each other, not legally binding, as there was no intention to create legal relations, the court stating at p 496 per Lane J:

'Agreements such as these, composed largely of optimistic aspirations presenting grave practical problems of enforcement and reached against a background of opinion adverse to enforceability, are . . . not contracts in the legal sense and are not enforceable at law.'

In *Goulding* at p 237, per Kenny J, the Supreme Court expressed reservations about the *Ford* decision. The Supreme Court analysed the nature of the particular agreement at issue in *Goulding* and held that it was 'a business-like document and had all the appearances of being intended to create legal relations'.

In *O'Rourke v Talbot* [1984] ILRM 587 Barrington J also referred to *Edwards* and to the leading textbooks on the law of contract which maintain that the test of intention to create or not to create legal relations is an 'objective' test. He held that in the case before him, the conditions of the objective test had been met and that Talbot could not rebut the presumption that the agreement they reached with the trade unions and the workforce was one intended to create legal relations. He held that the agreement was binding on the company and that it was in breach of agreement in making the plaintiffs redundant prior to the date after which employment had been guaranteed. The conclusion reached by the Supreme Court in *Goulding* on the general issue of whether a collective agreement is legally binding was effectively that regard must be had to the circumstances in which the agreement was concluded, and its contents which might suggest it was not intended to be legally binding, but concluded on the first issue:

'I would regard the agreement resulting from the acceptance of these proposals as being similar in effect to that dealt with in *Edwards v Skyways Ltd* [1964] 1 WLR 349 and, there being nothing to suggest the contrary, in my view a valid contract is thereby created between these unions and the plaintiff' (p 231 per O'Higgins CJ).

He went on to refer to 'this valid enforceable agreement'. In *Goulding* Kenny J held (at p 236):

'An agreement between parties is enforceable by the law unless the agreement itself or the surrounding circumstances show that the parties did not intend to enter into legal relations.'

In reviewing the authorities Kenny J stated: 'I have considerable doubts about the correctness of the decision in the *Ford Motor Company Ltd* case'. In relation to the agreement concluded between the company and trade unions within *Goulding* he said:

'It seems to me that the six-point agreement was intended to create legal relations and was intended to be a contract between the plaintiffs and the unions engaged in the negotiations . . . when an apparent agreement in relation to business relations is entered into the onus on the party who asserts that it was not intended to have legal effect is a heavy one. In my opinion the six-point statement and its acceptance created a valid enforceable contract between the plaintiffs and the unions who took part in the negotiations.'

On the second issue, as to whether, in the circumstances of this particular case where the defendants rejected an agreement accepted by the majority membership of the trade unions concerned and made this rejection clear to their employers, the members were or should be bound by the terms of the agreement which in itself the court had found to be binding on the company and trade unions, O'Higgins CJ stated (at p 231):

'I find it hard to accept . . . the defendants can be bound by an agreement which they have expressly repudiated and opposed. It seems to me that to hold them bound would be contrary to all principle.'

On this point Kenny J stated (at p 237):

'Membership of a corporate body or of an association does not have the consequence that every agreement made by that corporate body or association binds every member of it. None of the defendants are parties to the agreement and as they consistently opposed it no question of their being bound by acquiescence can arise.'

See also *Holland v London Society of Compositors* [1924] TLR 440 and *Young v Canadian Northern Railway Company* [1931] AC 83.

9.2.3 INCORPORATION INTO CONTRACT OF EMPLOYMENT

If a collective agreement is legally binding then in itself it constitutes a contract by which employer and employee and, in certain circumstances, the trade union, will be legally bound to each other. Even if the collective agreement is not in itself legally binding it may be incorporated into the contract of employment as referred to in *Whent v T Cartledge Ltd* [1997] IRLR 153 and the cases of *Robertson v British Gas Corporation* [1983] IRLR 302 and *National Coal Board v National Union of Mineworkers* [1986] IRLR 439.

Whent v Cartledge involved the transfer of an undertaking. Prior to the transfer the employees had their rates of pay determined under the terms of a collective agreement by a body known as the NJC. The individual contracts of employment provided that the employees' pay would be that set by the NJC. On 11 April 1994 the undertaking was transferred. On 21 April 1994 the transferee wrote to the trade union concerned withdrawing recognition and from the agreement stating that any collective agreements relating to employees transferred would no longer have effect. The employees were individually advised of the discontinuance of 'any formal or implied recognition arrangements or collective agreements or related arrangements' which were stated to no longer have any effect and to have ended with immediate effect. The employees claimed that despite these letters their pay was still to be ascertained by reference to the rates agreed and established from time to time by the NJC for their respective grades. The transferee contended that pay for the relevant employees was frozen at the level last fixed before the employers withdrew from the collective agreement. The EAT held:

'The transferee employers were still bound by the NJC agreement so far as incorporated in individual contracts of employment notwithstanding their withdrawal from the collective agreement. Until the transfer it was undisputed that the appellants' contracts incorporated the result of the annual round of negotiations and there were no grounds for holding that the transfer caused any change in the meaning of the words.'

In *Whent v Cartledge* the industrial tribunal, whose decision was overturned by the EAT, had reasoned 'it cannot be right that an employer is bound *ad infinitum* by the terms of the collective agreement negotiated by bodies other than themselves'. The EAT described that as 'fallacious reasoning' and stated (at p 154):

> 'The employer was not bound *ad infinitum* since it could at any time without breach of contract negotiate variations of contract with individual employees or terminate their contracts on due notice and offer fresh ones. In any event there was no reason why the parties should not if they choose agree that matters such as remuneration be fixed by processes in which they do not themselves participate.'

9.3 CONSTITUTIONAL POSITION

Article 40.6.1 of the Constitution states:

> 'The State guarantees liberty for the exercise of the following rights subject to public order and morality.'

Subsection (iii) provides:

> 'The right of the citizens to form associations and unions. Laws, however, may be enacted for the regulation and control in the public interest of the exercise of the foregoing rights.'

The scope of this constitutional provision has been examined in a number of cases, notably *National Union of Railwaymen v Sullivan* [1947] IR 77; *Educational Company of Ireland v Fitzpatrick* [1961] IR 345; *Murphy v Stewart* [1974] IR 97 and *Meskell v CIE* [1973] IR 121 and is most succinctly summarised in the words of Finlay J, the then President of the High Court, in *Rogers v ITGWU* [1978] ILRM 51 when he stated in reference to Article 40.6.1(iii):

> 'The constitutional right to the formation of trade unions involves of necessity the right to join or not to join existing trade unions.'

Employees have therefore a constitutional right to join a trade union, be a member and with some exceptions (see *Rodgers v ITGWU*) to enjoy the full benefits of membership and involvement in trade union affairs within their union. If an employee chooses to exercise his constitutional right to join a trade union, the employer is not, however, under any obligation to recognise that union and negotiate with it.

While the right of association applies throughout the European Union, the right of freedom of association has been enshrined in the constitutions of Belgium, Denmark, France, Germany, Greece, Ireland, Italy, Luxembourg, the Netherlands, Portugal and Spain.

9.4 UNION RECOGNITION

9.4.1 UNILATERAL RIGHT TO JOIN UNION

Employees who exercise a constitutional right to join a trade union cannot insist that they enjoy the full benefit of such membership, by in turn insisting that the employer recognise their union. The right conferred by the Constitution is an individual personal right and does not carry with it the concomitant obligation on an employer to recognise that trade union according to the judgment of McWilliam J in *Abbott and Whelan v ATGWU* [1982] 1 JISLL 56. The plaintiffs were members of a trade union, the ATGWU. Their employer, the Southern Health Board, did not have a formal recognition agreement with the ATGWU. The plaintiffs sought to insist that their employer deal with the trade union of their choice, and when the board refused the plaintiffs brought the matter to the High Court claiming inter alia that the defendants were interfering with or obstructing them in the exercise of their constitutional right to join the trade union of their choice and what they claimed was the further right to be represented by such trade union in the conduct of negotiations with their employers, concerning wages and other conditions of employment. In his judgment McWilliam J referred to Article 40.6.1(iii) and the rights conferred on the plaintiffs and other citizens by that provision and considered *Meskell v CIE* [1973] IR 121 and *Educational Company of Ireland v Fitzpatrick* [1961] IR 345, where active steps were taken to compel the citizens to forgo their constitutional rights. He held that there was no attempt to compel the plaintiffs to forgo their constitutional rights in this particular case in holding (at p 60):

'Insofar as the Board is concerned it appears to me to be clear that the plaintiffs have no constitutional right to compel the Board to engage in negotiations either with them or with their union. . . .

'In the present case, the plaintiffs have joined ATGWU without first ascertaining whether that trade union would or would not be in a position to negotiate with the Board. Employers must frequently have refused to negotiate with employees or their unions and this may have led to industrial action but, outside the terms of the contract of employment, employers are not bound to take part in any, or any particular form of, negotiations.

'On the facts of this case I am of the opinion that the refusal of the Board to negotiate with ATGWU is not coercion to forgo a constitutional right within the principles which have been enunciated.'

In the earlier case of *EI Company Ltd v Kennedy* [1968] IR 69 Walsh J stated in an obiter dictum:

'In law an employer is not obliged to meet anybody as the representative of his worker, nor indeed is he obliged to meet the worker himself for the purpose of discussing any demand which the worker may make.'

9.4.2   IMPLIED RECOGNITION

In the absence of a specific contractual provision that the employee's trade union will be recognised it is arguable that, where an employee is a member of a trade union and the employer is dealing with or had dealt with that union, there is an implied term in the contract between the employer and the employee to the effect that the employee's union will be recognised. In the context of a transfer of an undertaking the employees could then seek to rely on the provisions of article 3 of the Directive by claiming that their right to have their union recognised is something that arises from the existence of an employment relationship at the date of transfer. In this regard, article 3 refers to 'rights and obligations . . . arising from . . . an employment relationship'. The employment relationship could be deemed to involve a trade union where a person is a member and is actively represented by such union.

The absence of a system of formal recognition in Ireland allows that recognition may arise by express agreement but also by implied agreement. Recognition could be implied from a course of dealing between the parties and by the recognition, albeit in limited ways, of a trade union for certain purposes such as in disciplinary hearings. In *National Union of Tailors and Garment Workers v Charles Ingram and Co Ltd* [1977] IRLR 147 the UK EAT, in a case relating to recognition of a trade union for the purpose of redundancy consultations, held in relation to recognition:

'Recognition implies agreement which involves consent. Where, as in the present case, there is neither a written agreement that the union should be recognised nor an express agreement which is not in writing it is sufficient if the established facts are clear and unequivocal and give rise to the clear inference that the employers have recognised the union. This will normally involve conduct over a period of time and the longer that state of facts has existed the easier it is to reach a conclusion that the employers have recognised the union' (at p 147).

The Court of Appeal took a similar but stricter line on implied union recognition in the later case of *National Union of Gold, Silver and Allied Trades v Albury Brothers Ltd* [1978] IRLR 504. In that case the respondents dismissed four of their employees on grounds of redundancy without consulting with the trade union. There was no formal recognition agreement between the company and the union. The company was, however, a member of a trade association which had negotiated a number of agreements relating to terms and conditions of employment with the appellant trade union. On 5 May 1976, eight employees of the company joined the union and on 7 May the union's district secretary wrote to the company looking for a meeting to discuss rates of pay. That meeting took place on 20 May at which wages of one employee were discussed but no agreement was reached. Four of the employees were dismissed on grounds of redundancy on 28 May 1976. The union complained that this was in contravention of its statutory entitlement to be consulted in advance of redundancies The industrial tribunal held that the company had not recognised the union so as to impose an obligation to consult under the relevant statutory provision. The union's appeal was dismissed by the EAT. The union's appeal to the Court of Appeal was also rejected on the basis that the union had not been recognised. The Court of Appeal held:

'An act of recognition is such an important matter that it should not be held to be established unless the evidence is clear either by an actual agreement of recognition or clear and distinct conduct showing an implied agreement to recognise the trade union for the purposes of collective bargaining. Discussion between trade union representatives and management concerning matters referred to in [the appropriate legislation] is not sufficient in itself to constitute "recognition"; thus in the present case that discussions concerning wages took place on a particular occasion between the employer and the trade union was not sufficient to establish the employer had recognised the union particularly where the employer's attitude was one of refusing to bargain. Nor could it be held that recognition of the trade union came about by virtue of the employer's membership in an employers' association which recognised the union. The association was in no way the agent of the employers and the fact that there was an agreement between the employers' association and the union did not impose recognition on the members of the association.'

As there is no system of formal recognition provided for in Irish law there is also no system of derecognition. An employer wishing to derecognise a trade union must have regard to the contractual position the employer has with the trade union and with its own employees as referred to above.

9.5   RELATIONSHIPS BETWEEN TRADE UNIONS

For trade unions who are affiliated to the Irish Congress of Trade Unions (ICTU) the constitution of the ICTU contains regulations for dealing with the maintenance of good relationships between its affiliated unions and has a disputes procedure which can be invoked to deal with disputes and rule on their resolution. Clause 47(d) of the constitution of ICTU provides:

'Where any grade, group or category of workers, or the workers in any establishment, form a negotiating unit and their wages or conditions of work are determined by negotiations conducted by a single union of which the majority, or a substantial proportion of the workers concerned, are members, no other union shall organise or enrol as members any workers within that negotiating unit (that is workers within the grade, group, category or establishment) save only with the consent of the union concerned.'

The provisions of this rule were considered against the backdrop of an individual's constitutional right to join or not to join a trade union by McWilliam J in his judgment in *Abbott and Whelan v ATGWU* [1982] 1 JISLL 56 where he was invited to hold that the provisions of clause 47 were unconstitutional given the similarity between rule 47 and s 26 of the Trade Union Act, 1941 which had been held to be unconstitutional in *National Union of Railwaymen v Sullivan* [1947] IR 77. McWilliam J held that as clause 47(d) applied only between the trade unions concerned, the rule could not operate to deny the plaintiffs their constitutional rights which would remain enforceable 'despite any agreements to the contrary made between the two unions or anyone else'(at p 60).

9.6 CLOSED SHOP PROVISIONS

9.6.1 GENERALLY

Even where an employer does not recognise a union there is nothing to prevent the employees in their personal capacity being members of the trade union. While the judgment in *Abbott and Whelan v ATGWU* [1982] 1 JISLL 56 would indicate that in many situations the employees do not have the legal right to have their trade union recognised, they may still retain their membership, albeit in a situation where their trade union is very restricted as to what it can do for them. In European law an employee also has the right not to join a trade union and in the pre-entry closed shop case, *Sigurjonsson v Iceland* (1993) 16 EHRR 462, the European Court of Human Rights held that article 11 of the European Convention on Human Rights encompassed 'a negative right of association'. In addition, any attempt to have transferred employees give up membership of their trade union of choice would be seen as an attempt to get them to surrender their constitutional right to join the trade union of their choice and is likely to be held as unconstitutional as per *Meskell v CIE* [1979] IR 121. See also *Young, James and Webster v UK* [1983] IRLR 35 in relation to the post-entry closed shop.

The only course of action open to employees who have such a difficulty would be to seek to put pressure on either the employer or, indirectly, on their fellow employees by way of a trade dispute. A trade dispute engaged in by any party seeking to force membership of a particular trade union on any employee would itself be unconstitutional (see *Murtagh Properties Ltd v Cleary* [1972] IR 330). Where an employee has a constitutional right to be, and remain, a member of a trade union any attempt to have that person surrender that right would fall foul of *Murtagh Properties* and the judgment of Budd J in *Educational Company of Ireland Ltd v Fitzpatrick (No 2)* [1961] IR 345 where he stated inter alia (at p 368):

> 'The Court will therefore assist and uphold a citizen's constitutional rights . . . and it follows that if one citizen has a right under the Constitution there exists a correlative duty on the part of other citizens to respect that right and not to interfere with it.'

9.6.2 THE RIGHT TO STRIKE

The law of the European Union recognises the right to strike as enshrined in article 13 of the European Community Social Charter 1989. In Ireland there is no right to strike but rather there is a freedom in certain circumstances to strike in that immunities from legal restrictions on strikes and industrial actions will be conferred, provided certain conditions are met. The legal system of the European Union goes a stage further and confers a right which implies an entitlement to infrastructural, legal and state support for the right to strike. It is suggested that the right to strike values the collective interest more than it values the individual interest which may be overridden by the collective (see Barnard, *EC Employment Law*, pp 446–447).

9.7 TRADE DISPUTES

9.7.1 GENERALLY

Irish law is still based on the individual contract, and trade dispute law is no different although it recognises the position of trade unions, but more as supporters and advisers of the individual rather than the leaders of collective action, a position which was given particular importance in relation to secret ballots in *Nolan Transport (Oaklands) Ltd v Halligan* [1998] ELR 177 as dealt with in more detail at **9.10.3** below. In many employments, particularly those with larger numbers of employees and which are unionised, employers deal with their employees on a collective basis and conclude agreements either with a group of employees or a trade union or staff association acting on their behalf. In this way terms and conditions of employment, pay rises etc are dealt with rather than meeting and dealing with each individual employee. There would still be individual contact, perhaps in relation to performance appraisal and performance issues, but in the main the employers deal with the employees on a collective basis. Employers must keep in mind at all times that they have an individual contract with the employee and when it comes to terms, conditions, grievances and disciplinary matters regard must always be had to the individuality of the employees and their individual rights, entitlements, obligations and duties.

9.7.2 MAHER v ALLIED IRISH BANKS PLC

In 1991–92 AIB was in dispute with its employees represented by the IBOA. The IBOA issued a directive to members to work strict office hours without overtime and to decline to handle insurance and insurance-related business. AIB tolerated that restriction. The union later escalated the dispute by issuing a directive to its members not to carry out a substantial number of important bank procedures. This caused AIB considerable difficulty and it was not prepared to tolerate such a refusal on the part of its employees. Mary Maher worked for AIB and was a member of IBOA. She was approached by her manager and was asked to choose between carrying out her contractual duties to AIB or obeying the IBOA directive. She did not give a clear answer but asked if she could have representation from her trade union. She was then handed a pre-printed letter indicating that she had confirmed that she would not honour her professional contract and she was suspended without pay. She subsequently sued AIB, claiming damages for her loss of salary during the period of unpaid suspension. She also sought general damages. The matter came before the President of the District Court who allowed her claim in respect of the period of unpaid suspension but refused general damages in the case of *Maher v Allied Irish Banks plc* [1998] ELR 204 when he held:

(a)   The bank is entitled to adopt a measure of self-preservation. Where a unilateral decision has been made by employees to refuse performance of a significant part of their duties, the bank may treat same as a repudiatory breach of contract and in response may either terminate the contract or decline to accept proffered partial performance.

(b)   The bank has two options open to it in the circumstances. It can operate the suspension procedure in the contract of service or it can cease to employ temporarily any employee who refuses to carry out his or her full duties.

(c)   The bank could not, however, assume in this case that the plaintiff was going to side with the IBOA. The bank should have given the plaintiff the opportunity to be represented by her union as she requested and should not have 'jumped the gun'. Accordingly the purported suspension of the plaintiff was not justified and the plaintiff was entitled to be put back in the position as if she had not been suspended.

9.7.3 O'DONOVAN v ALLIED IRISH BANKS PLC

Some four months later the President of the District Court issued a similar judgment in *O'Donovan v Allied Irish Banks plc* [1998] ELR 209. In that case Mr O'Donovan was similarly approached by AIB, again with a pre-prepared letter effectively anticipating that Mr O'Donovan was going to confirm that he would follow the IBOA directive. The President of the District Court held that on the evidence before him AIB had no other objective evidence to show that Mr O'Donovan was not carrying out his normal duties or that he would have taken any steps consistent with a position of not carrying out his duties. It was held that AIB effectively approached their dealings with Mr O'Donovan with an element of pre-judgment and did not wait to see what he did which they then could have relied upon as evidence of his unwillingness to carry out his duties. In the course of his judgment the President stated:

'I think the bank had a serious duty to look at each case individually. These cases were not looked at individually. A decision was arrived at before the conversation with . . . Mr O'Donovan that unless there was an unequivocal declaration by him that he would not obey the IBOA directive he would be suspended. No consideration was given to the possibility that in fact the directive might not have affected him. The manager could have waited until there was one instance by Mr O'Donovan that he did not carry out something and this course of action then would result in a loss to the bank.'

The President went on to allow the plaintiff's claim in respect of his unpaid salary and held:

'The bank was legitimately seeking to protect its own interests and in so doing it has a duty to be fair and reasonable. The bank has a serious duty to look at each case individually and is not entitled to simply hand an employee a pre-printed letter, suspending the employee without having considered the possibility that the IBOA directive might not have affected the employee or having tangible proof of a particular instance where the employee had caused loss to the bank. Accordingly the plaintiff was entitled to his salary for the period during which he was suspended without pay.'

9.7.4 STATUTORY DEFINITIONS

The law in relation to trade disputes in Ireland is contained in the Trade Union and Industrial Relations Acts and principally the Industrial Relations Act, 1990. Part II of the 1990 Act contains practical provisions relevant to trade disputes. Section 8 contains a number of definitions including:

' "Trade dispute" means any dispute between employers and workers which is connected with the employment or non-employment or the terms or conditions of or affecting the employment of any person.

' "Employer" means a person for whom one or more workers work or have worked or normally work or seek to work having previously worked for that person.

' "Worker" means any person who is or was employed whether or not in the employment of the employer with whom a trade dispute arises but does not include a member of the Defence Forces or of the Garda Síochána.'

9.8 PRECONDITIONS TO LAWFUL INDUSTRIAL ACTION

In order for workers and their trade unions to engage in an effective and lawful trade dispute within the terms of the 1990 Act the following conditions must be satisfied.

The immunities in the Act only apply to members and officials of authorised trade unions (s 9(1)). Given the constitutional right to join or not to join a trade union it appears that the exclusion of persons who are not members of an authorised trade union from significant immunities conferred by the 1990 Act is constitutionally suspect but to date has not been challenged.

If the dispute relates to an individual worker any agreed procedures in existence or normally availed of by custom or in practice, in the employment concerned, or provided for in a collective agreement, for the resolution of individual grievances, must be adhered to before the immunities may be relied on (s 9(2)–(4)).

If the strike or industrial action is to be supported, organised or participated in, by a trade union the union must hold a secret ballot as provided for in s 14 of the Act. This does not preclude workers from taking unofficial action without a secret ballot or without the support or involvement of their trade union. If they do so, however, the restrictions on an employer obtaining injunctive relief as provided for in s 19 of the Act will not apply (see decision in *Nolan Transport (Oaklands) Ltd v Halligan* [1998] ELR 177).

9.9 THE GOLDEN FORMULA

9.9.1 INTRODUCTION

The Industrial Relations Act, 1990 confers the immunities on workers and their representatives only if they are acting within what is known as the 'golden formula' (see Wedderburn, *The Worker and the Law*, p 222). This 'golden formula' is repeated in many sections of the 1990 Act and is the principal condition workers and their representatives must satisfy in order to benefit from the immunities, and be entitled to engage in industrial action, as provided in the 1990 Act and other industrial relations legislation. The formula provides that the actions of such persons must be 'done in contemplation or furtherance of a trade dispute'.

9.9.2 STATUTORY DEFINITIONS

9.9.2.1 Generally

Part II of the 1990 Act commences with a definition section (s 8) which provides as follows:

'In this Part, save where the context otherwise requires—

' "employer" means a person for whom one or more workers work or have worked or normally work or seek to work having previously worked for that person;

' "trade dispute" means any dispute between employers and workers which is connected with the employment or non-employment, or the terms or conditions of or affecting the employment, of any person;

' "trade union" means a trade union which is the holder of a negotiation licence under Part II of the Trade Union Act, 1941;

' "worker" means any person who is or was employed whether or not in the employment of the employer with whom a trade dispute arises, but does not include a member of the Defence Forces or of the Garda Síochána;

' ''industrial action'' means any action which affects, or is likely to affect, the terms or conditions, whether express or implied, of a contract and which is taken by any number or body of workers acting in combination or under a common understanding as a means of compelling their employer, or to aid other workers in compelling their employer, to accept or not to accept terms or conditions of or affecting employment;

' ''strike'' means a cessation of work by any number or body of workers acting in combination or a concerted refusal or a refusal under a common understanding of any number of workers to continue to work for their employer done as a means of compelling their employer, or to aid other workers in compelling their employer, to accept or not to accept terms or conditions of or affecting employment.'

9.9.2.2   Employer

The Trade Disputes Act, 1906 did not define the word 'employer'. The Act did use the word and it was considered in the notorious case of *Roundabout Ltd v Beirne* [1959] IR 423. A pub was purchased by Roundabout Ltd and all unionised staff were dismissed. When the pub opened under its new ownership it was run by officers of the company and not employees. An injunction was granted on the basis that as the company employed no employees it could not be an employer. It is likely nowadays that a court would take a more liberal view and if necessary lift the corporate veil (see *Examite Ltd v Whitaker* [1977] IRLR 312).

In *McHenry Brothers Ltd v Carey* [1984] 3 JISLL 80 seasonal workers who worked for McHenry Brothers Coal Merchants were refused employment when the new season commenced and they then engaged in a picket. The company argued that as they were at that time unemployed they were not employees. The court did not accept that contention and held that as they were habitually engaged in employment and, in this particular case, with the company they were picketing then they were workers within the meaning of the 1906 Act and entitled to picket. The definition of worker in this section allows that a worker can be a person who is not in the employment of the employer with whom the trade dispute arises. The definition of 'employer' was enacted to give effect to the reasoning in the *McHenry Brothers* case. In *J Bradbury Ltd v Duffy* [1984] 3 JISLL 86 McWilliam J held that there had to be some restriction on who could picket an employer and he looked at the extreme case, which had very often been quoted by employers as being offensive to them, of a number of new job applications being received by an employer and the employer quite legitimately only having a set number of positions and rejecting some of the people concerned. If those people rejected were to picket there was no logic or fairness in treating that picket as being valid. It is suggested that the definition of 'employer', where it states that a person must be deemed in seeking work to have 'previously worked for that person', gives effect to the reasoning behind the *McHenry Brothers* decision but does not allow a person initially seeking employment, who fails, to engage in a valid trade dispute.

9.9.2.3   Trade dispute

The definition of 'trade dispute' is more restricted than that in the 1906 Act. The 1906 Act definition allowed disputes between worker and worker which were also most unpopular with employers. It is hard to argue with the logic of an employer's position where a dispute arises between two groups of workers and the employer's business can be validly and legally limited or totally restricted. At the same time, however, a trade dispute may now exist between an employer and persons who are not his employees as the definition states that the dispute may be with persons 'whether or not in the employment of the employer with whom a trade dispute arises'. Again it seems that this is more in the way of allowing secondary disputes than allowing that an employer's business be affected by total strangers with no nexus whatever. Considerable restrictions have been put on secondary picketing in s 11 (see **9.9.5.6** below).

The phrase 'connected with' in the definition of a trade dispute appears to allow for an indirect connection between the matters in dispute and the 'target' employer. The decision of Barron J in the High Court in *Nolan Transport (Oaklands) Ltd v Halligan* [1995] ELR 1 examined a number of aspects of the 1990 Act which are referred to throughout this chapter but, in relation to the definition of 'trade dispute', Barron J commented that the definition 'permits as a dispute anything affecting a worker in the course of his employment'.

9.9.2.4 Observations on the definitions

On the definitions generally Barron J made the interesting observation

> 'it seems to me, that so far as the law is to be applied to industrial relations disputes, the right to take industrial action including the right to picket has been restricted essentially to a right to workers to take action against their own employer and no-one else'.

He then allowed for the exception provided in s 11 which is dealt with at **9.9.5** below but commented on how restricted the right to secondary picketing is.

Barron J also held that 'it is now clear that as between employers and workmen everything which pertains to the terms and conditions of employment may be the subject of a trade dispute'. It is not a matter for a court to determine the reasonableness or otherwise of a dispute or a position either party might take in a dispute simply to determine whether there is a dispute and that it comes within the statutory definition. Section 5 of the Unfair Dismissals Act, 1977 (as amended) affords certain protections to employees dismissed for engaging in industrial action. In *Tuke v Coillte Teoranta* [1998] ELR 324 the claimants were held to have behaved unreasonably but it was determined that even though their actions were unreasonable, such actions did constitute industrial action within the meaning of the Unfair Dismissals Act, 1977 and they had available to them the protections afforded by the relevant sections. The EAT in that case, in examining the definition of industrial action in the Unfair Dismissals Acts, which is quite similar to the definition in the Industrial Relations Act, 1990, noted that the word 'lawful' was not used in the definition of 'strike' in the 1977 Act and went on to state 'a strike does involve a breach of contract (albeit a breach that is protected by law in certain circumstances)'.

It appears that a trade union cannot have a dispute with an employer within the meaning of the 1990 Act (see *Ryan v Cooke and Quinn* [1938] IR 512; *Doran v Lennon* [1945] IR 315; and *Sheriff v McMullen* [1952] IR 236). The *Sheriff* case was referred to in the *Nolan* decision and Barron J held 'at the time when it is sought to rely upon the existence of a trade dispute there must be a member of the union employed by the employer *on whose behalf the union is acting*'.

9.9.3 PROTECTION FOR TRADE UNIONS

The definitions of 'industrial action' and 'strike' are new. Both definitions require 'a common understanding' and are framed in such a way as to exclude action by individual workers. This is mirrored in further provisions below. Picketing comes within the definition of industrial actions. Section 9 of the 1990 Act provides:

> '(1) Sections 11, 12 and 13 shall apply only in relation to authorised trade unions which for the time being are holders of negotiation licences under the Trade Union Act, 1941, and the members and officials of such trade unions, and not otherwise.
> (2) Where in relation to the employment or non-employment or the terms or conditions of or affecting the employment of one individual worker, there are agreed procedures availed of by custom or in practice in the employment concerned, or provided for in a collective agreement, for the resolution of individual grievances, including dismissals, sections 10, 11 and 12 shall apply only where those procedures have been resorted to and exhausted.

(3)   Procedures shall be deemed to be exhausted if at any stage an employer fails or refuses to comply with them.

(4)   The procedures referred to in subsection (2) may include resort to such persons or bodies as a Rights Commissioner, the Labour Relations Commission, the Labour Court, an Equality Officer and the Employment Appeals Tribunal but shall not include an appeal to a court.'

Subsection (1) mirrors the provisions of s 11 of the Trade Union Act, 1941 and as a result persons who are not union members cannot picket and do not have the protection of s 12 of the 1990 Act. They are, however, protected by s 10 which deals with conspiracy. It is only required that persons be members or officials of trade unions, not that they have specific trade union sanction, although sanction in essence is required by s 17 of the 1990 Act referred to at **9.9.9** below. The definition section does not define who is a trade union official but there is a definition given in s 11(5) at **9.9.5.1** below. That definition limits cover to paid officials as opposed to shop stewards.

Section 9(2) is the legislature's attempt to direct disputes through the voluntary problem-solving mechanism and provides that immunities will not be available unless agreed procedures, or those normally provided for 'by custom or in practice', for the resolution of individual grievances are resorted to *and* exhausted. An injunction was granted in 1991 in the case of *Iarnrod Eireann v Darby and O'Connor* Irish Times, 23 March 1991 which was a dispute relating to an individual worker who had not gone through agreed procedures and the picket was held not to enjoy any immunities under the 1990 Act. Subsection (4) allows for reference to a number of bodies but specifically excludes 'an appeal to a court'. It must be taken therefore that if the Labour Court were to be subject to a judicial review or an EAT subject to appeal to the Circuit Court that an individual involved will not be deprived of the immunities by virtue of s 9(2).

9.9.4   THE GOLDEN FORMULA

9.9.4.1   Statutory provision

The golden formula appears for the first time in s 10 and from this section on the Act deals with the mechanics of actually taking industrial action. The golden formula has been considered in some detail by the courts here and in the UK. Section 10 provides:

'(1)   An agreement or combination by two or more persons to do or procure to be done any act in contemplation or furtherance of a trade dispute shall not be indictable as a conspiracy if such act committed by one person would not be punishable as a crime.

(2)   An act done in pursuance of an agreement or combination by two or more persons, if done in contemplation or furtherance of a trade dispute, shall not be actionable unless the act, if done without any such agreement or combination, would be actionable.

(3)   Section 3 of the Conspiracy, and Protection of Property Act, 1875, and subsections (1) and (2) of this section shall be construed together as one section.'

9.9.4.2   Case law

For a dispute to be in 'contemplation' the dispute must be either imminent or actual. Action may not be taken because of a possible dispute at some time in the future (see *Esplanade Pharmacy Ltd v Larkin* [1957] IR 285 and *Crazy Prices (Northern Ireland) v Hewitt* [1980] NI 150). The use of the word 'furtherance' has given rise to consideration as to whether or not the actions of persons involved in the dispute are to be measured objectively or subjectively. The House of Lords held in *Express Newspapers Ltd v MacShane* [1980] AC 672 that immunity depends on the bona fides of a defendant and that what must be examined is the defendants' belief as to whether or not they were acting in furtherance of their dispute by engaging in the action complained of. The 1990 Act touches on the problem in s 13(2) dealing with immunity against action in tort where it provides that there is a defence available where a trade union can show that the act 'was done in the reasonable belief that it was done in contemplation or furtherance of a trade dispute'.

Although a trade dispute cannot be anticipated, it was held in *General Aviation Services (UK) Ltd v TGWU* [1985] ICR 615 that an action taken through fears for job security after an employer contracted services to an outside party was related to termination or suspension of employees and so it was taken in furtherance of a trade dispute with the employer even though redundancy notices had not been served at the time the dispute was engaged in.

The consequences of a conspiracy have been dealt with in Ireland and England in recent decisions. The English Court of Appeal held in *Metall und Rohstoff AG v Donaldson Lufkin & Jenrette Inc* [1991] QB 391 that where two parties agreed to pressure a third party to cause that party economic loss, their actions do not give rise to liability unless their sole or predominant purpose is to injure the third party's interest. If their sole or predominant purpose is to advance their own commercial interests they are not liable. The Supreme Court took a different line in *Taylor v Smyth* 5 July 1990 (unreported) that liability for conspiracy would lie if what was done, if it was done by an individual, would be unlawful, regardless of the motive being solely of self interest.

In *Middlebrook Mushrooms Ltd v TGWU* [1993] IRLR 232 a trade union was in dispute with the plaintiffs who were mushroom producers. The union engaged in the distribution of leaflets urging supermarket customers to boycott the plaintiff's produce. The plaintiff sought an injunction against the union inducing breach of contract between it and its customers—the supermarkets—or from interfering with any such contract. The Court of Appeal held that in order for an action to amount to a direct inducement to break a contract it had to be aimed directly at one of the contracting parties. The action in this case had been aimed at shoppers and the effect such action had on the minds of the retailers was indirect and, there being no suggestion of any unlawful means, the union's actions were not therefore tortious. The court went on to hold that there was no evidence of any existing contracts between the supermarkets and the plaintiffs with which the union's actions could have interfered and this was not a situation in which the existence of contractual relations could or should be inferred from the surrounding facts.

9.9.5 PICKETING

9.9.5.1 Statutory provisions

Section 11 provides:

'(1) *It shall be lawful for one or more persons, acting on their own behalf or on behalf of a trade union in contemplation or furtherance of a trade dispute, to attend at, or where that is not practical, at the approaches to, a place where their employer works or carries on business, if they so attend merely for the purpose of peacefully obtaining or communicating information or of peacefully persuading any person to work or abstain from working.*

(2) *It shall be lawful for one or more persons acting on their own behalf or on behalf of a trade union in contemplation or furtherance of a trade dispute, to attend at, or where that is not practicable, at the approaches to, a place where an employer who is not a party to the trade dispute works or carries on business if, but only if, it is reasonable for those who are so attending to believe at the commencement of their attendance and throughout the continuance of their attendance that the employer has directly assisted their employer who is a party to the trade dispute for the purpose of frustrating the strike or other industrial action, provided that such attendance is merely for the purpose of peacefully obtaining or communicating information or of peacefully persuading any person to work or abstain from working.*

(3) *For the avoidance of doubt any action taken by an employer in the health services to maintain life-preserving services during a strike or other industrial action shall not constitute assistance for the purposes of subsection (2).*

(4)   It shall be lawful for a trade union official to accompany any member of his union whom he represents provided that the member is acting in accordance with the provisions of subsection (1) or (2) and provided that such official is attending merely for the purpose of peacefully persuading any person to work or abstain from working.

(5)   For the purposes of this section ''trade union official'' means any paid official of a trade union or any officer of a union or branch of a union elected or appointed in accordance with the rules of a union.'

No steps have been taken in this section to limit unofficial pickets. It may be seen that picketers must be acting 'in contemplation or furtherance of a trade dispute' and 'acting on their own behalf *or* on behalf of a trade union'.

9.9.5.2   Number of pickets

No attempt was made to limit the number of pickets but the courts have traditionally held that a dispute is not bona fide if excessive numbers of picketers 'go beyond what is reasonably permissible for the communication of information' or 'may amount to obstruction or nuisance or give rise to a reasonable apprehension of a breach of the peace' (see *EI Company Ltd v Kennedy* [1968] IR 69 at p 91). The courts have granted a number of injunctions over the years where pickets were strategically located to cause maximum nuisance or where the numbers deployed in picketing were such as to interfere with day-to-day activity.

In *Tynan v Balmer* [1966] 2 WLR 1181 it was held that where a group of pickets walking in a circle in the road outside a factory entrance blocked the highway and caused vehicles approaching to stop they were guilty of an unreasonable user of the highway and a nuisance at common law which overrode their possible immunities in respect of a trade dispute.

9.9.5.3   Place

The place at which picketing may be carried on has been limited in s 11(1). The 1906 Act allowed picketing 'at or near a house or place where a person resides or works or carries on business or happens to be'. It may be seen that picketing may now only be carried on 'at, or where that is not practicable, at the approaches to, a place where their employer works or carries on business'. Under the 1906 Act this right was limited despite the apparently explicit statutory provisions (see *Irish Dunlop Ltd v Power* 10 and 23 September 1981, High Ct (unreported). A problem can arise where the place sought to be lawfully picketed is located on private property to which access may be required but cannot be gained because the Act does not allow trespass. That situation has not changed in the 1990 Act.

Rathmines Town Hall Shopping Centre was picketed in 1982 as a result of a dispute between Power Supermarkets (Quinnsworth) and some of its employees. The employees picketed, on public property, all entrances to the shopping centre. The owners and one of the tenants sought an injunction given the effect of the picket on other businesses in the shopping centre which were not involved in the dispute. An injunction was granted but on the basis of an undertaking by New Ireland to permit access to the complex for the purposes of picketing Quinnsworth. The 1990 Act does not resolve the conflict between the right of employees to picket their employers and the right of the employers and/or others to refuse to allow trespass. In *Rayware Ltd v Transport and General Workers Union* [1989] IRLR 134 it was held that the phrase 'at or near' a place of work had to be considered in the geographical sense having regard to the purpose of the legislation and the modern context in which the picketing arose. Picketing at the entrance to a trading estate almost a mile away from the employer's actual premises was conducted 'near' the place of work and was lawful within the statute, particularly given that the only means of access to the premises to be picketed were by way of a private road which could not be trespassed upon.

9.9.5.4   Placards and documentation

Placards or documentation handed out on the picket line must be true and accurate, otherwise the validity of the picket might be affected (see *Brendan Dunne Ltd v Fitzpatrick* [1958] IR 29). See also the observations of Barron J in *Nolan Transport* referred to at **9.10.3** below.

9.9.5.5   Interpretation of 'employer'

The High Court and Supreme Court took a surprisingly strict line on the use of the words 'their employer' in s 11(1) in *Westman Holdings Ltd v McCormack* [1992] 1 IR 151; [1991] ILRM 833. The defendants had been employed as bar staff in a Dublin pub. The pub was sold to the plaintiff. Prior to the completion of the sale all the staff were dismissed by reason of redundancy. When the plaintiffs reopened the premises the staff sought employment and when this was refused they placed an official picket on the premises. It was argued that as the staff had never been employed by the plaintiff, the plaintiff was not 'their employer' within the meaning of s 11(1) and an injunction was granted by the High Court and upheld by the Supreme Court on the basis that there was a fair question to be tried at the full hearing and because the balance of convenience favoured the plaintiff. While the decision is in itself restrictive, it appears to ignore the provisions of the Acquired Rights Regulations.

9.9.5.6   Secondary picketing

The 1906 Act did not specifically deal with secondary picketing. The right to engage in secondary picketing was distilled from the various definitions in the Act and the scheme of the Act itself. The 1990 Act addresses secondary picketing directly in s 11(2). It can be seen that the secondary dispute has been greatly circumscribed.

The subsection may be paraphrased as follows:

> Action can be taken against an employer who is not a party to the trade dispute **if but only if it is reasonable** to believe at the commencement of attendance and **throughout the continuance of attendance** that that employer has **directly** assisted their employer who is a party to the trade dispute for the **purpose of frustrating the strike or other industrial action.**

It will undoubtedly prove difficult for secondary picketers to show that the employer they are picketing has directly assisted the employer with whom there is a dispute for the purpose of frustrating their action. Employers' support for each other tends to be commercial and not out of any sense of idealism or brotherhood. A third party employer may, however, by its actions constitute a considerable barrier to the resolution of a dispute in favour of the workers.

In *Nolan Transport (Oaklands) Ltd v Halligan* [1995] ELR 1 Barron J stated:

> 'it seems to be that so far as the law is to be applied to industrial relations disputes the right to take industrial action including the right to picket has been restricted essentially to a right to workers to take action against their own employer and no one else. An exception to that does exist in s 11 but it is only intended to permit secondary picketing when the person being picketed has acted out of its ordinary course of business and solely for the purpose of making the primary picketing ineffective. It is not applicable in the present case nor is it submitted that it is. The right which emerges is that workmen may take action against their employer in relation to a dispute between others. In other words workmen may picket their own employer in order to urge that employer to bring pressure on the employer involved in the primary dispute.'

9.9.6 INDUCING OR THREATENING BREACH OF CONTRACT

Section 12 is effectively a re-enaction of s 3 of the 1906 Act but, in addition, deals with the previously grey area of those who threaten to induce breach of contract of employment or threaten to breach their own contracts of employment. Section 12 provides:

'An act done by a person in contemplation or furtherance of a trade dispute shall not be actionable on the ground only that—

(a)   it induces some other person to break a contract of employment, or

(b)   it consists of a threat by a person to induce some other person to break a contract of employment or a threat by a person to break his own contract of employment, or

(c)   it is an interference with the trade, business, or employment of some other person, or with the right of some other person to dispose of his capital or his labour as he wills.'

It should be noted from this section that protection is only afforded where there is a threat to break one's own contract of employment and inducing breach of or threatening to induce breach of a commercial contract is not protected.

The section does not specifically address itself to indirect inducement of the breach of a commercial contract. It remains the case that lawful industrial action may, and often does, result in the breach of a commercial contract. The question must still be addressed as to whether or not that is actionable.

British decisions indicate a division of opinion (see *J T Stratford & Son Ltd v Lindley* [1965] AC 269 and *Hadmor Productions Ltd v Hamilton* [1983] 1 AC 191).

In *The Trade Union and Industrial Relations Acts of Ireland* by Tony Kerr he gives an example as follows:

B Limited is in dispute over terms and conditions of employment with its employees.

B Limited is party to a commercial contract with A Limited whereby A Limited has agreed to deliver goods to B Limited.

A trade union official representing employees of B Limited induces A Limited's employees to break their contracts of employment by persuading them to refuse to deliver the goods to B Limited. Consequently there is breach of the commercial contract.

Can either party sue the trade union official? If there has been inducement it is indirect and it relates to the context of employment of A Limited's employees.

Section 12 renders the inducement of breach of the contracts of employment 'not actionable'.

The trade union official appears immune in respect of an action by A Limited.

Is the trade union official immune in respect of an action brought in respect of the indirect inducement of the breach of the commercial contract?

The Supreme Court ruling at injunction stage in *Talbot (Ireland) Ltd v Merrigan* 1 May 1981, Supreme Ct (unreported) appears to have taken the view that the trade union official would possess no immunity as against either A Limited or B Limited. As Tony Kerr states at p 194, in the Dáil Debate on this Bill the phrase 'shall not be actionable' was stated to mean that it shall not be actionable *'by any person'*.

9.9.7 IMMUNITY IN TORT

Section 13 is substantially a re-enactment of s 4 of the 1906 Act but this time the immunity in tort is limited to torts committed in contemplation or furtherance of a trade dispute. The immunity in s 4 of the 1906 Act was against all actions in tort regardless of how they occurred. The immunity is strictly limited to actions in tort and not any of the other areas of law. Section 13 provides:

'(1) *An action against a trade union, whether of workers or employers, or its trustees or against any members or officials thereof on behalf of themselves and all other members of the trade union in respect of any tortious act committed by or on behalf of the trade union in contemplation or furtherance of a trade dispute, shall not be entertained by any court.*

(2) *In an action against any trade union or person referred to in subsection (1) in respect of any tortious act alleged or found to have been committed by or on behalf of a trade union it shall be a defence that the act was done in the reasonable belief that it was done in contemplation or furtherance of a trade dispute.'*

It may be seen that s 13(2) uses the subjective approach favoured in *Express Newspapers Ltd v McShane* [1980] AC 672 that the immunity will lie where the act was done 'in the reasonable belief' that it was in contemplation or furtherance of a trade dispute.

In *Nolan Transport (Oaklands) Ltd v Halligan* [1995] ELR 1 the union sought to avoid liability by relying on s 13. Barron J dealt with it by reference to both subsections as follows:

(a)   in relation to s 13(1) it did not avail the union because he held that there was no bona fide trade dispute in existence and the protection of this subsection was therefore lost; and

(b)   under s 13(2) he held that the defence lay under two different circumstances. He said on the facts there may have been a doubt about reasonable belief but, he emphasised, where there was no trade dispute how could there be a reasonable belief that a dispute existed? He commented that the fact that the creation of the dispute and the commencement of the industrial action in this particular case was not bona fide did not of itself mean that subsequent action by the union or branches of the union were necessarily mala fide. He held that the onus of proof lay on the union to establish such a reasonable belief and that there was no evidence available to him on this point and held that as a result the union was liable for the tortious activity established.

In considering the whole question of reasonableness regard must be had to the position, which has always been the case with the courts, that it is not a matter for the courts to examine whether or not a trade dispute has any merit. It is simply the function of the courts to establish the fact of a dispute no matter how outrageous the position of either party might be. Barron J in the *Nolan* case stated:

'[I]t is no function of this court to determine whether or not the conditions under which the drivers of the plaintiff company worked were fair or unfair, were favourable or unfavourable, having regard to other employments of a similar nature.'

Presumably, however, in now having to assess the reasonable belief of the existence of a trade dispute regard might well be had to the nature of the dispute and its bona fides. It will be very difficult for judges to avoid the temptation of taking that route towards a decision.

It was also held in *NWL Ltd v Woods and Nelson* [1979] 3 All ER 614 that a demand is not prevented from being a dispute or being the basis for a dispute connected with terms and conditions of employment by reason of the fact that it is unreasonable and commercially impracticable.

9.9.8   SECRET BALLOTS

9.9.8.1   Statutory provisions

Section 14 of the Act came into effect on 18 July 1992 as provided for in s 14(1). Section 14 provides inter alia:

'(2)   The rules of every trade union shall contain a provision that—

(a)   the union shall not organise, participate in, sanction or support a strike or other industrial action without a secret ballot, entitlement to vote in which shall be accorded equally to all members whom it is reasonable at the time of the ballot for the union concerned to believe will be called upon to engage in the strike or other industrial action;

(b)   the union shall take reasonable steps to ensure that every member entitled to vote in the ballot votes without interference from, or constraint imposed by, the union or any of its members, officials or employees and, so far as is reasonably possible, that such members shall be given a fair opportunity of voting;

(c)   the committee of management or other controlling authority of a trade union shall have full discretion in relation to organising, participating in, sanctioning or supporting a strike or other industrial action notwithstanding that the majority of those voting in the ballot, including an aggregate ballot referred to in paragraph (d), favour such strike or other industrial action;

(d)   the committee of management or other controlling authority of a trade union shall not organise, participate in, sanction or support a strike or other industrial action against the wishes of a majority of its members voting in a secret ballot, except where, in the case of ballots by more than one trade union, an aggregate majority of all the votes cast, favours such strike or other industrial action;

(e)   where the outcome of a secret ballot conducted by a trade union which is affiliated to the Irish Congress of Trade Unions or, in the case of ballots by more than one such trade union, an aggregate majority of all the votes cast, is in favour of supporting a strike organised by another trade union, a decision to take such supportive action shall not be implemented unless the action has been sanctioned by the Irish Congress of Trade Unions;

(f)   as soon as practicable after the conduct of a secret ballot the trade union shall take reasonable steps to make know to its members entitled to vote in the ballot:

(i)   the number of ballot papers issued;

(ii)   the number of votes cast;

(iii)   the number of votes in favour of the proposal;

(iv)   the number of votes against the proposal, and

(v)   the number of spoilt votes.

(3)   The rights conferred by a provision referred to in subsection (2) are conferred on the members of the trade union concerned and on no other person.

(4)   Nothing in this section shall constitute an obstacle to negotiations for the settlement of a trade dispute nor the return to work by workers party to the trade dispute.

(5)   The First Schedule to the Trade Union Act, 1871, is hereby extended to include the requirement provided for in subsection (2).'

This section is one of the more novel provisions of the 1990 Act. Although similar in intent to UK balloting provisions it is not similar in terms of the draftsmanship.

9.9.8.2   Deficiencies in statutory provisions

While a secret ballot is now required to sanction industrial action the blessing of the union is still not required, so unofficial action is still valid industrial action in Irish law. The whole process of balloting was examined closely in the *Nolan* decision and some of the evidence given in relation to the ballot and, in particular, its outcome in that case attracted very considerable attention. It is a constant source of frustration with Irish legislation that provisions are enacted setting out legal theory without proper regard being had to the practical consequences of the legislative provisions. It is difficult to understand why the legislature in this case did not seek to deal with the mechanics of balloting. Simply to provide that a ballot should take place and not deal with how it should take place, or the consequences of it not taking place in accordance with the statutory requirements, is most unsatisfactory and has already given, and will continue in the future to give, rise to problems.

9.9.8.3   Irregularities in balloting procedures

Section 14(3) provides that the rights conferred by the previous subsection dealing with the mechanics of a secret ballot are conferred only on members of the trade union concerned and on no other person. What is to happen therefore if a trade union ignores some or all of the provisions of a secret ballot and an employer is on the receiving end of what is effectively unlawful action by virtue of the breach of s 14?

Barron J went some way towards addressing this difficult issue. He stated that the protections of ss 10, 11 and 12 are lost when the action is in disregard of the outcome of a secret ballot (see s 17 at **9.9.9** below). He then said: 'These latter words are significant and suggest that the validity of the secret ballot is dependent upon proof that those voting were aware of the issue or issues involved'. Who is to provide this proof and who may call for such proof?

Barron J went on to state that the defendants made the case that the declared result of a secret ballot cannot be questioned by the plaintiff (s 14(3)). Barron J admitted evidence as to how the secret ballot was carried out in the *Nolan* case and as to how individuals voted. He stated:

> 'There are both rights conferred and obligations imposed on the union for the benefit of its members. Although no-one else can claim such benefits the subsection does not mean that a secret ballot could only be investigated at the instance of the members. In so far as there are rights conferred upon the members voting "and no other person" the members by giving sworn evidence are availing of such rights there is no proviso on the subsection that such rights can only be availed of in proceedings to which they are parties. Nor can the union avoid the obligation imposed upon it as to how the ballot should be conducted. Finally the allegation that the result was not properly declared is an allegation of fraud. In my view a section in an enactment cannot be used as an instrument of fraud so that the defendants will not be entitled in refuting the allegation of fraud to rely solely upon subsection (3).'

Barron J was reversed by the Supreme Court in its decision in *Nolan Transport (Oaklands) Ltd v Halligan* [1998] ELR 177 where the court accepted Barron J's findings as to the facts that the declared result of the ballot did not properly reflect the votes cast and that there was an irregularity in the ballot but held, despite the provisions of s 17 which provide that individuals lose immunities when they act in disregard of, or contrary to the outcome of secret ballot, the defendants in this case individually did not lose the benefits of the immunities. While the irregularities may have been a matter for the union it was held by the Supreme Court that the union did not lose immunity from actions in tort conferred by s 13 since that immunity is not made conditional upon a secret ballot, and the individual defendants, who were engaged in the picketing, could not be held liable for irregularities in the ballot carried out by the trade union.

In *RJB Mining (UK) Ltd v National Union of Mineworkers* [1997] IRLR 621 the RJB Group operated a number of coal mines. RJB did not formally recognise the NUM which had a substantial membership amongst RJB employees. The union proposed a series of one-day strikes by all of their members working at RJB collieries in support of its claim for recognition and conducted a secret ballot on the question of industrial action. Section 227(1) of the UK Trade Union and Labour Relations (Consolidation) Act 1992 provides:

> 'Entitlement to vote in the ballot must be accorded equally to all members of the trade union who it is reasonable at the time of the ballot for the union to believe will be induced to take part or, as the case may be, to continue to take part in the industrial action in question, and to no others.'

The Act also provides that where there are employees at different work locations, separate ballots should be held for each location. The results of the ballot may, however, be aggregated in a single ballot which was done by the NUM. The ballot took place and resulted in a decision in favour of strike action and strike notice was served. The employers sought an injunction on the basis of irregularities in the ballot arguing that the statutory balloting requirements had been contravened. One section of the workforce, members of the Colliery Officials and Staff Association (COSA), a part of the NUM, were not balloted. The employers argued that they should have been balloted. The union argued they did not have to be balloted but the employers countered that if that was the case then why were some 200 members of COSA balloted? The High Court granted an interlocutory injunction on the following basis:

'1   [I]t was at least highly arguable that the union was in breach of the requirements of [the 1992 Act] in omitting from the ballot on the proposed industrial action a significant number of its members who would be called on to take part in the action and including in the ballot a number of others who would not.

2.   It is the duty of the union to ensure that all those and only those entitled to vote in a ballot on industrial action are given the opportunity of doing so. A union is not expected to achieve 100 per cent perfection in conducting such ballots and has the protection of the de minimis rule and the test of reasonable practicability since there will always have been some changes with which the best of paper work or computer systems will not have kept pace. However the fact that the structure of a particular union is likely to be more productive of error than a different structure of another union is not an acceptable excuse for non-compliance with the statutory requirements. If the structure of an organisation makes it impossible or difficult to comply with new legislation the organisation must give consideration to how compliance can be better achieved.'

In *West Midlands Travel Ltd v Transport and General Workers Union* [1994] IRLR 578 a ballot paper asked two questions:

(1)   Are you prepared to take part in strike action?

(2)   Are you prepared to take part in industrial action short of a strike?

In relation to question (1) 1,265 answered yes, 1,225 answered no with 147 blanks. On the second question 1,059 voted yes and 1,156 voted no and there were 427 blanks. The total members who took part was 2,642.

The employers claimed that 1,265 was not a majority in favour of strike action and claimed that the action was not valid. The Court of Appeal held that the action was valid where there was a majority who answered question (1) in favour of strike action.

9.9.8.4   Who may be balloted

Section 14(2)(a) seems to allow a fairly wide electorate for a strike ballot and does not appear to limit the right to ballot to those employed by the employer or in the place where the dispute is proposed to take place. In *University of Central England v National and Local Government Officers Association* [1993] IRLR 81 the plaintiffs were former polytechnics. They negotiated with NALGO on terms and conditions of employment of their employees. A dispute arose and the union balloted all of its members affected by the negotiations who were employed in all the former polytechnics and colleges covered by the plaintiffs' organisation. The ballot allowed industrial action and allowed it against any of the individual employers. The plaintiffs sought an injunction against the union on the grounds that the ballot did not comply with the statutory requirements and that in order to do so, the ballot had to be a ballot of each individual employer's employees. The High Court rejected the plaintiffs' contention and held that the union was entitled to ballot the wider electorate provided that in the terms of the statute

'the union could show that it was reasonable for it to believe and it did believe that there was some common factor relating to the terms and conditions of employment in respect of which the industrial action was called, it was entitled to hold a ballot of all its members affected by that factor, whether or not they were employed by the same employer'.

Section 14(2)(a) also provides that a union 'shall not organise, participate in, sanction or support a strike or other industrial action without a secret ballot'. It would appear that this does not place the union in a neutral position and that the union is entitled to actively involve itself in preparation for such action prior to the taking of a ballot. See *London Borough of Newham v National and Local Government Officers Association* [1993] IRLR 83 where NALGO was involved in a wide-ranging dispute with the borough and held various ballots of various branches. Some ballots took place at a time when other branches were already in dispute and NALGO had involved itself in direct support of the other employees in dispute and was not obliged to call off all existing industrial action until the final of the ballots was completed. The court stated that where there was a series of disputes 'the fact that the earlier action would be subsumed in a broader industrial action did not mean that the later ballot was in any way concerned with the earlier action'.

In *London Underground Ltd v NUR* [1989] IRLR 341 a ballot paper referred to four areas of dispute, only one of which constituted a current dispute with the employers. The court held that the wording of a ballot of whether or not to take industrial action must not refer to matters which do not constitute a current trade dispute with an employer. Although it is permissible to gather into one general question separate issues which form separate trade disputes it is not permissible to refer to extraneous issues even if the ballot paper does also refer to a genuine and existing trade dispute.

In *Post Office v Union of Communication Workers* [1990] IRLR 143 the question was asked on a ballot as to whether or not members were willing to take industrial action up to and including strike action. There is a statutory provision in the UK to the effect that unions must ask separate questions in this regard and the court held that separate questions must be set down on the ballot form and, following the ballot, the union could then legally endorse only the type of action for which they secured a yes vote from the majority of members.

In *British Railways Board v NUR* [1989] IRLR 349 200 members of the NUR were accidentally not given the opportunity to vote. The court held that this did not render the ballot invalid.

9.9.8.5 Miscellaneous

Section 14(2)(c) allows that the officers of a trade union are not obliged to take industrial action simply because a secret ballot sanctions it.

Subsection (2)(d) allows a second trade union to support another trade union's dispute where that other trade union has had a valid secret ballot in favour of such dispute but where the first union does not.

Subsection (2)(e) requires the Irish Congress of Trade Unions to sanction its 'All Out Picket' before another trade union actively supports a dispute. The ICTU policy is that if a trade union wants to call on members of another union or unions to support strike action it must make its request through ICTU. Congress circulates this request to all affiliated unions and those directly concerned and the matter is given consideration by the Industrial Relations Committee of Congress. The provision provides therefore in multi-union disputes or wide-ranging disputes that not only must a secret ballot take place but ICTU authorisation must be given, which is again an indication of the support the 1990 Act gives to existing structures and practices which have proven useful in trade disputes.

9.9.9 UNION ROLES

Section 15 provides:

> '(1) *The committee of management or other controlling authority of a trade union shall, notwithstanding anything in the rules of the union, have power by memorandum in writing to alter the rules of the union so far as may be necessary to give effect to section 14.*

(2) In the case of a trade union which is a trade union under the law of another country having its headquarters control situation in that country, the committee of management or other controlling authority referred to in the Part shall have the same meaning as in section 17(2) of the Trade Union Act, 1975.

Section 16 provides:

(1) Every trade union registered under the Trade Union Acts, 1871 to 1975, or a trade union under the law of another country shall, not later than the operative date, forward to the Registrar of Friendly Societies a copy of its rules incorporating the provisions referred to in subsection (2) of section 14.

(2) A trade union failing to comply with subsection (2) of section 14 or subsection (1) of this section shall cease to be entitled to hold a negotiation licence under Part II of the Trade Union Act, 1941, and its existing licence shall stand revoked on the operative date.

(3) A body of persons shall not be granted a negotiation licence unless, in addition to fulfilling the relevant conditions specified in section 7 of the Trade Union Act, 1941, and section 2 of the Trade Union Act, 1971, as amended by section 21 of this Act, it complies with subsection (2) of section 14 and for this purpose that subsection shall have effect from the passing of this Act.

(4) A body of persons which is a trade union under the law of another country shall not be granted a negotiation licence unless, in addition to fulfilling the conditions referred to in subsection (3) and section 17 of the Trade Union Act, 1975, it forwards, at the time of application for a negotiation licence, a copy of its rules incorporating the provisions referred to in subsection (2) of section 14 to the Registrar of Friendly Societies.

(5) Where the Registrar of Friendly Societies is satisfied, after due investigation, that it is the policy or practice of a trade union registered under the Trade Union Acts, 1871 to 1975, or a trade union under the law of another country persistently to disregard any requirement of the provisions referred to in subsection (2) of section 14 he may issue an instruction to the trade union to comply with the requirement. Where such an instruction is disregarded, the Registrar of Friendly Societies shall inform the Minister and the Minister may revoke the negotiation licence of the trade union concerned.

Section 17 provides:

(1) Sections 10, 11 and 12 shall not apply in respect of proceedings arising out of or relating to a strike or other industrial action by a trade union or a group of workers in disregard of or contrary to, the outcome of a secret ballot relating to the issue or issues involved in the dispute.

(2) In the case of ballots by more than one trade union, the outcome of a secret ballot referred to in subsection (1) shall mean the outcome of the aggregated ballots.

(3) Where two or more secret ballots have been held in relation to a dispute, the ballot referred to in subsection (1) shall mean the last such ballot.'

As referred to above, s 17 ties the secret ballot to the immunities available under ss 10, 11 and 12. Again, however, the mechanics of secret ballots are not given sufficient attention and s 17(3) allows for any number of ballots to take place with the last of such ballots being the dominant deciding one.

9.9.10 EMPLOYERS' ASSOCIATIONS

Section 18 provides inter alia:

'(1) Sections 14 to 17 shall not apply to a trade union of employers.'

There are apparently some sixteen employers' associations registered as trade unions with the Registrar of Friendly Societies.

9.9.11 EMPLOYERS' RIGHTS TO INJUNCTIONS

Section 19 provides:

> '(1) Where a secret ballot has been held in accordance with the rules of a trade union as provided for in section 14, the outcome of which or, in the case of an aggregation of ballots, the outcome of the aggregated ballots, favours a strike or other industrial action and the trade union before engaging in the strike or other industrial action gives notice of not less than one week to the employer concerned of its intention to do so, that employer shall not be entitled to apply to any court for an injunction restraining the strike or other industrial action unless notice of the application has been given to the trade union and its members who are party to the trade dispute.
>
> (2) Where a secret ballot has been held in accordance with the rules of a trade union as provided for in section 14, the outcome of which or, in the case of an aggregation of ballots, the outcome of the aggregated ballots, favours a strike or other industrial action and the trade union before engaging in the strike or other industrial action gives notice of not less than one week to the employer concerned of its intention to do so, a court shall not grant an injunction restraining the strike or other industrial action where the respondent establishes a fair case that he was acting in contemplation or furtherance of a trade dispute.
>
> (3) Notice as provided for in subsection (1) may be given to the members of a trade union by referring such members to a document containing the notice which the members have reasonable opportunity of reading during the course of their employment or which is reasonably accessible to them in some other way.
>
> (4) Subsections (1) and (2) do not apply—
>
> (a) in respect of proceedings arising out of or relating to unlawfully entering into or remaining upon any property belonging to another, or unlawfully causing damage or causing or permitting damage to be caused to the property of another, or
>
> (b) in respect of proceedings arising out of or relating to any action resulting or likely to result in death or personal injury.
>
> (5) Where two or more secret ballots have been held in relation to a dispute, the ballot referred to in subsections (1) and (2) shall be the last such ballot.

Under the 1906 Act a large number of injunctions were granted to employers, due consideration having been given to the two determining factors governing the grant of all injunctions be they in trade dispute situations or otherwise:

(a) Had the applicant established that there was a fair issue to be tried?

(b) Whom did the balance of convenience favour?

It is difficult to conceive in any trade dispute situation where the balance of convenience would not favour the employer. Employees choose to take action and give up their rights to remuneration and therefore bring about their own loss, whereas the employer may be seen as the victim whose business could be irreparably damaged if a trade dispute was to be effective. The workers' position was more difficult where employers made applications for ex parte injunctions. McCarthy J was particularly critical of the situation in *Bayzana Ltd v Galligan* [1987] IR 241 where he made the point that the granting of an ex parte injunction and the consequent removal of a picket at its early stages could prove fatal to the entire industrial action sought to be engaged in and that the injunction was therefore resolving the dispute which was not the intention of the court or the purpose of the injunction. This was a view shared by Lardner J in *Draycar v Whelan* [1993] ELR 119 referred to in more detail at **9.10.1** below.

Section 19 has sought to limit an employer's right to apply for an injunction to a situation where the employer has given notice of application to the trade union and the members and where there has been a secret ballot. Then the court cannot grant an injunction as long as the trade union can establish 'a fair case' that it was 'acting in contemplation or furtherance of a trade dispute'. Subsection (2) alters the normal legal rules relating to interlocutory injunctions in so far as they apply to trade dispute situations. Once the applicant establishes there is a fair question to be decided the court must then establish whether the defendants can establish a fair case that they were acting in contemplation or furtherance of a trade dispute, in which event the injunction will not be granted. If the defendants cannot establish that they were acting in contemplation or furtherance of a trade dispute, then and only then will the court consider the balance of convenience.

9.10 THREE CASE STUDIES

9.10.1 DRAYCAR LTD v WHELAN

9.10.1.1 The facts

The defendants were originally employed by a company, Barry & Sons (Navan) Ltd which was restructured resulting in the incorporation of a number of other companies which traded at different locations. There were trading links between the various companies. The company Draycar Ltd, which traded as 'Japan', traded in the Ilac Centre. Another company 'Akala Ltd', also trading as 'Japan', traded from premises in Henry Street. Consequent on the restructuring some employees changed employer to one of the other linked companies. Following the restructuring the first-named defendant was made redundant and the other defendants, who had been full-time employees, were reduced to a three-day week. Proper procedures were followed under the 1990 Act and strike notice was served, after which the defendants placed pickets at the entrance to the plaintiff's premises at the Ilac Centre. The plaintiff sought injunctive relief on the grounds inter alia that the defendants did not have any trade dispute with it as it did not employ the defendants whom, it claimed, were employed by other companies and, further, that the defendants had an improper motive behind their picketing which was to force other employees in the Henry Street shop to join the trade union of which they were members.

9.10.1.2 The decision

Lardner J in the High Court [1993] ELR 119 refused the injunctive relief sought. It was held that there was a genuine trade dispute within the meaning of the Industrial Relations Act, 1990 and that there was some confusion as to who the employer of the defendants actually was. He held there was a fair question to be tried as to who was the real employer of the defendants but this was in favour of the defendants and not the employer, which had sought to argue that it was not the employer and therefore should not have been the target of the industrial action. Lardner J held in favour of the defendants on both primary picketing and secondary picketing issues stating:

> 'The entitlement to strike under the Industrial Relations Act, 1990 is primarily given in s 11(1). If the employer of the defendants is running the business of both boutiques and if the employees in the Ilac Centre boutique are under the same management as the employees in the Henry Street boutique, that would, I am satisfied, entitle the defendants to picket the Ilac Centre boutique. If however the defendants in truth and in fact are not employed by the same employer as the employees of the Ilac Centre boutique their entitlement to picket the Ilac Centre boutique would depend upon whether they can bring themselves within s 11(2) of the Act which authorises secondary picketing in certain circumstances. Under that subsection they are entitled to picket "a place where an employer who is not a party to the trade dispute, works or carries on business if, but only if, it is reasonable for those who are so attending to believe at the commencement of their attendance and throughout the continuance of their attendance that that employer

has directly assisted their employer who is a party to the trade dispute for the purpose of frustrating the strike or other industrial action".'

He then held that it was reasonable for the defendants in this case to believe that their employer at the Ilac Centre shop had directly assisted their employer at the Henry Street shop, who was a party to the dispute, and that this was done for the purpose of frustrating the strike. He was of the view that the defendants were entitled 'reasonably to hold that belief'.

On the balance of convenience Lardner J held that the defendants' bargaining position would undoubtedly be weakened if an injunction was granted as the full action was unlikely to be heard for more than twelve months. The affidavit on behalf of the plaintiff made very strong statements about the effect of the pickets resulting in a drastic deterioration in the plaintiff's sales, the inevitable closure of the plaintiff's store in Ilac, the termination of employment of the entire workforce and the consequent impact on the plaintiff's ability to honour its liabilities to its creditors. Lardner J stated, however, that these matters were deposed to

'by way of simple assertion and are unsupported by any facts on which the assertion can be said to be based. If there was a reduction in trading following upon the placing of the picket it should have been possible to give figures showing that reduction rather than to just assert that people would not pass the picket and come into the shop. The result is that I am left in grave doubt as to the correctness of these assertions.'

The court held:

'1.   The defendants are in dispute with their employer relating to the dismissal/ redundancy of the first named defendant and the reduction to a three-day week of the other defendants, coming within the terms of the Industrial Relations Act, 1990.

2.   There is a fair question to be tried as to who is the real employer of the defendants and whether or not the Ilac Centre and Henry Street's outlets are managed by the same employer.

3.   There is a body of fact from which the defendants might reasonably believe that the changes of employment which are alleged to have taken place, if they occurred, were made at least in part, for the purpose of frustrating the industrial action taken by the employees of the Henry Street shop.

4.   The defendants have established that the balance of convenience falls in favour of refusing the injunction.'

9.10.2   G & T CRAMPTON LTD v BUILDING AND ALLIED TRADES UNION

9.10.2.1   The facts

The plaintiff, Crampton, was building a science block at Dublin City University. Crampton had contracted for a specific completion date and was subject to penalty clauses providing for payment of £30,000 per week in the event of default on its part in completing the building on time. Certain of the defendants were employed as bricklayers on the site by a sub-contractor M J Lambe & Sons Ltd. Lambe had a specific sub-contract which it completed, and then terminated the employment of all of its bricklayers on the site. A second sub-contractor, Colm Murphy, was then engaged on a further sub-contract for other works but did not re-employ the bricklayers who had previously worked for Lambe on the site. The defendant trade union, BATU, contended that the bricklayers were actually employees of Crampton at all material times. Laffoy J in the High Court stated that the core issue between Crampton and BATU was BATU's objection to Crampton's practice of sub-contracting blocklaying and bricklaying work on its construction sites and of not employing blocklayers and bricklayers, members of BATU, directly. The union placed a picket at the entrance to the DCU site which effectively brought a stop to all work on the site. Crampton sought an injunction against the industrial action engaged in by BATU and some of its members who, in turn, relied on s 11 of the 1990 Act and contended that the court was precluded from granting the relief sought by virtue of s 19 of the Act. Laffoy J quoted s 19(2) in relation to secret ballots and stated that in applying that provision:

> 'I must determine whether three pre-conditions—that a secret ballot was held, that its outcome favoured industrial action and that the requisite notice was given—stipulated in the provision have been fulfilled and, if they have, I must then decide whether the defendants have established a fair case that they were acting in contemplation or furtherance of a trade dispute and if they have I must refuse the plaintiff's application.'

9.10.2.2   High Court decision

In giving her decision Laffoy J referred to a decision of Keane J in an early interlocutory application in the *Nolan Transport* case (22 March 1994) where Keane J commented that there appeared to be no authority on s 19 but that as a matter of first impression the onus must be on the person resisting an injunction application to establish that the provisions of s 14 have been complied with and that the court must be satisfied on the evidence before it that s 14 has been complied with. Laffoy J agreed with Keane J.

In a grounding affidavit on behalf of Crampton it was stated that not all of the members likely to be affected by the strike had been balloted, that union members employed by Murphy on the site had not been balloted, and if they had the result may well have been different. It was also claimed that although notification of the intention of the union to ballot its members was issued in advance of a Labour Court recommendation, one of the grounds claimed to justify the picket was the rejection by the union of the said Labour Court recommendation. In a replying affidavit on behalf of the defendants there was what Laffoy J called 'a bald statement' simply to the effect that the ballot had been carried out in accordance with the rules of the union as required by the 1990 Act. Given the conflicting statements in various affidavits Laffoy J concluded:

> 'there is no evidence whatsoever before the court as to the outcome of the secret ballot conducted by the union and, in particular, there is no evidence that the outcome favoured picketing the site. On this ground alone I am satisfied that there is no evidence before the court, that one of the pre-conditions stipulated in s 19(2) has been complied with. . . . Accordingly the defendants have not established that they are entitled to rely on s 19(2) and the plaintiff's application falls to be decided on the basis of the ordinary principles applicable to applications for interlocutory injunctions.'

Laffoy J went on to hold that there was a fair issue to be tried, the picketers were not entitled to the protection of s 11 and, on the balance of convenience, held that damages would not adequately compensate Crampton for loss suffered between the time of the application and the trial of the action. Conversely, if an injunction was granted, damages would adequately compensate the defendants should they be successful at the trial in respect of any loss suffered due to the injunction being in force pending the trial.

9.10.2.3   On appeal to the Supreme Court

The matter then went to the Supreme Court on appeal ([1998] ELR 4). Chief Justice Hamilton delivered a judgment with which Flaherty J and Barrington J concurred. Reference was made by the Supreme Court to the letter giving strike notice to Crampton which was notice of 'strike or other industrial action' and did not purport to particularise the nature of the industrial action sought to be taken. A question arose therefore on the interpretation of ss 14 and 19 as to whether it is sufficient merely to have a proposal before members on the question of strike or other industrial action without specifying the nature of the action for which the members' approval is sought and necessary by virtue of the terms of ss 14 and 19. The court held 'on this issue alone there is a fair question to be tried'. The court also held there is a fair question to be tried as to the need for the entire circumstances of the ballot to be investigated for the purpose of ascertaining whether or not the members whom it was reasonable to expect at the time would be called upon to engage in the strike or other industrial action were given a fair opportunity of voting. While it was alleged on behalf of the defendants that all members who were likely to be affected were notified, it was contended on behalf of Crampton that they were not all given an opportunity of voting and that there was an issue to be tried therefore as to the adequacy of the ballot. The adequacy of the ballot paper was also questioned by the court because the ballot paper did not contain the details of any proposal upon which the members were being called to ballot. It was merely described as an official ballot on a proposal to engage in strike or other industrial action but there was no detail of the actual 'proposal' with members simply being asked to vote either 'in favour' or 'against'. The court held there was also a fair issue to be tried as to whether Crampton was or had been the employer of some of the defendants as provided for in the definition of employer in the 1990 Act, s 8. Citing the judgment of Finlay CJ in *Westman Holdings Ltd v McCormack* [1992] 1 IR 151, the court held that there was a fair question to be tried and 'the learned trial judge was entitled to come to the conclusion that the condition precedent to the implementation of s 19 was not established'.

The Supreme Court therefore held:

(a) The learned trial judge was entitled to conclude that the conditions precedent to the implementation of the 1990 Act, s 19 were not established.

(b) There was a fair issue to be tried as to whether the ballot satisfied the terms of ss 14 and 19 of the 1990 Act since the proposal before the members failed to particularise the kind of industrial action contemplated.

(c) There was a fair issue to be tried as to whether or not all members whom it was reasonable to expect at the time would be called upon to engage in the strike or other industrial action were given a fair opportunity of voting.

(d) There was a fair issue to be tried whether the provisions of s 11(1) applied to the defendants.

The learned trial judge was entitled to conclude that damages would be an inadequate remedy if an injunction were refused and that the balance of convenience was in favour of granting an injunction.

9.10.3 NOLAN TRANSPORT (OAKLANDS) LTD v HALLIGAN

9.10.3.1 Background

The first- and second-named defendants were employed as drivers by the plaintiffs with a family-run haulage company. They were both members of SIPTU. A dispute arose over pay and conditions. Some of the drivers in the employ of the company joined SIPTU. SIPTU wrote to the company seeking a meeting 'to set in train the necessary steps to establish what we hope will be a good working relationship'. The day after the letter was sent three of the drivers met the father of the Nolan family and on the following day met other members of the family involved in running the company. As a result of the discussions with the father and the conduct of the father and other members of the family on those days the drivers contended that they had been dismissed from employment with the company. This contention, however, was rejected in the High Court by Barron J who held also that the father did not have authority to dismiss and the defendants 'recognised that this was so'. Subsequently meetings of the membership of the trade union were held, attended by only a small number of persons, and a decision was made to hold a ballot for industrial action. The ballot was held over a number of days at locations where the company traded or where their drivers were located. Twenty-three members of the union voted in the ballot. The union initiated a trenchant campaign in support of the planned industrial action but the overwhelming majority of the drivers (forty-eight) expressed dissatisfaction with it. Eleven of the drivers subsequently claimed that they had voted against industrial action and evidence was adduced to the High Court that a twelfth driver had also voted against industrial action which would have given a majority against such industrial action. The Supreme Court stated 'as the evidence of the drivers was accepted by the learned trial judge it necessarily followed that the result of the ballot . . . was dishonest and the inescapable conclusion reached that the ballot had been "rigged"'. A bitter dispute followed, some drivers working, others striking and bitter claims, counterclaims and allegations passing between those involved.

Following a twenty-eight-day hearing of nearly 100 witnesses Barron J held in the High Court [1995] ELR 1 that there was no bona fide trade dispute and that the union was not entitled to authorise strike action on the basis of what he found as a fact to be a false ballot result. Substantial damages were awarded to the company attributed to defamation and malicious falsehood, loss of profits and additional costs. The Supreme Court per Murphy J (Denham Barrington and Lynch JJ concurring) and per O'Flaherty J considered the following issues:

9.10.3.2 Was there a trade dispute?

The court held that the issue of whether there was a trade dispute depended on the question as to whether Halligan, Nolan or their union believed that the three employees, or some of them, had been dismissed as claimed. The court accepted that Barron J had effectively held that Mr Halligan had an honest belief that he had been dismissed but went on to state that the existence of a trade dispute based on that belief did not in the circumstances confer immunities under the 1990 Act on the employees and trade unions because he was of the view that the dispute was not

'in truth or in substance the injustice which the union sought to remedy by the industrial action and secondly that the true purpose of that industrial action was to coerce all of the employees of the plaintiff into membership of the union.'

The Supreme Court disagreed with that conclusion stating:

'Part of the difficulty arises from the fact that lawyers and judges have used the words "bona fide trade dispute" with different meanings and in different contexts. If employers and workers both acknowledge themselves to be engaged in a trade dispute there is no difficulty in describing it as a bona fide trade dispute. A bona fide trade dispute may also exist where one party denies that there is any dispute and the other believes that he has been wronged and is in dispute as a result. On the other hand an outside party or "meddler" who had no legitimate interest of his own to protect but who stirred up trouble in a business for reasons of malice or spite could not claim to be engaged in a bona fide trade dispute.'

The court went on to state:

'If however a bona fide trade dispute does exist between an employer and workers, some of whom happen to be members of a trade union the trade union is entitled within the Constitution and the law to support its members who are in dispute. That, in doing this, it may be partly motivated by the aim of impressing its members and other workers and enhancing its own reputation and membership appears to me to be quite irrelevant as long as it acts within the law and does not attempt to infringe the constitutional right of each worker to join or not to join a trade union as he himself thinks best.'

On this reasoning the court held that the appellants were entitled to the statutory immunities conferred by the 1990 Act.

9.10.3.3 Was the union entitled to authorise strike action?

In considering whether the union was entitled to authorise strike action the court examined the provisions of the 1990 Act in relation to the carrying out of secret ballots, the effect of a secret ballot and how the immunities provided for in the 1990 Act would be affected or not as a result of an impugned secret ballot. Reference was made to the decision reached at the interlocutory stage in the *Nolan* case by Keane J on 22 March 1994 where he held that there was not evidence before him of sufficient weight to indicate that s 14 had been complied with and therefore the benefit of s 19(2) was unavailable to the trade union. It was emphasised by Murphy J, however, that he made that determination on the balance of probabilities and in relation to the substantive issue between the parties and that he was merely concerned to determine whether there was a serious issue to be tried. Reference was also made to *G & T Crampton v Building and Allied Trades Union*, the judgment of Laffoy J and the fact that it was upheld by the Supreme Court but this was qualified by stating that those judgments related to particular and limited circumstances and Murphy J went on to state:

> 'In the circumstances it may be said that there has not been a definitive interpretation of s 19(2) of the 1990 Act but I would find it difficult to escape the conclusion reached by Keane J and accepted by Laffoy J that the onus lies upon the party resisting an application for an interlocutory injunction to show that a secret ballot as envisaged by s 14 has been held.'

9.10.3.4 Supreme Court decision

Murphy J went on to state that compliance with s 14 on the part of the trade union movement would obviate any problems in relation to the interpretation of s 19 but he reserved his position as to the interpretation of s 19 'until a case directly involving it comes before the Court'.

Murphy J concluded that a trade dispute existed in the *Nolan* case and that the statutory immunities were available to the appellants and overturned the decision of the High Court.

O'Flaherty J in his judgment made a number of interesting comments. On the two questions he held:

(a) Whether or not a trade dispute existed: 'The evidence is clear that there was a trade dispute. The men, at the very least, had good grounds for thinking themselves dismissed'.

(b) On whether or not the union was entitled to authorise strike action, having regard to the manner in which the 'secret ballot' was conducted and the manner in which those voting actually voted, he stated in the course of his judgment that s 14 was designed primarily to strengthen the role of union management against the actions of maverick members. He said this was borne out by the wording of subsection (3) which refers to the rights being conferred by subsection (2) on the members of the trade union *and on no other person*.

He went on to state that s 13 is unaffected by whether there has or has not been a ballot as the trade union immunity in tort is conferred regardless of whether there has been a ballot. On the status of secret ballots and in particular faulty or improper secret ballots he stated:

> '[W]hile I agree that the legislation touching the holding of secret ballots is there primarily as a matter of internal trade union management, I reject the submission that once such a shambles, as is disclosed as regards the ballot that was held here occurs, that we should simply turn a blind eye to it. The duty to observe the law devolves on everyone—I have already said that simply because the obligation comes through the rules rather than directly from the legislation is of no great importance—so there is a serious obligation on union management to give proper example to the rest of the people by ensuring that the requirements concerning the holding of a proper secret

ballot are always observed. . . . the legislation solidifies and, indeed, expands the privileged position afforded by the law to trade unions. Privilege carries duties as well as rights. That said however the essential position is that there was here a trade dispute and those engaged in it are protected and the union has its statutory immunity from suit.'

The Supreme Court ([1998] ELR 177) held:

(1) The court would not set aside any of the findings of primary fact made by the trial judge. The judge had ample evidence on which to base his conclusions and enjoyed the benefit of judging the credibility of witnesses.

(2) The contention made by the plaintiff that the dismissals were contrived by the employees was not supported by any version of the facts.

(3) The finding that the union was conducting affairs with the sole purpose of getting a foothold in the company to unionise the whole workforce could not stand. Such an inference was unjustified. The expressed aims of the industrial action and the mandate expressly sought by the union related to the reinstatement of employees who the union claimed were dismissed.

(4) If a bona fide trade dispute exists between an employer and employees, some of whom happen to be members of a trade union, the trade union is entitled, within the Constitution and the law, to support its members who are in dispute. That in doing this it may be partly motivated, in engaging in successful industrial action, by the aim of impressing its members and other workers and enhancing its own reputation and membership, is irrelevant as long as the union acts within the law and does not attempt to infringe the constitutional right of each worker to join or not to join a trade union as he himself thinks best.

(5) In determining whether a bona fide trade dispute exists the court is not entitled to review the conduct of those engaged in industrial action to determine their motivation or ultimate ambitions. The court's function is to decide whether there is a reasonable basis for an honest belief in the existence of a trade dispute.

(6) The trade dispute in the instant case was bona fide. There was evidence which justifies the employees' and the union's belief that they had been wrongfully dismissed and it was genuine in that it represented the immediate quarrel between the parties.

(7) The employees did not lose the benefits of the statutory immunities of the 1990 Act pursuant to s 17 of the Act. Either no secret ballot was held or else the secret ballot in its outcome authorised the industrial action. Obiter: even if the evidence justified the conclusion that the majority of the employees who were members of the union voted against industrial action the reconstruction of the resolution in pursuance of the decision of the court would not be 'the outcome' of the ballot and it could not be suggested that striking union members acted in disregard of it.

(8) Neither did the union lose the benefit of the statutory immunity given by s 13 of the 1990 Act. Under s 17 of the Act the union's immunity under s 13 would remain unaffected whether or not a secret ballot were held and regardless of the manner in which the ballot was held. It might, however, risk the loss of its negotiating licence in accordance with s 16 of the Act.

9.11 INDUSTRIAL RELATIONS

9.11.1 INSTITUTIONS

Ireland has a well-established and effective tradition of dispute resolution based largely on the voluntary structure created and governed, by the Industrial Relations Acts, 1946–1990.

The legislation established the existing structures of Irish industrial relations—initially the Labour Court, Joint Labour Committees and Joint Industrial Councils, the establishment of the function of rights commissioner in 1969 and later the Labour Relations Commission under the 1990 Act. Trade disputes, low pay and the necessity for flexible forms of conciliation and arbitration, are all dealt with within the framework established by this legislation.

The 1946 Act established the Labour Court and defines its functions and those of its various officers, set up Joint Labour Committees and Joint Industrial Councils and provides for the registration of certain employment agreements. The 1969 Act extended the functions of the Labour Court and created the office of rights commissioner. The 1976 Act brought agricultural workers within the scope of the two earlier Acts.

9.11.2 SCOPE

The Acts apply to any person aged 15 years or more who has 'entered into or works under a contract with an employer' to do any form of work—clerical, manual or otherwise. Excluded are various public service employees (see Industrial Relations Act, 1990, s 23) (civil servants, members of the Defence Forces and the Garda Síochána, officers of vocational education committees, teachers, etc) who have their own conciliation and arbitration schemes on agreements.

9.12 THE LABOUR COURT

9.12.1 GENERALLY

Established by the 1946 Act and extended in both size and functions by the 1969 and 1976 Acts, the Labour Court sits in divisions of three, consisting of an independent chairman and one employer and one trade union representative. The members of the court are full-time. The court has extensive powers to summon witnesses, to require evidence on oath if it wishes and to determine its own working procedures. It is obliged to submit a general report to the government each year. Labour Court hearings are relatively informal and normally consist of the parties making a written submission in advance of the hearing which is exchanged at, or immediately prior to, the hearing and then at the hearing itself one representative for each side acts as spokesperson taking the court through their submission and responding to the other side's submission and dealing with any questions or points of information raised by the members of the court.

The court does not apply rules of evidence such as would be applied in a court of law or at EAT hearings but will have regard to fair procedures and the rules of natural and constitutional justice and is very protective of the interests of all parties appearing before it. Decisions of the court are not legally binding (see *State (St Stephen's Green Club) v Labour Court* [1961] IR 85). Under the normal law of contract there is nothing to prevent the parties to a Labour Court reference agreeing in advance of the hearing to be bound as between themselves by the recommendation of the court. While the recommendation would not of itself thereby become legally binding it could be open to one or other of the parties to seek to enforce its terms by bringing a breach of contract action against the other party. Some confusion over the legal status of Labour Court recommendations has arisen in light of the provisions of s 13(9)(a) of the Industrial Relations Act, 1969. Section 13 creates the office of rights commissioner and sets out the functions of, and procedures to be adopted by, rights commissioners including the right to appeal a rights commissioner's recommendation to the Labour Court. Section 13(9)(a) provides:

'A party to a dispute in relation to which a Rights Commissioner has made a recommendation may appeal to the Court against the recommendation and the parties to the dispute shall be bound by the decision of the Court on the appeal.'

There is no legal mechanism to enforce the decision of the Labour Court on appeal from a rights commissioner and, as the court has no jurisdiction to make legally binding recommendations, the parties are not bound in law by the decision of the court. It appears that this section was intended to indicate a finality to the court's recommendation rather than to confer on it a legal status it does not have.

The Labour Court is empowered to make legally binding decisions when ruling on appeals from equality officers under the terms of the Anti-Discrimination (Pay) Act, 1974 and the Employment Equality Act, 1977. Despite the fact that Labour Court recommendations are not legally binding in industrial relations matters it is usual for the parties to accept such recommendations as failure to do so tends to contribute to ongoing industrial relations difficulties and may be to the discredit of the party rejecting the recommendation. See Kerr, *The Trade Union and Industrial Relations Acts of Ireland Commentary*, pp 207–208.

9.12.2 FUNCTIONS OF THE COURT

The principal function of the court is to conduct investigations (in private) into trade disputes, both existing and anticipated. It then makes a recommendation setting forth its opinion on the merits of the dispute and the terms on which it should be settled. The court will have regard to the fairness of the terms to the parties concerned, and the prospects of the terms being acceptable to them (1946 Act, s 68; 1969 Act, s 19). The court will have regard to the public interest and promoting of industrial peace. (See Industrial Relations Act, 1946 Regulations, 1950 (SI 258/1950).)

Recommendations are communicated to the parties, and are normally made public by the court, in many instances keeping the names of the parties confidential.

The court's power to investigate a trade dispute is limited. It may not investigate if:

(a) the dispute is between parties to a Joint Industrial Council, unless the Council so requests;

(b) the dispute does not appear likely to lead to a stoppage of work;

(c) a trade union is involved and satisfies the court that an agreement is in force between the union and the other parties which provides another method of settling the dispute (the court may still intervene if a dispute appears likely);

(d) the dispute is between parties to a registered employment agreement but the court may still intervene if any party requests, or if a dispute appears likely (see below in relation to the registration of employment agreements);

(e) a rights commissioner has already issued a recommendation on the dispute, unless that recommendation has been appealed, as the court may hear an appeal against such a recommendation and its decision on appeal is final. No penalties are specified for non-compliance with that decision.

9.12.3   SPECIAL INVESTIGATION PROCEDURES

The court must consider any matter referred to it by the Minister for Enterprise, Trade and Employment concerning 'the employment conditions prevailing as regards the workers of any class and their employers' and must furnish a report on the results of its investigation to the Minister (1946 Act, s 24).

If the workers or their union, as party to a dispute, ask the court to investigate and undertake to accept the court's recommendation, the court must investigate and the union is bound to accept its conclusions. If all parties to a dispute ask the court to investigate, and if they all agree to be bound by the recommendation, the court must investigate and the parties are bound to accept its conclusions. These investigations are to be given priority over the other business of the court (1969 Act, s 20).

The court may, unasked, investigate a dispute in which no trade union is involved if a stoppage of work has already occurred. In such cases, the court must publish its intentions and take evidence from all persons wishing to testify. The court may then decide to issue a recommendation, or take no action, or make an award having force for three months and whose terms (as regards conditions of employment, including pay) are legally enforceable (1946 Act, s 71).

In exceptional circumstances, which the court feels warrant its direct intervention in a dispute without being asked to do so by a party, it may conduct an investigation and issue a recommendation (1946 Act, s 67; 1969 Act, s 18).

9.12.4   CONCILIATION

The court appoints industrial relations officers (known as conciliation officers under the 1946 Act, but renamed in the 1969 Act) who, as independent mediators between the parties to trade disputes, are responsible for seeking to reconcile them. Such conciliation is a necessary preliminary to most investigations by the court except in circumstances which the court considers require its direct intervention (1969 Act, s 18).

9.12.5   ARBITRATION

Where a trade dispute has occurred or is feared, the court may, with the consent of the parties refer the dispute to an arbitrator, or may itself arbitrate (1946 Act, s 70). This power has not yet been used by the court. Arbitration of employment disputes in Ireland is virtually unknown. Section 5 of the Arbitration Act, 1954 provides that the Act shall not apply to 'arbitration of any question relating to the terms or conditions of employment or the remuneration of any employees'. This appears to exclude all employment disputes from the scope of arbitration. Section 5 provides that the restrictions contained in that section do not apply to the 1946 Act, s 70.

9.12.6   FAIR EMPLOYMENT RULES

The court has power, after consulting the organisations representing the employers and workers in question, to make rules providing for 'fair employment conditions'.

9.12.7   STANDARD WAGES FOR AREAS

Having given due notice of its intention, the court may (on its own initiative or at the request of any interested party) fix a weekly wage which, in its opinion, should be paid to adult, unskilled workers in any given area.

9.12.8 APPEAL

If a party is in disagreement with a Labour Court recommendation, they may refer the matter to the High Court on a point of law only. Such reference is normally made by way of judicial review. This is a quick and relatively inexpensive procedure whereby administrative bodies such as the Labour Court are subject to having their decisions scrutinised (mainly for procedural fairness) by the High Court to ensure that they are legally correct. Questions of fact are determined by the Labour Court and cannot be reviewed by the High Court. If the Labour Court has determined the facts of a case the findings of fact are not subject to review (see *North Western Health Board v Martyn* [1987] IR 565; [1988] ILRM 519 and *State (St Stephen's Green Club) v The Labour Court* [1961] IR 85).

9.13 RIGHTS COMMISSIONERS

The 1969 Act created the office of rights commissioner and empowers the Minister for Labour to appoint rights commissioners.

Where a trade dispute other than a dispute connected with the rates of pay, hours or times of work, or annual holidays of a body of workers exists or is apprehended, a party to the dispute may refer it to a rights commissioner. A rights commissioner cannot investigate a trade dispute if:

(a)   the Labour Court has already made a recommendation on it; or

(b)   a party to the dispute notifies the commissioner in writing that he objects to the dispute being investigated by a rights commissioner (in which event either party is free to bring the dispute before the Labour Court).

In addition, rights commissioners have been conferred with functions and powers by other legislation in respect of which their decisions are legally binding, such as unfair dismissal legislation and the Payment of Wages Act, 1991. Rights commissioners have power to provide for the conduct of proceedings before them; in general, such proceedings tend to be less formal than proceedings in the Labour Court. Investigations are held in private. Although the recommendations of a rights commissioner are not legally binding on the parties to a dispute, they are frequently sufficient to resolve it. If either party is dissatisfied, however, they may appeal to the Labour Court. The decision of the Labour Court is then final, although no penalties exist for refusing to comply (see Industrial Relations Act, 1969, s 13(9)). Except by way of such appeal, the court cannot investigate a dispute on which a rights commissioner has already issued a recommendation. Rights commissioners have had their functions greatly expanded to cover the resolution of disputes under a much wider body of legislation (eg unfair dismissal claims).

9.14 JOINT LABOUR COMMITTEES

The 1946 Act empowers the Labour Court to set up Joint Labour Committees ('JLCs'), whose purpose is to regulate conditions of employment and minimum rates of pay for all workers engaged in the type of activity of which the members of the committee are representative. Joint Labour Committees tend to exist in sectors where wages and conditions have traditionally been below the general norm. Some twenty-six JLCs now exist. Once the Labour Court approves the creation of a JLC whose members (employers and workers) the court believes to be representative of employers and workers in that trade or industry, the JLC is free to submit proposals to the court for an employment regulation order setting down proposals for minimum rates of pay and for other minimum conditions of employment. These proposals are then published by the Labour Court which may then, at its discretion, make an employment regulation order. The wages or conditions specified in the order thereupon become the legal minimum for all employees in that trade or industry whether or not they took part in the process or are even aware of the making of the order. The observance by employers of relevant employment regulation orders is enforced by inspectors appointed by the Minister for Labour. The inspectors have power to examine any data on wages, conditions of work, etc relevant to such order (eg wage books or employee registers).

9.15 JOINT INDUSTRIAL COUNCILS

A Joint Industrial Council (JIC) is an association of persons which:

(a) is substantially representative of workers of a particular class, type or group and their employers;

(b) has the object of promoting harmonious relations between such employers and workers;

(c) provides by its rules that if a trade dispute arises, no strike or lockout will take place until the dispute has been considered by the association.

The Labour Court, when satisfied these conditions are fulfilled, registers the association as a 'Registered Joint Industrial Council' (1946 Act, Part V). Registration of a JIC facilitates the subsequent registration of employment agreements (see **9.16** below) and also authorises the JIC to engage in negotiations to fix wages and/or conditions of employment even though it has no negotiation licence.

9.16 REGISTERED EMPLOYMENT AGREEMENTS

9.16.1 GENERALLY

The parties to any agreement on pay and/or conditions of employment of any class or group of workers may apply to the Labour Court to 'register' the agreement.

Once registered, the agreement becomes a legally enforceable statement of minimum pay rates and/or conditions of employment and is directly applicable to every worker (and his employer) of the type, class or group to which it is expressed to apply including workers and employers within the type, class or group who are not parties to the agreement (see *National Union of Security Employers v Labour Court Ireland and Attorney General* 10 JISLL 97). The terms, conditions and provisions of a registered employment agreement would automatically transfer to a transferee under the provisions of article 3(1) and (2) of the Transfer of Undertakings Directive and regulations 3 and 4(1) of SI 306/1980.

9.16.2 CONDITIONS OF REGISTRATION

The Labour Court will register an agreement if satisfied that the employers and workers' representative of the class of employment concerned are in agreement as to registration. The agreement must provide that no strike or lockout will occur until the appropriate negotiating procedures have been utilised. Before registering an agreement, the court must first publish notice of it and hear any objections made by any person affected. Employment agreements and their registration are dealt with in Part III of the 1946 Act.

9.17 INDUSTRIAL RELATIONS ACT, 1990

Part I of the 1990 Act consists of seven sections dealing with preliminary issues and interpretation and repeals. Part II as has been seen, contains the law relating to trade disputes. Part III of the Act is headed 'Industrial Relations Generally'. It contains a definition of 'worker' in s 23 which is somewhat different from the definition adopted for the purposes of trade union and trade dispute laws contained in Part II of the same Act. It is not as wide a definition as the one contained in s 8 and defines the term 'worker' only for the purposes of the Industrial Relations Acts, 1946 to 1976 and Part III of the 1990 Act and contains the requirement that the contract is one whereby the worker contracts 'personally to execute any work or labour'. As personal service is an essential feature of a contract of service independent contractors are thereby by their nature excluded from the legislation relating to industrial relations.

The definition of a worker was expanded in July 1998 to include officers of local authorities and health boards by the deletion of the exclusion of such persons in the 1990 Act, s 23(1)(d). This brought officers of local authorities and health boards within the remit of the 1990 Act and gave them access to the Labour Relations Commission, Labour Court and Rights Commissioners in respect of industrial relations matters (Industrial Relations Act 1990 (Definition of Worker) Order 1998, SI 264/1998).

Section 24 established the Labour Relations Commission (LRC). The constitution of and ground rules for the LRC are contained in the 1990 Act, Sch 4.

Section 25 sets out the functions of the Commission which are to:

(a) provide a conciliation service;

(b) provide an industrial relations advisory service;

(c) prepare codes of practice relevant to industrial relations in consultation with the unions and employer organisations;

(d) offer guidance on codes of practice and help to resolve disputes concerning the implementation of such codes;

(e) appoint equality officers and rights commissioners and provide staff and facilities for those services;

(f) conduct or commission research into industrial relations matters and review and monitor developments in that area; and

(g) assist JLCs and JICs in the exercise of their function.

The section provides that except where there is specific provision for the direct reference of trade disputes to the Labour Court trade disputes must first be referred to the Commission or its appropriate services.

Section 26 helps to demarcate the functions of the Labour Court and the LRC. The Labour Court cannot investigate a trade dispute unless it receives a report from the Commission that it cannot do anything further to advance the resolution of the dispute and the parties request the court to investigate. The chairman of the Commission may, however, refer a matter to the court for investigation.

9.18   CODES OF PRACTICE

Section 42 of the 1990 Act obliges the LRC to prepare draft codes of practice concerning industrial relations for submission to the Minister and to seek the views of interested parties on behalf of workers and employers. The draft code of practice is submitted to the Minister who then, by order, declares the code a statutory code under this Act. After that, in any proceedings before a court, the Labour Court, the Commission, the EAT, rights commissioner or equality officer the code of practice is admissible in evidence and any of its provisions of relevance may be taken into account in determining the question at issue. Failure by a person to observe any provision of the code of practice is not of itself an offence and does not render a person liable to any civil or criminal proceedings but obviously a breach of the code will have considerable bearing on the outcome of the determination.

The Labour Court has a function under s 43 to give an opinion as to the interpretation of a code of practice on application by any party on notice to any other party. Like its normal functions the Labour Court only makes a recommendation in relation to breach of codes of practice and there is nowhere stated to be a legally binding function for the court in this regard. The Labour Relations Commission has issued a code of practice for dealing with trade disputes in order to avoid strikes or other similar industrial action and the Industrial Relations Act 1990 Code of Practice on Disciplinary Procedures (Declaration) Order, 1996 (SI 117/1996) sets out a model form of disciplinary procedure based on best practice.

CHAPTER 10

TRANSFER OF UNDERTAKINGS

10.1 LEGISLATIVE HISTORY OF THE BUSINESS TRANSFER (EMPLOYEE RIGHTS) DIRECTIVE

Commission

Draft directive finalised 29 May 1974 (COM (74) 357 Final) and 21 June 1974 (COM (74) 351 Final/2)

Submitted to Council 31 May 1974 (Parl Doc 149/74)

Assembly

Reports of Social Affairs and Employment Committee (Mr Yeats) 25 October 1974 and 22 January 1975 (Parl Docs 385/74 and 385/74 Rev)

Debate and opinion 8 April 1975 (Parl Proc, pp 47–66 and [1975] OJ C95/17)

Economic and Social Committee

Report of Section for Social Questions (Mr Muhr) 13 March 1975
Opinion 24 April 1975 [1975] OJ C255/25.

10.2 THE TRANSFER OF UNDERTAKINGS DIRECTIVE

10.2.1 INTRODUCTION

On 14 February 1977 pursuant to article 100 of the EC Treaty the Council of the European Community enacted the Transfer of Undertakings Directive (77/187/EEC) ('the Directive') for the purpose of protecting certain rights of employees in the event that the business in which they were employed was transferred to a new employer. The preamble to the Directive recites that the Council had regard to:

'Economic trends . . . bringing in their wake, at both national and Community level, changes in the structure of undertakings, through transfers of undertakings, businesses or parts of businesses to other employers as a result of legal transfers or mergers.'

The Council felt it necessary to provide for:

'the protection of employees in the event of a change of employer, in particular to ensure that their rights are safeguarded'.

At first the Directive appeared to be only of interest and relevance to employment lawyers; however, the full scope of the Directive and the extraordinary effect it has had on commercial practice has now become clearer after a number of decisions of the European Court of Justice ('ECJ') as applied in, and to, the law of Member States by courts and tribunals throughout the European Union. While the concept of granting to employees the right to transfer to a new employer, at their behest, and to have their employment rights and entitlements maintained unchanged following a commercial change of employer was known and recognised in some Member States, notably France where the concept had been recognised since 1928, and Italy, the concept was unknown in the UK and Ireland and was considerably more restricted in other Member States. The Directive became part of Irish domestic legislation by virtue of the European Communities (Safeguarding of Employees' Rights on Transfer of Undertakings) Regulations 1980 (SI 306/1980) ('the Regulations').

10.2.2 SCOPE OF THE DIRECTIVE

10.2.2.1 Application

The main points to note in relation to the Directive are as follows:

It applies to 'undertakings' or 'parts of undertakings'. This raises the question as to what is meant by an undertaking and what constitutes the transfer of part of an undertaking. The term 'undertaking' is not defined in the Directive or the Irish regulations.

It applies to a 'transfer' of an undertaking or a part thereof. What constitutes a 'transfer' within the meaning of the Directive? In many cases this will be easy to identify but in some instances a transfer may take place without the parties to the transfer being aware that what they or others have done constitutes a transfer within the meaning of the Directive and, therefore, they may remain in ignorance of the full implications, both legal and practical, of what has occurred.

The transfer must involve a change of employer. In most cases it is easy to identify that there has been a change of employer; however, in some cases it may be difficult to ascertain. It is essential to establish if there has been a change of employer; if not the Directive will not apply as a change of employer is a fundamental pre-requisite.

The change of employer may come about by the takeover by a new owner but may also apply where full ownership does not change but management responsibility transfers including management of subsidiary activities. This is of particular importance in the contracting out of certain services which form part of a business where the main business itself remains in place with the same ownership and therefore, of itself, not subject to the provisions of the Directive.

It keeps employee and trade union contractual entitlements alive post-transfer regardless of whether the purchaser is aware of the existence of such obligations or commitments. All rights and entitlements of employees who transfer must be honoured by the purchaser or transferee both individually and collectively.

The legislature and courts in Ireland have not become involved to any great degree in the relationships between employers and trade unions representative of their employees. This has left it to employers and trade unions to order their own affairs and clarify the various commitments and obligations as may exist between them. Employers and trade unions do not always do this with precision. Even where they have ordered their affairs in a careful and prudent fashion the nature of the relationship is such that over a period of time commitments will arise not only by specific agreement but by implication, acquiescence, or by custom and practice, which are not specific and therefore difficult to define or measure. Trade unions may make claims from time to time based on practices that occurred some considerable time in the past which the employer may have forgotten about. An employer who has purchased a business may not have been fully informed by their predecessor and therefore be unaware of the existence of a practice or prior commitment that might be relevant to some future claim or event. This gives rise to particular difficulties in the operation of the Directive.

It provides for continued recognition of employee representatives. In much the same way that employment relationships are entered into by agreement of the parties an employer in Ireland is only obliged to recognise a trade union where the employer confers specific recognition rights on that trade union. If a business is transferred the new employer could possibly, under the strict law of contract, claim that a union should be derecognised in that that new employer has not entered into a contractual commitment with the trade union. The Directive, however, provides for automatic continuance of trade union representation.

The parties to a transfer have obligations to notify, inform and possibly to consult with employees and their representatives before the transfer takes effect. Given the importance to employees of a change in their employer it is essential in order for employees to protect their own interests that they get advance notice of any proposed change and the Directive makes specific and wide-ranging provisions in this regard. These provisions are particularly important to anyone entering into negotiations for the purchase or transfer of a business.

Pension entitlements do not have to be continued by a transferee. Given the wide scope of the Directive and its purpose of protecting employees, and taking into account the importance to employees of their pension arrangements, it is somewhat surprising that the Directive does not oblige a new employer to continue to provide pension benefits although there is an obligation to ensure that pension entitlements accrued up to the date of transfer can and will be honoured in respect of both employees transferred and others who have pension entitlements at the date of transfer.

Where the Directive is breached liability, in the main, falls on the transferee or purchaser. It is not possible for the parties to a commercial agreement to anticipate all liabilities that may arise in the future. It is therefore usual for commercial agreements for the sale or transfer of a business to provide that the purchaser will be indemnified in respect of certain liabilities be they specifically anticipated or not. As the Directive places virtually all liability after the date of transfer on the purchaser indemnities come into sharp focus and a failure to make proper provision for future liabilities could mean a significant negative impact on the transferee or purchaser of a business. Proper advance planning and due diligence enquiries are particularly important.

It does not apply to transfers in the context of an insolvent transferor. If an employer ceases to trade by reason of insolvency and the business is subsequently transferred the provisions of the Directive will not apply.

10.2.2.2 How businesses change hands

Businesses usually change hands in one of three ways:

Sale of shares

Shares in an employing company may change hands frequently and in varying amounts and this will not affect the employees. Even where a controlling shareholding is sold and the practical reality is that the company is being run by new owners this has no effect, in law, on the employees. They are still employed by the company regardless of who controls or owns it. The law relating to the transfer of undertakings and employee rights does not therefore apply in the case of a share sale. It should not need to apply in any event, as where the employing company remains in existence it must continue to honour its contractual obligations to its staff, staff representatives and others with whom it has contractual relationships, there is no change of employer and the Directive does not therefore apply.

Sale of the assets and goodwill of business to a new operator

A business may be sold wholly or partly to a new owner, be it a person or a company, who continues to operate it even with certain changes. The employees of the business are consequently employed by a new person or legal entity, the Directive comes into effect and governs the rights and obligations of the parties to the transaction, the seller, the buyer, the employees and their representatives. There is a change of employer and the Directive applies.

Transfer of ownership by operation of law or indirect means

The legal ownership of a business may change on the occurrence of something that does not require the specific agreement of the contracting parties such as the surrender of a lease or franchise. In these circumstances case law on the Directive has shown that if the business is continued by the person or body to whom it is surrendered or transferred there is a transfer of an undertaking and the transferee becomes liable not only to the employees, but for the employees, and may have a duty to continue them in employment depending on how the transferee plans to run the business.

10.2.3 WHO IS COVERED BY THE DIRECTIVE?

10.2.3.1 Generally

The Directive uses the term 'employee' throughout but also refers to persons having an 'employment relationship', which must be taken to be intended to cover most categories of persons carrying out work for another. The Directive does not state, however, what categories of persons who carry out work for another are covered by its provisions and regard must be had to other sources to determine what persons are covered by the Directive. The EC Treaty uses the term 'workers'. The European Parliament, its committees and the ECJ use the terms 'employee' and 'worker' as if they were synonymous and they certainly appear to be interchangeable terms in the terminology of the European Union. None of the case law has laid down a firm definition of what is meant by 'employee' in the Directive. This appears to be because of the variety of protections afforded to different types of workers throughout the European Union and the fact that the Directive is intended only to achieve partial harmonisation of employment law throughout the EU. Guidance was given by Advocate-General Slynn in *Mikkelsen v Danmols Inventar A/S* [1986] 1 CMLR 316, which is referred to in more detail below, when he stated in his opinion:

> 'an employee is one who in return for remuneration agrees to work for another and who can as a matter of law be directed as to what he does and how he does it, whether pursuant to a contract of employment or an employment relationship.'

This accords with the distinctions recognised in common law jurisdictions between a contract of service and a contract for services. Advocate-General Slynn expanded on his views in the case of *Botzen v Rotterdamsche Droogdok Maatschappij BV* [1986] 2 CMLR 50, where he was dealing with the sale of part of a business and was seeking to ascertain whether an employee was 'wholly engaged' in the part of the business that was transferred, and allowed that both full-time and part-time workers are covered. It would appear therefore that for the purposes of the Directive an employee with a contract of service of whatever nature is covered by the Directive.

10.2.3.2 Public bodies

In *Henke v Gemeinde Schierke & Verwaltungsgemeinschaft 'Brocken'* [1996] IRLR 701 the ECJ examined a situation where a public administrative entity, the Municipality of Schierke, was transferred to a new local government body and the municipal administration of Schierke was dissolved. Ms Henke was secretary to the mayor of Schierke. One of the matters that arose for consideration in the case was whether or not Ms Henke and people like her, who were employees of a public body, came within the scope of the term 'employee' as used in the Directive. In the course of his opinion Advocate-General Lenz considered submissions made by the German government that a local authority was not an undertaking within the meaning of the Directive. The Advocate-General stated (at paragraph 22) 'It is not contested . . . that a municipality can generally carry out economic activities'. He went on to refer to a number of areas of normal economic activity engaged in by local authorities and said that:

'even if exercise of an economic activity were to be regarded as a pre-condition for the application of the Directive a municipality could definitely be treated as being an undertaking within the meaning of the Directive. It is therefore questionable whether the Municipality and its employees should be excluded from the scope of application of the Directive simply because the Municipality also acts in the exercise of powers of a public authority.'

The Advocate-General in his reasoning allowed that in its purest form a State agency or an emanation of the State could be excluded from the scope of the Directive when carrying out governmental or quasi-governmental or local authority functions which are not among the activities of the European Community governed by the EC Treaty. He did, however, point out the type of economic activities that may be engaged in by such bodies in respect of which they can or may employ 'employees' who would be covered by the Directive. He also pointed out the difficulty in ascertaining the type of bodies that may be excluded from the definition of undertaking and commented:

'[T]he criterion of activity in the exercise of public powers is very difficult to pin down since it is subject to cost and change. What is today regarded as purely public may in even only a few years be carried out by a private undertaking with a view to profit. It also cannot be ruled out that functions carried out by a private undertaking will not be regarded after a time as being again functions of the public authorities. It is therefore possible to justify the employees carrying out these activities being covered at one time by the protection of the Directive and then following a change of view as to the public character of their activities, no longer enjoying that protection. In addition it is questionable how an employee carrying out both activities in the exercise of public powers and economic activities would have to be classified.'

He went on to say that while an 'undertaking' must be defined having regard to whether or not it employs employees the definition of 'employee' cannot have regard to whether or not the persons are employed in an 'undertaking'. He referred to *Redmond Stichting v Bartol* [1992] IRLR 366 and *Mikkelsen v Danmols Inventar A/S* [1986] 1 CMLR 316 and stated that the applicability of the Directive must be decided 'based solely on the concept of an employee'. He concluded by stating:

'Accordingly, the Directive is applicable whenever employees within the meaning of the national protective provisions are employed in an undertaking or an organisational entity. It is irrelevant whether the undertaking is engaged in the sphere of public administration or in the private sector. This means that the Directive may also be applied to a municipality where workers are employed within the meaning of the national protective provisions.'

In its subsequent judgment in *Henke v Gemeinde Schierke* the ECJ appeared to be in little doubt that governmental or public functions did not of themselves come within the terms of the Directive. The court made reference to the preamble to the Directive where the protection of the Directive is stated to relate to 'changes in the structure of undertakings resulting from economic trends' and without any further analysis concluded: 'the reorganisation of structures of the public administration or the transfer of administrative functions between public administrative authorities does not constitute a "transfer of an undertaking" within the meaning of the Directive'.

The ECJ disagreed with the Advocate-General as to whether the local authority concerned was an undertaking within the meaning of the Directive. The court held that it was not an undertaking. The court did not make any observation on whether or not the status of the persons employed therein, as determined under national law, would disqualify them from the coverage of the Directive if they did not have a 'contract of service'. Regard must be had to article 3 of the Directive when it refers to 'employment relationships' and given that, while civil servants do not have coverage of all employment legislation in Ireland and indeed are excluded from much of it, they do have legal protections and it appears therefore that while they are not 'protected as an employee under the national legislation' as referred to by Advocate-General Van Gerven in *Redmond Stichting v Bartol* their employment relationship must transfer. It appears from the decision of the court in *Henke v Gemeinde Schierke* that if there is determined to be in existence an 'undertaking' within the meaning of the Directive and there is a 'transfer' within the meaning of the Directive then the persons employed in the undertaking to be transferred have the protection of the Directive.

If a civil servant were to be employed in an undertaking, the subject matter of a transfer, and the undertaking transferred from public ownership into private ownership practical difficulties would arise where the new private employer would be expected to meet the employment entitlements of a civil servant which, of course, would be impossible. The solution would appear to be the fact that the civil servant remains a servant of the State who was in reality seconded to the 'undertaking' prior to the transfer and must be deemed to remain seconded to the undertaking after the transfer. If the transferee had economic, technical or organisational reasons for no longer requiring the civil servant to continue working in the undertaking the civil servant would not become unemployed but would revert to his status prior to being seconded to the undertaking in the first place. It would be a matter for the State to redeploy its servant, which itself is liable to cause practical difficulties, but not for the transferee.

10.3   INTERPRETING THE DIRECTIVE

The long title of the Directive is:

> 'On the Approximation of the Laws of the Member States Relating to the Safeguarding of Employees' Rights in the Event of Transfers of Undertakings, Businesses or Parts of Businesses.'

10.3.1   THE PREAMBLE

The preamble makes reference to the manner in which the Directive became law, refers to article 100 of the EC Treaty and goes on to state:

> 'Whereas economic trends are bringing in their wake, at both National and Community level, changes in the structure of undertakings, through transfers of undertakings, businesses or parts of businesses to other employers as a result of legal transfers or mergers;

> 'Whereas it is necessary to provide for the protection of employees in the event of a change of employer, in particular, to ensure that their rights are safeguarded;

> 'Whereas differences still remain in the Member States as regards the extent of the protection of employees in this respect and these differences should be reduced;

> 'Whereas these differences can have a direct effect on the functioning of the common market;

> 'Whereas it is therefore necessary to promote the approximation of laws in this field while maintaining the improvement described in Article 117 of The Treaty.'

The preamble has been quoted in cases to assist in interpreting the scope of the Directive as in *Henke v Gemeinde Schierke* [1996] IRLR 701 where the ECJ referred to the use of the words 'economic trends' to support the view that the Directive does not apply to governmental or civil service activities. The applicability of the Directive is set out in articles 1 and 2 which provide:

'ARTICLE 1

1. *This Directive shall apply to the transfer of an undertaking, business or part of a business to another employer as a result of a legal transfer or merger.*
2. *This Directive shall apply where and, in so far as the undertaking, business or part of the business to be transferred is situated within the territorial scope of the Treaty.*
3. *This Directive shall not apply to sea-going vessels.*

ARTICLE 2

For the purposes of this Directive:

(a) *"transferor" means any natural or legal person who, by reason of a transfer within the meaning of Article 1(1), ceases to be the employer in respect of the undertaking, business or part of the business;*
(b) *"transferee" means any natural or legal person who, by reason of a transfer within the meaning of Article 1(1), becomes the employer in respect of the undertaking, business or part of the business;*
(c) *"representatives of the employees" means the representatives of the employees provided for by the laws or practice of the Member States, with the exception of members of administrative, governing or supervisory bodies of companies who represent employees on such bodies in certain Member States.'*

Regulation 1 of SI 306/1980 gives the title of the Regulations and the effective date of operation, being 3 November 1980. Regulation 2 refers to Directive 77/187/EEC and defines the Minister for the purposes of the Regulations as being the Minister for Labour, now the Minister for Trade, Enterprise and Employment.

Regulation 2(2) provides:

'A word or expression that is used in these Regulations and is also used in the Council Directive shall, unless the context otherwise requires, have the meaning in these Regulations that it has in the Council Directive.'

10.3.2 TERRITORIAL SCOPE

The territorial scope of the EC Treaty is as set out generally in the European Communities Act, 1972 and covers Ireland and its territorial waters. Article 1(2) provides that the undertaking must be within the territorial scope of the EC Treaty. The question of territorial waters and jurisdiction under the Directive and the UK regulations was considered by the Scottish EAT in *Addison v Denholm Ship Management (UK) Ltd* [1997] IRLR 389. Article 1(3) excludes sea-going vessels from the scope of the Directive and the definition of what constitutes a sea-going vessel was also considered in *Addison* when North Sea oil vessels known as flotels were considered to be sea-going vessels and therefore excluded from the terms of the Directive and Regulations. The purpose of a flotel is to provide accommodation for tradesmen, caterers, labourers and others required during the construction and commissioning of fixed oil and gas installations offshore. They consist of a platform, which is floating on the water, and carries accommodation for a large number of people together with offices, workshops and storage areas. They carry large cranes and helicopter landing facilities and can supply power to the installations. Flotels are taken to locations of installations, possibly under their own power but more usually under tow. While working on the installations they are anchored in position and they carry a maritime crew. The EAT in *Addison* was also asked to consider where employees employed on the flotels ordinarily worked for the purpose of jurisdiction under unfair dismissals legislation. Under Irish unfair dismissal legislation employees who work outside the State are excluded from the provision of the legislation pursuant to the provisions of the Unfair Dismissals Act, 1977, s 2(3) which provides:

(a) *'This Act shall not apply in relation to the dismissal of an employee who, under the relevant contract of employment, ordinarily worked outside the State unless—*
   (i) *he was ordinarily resident in the State during the term of the contract, or*
   (ii) *he was domiciled in the State during the term of the contract, and the employer—*
      (I) *in case the employee was an individual, was ordinarily resident in the State during the term of the contract, or*
      (II) *in case the employer was a body corporate or an unincorporated body of persons, had its principal place of business in the State during the term of the contract.*
(b) *In this subsection ''term of the contract'' means the whole of the period from the time of the commencement of work under the contract to the time of the relevant dismissal.'*

The question of residence in Ireland was considered in *Roche v Sealink Stena Line Ltd* [1993] ELR 89. See also *Davis v Sealink Stena Line Ltd* UD 874/93.

10.3.3 THE PURPOSIVE APPROACH

The Directive and Regulations are broadly drafted and, in the absence of clear definitions, interpretation has been difficult. The approach adopted by courts and tribunals has been to ensure the social purpose of the Directive is met, albeit thereby causing difficulty for employers, employees and their advisers in trying to interpret the precise scope and application of the Directive's provisions and ordering their affairs accordingly. Rather than limiting themselves to the interpretation of the precise words and phrases used in the Directive the courts have adopted what is called the 'purposive approach'. In his opinion in *JMA Spijkers v Gebroeders Benedik Abattoir CV* [1986] 2 CMLR 296 Advocate-General, Sir Gordon Slynn stated (at p 489):

'It is clear that the overriding objective of the Directive is to protect workers in a business which is transferred. . . . In deciding whether there has been a transfer . . . all the circumstances have to be looked at. Technical rules are to be avoided and the substance matters more than the form.'

In *Spijkers* the full court (at p 492) also made reference to the aim and context of the Directive which is referred to in the preamble to the Directive as being:

'To provide for the protection of employees in the event of a change of employer, in particular, to ensure that their rights are safeguarded.'

In *Landsorganisationen i Danmark v Ny Molle Kro* [1989] IRLR 37 the court stated again in quoting the preamble and referring to articles 1(1), 3(1), (2) and 4(1) of the Directive:

'[T]he purpose of the Directive is to safeguard, as far as possible, the rights of workers in the event of a change of employer by enabling them to remain in employment with the new employer on the same conditions agreed with the transferor' (p 39).

Also in *Ny Molle Kro* the court, referring to its decision in *Mikkelsen v Danmols Inventar A/S* [1986] 1 CMLR 316, stated (at p 40):

'The objective of the Directive is to ensure as far as possible the continuation without change of the contract of employment or the employment relationship with the transferee in order to avoid the worker concerned being placed in a less favourable position by reason of the transfer alone.'

The courts in Ireland have, in common with courts in the UK, adopted this purposive approach which is not their traditional approach to the interpretation of legislation.

Blaney J in *Bannon v Employment Appeals Tribunal and Drogheda Town Centre Ltd* [1992] ELR 203 quoted the ECJ in its reference to the aim and context of the Directive as being to protect employees, and went on to find that there was a transfer in that particular case and the employee concerned was protected by the provisions of the Directive and Regulations.

Irish law must have regard to the ECJ interpretation of Directives to ensure that the implementation of the domestic equivalent of the relevant European law meets the requirements of the European Union. The Transfer of Undertakings Directive, however, is imprecisely and broadly drafted and, after much judicial examination, it may now be seen that it did not have regard to all of the circumstances to which it might apply, as a result of which it has been left to the courts not only to interpret the intention of the legislature but also to flesh out the provisions of the Directive and adapt and adopt it to practical commercial situations which have been referred for consideration. This has caused practical difficulties for employers, employees and advisers and has led to considerable confusion as to when and how the Directive applies to commercial transactions.

In *Henke v Gemeinde Schierke* [1996] IRLR 701 Advocate-General Lenz referred to the purposive approach in seeking to decide whether or not public servants, being employees of a public administration, were covered by the Directive and held:

'If regard is had to the protective purpose of the Directive it cannot be seen why employees of the public administration . . . should be excluded from the protective ambit of the Directive merely because their authority acts also in the exercise of public authority. To my mind this would clearly be at odds with the protective purpose of the Directive. . . . Moreover, a distinction should not be made between employees in the public service and employees in the sphere of private law. This would produce results which would conflict with the protective purpose of the Directive especially since such a distinction does not exist in all the Member States.'

The full court in *Henke* held, however, that the public administration concerned was not an undertaking within the meaning of the Directive.

In cases where the Directive has been held not to apply the Advocates-General and the court have had difficulty in indicating how the purposive approach was being applied. For example, in *Ledernes Hovedorganisation (Rygaard) v Dansk Arbejdsgiverforening (Stro Mølle Akustik) A/S* [1996] IRLR 51 ('*Rygaard*') a carpentry sub-contract was transferred from one employer to another. The Advocate-General recited the precedents in respect of the purposive approach to be taken and went on to hold that the transfer in that particular case could come within the Directive but it was a matter for the national court to decide whether the Directive in fact applied. The ECJ, however, took a simpler but contrary view. Without making any reference to the purpose of the Directive the court held that taking over a sub-contract with the consent of the main awarder of the contract 'does not constitute a transfer of an undertaking . . . within the meaning of . . . Directive 77/187/EEC'. No explanation was given as to why the purpose of the Directive was not or could not be met in that situation.

10.3.4 IRISH POSITION

Blayney J commented in *Bannon v Employment Appeals Tribunal and Drogheda Town Centre Ltd* [1992] ELR 203 at p 207, referring to both *Spijkers v Gebroeders Benedik Abattoir CV* [1986] 2 CMLR 296 and *Landsorganisationen i Danmark v Ny Molle Kro* [1989] IRLR 37:

'[T]he Court has indicated very clearly what the objective of the Directive is and it has also set out the criteria in the light of which the National Courts should determine if the Directive is applicable.'

He also quoted with favour (at p 209) the ECJ's judgment in *Ny Molle Kro* on the purposive approach to be adopted in Irish law.

The EAT took a wide and purposive approach in its determination in *Morris v Smart Brothers Ltd* UD 688/93. In that case the EAT was faced with a factual situation where on the transfer of a business certain employees had their employment terminated by the transferor by reason of redundancy and claimed unfair dismissal against the transferor and the transferee. In the absence of proper Irish regulations implementing the Directive and interlinking it with existing Irish employment law, the EAT was left to wrestle with the difficulties posed in giving effect to the Directive. The EAT quoted Barrington J in *Mythen v Employment Appeals Tribunal* [1990] ELR 1 when he commented that the provisions of the Directive and Regulations 'have revolutionary implications for the relationship between employers and employees' and went on to state in relation to the effect of the Directive on Irish employment law:

'In using the word "revolutionary" Barrington J did not under-state the significance of the changes to the law involved in the Directive. [It] did indeed revolutionise the law in relation to contracts of employment. In effect it obliges the new owner of a business to enter a contract of employment with any employee who was working in the business at the date of transfer. This obligation flies in the face of the Common Law principles governing the creation of contracts of any kind. Given the primacy of EC law the Common Law must, of course, give way.

'Moreover, if the new owner of a business does not engage such an employee his failure to do so may be regarded as dismissal. This leads to the major conceptual problem that one is deemed to have dismissed someone whom one never employed. In Common Law terms one is deemed to have terminated a contract that never existed.

'There are other conceptual problems involved in the Directive's use of the word "dismissal". Apart from the liability placed on the new owner of a business who never engaged the employee concerned there is another difficult legal question. If the transferee declines to engage the employee what is the position of the transferor? Closely related to this is another question as to the separate liabilities of the old employer and the new employer.'

10.4 UNDERTAKINGS

The Directive and Regulations apply only to the transfer of an 'undertaking'. There is no definition given of the term 'undertaking' in the Directive or the Regulations, nor is there any definition given in any of the EU Treaties. The term is, however, used in article 85 of the EC Treaty which deals with competition law and provides:

'The following shall be prohibited as incompatible with the common market: all agreements between undertakings, decisions by associations of undertakings and concerted practices which may affect trade between Member States and which have as their object or effect the prevention, restriction or distortion of competition within the common market.'

In considering the scope and extent of article 85 the ECJ held in *Hofner & Elsner v Macrotron* [1991] ECR I-1979 (at para 21):

'It must be observed, in the context of competition law, first that the concept of an undertaking encompasses every entity engaged in economic activity, regardless of the legal status of the entity and the way in which it is financed and, secondly that employment procurement is an economic activity.'

In *SAT Fluggesellschaft v Eurocontrol* [1994] ECR I-43 Eurocontrol collected route charges, as a result of which the applicant in the case maintained that Eurocontrol was engaged in an economic activity, even though Eurocontrol was financed by contributions of various

Member States which supported its existence. The ECJ held that the collection of route charges could not be separated from the organisation's other activities and that the activities taken as a whole constituted the exercise of powers of a public authority as opposed to trading of an economic nature and excluded Eurocontrol from the definition of an undertaking under competition law.

In *Fédération Francaise des Sociétés D'Assurance v Ministère de l'Agriculture et de la Pêche* [1996] 4 CMLR 536 a non-profit-making organisation established to provide a pension system intended to supplement the basic state scheme funded by contributions from members of the scheme was held to constitute an 'undertaking' within the meaning of article 85 of the EC Treaty.

Economic activity is not to be equated with profitable, or profit-making, activity. In order for an economic entity to be regarded as an undertaking it does not have to be engaged in activity which is carried on with a view to making a profit. This definition has the effect of allowing within the ambit of the Directive/Regulations:

(a)   charities;

(b)   local authorities;

(c)   health boards;

(d)   State and semi-State bodies;

(e)   schools, colleges, educational and medical establishments and foundations;

(f)   trade associations; and

(g)   trade unions.

10.5   ECONOMIC ENTITY/UNDERTAKING

10.5.1   INTRODUCTION

The way in which the ECJ has approached the concept of an economic entity indicates that the term 'economic entity' is interchangeable with the term 'undertaking'. Undertakings are economic entities and vice versa. In *Suzen v Zehnacker Gebaudereinigung GmbH Krankenhausservice* [1997] IRLR 255 the ECJ observed:

'The aim of the Directive is to ensure continuity of employment relationships within an economic entity. . . . The decisive criterion for establishing the existence of a transfer within the meaning of the Directive is whether the entity in question retains its identity as indicated inter alia by the fact that its operation is actually continued or resumed. For the Directive to be applicable the transfer must relate to a stable economic entity whose activity is not limited to preforming one specific works contract. The term entity thus refers to an organised grouping of persons and assets facilitating the exercise of an economic activity which pursues a specific objective.'

In the UK case of *Isles of Scilly Council v Brintel Helicopters Ltd and Ellis* [1995] IRLR 6 the EAT observed:

'An economic entity may well just comprise activities and employees. In the service industry tangible assets may be unimportant or possibly non-existent. Thus for example the economic entity may consist of the provision of services where the real asset may be goodwill or possibly just the right to provide the service in question.'

10.5.2   STABLE ECONOMIC ENTITY

In *Ledernes Hovedorganisation (Rygaard) v Dansk Arbejdsgiverforening (Stro Mølle Akustik) A/S* [1996] IRLR 51 the ECJ created the concept of the transfer of an undertaking of part of a business needing to be a transfer of 'a stable economic entity'—see the decision in *Suzen*, referred to at **10.5.1** above, also dealt with in more detail at **10.9.8.2**.

An undertaking or economic entity the subject matter of a transfer comes within the scope of the Directive and Regulations. Where a transaction involves the transfer of the whole or a substantial part of a business or economic entity it may be easily observed that there is a transfer of an undertaking involved. Where part of the economic entity or undertaking transfers the question arises as to whether that part of itself forms an economic entity and is a severable part of the undertaking. This topic is dealt with in more detail at **10.9** below, which deals with service providers and highlights the difficulties associated with carving out part of an economic entity or undertaking, transferring it, and then seeking to determine whether or not the Directive and Regulations apply in establishing whether or not there is an economic entity which is capable of being the subject of a transfer. In *Botzen v Rotterdamasche Droogdok Maatschappij BV* [1986] ECR 519 certain departments of the main undertaking transferred and those departments were held to be in themselves an economic entity forming part of an undertaking capable of being the subject matter of a transfer for the purposes of the Directive and Regulations. That was a straightforward and predictable decision. The position was far less straightforward and less predictable in *Schmidt v Spar und Leihkasse der Fruheren Amter Bordesholm* [1994] IRLR 302, which is also examined at **10.9.3**. In that case Ms Schmidt was employed by the bank concerned as a full-time employee to carry out cleaning of the branch that employed her. She was the only cleaner. The bank subsequently contracted out its cleaning work to an independent contract cleaning company. In the *Schmidt* case the question arose as to whether the cleaning activity of a branch of a bank constituted an economic entity or part of a business. Quite clearly the bank was itself an economic entity.

The question arose as to whether part of that economic entity transferred. Basic logic suggests that there is a transfer of part of the economic entity in such circumstances. The *Schmidt* case was therefore determined more on the question of part of the banking economic entity rather than by classifying the cleaning operations as an economic entity in themselves capable of being the subject matter of a transfer. The ECJ held (at p 303):

'The decisive criterion for establishing whether there is a transfer for the purposes of the Directive is whether the business in question retains its identity. This is indicated, inter alia, by the actual continuation or resumption by the new employer of the same or similar activities. In the present case the similarity in the cleaning work performed before and after the transfer, which was reflected in the offer to re-engage the employee in question, was typical of an operation which comes within the scope of the Directive.'

10.6   TRANSFER

10.6.1   INTRODUCTION

Article 1 of the Directive requires that there be a transfer of some nature, of the whole or part of an undertaking. The rights, duties and obligations governed by the Directive crystallise, or are triggered, by the occurrence of a transfer.

The 1980 Regulations provide at regulation 3:

'The rights and obligations of the transferor arising from a contract of employment or from an employment relationship existing on the date of a transfer shall, by reason of such transfer, be transferred to the transferee.'

See also article 3 of the Directive referred to at **10.9.8.8** below.

One of the earliest decisions of the ECJ interpreting the terms of the Directive, and one which continues to maintain seminal importance in the law relating to the transfer of undertakings, is the decision given by the court on 18 March 1986 in *JMA Spijkers v Gebroeders Benedik Abbatoir CV* [1986] 2 CMLR 296. Mr Spijkers worked for a company known as Colaris at their slaughterhouse located in the inappropriately named Ubach über Worms. Colaris agreed to sell the slaughterhouse together with offices, land and specified equipment to Benedik CV on 27 December 1982. From that date Colaris ceased trading. No trading was carried out until Benedik commenced trading on 7 February 1983. There was, therefore, at the time Benedik commenced business, no goodwill in the business. Benedik did not commence the identical trade as Colaris but carried on a similar type of trade using all of the Colaris employees, whom it re-employed under contracts agreed with those employees, with the exception of Mr Spijkers and one other employee who was too ill to work. Spijkers claimed that there had been a transfer of an undertaking and that Benedik should pay him from 27 December 1982 and provide him with work. Advocate-General Slynn made the following observations in his opinion (at pp 120–121):

'It is clear that the overriding objective of the Directive is to protect workers in a business which is transferred. In deciding whether there has been a transfer . . . all the circumstances have to be looked at. Technical rules are to be avoided . . . the substance matters more than the form. The essential question is whether the transferee has obtained a business or an undertaking (or a part thereof) which he can continue to operate. That at the time of transfer the business is still active, that machinery is being used, customers supplied, workers employed and that all the physical assets and goodwill are sold are strong indications that a transfer . . . has taken place. But these are not all necessary pre-requisites of a transfer in every case . . . the fact that at the date of transfer trading has ceased or has been substantially reduced does not prevent there being a transfer of a business if the wherewithal to carry on the business such as plant, building and employees are available and are transferred. Nor is the fact that goodwill or existing contracts are not transferred conclusive against there being a transfer.'

The court followed that line of reasoning and held that in order for a business activity to come within the definition of the transfer of an undertaking *'the business in question . . . [must] . . . retain its identity'*. The court held that there did not need to be a transfer of goodwill and that there could be cessation and resumption of the same or similar economic activities and stated (at p 493):

'Consequently it cannot be said that there is a transfer of an enterprise, business or part of a business on the sole ground that its assets have been sold. On the contrary, in a case like the present, it is necessary to determine whether what has been sold is an economic entity which is still in existence and this will be apparent from the fact that its operation is actually being continued or has been taken over by the new employer, with the same economic or similar activities.

'To decide whether these conditions are fulfilled it is necessary to take account of all the factual circumstances of the transaction in question including the type of undertaking or business in question, the transfer or otherwise of tangible assets such as buildings and stocks, the value of intangible assets at the date of transfer, whether the majority of the staff are taken over by the new employer, the transfer or otherwise of the circle of customers and the degree of similarity between activities before and after the transfer, and the duration of any interruption in those activities. It should remain clear however that each of these factors is only a part of the overall assessment which is required and therefore they cannot be examined independently of each other.'

While reference is made to the transfer of assets, as is seen at **10.9.7** below, asset transfer is not essential in order for there to be a transfer of an undertaking or part of an undertaking.

In *Schmidt v Spar und Leihkasse* [1994] IRLR 302 no assets transferred and in *Merckx and Neuhuys v Ford Motor Co Belgium SA* [1996] IRLR 467 the ECJ said (at p 467):

'That there had been no transfer of tangible assets did not prevent the application of the Directive.'

The *Spijkers* tests for identifying the existence of a transfer have survived the passage of time and are still relevant but it must be kept in mind that each of the tests is in itself merely for guidance and when each test has been answered the totality has to be assessed to see whether or not it adds up to there being a transfer.

10.6.2 CESSATION AND LATER RESUMPTION

The fact that a transferor ceases the business entirely and there is then a lapse of time before the transferee resumes the business does not prevent there being a transfer of the undertaking or business concerned. Advocate-General Slynn went on to observe in *Spijkers* (at p 489):

'That after the sale there is a gap before trading is resumed is a relevant fact but it is not conclusive against there being a transfer within the meaning of the Directive. The transferee may well want to spend time reorganising or renovating the premises or equipment . . . the fact that the business is carried on in a different way is not conclusive against there being a transfer—new methods, new machinery, new types of customer are relevant factors but they do not of themselves prevent there being in reality a transfer of a business or undertaking. Though it is plain that a sale may take place simply of the physical assets or part of them with no intention in any real sense that the business should thereafter be carried on care must be taken to ensure that such a sale is not a disguise to avoid obligations to the workers.'

10.6.3 CHANGE OF OWNERSHIP

10.6.3.1 Daddy's Dance Hall

Spijkers is a straightforward case of a business changing hands and it was understood initially that it was only on a change of ownership that the Directive applied. The decision in *Daddy's Dance Hall* delivered by the ECJ on 10 February 1988 showed that the Directive could apply where there was no change in the legal owner of a business but rather a change in the person or body responsible for the management or day-to-day operation of the business which the court held constituted a transfer for the purposes of the Directive.

The full name of the case is *Foreningen af Arbejdsledere i Danmark v Daddy's Dance Hall A/S* [1988] IRLR 315. Irma Catering, a company, leased restaurants and bars from another company, Palads Teatret. The lease was determined on 28 January 1983 with effect from 25 February 1983. Mr Tellerup was an employee of the business operated by Irma Catering and was dismissed on notice to expire on 30 April 1983. On 25 February 1983, a new lease was granted by Palads Teatret to a different company, Daddy's Dance Hall. Mr Tellerup was re-engaged by Daddy's Dance Hall. He was later dismissed by Daddy's Dance Hall on 26 April 1983. A dispute arose about the terms of Mr Tellerup's employment at the date of termination and the length of notice to which he was entitled from Daddy's Dance Hall. It was held that Daddy's Dance Hall must carry the liabilities of Irma Catering to Mr Tellerup. The ECJ held that the Directive applies to a situation where, after the termination of a lease, the owner of the undertaking leases it to a new lessee who continues to run the business and held '*It is of no importance to know whether the ownership of the undertaking has been transferred*'. It should be noted that there was no contractual nexus between Irma Catering and Daddy's Dance Hall. The court held:

'The Directive therefore applies as soon as there is a change, resulting from a conventional sale or from a merger, of the natural or legal person responsible for operating the undertaking who consequently enters into obligations as an employer towards the employees working in the undertaking and it is of no importance to know whether the ownership of the undertaking has been transferred.

'It follows that when the lessee who has the capacity of proprietor of the undertaking at the termination of the lease loses this capacity and a third person acquires it under a new lease concluded with the owner the resulting operation is capable of falling within the scope of application of the Directive as defined in Article 1(1). The fact that in such case the transfer takes place in two phases in the sense that as a first step the undertaking is transferred back from the original lessee to the owner who then transfers it to the new lessee, does not exclude the applicability of the Directive as long as the economic unit retains its identity. This is the case in particular when as in the instant case the business continues to be run without interruption from the new lessee with the same staff that was employed in the undertaking before the transfer' (at paras 9 and 10, p 317).

10.6.3.2 Ny Molle Kro

A similar line of reasoning to the *Daddy's Dance Hall* decision was followed in two further cases. In *Landsorganisationen i Danmark v Ny Molle Kro* [1989] IRLR 37 the owner of a tavern business, Mrs Hannibalsen, leased the tavern to Mrs Larsen. Mrs Larsen ran the tavern until such time as she was in breach of the lease whereupon the business reverted to the owner. The owner continued to manage the business without interruption to the employees. The reversion to the owner took place in January 1981. In May 1983 an employee was taken on and later that year when she left employment she claimed that she was entitled to a higher rate of wages than were actually paid to her by virtue of a collective agreement to which the lessee had been party. The question arose as to whether or not the lessee's obligations under the collective agreement transferred to the owner on her taking back the operation of the tavern business from Mrs Larsen. The court held that the resumption of the business by the owner constituted a transfer in so far as the lessee lost the capacity of employer and that capacity was reacquired by the lessor. The court held that there was a transfer within the meaning of the Directive 'whenever as a result of a legal transfer or merger there was a change in the natural or legal person responsible for the running of the undertaking'.

This applies regardless of whether ownership of the undertaking has been transferred. The employees of an undertaking in which the employers change, without a transfer of ownership, are in need of the same protection afforded to employees of an undertaking which has been sold. Following that line of reasoning the court held that the takeover by Mrs Larsen as managing lessee meant that under the terms of the lease she acquired the capacity of employer and that in turn constituted a transfer of an undertaking and, further, that where the owner of the lease took back the running of the undertaking that resumption also constituted a transfer in so far as the lessee lost the capacity of employer and that capacity was reacquired by the lessor.

10.6.3.3 Berg and Busschers v Besselsen

In *Berg and Busschers v Besselsen* [1989] IRLR 447 Berg was employed as the manager of a bar/disco owned by Besselsen. In 1983 Besselsen transferred the operation of the establishment to a commercial partnership by means of a lease purchase agreement. Under Dutch law this type of transaction is defined as a 'sale of deferred payments by which the parties agree that objects sold shall not become the property of the purchaser by mere transfer'. This involves a change of management but no change of ownership until the deferred payments have been made, not dissimilar to a retention of title clause in the sale of goods. The commercial partnership in this case failed to perform its obligations under the lease purchase agreement, which was consequently terminated on foot of a court ruling obtained by Besselsen. The court ordered the restoration of the bar/disco to Besselsen. Following the logic of *Ny Molle Kro* referred to at **10.6.3.2** above the court held that the transfer of an undertaking pursuant to a lease purchase agreement such as that recognised under Netherlands law and to the retransfer of that undertaking on the termination of the agreement by a judicial decision came within the scope of the Directive.

10.6.3.4 Guidon v Hugh Farrington

In *Guidon v Hugh Farrington and Ushers Island Petrol Station* [1993] ELR 98 the claimant worked with Local Stores (Trading) Ltd trading as Seven-Eleven. Seven-Eleven had a branch in the Ushers Island Petrol Station which was owned by Mr Farrington. Seven-Eleven went into receivership and its lease at Ushers Island was surrendered on 14 June 1991, which was a Friday and a normal day of work for the claimant. The claimant returned to work at Ushers Island on 17 June 1991 and was advised that her employment had terminated. She claimed unfair dismissal against the respondent and claimed he was a transferee within the meaning of the Directive and Regulations, the lease having been surrendered and the business reverting to him. The EAT had regard to the decisions of the ECJ in *Ny Molle Kro* and *Berg v Besselsen* and held that there had been a transfer of the undertaking of the Seven-Eleven shop to the respondent Mr Farrington and that the dismissal of the claimant on the grounds of transfer was prohibited by the Directive and Regulations and in the circumstances was deemed to be unfair.

10.6.4 CONTRACTUAL NEXUS BETWEEN TRANSFEROR AND TRANSFEREE

The *Daddy's Dance Hall, Ny Molle Kro* and *Berg* cases illustrate how a transfer may result from actions of or affecting the parties without there being a contractual nexus between them. This lack of a contractual nexus came into even sharper focus in *Redmond Stichting v Bartol* [1992] IRLR 366. The Dr Sophie Redmond Foundation provided assistance to drug addicts, including those of a particular ethnic origin, in the Netherlands. The foundation was funded by grants from the Groningen local authority. The local authority terminated the grants to the Redmond Foundation and instead funded another foundation, the Sigma Foundation, which provided general assistance to those who had problems with drug dependency on condition that that foundation would be accessible to drug addicts. The clients/patients of the Redmond Foundation were transferred to the Sigma Foundation. The local authority had been leasing a building to the Redmond Foundation which they transferred to Sigma. Some of the Redmond employees transferred to the Sigma Foundation on foot of offers of new contracts of employment from Sigma.

Some of those employees not transferred to the Sigma Foundation who had been employed by the Redmond Foundation claimed that there had been a transfer of an undertaking within the meaning of the Directive and that their employment should transfer also. The ECJ held that the Directive did apply. The main points to note from the judgment are:

(1) There is a transfer where a public body terminates a subsidy paid to one legal entity as a result of which the activities of that entity are terminated and transferred to another legal entity with similar aims.

(2) The Directive does not exclude non-profit-making bodies such as charities or foundations. The Directive applies to all employees who are covered by protection against dismissal under national law even if it be limited.

(3) The fact that the termination of the subsidy to the Redmond Foundation was a unilateral act of the local authority does not affect the determination as to whether or not there has been a transfer. *This finding is of particular relevance to transfers of parts of undertakings such as canteen and cleaning services as was highlighted in more detail in the Christel Schmidt cases dealt with at 10.9.3.*

(4) The decisive criterion for establishing whether there is a transfer of an undertaking is whether the unit in question retains its identity after the transfer. In order to ascertain whether or not there is a transfer it is necessary to determine whether the functions performed are in fact carried out or resumed by the new legal entity with the same or similar activities. *This provision has had the effect of bringing the whole area of privatisation of hitherto publicly provided services within the scope of the Directive and Regulations.*

The *Redmond* case focused attention on the fact that employees may follow the activity upon which they were working if that activity transfers from one employer to another. This could be the case even where their employer did not sell the business as a going concern and indeed may have played no active part in the transfer. The transfer of its activities was not effected by the foundation itself but by the funding authority. The activity then followed the funding and the employees followed the activity. These concepts did not fit easily into Irish law. In Irish law, prior to the Directive taking effect, ownership and the status of employer and employee only changed or varied by or as a result of the conclusion of a specific agreement between the parties or implied in a situation or transaction where the parties were active. The *Redmond* case showed how the obligations of an employer towards an employee could transfer from one employer to another as a result of actions taken, not by those parties or in circumstances in which they had an input, but by others over whom they may have had no influence, or as result of a decision into which they had no input, and possibly against their wishes. However, in order to give full effect to the purpose of the Directive, the transfer must be looked at from the level of the employee and the effect on the employee rather than at the level of the employer and what the employer might seek or wish to do. As was seen at **10.3.1** article 1 of the Directive requires that there be the transfer of an undertaking or part of an undertaking 'as a result of a legal transfer or merger'. This would seem to imply that there must be a contractual nexus between the parties to a transfer. No guidance is given in the Directive as to what is meant by 'a legal transfer or merger', nor is there any reference to the term in the explanatory memorandum. Case law has shown that a very loose definition will be applied requiring, not that there be any legal formality to the transfer, but rather that the transfer take place within the context of an arrangement which has aspects of legality and enforceability to it. Advocate-General Van Gerven in *Redmond* stated:

> 'I would like to stress that, in assessing the question whether, in a given situation, there has been a transfer resulting from a "legal transfer or merger" within the meaning of the Directive, the Court has generally taken as its starting point the principle that the question must be examined in the light of the final result of the operation in question' (at p 373, para 18).

10.6.5 TRANSFER OF ACTIVITY

Advocate-General Van Gerven has indicated in *Redmond Stichting v Bartol* the thinking that will apply, which is to ascertain what is the activity for which the employees were employed in the first place, and examine it then in light of what has occurred. If the activity is seen to be continuing, even with some differences, there is likely to be deemed to be, or have been, a transfer of an undertaking within the meaning of the Directive. Not all of the activity has to transfer. It was argued in *Redmond* that Sigma did not do everything the Redmond Foundation had done, nor did all of the Redmond employees transfer, and that there were differences in the way in which certain other services would or would not be provided. In light of this it was argued that as the activity that transferred was not identical to that carried out by Redmond the Directive then did not apply. The court rejected that argument and indicated that what did and did not transfer must be examined and weighed within the overall context of what occurred to determine on balance whether or not the business retained its identity and was transferred. The court set out a list of criteria to be examined but stressed that each criterion is merely a single factor in the overall assessment and none of them are determining factors. When the factors are weighed it is for the national court to decide in light of that exercise whether or not the business in question retained its identity. In quoting its own judgment in *Spijkers v Gebroeders Benedik Abbatoir CV* [1986] CMLR 296 the Court held in *Redmond*:

'[T]he decisive criterion for establishing whether there is a transfer within the meaning of the Directive is whether the business in question retains its identity as would be indicated, in particular, by the fact that its operation was actually continued or resumed.

'. . . in order to determine whether those conditions are fulfilled, it is necessary to consider all the factual circumstances characterising the transaction in question, including the type of undertaking or business concerned, whether the business's tangible assets such as buildings or moveable property are transferred, the value of its intangible assets at the time of the transfer, whether or not the majority of its employees are taken over by the new employer, whether or not its customers are transferred and the degree of similarity between the activities carried on before and after the transfer and the period, if any, for which those activities are suspended. It should be noted, however, that all those circumstances are merely single factors in the overall assessment which must be made and cannot therefore be considered in isolation' (at p 369, paras 23 and 24).

10.7 FRANCHISES OR DEALERSHIPS

When a franchise or dealership changes hands is this transfer of an undertaking? In *Merckx and Neuhuys v Ford Motor Co Belgium SA* [1996] IRLR 467 Mr Merckx and Mr Neuhuys were employed as salesmen with Anfo Motors which sold motor vehicles as a Ford dealer in and around Brussels. Ford was the main shareholder in Anfo Motors. On 8 October 1987 Anfo Motors informed Mr Merckx and Mr Neuhuys that it would discontinue all its activities on 31 December 1987 and that with effect from 1 November 1987 Ford would have its interests looked after by an independent dealership, Novarobel, which was then in existence and trading. Novarobel took on fourteen of the sixty-four employees of Anfo. Anfo wrote to all of its customers informing them of the discontinuance of its activities and recommending the services of Novarobel. Mr Merckx and Mr Neuhuys were proposed to move to the employment of Novarobel but for various reasons they objected and sought compensation for breach of contract, unlawful dismissal and redundancy together with outstanding bonus payments. Anfo counterclaimed. The court stated that there were two questions to be dealt with. The first question was:

Whether article 1(1) of the Directive must be interpreted as applying where an undertaking holding a motor vehicle dealership for a particular territory discontinues its business and the dealership is then transferred to another undertaking which takes on part of its staff and is recommended to customers, without any transfer of assets.

Reaching its decision the court had regard to a number of decisions including *Redmond Stichting v Bartol* [1992] IRLR 366, and *Foreningen af Arbejdsledere i Danmark v Daddy's Dance Hall A/S* [1988] IRLR 315. In answer to the first question the court stated inter alia (at p 474):

'It is clear from the case law that for the Directive to apply it is not necessary for there to be a direct contractual relationship between the transferor and the transferee. Consequently, where a motor vehicle dealership concluded with one undertaking is terminated and a new dealership is awarded to another undertaking pursuing the same activities the transfer of undertaking is the result of a legal transfer for the purposes of the Directive as interpreted by the Court.'

On the facts of this particular case it was found that Ford had concluded an agreement and guarantee with Novarobel under which Ford undertook 'to bear the expenses relating to certain payments for breach of contract, unlawful dismissal or redundancy which might be payable by Novarobel to members of the staff previously employed by Anfo Motors'. The court held that fact confirmed there was a legal transfer within the meaning of the Directive. The court answered the first question by determining that the Directive did apply. See also *Clark and Tokeley Ltd (t/a Spellbrook) v Oakes* [1997] IRLR 564.

10.8 TRANSFER OF EMPLOYEES

10.8.1 UNDERLYING PHILOSOPHY

The underlying philosophy of the Directive was well explained by the English EAT in *Birch v Nuneaton and Bedworth Borough Council* [1995] IRLR 518 when it stated:

'If similar activities are continued in different hands the identity of the undertaking is retained, a transfer occurs, the employees follow the work and protection is enjoyed by the employees.'

10.8.2 TRANSFER OF PART OF AN UNDERTAKING

Article 1(1) of the Directive provides that it shall apply not just to the transfer of an undertaking or business but to the transfer of part of an undertaking or business. It has been seen that where part of a business is an economic entity in itself that part may be easily identifiable as the subject matter of a transfer of part of a business. Difficulties may arise where the part sold off or transferred was not a readily identifiable economic entity prior to the transfer as it depended for its existence on being part of a larger economic entity. Difficulty may arise in identifying the transferor and whether particular employees are employed in the part of the business transferred. In *Michael Peters Ltd v Farnfield and Michael Peters Group plc* [1995] IRLR 190 Mr Farnfield was chief executive of the Michael Peters Group plc, a holding company for some twenty-five subsidiaries. When the parent company and its subsidiaries went into receivership and four subsidiaries were sold off, the parent company was not a party to the sale agreement. It was held, however, by an industrial tribunal that Mr Farnfield's employment transfer was on the basis that in reality the four subsidiary companies, together with that part of the parent company's assets belonging to those companies, formed part of a 'single economic unit'. Part of the parent company was transferred and Mr Farnfield was protected because he was employed by the transferor of the business. The EAT, however, overruled the industrial tribunal, holding that it was inappropriate to apply a concept of a 'single economic unit' that the transferors were not the parent company and Mr Farnfield was not therefore an employee of the transferor.

In *Sunley Turriff Holdings Ltd v Thomson* [1995] IRLR 184 there was a detailed analysis of the particular transfer concerned and it was decided that the part of the business in relation to which Thomson was employed by the transferor was actually transferred, and therefore the Directive/Regulations applied. The twist in this case was that Thomson continued to work for the transferor after the transfer. He was not designated as one of the employees transferred and continued to work for a receiver for some two months after the transfer until he was dismissed. The tribunal held that a mistaken belief of the employee cannot defeat the principle of automatic transfer under the Directive/Regulations. The contract transferred as a matter of law and there was no actual dismissal by the transferees or resignation from their employment.

In *Botzen v Rotterdamsche Droogdok Maatschappij* [1986] ECR 519 the ECJ considered a situation where Mr Botzen and his seven co-plaintiffs were assigned to parts of a business which were not the subject matter of transfer. One of the questions addressed to the court was:

'Does the scope of the Directive also extend to the rights conferred upon and the obligations imposed upon the transferor by contracts of employment which exist at the date of transfer and which are made with employees whose duties are not performed exclusively with the aid of assets which belong to the transferred part of the undertaking.'

Advocate-General Slynn dealt with the transfer of a part of an undertaking in *Botzen* at p 521 as follows:

'I do not consider that it is necessary or desirable in this case to seek to define comprehensively what is "part of" a business. That is largely a question of fact though it will usually involve the transfer of a department or factory or facet of the business. It may perhaps also involve the sale of a fraction of a single unit of business. Once it is decided as a fact that part of the business is transferred then those workers who during their working hours are wholly engaged in that part are entitled to rely on the terms of the Directive. It will of course cover the full-time and part-time workers. A basic working test, it seems to me, is to ask whether, if that part of the business had been separately owned before the transfer the worker would have been employed by the owners of that part over the owners of the remaining part. The only exception I would admit to the requirement that an employee must be "wholly" engaged in that part of the business would be where an employee was required to perform other duties to an extent which could fairly be described as *de minimis*. On the other hand if a worker in fact is engaged in the activities of the whole business or in several parts then he cannot be regarded for the purpose of the Directive as an employee "of" the part of the business transferred.'

The decision of the full court in *Botzen* is not particularly helpful in that the court held that the test to be applied was whether or not there had been a transfer of the part of the business for which the employee was 'assigned and which formed the organisational framework within which their employment relationship took effect'.

10.8.3   PART OF AN UNDERTAKING OR A MERE ACTIVITY?

The subject matter of a transfer is not always easily distinguishable as being part of the undertaking from which it is transferred. The question may arise as to whether or not it is an integral part of the economic entity constituting the undertaking or, alternatively, whether it is merely an activity of the undertaking which activity in itself is not an economic activity capable of being the subject matter of a transfer within the meaning of the Directive. In *Schmidt v Spar und Leihkasse der Fruheren Amter Bordesholm* [1994] IRLR 302, the bank which employed Ms Schmidt, which of itself was clearly an 'undertaking', decided that it no longer wished to employ Ms Schmidt as an employee to carry out the daily cleaning work of the bank and decided to contract out the work to a contract cleaning company. This case is dealt with in more detail at **10.9.3** below. The question arose, however, as to whether or not the cleaning work constituted part of the undertaking of the bank so transferred. The bank contended that the performance of the cleaning operations was neither the main function nor an ancillary function of the undertaking and therefore did not involve the transfer of an economic unit and did not come within the definition of transfer of an undertaking within the terms of the Directive. In its submissions to the court the Commission took the view that if the cleaning was carried out by staff of the undertaking it was a service which the undertaking itself performed and the fact that such work was merely an ancillary activity not necessarily connected with the main objects of the undertaking could not have the effect of excluding the transfer from the scope of the Directive. The court held in this regard:

'The cleaning operations of a branch of an undertaking can be treated as a "part of an undertaking" within the meaning of the Directive.

'The decisive criterion for establishing whether there is a transfer . . . is whether the business in question retains its identity. This is indicated inter alia by the actual continuation or resumption by the new employer of the same or similar activities.

'The fact that the activity in question was performed by a single employee prior to the transfer is not sufficient to preclude application of the Directive' (p 636).

10.8.4 STABLE ECONOMIC ENTITY

What might in day-to-day terminology be termed as an ancillary activity of an undertaking may be deemed to be part of the undertaking and therefore be classified as a transfer within the terms of the Directive. The activity must, however, be classifiable as a stable economic entity as per *Ledernes Hovedorganisation (Rygaard) v Dansk Arbejdsgiverforening (Stro Mølle Akustik) A/S* [1996] IRLR 51 ('*Rygaard*') which is dealt with in detail at **10.9.6**. See also *Wynnwith Engineering Co Ltd v Bennett* [2002] IRLR 170 and *Temco Service Industries SA v Imzilyen* [2002] IRLR 214.

10.8.5 SPIJKERS CRITERIA

In ascertaining whether or not there has been a transfer of an undertaking, and keeping in mind that it must be a stable undertaking with an ongoing life rather than a short-term contractual enterprise as per *Rygaard*, the following are the *Spijkers* criteria to be judged in an overall context in ascertaining has there been a transfer:

–   Has the entity retained its identity?

–   Have assets transferred? (not essential that they do so)

–   What has happened to the intangible assets, such as goodwill, and have they transferred?

–   Have some or all of the staff been taken over by the new employer?

–   Has the customer base transferred?

–   Are the activities carried on post-transfer similar to those carried on pre-transfer?

–   An interruption in the operation of the undertaking or economic entity is not fatal to the fact of transfer, but a consideration, and dependent on the duration and effect of such interruption.

–   If there is no transfer of assets and the transferee does not take over a major part of the workforce and the combined entity of the group of employees and assets they used to carry on the economic activity is not transferred, in circumstances where the economic entity needs assets to continue in existence there may not be a transfer as per the qualifications laid down by the ECJ in *Suzen v Zehnacker Gebaudereinigung GmbH Krankenhausservice* [1997] IRLR 255.

10.9 SERVICE PROVIDERS

10.9.1 GENERALLY

Many businesses have services provided for them by outside agencies, companies or individuals none of whom are, or can be, classified as employees but which themselves have employees who may be committed wholly or in substantial part to the provision of the services. These services also can be in respect of core activities or ancillary activities. They could be core activities in the sense of having sub-contract manufacturing done, or ancillary activities, such as the provision of canteen services to employees of the business, the cleaning of the premises or the provision of security services.

Whether subsidiary or ancillary activities which are transferred are covered by the Directive/Regulations will depend on whether or not they are classified as an economic entity or a mere activity. What constitutes an economic entity has proven to be particularly difficult to distinguish from a mere activity in the area of service providers and subsidiary or ancillary services. The starting point in determining the tests to be applied has to be *JMA Spijkers v Gebroeders Benedik Abbatoir CV* [1986] 2 CMLR 296. The *Spijkers* criteria are merely indiciae of what might be an economic entity or an economic unit within or attached to an undertaking. While *Spijkers* is the starting point subsequent case law has both fine-tuned the definition of the economic entity or activity that may be the subject of a transfer of an undertaking or part of an undertaking and has added new tests, most notably in *Ledernes Hovedorganisation (Rygaard) v Dansk Arbejdsgiverfovenig Stro Mølle Akinskik A/S* [1996] IRLR 51.

The position of service providers and the transfer or movement of services and service contracts and whether they are covered by the Directive and Regulations will depend on the facts of the situation and how employees are affected.

The position of employees affected by the contracting out of services is governed in the main by two fact situations that may arise:

(a) where the principal is providing the service itself and determines to transfer the service to an outside agency, which henceforward will provide the service, as an independent contractor, usually a company that is in the particular line of business providing a service to a number of principals; or

(b) where a company is already contracting out services, which it may or may not have itself provided in the past, to an independent contractor and changes independent contractors. The question arises as to what happens to staff providing the service where their employer loses the contract to provide the service and the contract is awarded to another independent contractor employer, who is not the principal.

10.9.2 RASK AND CHRISTENSEN v ISS KANTINESERVICE A/S

The first situation arose and was considered by the ECJ in *Rask and Christensen v ISS Kantineservice A/S* [1993] IRLR 133.

The principal, Philips A/S, a Danish company which had provided a canteen service for its staff and employed a number of people to provide that canteen service, decided to contract out the running of its staff canteen to ISS, which was an independent catering company providing canteen services to various companies. Philips agreed to pay ISS a fixed monthly fee to cover costs relating to management, wages, insurance and the provision of work clothing. Philips also agreed to provide, free of charge, premises, equipment, electricity and certain other services. Some basic assets such as tableware were sold at cost price to ISS. ISS undertook to offer employment on the same rates of pay to the Philips' staff who were engaged in the provision of the service and would transfer into the employment of ISS consequent on the awarding of the contract. Rask and Christensen transferred to ISS but complained about certain changes in their working conditions made by ISS. Following on from that dispute Rask refused to work under the new conditions and as a consequence was dismissed. Rask and Christensen claimed compensation for the changes in their terms and conditions and Rask also claimed compensation in respect of her dismissal. They claimed against ISS and the question as to whether or not the transfer between Philips and ISS came within the meaning of Directive 77/187 (and the domestic Danish law implementing that Directive) was referred to the ECJ for consideration. ISS put forward two main arguments to the court.

(a) An agreement of the type concluded with Philips A/S does not effect any transfer within the meaning intended by the Directive since it does not confer either full and entire responsibility for the provision of the services, particularly in so far as the customers and the fixing of prices is concerned, nor does it confer legal ownership of assets necessary for the provision of the services.

(b) An agreement such as concluded between ISS and Philips A/S relates to services which themselves could not be described as an 'undertaking' within the meaning of the Directive by reason of the fact that they are ancillary activities and not part of the main core activity of the transferor.

In addressing the two points the ECJ referred to its decision in *Berg and Busschers v Besselsen* [1989] IRLR 447 where it held that the Directive was applicable in any case where, following a legal transfer or merger, there is a change in the legal or natural person responsible for carrying on the business and who, by virtue of that fact, incurs the obligation of an employer vis-à-vis the employees of the undertaking, regardless of whether or not ownership of the undertaking is transferred. The ECJ also referred to *Botzen v Rotterdamsche Droogdok Maatschappij* [1986] ECR 519 and its finding that the employment relationship 'is essentially characterised by the link existing between the employee and the part of the undertaking to which he is assigned to carry out his duties'. The ECJ went on to state that the fact that the activity transferred 'is only an ancillary activity of the transferor undertaking not necessarily related to its objects cannot have the effect of excluding that transaction from the scope of the Directive'. The court also held that the restricted form of agreement between the transferor and the transferee was not such as could operate to exclude the provisions of the Directive either.

On the principal question referred to it the ECJ held inter alia:

Where the responsibility for providing a service is, by agreement, entrusted by the owner of an undertaking to the owner of another undertaking who assumes the obligations of an employer in respect of the employees who are engaged in the provision of that service, that transaction is capable of falling within the scope of article 1(1). Neither the fact that the activity transferred is only an ancillary activity of the transferor nor the fact that the agreement relates to the provision of services provided exclusively for the benefit of the transferor in return for a fee the form of which is fixed by the agreement, prevents the Directive from applying.

10.9.3   SCHMIDT v SPAR

The issue of the contracting-out of services came into sharper focus in another decision of the ECJ some two years later in *Schmidt v Spar und Leihkasse der Fruheren Amter Bordesholm,* [1994] IRLR 302. In this case a branch of a bank employed Schmidt to do the cleaning work required by that branch. Following refurbishment and extension the bank decided to terminate the employment of Schmidt and contract out the cleaning work to a contract cleaning company which was already responsible for cleaning most of the other branches of the bank. Schmidt was offered employment by the contract cleaning company at a higher monthly wage but she turned down the offer on the grounds that she would be receiving in essence a lower hourly wage, since there was a larger area to clean as a result of the extension of the premises.

Schmidt claimed under the terms of the Directive. It was argued by the German government and the bank that cleaning was not a business carried on by the bank and that there was not therefore a transfer of an undertaking or part of an undertaking. The bank contended that the cleaning operations were neither the main function nor an ancillary function of the undertaking. What occurred in *Schmidt* was similar in principle to what happened in *Rask and Christensen v ISS Kantineservice A/S* [1993] IRLR 133 and, not surprisingly therefore, the court held that there had been a transfer. What caused the surprise expressed at the time the *Schmidt* decision issued was the fact that the actual work done by Schmidt was not as substantial as that done by the employees in *Rask and Christensen* and there was no transfer of assets or infrastructure surrounding *Schmidt*, but rather a transfer of the actual service itself which was provided by one individual employee. Many commentators construed the work done by Schmidt as merely an activity carried on in or by the bank. Many could not understand how such an activity could be in itself deemed an economic entity or part of a larger economic entity being the bank itself. The ECJ held in *Schmidt*:

(a) the cleaning operations of a branch of an undertaking may be treated as part of the business of that undertaking within the meaning of the Directive;

(b) where a transfer relates only to part of a business, the protection provided by the Directive applies to employees assigned to that part of the undertaking;

(c) when an undertaking contracts out the responsibility for operating one of its services, such as cleaning, to another undertaking which thereby assumes the obligations of an employer towards employees assigned to those duties, that operation may come within the scope of the Directive;

(d) the decisive criterion for establishing whether there is a transfer for the purposes of the Directive is whether the business in question retains its identity. This is indicated, inter alia, by the actual continuation or resumption by the new employer of the same or similar activities, as the ECJ had held in both *Spijkers v Gebroeders Benedik Abbatoir CV* [1986] 2 CMLR 296 and *Redmond Stichting v Bartol* [1992] IRLR 366; and

(e) the fact that only one employee was assigned to the part of the undertaking transferred does not preclude the application of the Directive, nor does the absence of any transfer of tangible assets even though this is normally a factor taken into account by national courts in assessing when there has in fact been a transfer of an undertaking.

In its decision the ECJ refers to the cleaning work of the bank being part of the undertaking of the bank. It based its decision on the applicability of the Directive to the transfer of part of an undertaking. Previous case law, however, had distinguished parts of an undertaking so covered by the Directive by reference to there being an economic entity in itself capable of being transferred. In *Schmidt* the ECJ made reference to its decision in *Botzen*. Most of the confusion in the minds of commentators on *Schmidt*, and the difficulties caused by the subsequent application of the *Schmidt* criteria, have been caused by the failure to accept or understand that the cleaning work carried out in *Schmidt* was in itself an economic entity which became the subject of a transfer.

10.9.4 ECONOMIC UNIT

Using a term such as 'economic entity' to describe the cleaning services provided by *Schmidt* has caused confusion. It is difficult for many people to understand how the activity of cleaning one branch of a bank by one person could constitute an economic entity within the scope of the Directive. A somewhat more understandable and acceptable term 'economic unit' was adverted to by Advocate-General Van Gerven in his opinion in *Schmidt* when he stated:

'the Court recognises a common denominator underlying three concepts of "undertaking", "business" and "part of a business", namely that of an "economic unit" or a "business", terms which, in my opinion, refer to a unit with a minimum level of organisational independence which can exist by itself or constitute part of a larger undertaking.'

He also stated:

'From all this I infer that the phrase "undertaking, business or part of a business" within the meaning of the Directive is underpinned by the concept of an economic unit which refers to an organised whole consisting of persons and (tangible and/or intangible) assets by means of which an economic activity is carried on having an objective of its own, albeit one that is ancillary to the objects of the undertaking; a whole which, more over, can be part of an even larger corporate whole.'

Advocate-General Van Gerven was of the view that cleaning operations constituted an economic activity within the meaning of the Directive. He also emphasised in reaching his decision that the fact situation in *Schmidt* involved an undertaking ceasing cleaning operations previously performed by its staff in order to contract them out to a separate undertaking. It must be kept in mind in any analysis of the *Schmidt* decision that that is the particular fact situation giving rise to the decision. In *Schmidt* it was also argued to the ECJ that entrusting cleaning operations to an outside firm did not involve the transfer of an economic unit. In arriving at its decision the ECJ quoted with favour the argument put forward on behalf of the Commission which was:

'[I]f the cleaning is carried out by the staff of the undertaking, it is a service which the [undertaking] performs itself and the fact that such work is merely an ancillary activity not necessarily connected with the objects of the undertaking cannot have the effect of excluding the transfer from the scope of the Directive.

'According to the case law of the Court . . . the Directive is applicable where, following a legal transfer or merger, there is a change in the legal or natural person who is responsible for carrying on the business and who by virtue of that fact incurs the obligations of an employer vis-à-vis the employees of the undertaking, regardless of whether or not ownership of the undertaking is transferred.'

The protection provided by the Directive applies in particular by virtue of article 1(1) where the transfer relates only to a business or part of a business; that is to say, a part of an undertaking. In those circumstances the transfer relates to employees assigned to that part of the undertaking since, as the ECJ held in its judgment in *Botzen v Rotterdamsche Droogdok Maatschappij* [1986] 2 CMLR 50, an employment relationship is essentially characterised by the link between the employee and the part of the undertaking or business to which he is assigned to carry out his duties.

Thus, when an undertaking entrusts by contract the responsibility for operating one of its services, such as cleaning, to another undertaking which thereby assumes the obligations of an employer towards employees assigned to those employees, that operation may come within the scope of the Directive. As the ECJ held at paragraph 17 of its judgment in *Rask and Christensen v ISS Kantineservice* [1993] IRLR 133 the fact that in such a case the activity transferred is for the transferor merely an ancillary activity not necessarily connected with its objects cannot have the effect of excluding that operation from the scope of the Directive.

In retrospect, and in particular in light of its subsequent decision in *Suzen v Zehnacker Gebaudereinigung GmbH Krankenhausservice* [1997] IRLR 255, it would have been more helpful had the ECJ specifically referred to the cleaning activity as being an economic entity in itself and how it was held to be so.

10.9.5 RESTRICTING TRANSFERS

In view of the wide and purposive approach taken by the courts to the application of the Directive employers and their advisers were finding that it was becoming increasingly difficult to ascertain exactly where the Directive did or did not apply. Apart from the very many obvious cases when it would apply it was being found that its provisions were arising in situations that no-one had anticipated as being relevant to them. The application to service contracts and service providers caused enormous practical difficulties and business people were becoming more and more vocal in their criticism of the Directive and the domestic regulations in the Member States. It appears that the members of the ECJ became aware of the practical difficulties their decisions were causing. Their response was to issue two judgments which introduced fine, and indeed not so fine, points of distinction as to what would or would not constitute a transfer of an undertaking, thereby restricting the application of the Directive and domestic regulations and leading in *Betts v Brintel Helicopters Ltd* [1997] IRLR 361 to a reversal of the High Court decision.

10.9.6 STABLE ECONOMIC ENTITY—RYGAARD

In *Ledernes Hovedorganisation (Rygaard) v Dansk Arbejdsgiverforening (Stro Mølle Akustik) A/S* [1996] IRLR 51 Rygaard was employed by Svend Pedersen A/S, a firm of carpenters. Pedersen had a contract with SAS Service Partner to build a canteen. Pedersen informed SAS that it wanted part of the work it was contracted to do to be completed by Stro Mølle Akustik. Stro Mølle submitted a tender to SAS and it was accepted. Pedersen and Stro Mølle then entered into an agreement to effect a takeover of the works transferred. The agreement provided that Stro Mølle was liable to reimburse Pedersen the expenditure, including wages, which Pedersen had already incurred with regard to the works trans-ferred. It also provided that two of Pedersen's apprentices would be transferred to Stro Mølle. On the day after the agreement Pedersen terminated Rygaard's contract of employ-ment. Rygaard continued to work for Stro Mølle until he was given notice of dismissal by them. Meanwhile Pedersen was declared bankrupt. Rygaard brought wrongful dismissal proceedings against Stro Mølle and the question arose as to whether or not the Directive applied to the transfer of Rygaard's employment from Pedersen to Stro Mølle. The ECJ held that:

(a) The taking over with the view to completing, with the consent of the awarder of the main building contract, works started by another undertaking, consisting of two apprentices and an employee together with the materials assigned to those works, does not constitute a transfer of an undertaking within the meaning of the Directive;

(b) In order to be a transfer of an undertaking the transfer must relate to a stable economic entity whose activity is not limited to performing one specific works contract. That is not the case where there is a transfer from one undertaking to another of building works with a view to their completion and the transferor undertaking merely makes available to the new contractor certain workers and material for carrying out the works in question. Such a transfer could come within the terms of the Directive only if it included the transfer of a body of assets enabling activities of the transferor undertaking to be carried on in a stable way.

10.9.7 ASSET TRANSFER

In *Spijkers v Gebroeders Benedik Abattoir CV* [1986] 2 CMLR 296 the ECJ had held that the fact that physical assets were sold was a strong indication that a transfer within the meaning of the Directive had taken place. In *Rask and Christensen v ISS Kantineservice* [1993] IRLR 133 the ECJ held that consideration of whether a business's tangible assets were transferred is one of the circumstances to be considered in determining whether or not there was a transfer of undertaking but was merely a single factor in the overall assessment which must be made and could not be considered in isolation. In *Schmidt v Spar und Leihkasse der Fruheren Amter Bordesholm* [1994] IRLR 302 the ECJ also confirmed that the transfer of assets was one of the factors to be considered in the overall judgment as to whether or not an undertaking has in fact been transferred but stated that the absence of a transfer of assets does not preclude the existence of part of the undertaking. In *Ledernes Hovedorganisation (Rygaard) v Dansk Arbejdsgiverforening (Stro Mølle Akustik) A/S* [1996] IRLR 51 ('*Rygaard*') the ECJ, reaffirming its view on the transfer of assets as being one of the factors to be considered, then gave the 'asset test' a particular importance in the circumstances of this by holding that the cases of *Spijkers* and *Schmidt* presupposed that the transfer related to a stable economic entity whose activity was not limited to performing one specific works contract. In *Schmidt* the cleaning work needed to be done for as long as the bank was in use. In *Rygaard*, however, once the carpentry sub-contract had come to an end the economic entity effectively ceased to be. In determining whether or not an economic entity was stable and long term the ECJ held that the transfer of a specific works contract 'would only come within the terms of the Directive if there was a transfer of a body of assets' but further qualified that requirement by stating 'the assets must enable the activities of the transferor undertaking, or the part transferred, to be carried on in a stable way'. It must be taken that what is meant by 'stable' in this context is the same as 'long term' or 'ongoing'.

10.9.8 LEGAL TRANSFER OR MERGER AND SERVICE PROVIDER

10.9.8.1 What is legal transfer?

Article 1(1) of the Directive states that it shall apply to the transfer of an undertaking 'as a result of a legal transfer or merger'.

In *Rygaard* Advocate-General Cosmas examined the facts in the case in detail in light of the case law and his views may be summarised as follows.

(a) The case law of the ECJ has established that there must be a change in the person responsible for the operation of the undertaking in order for there to be a transfer.

(b) The economic entity transferred must continue to exist and retain its identity. The ECJ has accepted that an undertaking retains its identity where its operation is in fact continued or taken over by the new employer with the same economic activities or analogous activities.

(c) The Directive is applicable only when the change in the person responsible for the operation of the undertaking is based on a contract, that is to say, stems from a contractual transfer or from a merger and transfers by operation of the law or resulting from a unilateral act of dispositions are thus excluded. This is a questionable finding given the approach taken by the ECJ in *Redmond Stichting v Bartol* [1992] IRLR 366 where it could be said that the Redmond Stichting played no part in the transfer and from where they stood the transfer was a unilateral act. In *Redmond* the ECJ held that the term 'legal transfer' covers the situation in which a public body decides to terminate a subsidy paid to one legal person as a result of which the activities of that legal person are fully and definitively terminated and to transfer to another legal person with similar aims.

10.9.8.2 The Suzen case

On 11 March 1997 the ECJ issued a decision directly relating to change of service providers which greatly qualified the general understanding of previous decisions of the court. The case was *Suzen v Zehnacker Gebaudereinigung GmbH Krankenhausservice* [1997] IRLR 255. Two questions were referred to the court and were considered together. They asked whether the Directive applies to a situation in which a person, who had entrusted the cleaning of his premises to a first undertaking, terminates that contract and for the performance of similar work enters into a new contract with a second undertaking without any concomitant transfer of tangible or intangible business assets from one undertaking to the other. The following points were made by the court.

(a)   The aim of the Directive is to ensure continuity of employment relationships within an economic entity irrespective of any change of ownership.

(b)   For the Directive to be applicable the transfer must relate to a stable economic entity whose activity is not limited to performing one specific works contract (see *Rygaard*).

(c)   The mere fact that the service provided by the old and the new awardees of a contract is similar does not support the conclusion that an economic entity has been transferred. An entity cannot be reduced to the activity entrusted to it. Its identity also emerges from other factors, such as its workforce, its management staff, the way in which its work is organised, its operating methods or, indeed, where appropriate, the operational resources available to it.

(d)   The mere loss of a service contract to a competitor cannot therefore by itself indicate the existence of a transfer within the meaning of the Directive. In those circumstances the service undertaking previously entrusted does not, on losing a customer, cease fully to exist, and a business or part of a business belonging to it cannot be considered to have been transferred to the new awardee of the contract.

(e)   Since, in certain labour-intensive sectors, a group of workers engaged in a joint activity on a permanent basis may constitute an economic entity it must be recognised that such an entity is capable of maintaining its identity after it has been transferred where the new employer does not merely pursue the activity in question but also takes over a major part in terms of the numbers and skills of the employees specially assigned by his predecessor to that task. In those circumstances the new employer takes over a body of assets enabling him to carry on the activities or certain activities of the transferor undertaking on a regular basis.

The ECJ held:

'The Directive . . . is to be interpreted as meaning that the Directive does not apply to a situation in which a person who had entrusted the cleaning of his premises to a first undertaking terminates his contract with the latter and for the performance of similar work enters into a new contract with a second undertaking, if there is no concomitant transfer from one undertaking to the other of significant tangible or intangible assets or taking over by the new employer of a major part of the workforce in terms of their numbers and skills assigned by his predecessor to the performance of the contract.'

The application of the principles and the finding in *Schmidt v Spar und Leihkasse der Fruheren Amter Bordesholm* [1994] IRLR 302, together with the guidance given in other cases, had led to the conclusion that, in both example situations as set out above where service providers were retained or changed, the Directive would apply. That was greatly qualified by the decision in *Suzen*. The *Schmidt* case had set out general principles of interpretation but its finding was based on the particular facts.

The *Suzen* decision caused considerable confusion when it first issued. Many commentators thought that the ECJ had overruled itself. Advocate-General La Pergola in *Suzen* certainly invited the court to contradict previous findings, but the court took a more subtle approach and found on the particular facts of the case leaving *Schmidt* intact.

In *Schmidt* the bank was clearly an economic entity. The cleaning of the bank was held to be part of that economic entity. That part of the undertaking transferred to the outside cleaning company retained to do the cleaning work. That outside cleaning company took over part of the economic entity and it did not take a great jump of logic to conclude that the employee assigned to the part transferred came within the Directive and was herself transferred.

In *Suzen* the cleaning work did not form part of the economic entity that was the school. The school had separated it and given it to an outside company. When the contract between them came to an end, a new contract was granted to a new service provider. The new service provider was in the cleaning business and simply got the commercial benefit of being able to use its existing assets and workforce to do the cleaning. The first cleaning company who had lost the contract remained in existence and continued working. Its contract with the school could not be deemed to be part of its undertaking, merely one of its assets. When the contract transferred it was therefore not a transfer of part of the undertaking of that first contract cleaning company but a transfer of one of its assets and, as Advocate-General Cosmas stated in *Rygaard*, 'the mere disposal of assets of an undertaking does not constitute a transfer of that undertaking within the meaning of the Directive'.

10.9.8.3   Cannon v Noonan Cleaning Ltd

The EAT considered the scope of the *Suzen* decision in *Cannon v Noonan Cleaning Ltd and CPS Cleaning Services Ltd* [1998] ELR 153. Noonan Cleaning Ltd had a contract with the Department of Justice for the cleaning of Balbriggan Garda Station. The cleaning contract was put out to tender and CPS Cleaning Services Ltd succeeded in obtaining the contract. When Noonan Cleaning were advised that they were losing the contract they wrote to CPS giving details of all persons employed by them in the cleaning of Balbriggan Garda Station and stating that under the terms of the Directive the staff would become the responsibility of CPS. Noonan also advised the claimant and her fellow employees that under the terms of the Directive, CPS would be responsible for the continuation of their employment on the same terms and conditions as they had enjoyed with them. When the claimant presented for work with CPS she was refused employment and advised that the Directive did not apply as a consequence of which she brought claims against both Noonan and CPS under the Redundancy Payments Acts, Minimum Notice and Terms of Employment Acts and Unfair Dismissals Acts.

In the course of its determination the EAT cited all of the relevant authorities and, in particular, *Foreningen af Arbejdsledere i Danmark v Daddy's Dance Hall A/S* [1988] IRLR 315 and *Suzen*. In relation to *Suzen* the EAT stated:

'It was agreed that the legal situation prior to the case cited above was that the circumstances obtaining in the case before the Tribunal were that the Directive would probably have applied. Counsel for the second-named respondent argued that this case now changed the position claiming that in a situation where a contract is withdrawn from one contractor at the end of the contract period tenders having been invited and the contract then awarded to another contractor and where the assets of the undertaking do not pass or where the workforce or part thereof are not taken on by the new contractor then there is no transfer of undertaking.'

In examining what transferred in this case the EAT made the following observations:

'The nature of this undertaking is that of cleaning. The equipment used by Noonan was not transferred to the new contractor. The same premises had to be cleaned by both contractors and each was under the control of the Department of Justice. The staff did not transfer when the contract was withdrawn and given to the new contractor. There was no goodwill as such to be transferred. The undertaking could be said to have retained its identity. While there was no apparent transfer of tangible assets, however, it could be said that there was a transfer of an intangible asset, ie the likely profit to be made from the contract. This must have existed; otherwise why was there competition for the contract?'

The EAT referred to the fact that the Department of Justice had withdrawn the contract from one contractor and given it to another and equated that transaction with the situation that pertained in *Daddy's Dance Hall*. The EAT also noted that there is no need for a direct contractual relationship to exist between the old and the new contractor for the Directive to apply. In referring to *Suzen* the EAT noted that the ECJ had drawn a distinction between a first generation transfer and a second and subsequent generation transfer. The EAT, however, had a difficulty in distinguishing between a first generation transfer, as per *Schmidt*, which is covered by the Directive and the second or subsequent generation transfer, as in *Suzen*, which is not covered by the Directive on the basis that the same 'undertaking' would be involved in each transfer. The EAT observed:

'It appears that where the new contractor refuses to take on a major part of the workforce in circumstances of a second generation transfer where a third party is responsible for the transfer, the Directive does not apply, ie there is no transfer of undertaking.

'There is no doubt that in a service undertaking, the workforce and its expertise constitute a major aspect of the undertaking but it is difficult to understand how, where an employer refuses to take on the workers of the previous contractor, he can escape the rigours of the Directive while a contractor who takes on a major part of the workforce, perhaps out of magnanimity, will be caught by it. It would seem that the Directive in the former instance has not addressed the mischief in the law that it was intended to do. The sensible course for a transferee to take then is to refuse to employ any of the workforce of the transferor in such a situation.'

The EAT went on to hold that the possible transfer of the intangible profit margin in the contract was not of sufficient significance of itself to be a major factor in the transfer and as a consequence, and in light of the ruling of the ECJ in *Suzen*, held that this transfer was not 'caught by the Directive as it does not constitute a transfer of undertaking'.

10.9.8.4 Schmidt and Suzen distinguished

Subsequent decisions in Ireland and the UK have helped to clarify the distinction between *Schmidt* and *Suzen*, most notably by the Irish EAT in *Power v St Paul's Nursing Home and T & M Cleaning Ltd* [1998] ELR 212 and the UK EAT in *ECM (Vehicle Delivery Service Ltd) v Cox* [1998] IRLR 416.

In *Power* the claimants were employed as cleaners at St Paul's Nursing Home. The nursing home decided to contract out the cleaning duties in respect of which the claimants were employed. The claimants were made redundant. St Paul's then entered into a contract with T & M Cleaning Ltd to carry out the cleaning duties. Cleaning equipment and other ancillary minor assets which St Paul's utilised in the cleaning operations were transferred to T & M Cleaning Ltd. The respondents submitted the basis of case law, including the *Suzen* decision, that they had no liability for the claimants whom, they maintained, had no rights under the Directive and Regulations as a result of the transfer of the cleaning activities. In referring to the *Suzen* decision the EAT held:

'For the Directive to be applicable the Court held that the transfer must relate to a stable economic entity whose activity is not limited to performing one specific works contract and the term entity referring to an organised grouping of persons and assets . . . there were tangible assets such as any could be identified in cleaning services. Employees would have been taken over by the new employer, the activities were exactly the same before and after the transfer. . . . It is the opinion of this Tribunal that the Directive applies to these particular sets of circumstances and in fact it would be most artificial if it was held that the case was otherwise.'

The most succinct explanation of the distinction between the ECJ decisions in *Schmidt* and *Suzen* was given by the UK EAT in *ECM (Vehicle Delivery Service Ltd) v Cox*. Axial Ltd employed the applicants as drivers and yardmen. Axial had a contract with VAG Ltd to deliver cars imported into the UK. VAG changed service provider and Axial lost the contract which was given by VAG to ECM. ECM carried out the contract from a different site and used a different delivery system with different administrative arrangements. ECM did not employ any of the applicants who had worked on the contract prior to the change of the contractor. The applicants claimed that the transfer was covered by the Directive and Regulations and that they had been unfairly dismissed as a consequence. The industrial tribunal held in their favour. The tribunal found that there was a relevant transfer within the meaning of the appropriate UK Regulations and stated that the 'undertaking which was transferred amounted to the VAG contract itself and the activities that surrounded that contract'. Subsequent to the industrial tribunal decision the ECJ issued its decision in *Suzen*. On appeal to the EAT it was argued, on behalf of the employers, that in light of the *Suzen* decision the industrial tribunal had erred in equating the transfer of a service contract with the transfer of an undertaking and that all that had been transferred in this particular case was a particular activity. The EAT under the chairmanship of Morison J dismissed the appeal and held inter alia:

The industrial tribunal did not err in finding that there was a transfer of an undertaking when the applicants' employers lost a car delivery contract on which they were employed to ECM and the applicants were not employed by ECM.

10.9.8.5 Factors to be considered

The following factors should be considered in measuring a given fact situation as being a transfer or not as the case may be.

Assets or resources

It is relevant to consider whether or not assets or resources are taken over (see the judgment of the Court of Appeal in *Betts v Brintel Helicopters* [1997] IRLR 361). The ECJ, however, in *Merckx and Neuhuys v Ford Motor Co* [1996] IRLR 467 held that there could still be a transfer even though the premises at which the motor dealership was carried on did not change hands, and stated that it was 'irrelevant that the principal place of business is situated in a different area of the same conurbation provided that the contract territory remains the same'. It should also be noted that there were no assets involved in *Schmidt*.

Transfer of goodwill

Goodwill is such an intangible thing, and so limited in many modern situations where the goodwill may be invested in customers who could disappear on a transfer of a business, that while consideration must be given to the transfer of goodwill and/or customers not a lot of weight will be given to this particular test. The Court of Appeal did, however, suggest, in *Betts* that the right to provide a service which is an intangible asset comparable to goodwill, is a 'significant asset', and is probably at the very least a 'reserve'.

Employees

Following *Suzen* consideration will now have to be given to whether or not a major part of the workforce has been taken over by the new employer. The ECJ, in referring to what is or is not a major part of the workforce, stated in its judgment:

'In labour-intensive sectors a group of workers engaged in the joint activity on a permanent basis may constitute an economic entity and such an entity is capable of maintaining its identity after it has been transferred where the new employer does not merely pursue the activity in question but also takes over a major part in terms of the numbers and skills of the employees specially assigned by his predecessor to that task. In those circumstances the new employer takes over a body of assets enabling him to carry on activities of the transferor undertaking on a regular basis.'

It would appear, therefore, that a major part of the workforce may be defined as being a numerical minority of the workforce where the skills of that minority are the determining factor in their retention. Failure or refusal to take on part of the workforce in an attempt to circumvent the Directive and Regulations will not avail a transferee as held in *Power v St Paul's Nursing Home and T & M Cleaning Ltd* [1988] ELR 212 and *ECM (Vehicle Delivery Service Ltd) v Cox* [1998] IRLR 416.

Existence of organisational structure or organised grouping of resources

The assets, goodwill, resources and employees must be underpinned or marked out by an organisational structure giving them a unity or making them capable of being construed as an economic entity or unit in themselves. The infrastructure of management operating methods and operational resources will act as the glue to bind assets, goodwill and employees together as an identifiable entity capable of being the subject matter of a transfer, as highlighted in the *Suzen* decision. The infrastructure and method of operation may change, provided there remains an organisational structure marking out the business or part of the business transferred as an economic entity in itself.

The interesting concept of a 'grouping of resources' was introduced, for the first time, in article 1(1)(b) of the amending Directive.

10.9.8.6 Further case law

The ECJ recently issued decisions in five service provider cases consolidated into two separate decisions.

The first case was *Hernandez v Gomez Perez* [1999] IRLR 132. This case involved bringing back in-house cleaning work which had previously been contracted out. The question arose as to whether the employees of the service provider were entitled to transfer into the employment of the principal when the principal terminated the service contract and took upon itself the carrying out of the work previously contracted out. The ECJ held:

> 'Directive 77/187 applies to a situation in which an undertaking which contracted out the cleaning of its premises to another undertaking decides to terminate the contract which it had with that other undertaking and to carry out that cleaning work itself provided that the operation is accompanied by the transfer of an economic entity between the two undertakings.

> 'The aim of Directive 77/187 is to ensure continuity of employment relationships within an economic entity irrespective of any change of ownership. The term "economic entity" refers to an organised grouping of persons and assets enabling an economic activity which pursues a specific objective to be exercised. While such an entity must be sufficiently structured and autonomous it will not necessarily have significant tangible or intangible assets. In certain sectors such as cleaning the activity is essentially based on manpower. Thus an organised grouping of wage earners who are specifically and permanently assigned to a common task may, in the absence of other factors of production, amount to an economic entity.

> 'It is for the national court to determine whether the maintenance of the premises of the undertaking which awarded the contract was organised in the form of an economic entity within the outside cleaning firm before the firm awarding the contract decided to carry out the work itself.'

The second decision was in the cases of *Sanchez Hidalgo v Associacion de Servicios Aser* and *Ziemann v Ziemann Sicherheit GmbH* [1999] IRLR 136, the first of which involved two cases on the change of one service provider for another on the ending of a contract. Mrs Sanchez Hidalgo was one of five employees employed by a contracting firm which provided home-help services to persons in need on foot of a contract it held with the municipality of Guadalajara. When the contract expired the municipality awarded a new contract to Aser. The ECJ was posed the question as to whether there was a transfer of undertaking as between the first company, Minerva, and the second company, Aser. The second case involved the transfer of security or surveillance services between service providers. The ECJ held:

> 'Directive 77/187 applies to a situation in which a public body which contracted out its home-help service for people in need or awarded a contract for the surveillance of some

of its premises, decides on expiry of the contract or its termination to contract out the service to a different undertaking provided that the operation is accompanied by the transfer of an economic entity between the two undertakings.

'The aim of Directive 77/187 is to ensure continuity of employment relationships within an economic entity irrespective of any change of ownership. The term "economic entity" refers to an organised grouping of persons and assets enabling an economic activity which pursues a specific objective to be exercised. Whilst such an entity must be sufficiently structured and autonomous it will not necessarily have significant tangible or intangible assets. In certain sectors such as cleaning and surveillance the activity is essentially based on manpower. Thus an organised grouping of wage earners who are specifically and permanently assigned to a common task may, in the absence of other factors of production, amount to an economic entity.

'It is for the National Court to determine whether the home-help service and the surveillance of the medical supplies depot were organised in the form of an economic entity within the first undertaking, to which provision of the service in question was contracted out.'

10.9.8.7   Keenan v Professional Contract Services Ltd

The EAT appears to have changed the position it took in *Cannon v Noonan Cleaning Ltd* in the recent decision of *Keenan v Professional Contract Services Ltd* UD 454/455/456/98. The facts of the case were that Professional Contract Services Ltd took over a cleaning contract from Grosvener Cleaning at Dublin City University. Meetings were held prior to the takeover which the claimants attended. The facts are not set out in any particular detail in the EAT determination but it appears that the employees of Grosvenor were asked to fill out forms to confirm their interest in transferring but it is not stated in the determination why it was that the three claimants did not transfer. The respondents submitted to the EAT that they required forms to be filled out because of certain restrictions being placed on them by the university and the need to change the work rota from a two-shift to a one-shift operation. It appears that the claimants' failure to submit the forms referred to 'left the respondents with the impression that for some reason . . . the claimants no longer wished to work for them'. Following the late submission of the forms the respondents offered alternative employment to the claimants but this was rejected. The EAT held:

'The Tribunal determines that there was a transfer of undertaking in this case which was accepted by the respondents. The recommendation of the Rights Commissioner is therefore overturned. The Tribunal is not satisfied that the claimants were made sufficiently aware of their entitlements under the transfer of undertaking to the extent that the respondents did not fulfil their obligation to their employees. Consequently the Tribunal finds that the claimants were unfairly dismissed. The Tribunal is however unanimous in finding that the claimants contributed substantially by not making their position sufficiently clear to the employer.'

The employees' contribution was taken into account in calculating the modest amounts of compensation awarded by the EAT.

10.9.8.8   What is transferred?

Regulation 3 of SI 306/1980 provides

'The rights and obligations of the transferor arising from a contract of employment or from an employment relationship existing on the date of a transfer shall, by reason of such transfer, be transferred to the transferee.'

These provisions give rise to the question as to what precisely is transferred when the transfer of an undertaking occurs. Contracts of employment and the terms and conditions that apply between an employer and an employee or worker are not easily ascertainable. The nature of employment relationships is such that the terms, conditions, rights and obligations of the parties are rarely clearly laid out and arise from a number of sources, some giving rise to legal rights and obligations which may only be altered at the instance of, and with the consent of, both parties, and others which are merely prescriptive or arise for administrative convenience which may be altered, varied or removed at the instance of one of the parties, often the employer.

In order to appreciate the full scope of the Directive and Regulations regard must be had to existing Irish law and practice on terms and conditions of employment and how they can be changed or varied.

In *Rask and Christensen v ISS Kantineservice A/S* [1993] IRLR 133 ISS had made some relatively minor changes to the terms and conditions of employment of the plaintiffs when they transferred. Instead of paying salaries on the last Thursday of the month they paid them on the last working day of a month and employees no longer received allowances for laundry or for shoes, which they claimed were part of their pay prior to the transfer. In *Rask* the ECJ held (at p 134):

'Article 3 of the Directive must be interpreted as meaning that on the transfer the terms of the contract of employment or of the employment relationship relating to salary, and in particular to its date of payment and composition, may not be varied, notwithstanding that the total amount remains unchanged.

'The Directive does not however preclude a variation of the employment relationship with the new employer insofar as national law allows the employment relationship to be altered in a manner unfavourable to employees in situations other than the transfer of an undertaking provided that the transfer of the undertaking itself is not the reason for the alteration. The Directive is intended to extend the protection guaranteed to workers independently by the laws of Member States to cover the case where an undertaking is transferred. It is not intended to establish a uniform level of protection throughout the Community. Thus the Directive can be relied on only to ensure that the employee concerned is protected in his relations with the transferee to the same extent as he was in his relations with the transferor under national law.'

It may be seen therefore that where the laws of Member States within the European Union allow for contracts, terms or conditions of employment to be changed or alterations made in employment relationships, then, provided that the transferor could do so, there is nothing to prevent the transferee doing so. Regard must be had, however, to regulation 5 as dealt with at **10.10.1** below which precludes changes arising directly as a result of the fact of the transfer. These situations will, however, be rare.

10.9.9   DATE OF TRANSFER AND EXISTENCE OF RIGHTS AND OBLIGATIONS

The rights of employees which become subject to transfer and the obligations of the transferee consequent on the transfer depend on what rights and obligations were in existence as of the date of transfer as per article 3(1). In order to ascertain the full extent of such rights and obligations the existence of a contract of employment or employment relationship as of the date of transfer must be established and there must then be an analysis of the terms and conditions applying as between the parties to ascertain what exactly transfers.

In *Secretary of State for Employment v Spence* [1986] IRLR 248 the Court of Appeal held that where a company was in receivership and employees were dismissed at 11.00 am on 28 November 1983 and an agreement for the sale of the business was concluded at 2.00 pm on 29 November 1983, the contracts of employment of the employees did not subsist at the moment of transfer and their contracts of employment did not therefore transfer on the sale of the business. This decision was greatly qualified in *Litster v Forth Dry Dock and Engineering Co Ltd* [1989] IRLR 161 referred to at **10.9.10.1** below, albeit directly related to the interpretation of UK regulation 5. The ECJ has effectively confirmed *Litster* and the potential liability of a transferee for dismissals effected immediately before transfer by a transferor in *Dethier v Dassy and Sovam SPRL (in liquidation)*12 March 1998 (unreported).

Where an employment relationship does not exist at the date of transfer the transferee has no liability for the former employee of the transferor. In *Wendelboe v LJ Music ApS (in liquidation)* [1985] ECR 457 Mr Wendelboe and two colleagues were employed by LJ Music, a company which made cassette recordings, until 28 February 1980 on which date they were made redundant with immediate effect as the company was in financial difficulty. On 4 March 1980 the company was declared insolvent. At the bankruptcy hearing on 4 March a director of the company, who had been one of its employees, proposed that the business including premises, stock and machines be purchased by another company, SPKR. The final agreement on the transfer was concluded on 27 March 1980. The Bankruptcy Court did, however, authorise SPKR to use the insolvent business's premises and equipment as and from 5 March 1980. The final agreement of 27 March specified that the company's business was deemed to have been carried out on behalf of and at the risk of SPKR from 4 March 1980. On 6 March 1980, six days after their dismissal, Mr Wendelboe and his two colleagues were engaged by SPKR. Wendelboe and his colleagues brought an action against the insolvent company which argued inter alia that as there was a continuing employment relationship the transferee company, SPKR, was liable in respect of any damages for unfair dismissal. In considering the issues put to it the ECJ in the course of its judgment held that the Directive does not apply to rights and obligations of workers whose contract of employment or employment relationship had terminated or ceased at the time of transfer. The court in *Wendelboe* did not analyse the actual date of transfer in any particular detail but it is implicit from the judgment that the date of transfer must have been held to be 27 March. The judgment is a general one and does not specifically deal with Mr Wendelboe but does make it clear that if an employee is not employed in an undertaking on the date of transfer—and date of transfer is a matter of fact to be decided by national courts—there is then no obligation on the transferee in respect of rights or obligations arising from the contract of employment or employment relationship with the transferor.

10.9.10 TIME OF TRANSFER OR DATE OF TRANSFER?

10.9.10.1 Time of transfer and date of transfer distinguished

In *Wendelboe* the ECJ used the expressions 'date of transfer' and 'time of transfer' as if they were identical terms. They are clearly not. Commercial arrangements and transfers may take place in phases or in stages rather than at a precise moment. In order to ensure that the purpose of the Directive is achieved it would appear that 'time of transfer' would allow more scope than the more precise term 'date of transfer'. Article 3(1) is, however, quite clear in its use of the term 'date of transfer'. The Irish Regulations also use the term date of transfer. A more purposive approach than that taken in *Secretary of State for Employment v Spence* [1986] IRLR 248 was taken by the House of Lords in *Litster v Forth Dry Dock and Engineering Co Ltd* [1989] IRLR 161. In *Litster* the transferor and transferee arrived at an agreement prior to the transfer that the transferor would dismiss employees in order that the transferee would benefit from the hiring of other and cheaper labour after the transfer. In order to continue the business employees were needed and therefore, under regulation 5, the employees were held to be entitled to transfer and liability under the Directive and UK Regulations was held to be that of the transferee. As of the actual date of transfer there were no contracts of employment or employment relationships in existence. Adopting the 'date of transfer' terminology in the Directive would have allowed the aim of the Directive to be defeated in situations such as arose in *Litster*. To ensure that the purpose of the Directive was met the House of Lords was prepared to imply into the terminology of the UK

Regulations a term that the rights conferred by those regulations on persons 'employed immediately before the transfer' also cover persons who 'would have been so employed if they had not been unfairly dismissed in the circumstances'.

10.9.10.2 Transfer over period of time

Case law indicates that courts and tribunals are prepared to allow that a transfer may take place over a period of time, thereby giving the coverage of the Directive and Regulations to employees who were employed in the undertaking at any time over that period (see *A & G Tuck Ltd v Bartlett* [1994] IRLR 162 and *Dabell v Vale Industrial Services (Nottingham) Ltd* [1988] IRLR 439). In *Dabell* there had been dealings between the proposed transferor and transferee over a period of time but the proposed transfer was subsequently abandoned. Dabell was employed by Vale Industrial Services which became technically insolvent. Nofotech made an offer for the purchase of Vale's business. An agreement was reached in principle and various assets, machines, materials, orders and debtors transferred. Three employees of Vale, including Mr Dabell, worked for Nofotech for a short period during which time they were paid by Nofotech. A short time later Dabell tendered his resignation to Nofotech claiming constructive dismissal. The negotiations between Nofotech and Vale subsequently ran into difficulty and the proposed merger was abandoned. Dabell maintained his claim against Nofotech. In the circumstances of that case the Court of Appeal held:

> '[T]here had been a transfer of the business of Vale Industrial Services to Nofotech prior to the appellant's resignation from Nofotech notwithstanding that the merger was subsequently called off.

> 'Whether or not there has been a transfer of a business must be decided as at the date when the act of which the employee complains occurred. In the present case at the date of the appellant's resignation Vale had closed its premises and everything had been handed over to Nofotech—machines, customer connection, goodwill, existing contracts and employees. There was clearly a transfer of the undertaking on the ordinary meaning of the words.'

In *Dabell* Balcombe LJ in an obiter dictum stated (at p 443):

> 'The argument on behalf of the respondents that there had not been a final and conclusive transfer of ownership at the date of the appellant's resignation would mean that, even if the deal had come to full fruition as in most cases it probably would have, the appellant would not have been entitled to claim unfair dismissal by Nofotech. That would make no kind of sense on the facts of the present case.'

In *Longden and Paisley v Ferrari Ltd* [1994] IRLR 157 the second-named respondent purchased the business of Ferrari Ltd from receivers by way of a single sale of assets agreement which had been concluded on foot of a course of dealing over a period of weeks. At the time of the conclusion of the sale of assets agreement the appellants were not employed in the business. Their claims under the Transfer of Undertaking Regulations failed because they were not employed in the transfer of business 'immediately before' the transfer of the undertaking. In this case the EAT looked at the transactions engaged in between the transferee and the receivers and held that, while there existed a series of linked transactions, the transfer of the undertaking was not 'effected' by the series of transactions but was effected by the conclusion of the final agreement and at the time it was effected the appellants were not in employment and therefore not subject to transfer. The EAT held inter alia:

> 'In the present case although there was a succession of events which could be described as causally linked to one another and to the ultimate conclusion of the sale agreement the transfer was not effected by those earlier transactions. The transfer took place on completion of the agreement.'

10.9.10.3 Purposive approach by courts

Courts and tribunals have tended to take a more purposive approach to the construction of the date of transfer then was taken in the *Longden and Paisley* case following the lead given by the House of Lords in *Litster*. In *Macer v Abafast Ltd* [1990] IRLR 137 a transfer took place through a series of transactions which involved a twelve-day gap in employment for Mr Macer. The EAT closed that gap by following *Litster* and as it had been admitted by Abafast Ltd that it had engineered the twelve-day gap in employment to break Mr Macer's statutory continuity of service which was not allowed by the EAT. What the employee actually does during the gap in service may be relevant to the determination as to whether or not he was employed at the date or time of transfer. In *Justfern Ltd v Skaife D'Ingerthorpe* [1994] IRLR 164 the EAT held that where an employee was in receipt of unemployment benefit for a period of one week between the closing of a business and its subsequent purchase he was on a liberal construction of the words 'at the time of the transfer' available for work and therefore effectively still in employment and stated:

'The receipt of unemployment benefit is not inconsistent with availability for employment in the business in which an employee had been lately employed. A liberal construction of the words "at the time of the transfer" accords wth the evident policy of the legislature to preserve continuity of employment . . . regulation 17(2) is capable of operating a cross and interval greater than a week. It followed that it is capable of bridging a similar period of uncertainty as to whether or not an employee will be re-employed by the purchaser of the business. The receipt of unemployment benefit does no more than create such uncertainty. It does not eliminate the possibility even on a short term basis of such employment. There is a major distinction between applying for and receiving unemployment benefit because wages have ceased and taking on another job. Accordingly, the employee's application for and receipt of unemployment benefit did not result in an interruption in his employment such as to make it impossible to treat his employment with the [transferee] . . . as continuous with his employment with the [transferor].'

Article 3(3), in referring to pension rights and the necessity to protect the interest of employees and of persons no longer employed, refers to 'at the time of the transfer'. The wording of the Directive does not therefore draw a distinction between the terms 'date of transfer' and 'time of transfer' and it appears to be left to the ECJ to give some further interpretation as to how strictly the term 'date of transfer' will be applied and whether or not the expression 'time of transfer' allows for a widening of the timing of the occurrence of the transfer from the twenty-four-hour period clearly provided within the expression 'date of transfer'.

10.9.11 CAN EMPLOYEES AGREE CHANGES PRIOR TO OR AT TIME OF TRANSFER?

10.9.11.1 Introduction

While it may appear commercially desirable, and indeed desirable in the context of on-going industrial relations, that the parties to an employment relationship should remain free to agree changes in terms and conditions of employment regardless of whether or not a transfer is or has taken place within the meaning of the Directive, the legality of agreed changes in the event that there is a transfer within the meaning of the Directive is unclear. While there are no contracting-out provisions in the Directive or Regulations the application of the Directive is mandatory and therefore it is not open to the parties to a transfer to avoid its provisions. If the parties reach agreement that something should occur, such as a variation in terms and conditions, which the transferor and transferee are prohibited by the Directive from doing themselves, is such variation valid ?

In *Foreningen af Arbejdsledere i Danmark v Daddy's Dance Hall A/S* [1988] IRLR 315 the ECJ set out the general principle which suggests that an employee cannot agree a change even where it may be advantageous holding as referred to above and qualified in *Rask and Christensen v ISS Kantineservice A/S* [1993] IRLR 133, also referred to at **10.9.2** above.

In two joined appeals the UK Court of Appeal considered whether or not the Directive prohibited agreed changes in terms and conditions between the transferee and the employees whose employment had been or was about to be transferred. The court considered the question in the cases of *Wilson v St Helens Borough Council* and *Meade and Baxendale v British Fuels Ltd* [1977] IRLR 505.

The facts of the two cases were different and, while the appeals were joined as one, different conclusions were reached in each case.

10.9.11.2 Wilson v St Helens Borough Council

In *Wilson v St Helens Borough Council* the employees were employed in a home for boys with behavioural problems. They were employed by Lancashire County Council which gave notice, to the trustees of the home, that they would cease to manage the home due to funding problems. St Helens Council agreed to take over responsibility on certain terms. Lancashire County Council entered into negotiations with the trade union which was representative of the staff and it was agreed that staff numbers would be reduced from 162 to 72 and that those transferring to St Helens would be appointed to new posts with different job descriptions. Those not transferring were redeployed by Lancashire. The staff to be transferred were dismissed by Lancashire by reason of redundancy and were re-employed with immediate effect by St Helens Council but on different terms and conditions from they had enjoyed with Lancashire. Some of the employees brought claims that the changed terms and conditions worked a detriment on them as compared to the terms and conditions they had enjoyed. The EAT held that if the operative reason for an agreed variation in terms and conditions is the transfer of an undertaking the variation is ineffective and the terms of the original contract of employment remain in force. The EAT held that the principle of automatic transfer contained in the Directive is mandatory and precludes even a consensual variation. The Court of Appeal, however, did not address that very important issue and took a different approach to the facts of the situation. The court focused on the reason for the change and sought to categorise it within the category of 'economic, technical or organisational reasons entailing changes in the workforce' which allows, in certain circumstances, for termination of employment in the context of a transfer within the meaning of the Directive. In doing so the Court of Appeal avoided answering the question as to whether terms and conditions may be consensually varied at the time of or immediately after a transfer. The court held that the termination by Lancashire County Council of the employment of Wilson and the other applicants was a permissible termination and therefore St Helens Council was starting from a position of having no obligations transferred to it. There was therefore not a variation but rather a termination by Lancashire, which was permitted within the terms of the Directive, and the creation of new contracts on new terms and conditions between St Helens and the employees concerned. St Helens therefore did not have liability to the employees for detriment suffered arising from or in comparison with the terms and conditions they enjoyed with Lancashire.

10.9.11.3 Meade and Baxendale v British Fuels Ltd

Meade and Baxendale had similar facts but arrived at a different conclusion. The two men worked for National Fuel Distributors (NFD) which merged with the British Fuels Group to form British Fuels Ltd (BFL). NFD gave notice of dismissal on grounds of redundancy to both men. On the same day they received notice they were offered employment with BFL on less favourable terms and conditions including a lower rate of pay. The letter of offer noted that their previous service had been 'bought out' by the redundancy and severance payments made by NFD. BFL were unaware that the Directive applied. Meade and Baxendale took up employment with BFL and some months later signed statements of terms and conditions reflecting their new terms. A year later they sought declarations that they were still employed on the terms and conditions they had enjoyed with NFD.

The Court of Appeal held that, on the evidence, the transfer of the undertaking itself was the reason for the dismissal of both Meade and Baxendale. The purported dismissal was ineffective within the terms of the Directive and the original contracts of employment continued as if made with the transferee BFL. Subsequent agreement with BFL on different terms and conditions could not limit the operation of the terms of the Directive since the transfer or a reason connected with it remained the principal reason for the alteration.

While the ECJ appears to have left some discretion to courts in Member States to determine whether or not changes to a contract are allowable within the law of that Member State, *Meade and Baxendale* was not determined on whether or not the employees had validly agreed changes to their contract within the contract law of the UK but rather allowed the two employees to argue either that there was no real intention to change their contracts, or they did so under a mistaken belief that they may have had no option or, indeed, even been obliged to do so and the Directive applied to set aside their apparent consensual variation in their contracts of employment. The Court of Appeal reasoned that there was a direct causal link between the transfer and the dismissal of Meade and Baxendale; therefore the dismissal was a nullity as also effectively was the variation of terms and conditions, which was, on the face of it, valid at common law, because it too had a causal link to the transfer.

10.9.11.4 Conclusion

It appears therefore that changes may only be agreed or imposed where the first pre-transfer contract has come to an end for economic, technical or organisational reasons. Following this line of reasoning employers will encounter considerable practical difficulties where the terms and conditions of a workforce which is merged with or added to an existing workforce are considerably different from the existing workforce and it will take considerable time and effort to reach a position of harmonisation of both. It would appear, however, following *Wilson* and *Meade and Baxendale* that the employer is not in a position to negotiate or agree changes with employees unless their contracts are validly terminated within the terms of the Directive and domestic regulations prior to the transfer in which event the transferee is starting with a clean slate. See the House of Lords decision in these joined cases: *Wilson v St Helens Borough Council* and *British Fuels Ltd v Baxendale and Meade* [1998] IRLR 706.

10.9.12 NO OBLIGATION ON EMPLOYEES TO TRANSFER

It should be kept in mind at all times in contemplating a purchase of a business or effecting a transfer that employees are not obliged to transfer. In *Katsikas v Konstantinidis and Skreb* [1993] IRLR 179 the ECJ held that, in the event of a transfer, employees were entitled to object to the transfer. What then happens to the contract of employment is a matter for each Member State to determine. The ECJ has made its view as to what happens very clear in a number of cases, notably *Mikkelsen v Danmols Inventar A/S* [1986] 1 CMLR 316 where the court stated (para 16):

> 'The protection which the Directive is intended to guarantee is however redundant where the person concerned decides of his own accord not to continue the employment relationship with the new employer after the transfer. That is the case where the employee in question terminates the employment contract or employment relationship of his own free will with effect from the date of the transfer or where that contract or relationship is terminated with effect from the date of the transfer by virtue of an agreement voluntarily concluded between the worker and the transferor or the transferee of the undertaking. In that situation Article 3(1) of the Directive does not apply.'

The ECJ further stated in *Merckx and Neuhuys v Ford Motor Company Belgium SA* [1996] IRLR 467:

> 'Article 3(1) of Directive 77/187 does not preclude an employee employed by the transferor at the date of the transfer of an undertaking from objecting to the transfer to the transferee of the contract of employment or the employment relationship. In such a case it is for the Member States to determine what the fate of the contract or employment relationship with the transferor should be.'

10.10 TRADE UNIONS

10.10.1 LEGISLATIVE PROVISIONS

The status and rights of trade unions and employee representatives are sought to be protected in the transfer of undertakings by virtue of the provisions of article 5 of the Directive, which the explanatory note states was intended not to interfere 'with existing national arrangements and structures of workers' representative bodies'. Article 5 provides as follows:

'1.   'If the business preserves its autonomy, the status and function, as laid down by the laws, regulations or administrative provisions of the Member States, of the representatives or of the representation of the employees affected by the transfer within the meaning of Article 1(1) shall be preserved.

The first sub-paragraph shall not apply if, under the laws, regulations, administrative provisions or practice of the Member States, the conditions necessary for the re-appointment of the representatives of the employees or for the reconstitution of the representation of the employees are fulfilled.

2.   If the term of office of the representatives of the employees affected by a transfer within the meaning of Article 1(1) expires as a result of the transfer, the representatives shall continue to enjoy the protection provided by the laws, regulations, administrative provisions or practices of the Member States.'

Regulation 6 of SI 306/1980 provides as follows:

'Where an undertaking or business or part of a business the subject of a transfer preserves its autonomy after the transfer the status and function as laid down by the laws, regulations or administrative provisions of the State, of the representatives or of the representation of the employees affected by the transfer shall be preserved by the transferee concerned.'

10.10.2 UNION RECOGNITION

Employees who exercise a constitutional right to join a trade union cannot insist that they enjoy the full benefit of such membership by in turn insisting that the employer recognise their union. The right conferred by the Constitution is an individual personal right and does not carry with it the concomitant obligation on an employer to recognise that trade union, according to the judgment of McWilliam J in *Abbott and Whelan v ATGWU* [1982] 1 JISLL 56. The plaintiffs were members of a trade union, the ATGWU. Their employer, the Southern Health Board, had a formal recognition agreement with the ITGWU. The plaintiffs sought to insist that their employer deal with the trade union of their choice and, when the board refused, the plaintiffs brought the matter to the High Court claiming inter alia that the defendants were interfering with or obstructing them in the exercise of their constitutional right to join the trade union of their choice and what they claimed was the further right to be represented by such trade union in the conduct of negotiations with their employers concerning wages and other conditions of employment. In his judgment McWilliam J referred to Article 40.6.1(iii) of the Constitution and the rights conferred on the plaintiffs and other citizens by that provision, considered in *Meskell v CIE* [1973] IR 121 and *Educational Company of Ireland v Fitzpatrick* [1961] IR 345 where active steps were taken to compel the citizens to forgo their constitutional rights, and held that there was no attempt to compel the plaintiffs to forgo their constitutional rights in this particular case stating (at p 60):

> 'Insofar as the Board is concerned it appears to me to be clear that the plaintiffs have no constitutional right to compel the Board to engage in negotiations either with them or with their union. . . .

> 'In the present case, the plaintiffs have joined ATGWU without first ascertaining whether that union would or would not be in a position to negotiate with the Board. Employers must frequently have refused to negotiate with employees or their unions and this may have led to industrial action but, outside the terms of the contract of employment, employers are not bound to take part in any, or any particular form of, negotiations.

> 'On the facts of this case I am of the opinion that the refusal of the Board to negotiate with ATGWU is not coercion to forgo a constitutional right within the principles which have been enunciated.'

In the earlier case of *EI Company Ltd v Kennedy* [1968] IR 69 Walsh J stated in an obiter dictum:

> 'In law an employer is not obliged to meet anybody as the representative of his worker, nor indeed is he obliged to meet the worker himself for the purpose of discussing any demand which the worker may make.'

10.10.3 IMPLIED RECOGNITION

In the absence of a specific contractual provision that the employee's trade union will be recognised it is arguable that, where an employee is a member of a union and the employer is dealing with or had dealt with that union, there is an implied term in the contract between the employer and the employee to the effect that the employee's union will be recognised. In the context of a transfer of an undertaking the employee could then seek to rely on the provisions of article 3 of the Directive by claiming that his right to have his union recognised is something that arises from the existence of an employment relationship at the date of transfer. In this regard article 3 refers to 'rights and obligations . . . arising from . . . an employment relationship'. The employment relationship could be deemed to involve a trade union where a person is a member and is actively represented by such union.

The absence of a system of formal recognition in Ireland allows that recognition may arise by express agreement but also by implied agreement. Recognition could be implied from a course of dealing between the parties and by the recognition, albeit in limited ways, of a trade union for certain purposes such as in disciplinary hearings. In *National Union of Tailors and Garment Workers v Charles Ingram & Co Ltd* [1977] IRLR 147, the UK EAT, in a case relating to recognition of a trade union for the purpose of redundancy consultations, held in relation to recognition:

> 'Recognition implies agreement which involves consent. Where, as in the present case, there is neither a written agreement that the union should be recognised nor an express agreement which is not in writing it is sufficient if the established facts are clear and unequivocal and give rise to the clear inference that the employers have recognised the union. This will normally involve conduct over a period of time and the longer that state of facts has existed the easier it is to reach a conclusion that the employers have recognised the union.'

10.10.4 PICKETING BY EMPLOYEES OF A TRANSFEROR

The High Court, and on appeal the Supreme Court, granted an interlocutory injunction to the purchaser of a pub to restrain a picket placed by employees of the former owners in *Westman Holdings Ltd v McCormack* [1992] 1 IR 151. The defendants in the case had been employed in a pub which was sold to the plaintiff. Before the completion of the sale the defendants and all other members of staff were dismissed. The defendants sought employment with the new owner, the plaintiff, but were refused. When the new owners re-opened the premises an official picket was placed on the pub. As none of the defendants had ever been employed by the new owner, the plaintiff, it was argued that the plaintiff could not constitute their 'employer' within the meaning of s 11(1) of the 1990 Act. The High Court granted an interlocutory injunction restraining the picketing on the basis that the plaintiff had raised a fair question and because the balance of convenience was in its favour. That decision was upheld by the Supreme Court. The case did not appear again before either the High Court or the Supreme Court and therefore the benefit of their observations on the effect of the Directive and Regulations on the transfer of a trade dispute is not available. From the available information it is not clear if the Directive and Regulations were referred to at all in either hearing and it appears that the case was dealt with purely as a trade dispute under the 1990 Act. It appears that following the ECJ decisions *d'Urso v Ercole Marelli Elettromeccanica Generale SpA* [1992] IRLR 136 and *Rotsart de Hertaing v J Benoidt SA (in liquidation)* [1997] IRLR 127 picketing by employees of a transferor directed against a transferee must be held to be valid and protected, provided all of the other requirements of the 1990 Act are complied with. Injunctive relief may still be available to a transferee under the 1990 Act provided the applicant for injunctive relief can establish that there is a fair question to be tried at the hearing of the action and that the balance of convenience is in favour of granting such relief (see *Bayzana Ltd v Galligan* [1987] IR 241).

Article 4 of the Directive provides as follows:

'1.   *The transfer of an undertaking, business or part of a business shall not in itself constitute grounds for dismissal by the transferor or the transferee. This provision shall not stand in the way of dismissals that may take place for economic, technical or organisational reasons entailing changes in the workforce. Member States may provide that the first sub-paragraph shall not apply to certain specific categories of employees who are not covered by the laws or practice of the Member States in respect of protection against dismissal.*

2.   *If the contract of employment or the employment relationship is terminated because the transfer [within the meaning of Article 1(1)] involves a substantial change in working conditions to the detriment of the employee, the employer shall be regarded as having been responsible for termination of the contract of employment or of the employment relationship.'*

Regulation 5 of the Irish Regulations provides similar protection but with some important difference in wording and emphasis as follows:

'(1) *The transfer of an undertaking, business or part of a business shall not in itself constitute grounds for dismissal by the transferor or the transferee and a dismissal, the grounds for which are such a transfer, by a transferor or a transferee is hereby prohibited. However, nothing in this Regulation shall be construed as prohibiting dismissals for economic, technical or organisational reasons entailing changes in the work-force.*

(2)   *If a contract of employment or an employment relationship is terminated because a transfer involves a substantial change in working conditions to the detriment of the employee concerned the employer concerned shall be regarded as having been responsible for termination of the contract of employment or of the employment relationship.'*

10.10.5 TRANSFER RELATED DISMISSALS AND ORGANISATIONAL CHANGES ARISING FROM TRANSFER

In the original draft Directive article 4 allowed for dismissals to take place where there existed what were described as 'pressing business reasons'. The draft Directive did not list what might be acceptable or justifiable reasons. The wording of the Directive as passed into law simply provides that dismissals 'may take place for economic, technical or organisational reasons entailing changes in the workforce'. No guidance is given as to what is meant by any of the terms 'economic', 'technical' or 'organisational', nor is there any guidance given as to the extent of 'changes in the workforce' which may or must result following on such dismissals. It is left to the individual Member States and their courts and tribunals to determine what is or is not allowable. The operation of this facility or freedom to avoid the obligation of having to retain all post-transfer employees in employment must be linked to the information and consultation provisions of the Directive and Regulations which themselves set up a framework for all interested parties to seek to avoid dismissals and to put employees on notice of plans and proposals in order that they may take whatever actions are available to them. Each of the Member States of the EU is bound by the EU Directive on collective redundancies and most of the Member States have domestic laws on the restructuring of businesses and consequent redundancy of employees.

Article 4 does not provide for sanctions against an employer who breaches its terms. That is again left to the Member States and courts and tribunals within those Member States.

10.10.6 TRANSFER RELATED DISMISSALS

It is not uncommon in trying to circumvent the Directive and Regulations that the transferee of a business will require that the transferor terminate the employment of some or all of the employees prior to the transfer. The ECJ held in *P Bork International A/S (in liquidation) v Foreningen af Arbejdsledere i Danmark* [1989] IRLR 41 that where employees were dismissed on 22 December 1981, when a company ceased operation, and were re-employed on 30 December 1981 by the purchaser of the business the reason for the termination was the transfer itself. The court found this as a fact in light of the evidence to the effect that the dismissals took place at a time close to the date of transfer and the workers concerned were subsequently re-engaged. The court held that in order to give effect to the Regulations the workers must be considered as still employed in the undertaking on the date of the transfer with the consequent effect that the Regulations/Directive apply to them. The ECJ stated in its judgment:

'[I]t is appropriate to take account of all the factual circumstances surrounding the transaction which may include in particular whether the tangible and intangible assets have been transferred as well as a major part of the staff of the undertaking, the degree of similarity between its activities before and after the transfer and the duration of any period of stoppage connected with the transfer. The fact that the undertaking was temporarily closed and did not have any employees at the time of the transfer was a factor to be taken into consideration for the purpose of determining whether an economic entity which was still in existence had been transferred. However it was not in itself sufficient to preclude the existence of a transfer within the meaning of Article 1(1) particularly in a situation such as the present case in which the undertaking ceased its operations for only a short period which also coincided with the end-of-the-year holidays.'

'Hiving-down' or requiring pre-transfer dismissals is prohibited.

10.10.7 SLIMMING DOWN AND LIABILITY FOR SEVERANCE COSTS

Any attempt by a purchaser or transferee to negotiate or deal with a transferor and procure that the transferor bring about structural or organisational changes in order that the transferee can take over a slimmed-down or reduced workforce will clearly impact on the transferee and, having regard to the automatic transfer of liabilities as referred to in *Rotsart de Hertaing v J Benoidt SA* [1997] IRLR 127, the only possibility the transferee has of mitigating the effect of these provisions is to secure sufficient effective indemnities. Such indemnities will only apply as between the transferor and the transferee. As far as the employees are concerned the transferee is the one who will carry liability to them. It is therefore advisable that reorganisation, restructuring or reduction of a workforce should be carried out by the transferee, leaving the transferee in the best position to justify its own actions in terminating the employment of certain of the workforce. That will not help the transferee, however, in costing the takeover of the business from the transferor. The transferee will not want to carry potentially substantial severance payments immediately after purchasing a business but again this is a matter it will have to plan for in its negotiations with the transferor. A transferee should not seek to have liability for such payments imposed on the transferor by having the transferor reduce or reorganise the workforce on the basis of someone else's (the transferee's) reasons or plans for doing so. The transferee is better placed to deal with all issues arising consequent on termination of employment of any of the workforce as a result of the transfer. If the transferee does not want to be exposed to the cost of having to do so, provision may be made to recover the cost from the transferor or make some provision for the reservation of sufficient funds for this purpose; however, the level of severance payments the workforce might seek may not be easily predictable. If the workforce were to hold out for substantially higher payments than may have been paid in the past, and the parties have done their calculations based on such historical payments, difficulties may arise and great care must be taken by both parties in planning for the costs of rationalisation or reduction in the workforce consequent on a transfer.

10.11 THE ETO DEFENCE

10.11.1 GENERALLY

Article 4 is qualified by providing that nothing in the article shall prohibit dismissal for economic, technical or organisational ('ETO') reasons entailing changes in the workforce. In the main this may be construed as coming within the statutory definition of redundancy. It does, however, appear to go a stage further. In *Anderson v Dalkeith Engineering Ltd* [1984] IRLR 429, on similar facts to *Litster v Forth Dry Dock and Engineering Co Ltd* [1989] IRLR 161, new owners employed many of the workforce dismissed by a receiver prior to a transfer. Those not re-employed complained of unfair dismissal. It was held that the dismissals were not unfair. It was held that the motives of the purchaser in seeking the dismissals were irrelevant to the consideration of whether the vendor had acted fairly. The EAT held that what was relevant was the reasons of the receiver, not the acquiring company. The reasons of the receiver were economic. In order to get the best price for the business the receiver was obliged to dismiss the workforce. It appears the effect of this decision is that if the transferor can satisfactorily show that in order to sell the business he had no option but to dismiss some or all of the workforce those dismissals will not be unfair. It may well be that the transferor/vendor of the business can anticipate generally what a, as yet unknown, transferor or purchaser would look for in such a business and, indeed, if the business is in poor commercial health it may be prudent to make such changes regardless of whether the business is ever sold or transferred, but in many cases the vendor or transferor will know who the likely purchaser/transferee is. They will very often have discussions and negotiations with that party and the prospective purchaser/transferee is very likely to give an indication as to the type of business structure or numbers employed that they would consider to be ideal. In that instance it would be very difficult for a vendor/transferor to claim, as their own, the reasons for restructuring and effecting dismissals albeit within domestic redundancy laws. The best practice would seem to be for the transferee to effect the necessary changes and accommodate the cost of doing so in their contract with the vendor/transferor.

Where a transferee requires the imposition of pre-transfer manpower structures or requirements it is prudent that a transferor enquire into the reasons of the transferee for doing so; otherwise it may well be held that the transferor did not have a reason of substance by virtue of his unquestioning acceptance of the requirements of the transferee. The change in judicial approach to, and interpretation of, the Directive and Regulations in recent years is such that liability will almost always be deemed to be that of the transferee. The reasoning should therefore be that of the transferee. Employers have found it difficult to justify making changes prior to a transfer in order to make their business more saleable or more attractive (see *Wheeler v Patel* [1987] IRLR 211; *Gateway Hotels Ltd v Stewart* [1988] IRLR 287 and *Ibex Trading Co Ltd v Walton* [1994] IRLR 564).

10.11.2 CHANGES IN THE WORKFORCE

10.11.2.1 Harmonisation of terms and conditions

It is essential that the ETO reasons must entail *'changes in the workforce'*. This normally requires a change in the numbers of people employed to perform particular functions, not merely a change in their terms and conditions (see *Berriman v Delabole Slate Ltd* [1985] IRLR 305). Where a transferee purchases a business or part of a business to add to a pre-existing business, difficulties may arise where attempts are made to harmonise terms and conditions as between the two groups of employees. There appears to be very little scope for employers to do other than improve all terms and conditions to the best available or, at the very least, to *'red circle'* the less attractive terms and conditions in so far as they apply to some employees within the total workforce. The UK EAT, however, did allow that numbers may remain the same and yet there could be an organisational change which might justify the termination of employment of one or more employees, and presumably their replacement by others engaged in significantly different functions. In *Crawford v Swinton Insurance Brokers Ltd* [1990] IRLR 42 Mrs Crawford was required to change from the typing and clerical job to working as an insurance salesperson. In the headnote to its judgment (at pp 42–43) the EAT held:

> '[T]here does not have to be a change in the identity of at least one of the workers who constitute the workforce in order for there to be an organisational reason for dismissal entailing "changes in the workforce" within the meaning of . . . the Regulations.

> 'There can be a "change in a workforce" . . . if the same people are kept on but they are given entirely different jobs to do. In accordance with the decision of the Court of Appeal in *Berriman v Delabole Slate Ltd* the "workforce" connotes the whole body of employees as an entity and corresponds to the "strength" or the "establishment". Therefore what has to be looked at is the workforce as a whole separate from the individuals who make it up. It then has to be determined whether the reason in question is one which involves a change in that workforce strength or establishment. If as a result of an organisational change on a relevant transfer a workforce is engaged in a different occupation there is a change in the workforce for the purpose of [the Regulations].'

It is to be expected that where an employer seeks to impose such fundamental changes on an employee that the reason for doing so will be examined very carefully, as was done in *Crawford*, and the transferee who seeks to impose such changes will be considerably more exposed to unfair dismissal claims or claims for breach of the Directive/Regulations than the transferee who reduces numbers as in *Berriman*.

10.11.2.2 Employees surplus to requirements

If, after a transfer, employees are surplus to the transferee's requirements and could in a non-transfer situation be properly regarded as redundant, then the ETO defence will apply, see *Gorictree Ltd v Jenkinson* [1984] IRLR 391 and *Trafford v Sharpe & Fisher (Building Supplies) Ltd* [1994] IRLR 325.

10.11.2.3 Economic reasons

Where an employer seeks to justify changes on economic grounds this does not entitle the employer to reduce the employee's remuneration. In *Meikle v McPhail* [1983] IRLR 351 the new owner of a pub, who had accepted liability for existing employees when he took over the premises, realised after he took control of the business that substantial economies would have to be made and, as a result, made all of the staff, with one exception, redundant. Mrs Meikle challenged the decision to make her redundant and, in the absence of being able to show that she should have had preference over an employee who was retained, she failed in her claim as the employer relied on the economic defence available in the Directive and Regulations.

The UK EAT has held that the economic reason for the dismissal must relate to the conduct of the business, and therefore a desire to obtain an enhanced price for the business or to achieve a sale is not a reason which relates to the conduct of the business, and is therefore not an economic reason. In that particular case the reason for the dismissal was the vendor's wish to comply with the requirements of the intending purchaser who wanted the workforce reduced and this was held not to be capable of coming within the term 'economic'. The EAT also stated in that case that the word 'economic' cannot be read on its own as to do so would be to give the term very wide meaning and would allow for dismissals in far more situations than had been envisaged by the Directive and Regulations. The EAT suggested that the approach that might be taken would be to limit the meaning of the word and stated 'the adjective economic' must be construed ejusdem generis with the adjectives 'technical' and 'organisational'. The approach to the construction of the word 'economic' adopted in *Wheeler v Patel* [1987] IRLR 211 was followed by the UK EAT in *Gateway Hotels Ltd v Stewart* [1988] IRLR 287.

Gateway operated a hotel which was making a loss and they agreed the sale of the hotel as a going concern to another company which made it a condition of the sale that Gateway would terminate the employment of all of the employees in the business prior to takeover. Gateway were very unhappy with this and tried to persuade the purchaser to remove the condition, but as they were anxious not to lose the sale, they ultimately had to agree to the term and dismissed all of the staff. The staff claimed against Gateway on the basis of their belief that there should have been an automatic transfer of their employment to the purchaser. Gateway pleaded that there was an 'economic' reason for the terminations. The EAT upheld the decision of the industrial tribunal that the reason for the dismissals was the transfer of the undertaking and not on 'economic' grounds.

Attempts by transferors to facilitate transferees by dismissing staff before the transfer are unlikely to survive the tests laid down by the ECJ, particularly in *Rotsart de Hertaing v J Benoidt SA* [1997] IRLR 127 coupled with *Litster v Forth Dry Dock and Engineering Co Ltd* [1989] IRLR 161, and even if the employees were to be re-engaged it could still be held to be a breach of the Directive as commented on by Advocate-General Slynn in *Wendelboe v LJ Music ApS* [1985] ECR 457 when he stated:

> 'When employees are dismissed, with a view to, and before, a transfer falling within the Directive and are re-engaged immediately by the transferee thereafter, their dismissal must be regarded as contrary to Article 4(1) subject to the exceptions specified in that paragraph.'

10.11.3 REASON FOR DISMISSAL—TRANSFER OR ETO?

It is a feature of many of the cases where the ETO defence is pleaded that employees claim the reason for their dismissal was the transfer per se and therefore their dismissal was prohibited, whereas the transferor or transferee claims that the reasons were economic, technical or organisational. In *Porter and Nanayakkara v Queens Medical Centre* [1993] IRLR 486 the plaintiffs were employed by a health authority as consultant paediatricians. The authority had contracts with two hospitals for the provision of paediatric services. The authority decided to reorganise the service and terminated the arrangement with the two hospitals, entering into a new contract with the defendants. The defendants looked at alternative ways of providing the paediatric service and decided to restructure by creating four new consultant paediatrician posts. These posts carried different responsibilities and obligations from the consultant posts previously held by the plaintiffs with the health authority. The plaintiffs applied for two of the 'new' posts but were unsuccessful. As a result of the restructuring of the transferee the plaintiffs were made redundant. The plaintiffs claimed that they were dismissed by reason of the transfer of the undertaking. The High Court held that the transfer of the service to the defendants was a transfer of an undertaking stating:

'Although the dismissal of the plaintiffs on the grounds of redundancy was a consequence of the transfer of the undertaking the termination was not invalidated by Article 4(1) of the Directive which provides that the transfer of an undertaking "shall not in itself constitute grounds for dismissal by the transferor or the transferee".

'The changed methods which the defendants intended to introduce to provide the services required amounted to a reorganisation entailing changes in the workforce. Since the defendants were introducing a new organisation which required that they should be free to make an uninhibited choice in filling the posts concerned the change in the workforce which was entailed by organisational reasons was the termination of the existing contracts.' (See also *Ibex Trading Co Ltd v Walton* [1994] IRLR 564.)

10.11.4 MOTIVATION FOR CHANGE

In order for employers to rely on the ETO defence they must be able to show that their decision was a bona fide decision to make changes and that those changes entailed changes in the workforce. The motivation factor mirrors the requirement in redundancy law that the dismissal must be 'wholly or mainly' by reason of redundancy (Redundancy Payments Act, 1967, s 7(2)).

10.11.5 ETO AND REDUNDANCY

10.11.5.1 Morris v Smart Brothers Ltd

The Irish cases have tended to equate the ETO defence with the concept of redundancy, particularly decisions of the EAT. In *Morris v Smart Brothers Ltd* UD 688/93 the EAT examined a situation where Smart Brothers had operated eight retail clothing outlets in Dublin together with a head office, warehouse and wholesale business. When the company ran into trading difficulties it was broken up and various of the shops were sold off, some to co-respondents of Smart Brothers in this particular case. The EAT had to consider the position of employees in some of the stores which had changed hands and continued to operate and where the employees had claimed they were entitled to remain in employment in the stores by reason of the protections afforded by the Directive and Regulations. The EAT held that there had been transfer of an undertaking in the sale of shops to some of the co-respondent companies by Smart Brothers, which itself ceased to trade, and the EAT held inter alia:

(a)   The employment of all of the staff ended by reason of redundancy when Smart Brothers ceased to carry on business. There was therefore no claim of unfair dismissal against Smart Brothers as redundancy is a substantial ground justifying dismissal under unfair dismissal legislation.

(b)   Individual shops which had been subsidiaries of Smart Brothers continued operating as clothing shops under various new owners. The EAT held that, notwithstanding the application of the Directive and Regulations, in those circumstances no liability for staff remained with Smart Brothers in respect of the failure of transferees to engage staff who previously had worked at those locations. The dismissal of the employees by Smart Brothers was not grounded in the transfer 'in itself' but arose because that company ceased trading, leading to the redundancy of its employees. That is an economic reason as permitted by the Directive.

(c)   While one of the shops retained its identity it retained a greatly reduced workforce and moved from being 100 per cent retail to 50 per cent retail, 50 per cent wholesale. Two people remained employed in the business; one was the owner and the other was an individual moved from another branch because of his experience of the wholesale trade. The EAT held that the reduction in staff numbers on the retail side and the introduction of wholesale business amounted to 'economic, technical or organisational reasons entailing changes in the workforce'.

(d)   In respect of one of the shops that retained its identity with the same trade as had been carried on by Smart Brothers, an employee succeeded in his claim of unfair dismissal when he was not engaged by the transferee whom the EAT held had failed to show an economic, technical or organisational reason to justify the non-employment of the individual concerned.

10.11.5.2   Cunningham v Oasis Stores Ltd

In another EAT case, *Cunningham v Oasis Stores Ltd* [1995] ELR 183, the EAT examined a complicated factual situation where a retail clothing business had been run by a succession of companies operating retail shops. The last transfer involved the purchase of four of the shops by Oasis Stores Ltd, a British company, which operated its own retail clothing business. Oasis planned to add the four shops to its chain of stores. Mrs Cunningham and Mrs O'Connor, the claimants in the case, were senior executives involved in managing the business and operating the four shops. The legal owners of the shops licensed them to the operators who employed Mrs Cunningham and Mrs O'Connor. Oasis purchased the legal interest in the shops and the licences were in due course surrendered to Oasis. On assuming ownership and responsibility for the shops Oasis managed them from an area office in the north of England. Senior management functions were based at the Oasis head office in London. The claimants argued that there was a transfer of an undertaking and that the failure to retain them in employment was a prohibited dismissal. The respondents argued that there was no transfer because Oasis had most of its clothing stock specially manufactured to its own specification, but that if there was a transfer the claimants' work was not referable solely to the part of the business transferred, and, further that the manner in which Oasis structured the management of the business and carried it on from a different location by persons who were already working for them was an economic, technical or organisational justification for the termination of the claimants' employment.

10.11.6   SCOPE OF THE ETO DEFENCE

- The reasons must be those of the transferee.

    - Dismissal by a transferor at the request or behest of a transferee immediately prior to the transfer in circumstances where it is abundantly clear that there is an obvious ETO reason why the employee should not physically transfer on the basis that his employment would inevitably be terminated by the transferee may constitute a valid defence.

- There must be a change or changes in the workforce.
  - Normally numbers will reduce but not necessarily. If a function is done away with this could be a change in the workforce but if a new function is created the numbers may not drop and yet the ETO defence could justify the termination of the employment of the employee carrying out the function which has been done away with.
  - A transferee cannot use the ETO defence to simply change terms and conditions of employment. If an employee's function is no longer required the employment of that employee may come to an end. In the employer's restructuring a new post could be created with different terms and conditions.

- Economic grounds must relate to the conduct of the business post-transfer and will relate to the cost of running the business.

- Technical grounds must also relate to the conduct of the business after transfer and will relate to skills and manner of operation of the business and the use of technical skills, be they abilities and qualifications, be they mental or physical.

- Organisational grounds again must relate to the business post-transfer and must be linked to the manner in which the business is run in terms of structural, departmental, administrative or managerial functions.

- Redundancy as recognised by Irish law will meet the requirements of the ETO defence.

10.12 INFORMATION AND CONSULTATION

10.12.1 LEGISLATIVE REQUIREMENTS

Article 6 of the Directive takes up all of section III of the Directive and is headed 'Information and Consultation'. It confers joint obligations on the transferor and the transferee to inform employee representatives of the reasons for transfer, the legal, economic and social implications of the transfer for the employees, and of any measures envisaged in relation to the employees. This information is to be given in good time before the transfer is carried out and, in any event, before the employees are directly affected by the transfer 'as regards their conditions of work and employment'.

Regulation 7 of the Irish Regulations gives effect to article 6 of the Directive and provides as follows:

'(1) The transferor and transferee concerned in a transfer shall inform the representatives of their respective employees affected by the transfer of—
 (a) the reasons for the transfer;
 (b) the legal, economic and social implications of the transfer for the employees, and
 (c) the measures envisaged in relation to the employees.
   and the information shall be given—
   (i) by the transferor to the representatives of his employees in good time before the transfer is carried out, and
   (ii) by the transferee, to the representatives of his employees in good time, and in any event before his employees are directly affected by the transfer as regards their conditions of work and employment.
(2) If the transferor or the transferee concerned in a transfer envisages measures in relation to his employees, he shall consult his representatives of the employees in good time on such measures with a view to seeking agreement.

> *(3)   Where, in the case of a transfer, there are no representatives of the employees in the undertaking or business of the transferor or, as the case may be, in the undertaking or business of the transferee, the transferor or transferee, as may be appropriate, shall cause—*
>
> *(a)   a statement in writing containing the particulars specified in subparagraphs (a), (b) and (c) of paragraph (1) of this Regulation to be given in good time before the transfer is carried out to each employee in the business or undertaking, and*
>
> *(b)   notices containing the particulars aforesaid to be displayed prominently in good time before the transfer is carried out at positions in the workplaces of the employees where they can be read conveniently by the employees.'*

Regulation 7 may be summarised as providing the following:

(1)   An obligation to inform:

    (a)   The obligation lies on both the transferor and transferee.

    (b)   Both transferor and transferee must inform the employee representatives of the employees who are affected by the transfer.

    (c)   Where there are no employee representatives in either or both workforces the employer concerned must inform the employees directly.

    (d)   The information must cover the following:

        (i)   the reasons for the transfer;

        (ii)   the legal, economic and social implications of the transfer for the employees; and

        (iii)   the measures envisaged in relation to the employees.

    (e)   The information must be given in good time before the transfer is carried out but, in any event, before the employees are directly affected as regards their conditions of work and employment.

(2)   An obligation to consult:

    (a)   applies only where there are measures envisaged by either the transferor or the transferee in relation to his employees;

    (b)   the obligation is only to consult the representatives of employees;

    (c)   consultation must be in good time and relate to the measures envisaged; and

    (d)   consultation must be carried out 'with a view to seeking agreement'.

10.12.2   TIMING

Regulation 7(1) provides a joint liability on both the transferor and the transferee to 'inform' all employees of the matters referred to therein 'in good time' before the transfer. Regulation 7(2) provides that if measures are envisaged in relation to the employees then the transferor or the transferee, whichever is appropriate, shall consult with the employee representatives, again 'in good time', on such measures but, very importantly, must do so 'with a view to seeking agreement' as provided for in article 6(2) of the Directive. As to when information should be given, both the Directive and the Regulations differentiate as between the transferor and the transferee. The transferor is obliged to inform employee representatives 'in good time before the transfer is carried out', while the transferee must furnish the information, 'in good time, and in any event before his employees are directly affected by the transfer as regards their conditions of work and employment'.

Do these obligations crystallise when the transfer is a possibility or a probability? Does there have to be a legally binding agreement in place in order for the obligations to crystallise? If heads of agreement are signed, does the obligation crystallise, even though the heads of agreement are not legally binding and the transfer may never take place, as happened in *Dabell v Vale Industrial Services Ltd* [1988] IRLR 439? Some assistance can be derived from the decision of the UK High Court, in *Griffin v South West Water Services Ltd* [1995] IRLR 15. In that case, the court considered the EC Collective Redundancies Directive (75/129/EEC) (as amended). Article 2 of that Directive provides, in language which is almost identical to the language used in regulation 7 of the Irish Regulations:

> *'Where an employer is contemplating collective redundancies, he shall begin consultations with the workers' representatives in good time with a view to reaching an agreement.'*

The court, when considering the obligation to consult with workers' representatives, in that context, stated that

> 'The obligation to consult only arises when the employer's contemplation of redundancies has reached the point where he is able to identify the workers likely to be affected and can supply the information which the Article requires him to supply. Provided he does this in sufficient time to enable consultation to take place with the workers' representatives "with a view to reaching an agreement" (or, as it is put in the amended Article, "in good time with a view to reaching an agreement") I cannot see that the Article requires the employer to embark upon the process of consultation at any particular moment, much less as soon as he can be said to have in mind that collective redundancies may occur. The essential point, to my mind, is that the consultation must be one where, if they wish to do so, the workers' representatives can make constructive proposals and have time in which to do so before the relevant dismissal notices are sent out.'

It may be open to employers who have compelling reasons not to comply with regulation 7, and where those compelling reasons constitute emergency or force majeure, to seek a type of exemption afforded by the ECJ in the collective redundancies case of *Dansk Metalarbeijderforbund v Nielsen* [1985] ECR 553 as referred to at **6.16.9.4**. The Scottish EAT in *Association of Patternmakers and Allied Craftsmen v Kirvin Ltd* [1978] IRLR 318 considered a situation where the employer in the face of financial difficulties continued to trade in what was held to be 'the genuine and reasonable expectation that redundancies will be avoided' and in that case that was held to be a 'special circumstance' which absolved the employer from the obligation to inform and consult under the UK Employment Protection Act 1975. These cases, however, were cases where redundancies were forced on the employers by circumstances outside their control. It is hard to envisage a situation where a transfer could affect an employer so quickly and with a suddenness that would justify failure to inform and consult employees to be affected by the transfer. Employers may well have a dilemma where commercial confidentiality is essential; they inform and consult their employees at the first available opportunity but the transfer takes effect immediately or very soon thereafter.

10.12.3 NOTICES

The Irish Regulations provide a method of notifying employees directly where they do not have representatives. Regulation 7(3) requires the transferor and/or the transferee, as appropriate, to furnish each employee with written notices containing particulars, in terms of subparagraphs (a), (b) and (c) of regulation 7(1) and to display similar notices 'prominently' in the workplaces 'in good time before the transfer is carried out', in circumstances where there are no representatives of the employees.

10.12.4 INJUNCTIVE RELIEF

One of the most effective remedies for an employee is to obtain injunctive relief preventing any steps being taken in the transfer by either or both of the transferor and transferee until the employee's rights under regulation 7 are honoured. The question of injunctive relief as an effective remedy under the Collective Redundancies Directive was sought to be referred to the ECJ in *Griffin v South West Water Services Ltd* [1995] IRLR 15 but the Court of Appeal refused to refer questions to the ECJ when requested to do so by the union in that case.

Where an employer fails to comply with the requirements of regulation 7, it may be open to an employee or a representative union to obtain injunctive relief, preventing the implementation of the transfer, pending compliance with regulation 7. In the decision of Blayney J in *Maybury v Pump Services Ltd and Eldea Ltd* 2 May 1990, High Ct (unreported) the first-named defendant had encountered financial difficulties. The second-named defendant was a company specifically formed with the intention of purchasing the assets, business and goodwill of the first defendant. The plaintiff was advised by his employer, Pump Services Ltd, that his employment would not continue after the transfer, unless he was offered employment by the second-named defendant, the purchaser of the business. The second-named defendant was unable to give the plaintiff any assurances regarding the terms of continued employment or any indication of the implications of the transfer of the business for him personally. The plaintiff made an ex parte application to the High Court, seeking injunctive relief on the grounds that both defendants had failed to comply with regulation 7. The High Court made an interim order, restraining the first-named defendant from selling or completing the sale of the assets and goodwill of the business to the second-named defendant until further order. The case settled at the interlocutory stage without any further order.

Since then the UK High Court has refused to grant injunctive relief in *Betts v Brintel Helicopters Ltd; Betts v KLM ERA Helicopters (UK) Ltd* [1997] IRLR 361, which was based on an interpretation of the relevant UK regulations which specifically provide that the remedy for a breach of the relevant section referring to transfer of undertakings be by way of complaint to an industrial tribunal. The court refused the injunction in *Betts* on the basis that the remedy available to the employee was by way of complaint to an industrial tribunal. There are no remedies for employees provided for in the Irish Regulations. It is a matter for the State to impose the penalties provided for in the Regulations. Employees may plead the Regulations in seeking to enforce the rights created thereunder but there is no right to any remedy. Whatever about employees covered by unfair dismissal legislation, employees who are refused information or consultation and whose employer simply ignores regulation 7 cannot be left without any remedy, which would be the case were injunctive relief to be refused in all cases. The High Court in Ireland refused injunctive relief in *Hyland Shipping Agencies* 2 February 1996, High Ct (unreported) but not in a situation involving article 6 or regulation 7. Various reliefs were sought in *Hyland*, one of which was a mandatory injunction directing the defendants to comply with their obligations to inform and consult; however, at the time of the hearing the transfer had taken place and the judgment was therefore taken up with consideration of the failure to employ, or dismiss the plaintiffs consequent on the transfer. Seeking to injunct a dismissal is a considerably more complicated matter than seeking to injunct a transfer, at least until such time as information is furnished and/or consultation takes place. The courts might in time prove to be more amenable to regulation 7 injunctions given that employers are well placed to have the injunction removed by the relatively simple act of complying with the regulation and, in many cases, would be in a position to furnish an undertaking to this effect on the making of an injunction application.

It should also be remembered that no consultation, or inadequate consultation, in breach of regulation 7, may give rise to valid industrial action protected by the provision of the Industrial Relations Acts.

10.12.5 TRANSFER OF RESTRICTIVE COVENANTS

Given that the Directive and Regulations are clear in both article 3 and regulation 3 that the rights of a transferor arising from a contract of employment or from an employment relationship transfer to the transferee then it is to be expected that if restrictive covenants are otherwise effective in law the benefit of those restrictive covenants and contractual obligations must pass to the transferee. This is a comparatively rare situation in which an employer may seek to invoke the terms of the Directive and Regulations in its favour. The impact of the Directive on this area of employment law has yet to be considered in Ireland. In the UK case of *Morris Angel & Son Ltd v Hollande* [1993] IRLR 169, the Court of Appeal considered what happens to a clause prohibiting employees from soliciting the employer's customers, on the transfer of a business. In such circumstances, the transferor and the transferee inevitably will have different customer lists. There are two issues to be considered:

(1)   Does the restriction transfer automatically?

(2)   If it transfers what does it restrict? If, for example, a restriction applied to customers of the transferor it would appear that after the transfer, and provided the transferee has acquired the part of the business which still deals with those customers, the restriction will apply in respect of those customers. If, however, the employee has started to deal with customers of the transferee in his new employment can the restriction he had with the transferor be read as including the transferee's customers? It would seem logical and practical that it must do so but given the strict interpretation applied to restrictive covenants this is unlikely to be the case. The covenant is likely to be interpreted exactly as it was drafted with the transferor and only be effective in the context in which it was actually put in place.

In *Morris Angel & Son Ltd v Hollande* the Court of Appeal considered regulation 5(1) of the UK Regulations which provides:

'A relevant transfer shall not operate so as to terminate the contract of employment of any person employed by the transferor in the undertaking or part transferred but any such contract which would otherwise have been terminated by the transfer shall have effect after the transfer as if originally made between the person so employed and the transferee.'

The equivalent Irish regulation 3, as has been seen at **10.9.8.8** above provides:

'The rights and obligations of the transferor arising from a contract of employment or from an employment relationship existing on the date of a transfer shall, by reason of such transfer, be transferred to the transferee.'

The Court of Appeal, in overturning the earlier High Court decision, interpreted regulation 5(1) as having a retrospective effect, in the sense that it should be 'read as referring to the transferee as the owner of the undertaking transferred or in respect of the undertaking transferred'. The practical result, where the employee continues in the transferee's employment, is that, in most cases, the new owners will have to renegotiate restrictive covenants with the employees concerned. Otherwise, it appears that the scope of the prohibition could remain frozen as at the date of transfer, despite the employee's ongoing dealings with customers of the transferee. The alternative interpretation would give rise to a situation whereby an employee who, having joined a small company and having undertaken not to solicit that company's customers, could find himself in a position where a much larger entity takes over his company and, consequently, the prohibition on soliciting customers covers a much larger number of such customers. The court pointed out that such interpretation would:

'turn the obligation on the employee . . . into a quite different and possibly much wider obligation than the obligation which bound him before the transfer. . . . Such an obligation was not remotely in contemplation when the service agreement was entered into.'

The Court of Appeal would not allow the covenant to operate to cover the business of the transferee which had not been in contemplation or existence at the time the restriction was concluded with the transferor but did allow that the restriction would continue to apply post-transfer in relation to the clients of the transferor stating:

> 'The better construction is that the covenant can be enforced in respect of clients of the undertaking transferred of which Morris Angel Ltd are deemed as a result of the transfer retrospectively to have been the owner.'

The Court of Appeal held that restrictive covenants do transfer but only in certain circumstances and subject to certain qualifications.

10.12.6 EXTENT OF RESTRICTION

In *Morris Angel & Son Ltd v Hollande* [1993] IRLR 169 the restriction took effect after employment ended and restricted the employee for a period of one year after ceasing to be employed from directly or indirectly seeking to procure orders from or do business with 'any person, firm or company who has at any time during the one year immediately preceding such cesser done business with the group'. When the business transferred Mr Hollande was dismissed. The transferee then sought to enforce the restrictive covenant in respect, not only of persons, firms or companies Mr Hollande had done business with while employed by the transferors, but also sought to restrain him from doing or seeking to do business with anyone who had done business with the plaintiffs during the relevant period. That clearly was an extension of the obligation Hollande had entered into. But could an employee who remains in employment with the transferee seek to avoid the restriction continuing into his future employment with the transferee? It appears that this will largely depend on the wording of the restriction transferred. If somebody in Hollande's position, for example, worked for a period of six months with the transferee and then left employment could the transferee restrict him from doing business with everyone with whom he had dealt in the twelve months prior to the termination? This would include, in the example given, six months of the transferor's customers and six months of the customer base of the merged business of the transferor and the transferee. It is unlikely that a difficulty will arise if the post-transfer customer base is largely the same or similar to the pre-transfer base but if the transferee is a larger company and mixes the transferor's business with its own thereby giving the restriction much wider scope will it still be upheld? It is to be expected that the temporal, product and geographical restrictions on restrictive covenants will continue to apply but could the employee argue that at the time he agreed the original restriction he did not contemplate there being a transfer, and the consequent widening of its scope, thereby escaping its effects? That question remains to be answered. One answer would be to follow the line of the Court of Appeal in *Morris Angel v Hollande* and strike down the restriction as applying to the wider business on the grounds that it constituted 'an obligation . . . not remotely in contemplation when the service agreement was entered into' but upholding the general concept that such a covenant, indeed all contractual covenants, prima facie do transfer.

10.13 AUTOMATIC TRANSFER OF LIABILITIES

10.13.1 GENERALLY

The ECJ held in *Berg and Busschers v Besselsen* [1989] IRLR 447 that, in circumstances where Member States have not determined that the transferor and the transferee shall be severally liable after the transfer, article 3(1) must be interpreted as meaning that, after the date of a transfer, the transferor is, by virtue of the transfer alone, discharged from liability. In *Rotsart de Hertaing v J Benoidt SA (in liquidation)* [1997] IRLR 127 the ECJ held that there was an automatic transfer of obligations, independent of the actions of the parties, and that the transfer necessarily takes place on the date of the transfer and may not be postponed or altered at the instance of any of the parties. The ECJ held:

(1) Article 3(1) of the Directive is to be interpreted as meaning that the contracts of employment and employment relationships existing on the date of the transfer of an undertaking, between the transferor and the workers employed in the undertaking transferred, are automatically transferred from the transferor to the transferee by the mere fact of the transfer of the undertaking, despite the contrary intention of the transferor or transferee and despite the latter's refusal to fulfil his obligations.

(2) The transfer of the contracts of employment and employment relationships necessarily takes place on the date of the transfer of the undertaking and cannot be postponed to another date at the will of the transferor or transferee.

On the automatic transfer of liability to a transferee see also *Allan v Sterling District Council* [1995] IRLR 301 and *Ibex Trading Co Ltd v Walton* [1994] IRLR 564. While the Irish EAT did not made any specific comment on the automatic transfer of obligations to a transferee in *Gray v ISPCA David Prenderville and Dublin Corporation* [1994] ELR 225, the EAT held the ultimate transferee to be liable to the employees concerned. The decision in that case issued on 28 October 1994. The EAT in *Morris v Smart Brothers* UD 688/93 had earlier issued its judgment on 16 August 1994 and on the question of the transfer of liability expressed uncertainty as follows:

'Where employment is not continued after a transfer it remains therefore a vexed question whether the liability for a prohibited dismissal rests on the old employer who must inevitably dismiss (in the sense of terminating the contract of employment) on ceasing to carry on business or on the transferee who cannot dismiss (in the sense that he cannot terminate a contract that never began). And if "dismissal" under the Directive means not termination of a contract of employment but failure to offer a new contract is the old employer liable for the transferee's failure?'

10.13.2 BENEFITS TRANSFERRED

The extent of potential liabilities that may be the subject of a transfer is considerable and includes all contractual liabilities such as remuneration, holidays and other benefits including benefits-in-kind. In *O'Donovan v Ryanair Ltd and Servisair (Ireland) Ltd* [1997] ELR 63 the claimant claimed in respect of the loss of travel concessions when moving from the employment of Ryanair to Servisair. The EAT did not give any definitive views on whether or not travel concessions were transferred by the Directive/Regulations but did accept that the claimant had a grievance regarding the withdrawal of travel concessions. His claim failed on other grounds.

Neither the Directive nor the Regulations nor any of the existing case law deal with the problem posed to a transferee where the transferee is incapable of meeting all of the contractual terms and conditions existing on the date of transfer. If an airline carried out its own baggage handling and employed baggage handlers to do that work and those baggage handlers enjoyed travel concessions what would be the position if the baggage handling transferred to another independent company which was not an airline and could not provide, and did not have access to, travel concessions which it could confer on its employees? None of the existing case law answers such a troublesome question. If the line were to be taken that the liability to provide all benefits and benefits-in-kind transfer and the obligation to provide travel concessions transfers to the transferee is the transferee obliged to subsidise travel engaged in by its new employees?

If one employee never travels and another employee, on identical remuneration and doing identical work, travels at every opportunity is the transferee bound to incur considerable cost for one employee and not the other? If a transferor is a public company with a share option scheme and part of its business transfers to an individual or partnership is the individual or partnership transferee obliged to make share option benefits or the cash value of same available to the transferring employees? If there is such an obligation how is the value to be measured? Shares may go up in value or down in value: what is the transferee to do? These problems remain to be answered. There have not been any cases under the Directive and Regulations relating to share option schemes or similar benefits. The case law on share options tends to relate to the construction as to whether the option is contractual or discretionary and how such schemes should operate, as in *Thompson v Asda MFI Group plc* and *Micklefield v SAC Technology Ltd* [1988] IRLR 340 but the construction applied to the share option schemes in those cases, being a contractual construction, would not be the correct construction under the Directive which covers not just rights and obligations arising from a contract of employment but also 'from an employment relationship'. (See also *Inland Revenue Commissioners v Burton Group plc* The Times, 5 February 1990.)

10.14   PENSIONS

10.14.1   GENERAL EXCLUSION FOR PENSIONS

Article 3(3) of the Directive qualifies the general principle set out in article 3(1) and (2) that all rights and obligations arising from the contract of employment or the employment relationship shall transfer by providing:

> *'Paragraphs 1 and 2 shall not cover employees' rights to old-age, invalidity or survivors' benefits under supplementary company or inter-company pension schemes outside the statutory social security schemes in Member States.*

> *'Member States shall adopt the measures necessary to protect the interests of employees and of persons no longer employed in the transferor's business at the time of the transfer within the meaning of Article 1(1) in respect of rights conferring on them immediate or prospective entitlement to old-age benefits, including survivors' benefits under supplementary schemes referred to in the first subparagraph.'*

The first part of article 3(3) has been considered in a number of cases, the conclusion being reached that all rights and obligations arising from private or individual pension schemes are not covered by the Directive and there is no obligation on a transferee to continue them.

In *Adams v Lancashire County Council and BET Catering Services Ltd* [1997] IRLR 436 the UK Court of Appeal considered the provisions of the Directive in relation to pensions against the background of the domestic UK regulations implementing the terms of the Directive in light of the then relevant transfer of undertakings regulations in the UK. In relation to the Directive it was held that the exclusion of employees' rights to benefits under company pension schemes provided in article 3(3) was unlimited. The court held that there was no obligation on a transferee to continue a pension scheme, even having regard to the purpose of the Directive and the purposive approach required in interpretation of the provisions of the Directive and that the employees in the case were not entitled to comparable pension rights from a transferee as they had enjoyed while in the employment of the transferor prior to the transfer of the undertaking.

It was held, however, that the Directive required Member States to protect the interests of employees and ex-employees '*in respect of rights conferring on them immediate or prospective entitlement to old age benefits including survivors' benefits*'.

In the course of his judgment Morritt LJ stated (at p 441, para 26):

> '[T]he plaintiffs did not contend that there was a general obligation on an employer to set up and fund and thereafter at all times to maintain a pension scheme for the benefit

of its workforce. If there is no such general obligation in respect of the transferee's existing workforce then there seems to be no good reason to assume that it was intended that the transferee of the undertaking should be subjected to such an obligation in respect of those employees whose employment is transferred.'

10.14.2 ACCRUED PENSION RIGHTS UP TO DATE OF TRANSFER

The second limb of article 3(3), which obliges Member States to protect the interests of employees and former employees in respect of pension rights, was considered by the EAT in Britain in *Walden Engineering v Warrener* [1993] IRLR 420. Wood J stated (at p 422) that a proper reading of the second part of the article:

'indicates a duty on Member States to protect the interests which crystallise at the time of transfer in respect of the rights therein referred to. Unless so read, the wording would be in conflict with the clear words of [the earlier part of article 3(3)].'

In Ireland SI 306/1980 gives effect to article 3(3) of the Directive in regulation 4(2) by providing:

'Regulation 3 of these regulations and paragraph (1) of this Regulation shall not apply in relation to employees' rights to old-age, invalidity or survivors' benefits under supplementary company or inter-company pension schemes outside the Social Welfare Acts 1952–1979, but the transferee shall ensure that the interests of employees and of persons no longer employed in the transferor's business at the time of the transfer in respect of rights conferring on them immediate or prospective entitlement to old-age benefits including survivors' benefits under such supplementary company pension schemes are protected.'

This was the Irish government's method of implementing both the exclusion of pension schemes in the first part of article 3(3) of the Directive and, at the same time, adopting the measures required by the second part of article 3(3). None of the case law to date has focused on the use of the words in the Directive and the Regulations *'and of persons no longer employed in the transferor's business at the time of the transfer'*. Does this mean all persons subject to the transferor's pension scheme who may have retired or left service? If it does then there would appear to be a specific obligation on a transferee to effectively guarantee pensions to three categories of person:

(a) employees in the business of the transferor who are not transferred into the employment of the transferee in that regulation 4(2) refers to the 'interests of employees . . . in the transferor's business at the time of the transfer';

(b) employees who are subject to transfer and who do take up employment with the transferee; and

(c) anyone who had at any time worked for the transferor and who does or should enjoy an entitlement to pension rights or is actually in receipt of pension rights.

10.15 INSOLVENCY

The Regulations do not apply to the transfer of undertakings, businesses or parts of businesses which occur in the context of insolvency proceedings instituted with a view to the liquidation of the assets of the transferor (see *HBM Abels v Administrative Board of Bedrijfsvereniging Voor de Metaal-Industrie en de Electrotechnische Industrie* [1987] 2 CMLR 406). The Irish High Court has confirmed this view in *Re Castle Brand Ltd (in liquidation)* and *Re the Companies Acts, 1963 to 1983* 25 March 1995, Hamilton J (unreported). In *Abels* the transferor had been adjudged insolvent but the court did not elaborate to confirm whether or not the

Regulations applied to a voluntary winding-up. It appears that the Regulations could apply to a creditors' voluntary winding-up in that there is an element of enforced closure in such a case. In *Abels* the ECJ made it clear, however, that the Directive applies where a business is transferred to another employer in the course of semi-insolvency proceedings such as judicially sanctioned suspension of payments, or what is known in Europe as the 'surseance van betaling'. The surseance includes among its objectives the protection of a business with a view to ensuring its future. This appears to directly mirror a receivership in this jurisdiction to which it is clear that the Regulations apply. In the UK the regulations have been applied to receivers in a number of cases: see *Angus Jowett & Co v Tailors and Garment Workers Union* [1985] IRLR 326 and *Secretary of State for Employment v Spence* [1986] IRLR 248. The Directive would also apply where a court has appointed an examiner under the Companies (Amendment) Act, 1990. In *d'Urso v Ercole Marelli Elettromeccanica Generale SpA* [1992] IRLR 136 Ercole Marelli ('EMG') was placed under special administration which is governed under Italian law by specific provisions on urgent measures for the special administration of large undertakings in critical difficulties. In order to assist EMG in its difficulties a new company was formed and the bulk of the workforce was transferred into that new company. D'Urso and his fellow claimants did not transfer. They claimed that there had been a transfer of undertaking within the meaning of the Directive. The ECJ and Advocate-General Van Gerven referred to *Abels* and stated that the Directive did not apply to transfers effected in bankruptcy proceedings designed to liquidate the transferor's assets under the supervision of a competent judicial authority. The bankruptcy proceedings in *Abels* under Dutch law, being the surseance or suspension of payments, was compared with the procedure applied to EMG under Italian law. In examining the applicable Italian law the ECJ had regard to the fact that the law was sufficiently wide to allow for different actions to be taken depending on the sort of difficulties encountered by the company concerned. In certain situations of irretrievable difficulties there is a compulsory liquidation but in others a restructuring and a provision of assistance to rescue the company. The ECJ held that article 1(1) of the Directive:

'does not apply to transfers of undertakings made as part of a creditors' arrangement procedure of the kind provided for in the Italian legislation on compulsory administrative liquidation . . . on special administration for large undertakings in critical difficulties. However that provision of that Directive does apply when in accordance with a body of legislation such as that governing special administration for large undertakings in critical difficulties it has been decided that the undertaking is to continue trading for as long as that decision remains in force.'

The EAT in Ireland has taken the view that a voluntary liquidation does not come within the exclusion of insolvent undertakings from the terms of the Directive and Regulations. In *Kelly v Cavanagh Hiester Ltd (in liquidation) and Dubshad Ltd* UD 222–224/96 the EAT held inter alia:

'As the liquidation of Hiester Ltd was a voluntary liquidation the Tribunal holds that the . . . Regulations SI 306/1980 apply and in this instance there was a transfer of the business to Mr Brian Cavanagh when Hiester Ltd went into liquidation. Accordingly there was no break in the claimant's service.'

The High Court in *Mythen v Employment Appeals Tribunal* considered the scope of the *Abels* decision and, while not making a definitive statement, did indicate that *Abels* would be restricted to a sale by a liquidator when holding (at p 2):

'It could not be assumed that because the Court of Justice of the European Communities had held that the Directive does not apply to a sale by a liquidator, it would also hold that the Directive would not apply to a sale by a receiver appointed by a debenture holder—*Abels* considered.'

In *Mythen* Barrington J analysed the views of Advocate-General Sir Gordon Slynn and the reasoning of the ECJ in *Abels* and appeared to take the view that the *Abels* principle could only apply in an enforced liquidation of a bankrupt company and stated (at p 10):

'It follows that the reasons for not applying the directive to transfers of undertakings taking place in liquidation proceedings are not applicable to proceedings of this kind taking place at an earlier stage.'

See also the ECJ decision in *Dethier v Dassy and Sovam SPRL (in liquidation)* 12 March 1998 (unreported).

10.16 DUE DILIGENCE

10.16.1 INTRODUCTION

Having formed the preliminary intention to transfer the undertaking the transferor and transferee must at an early stage have regard to their obligations under article 6 and regulation 7 and carry out detailed preparatory work to ascertain the full nature and extent of the obligations arising under the Directive and Regulations consequent on the proposed transfer.

The sort of practical difficulties that may arise in the sale of a business and transfer of employees are indicated by the case of *Walsh and Cotter v Demford Taverns Ltd and Bowler* UD 436/437/97. Demford Taverns ran a pub which they agreed to sell to John Bowler. The claimants were barmen employed by Demford. After the sale the claimants reported for work with Mr Bowler who told them that they would have to apply for any jobs that might be available. Mr Bowler believed that the employees were the responsibility of Demford as they were their employees and believed that Demford had 'taken care' of them. The claimants sued both the transferor, Demford, and the transferee, Bowler, for unfair dismissal. Mr Bowler argued that the business he had purchased and was operating was very different from the business that had been carried out by Demford prior to the sale because he had modernised it, refurbished the building and was carrying it out in a very different fashion. The EAT, however, held that the identity of the business was still the same and had not changed as a result of the transfer. It was still a pub serving both food and drink and running a late-night bar in a similar fashion to its operation by Demford Taverns. The EAT accordingly held that there had been a transfer of undertaking within the meaning of the Directive and Regulations and that the claimants should succeed in their claim.

Some suggested steps to be followed in order to assist with complying with the obligations under the Directive and Regulations and to ensure that the transferee is fully informed and in a position to deal with all eventualities that may arise are set out below.

10.16.2 PRELIMINARY PERSONNEL AUDIT

A comprehensive audit of the target business should be carried out at an early stage, *prior* to the due diligence process, and a listing of the transferring employees should be made, with as much consideration as possible given individually to each of the employees concerned, as regards his/her future in the new entity. Where it is not possible to plan for individual employees or specific numbers a general assessment of manpower requirements must be carried out.

A similar audit of the transferee's business should be carried out in order to see whether there will be duplication of function, as the addition of the 'new' employees may impact on the purchaser's own staff.

This exercise will assist the transferee to put a shape on the appearance of the new entity into the future and should allow generation of enough information and plans to allow compliance with regulation 7. In complying with regulation 7, it is advisable to inform the employees and/or their representatives that due diligence has not been carried out and while a comprehensive and open account of the plans is being given, the parties must reserve their position, in the event that they feel that other changes are commercially necessary, but that such changes will be notified as soon as is practicable.

10.16.3 THE DUE DILIGENCE PROCESS

Legal and financial advisers will play a significant role with their clients in the due diligence process itself, and it is incumbent on them to obtain from their opposite number, or the transferor directly, as much necessary information as possible. Where queries are raised and answered, the transferee will have secured representations from the transferor, which may be relied on in the future, in the event of difficulties arising. Failure to raise the queries may fix the transferee with additional liability or cause confusion, where liability cannot be established, at a later stage. The nature of the business will dictate the type of employee requisitions raised. The general structure will be the same in most cases, but the specific level of detail will vary, depending on the nature of the business. Businesses with highly skilled employees of a technical or professional nature, will require more in-depth enquiry than might otherwise be the case.

The transferee should seek confirmation that the transferor has complied with his obligations under regulation 7.

10.16.4 TRADE UNIONS

While trade union involvement in the undertaking may be dealt with in the queries raised regarding each individual employee, it is better to categorise union affairs on a separate basis. Most unionised companies have various agreements with trade unions and tend to keep this sort of information on separate files, which must be opened to the purchasers. Queries should be raised as to meetings held with the trade unions in the months, and indeed years, prior to the transfer, in order to establish the type of issues that tend to be raised by the unions. It might be the case that individual employees have contractual obligations, and answers given to queries in that context might indicate that the employees perform those obligations without difficulty. However, if it transpired that the unions had been making various claims, prior to the transfer, to have the situation changed, it is most important that a transferee be on notice of that fact. It could have a significant effect on the manner in which the work is done and the cost of having it done. In particular, where a target undertaking is in some difficulty, trade unions may have gone quiet, immediately prior to the transfer, not wishing to rock the boat. The arrival of a potential transferee who is bigger and wealthier, may lead to the resurrection of claims which had been thought to have disappeared. There are loose traditions in certain industries and services that an employer who sells out gives the employees who remain some form of 'bonus'. That has to be anticipated, where at all possible, and steps taken to ensure that the purchaser does not, unknowingly, become liable for such payments or unwittingly purchase the business, without an indemnity against any such claim being made.

10.16.5 INDEMNITIES AND WARRANTIES

The actual nature of indemnities and warranties sought and obtained will vary from case to case. While it is easy to advise that indemnities and warranties be obtained, in practice, they can be very difficult to secure. Where they are secured, it is vitally important to ensure that the wording is correct. A transferee might be indemnified against any award that might be made to an employee, but may not be indemnified against the legal costs of having to defend themselves. Where, for example, there are redundancies to be effected as a result of the transfer and given that the ETO defence is likely to be more available to the transferee than the transferor it being the reasons of the transferee that have given rise to termination, the question of meeting the cost of redundancy payments, both statutory and ex gratia, will have to be considered. In practice it is more likely that the transferee will have to carry such cost and it may require to provide for the cost in consideration paid to the transferor, if any. It may not be possible to measure the full extent of such costs at the time of transfer and therefore some form of indemnity will usually be sought from the transferor. The transferor, on the other hand, will not wish to furnish an open-ended indemnity and allow the transferee to spend his money at will so the nature, extent and effectiveness of these indemnities and warranties will usually fall to negotiations between the parties. Having followed the above steps the parties and, in particular, the transferee will be better able to assess what is required by way of indemnity and warranty.

10.16.6 SOCIAL PLAN

Having followed the above steps the transferee may need to prepare a social plan, particularly where there are measures envisaged that may impact negatively on employees, either those transferred or those not being transferred or, in certain circumstances, the existing workforce of the transferee. The type of social plan to be drawn up should be similar to that required in the case of collective redundancies as provided for in the Protection of Employment Order, 1996 (SI 370/1996).

10.16.7 INSURANCE

It is essential that a transferee carry out a comprehensive review of its existing insurance arrangements and what insurance may be required in the future consequent on the transfer of the responsibilities and liabilities created by the Directive and Regulations. With the transfer of all tort liabilities to a new workforce the transferee's existing insurance arrangements may not allow for the addition of such persons under insurance cover and may indeed, in certain circumstances, exclude them. The transferee should therefore ensure that its insurance arrangements are such as to meet all liabilities arising consequent on the transfer taking place.

10.16.8 ENFORCEMENT OF AND REMEDIES UNDER SI 306/1980

Regulation 8 of the Irish Regulations provides that an officer of the Minister who is of the opinion that a transaction constitutes a transfer may request the parties to furnish him with such information as he requires for the purpose of determining whether the transaction does constitute a transfer and also to make available to him books and documents for inspection and where appropriate copying. Regulation 8(1) also provides that the officer:

> 'for the purpose of his functions under this regulation . . . may at all reasonable times enter any place where there are kept books or documents to which a request by him under this regulation relates.'

Regulation 9 provides that any person who contravenes any provision of the Regulations shall be guilty of an offence and shall be liable 'on summary conviction' to a fine not exceeding £500. The breach of regulation 8 attracts a fine on summary conviction not exceeding £300, per regulation 9(1)(b). The time limit for bringing proceedings for breach of regulations is twelve months from the date of the offence as per regulation 9(3).

Regulation 10, which is the last of the Regulations, provides that where an offence is committed by a body corporate and the offence is proved to have been committed with the consent or approval, or have been facilitated by any neglect on the part of any person who was a director or member of the committee of management or other controlling authority that person shall be deemed to have committed an offence under the Regulations.

The Regulations do not provide any remedies for employees, either individually or collectively, or trade unions whose rights under the Directive and Regulations may be disregarded. The European Commission has taken proceedings against the UK for not having effective remedies for employees in respect of breaches of transfer of undertakings law and regulations and collective redundancies laws and regulations in *Commission v United Kingdom* (Case C-382/1992) [1994] IRLR 392 in respect of the former and Case C-383/1992 in respect of the latter. The ECJ held that truly deterrent penalties would have to be provided in order to give proper effect to the respective Directives. Ireland has not introduced any effective remedies for employees or their representatives in respect of breach of the Directive and Regulations. The Regulations themselves are clearly inadequate in this regard. While injunctive relief remains a possibility it is not ideal in all situations and can be quite cumbersome in others.

10.16.9 PROPOSALS FOR REFORM

In December 1997 a Private Member's Bill was initiated by Labour Party Deputy, Tommy Broughan, seeking to provide remedies for employees where their rights have not been honoured under collective redundancy legislation and the transfer of undertakings regulations. The regulations, if made law, would constitute a very considerable advance on the total absence of remedy at present. The Bill, however, lacks subtlety and, in seeking to have all disputes referred initially to a rights commissioner, under-estimates the complexity and importance of such disputes and, in particular, does not allow for the proper enforcement of the information and consultation provisions, but rather provides penalties for their breach. The following are the main provisions of the Bill:

(1) Any dispute arising in respect of collective redundancy or transfer of undertakings law may be referred to a rights commissioner within six months of the date on which the event complained of occurred. In exceptional circumstances the rights commissioner may extend that period to twelve months.

(2) Hearings before a rights commissioner shall be in private.

(3) Appeal from a decision of a rights commissioner lies to the EAT to be made within four weeks of the date of notification of the rights commissioner's decision.

(4) There are no provisions for witnesses to appear before a rights commissioner but witnesses who appear before the EAT on appeal have immunities and privileges as apply to witnesses in the High Court.

(5) Appeal beyond the EAT is only to the High Court on a point of law.

(6) Redress available under the Bill consists of reinstatement, re-engagement or an award of 'compensation' such as is deemed to be just and equitable to a maximum of the equivalent of 104 weeks' remuneration of the employee concerned. It should be noted that the proposal is for compensation not damages. If a transferor or transferee fails to inform or consult in advance of a transfer but the employee does not suffer any loss there is no effective redress available.

(7) The rights commissioner or EAT may also provide in their decision or determination that such 'other steps' as they specify in their decision should be taken 'by the relevant employer'. This could cover the information and consultation provisions; however, with the immediacy of the time scale of most transfers it would appear unlikely that this remedy could be made available in time to make the information and consultation process effective. The rights commissioner and the EAT do not have the status of the civil courts and even if they were to order a transferor or transferee or both to take specific steps there is no effective method of ensuring that

they do so other than to refer the matter to the Circuit Court as is provided in clause 7 of the Bill. This again emphasises the lack of an immediate and effective remedy in respect of information and consultation if it is the case that the employees may have to go through three stages before they get an effective order. Clause 7 does allow a reference of the failure of an employer to carry out the terms of a decision of a rights commissioner to be made directly to the Circuit Court but only when a period of four weeks has elapsed from the notification of the decision.

(8)   The penalties in regulation 9 of £500 and £300 are both proposed to be increased to £1,500. In addition, imprisonment for not less than six months, possibly in addition to the financial penalty, is also provided for.

(9)   The Regulations adopt the definition of employer and employee contained in the Maternity Protection Act, 1994 which as has been seen at **1.2.6.3**, contains the definition of 'deemed employer' in making reference to the Employment Agency Act, 1971. Quite how the Bill proposes to impose that definition on the Regulations is unclear. Is it intended that references to 'employer' and 'employee' in the Regulations are now to be amended to include 'deemed employer' and 'deemed employee'? That would be a substantial amendment of the original regulations unrelated to the issue of redress sought to be addressed by the Bill. It is also doubtful whether the Bill as drafted could achieve that aim. In any event the Regulations use the term 'transferor' and 'transferee' rather than employer and the word employee only appears in a few places within the regulations. The reference in the Bill to the Maternity Protection Act definitions does therefore appear to be unworkable and to make little sense. There have been problems since 1980 in deciphering what the Regulations mean and it would do nothing to assist the position if new legislation is to be enacted superimposing terms or definitions on the Regulations where they do not fit easily into the existing wording.

10.17 APPENDIX: DIRECTIVE 98/50/EC

EC Council Directive 98/50/EC of 29 June 1998 amending Directive 77/187/EEC on the approximation of the laws of the Member States relating to the safeguarding of employees' rights in the event of transfers of undertakings, businesses or parts of businesses.

'THE COUNCIL OF THE EUROPEAN UNION

'Having regard to the Treaty establishing the European Community, and in particular Article 100 thereof,

'Having regard to the proposal from the Commission,

'Having regard to the opinion of the European Parliament,

'Having regard to the opinion of the Economic and Social Committee,

'Having regard to the opinion of the Committee of the Regions,

'(1) Whereas the Community Charter of the fundamental social rights of workers adopted on 9 December 1989 ("Social Charter") states, in points 7, 17 and 18 in particular that: "The completion of the internal market must lead to an improvement in the living and working conditions of workers in the European Community. The improvement must cover, where necessary, the development of certain aspects of employment regulations such as procedures for collective redundancies and those regarding bankruptcies. Information, consultation and participation for workers must be developed along appropriate lines, taking account of the practices in force in the various Member States. Such information, consultation and participation must be implemented in due time, particularly in connection with restructuring operations in undertakings or in cases of mergers having an impact on the employment of workers;

'(2) Whereas Directive 77/187/EEC promotes the harmonisation of the relevant national laws ensuring the safeguarding of the rights of employees and requiring transferors and transferees to inform and consult employees' representatives in good time;

'(3) Whereas the purpose of this Directive is to amend Directive 77/187/EEC in the light of the impact of the internal market, the legislative tendencies of the Member States with regard to the rescue of undertakings in economic difficulties, the case law of the Court of Justice of the European Communities, Council Directive 75/129/EEC of 17 February 1975 on the approximation of the laws of the Member States relating to collective redundancies and the legislation already in force in most Member States;

'(4) Whereas considerations of legal security and transparency require that the legal concept of transfer be clarified in the light of the case law of the Court of Justice; whereas such clarification does not alter the scope of Directive 77/187/EEC as interpreted by the Court of Justice;

'(5) Whereas those considerations also require an express provision, in the light of the case-law of the Court of Justice, that Directive 77/187/EEC should apply to private and public undertakings carrying out economic activities, whether or not they operate for gain;

'(6) Whereas it is necessary to clarify the concept of "employee" in the light of the case law of the Court of Justice;

'(7) Whereas, with a view to ensuring the survival of insolvent undertakings, Member States should be expressly allowed not to apply Articles 3 and 4 of Directive 77/187/EEC to transfers effected in the framework of liquidation proceedings, and certain derogations from that Directive's general provisions should be permitted in the case of transfers effected in the context of insolvency proceedings;

'(8) Whereas such derogations should also be allowed for one Member State which has special procedures to promote the survival of companies declared to be in a state of economic crisis;

'(9) Whereas the circumstances in which the function and status of employee representatives are to be preserved should be clarified;

(10) Whereas, in order to ensure equal treatment for similar situations, it is necessary to ensure that the information and consultation requirements laid down in Directive 77/187/EEC are complied with irrespective of whether the decision leading to the transfer is taken by the employer or by an undertaking controlling the employer,

(11) Whereas it is appropriate to clarify that, when Member States adopt measures to ensure that the transferee is informed of all the rights and obligations to be transferred, failure to provide that information is not to affect the transfer of the rights and obligations concerned;

(12) Whereas it is necessary to clarify the circumstances in which employees must be informed where there are no employee representatives;

(13) Whereas the Social Charter recognises the importance of the fight against all forms of discrimination, especially based on sex, colour, race, opinion and creed,

HAS ADOPTED THIS DIRECTIVE.

Article 1

Directive 77/187/EEC is hereby amended as follows:

1. *The title shall be replaced by the following:*

   "Council Directive 77/187/EEC of 14 February 1977 on the approximation of the laws of the Member States relating to the safeguarding of employees' rights in the event of transfers of undertakings, businesses or parts of undertakings or businesses";

2. *Articles 1 to 7 shall be replaced by the following:*

   "SECTION 1: SCOPE AND DEFINITIONS

   Article 1

   1(a) This Directive shall apply to any transfer of an undertaking, business, or part of an undertaking or business to another employer as a result of a legal transfer or merger."'

Transfer. Article 1 of the Directive requires that there be a transfer of some nature, of the whole or part of an undertaking. The rights, duties and obligations governed by the Directive crystallise, or are triggered by, the occurrence of a transfer.

Transfer of part of an undertaking. Article 1(1) of the Directive provides that it shall apply not just to the transfer of an undertaking or business but to the transfer of part of an undertaking or business. Where part of a business is an economic entity in itself, that part may be easily identifiable as the subject matter of a transfer of part of a business. Difficulties can arise where the part sold off or transferred was not a readily identifiable economic entity prior to the transfer as it depended for its existence on being part of a larger economic entity. Difficulty may arise in identifying the transferor and whether particular employees are employed in the part of the business transferred. In *Michael Peters Ltd v Farnfield and Michael Peters Group plc* [1995] IRLR 190 Mr Farnfield was chief executive of the Michael Peters Group plc, a holding company for some twenty-five subsidiaries. When the parent company and its subsidiaries went into receivership and four subsidiaries were sold off, the parent company was not a party to the sale agreement. It was held, however, by an industrial tribunal that Mr Farnfield's employment transfer was on the basis that in reality the four subsidiary companies, together with that part of the parent company's assets belonging to those companies, formed part of a 'single economic unit'. Part of the parent company was transferred and Mr Farnfield was protected because he was employed by the transferor of the business. The EAT, however, overruled the industrial tribunal, holding that it was inappropriate to apply a concept of a 'single economic unit', that the transferors were not the parent company, and that Mr Farnfield was not therefore an employee of the transferor. In *Sunley Turriff Holdings Ltd v Thomson* [1995] IRLR 184 there was a detailed analysis of the particular transfer concerned and it was decided that the part of the business in relation to which Thomson was employed by the transferor was actually transferred, and therefore the Directive/Regulations applied. The twist in this case was that Thomson continued to work for the transferor after the transfer. He was not designated as one of the employees transferred and continued to work for a receiver for some two months after the transfer until he was dismissed. The EAT held that a mistaken belief of the employee cannot defeat the principle of automatic transfer under the Directive/Regulations. The contract transferred as a matter of law and there was no actual dismissal by the transferees or resignation from their employment.

In *Botzen v Rotterdamsche Droogdok Maatschappij BV* [1985] ECR 519 the ECJ considered a situation where Mr Botzen and his seven co-plaintiffs were assigned to parts of a business which were not the subject matter of transfer. One of the questions addressed to the court was:

> 'Does the scope of the Directive also extend to the rights conferred upon and the obligations imposed upon the transferor by contracts of employment which exist at the date of transfer and which are made with employees whose duties are not performed exclusively with the aid of assets which belong to the transferred part of the under-taking?'

Advocate-General Slynn dealt with the transfer of a part of an undertaking in *Botzen* as follows:

> 'I do not consider that it is necessary or desirable in this case to seek to define comprehensively what is part of a business. That is largely a question of fact though it will usually involve the transfer of a department or factory or facet of the business. It may perhaps also involve the sale of a fraction of a single unit of business. Once it is decided as a fact that part of the business is transferred then those workers who during their working hours are wholly engaged in that part are entitled to rely on the terms of the Directive. It will of course cover the full-time and part-time workers. A basic working test, it seems to me, is to ask whether, if that part of the business had been separately owned before the transfer the worker would have been employed by the owners of that part over the owners of the remaining part. The only exception I would admit to the requirement that an employee must be "wholly" engaged in that part of the business would be where an employee was required to perform other duties to an extent which could fairly be described as *de minimis*. On the other hand if a worker in fact is engaged in the activities of the whole business or in several parts then he cannot be regarded for the purpose of the Directive as an employee of the part of the business transferred.'

The decision of the full court in *Botzen* is not particularly helpful in that the court held that the test to be applied was whether or not there had been a transfer of the part of the business for which the employee was 'assigned and which formed the organisational framework within which their employment relationship took effect'.

> ' "1(b)   *Subject to sub-paragraph (a) and the following provisions of this Article, there is a transfer within the meaning of this Directive where there is a transfer of an economic entity which retains its identity, meaning an organised grouping of resources which has the objective of pursuing an economic activity, whether or not that activity is central or ancillary."*

Undertakings. The Directive and Regulations apply only to the transfer of an 'undertaking'. There is no definition given of the term 'undertaking' in the Directive or the Regulations nor is there any definition given in any of the EU Treaties. The term is, however, used in article 85 of the EC Treaty which deals with competition law and provides:

> *'The following shall be prohibited as incompatible with the common market: all agreements between undertakings, decisions by associations of undertakings and concerted practices which may effect trade between Member States and which have as their object or effect the prevention, restriction or distortion of competition within the common market'.*

In considering the scope and extent of article 85 the ECJ held in *Hofner & Elsner v Macrotron* [1993] 4 CMLR 306:

> 'It must be observed, in the context of competition law, first that the concept of an undertaking encompasses every entity engaged in economic activity, regardless of the

legal status of the entity and the way in which it is financed and, secondly that employment procurement is an economic activity.'

> ' ''1(c)   This Directive shall apply to public and private undertakings engaged in economic activities whether or not they are operating for gain. An administrative reorganisation of public administrative authorities, or the transfer of administrative functions between public administrative authorities, is not a transfer within the meaning of this Directive.''

In *Henke v Gemeinde Schierke & Verwaltungsgemeinschaft, 'Brocken'* [1995] IRLR 6 the ECJ examined a situation where a public administrative entity, the municipality of Schierke, was transferred to a new local government body and the municipal administration of Schierke was dissolved. Ms Henke was secretary to the mayor of Schierke. One of the matters that arose for consideration in the case was whether or not Ms Henke and people like her, who were employees of a public body, came within the scope of the term 'employee' as used in the Directive. In the course of his opinion Advocate-General Lenz considered submissions made by the German government that a local authority was not an undertaking within the meaning of the Directive. The Advocate-General stated: 'It is not contested ... that a Municipality can generally carry out economic activities'. He went on to refer to a number of areas of normal economic activity engaged in by local authorities and said that:

> 'even if exercise of an economic activity were to be regarded as a pre-condition for the application of the Directive a municipality could definitely be treated as being an undertaking within the meaning of the Directive. It is therefore questionable whether the municipality and its employees should be excluded from the scope of application of the Directive simply because the municipality also acts in the exercise of powers of a public authority.'

> ' ''1.2   This Directive shall apply where and insofar as the undertaking, business or part of the undertaking or business to be transferred is situated within the territorial scope of the Treaty.
>
> 1.3   This Directive shall not apply to sea-going vessels.

Article 2

> 1.   For the purposes of this Directive:
>
> (a)   'transferor' shall mean any natural or legal person who, by reason of transfer within the meaning of Article 1(1) ceases to be the employer in respect of the undertaking, business or part of the undertaking or business;
>
> (b)   'transferee' shall mean any natural or legal person who, by reason of transfer within the meaning of Article 1(1), becomes the employer in respect of the undertaking, business or part of the undertaking or business;
>
> (c)   'representatives of employees' and related expressions shall mean the representatives of the employed provided for by the laws or practices of the Member States;
>
> (d)   'employee' shall mean any person who, in the Member State concerned, is protected as an employee under national employment law.
>
> 2.   This Directive shall not be without prejudice to national law as regards the definition of contract of employment or employment relationship. However, Member States shall not exclude from the scope of this Directive contracts of employment or employment relationships solely because:
>
> (a)   of the number of working hours performed or to be performed,
>
> (b)   they are employment relationships governed by a fixed-duration contract of employment within the meaning of Article 1(1) of Council Directive 91/383/EEC of 25 June 1991 supplementing the measures to encourage improvements in the safety and health at work of workers with a fixed-duration employment relationship or a temporary employment relationship or
>
> (c)   they are temporary employment relationships within the meaning of Article 1(2) of

Directive 91/383/EEC, and the undertaking, business or part of the undertaking or business transferred is, or is part of, the temporary employment business which is the employer.

SECTION II. SAFEGUARDING OF EMPLOYEES' RIGHTS

Article 3

1. *The transferor's rights and obligations arising from a contract of employment or from an employment relationship existing on the date of a transfer shall, by reason of such transfer, be transferred to the transferee. Member States may provide that, after the date of transfer, the transferor and the transferee shall be jointly and severally liable in respect of obligations which arose before the date of transfer from a contract of employment or an employment relationship existing on the date of the transfer.*

2. *Member States may adopt appropriate measures to ensure that the transferor notifies the transferee of all the rights and obligations which will be transferred to the transferee under this Article, so far as those rights and obligations are or ought to have been known to the transferor at the time of the transfer. A failure by the transferor to notify the transferee of any such right or obligation shall not affect the transfer of that right or obligation and the rights of any employees against the transferee and/or transferor in respect of that right or obligation.''*

What transfers? While liability automatically transfers to a transferee when there has been a transfer of an undertaking, one of the biggest problems for a transferee has been ascertaining or measuring the exact extent of the liabilities transferring. While in normal commercial transactions it is possible to raise requisitions, seek indemnities and warranties etc, in many transactions, particularly those where a transfer takes place effectively by operation of law, such as the reversion of a lease, the transferee has no negotiating or commercial power to require that information be given to him. This has led to considerable difficulties for transferees who have taken over employees without knowing the full extent of liabilities transferring with them. It is to be hoped that the Irish government will exercise the option provided for in this sub-article and enact appropriate regulations to oblige transferors to furnish all information to a transferee. The provision emphasises that even in the event of the failure by a transferor to comply with any regulation made thereunder this cannot affect the position of the employees but is simply a matter between transferor and transferee.

' ''3. *Following the transfer, the transferee shall continue to observe the terms and conditions agreed in any collective agreement on the same terms applicable to the transferor under that agreement, until the date of termination or expiry of the collective agreement or the entry into force or application of another collective agreement. Member States may limit the period for observing such terms and conditions with the proviso that it shall not be less than one year.*

4 (a) *Unless Member States provide otherwise, paragraphs 1 and 3 shall not apply in relation to employees' rights to old-age, invalidity or survivors' benefits under supplemental company or inter-company pension schemes outside the statutory social security schemes in Member States.*

(b) *Even where they do not provide in accordance with subparagraph (a) that paragraphs 1 and 3 apply in relation to such rights, Member States shall adopt the measures necessary to protect the interests of employees and of persons no longer employed in the transferor's business at the time of the transfer in respect of rights conferring on them immediate or prospective entitlement to old age benefits, including survivors' benefits, under supplementary schemes referred to in subparagraph (a).'' '*

While article 3(4) is new it reflects the similar provision in article 3(3) of the original Directive.

' ''**Article 4**

1. *The transfer of the undertaking, business or part of the undertaking or business shall not in itself constitute grounds for dismissal by the transferor or the transferee. This*

provision shall not stand in the way of dismissals that may take place for economic, technical or organisational reasons entailing changes in the workforce.

Member States may provide that the first subparagraph shall not apply to certain specific categories of employees who are not covered by the laws or practice of the Member States in respect of protection against dismissal.

2. *If the contract of employment or the employment relationship is terminated because the transfer involves a substantial change in working conditions to the detriment of the employee, the employer shall be regarded as having been responsible for termination of the contract of employment or of the employment relationship.*

Article 4a

1. *Unless Member States provide otherwise, Articles 3 and 4 shall not apply to any transfer of an undertaking, business or part of an undertaking or business where the transferor is the subject of bankruptcy proceedings or any analogous insolvency proceedings which have been instituted with a view to the liquidation of the assets of the transferor and are under the supervision of a competent public authority (which may be an insolvency practitioner authorised by a competent public authority).*

2. *Where Articles 3 and 4 apply to a transfer during insolvency proceedings which have been opened in relation to a transferor (whether or not those proceedings have been instituted with a view to the liquidation of the assets of the transferor) and provided that such proceedings are under the supervision of a competent public authority (which may be an insolvency practitioner determined by national law) a Member State may provide that:*

(a) *notwithstanding Article 3(1), the transferor's debts arising from any contracts of employment or employment relationships and payable before the transfer or before the opening of the insolvency proceedings shall not be transferred to the transferee, provided that such proceedings give rise, under the law of that Member State, to protection at least equivalent to that provided for in situations covered by Council Directive 80/987/EEC of 20 October 1980 on the approximation of the laws of the Member States relating to the protection of employees in the event of the insolvency of their employer;*
and, or alternatively, that

(b) *the transferee, transferor, or person or persons exercising the transferor's functions, on the one hand, and the representatives of the employees on the other hand may agree alterations, insofar as current law or practice permits, to the employees' terms and conditions of employment designed to safeguard employment opportunities by ensuring the survival of the undertaking, business or part of the undertaking or business.*

3. *A Member State may apply paragraph 2(b) to any transfers where the transferor is in a situation of serious economic crisis, as defined by national law, provided that the situation is declared by a competent public authority and open to judicial supervision, on condition that such provisions already exist in national law by 17 July 1998.*
The Commission shall present a report on the effects of this provision before 17 July 2003 and shall submit any appropriate proposals to the Council.

4. *Member States shall take appropriate measures with a view to preventing misuse of insolvency proceedings in such a way as to deprive employees of the rights provided for in this Directive.'' '*

The High Court in *Mythen v Employment Appeals Tribunal* [1990] ELR 1 considered the scope of the decision in *HBM Abels v Administrative Board of Bedrijfsvereniging voor de Metaal-Industrie* [1987] 2 CMLR 406 and, while not making a definitive statement, did indicate that *Abels* would be restricted to a sale by a liquidator when holding:

'It could not be assumed that because the Court of Justice of the European Communities had held that the Directive does not apply to a sale by a liquidator, it would also hold that the Directive would not apply to a sale by a receiver appointed by a debenture holder—*Abels* considered.'

This new and expanded article gives Member States more flexibility to deal with the various types of insolvency procedures and protections in their jurisdiction provided the various safeguards set out in the article are met.

'"*Article 5*

1. *If the undertaking, business or part of an undertaking or business preserves its autonomy, the status and function of the representatives or of the representation of the employees affected by the transfer shall be presented on the same terms and subject to the same conditions as existed before the date of the transfer by virtue of law, regulation, administrative provision or agreement, provided that the conditions necessary for the constitution of the employees' representation are fulfilled.*

   The first sub-paragraph shall not apply if, under the laws, regulations, administrative provisions or practice in the Member States, or by agreement with the representatives of the employees, the conditions necessary for the reappointment of the representatives of the employees or for the reconstitution of the representation of the employees are fulfilled.

   Where the transferor is the subject of bankruptcy proceedings or any analogous insolvency proceedings which have been instituted with a view to the liquidation of the assets of the transferor and are under the supervision of a competent public authority (which may be an insolvent practitioner authorised by a competent public authority), Member States may take the necessary measures to ensure that the transferred employees are properly represented until the new election or designation of representatives of the employees. If the undertaking, business or part of an undertaking or business does not preserve its autonomy, the Member States shall take the necessary measures to ensure that the employees transferred who were represented before the transfer continue to be properly represented during the period necessary for the reconstitution or reappointment of the representation of employees in accordance with national law or practice.

2. *If the term of office of the representatives of the employees affected by the transfer expires as a result of the transfer, the representatives shall continue to enjoy the protection provided by the laws, regulations, administrative provisions or practice of the Member States."* '

Article 11 of the European Community Social Charter 1989 provides:

'*Employers and workers of the European Community shall have the right of association in order to constitute professional organisations or trade unions of their choice for the defence of their economic and social interests. Every employer and every worker shall have the freedom to join or not to join such organisations without any personal or occupational damage being thereby suffered by him.*'

Ireland is a member of the International Labour Organisation (ILO). As a member of the ILO Ireland is subject to Convention No 98, article 4 of which provides:

'Measures appropriate to national conditions shall be taken where necessary to encourage and promote the full development and utilisation of machinery for voluntary negotiation between employers or employers' organisations and workers' organisations with a view to the regulation of terms and conditions of employment by means of collective agreements.'

In Irish law employees have a constitutional right to join a trade union or not to join a trade union as they see fit but no legal right to have their trade union recognised by their employer. The purchase or transfer of a business or the merger or amalgamation of two or more businesses can give rise to all sorts of problems where there may be a multiplicity of trade unions where previously there might have been only one or two. These difficulties are not addressed in the Directive or the Irish Regulations which provide for limited rights and obligations in the area of collective employment law and industrial relations. The ECJ stated in *Foreningen af Arbejdsledere i Danmark v Daddy's Dance Hall* [1988] IRLR 315 that the Directive only aims at partial harmonisation of employment law in the Member States of the EU but is intended to extend the protection workers enjoy under the law of the Member State in which they work to a situation where the undertaking in which they work is the subject matter of a transfer within the meaning of the Directive. The starting-point therefore of analysis of trade union rights in the transfer of an undertaking is to examine what rights, duties and obligations apply to the parties in Irish law and then to extend that to the transfer of an undertaking.

' ''SECTION III. INFORMATION AND CONSULTATION

Article 6

1. *The transferor and transferee shall be required to inform the representatives of their respective employees affected by the transfer of the following:*

   – the date or proposed date of the transfer,
   – the reasons for the transfer,
   – the legal, economic and social implications of the transfer for the employees,
   – any measures envisaged in relation to the employees.

   The transferor must give such information to the representatives of his employees in good time before the transfer is carried out.
   The transferee must give such information to the representatives of his employees in good time, and in any event before his employees are directly affected by the transfer as regards their conditions of work and employment.

2. *Where the transferor or the transferee envisages measures in relation to his employees, he shall consult the representatives of his employees in good time on such measures with a view to reaching an agreement.*

3. *Member States whose laws, regulations or administrative provisions provide that representatives of the employees may have recourse to an arbitration board to obtain a decision on the measures to be taken in relation to employees may limit the obligations laid down in paragraphs 1 and 2 to cases where the transfer carried out gives rise to a change in the business likely to entail serious disadvantages for a considerable number of the employees.*
   The information and consultations shall cover at least the measures envisaged in relation to the employees.
   The information must be provided and consultations take place in good time before the change in the business as referred to in the first sub-paragraph is effected.

4. *The obligations laid down in this Article shall apply irrespective of whether the decision resulting in the transfer is taken by the employer or an undertaking controlling the employer.*
   In considering alleged breaches of the information and consultation requirements laid down by this Directive, the argument that such a breach occurred because the information was not provided by an undertaking controlling the employer shall not be accepted as an excuse.

5. *Member States may limit the obligations laid down in paragraphs 1, 2 and 3 to undertakings or businesses which, in terms of the number of employees, meet the conditions for the election or nomination of a collegiate body representing the employees.*

6. *Member States shall provide that, where there are no representatives of the employees in an undertaking or business through no fault of their own, the employees concerned must be informed in advance of:*

   – the date or proposed date of the transfer,
   – the reason for the transfer,
   – the legal, economic and social implications of the transfer for the employees,
   – any measures envisaged in relation to the employees.'' '

Application of these provisions. In Ireland the meaning of the words 'legal, economic and social implications' has not been addressed, nor do we know how the courts will interpret the words 'measures envisaged'. The UK equivalent of regulation 7 was considered by the UK High Court in *Institution of Professional Civil Servants v Secretary of State for Defence* [1987] IRLR 373 which interpreted 'legal, economic and social implications', as simply meaning 'consequences'. The court analysed the words 'measures envisaged' more closely, albeit in the context of the UK regulations, which are phrased somewhat differently from the Irish regulations and stated that:

> 'It was common ground that "measures" is a word of the widest import and includes any action, step or arrangement, while "envisages" simply means "visualises" or "foresees". Despite the width of these words, it is clear that manpower projections are not "measures" at all; though positive steps to achieve planned reductions in manpower levels otherwise than through natural wastage would be.'

In that case, in considering the extent of information to be furnished by an employer and the type of consultations that should take place, the court observed:

> 'Parliament can hardly have intended to compel the employer in the private sector to consult the unions on the desirability of the transfer itself or the sufficiency of the reasons for it. These are matters of business policy for the transferring employer to decide, and the unions cannot expect to participate in the decision.'

The court went on to state:

> 'In an ordinary case in the private sector under the ... Regulations an Industrial Tribunal ought, in my judgment, to look at the matter broadly. It ought not to conduct a minute line by line examination of the information available to, and provided by the employer. And it ought not to grant relief unless the employer has plainly been recalcitrant or neglectful of his statutory obligations.'

In *Banking Insurance and Finance Union v Barclays Bank plc* [1987] ICR 495 the UK Employment Appeal Tribunal held that the duty to inform employees applies to a 'proposed' transfer and therefore crystallises at an earlier stage than when the transfer becomes an actuality or a reality. No guidance is given in that case as to exactly when a transfer becomes a 'proposed' transfer but the case does allow for the obligation to arise at an early stage of transfer negotiations.

Timing. Article 6 and regulation 7(1) provide a joint liability on both the transferor and the transferee to 'inform' all employees of the matters referred to therein 'in good time' before the transfer. Regulation 7(2) provides that if measures are envisaged in relation to the employees then the transferor or the transferee, whichever is appropriate, shall consult with the employee representatives again 'in good time' on such measures but, very importantly, must do so 'with a view to seeking agreement' as provided for in article 6(2) of the Directive. As to when information should be given, both the Directive and the Regulations differentiate as between the transferor and the transferee. The transferor is obliged to inform employee representatives 'in good time before the transfer is carried out', while the transferee must furnish the information, 'in good time, and in any event before his employees are directly affected by the transfer as regards their conditions of work and employment'.

In the absence of any Irish cases on the transfer of undertakings obligations to inform and consult, and as the *Institution of Professional Civil Servants* case is the only UK case, a parallel must be sought in the law on redundancy, and collective redundancies in particular, which has similar provisions and obligations. There have been a number of decisions of UK courts and tribunals in that area which are of assistance. In *Orr v Secretary of State, ex parte Vardy* [1993] IRLR 104 it was held that an announcement to close thirty-one pits which was made prior to there being any consultation was a breach of the Collective Redundancies Directive— and also *Re Hartlebury Printers Ltd* [1992] IRLR 516 and *GMB v Rankin & Harrison* [1992] IRLR 514. In *Griffin v South West Water Services Ltd* [1995] IRLR 15 Blackburne J stated inter alia:

'The essential point to my mind is that the consultation must be one where if they wish to do so the workers representatives can make constructive proposals and have time in which to do so.'

'"SECTION IV. FINAL PROVISIONS

Article 7

This Directive shall not affect the right of Member States to apply or introduce laws, regulations or administrative provisions which are more favourable to employees or to promote or permit collective agreements or agreements between social partners more favourable to employees.

Article 7a

Member States shall introduce into their national legal systems such measures as are necessary to enable all employees and representatives of employees who consider themselves wronged by failure to comply with the obligations arising from this Directive to pursue their claims by judicial process after possible recourse to other competent authorities

Article 7b

The Commission shall submit to the Council an analysis of the effects of the provisions of this Directive before 17 July 2006. It shall propose any amendment which may seem necessary."

'Article 2

1. *Member States shall bring into force the laws, regulations and administrative provisions necessary to comply with this Directive by 17 July 2001 at the latest or shall ensure that, by that date, at the latest, the employers' and employees' representatives have introduced the required provisions by means of agreement, Member States being obliged to take the necessary steps enabling them at all times to guarantee the results imposed by this Directive.*

2. *When Member States adopt the measures referred to in paragraph 1, they shall contain a reference to this Directive or shall be accompanied by such reference on the occasion of their official publication. The methods of making such reference shall be laid down by Member States.*
    Member States shall inform the Commission immediately of the measures they take to implement this Directive.

Article 3

This Directive shall enter into force on the day of its publication in the Official Journal of the European Communities.

Article 4

This Directive is addressed to the Member States.

Done at Luxembourg, 29 June 1998.'

CHAPTER 11

HEALTH AND SAFETY LAW*

11.1   INTRODUCTION

The focus of this chapter is on the legislative and common law positions relating to health and safety and the consequent implications for employers and employees. It reviews in particular the Safety, Health and Welfare at Work Act, 1989 and the regulations implemented under that Act. It also considers the duty of care likely to be imposed on employers in the future.

The burden or liability placed upon employers has significantly altered in the past two hundred years. It is clear from any examination of this area that the process must be viewed as a continuum, with all developments broadly moving in one direction, generally favouring employees. The regime of protection established may be classified under two general headings: obligations imposed by the legislature; and obligations imposed by the judiciary under the common law.

11.2   STATUTORY REGULATION

Until the nineteenth century there was little or no statutory intervention by the legislature which was composed, in the main, of property owners and employers, to afford protection to employees. However, in the early nineteenth century specific limited intervention was demanded to remedy glaring injustices. One of the earliest examples of legislative intervention to stem this clamour for reform was the Act of 1802 entitled 'An Act for the Preservation of the Health and Morals of Apprentices and Others Employed in Cotton and Other Mills and Cotton and Other Factories' (42 Geo III c 73). This first Act to regulate the operation of factories provided, inter alia, that the rooms in mills or factories to which the Act applied should be washed with quicklime and water twice a year and that care should be taken to admit fresh air. It also provided that no apprentice should be employed or compelled to work for more than twelve hours (excluding meal times) in any one day, as well as requiring that no more than two apprentices should sleep in the one bed. Progress continued apace with further reforming legislation which, in the main, sought to improve the safety and working conditions of employees.

Major reform, so far as factories were concerned, was introduced in the Factories and Workshop Act, 1878. This Act consolidated and amended all earlier statute law governing factories and introduced additional sanitary and safety provisions. It limited the hours that might be worked by children, young persons and women and it prohibited children under

---

* The law and practice alluded to in this chapter are stated as at February 2002.

the age of 10 years from being employed in a factory or workshop (Factories and Workshop Act, 1878, s 20). This Act, and subsequent amending measures, were repealed by the Factories and Workshop Act, 1901. Following the now established practice, the 1901 Act brought all previous legislation in the area within the ambit of the one enactment. Further, it expanded both in substance and application, the provisions relating to health and safety. It still, however, continued only to apply to factories and workshops. Importantly, s 79 of the 1901 Act provided the Secretary of State with the power to make special regulations for health and safety in respect of factories, workshops, building operations, operations at docks, quays and warehouses. The importance of this procedure will be evidenced later as it is under this procedure that all modern regulations are introduced.

The next significant enactment was the Factories Act, 1955. This repealed and replaced the 1901 Act in Ireland. Unlike previous legislation it did not seek to ameliorate or eliminate specific hazards. Rather, it provided a code to ensure the safety, health and welfare of factory employees. Section 3(1) of the Factories Act, 1955 provided a primary definition of the term 'factory':

> 'Subject to the provisions of this section, in this Act ''factory'' means any premises in which, or within the close or curtilage or precincts of which, persons are employed in manual labour in any process for or incidental to any of the following purposes:
>
> (a) the making of any article or part of any article;
> (b) the altering, repairing, ornamenting, finishing, washing, or the breaking up or demolition, of any article;
> (c) the adapting for sale of any article,
>
> being premises in which, or within the close or curtilage or precincts of which, the work is carried on by way of trade or for purposes of gain and to or over which the employer of the persons employed therein has the right of access or control.'

If a place of work fell within the ambit of the primary definition, then it was deemed a 'factory' within the meaning of the Act. Further, s 3(1) also provided for and extended the definition of factory to include places which would not otherwise have fallen within that definition. In addition, the Act contained the proviso that its provisions would also apply to places not otherwise falling within s 3(1). These 'notional factories' included, inter alia, docks, warehouses, building operations and electrical stations.

There were further Acts, including the Office Premises Act, 1958, the Mines and Quarries Act, 1965, the Safety in Industry Act, 1980 and the Safety, Health and Welfare at Work (Offshore Installations) Act, 1987 as well as various regulations made under these Acts. All these legislative interventions went a long way towards improving the safety, health and welfare of employees. However, three major difficulties remained. First, the piecemeal approach to legislation, with each new Act superseding and amending prior legislation, rendered the law both inaccessible and confusing. Secondly, despite the volume of legislation many premises and places of work were entirely excluded from regulation. Consequently, those employees were deprived of protection granted as a matter of course to others. Finally, the myriad of statutory provisions had entirely failed in the preceding years to reduce the level of accidents. Allied to the realisation of the foregoing considerations was the requirement to introduce into domestic law the terms of the 1989 Framework Directive on Safety and Health (89/391/EEC). A central feature of this directive was the setting down of a minimum level of protection for all employees throughout the Member States. It established general rules on occupational health and safety that employers were required to conform to and set out worker obligations and responsibilities. The Framework Directive was followed by six further directives, all of which were required to be implemented by 1 January 1993.

11.3   COMMON LAW

11.3.1   GENERALLY

As well as obligations under statute law, employers have a common law duty of care to their employees. For example, employers owe a specific duty to their employees to provide them with a safe premises, independently of any duty they may owe to them under the health and safety legislation. The common law rules are laws extracted from several hundred years of judicial experience and decisions. Over the centuries remedies and, more importantly, compensation were available to an injured employee. However, the grounds for recovery in the eighteenth and nineteenth centuries were extremely circumscribed. In the nineteenth century 'fault' or negligence fell to be the main basis upon which liability was to be decided. To recover against an employer an injured employee had to prove that his employer failed to act in the same manner as a reasonable employer would have in the circumstances. He also had to demonstrate that this failure caused the loss or damage of which he complained. Further, even were he to so demonstrate, he still had to surmount the infamous triumvirate of defences created by the judiciary and relied upon by employers, *volenti non fit injuria* (voluntary assumption of risk), the doctrine of common employment and the preclusion from recovery of a finding of contributory negligence on the part of the employee. These defences have now been considerably relaxed as a result of legislative intervention.

11.3.2   *VOLENTI NON FIT INJURIA*

The defence of *volenti non fit injuria* equated knowledge on the part of the employee of the risk of harm with the consent of the employee to accept that risk. As Hawkins J in *Thrausser v Handyside* (1880) 20 QBD 359 at p 364 commented, the employee's 'poverty, not his will, consented to incur the danger'. This defence was only finally emasculated in this jurisdiction by virtue of s 34(1)(b) of the Civil Liability Act, 1961. It is important to note, however, that this defence was never accepted in actions for breach of statutory duty. This obviously increased the importance of statutory duties being imposed on employers.

11.3.3   DOCTRINE OF COMMON EMPLOYMENT

The doctrine of common employment operated to oust the doctrine of vicarious liability in circumstances where an employee was injured through the negligence of a fellow employee (*Priestly v Fowler* [1837] 3 M & W 1). Vicarious liability arises where an employer is liable for the wrongs of his employees. In summary, the doctrine of common employment provided that where one employee was injured through the negligence or wrongdoing of another employee, and where both employees were employed by the same employer, the employer could not be held liable for that wrong. This doctrine was curtailed over the years, surviving, albeit in a limited form, until the enactment of the Law Reform Personal Injuries Act, 1958.

11.3.4   CONTRIBUTORY NEGLIGENCE

Until the enactment of the Civil Liability Act, 1961 contributory negligence was a complete bar to recovery. Section 34 of the 1961 Act provided that contributory negligence could only operate to reduce the amount of damages awarded, having regard to the respective degrees of fault of both the plaintiff and defendant.

11.3.5 EVOLUTION OF MODERN DUTY OF CARE OWED BY EMPLOYER TO EMPLOYEE

It was not until 1937, with the decision of the House of Lords in England in *Wilson and Clyde Coal Co Ltd v English* [1937] 3 All ER 628, that the modern duty of care owed by an employer to an employee was established. In summary, an employer was deemed to owe a duty of care to his employees, which was personal to the employer and was not capable of being discharged merely by delegating its performance to another apparently competent person. This duty included the provision of a safe place of work, a safe system of work, the provision of competent staff and proper equipment. These particular duties, in expanded form, were finally enacted into legislation in Part II of the Safety, Health and Welfare at Work Act, 1989.

McGuinness J considered the modern duty of care alluded to above in the High Court in the case of *Bradley v An Post*, 7 July 1998, High Ct (unreported). The case concerned an employee of the defendant company, who sustained back injury while delivering letters to low-level letterboxes in June 1993. He reported the matter to his supervisor and subsequently attended the company doctor. The injury resulted in an absence of two months by the plaintiff from the defendant's employment. His injury and consequent vulnerability were well known to his employers, yet in October 1993 he was dispatched on non-emergency overtime to deliver mail to a development where some 350 houses had low-level letterboxes. During the course of this delivery the plaintiff again suffered back injury. McGuinness J held that the defendant company's duty of care towards the plaintiff included a duty to ensure that, at least in the short term after his illness, he did not assume duties which would place undue and extraordinary strain on his back. Consequently, the defendant company was held liable as it did not properly discharge the employer's duty of care in the case of the plaintiff's second injury.

McGuinness J's approach to the employer's duty of care is consistent with the approach adopted in previous cases. These cases decided that an employer discharges his duty of care 'if he does what a reasonable or prudent employer would have done in the circumstances'. The employer's duty is therefore not an unlimited one and varies according to the employee's circumstances.

11.4 SAFETY, HEALTH AND WELFARE AT WORK ACT, 1989

The Safety, Health and Welfare at Work Act, 1989 ('the 1989 Act') is a groundbreaking piece of legislation. For the first time all places of work within the State are afforded protection under the umbrella of one statute. All persons involved with or connected to places of employment, including employers, employees, designers, builders and manufacturers are covered by the Act. Unlike previous Acts, which were aimed at defining the circumstances whereby liability was imposed, this Act is proactive in seeking to prevent accidents by obliging employers to assess and address potential risks in their place of work and by establishing a regulatory body with enforcement powers. Generally the 1989 Act provides only for criminal liability for breaches of its provisions. That said, s 28 of the Act allows for the making of regulations that attract civil liability.

11.5 GENERAL DUTIES IMPOSED BY THE 1989 ACT

Part II of the 1989 Act, ss 6–11, establishes the general duties owed by persons under the Act. Each of these duties will be considered in turn.

11.5.1   GENERAL DUTIES OF EMPLOYERS TO THEIR EMPLOYEES

Section 6(1) of the 1989 Act provides that it shall be the duty of every employer to ensure, so far as is reasonably practicable, the safety, health and welfare at work of all his employees. Ten specific matters, which an employer must consider when fulfilling the duty imposed by s 6(1) of the Act, are referred to in s 6(2). It is important to note that this list is not exhaustive and is merely an expanded statement of the existing common law position. (The common law duty owed by employers to employees is broadly stated as to provide a safe place of work, a safe system of work, proper equipment and competent staff.) Further, the duties imposed under the 1989 Act cannot be taken by employers as granting them a licence to implement draconian measures under the guise of purported compliance with the 1989 Act. The actions of the employer in each particular case must be reasonable in the circumstances. In *Donegal County Council v Porter and others* [1993] ELR 101, the county council sought to implement a December 1985 Department of Environment circular which recommended, inter alia, the introduction of a retirement age of 55 for all fire fighters and a compulsory annual medical examination 'on a uniform basis for all operational personnel'. Due to an industrial dispute, Porter and the other respondents refused to undergo a medical examination requested by the council. They were dismissed after refusing to undergo the medical examination for three years.

The council relied for its defence, in part, on *Maureen Heeney v Dublin Corporation*, 16 May 1991, High Ct (unreported). In this case the widow of a fire officer successfully sued Dublin Corporation for damages in negligence arising from her husband's death on 12 October 1987. Mr Heeney, a fire fighter, collapsed and died from a heart attack after entering a burning building on a number of occasions without breathing apparatus. On 12 March 1985 the Labour Court recommended the retirement of fire fighters for ill health at the age of 55 as well as annual medical examinations for all fire fighters over the age of 55. No such medical examinations were in place at the time of Mr Heeney's death. Mr Heeney suffered from hypertension and was aged in excess of 55 at his death.

Donegal County Council, in its case against Porter and others, claimed that the *Heeney* case demonstrated a clear risk to the safety, health and welfare of Porter and his fellow respondents that the council was seeking to avoid by requiring a medical examination. The council, relying on s 6 as aforesaid, in furtherance of complying with its duty to ensure the safety, health and welfare of the respondents, so far as it was reasonably practicable, argued that their dismissal was permitted under the Unfair Dismissals Act, 1977. Flood J, however, held that the respondents' dismissal was unfair:

> 'Dismissal, as I see it, would be a blanket performance [of] the said statutory duty under section 6 of the Safety, Health and Welfare at Work Act, 1989. In my view there is undoubtedly a statutory duty to observe. The council can observe it by a much less draconian measure than dismissal at the age of 55 and one which does not involve a blatant disregard for the council's contractual obligations to the respondents and others in their category.'

It is clear, therefore, that an employer, in endeavouring to comply with the general duty imposed upon him by virtue of s 6(1), must take into account all the circumstances of each case and act accordingly. (See also *Scally v Westmeath County Council* [1996] ELR 96.) If an employee's conditions and terms of employment are to be affected, only the minimum intrusion possible will be countenanced (see *Deborah Timmons v Oglesby & Butler Ltd* [1999] ELR 119).

11.5.2   GENERAL DUTIES OF EMPLOYERS AND SELF-EMPLOYED TO PERSONS OTHER THAN THEIR EMPLOYEES

Section 7 addresses the general duties of employers and the self-employed to persons other than their employees. In effect, this refers to employees of sub-contractors and independent contractors. This would seem to have particular relevance to construction sites where many of the skilled craftsmen and artisans would be independent contractors and thus self-employed. Therefore, an obligation is imposed under the Act on such independent contractors to have regard for the health and safety of employees of the main contractor and other sub-contractors.

11.5.3 GENERAL DUTIES OF PERSONS CONCERNED WITH PLACES OF WORK TO PERSONS OTHER THAN THEIR EMPLOYEES

Section 8 deals with the general duties of persons concerned with places of work to persons other than their employees. In essence, this provision regulates the duties of those who control to any extent a place of work. To some degree there is an overlap between this section and the preceding section.

11.5.4 GENERAL DUTIES OF EMPLOYEES

Section 9 sets down the duties owed by all employees while at work. This is a new departure. Hitherto, legislation conferred rights upon employees. Under this section employees now have duties as well as rights. The employee's primary duty is to take reasonable care for their own and others' safety, health and welfare. There is also a duty on an employee to co-operate with his employer, to use the protective equipment and clothing provided to him and to report dangerous risks of which he becomes aware. As noted at **11.6** below, the sanction under this section is criminal only. The section is also of some use in defending claims as it enables an employer to possibly reduce his liability by claiming that an employee failed to comply with the obligations imposed upon him under this section and was thus guilty of contributory negligence. Therefore, the section offers considerable assistance to employers, at least in so far as discipline is concerned. This section would also appear to strengthen the position of employers defending cases before the Employment Appeals Tribunal in the instances of employees dismissed for serious breaches of safety rules. In *Michael Kellegher v Power Supermarkets Ltd* UD 720/89 the dismissed employee lifted the forks on a forklift some seventeen to twenty feet in the air, while another employee was perched on them. He then drove back and forth, stopping quickly, thereby causing the forks to rattle. The night manager observed the claimant's actions and he was dismissed. Subsequently the EAT unanimously held the applicant's dismissal for a breach of the safety procedure to have been justified in the circumstances.

Mr Eamon Leahy, Chairman of the EAT, summarised the position in the following terms:

> '[H]aving regard to the seriousness of the incident which brought about the dismissal, it is the unanimous view of the Tribunal that the respondent acted reasonably in dismissing the appellant.'

11.5.5 GENERAL DUTIES OF DESIGNERS, MANUFACTURERS, IMPORTERS AND SUPPLIERS OF ARTICLES AND SUBSTANCES FOR USE AT WORK

Section 10 deals comprehensively with the duty owed by persons who design, manufacture, import or supply articles for use in the workplace. It is preventative in nature in that it attempts to ensure that all articles and substances used in the workplace are properly designed, constructed and tested prior to supply and use. The section also provides for the supply of adequate information concerning the dismantling and disposal of articles. Suppliers, therefore, have an ongoing obligation under the Act throughout the life of an article and beyond. Similar provisions are imposed upon manufacturers, importers and suppliers of substances. The extent of this duty is limited by virtue of subsection (7), which provides that the duty in the preceding provisions of s 10 shall extend only to things done by a person in the course of a trade or business and to matters within his control.

11.5.6 GENERAL DUTIES OF PERSONS WHO DESIGN AND CONSTRUCT PLACES OF WORK

Section 11 imposes a duty on any persons who design places of work to design them so that they are, so far as is reasonably practicable, safe and without risk to health. A similar duty is imposed on people who construct places of work. Again, this section is preventative in nature.

11.6 GENERAL OVERVIEW OF THE 1989 ACT, ss 6–11

A number of points require elaboration in respect of the general duties contained in ss 6–11 as discussed. The duties imposed by ss 6–11 are broad in nature. Under s 60 failure to comply with the duties imposed by or under ss 6–11 will not give rise to a cause of action in civil proceedings. Contravention of these sections merely attract criminal sanctions (1989 Act, s 48). Section 28, however, confers wide powers on the Minister to make regulations pursuant to the Act. These regulations may be made in respect of all work activities. Crucially, s 60(2) provides that a breach of a duty imposed by regulation under s 28, in so far as it causes damage and a link is established between the breach of that duty and the damage caused, shall be actionable in the civil courts, unless the regulation in question specifically provides otherwise.

Throughout ss 6–11 reference is made to what is 'reasonably practicable'. Asquith LJ classically defined the 'reasonably practicable' standard in *Edwards v National Coal Board* [1949] 1 All ER 743 (CA), in the following manner:

'"[R]easonably practicable" is a narrower term than "physically possible" and seems to me to imply that a computation must be made by the owner in which the *quantum* of risk is placed on one scale and the sacrifice involved in the measures necessary for averting the risk (whether in money, time or trouble) is placed in the other, and that, if it be shown that there is a gross disproportion between them—the risk being insignificant in relation to the sacrifice—the defendants discharge the onus on them. Moreover, this computation falls to be made by the owner at a point of time anterior to the accident.'

It is important to distinguish the concept of negligence from that of 'reasonably practicable'. A defendant may avoid liability in negligence for failing to fulfil certain duties merely by demonstrating that the burden imposed upon him (time and/or cost) by taking those precautions outweighs the scale of the loss, taking into account the chance of that loss occurring. It is clear from Asquith LJ in *Edwards* that reasonable practicability is an altogether different creature. For reasonable practicability there must be a gross disproportion. From this it is evident that the burden imposed by what is 'reasonably practicable' is set at a higher standard than that imposed by the general principle of negligence. In *Daly v Avonmore Creameries Ltd* [1984] IR 131, McCarthy J, in the Supreme Court, considered 'reasonably practicable' at p 131:

'I am not to be taken as supporting a view that, where lives are at stake, considerations of expense are any more than vaguely material.' (See also *Kirwan v Bray UDC*, 30 July 1969, Supreme Ct (unreported).)

It would appear, therefore, that in monetary terms the money required to be expended would have to be very significant before it would not be 'reasonably practicable' to take the precautions. That said, it would seem that what could be construed as 'reasonably practicable' for a multinational corporation might not necessarily pertain in a small corner shop. This is a matter for each individual employer, however, as pursuant to s 50 of the 1989 Act, in any prosecution for an offence consisting of a failure to comply with a duty to do something, so far as it was practicable or 'reasonably practicable', it is for the accused to prove that it was not practicable or was not 'reasonably practicable' to do more than was in fact done to satisfy this duty or requirement. The Supreme Court reinforced this view in *Boyle v Marathon Petroleum Ireland Ltd*, 12 January 1999, Supreme Ct (unreported). In that case, O'Flaherty J affirmed the view of the High Court (1 November 1995, McCracken J (unreported)) that the onus of proof was on the defendant to show that it was not 'reasonably practicable' to do more than was done to discharge his statutory duty under the health and safety legislation:

> 'I am . . . of the opinion that this duty is more extensive than the common law duty which devolves on employers to exercise reasonable care in various aspects as regards their employees. It is an obligation to take all practical steps. That seems to me to involve more than that they should respond that they, as employers, did all that was reasonably to be expected of them in a particular situation. An employer might sometimes be able to say that what he did by way of exercising reasonable care was done in the "agony of the moment", for example, but that might not be enough to discharge his statutory duty under the section in question.'

(See also the Scottish case of *Mains v Uniroyal Engelbert Tyres Ltd* [1995] IRLR 544, heard in the Court of Session before Lords Wylie, Sutherland and Johnston.)

It must be emphasised that, for the first time, all places of work fall within the parameters of the one Act. In the 1989 Act, s 2 'place of work' is defined as:

> *'[a] place, land or other location at, in, upon or near which, work is carried on whether occasionally or otherwise and in particular includes:*
> (a) *a premises;*
> (b) *any installation on land and any offshore installation including any offshore installation to which the Safety, Health and Welfare (Offshore Installations) Act, 1987 applies);*
> (c) *a tent, temporary structure or movable structure, and a vehicle, vessel or aircraft.'*

It is submitted, taking cognisance of the clear intention of the legislature and the spirit of the Act, that this definition will be very broadly construed.

11.7   SAFETY STATEMENTS

Under the 1989 Act, s 12 every employer must, as soon as possible, prepare or cause to be prepared a statement in writing which is known as a safety statement. This statement specifies the manner in which safety, health and welfare shall be secured in the workplace. It should contain a summary of the organisation's safety and health goals and objectives, assignment of responsibilities and means of achieving the aims and objectives. This safety statement should demonstrate how the employer intends to comply with the 1989 Act, s 6(2), which details the key duties of an employer as listed below:

- provide a properly designed and maintained place of work such that it is safe and without risk to health (s 6(2)(a));

- provide a properly designed and maintained means of egress and access to the place of work (s 6(2)(b));

- provide a properly designed and maintained plant and machinery such that it is safe and without risk to health (s 6(2)(c));

- provide a properly planned, organised, performed and maintained system of work such that it is safe and without risk to health (s 6(2)(d));

- provide such information, instruction, training and supervision as is necessary for ensuring the safety and health of his/her employees (s 6(2)(e));

- provide suitable protective equipment where it is not possible to eliminate or reduce a risk to a safe level as appropriate for ensuring the safety and health of his/her employees (s 6(2)(f));

- prepare and revise adequate plans to be followed in emergencies (s 6(2)(g));

- ensure the safety and health of persons working with an article or substance (s 6(2)(h));

- provide and maintain facilities to ensure the welfare of his/her employees (s 6(2)(i)); and

- obtain the services of a competent person for the purposes of ensuring the safety and health of employees (s 6(2)(j)).

The purpose of the safety statement is to require employers to assess the workplace over which they have control and to identify the hazards to safety, health and welfare at that place of work. In particular, it must specify the arrangements made and the resources provided for safeguarding persons employed at that place of work. A safety statement must also identify the co-operation required from employees and include the names of the persons responsible for the safety tasks assigned to them under the Act. The employer must bring the terms of the safety statement to the attention of both persons employed by him and others who may be affected by the safety statement. Interestingly, the annual report of a company under s 158 of the Companies Act, 1963 must include an evaluation of the extent to which the policy set out in the safety statement was fulfilled during the period of time covered by the report.

Failure to comply with the section 12 safety statement requirement is a criminal offence. Civil liability may also attach, as s 12 is not included in the embargo contained in s 60. Where there has been loss or damage suffered by an employee the mere failure of an employer to prepare a safety statement does not automatically impose liability on the employer for that loss or damage. In *Matthews v Irish Society of Autism*, 18 April 1997, High Ct, Laffoy J (unreported) it was held that the defendant's failure to prepare a safety statement was irrelevant in that case as the risk in question was not one that would have been averted to in the safety statement, had one been prepared.

11.8   CONSULTATION

Under the 1989 Act, s 13 every employer must consult with his employees on safety, health and welfare matters at work. In so far as is 'reasonably practicable' he must take into account representations made by his employees in this regard. The section confers the right on employees to make representations to their employer on matters of safety, health and welfare and to appoint a safety representative from among their number to act on their own behalf. This safety representative has a right to information and to investigate accidents, potential hazards and complaints. Failure to comply with this section constitutes a criminal offence under the 1989 Act, s 48(1). Section 13, in common with s 12, is not included in the embargo on civil liability contained in s 60. Presumably, however, following the rationale of the *Matthews* case, there would have to be some causal connection between the loss or damage sustained and the failure to comply with s 13 of the Act before civil liability would be imposed upon the employer.

11.9   REGULATIONS IMPLEMENTED UNDER THE 1989 ACT

Section 28 of the 1989 Act empowers the Minister to make regulations in respect of a very wide range of topics as well as any other matters necessary to give effect to the Act (see Schedule 4 to the 1989 Act). It is reasonable to suppose that in time very detailed regulations will be promulgated governing all parties in the workplace. Their primary importance derives from the fact that breach of the regulations incurs civil liability. Crucially, the nature of the duties imposed under certain regulations currently in force appear to be absolute in nature. That is to say they require the result imposed by virtue of the statutory provision to be achieved by the person or body upon whom the duty is imposed. It is not a defence to state that reasonable care was taken or, alternatively, that it was not 'reasonably practicable' or practicable to achieve the required result. At best this absolute standard of care might be considered unfair and, at worst, ultra vires the Act. After all, the duty imposed under the 1989 Act is, depending on the section, one of reasonable practicability or practicability.

The Safety, Health and Welfare at Work (General Application) Regulations, 1993 (SI 44/ 1993) supplanted many provisions found in or made under the Factories Act, 1955 and related legislation. Any remaining overlap between the Factories Act, 1955 and the Safety, Health and Welfare at Work (General Application) Regulations, 1993 was addressed in the Safety, Health and Welfare at Work Act, 1989 (Repeals and Revocations) Order, 1995 (SI 357/1995).

To date, numerous regulations have been implemented under the 1989 Act. The main regulations are the Safety, Health and Welfare at Work (General Application) Regulations, 1993 and the Safety, Health and Welfare at Work (Construction) Regulations, 1995 (SI 138/1995).

11.10 SAFETY, HEALTH AND WELFARE AT WORK (GENERAL APPLICATION) REGULATIONS, 1993

Despite the fact that these rules ('the 1993 Regulations') are implemented by way of regulation as opposed to an Act of the Oireachtas, they are probably the most important legal development relating to safety, health and welfare at work for the past forty years. The Safety, Health and Welfare at Work (General Application) Regulations 1993 (SI 44/1993) ('the 1993 Regulations') impose certain absolute duties and are divided into ten Parts, each of which now falls to be considered.

11.10.1 PART I: INTERPRETATION AND APPLICABILITY

The duties imposed under the 1993 Regulations are placed on employers and employees for the benefit of employees. The term 'employee', however, is not defined in the regulations. It seems clear that 'employee' in the regulations bears the same meaning as in the 1989 Act under which the regulations were enacted. Section 2(1) of the 1989 Act defined an employee as a person under a contract of service or apprenticeship. Part I of the regulations provides that they shall 'also apply in respect of the use by [the employer] of the services of a fixed-term employee or a temporary employee' (see regulation 4(2)). 'Fixed-term employee' and 'temporary employee' are defined in the regulations. The former is defined as an 'employee whose employment is governed by a contract of employment for a fixed term or for a specified purpose (being a purpose of a kind that the duration of the contract was limited but was, at the time of its making, incapable of precise ascertainment)' (see regulation 2(1)). The latter is defined as an 'employee in a temporary employment business which is the employer of that employee and where the employee is assigned to work for and under the control of another undertaking making use of his services' (see regulation 2(1)). It has been suggested that certain independent contractors, for example, an electrician employed to rewire a factory (and thus a fixed-term employee), would be governed by the regulations. However, the workman employed by the electrician performing identical work to the electrician is not entitled to the protection afforded such fixed-term employees, as his contract is a contract for services (White, J.P.M., *Civil Liability for Industrial Accidents* (Dublin: Oak Tree Press, 1993), vol 1, p 1021). This would not leave the employee of the electrician without protection as a duty of care would still be owed to him by the electrician as a deemed occupier under the Occupiers' Liability Act, 1995 as well as an employer at common law. It would, however, be fair to say that the level of protection afforded under the 1993 Regulations is greater. A further point to be made is that a person casually borrowed from another employer would not fall within the definition of temporary employee for the purpose of the regulations, even though he may qualify as an employee under the borrowing employer's liability insurance policy (MacNamee, M, 'Employers' Liability; Recent Legislative and Common Law Developments' (1997) *Irish Insurance Law Review*, vol 1, no 1, p 15).

11.10.2 PART II: GENERAL SAFETY AND HEALTH PROVISIONS

11.10.2.1 Generally

Part II of the 1993 Regulations, and in particular regulation 5, obliges every employer, in taking measures for the safety, health and welfare of his employees, to take into account 'the general principles of prevention' which are outlined in Schedule 1 to the regulations. Broadly, these relate to the evaluation and avoidance of risk, the adaptation of the workplace, system of work and the provision of safe equipment to the employee. Part II of the regulations imposes specific duties in respect of training, health surveillance, protective and preventative services, emergency duties, risk assessment, provision of information to employees and consultation with employees where safety measures are concerned. This Part has been criticised as presenting 'a problem of interpretation' due mainly to 'an appalling want of specificity'(White, *Civil Liability for Industrial Accidents*, p 1024).

11.10.2.2 Bullying and stress as a health and safety issue

The 1989 Act imposes an obligation on every employer to provide systems of work that are planned, organised, performed and maintained so as to be, as far as is reasonably practicable, safe and without risk to health. (See, in particular, the 1989 Act, s 6(2)(d).) That said, it is doubtful whether a successful action could be brought for bullying or stress under the 1989 Act. The real potential and value lies in the 1993 Regulations, and in particular Part II of these regulations, a breach of which can be used in civil litigation (see **11.6**). It is for this reason that bullying and stress fall for consideration under Part II of the 1993 Regulations.

An employer's duty of care to look after the health and safety of employees includes the reasonable prevention of bullying and stress-related injuries in the workplace. This duty of care is implied into the contract of employment by the 1989 Act and the 1993 Regulations. Breach of this duty may be treated as a breach of the contract of employment, enabling the employee to claim constructive dismissal (see Chapter 6: Unfair Dismissal Law). Constructive dismissal should only be availed of where an employee is left with no option other than to resign. Consequently, it is important that the employee exhausts any grievance procedure before adopting this course of action. In the recent determination of the EAT, *Liz Allen v Independent Newspapers (Ireland) Ltd*, 2 August 2001, UD 641/2000, the EAT awarded the claimant £70,500 compensation. Significantly, the EAT included compensation for stress suffered as a result of constructive dismissal.

11.10.2.3 Bullying

The 1989 Act provides that employers shall carry out a risk assessment at their place of work in the preparation of a safety statement. Such an assessment should include the risks associated with bullying. Procedures or preventative measures should follow this risk assessment in order to eliminate the risk or reduce the level of risk to an acceptable level. Regulation 10 of the 1993 Regulations requires employers to document the result of these risk assessments. A relevant and instructive case is that of *Michael Shanley v Sligo County Council*, 10 October 2001, High Ct (unreported). In this case the plaintiff was 'systematically abused, bullied, and belittled' over a protracted period of time (ie eight years) by a superior officer. The abuse had been so severe that the plaintiff had contemplated suicide. It was noted that the plaintiff had filed complaints with senior management, who failed to act. Butler J assessed damages at £65,000, the defendant council having admitted liability.

11.10.2.4 Stress

The Health and Safety Authority ('HSA') defines workplace stress as arising 'when the demands of the job and the working environment on a person exceeds their capacity to meet them'. The Authority identifies the following as situations that can cause stress in the workplace:

- poor communication at work
- poor working relationships
- poorly organised shiftwork
- faulty work organisation
- ill-defined work roles
- lack of personal control over work
- machine-paced work
- highly demanding tasks
- dull repetitive work
- dealing directly with the public

The HSA notes that stress can affect the individual at the emotional level (fatigue), the cognitive level (making mistakes), the behavioural level (excess drinking or over eating) and the physiological level (heart disease, reduced resistance to infection and skin problems). At the macro level, a company/organisation may be affected by someone who is suffering from stress through poor industrial relations, increased absenteeism, faulty decision-making and reduced productivity.

An employer's duty is not to provide a stress-free environment but to take reasonably practicable steps to shield employees from exposure to stress and from the consequences of unreasonably stressful working conditions. Employers have both a statutory and common law duty of care to protect their staff against stress. Whilst there have been few cases decided on this point, the potential for litigation in this area is growing. This can be seen from the case of *Saehan Media Ireland Ltd v A Worker* [1999] ELR 41, where the Labour Court acknowledged work-related stress as a health and safety issue and held that 'employers have an obligation to deal with instances of its occurrence which may be brought to their attention'. The issue of foreseeability has therefore been to the forefront in the evolution of the stress at work case law. Once an employer is on notice that a particular employee has a greater susceptibility to stress than others, the employer is under a higher duty as a work-related stress injury is more likely to occur.

The 1989 Act provides that all employers shall provide safe places and systems of work, including safe plant and equipment. This implies work activities and environments that minimise stress. However, it should be noted that some work is regarded as intrinsically containing certain stressors and the voluntary assumption of such jobs creates a degree of defence for the employer in civil law.

Health and safety law requires risks to be eliminated or reduced so far as is reasonably practicable, a concept previously discussed at length. The 1989 Act also requires employers to conduct risk assessments. Any such risk assessments should include assessments of activities that could potentially cause unreasonable stress to workers. Regulation 10 of the 1993 Regulations provides that the results of these assessments should be documented. Regulation 17 of and Schedule 2 to the 1993 Regulations cover a number of workplace standards on ventilation, room temperature, natural and artificial room lighting, space allocation and sanitary facilities that must be in place, and failure to do so could amount to contributing to stress at work.

The distinction between physical and psychiatric injury is no longer either medically or legally defensible. The 1989 Act no longer discriminates between physical and psychiatric injury. Section 2 of that Act defines 'personal injury' as including 'any disease and any impairment of a person's physical or mental condition'.

In the recent Circuit Court decision of *Curran v Cadbury (Ireland) Ltd* (2000) 18 ILT 140, McMahon J held that the duty of the employer towards his employee extends to protecting the employee from non-physical injury such as psychiatric illness or the mental illness that might result from negligence or from harassment or bullying in the workplace. He referred to *Walker v Northumberland County Council* [1995] 1 All ER 737, a case in which the English courts imposed liability where the plaintiff foreseeably suffered a nervous breakdown because of unreasonably stressful working conditions imposed on him by his employer, and stated that there was no reason to suspect that courts in Ireland would not adopt this approach. The learned judge held that the plaintiff could recover since her employer owed her a duty of care not to expose her to reasonably foreseeable psychiatric illness caused by the employer's negligence.

McMahon J also found that the defendant company had breached paragraph 13 of Schedule 5 to the 1993 Regulations, which states as follows:

> '(a) Where possible maintenance operations shall be carried out when equipment is shut down.
> (b) Where this is not possible, it shall be necessary to take appropriate protection measures for the carrying out of such operations or for such operations to be carried out outside the area of danger.'

The judge held that since the defendant company should have foreseen that the plaintiff might have suffered psychiatric illness as a result of its breach of the foregoing provision, the plaintiff was also entitled to recover on the ground of breach of statutory duty. Significantly, McMahon J held that in defining 'personal injury', s 2 of the 1989 Act included 'any disease and any impairment of a person's physical or mental condition'.

A recent relevant and instructive decision on stress at work from the Scottish Court of Session is *Cross v Highlands and Islands Enterprise* [2001] IRLR 336 wherein Lord Macfadyen stated that the duty on an employer to take reasonable care for an employee's safety and health, and to provide and maintain a safe system of work, includes a duty not to subject the employee to work conditions which are reasonably foreseeably likely to cause him or her psychiatric illness or injury. (See also *Ingram v Worcester County Council* (Health and Safety Review, March 2000, p 26) and *Howell v Newport County Borough Council* (The Times, 5 December 2000)).

11.10.2.5 Minimising liability to work-related bullying and stress claims

There is a detectable movement towards encouraging employers to manage health and safety issues and this is particularly pertinent when addressing the identification of bullying and stress in the workplace. Such an approach involves inter alia the employer carrying out a risk assessment on an ongoing basis. The risk assessment should form part of the safety statement. This statement should aver not merely to the physical hazards but also to the potential damages of stress and bullying.

In the Scottish case of *Cross v Highlands and Islands Enterprise* [2001] IRLR 336 Lord Macfadyen alluded to the many publications and guidelines on stress at work which emphasise that 'stress should be treated like any other health hazard'. Consequently he held that it is 'strongly arguable that today a reasonable employer would carry out assessments of the risk of injury to their employees of stress at work'.

Bullying policies are essential in the defence of a bullying and stress claim by an employee arising out of alleged bullying. For example, the sanctions to be taken against those found to be in breach of the anti-bullying policy should be clearly stated. Indeed, the HSA's booklet recommends that a bullying policy be incorporated into the company's safety statement. To be effective, bullying policies should be brought to the attention of every employee before he enters into a contract with the employer.

Formal grievance procedures should be put in place to ensure access to management. Such procedures are central to the avoidance of bullying and stress-related claims in that they impose an obligation on the employee to alert the employer of the existence of a bullying and stress-related problem. Each complaint must be comprehensively investigated.

Where an employer becomes aware that an employee is exposed to work-related stress, the employer should relieve the employee of his or her duties on full salary and obtain advice from health professionals. Such an approach will enable the employer to investigate the matter and discharge his/her duty to take reasonable care for his/her employees' health and safety. The foregoing procedure was adopted in *Nolan v Ryan Hotels plc (t/a The Gresham Hotel)* [1999] ELR 214, where the EAT held that 'the employer acted in a proper manner in investigating the matter'.

11.10.3 PART III: WORKPLACE

11.10.3.1 Meaning of workplace

Regulation 16 defines a place of work in the following manner:

'*"[p]lace of work" means a place of work intended to house workstations on the premises of the undertaking and any other place within the area of the undertaking to which an employee has access in the course of his employment but does not include:-*
(a)   means of transport used outside the undertaking or a place of work inside a means of transport;
(b)   construction sites;
(c)   extractive industries;
(d)   fishing boats;
(e)   fields, woods and land forming part of an agricultural or forestry undertaking but situated away from the undertaking's buildings.'

It is clear from the foregoing that certain areas are excluded. Workplaces such as schools and colleges are, however, regulated. Regulation 17 confines the scope of applicability by limiting the duty of an employer only to 'any place of work within his control'. The protection provided under these provisions has been criticised as being seriously deficient (White, *Civil Liability for Industrial Accidents*, p 1026). Part III of the 1993 Regulations and the attending schedules err principally in omission. In particular, the writer refers to the former duty imposed by the Factories Act, 1955, s 37, as amended by the Safety in Industry Act, 1980, s 12 with regard to access to and egress from the workplace. (Section 37 of the Factories Act, 1955, as amended by the Safety in Industry Act, 1980, s 12 has been repealed by the Safety, Health and Welfare at Work Act, 1989 (Repeals and Revocations) Order, 1995.) An employee, injured accessing or egressing the workplace, will now have to rely on the common law duty of care which imposes a lower standard of care upon the employer, the 1989 Act which attracts criminal, but not civil sanctions and the Occupiers' Liability Act, 1995.

11.10.3.2 Passive smoking claims

The employer's responsibility in respect of smoking arises both under the 1989 Act and Part III of the 1993 Regulations. In particular, s 6 of the 1989 Act requires all employers to provide safe places of work, which includes a working environment free from tobacco smoke. Part III and paragraph 10(3) of Schedule 3 to the 1993 Regulations offer further protection to the non-smoker employee in the following terms:

'In rest rooms appropriate measures shall be introduced for the protection of non-smokers against discomfort caused by tobacco smoke.'

See also *Working Together for Cleaner Air* (Department of Health, 1997).

While there is a deficit of case law on this topic in Ireland, the matter has been considered on a number of occasions in the neighbouring jurisdiction. A relevant and instructive case is *Rae v Strathclyde Joint Police Board* (OH) 1999 SCLR 793, where Lord Bonomy stated that:

'smoking is a non-industrial activity, indeed, a social activity indulged in by workers and tolerated by employers which has got absolutely nothing to do with the industrial process. If to the knowledge of an employer smoking in the workplace gives rise to the risk that an employee will contract illness through working regularly in close proximity to smokers, then it may well, depending on the circumstances, be very easy to regard the employer as under a duty to stamp out smoking, or at the very least mitigate the effects of smoking since there may well in the circumstances be no difficult issues of practicability or expense to be weighed against the risk.' (See also *Dryden v Greater Glasgow Health Board* [1992] IRLR 669; *Bland v Stockport Borough Council* (1993) New Law Journal, 13 February and *Waltons & Morse v Dorrington* [1997] IRLR 488.)

11.10.4 PART IV: USE OF WORK EQUIPMENT

11.10.4.1 Statutory regulation

Part IV of the 1993 Regulations addresses the issue and use of work equipment. Regulation 18 defines the use of work equipment as 'any activity involving work equipment'. Significantly, regulation 19 outlines the duties of employers, which cover responsibilities such as risk assessment (regulation 19(b)) and the provision of training relating to the proper use of the work equipment (regulation 19(e)). All work equipment acquired before 31 December 1992, for use by employees, at a place of work, must comply with certain minimum standards set out in Schedule 5 to the Regulations (see regulation 20). Schedule 5 details the minimum design standards, conditions of use and maintenance of all work equipment regardless of type, provided for use before 31 December 1992. Equipment provided after that date must comply with both the minimum requirements and any relevant and applicable EU directive (see regulation 20). An example of a regulation implementing a directive that would take precedence over the Schedule 5 requirements is the European Communities (Electricity Hydraulically or Oil-Electricity Operated Lifts) Regulations, 1991 (SI 41/1991). Accordingly, work equipment brought into use after 31 December 1992, and relating to electrically-operated lifts, must satisfy the minimum design standards set out in the above regulations and not Schedule 5.

The Safety, Health and Welfare at Work (General Application) (Amendment) Regulations, 2001 (SI 188/2001), which came into force in May 2001, set down new requirements, such as ergonomic risk assessments, in respect of all work equipment. Schedule 3 is also to be amended to outline the minimum requirements for mobile work equipment.

11.10.4.2 Case law

All equipment supplied must be maintained to the requisite standard throughout its life. In *Doherty v Bowaters Irish Wallboard Mills Ltd* [1968] IR 277 a load suspended from a travelling crane fell, injuring the plaintiff. The cause of the accident was a latent defect in the hook of which the defendant correctly protested he could not have been aware. The Supreme Court held that the requirement in s 34(1) of the Factories Act, 1955, that the hook be of adequate strength, was an absolute duty. The mere fact that the hook broke and caused injury was sufficient of itself to impose liability for the accident upon the employer. It can be seen from *Everitt v Thorsman (Irl) Ltd and Jumbo Bins and Sludge Disposals Ltd*, 23 June 1999, High Ct (unreported) that this absolute standard has been maintained in regulations 19 and 20 and paragraph 8 of Schedule 5 to the 1993 Regulations. In that case Kearns J stated:

'[W]hile there is no blameworthiness in any meaningful sense of the word on the part of the employers in this case, these Regulations do exist for sound policy reasons at least, namely, to ensure that an employee who suffers an injury at work through no fault of his own by using defective equipment should not be left without a remedy. . . . [A]n employer in such a situation may usually, though not always, be in a position to seek indemnity from the third party who supplied the work equipment.'

The handling, preparation and use of dangerous machinery which is a product of the workplace, as provided for in the Factories Act, 1955, s 23 has not been included in the fencing provision in Part IV of and Schedule 5 to the regulations. It should be noted that ss 21–23 of the Factories Act, 1955 have not been repealed by the Safety, Health and Welfare at Work Act, 1989 (Repeals and Revocations) Order, 1995. Regrettably, this means that the objective of consolidating all health and safety legislation into one statute has not been achieved.

The onerous duty imposed upon employers in relation to work equipment was addressed in the case of *Eamon Stakelum v Governor and Company of the Bank of Ireland*, 5 July 1999, High Ct (unreported). In summary, the High Court held in that case that employers have a duty to ensure that any equipment used by an employee in the course of his work is free from defects and suitable for the purposes for which it is used. O'Donovan J placed particular emphasis on the employer's duty to submit equipment used by an employee in the course of his employment to risk/safety assessment. A further relevant and instructive case is that of *Gilna v Maguire and 3M Ireland Ltd*, 19 May 1999, High Ct (unreported). In that case, the plaintiff, a 25-year-old radiographer employed at Beaumont Hospital, experienced a shock from a laser image processor, supplied by the second-named defendant, 3M Ireland Ltd. The shock catapulted her across the room causing her personal injury. Her injuries endured for some time notwithstanding extensive physical treatment. The High Court (Johnson J) held that the first-named defendant, who was the representative of Beaumont Hospital in the proceedings, had failed to provide safe equipment to the plaintiff. The court also held that the manufacturer had been negligent in selling a machine in a condition that caused the plaintiff to experience an electrostatic shock. Damages of £664,203 were awarded. (See also *Everitt v Thorsman (Irl) Ltd and Jumbo Bins and Sludge Disposals Ltd*, 23 June 1999, High Ct (unreported) discussed above.)

11.10.5 PART V: PERSONAL PROTECTIVE EQUIPMENT

Part V of the 1993 Regulations requires employers, where risk to health and safety cannot be avoided by technical measures and procedures, to provide personal protective equipment for use by their employees. Prior to the supply and use of personal protective equipment, the employer must ensure that the equipment is effective and compatible with other equipment. Further, every employer must also ensure that the personal protective equipment supplied by him is maintained at all times in good working order. The employer must also give information, training and instruction to the employee in the use of the personal protective equipment (see *Joseph P Magee v Ideal Cleaning Services Ltd* [1999] ELR 218). These duties are absolute in nature. It would appear that the regulations do not impose a duty on an employer to enforce the use of the personal safety equipment that he is obliged to provide to his employees. A common law duty is imposed on an employer in this regard, however, through the tort of negligence.

11.10.6 PART VI: MANUAL HANDLING OF LOADS

11.10.6.1 Statutory provisions

Lifting manual loads in the workplace was formerly regulated by the Factories Act, 1955 (Manual Labour)(Maximum Weights and Transport) Regulations, 1972 (SI 000/1972). By virtue of the Safety, Health and Welfare at Work Act, 1989 (Repeals and Revocations) Order, 1995, which came into force on 21 December 1995, Part VI and Schedules 8 and 9 of the 1993 Regulations now replace the 1972 Regulations. Regulation 27 defines what constitutes the manual handling of loads:

' ''Manual handling of loads'' means any transporting or supporting of a load by one or more employees, and includes lifting, putting down, pushing, pulling, carrying or moving a load, which, by reason of its characteristics or of unfavourable ergonomic conditions, involves risk, particularly of back injury, to employees.'

Part VI envisages the manual handling of loads by employees as a last resort. Where such handling is required an employer is obliged to minimise the risk involved and provide, where possible, information concerning the weight and centre of gravity of a load to the employee (see regulation 28). Schedule 8 details the four factors that must be taken into account by an employer for the manual handling of loads:

(a)   the characteristics of the load;

(b)   the physical effort required;

(c)   the characteristics of the working environment; and

(d)   the requirements of the activity.

Schedule 9 identifies individual risk factors in the manual handling of loads. This schedule provides that an employee may be at risk if he is physically unsuited to perform the task in question, is wearing unsuitable clothing and does not have the adequate or appropriate knowledge or training. (Schedule 9 provides that wearing unsuitable footwear or other personal effects may also put an employee at risk.)

On a literal interpretation of the regulation an employer would be under an absolute duty to eliminate all manual handling of goods. The logical consequence of such an interpretation would be to mechanise a system and remove the need for employees altogether. Perhaps the greatest defect in this Part is one of omission. Whereas the 1972 Regulations included a list of maximum weights, broken down by age and sex, the new regulations are silent on this point. (The 1972 Regulations were abolished by the Safety, Health and Welfare at Work Act, 1989 (Repeals and Revocations) Order, 1995.) This has resulted in considerable uncertainty, which will ultimately benefit neither employees nor employers.

11.10.6.2 Training

Regular manual handling training will reduce the exposure of an employer to a claim under this Part of the Act. A relevant and instructive case is *Gorry v British Midland Airways Ltd* (1999) 17 ILT 224. Dunne J, citing Part VI of the 1993 Regulations, noted that all reasonable precautions were required. The learned judge held that, even where employees were performing a task on a daily basis, they acquired bad habits and needed to be provided with regular training so as to carry out their tasks safely. For manual handling training prior to the 1993 Regulations, see *Catherine Firth v South Eastern Health Board*, 27 July 1993, High Ct (unreported).

11.10.6.3 Repetitive strain injury

It is worth noting that this Part, considering the characteristics specified in Part IV and Schedule 8, which refers, inter alia, to 'over-frequent or over-prolonged physical effort involving in particular the spine', could be pleaded in claims involving repetitive strain injury (RSI). RSI is a term covering all kinds of work-related injuries to the muscles, nerves and tendons of the upper limbs. While its recognition as a medical disorder has been slow, there is ample authority to conclude that its existence has been acknowledged at Circuit Court and High Court level in this jurisdiction. In *Sammon v Flemming GMBH* , 23 November 1993, High Ct (unreported) the plaintiff alleged that she was suffering tennis elbow as a result of her employment. Her work involved screwing caps by hand onto phials on a production line. Barron J accepted on the evidence that the repetitive nature of the work required of her was the probable cause of her condition. He dismissed the claim, however, on the basis that:

'[t]he Defendant acted reasonably and could not reasonably be expected to have anticipated that the particular work which the Plaintiff was doing would lead to such an abuse of the muscles of her forearm that she would sustain an injury.'

See, however, *Paul Bolger v Queally Pig Slaughtering Ltd*, 8 March 1996, High Ct, Barron J (unreported).

As this case pre-dated the 1993 Regulations they were not considered. The 1993 Regulations now oblige employers to evaluate the potential risk to their employees and review their safety policies. In the above case, the plaintiff first complained in 1987, six years prior to the enactment of the 1993 Regulations. Knowledge of RSI is now widely publicised. (This was a key factor in the decision of the judge in the English case of *McSherry and Lodge v British Telecommunications plc*, 1991, High Ct (unreported) in holding for the plaintiffs.) It may thus be said to be a known risk factor which should fall to be considered by an employer. It is contended that it would now be open to an employee in a similar situation to *Sammon* to claim and to utilise the higher standard imposed by statute (see regulations 5, 10, 11, 13 and 15 of the 1993 Regulations).

In *Brennan v Telemecanique Ltd* [1997] ILLW 254, a Circuit Court case heard in the Eastern Circuit by Lynch J in January 1997, RSI sustained during assembly work fell to be considered. Lynch J held that the overuse by the plaintiff of the middle finger caused the injury, the subject matter of the proceedings. Further, he held that the overuse of the finger was foreseeable by the defendant. Consequently, the employer was held to be in breach of his duty to provide a safe system of work. It is unclear whether the regulations and/or breach of statutory duty were pleaded or relied upon in this case.

In May 1999 a typist was awarded record damages (£100,000) by the English County Court in a landmark case (*McPherson v Camden Council* 19 May 1999 (unreported)). Thornton J, in the course of his judgment, stated that the council should have provided a wrist rest and a flat keyboard to prevent the onset of the plaintiff's condition and criticised it for its failure to ensure regular breaks from typing.

McPherson v Camden Council, while only of persuasive authority in this jurisdiction, shows that employers can now ill afford to ignore RSI. Indeed, in the short term and the medium term it is widely believed that the number of RSI claims will continue to rise.

In RSI cases much depends upon evidence of the system of work operated by an employer. It would be difficult for a judge, faced with evidence of repetitive work, few breaks and inadequate rotation (see Organisation of Working Time Act, 1997), to find, on the balance of probabilities, that work practices were not to blame. Employers must be proactive in risk prevention and control. Indeed, the 1989 Act and the 1993 Regulations have firmly placed the onus on the employer for analysis and prevention of RSI risks. The issue of RSI is not one that is likely to disappear and employers must take care in advising their staff. This is borne out by the English Court of Appeal decision in *Pickford v ICI* [1998] 3 All ER 462, where it was held that a typist who worked a seven-hour day could claim against her employer for injury caused by excessive typing for lengthy periods without proper breaks or rest periods because the employer had not given her the same instructions as he had other typists to take regular breaks.

From an insurance perspective it is the employer's liability insurance that will pay for any successful RSI claims. A policy will generally cover the compensation awarded by a court, all costs and expenses of litigation incurred by both the defendant and plaintiff and all other costs.

In line with the more onerous duties imposed upon employers by the 1989 Act and the regulations implemented thereunder, the future will undoubtedly result in a wider duty of care on the employer coupled with a more burdensome standard of care—an employer will be required to consider even more contingencies to an even greater depth. This is likely to impact upon the legal position of RSI and will necessitate the determination of a general date of knowledge. This is the date that the employer should have known that there was a danger to his or her employees and done something to protect them. Causation will, however, continue to be a significant obstacle to the employee asserting RSI. In short, the employee must not only establish a breach of duty on the part of his employer but must also satisfy the court that he is suffering from a clinically recognised condition caused by his employment.

11.10.7   PART VII: DISPLAY SCREEN EQUIPMENT

Part VII of and Schedules 10 and 11 to the 1993 Regulations impose new duties on an employer to protect an employee 'who habitually uses display screen equipment as a significant part of his normal work'. Regulation 30 excludes the following:

'(a)   drivers' cabs or control cabs for vehicles or machinery;
(b)   computer systems on board a means of transport;
(c)   computer systems mainly intended for public use;
(d)   portable display equipment not in prolonged use at a work-station;
(e)   calculators, cash registers and any equipment having a small data or measurement display required for direct use of the equipment; and
(f)   typewriters of traditional design, of the type known as "typewriter with window".'

It is obvious from the foregoing that portable or laptop computers as well as conventional typewriters are excluded from the remit of this section. Regulation 31 imposes specific duties on employers to, inter alia, assess the risk presented by display equipment, plan employees' activities to provide breaks and provide training, information and advice to employees on the proper use of the equipment. The provision of eye tests at regular intervals before, during and after work, and the provision of special corrective appliances, where necessary, are dealt with in regulation 32.

11.10.8   PART VIII: ELECTRICITY

Part VIII of the 1993 Regulations applies, inter alia, to the generation, storage, transmission and provision of electrical energy in most places of work. Regulation 36 is worthy of particular note in that it imposes absolute duties:

'All electrical equipment and electrical installations shall at all times be so—
(a)   constructed,
(b)   installed,
(c)   maintained,
(d)   protected, and
(e)   used so as to prevent danger.'

11.10.9   PART IX: FIRST AID

Part IX of the 1993 Regulations imposes a duty on an employer in respect of first aid.

11.10.10 PART X: NOTIFICATION OF ACCIDENTS AND DANGEROUS OCCURRENCES

Part X of and Schedule 12 to the 1993 Regulations impose requirements with respect to the notification of accidents, the maintenance of records relating to accidents and the examination and tests to be effected in their investigation. It is a defence, however, to any proceedings under this section, for a person to prove that he has taken all reasonable steps to have all incidence of accidents and dangerous occurrences brought to his notice and that he was not aware of the accident or dangerous occurrence the subject matter of the prosecution.

11.11 MATERNITY PROTECTION ACT, 1994

The Maternity Protection Act, 1994 provides that all employers shall carry out risk assessments taking particular account of risks to new and expectant mothers. It came into effect on 30 January 1995 (see SI 16/1995). The Act specifically provides for a reduction of risks where practicable, changes in working arrangements, the offer of suitable alternative employment or, if that is not possible, paid leave for the employee concerned for as long as is necessary to protect her health and safety or that of her child. It should be noted that regulation 17 of and Schedule 3 to the 1993 Regulations impose an obligation upon employers to provide suitable facilities for pregnant and nursing mothers. In summary, this involves the provision of a quiet and private area where rests may be taken during the working day, and where a breastfeeding mother may feed her baby during such a break.

11.12 SAFETY, HEALTH AND WELFARE AT WORK (CONSTRUCTION) REGULATIONS, 1995

The Safety, Health and Welfare at Work (Construction) Regulations, 1995 (SI 138/1995) were introduced to regulate and protect the safety, health and welfare of persons on construction sites and building projects. Construction work is very broadly defined in the regulations. It includes site clearance, excavation and the erection of a new structure, the demolition and removal of structures as well as extensions to and the maintenance of existing buildings. Window cleaning, painting and decorating projects as well as routine maintenance works are all, to some degree, affected by these regulations. The erection of a single private dwelling, a development akin to the development of the Financial Services Centre in Dublin, and all construction sites in between fall within the parameters of the regulations.

Regulation 3 requires the appointment of a project supervisor for the design stage and construction stage of every project. The one person may hold both positions if suitably qualified. Specific duties are imposed on both the design and project supervisors. Regulation 8 of and Schedules 4 and 5 to the 1995 Regulations impose general duties on contractors. The regulations provide for the co-operation and supply of information to the project supervisor. Any contractor who normally has more than twenty persons under his direct control at any one time on any one site is obliged under the regulations to appoint a qualified safety officer. (This figure includes sub-contractors, the self-employed and direct employees.) Particular provision is made in the regulations in respect of the erection, installation and modification of plant and equipment, and in particular scaffolding. Employees under these regulations must co-operate with the employer on matters affecting health and safety, report defects in plant and equipment and make proper use of the protective equipment provided.

In common with all regulations made pursuant to the 1989 Act, s 28, unless the regulations specifically provide otherwise, civil as well as criminal sanctions attach. Obviously in respect of civil actions, there must be a causal connection between the breach of the duty alleged and the loss or injury sustained.

It should be noted that the Safety, Health and Welfare at Work (Construction) Regulations 2001, which came into force on 1 January 2002, revoke the Safety, Health and Welfare at Work (Construction) Regulations 1995. The 2001 Regulations impose a mandatory requirement that each construction worker receive a basic health and safety course under the FAS Safe Pass training programme and is in possession of a registration card. In addition, workers who are obliged to carry out specified safety critical duties are required to be in possession of a Construction Skills Certification Scheme registration card indicating they have successfully completed training approved by FAS under the Construction Skills Certification Scheme.

11.13 OCCUPIERS' LIABILITY ACT, 1995

The occupier of a premises is obliged to take reasonable precautions in terms of the general condition of the premises. This is termed occupiers' liability and is largely governed by the Occupiers' Liability Act, 1995. Section 8(b) of this Act explicitly provides for the retention of the common law duty of care that an employer owes to an employee. For example, employers owe a specific duty to their employees to provide them with a safe premises, independently of any duty they may owe to them as occupiers. Section 8 of the 1995 Act makes it clear that the statutory prescription of occupiers' liability does not affect this type of duty. A relevant and instructive case is *McCarthy v Southern Health Board*, 1995, High Ct (unreported). The defendant employed the plaintiff. She slipped and fell on an icy patch while walking along a concrete footpath that formed part of the roadway leading to a hospital building controlled by the defendant. The plaintiff suffered personal injury and sued the defendant health board claiming, inter alia, that it was in breach of its duty of care to her as an employer and/or occupier. The court dismissed the claim holding that the most careful employer/occupier could never ensure that there would not be an occasional accumulation of water in such weather conditions.

11.14 SAFETY, HEALTH AND WELFARE AT WORK (MISCELLANEOUS WELFARE PROVISIONS) REGULATIONS, 1995

The Safety, Health and Welfare at Work (Miscellaneous Welfare Provisions) Regulations, 1995 (SI 358/1995) provide for a number of employer duties and repeal pertinent sections of the Office Premises Act, 1958 and the Safety in Industry Act, 1980. This statutory instrument, along with regulation 17 of and Schedule 2 to the 1993 Regulations, imposes an obligation on employers to provide a safe and comfortable place of work. The employer duties include, inter alia, the provision of adequate and suitable facilities for taking meals, facilities for sitting where practicable and an adequate supply of drinking water.

11.15 PROTECTION OF YOUNG PERSONS (EMPLOYMENT) ACT, 1996

The 1989 Act provides that employers must provide safe places and systems of work for all staff, including young persons. The Protection of Young Persons (Employment) Act, 1996 in effect limits the employment of young persons under the age of 18 but over 16 and restricts the employment of children under 16. In general, no child under the age of 13 is permitted to work without a licence from the Minister who must take cognisance of such matters as the safety, health, welfare and education of the child in granting such a licence. Likewise, a 13-year-old can only work under licence or by regulation. The Act requires the employer to receive a copy of the person's birth certificate and, in the case of children, written permission from the parent or guardian of the child, prior to the commencement of employment. The employer must maintain a register of employed young persons (including children) which outlines the times of attendance at work for each day, the rate of pay and the total amount paid in wages. Section 35 of the Organisation of Working Time Act, 1997 amends the Protection of Young Persons (Employment) Act, 1996 to extend to situations where a young person has more than one job.

11.16 SAFETY, HEALTH AND WELFARE AT WORK (CHILDREN AND YOUNG PERSONS) REGULATIONS, 1998

The Safety, Health and Welfare at Work (Children and Young Persons) Regulations, 1998 (SI 504/1998) elaborate on the basic requirements detailed in the 1989 Act and the 1993 Regulations. These regulations require the employer to carry out a risk assessment that takes cognisance of the particular risks to young persons or children if they are employed by the employer. The risk assessment is to include an assessment of the exposure to certain physical, chemical and biological agents as well as particular work activities, which are detailed in the schedule to the regulations. The assessment must not only take cognisance of the safety and health of the child or young person but should also take account of their physical and mental development. The employer is to provide protective and preventative measures and consult any child or young person employed of these measures and of the risks that they are being protected from. The parent or guardian is also to be informed of these risks and preventative measures taken if the person employed is a child. Where the results of a risk assessment confirm that particular work activities may cause harm to a child or young person, they shall not be employed in any such activity (regulation 3(d)). Further, where an assessment shows that a child or young person may be exposed to a risk to their physical or mental development, then health surveillance must be made available to them without charge.

If the work involves night work, the employer must provide health assessment without charge prior to the commencement on night work and at regular intervals thereafter. (However, under the Protection of Young Persons (Employment) Act 1996, young persons are expressly precluded from being employed after 11pm or before 7am. Similarly, children cannot be employed after 8pm or before 8am the next morning.) The parents or guardians of children must be informed of the results of health surveillances or assessments.

11.17 SAFETY, HEALTH AND WELFARE AT WORK (NIGHT WORK AND SHIFT WORK) REGULATIONS, 2000

The principal elements of the 1993 EC Working Time Directive, 93/104/EC, were implemented by the Organisation of Working Time Act, 1997. Articles 9 and 13 of the 1993 Directive were implemented by the Safety, Health and Welfare at Work (Night Work and Shift Work) Regulations, 1998 (SI 485/1998), which became operative on 1 February 1999. The Safety, Health and Welfare at Work (Night Work and Shift Work) Regulations,

2000 (SI 11/2000) revoke and replace the 1998 Regulations. Their purpose was to avoid any ambiguity as regards the application of the provisions of regulation 6 of the 1998 Regulations to night workers. The 2000 Regulations do not impose new obligations or conditions not intended in the 1998 Regulations.

In summary, the 2000 Regulations oblige employers to take such steps as, having regard to the nature of the work, are appropriate for the protection of the health and safety of night workers and shift workers. Regulation 6 of the 2000 Regulations requires an employer to carry out a risk assessment to determine if any night workers are exposed to special hazards or a heavy physical strain. (See also the Organisation of Working Time Act, 1997, s 16(2)(a), (b).) The risk assessment must take account of the specific effects and hazards of night work and have regard to the risk assessment requirements detailed in the 1989 Act, s 12 (see **11.7**). Regulation 7(1) of the 2000 Regulations obliges employers before an employee is employed to do night work and at regular intervals thereafter to make available to the employee, free of charge, an assessment of the effects, if any, on the employee's health. Regulation 7(2) states that the health assessment must be conducted by a registered medical practitioner or a person acting under his or her supervision. The employer and employee are to be advised by the person carrying out the assessment of his or her opinion as to whether the employee is fit or unfit to perform the night work concerned (regulation 7(3)(b)). If of the opinion that the employee is unfit for night work by virtue only of the particular conditions under which it is performed, the employer and employee are to be informed of the person's opinion of what changes could be made which would result in his or her being able to consider the employee fit to perform that work (regulation 7(3)(b). Regulation 7(4) makes clear that the health assessment must comply with requirements of medical confidentiality. Regulation 7(5) requires employers, whose night workers become ill or otherwise exhibit symptoms of ill-health which are recognised as being connected with the fact that they perform night work, to reassign such workers to day work suited to them whenever possible.

11.18 EUROPEAN COMMUNITIES (PROTECTION OF WORKERS) (EXPOSURE TO ASBESTOS) (AMENDMENT) REGULATIONS 2000

The European Communities (Protection of Workers) (Exposure to Asbestos) (Amendment) Regulations, 2000 (SI 74/2000) implement article 7 of Council Directive 87/217/EEC on the prevention and protection of environmental pollution by asbestos by amending the requirements of the plan provided for in article 12 of Directive 83/477/EEC which must be prepared prior to any demolition work involving asbestos. Regulation 4 of the 2000 Regulations also amends the length of time that medical records and the occupational health register must be maintained.

11.19 SAFETY, HEALTH AND WELFARE AT WORK (PREGNANT EMPLOYEES ETC) REGULATIONS 2000

The Safety, Health and Welfare at Work (Pregnant Employees etc) Regulations, 2000 (SI 218/2000) implement the occupational health and safety provisions of Council Directive 92/85/EEC of 19 October 1992 by the introduction of measures to promote improvement in the health and safety at work of pregnant workers and workers who have recently given birth. These regulations revoke and replace the Safety, Health and Welfare at Work (Pregnant Employees etc) Regulations 1994 (SI 446/1994). They require employers to take such steps as, having regard to the nature of the work, are necessary for the protection of the health and safety at work of pregnant workers and workers who have recently given birth or are breastfeeding. Regulation 4 requires an employer to carry out a risk assessment to determine any possible effects on the pregnancy of, or breastfeeding by, employees resulting from any activity at the employer's place of work. Regulation 5 states that if a pregnant employee is certified by a medical practitioner as not being able to perform night work during pregnancy or for fourteen weeks after childbirth, the employer shall find day employment for her. If this is not possible the employer must grant the employee leave or extend the period of maternity leave (see **00.0.0**). The introduction of the Safety, Health and Welfare at Work (Pregnant Employees etc) Regulations, 2000 has, however, had no material impact on the practical obligations previously imposed at the workplace under the 1994 Regulations.

11.20 ENFORCEMENT UNDER THE 1989 REGIME

11.20.1 HEALTH AND SAFETY AUTHORITY

The sanctions provided under the 1989 Act are primarily criminal. Given the fact that breaches would be technical in nature, it was logical to vest responsibility for enforcement in a new administrative body, namely the National Authority for Occupational Safety and Health, better known as the Health and Safety Authority. Part III of the 1989 Act establishes the Authority, while Parts V, VI, VII and VIII provide that body with its metaphorical teeth. Under s 16 of the Act the principal functions of the Authority include the enforcement of the relevant statutory provisions and the prevention of accidents. Under Part IV of the legislation the Authority is obliged to review on a regular basis all relevant safety legislation. Section 30 of the Act permits the Authority to issue codes of practice, with the consent of the Minister. These codes serve primarily as aids to understanding the purpose and desired result of the regulations, though they are not legally binding. Part V of the Act enables the Minister to prescribe persons, including local authorities, to be enforcement agents in lieu of the Authority (1989 Act, s 32(1)). To date, however, only the Authority itself has been so authorised to enforce the provisions of the Act.

Section 33 of the Act authorises the Authority (or a prescribed enforcement agency) to appoint inspectors to enforce the provisions of the Act. By virtue of s 34, very wide powers of entry, inspection, examination, search, seizure and analysis are entrusted to the appointed inspectors. Among the particular powers of the inspector is the authority to issue improvement directions and plans (1989 Act, s 35), improvement notices (1989 Act, s 36) and prohibition notices (1989 Act, s 37). Under s 39(1) of the 1989 Act the Authority may apply ex parte to the High Court for an order when it 'considers that the risk to the safety and health of persons is so serious that the use of the place of work or part thereof should be restricted or should be immediately prohibited until specified measures have been taken to reduce the risk to a reasonable level'. The High Court may make an interim or interlocutory order as it sees fit. In 1996, the Health and Safety Authority obtained, for the first time, a High Court order under this section. Two High Court orders were obtained in 1997, two again in 1998, four in 1999 and two in 2000.

Part VII of the Act invests the Authority with the power to direct any of its staff or any other competent person to investigate the circumstances surrounding any accident, disease, occurrence, situation or any other matters. Failure to comply with specified provisions of the Act or regulations made under s 28 is a criminal offence. The particular penalties are specified in s 49 of the 1989 Act. These include fines and terms of imprisonment. The maximum fine on summary conviction is £1,500 (increased from £1,000 by the Organisation of Working Time Act, 1997, s 41). On conviction on indictment the fine imposed is at the discretion of the court.

11.20.2 PROSECUTION OF OFFENCES

There is little possibility of escaping responsibility for breaches of the 1989 Act as employers (ss 6, 7 or 8), the self-employed (ss 7, 8), employees (s 9) and manufacturers, designers and builders (ss 10, 11) may all be prosecuted for breaches of the Act. Both individuals and bodies corporate may be prosecuted. In most cases the company itself will be prosecuted. However, s 48(19) of the 1989 Act specifically provides for the prosecution of the officers and management of a company or other body. Where an offence has been committed by a 'body corporate', and that offence is shown to 'have been committed with the consent or connivance of, or to have been attributable to any neglect on the part of any director', or other officer, that person may be prosecuted in addition to the corporate body. This approach has been taken in England since the introduction in that jurisdiction of a similar provision in 1974 (Health and Safety at Work Act 1974, s 37). In *R v Boal* [1992] QB 591, for example, an inspection of a bookshop identified serious breaches of the Fire Precautions Act 1971. That Act contained a provision similar to s 48(19) of the 1989 Act in this jurisdiction. Mr Boal held the position of assistant manager in the bookshop and was only in charge when the manager was absent. The manager was absent on the particular day of the inspection. However, the case against Mr Boal was dismissed, as it was held that, although he was in charge of the store on the particular day of the inspection, he had no control over the fire safety policy of the shop. That said, the owners were successfully prosecuted. (See also *Armour v Skeen* [1977] IRLR 310.) It would appear, therefore, that, for the imposition of personal liability on an officer or manager of a company, some element of control over corporate policy is required. The application of s 48(19) in this jurisdiction can be seen in the November 1998 case of *National Authority for Occupational Safety and Health v Noel Frisby Construction Ltd and Noel Frisby* (see Health and Safety Authority Annual Report 1998, p 17).

11.20.3 TIME LIMITS

Prosecutions must be brought, pursuant to the 1989 Act, s 51(3), within one year from the date of the offence. Section 51(4) provides that where a statutory report on foot of an investigation is required or where an inquest is held, summary proceedings must be brought within six months of the making of the report or the conclusion of the inquest. However, Murphy J in *National Authority for Occupational Safety and Health v Fingal County Council* [1997] 1 ILRM 128 held that, as the section was penal in nature, it must be construed in favour of the accused. In consequence s 51(3) was held to be limited by s 51(4). This limitation has now been removed by the Organisation of Working Time Act, 1997, s 38 which provides, inter alia, that the provisions in s 51(3) are not prejudiced by the provisions in s 51(4).

11.21 FUTURE OF HEALTH AND SAFETY LEGISLATION AND MANAGEMENT STANDARDS

11.21.1 GENERALLY

It is clear from the foregoing that there has been a powerful movement towards greater protection of the safety, health and welfare of employees at work. Certainly, there would be few that would disagree that we have come a long way from the 1802 Act for the Preservation of the Health and Morals of Apprentices and Others. It is probable that many more regulations affecting all aspects of the workplace and all those persons connected with it will be introduced pursuant to the 1989 Act, s 28. These regulations will, no doubt, impose more extensive obligations upon employers as a whole. The cost of complying with these regulations will also increase.

11.21.2 DUTY OF CARE

The leading question that remains to be addressed is what duty of care will be imposed on employers in the future. Currently, the protection afforded by statute is in excess of that presently afforded by the common law. Several provisions of the 1989 Act require the high standard of reasonable practicability from employers. Surprisingly, very few references are made to this standard of reasonable practicability in the 1993 Regulations. In fact, the 1993 Regulations impose certain absolute duties (see regulations 19, 20 and 36). Is it likely, therefore, that future regulations will impose a higher standard of care on employers than the 1989 Act?

It has been argued that the duty of care imposed under future regulations should be one of absolute liability. Strict liability is not to be equated with absolute liability. Defences may be pleaded in respect of a strict liability standard whereas no defence is available to a standard of absolute liability. This standard is higher than that of reasonable practicability under the 1989 Act. A number of reasons for this approach are proffered. Most regulations commence life as directives from Europe, which this State is obliged, pursuant to its Treaty obligations, to implement. Directives set down minimum standards not maximum ones and do not preclude the imposition of a higher duty of care. Accordingly, it is always open to a court to hold that the regulations impose a higher standard than that provided for under the 1989 Act. In addition, in some cases, absolute duties have already been in existence in Irish law since the Factories Act, 1955 and to withdraw or recoil from that now would be to reduce the level of protection available to employees under the 1989 Act. This would be totally contrary to the intention of the legislature and the spirit of the legislation. Further, many of the regulations are general in nature and, indeed, vague in parts. This would and should militate against too strict an interpretation of the regulations by the courts.

11.21.3 INCREASED EXPECTATIONS

With the passage of time, the 1989 Act, the regulations implemented under that Act and the Occupiers' Liability Act, 1995 will improve the health and safety standards which employees enjoy in the workplace. This should result in fewer accidents. Consequently, the number and cost of claims should fall. This increased protection may raise the expectations of society as a whole in so far as safety, health and welfare at work are concerned. It may serve in time to impact upon the common law duty of care. In other words, what is reasonable now may not be deemed reasonable in the future. In summary, the greater protection afforded by statute may become no more than merely declaratory of the common law position.

Society and the courts are already reflecting this increased awareness of health and safety. In a case heard in May 1998, namely *DPP v Cullagh* (Irish Times Law Reports, 31 May 1999), the operator of a funfair was prosecuted for and convicted of criminal negligence arising out of the death of a member of the public. This case was not taken under the health and safety legislation but rather under the common law. The initiation of manslaughter charges by the Director of Public Prosecutions against the managing director of a company (arising from the death of two employees at work) in a case in 1999 should be noted by employers as it signposts the fact that workplace deaths can no longer be discounted as a minor matter for the District Court.

11.21.4 CORPORATE RESPONSIBILITY

In the future it is likely that individual members of management will face criminal charges arising out of deaths and injuries at work where it is possible to connect the individual failures of senior executives with the corporate body. It is interesting to note that the former

British Home Secretary, Jack Straw, mooted the introduction of a new offence of 'corporate killing' in the United Kingdom. This offence would facilitate the prosecution of company directors and render them liable for unlimited fines and imprisonment in circumstances where they are found to have neglected the health and safety of those affected by their activities. (Such an offence was proposed in the United Kingdom by the Law Commission in 1996: Law Com No 237, 'Legislating the Criminal Code: Involuntary Manslaughter' (HMSO, 1996)). This writer takes the view that it will not be long before a similar approach is adopted in this jurisdiction.

INDEX

INDEX